2006
FUNK & WAGNALLS
NEW ENCYCLOPEDIA
YEARBOOK

A REVIEW OF THE EVENTS OF 2005

FUNK & WAGNALLS
Publishers Since 1876

An Imprint of World Almanac Education Group

Published 2006 by World Almanac Education Group, Inc.

Funk & Wagnalls and F&W are registered trademarks of World Almanac
Education Group, Inc.

This annual is also published under the title *The 2006 World Book Year Book*
© 2006 World Book, Inc.

Library of Congress Control Number: 62-4818
ISBN: 0-8343-0257-8

Printed in the United States of America.

STAFF

EDITORIAL

Executive Editor
Sara Dreyfuss

**Managing Editor,
The Year Book**
Scott Thomas

Senior Editor
Kristina A. Vaicikonis

Staff Editors
Heather McShane
S. Thomas Richardson
Marty Zwikel

Contributing Editors
Dan Blunk
Robert Knight
Barbara A. Mayes
Alfred J. Smuskiewicz

Editorial Assistant
Ethel Matthews

Cartographic Services
H. George Stoll, Head
Wayne K. Pichler, Manager,
Digital Cartography
John M. Rejba,
Staff Cartographer

Indexing Services
David Pofelski, Head
Aamir Burki, Staff Indexer

Statistics Editor
William M. Harrod

Permissions Editor
Janet Peterson

ART

Manager, Graphics and Design
Sandra M. Dyrlund

Project Design Coordinator
Brenda B. Tropinski

Senior Designers
Don Di Sante
Isaiah W. Sheppard

Senior Photographs Editor
Tom Evans

Photographs Editor
Kathryn Creech

**Production and
Administrative Support**
John Whitney

RESEARCH SERVICES

Manager, Research Services
Loranne K. Shields

Researchers
Madolynn H. Cronk
Lynn Durbin
Cheryl Graham
Karen A. McCormack

Library Services
Stephanie Kitchen,
Information Services Coordinator

PRODUCTION

**Director, Manufacturing
and Pre-Press**
Carma Fazio

Manufacturing Manager
Barbara Podczerwinski

Senior Production Manager
Madelyn S. Underwood

Production Manager
Anne Fritzinger

Proofreading
Anne Dillon, Head

Text Processing
Curley Hunter
Gwendolyn Johnson

MARKETING

Director, Direct Marketing
Mark R. Willy

Marketing Analyst
Zofia Kulik

Editor in Chief
Paul A. Kobasa

CONTRIBUTORS

Contributors not listed on these pages are members of the editorial staff.

ANDREWS, PETER J., B.A., M.S.; free-lance writer. **[Chemistry]**

APPLEBY, R. SCOTT, B.A., PH.D.; Professor of History and John M, Regan, Jr., Director of Joan B. Kroc Institute for International Peace Studies, University of Notre Dame. **[Deaths Special Report: John Paul II]**

BARNHART, BILL, B.A., M.S.T., M.B.A.; financial markets columnist, *Chicago Tribune*. **[Stocks and bonds]**

BARRETT, NORMAN, M.A.; free-lance writer. **[Soccer]**

BAYNHAM, SIMON, B.A., M.A., Ph.D.; Senior Research Associate, Centre for Defence & International Security Studies, University of Lancaster, U.K. **[Africa and African country articles]**

BERGER, ERIC R., B.A, M.A.; science writer, *Houston Chronicle*. **[Houston]**

BOYD, JOHN D., B.S.; Economics writer. **[Economics, U.S.; Economics, World; International trade]**

BRADSHER, HENRY S., A.B., B.J.; foreign affairs analyst. **[Asia and Asian country articles]**

BRETT, CARLTON E., B.A., M.S., Ph.D.; Professor of Geology, University of Cincinnati. **[Paleontology]**

CAMPBELL, GEOFFREY A., B.J.; free-lance writer. **[Human rights; U.S. government articles]**

CARDINALE, DIANE P., B.A.; Research Associate, Toy Industry Association, Incorporated. **[Toys and games]**

CARLSON, ROB, B.A., M.S.; Deputy Executive Director, Library and Information Technology Association, American Library Association. **[Library]**

CASEY, MIKE, B.S., M.A.; Assistant Editor, *Kansas City Star*. **[Automobile]**

DEEB, MARIUS K., B.A., Ph.D.; Professor, School of Advanced International Studies, Johns Hopkins University. **[Middle East and Middle Eastern country articles; North African country articles]**

DEEB, MARY-JANE, B.A., Ph.D.; Arab World Area Specialist, Library of Congress. **[Middle East and Middle Eastern country articles; North African country articles]**

DeFRANK, THOMAS M., B.A., M.A.; Washington Bureau Chief, *New York Daily News*. **[Armed forces]**

DELANEY, KEVIN, B.A.; staff reporter, *The Wall Street Journal*. **[Crime Special Report: Identity Theft: The New Face of Crime]**

DEVINE, MICHAEL J., B.A.. M.A., Ph.D.; Director, Harry S. Truman Presidential Library. **[United States, President of the, Special Report: Preserving Legacies]**

DILLON, DAVID, B.A., M.A., Ph.D.; architecture and design editor, *The Dallas Morning News*. **[Architecture]**

ELLIS, GAVIN, former Editor in Chief, *The New Zealand Herald & Weekend Herald*. **[New Zealand]**

FARR, DAVID M. L., D.Phil., LL.D.; Professor Emeritus of History, Carleton University. **[Canada; Canada, Prime Minister of; Canadian provinces; Canadian territories]**

FERRELL, KEITH, free-lance writer. **[Computer; Electronics]**

FISHER, ROBERT W., B.A., M.A.; free-lance writer. **[Labor and employment]**

FITZGERALD, MARK, B.A.; editor at large, *Editor & Publisher* magazine. **[Magazine; Newspaper]**

FRIEDMAN, EMILY, B.A.; health policy and ethics analyst. **[Health care issues; Social Security Special Report: Benefit of Doubt: How Secure Are American Entitlements?]**

GADOMSKI, FRED, B.S., M.S.; Meteorologist, Pennsylvania State University. **[Global warming; Weather]**

GATTY, ROBERT C., free-lance writer, *Gatty Edits*. **[Food]**

GOLDEN, JONATHAN J., B.A., M.J.Ed.; Chair, History Department at the Gann Academy, New Jewish High School of Greater Boston. **[Judaism]**

GOLDNER, NANCY, B.A.; free-lance dance critic. **[Dance]**

HARAKAS, STANLEY SAMUEL, B.A., B.Th., Th.D.; Archbishop Iakovos Professor (Emeritus) of Orthodox Theology, Holy Cross Greek Orthodox School of Theology. **[Eastern Orthodox Churches]**

HAVERSTOCK, NATHAN A., A.B.; affiliate scholar, Oberlin College. **[Latin America and Latin American country articles]**

HENDERSON, HAROLD, B.A.; staff writer, *Chicago Reader*. **[Chicago]**

HOFFMAN, ANDREW J., B.S., M.S., Ph.D.; Holcim Professor of Enterprise, University of Michigan. **[Environmental pollution]**

JOHANSON, DONALD C., B.S., M.A., Ph.D.; Director and Professor, Institute of Human Origins, Arizona State University. **[Anthropology]**

JOHNSON, CHRISTINA S., B.A., M.S.; free-lance science writer. **[Ocean]**

JOHNSON, JULIET, A.B., M.A., Ph.D.; Associate Professor of Political Science, McGill University. **[Russia Special Report: Russia in the Post-Soviet World; Russia and other former Soviet republic articles]**

KATES, MICHAEL, B.S.J.; Associate Sports Editor, *Chicago Tribune*. **[Sports articles]**

KENNEDY, BRIAN, M.A.; free-lance writer. **[Australia; Australia, Prime Minister of; Australian rules football]**

KILGORE, MARGARET, B.A., M.B.A.; free-lance writer, Kilgore and Associates. **[Los Angeles]**

KING, MIKE, reporter, *The (Montreal) Gazette*. **[Montreal]**

KLINTBERG, PATRICIA PEAK, B.A.; Director of Constituent Affairs, Office of Communications, U.S. Department of Agriculture. **[Agriculture]**

KOPSTEIN, JEFFREY, B.A., M.A., Ph.D; Professor of Political Science and Director, Centre for European, Russian, and Eurasian Studies, University of Toronto. **[Europe and Western European country articles]**

KRONHOLZ, JUNE, B.S.J.; staff reporter, *The Wall Street Journal.* **[Education]**

LAWRENCE, ALBERT, B.A., M.A., M.Ed.; Executive Director, World Chess Hall of Fame. **[Chess]**

LEWIS, DAVID C., M.D.; Professor of Medicine and Community Health, Brown University. **[Drug abuse]**

LIEBENSON, DONALD, B.A.; free-lance writer. **[Popular music; Television; Television portrait]**

LYE, KEITH, B.A., F.R.G.S.; free-lance writer and editor. **[Cricket]**

MARCH, ROBERT H., A.B., M.S., Ph.D.; Professor Emeritus of Physics and Liberal Studies, University of Wisconsin at Madison. **[Physics]**

MARSCHALL, LAURENCE A., B.S., Ph.D.; W.K.T. Sahm Professor of Physics, Gettysburg College. **[Astronomy]**

MARTY, MARTIN E., Ph.D.; Fairfax M. Cone Distinguished Service Professor Emeritus, University of Chicago. **[Protestantism]**

MAY, SALLY RUTH, B.A, M.A.; free-lance art writer. **[Art]**

McDONALD, ELAINE STUART, B.A.; free-lance public policy writer and editor. **[State government]**

McWILLIAM, ROHAN, B.A., M.A., D.Phil; Senior Lecturer in History, Anglia Polytechnic University, Cambridge, U.K. **[Ireland; Northern Ireland; United Kingdom; United Kingdom, Prime Minister of]**

MINER, TODD J., B.S., M.S.; Meteorologist, Pennsylvania State University. **[Weather]**

MORITZ, OWEN, B.A.; urban affairs editor, *New York Daily News.* **[New York City]**

MORRING, FRANK, Jr., B.A.; Senior Space Technology editor, *Aviation Week & Space Technology* magazine. **[Space exploration]**

MORRIS, BERNADINE, B.A., M.A.; free-lance fashion writer. **[Fashion]**

MULLINS, HENRY T., B.S., M.S., Ph.D.; Professor of Geology, Syracuse University. **[Geology]**

NGUYEN, J. TUYET, M.A.; United Nations correspondent, Deutsche Presse-Agentur. **[Population; United Nations]**

OGAN, EUGENE, B.A., Ph.D.; Professor Emeritus of Anthropology, University of Minnesota. **[Pacific Islands]**

PAETH, GREGORY, B.A.; business writer, *The Cincinnati Post.* **[Radio]**

REINHART, A. KEVIN, B.A., M.A., Ph.D.; Associate Professor of Religious Studies, Dartmouth College. **[Islam]**

RICCIUTI, EDWARD, B.A.; free-lance writer. **[Biology; Conservation; Zoos]**

ROBERTS, THOMAS W., Editor, *The National Catholic Reporter.* **[Roman Catholic Church]**

ROSE, MARK J., B.A., M.A., Ph.D.; Executive Editor, *Archaeology* magazine. **[Archaeology]**

RUBENSTEIN, RICHARD E., B.A., M.A., J.D.; Professor of Conflict Resolution and Public Affairs, George Mason University. **[Terrorism]**

RUSSELL, MARY HARRIS, B.A., M.A, Ph.D.; Professor of English, Indiana University. **[Literature for children]**

SARNA, JONATHAN D., Ph.D.; Joseph H. & Belle R. Braun Professor of American Jewish History, Brandeis University. **[Judaism]**

SAVAGE, IAN, B.A., Ph.D.; Associate Professor of Economics and Transportation, Northwestern University. **[Aviation; Transportation]**

SCHWARTZ, BERNARD, B.A.; Assistant to the Director, Unterberg Poetry Center. **[Literature]**

SHAPIRO, HOWARD, B.S.; staff writer and travel columnist, *The Philadelphia Inquirer.* **[Philadelphia; Washington, D.C.]**

SMUSKIEWICZ, ALFRED J., B.S., M.S.; free-lance writer. **[Physics Special Report: 1905—Einstein's Miracle Year]**

STEIN, DAVID LEWIS, B.A., M.S.; former urban affairs columnist, *The Toronto Star.* **[Toronto]**

STOS, WILLIAM, B.A., M.A.; free-lance writer. **[Canadian provinces; Canadian territories]**

TANNER, JAMES C., B.J.; former news editor—energy, *The Wall Street Journal.* **[Energy supply]**

TATUM, HENRY K., B.A.; retired Associate Editor, *The Dallas Morning News.* **[Dallas]**

THOMAS, PAULETTE, B.A.; free-lance writer. **[Bank]**

VAN, JON, B.A., M.A.; technology writer, *Chicago Tribune.* **[Telecommunications]**

von RHEIN, JOHN, B.A.; classical music critic, *Chicago Tribune.* [Classical music]

WHITAKER, CHARLES, B.S.J., M.S.J.; Director, Academy for Alternative Journalism, Medill School of Journalism **[Magazine portrait]**

WILSON, DAVE, B.A.; Producer, Cable News Network. **[Internet]**

WOLCHIK, SHARON L., B.A., M.A., Ph.D.; Professor of Political Science and International Affairs, George Washington University. **[Eastern European country articles]**

WRIGHT, ANDREW G., B.A.; Managing Senior Editor, *Engineering News-Record* magazine. **[Building and construction]**

WUNTCH, PHILIP, B.A.; film critic, *The Dallas Morning News.* **[Motion pictures]**

YEZZI, DAVID, B.F.A., M.F.A.; Executive Editor, *The New Criterion* magazine. **[Literature Special Report: The Graphic Novel: Drawing a New Audience; Poetry; Theater; Theater portraits]**

CONTENTS

8   **MAJOR NEWS STORIES**

The editors' pick of the most memorable, exciting, or important news stories of 2005.

11   **THE YEAR IN BRIEF**

A month-by-month review of the major news stories of 2005.

36   **UPDATE**

The major world events of 2005 are reported in more than 250 alphabetically arranged Update articles—from "Afghanistan" to "Zoos." Included are Special Reports that provide an in-depth focus on especially noteworthy developments.

SPECIAL REPORTS

126   CRIME
Identity Theft:
The New Face of Crime
by Kevin J. Delaney
An investigation into one of the fastest-growing crimes in the United States.

148   DEATHS
Pope John Paul II
(1920-2005)
by R. Scott Appleby
A remembrance of one of the Roman Catholic Church's longest-reigning and most revered pontiffs.

158   DISASTERS
The Second Battle of New
Orleans
A photo essay chronicles one of the worst disasters in U.S. history.

238   LITERATURE
The Graphic Novel
by David Yezzi
A relatively new literary form takes the publishing world by storm.

294   PHYSICS
1905—Einstein's Miracle Year
by Alfred J. Smuskiewicz
Einstein's theories continue to shape scientific thought and affect the reality of existence.

316   RUSSIA
Russia in the Post-Soviet World
by Juliet Johnson
President Vladimir Putin struggles to maintain Russian influence in the face of the so-called "colored revolutions."

334   SOCIAL SECURITY
Benefit of Doubt: How Secure
Are American Entitlements?
by Emily Friedman and Scott Thomas
A reexamination of U.S. "entitlement" programs—Social Security, Medicare, and Medicaid.

394   UNITED STATES, PRESIDENT OF THE
Preserving Legacies
by Michael J. Devine
The director of the Truman Library offers an insider's look at presidential libraries.

FOCUS ON

49 ARCHITECTURE
Spectacular new museums

68 AUTOMOBILE
2006 Models

194 GERMANY
Holocaust memorial

212 IRAQ
The war in 2005

216 ISRAEL
Israel pulls out of Gaza

260 MOTION PICTURES
Academy Awards

348 SPACE EXPLORATION
New Horizons in Space

410 WEATHER
Natural Disasters of 2005

PORTRAITS

202 HUMAN RIGHTS
Rosa Parks

236 LITERATURE
Saul Bellow

250 MAGAZINE
John H. Johnson

366 TELEVISION
Johnny Carson

373 THEATER
Arthur Miller

374 THEATER
August Wilson

417 **INDEX**

A cumulative index covering
the contents of the 2004,
2005, and 2006 editions of
the Yearbook.

From the death of one of the longest-reigning popes in history to the discovery of a possible new planet, 2005 was a year of extraordinary events. On these three pages are stories that the editors picked as some of the most important of the year, along with details on where to find more information about them in this volume.

The Editors

2005

A NEW SUPREME COURT

The death of the chief justice of the United States Supreme Court and the retirement of an associate justice brings sweeping changes to an institution that had remained constant for more than a decade. See **People in the news,** page 281; **Supreme Court of the United States,** page 359; **United States, Government of the,** page 389; **United States, President of the,** page 393.

DEATH OF A POPE

Pope John Paul II, one of the longest-reigning pontiffs in history, dies in April. A new pope, who chose the name Benedict XVI, is elected to succeed him. See **Deaths: A Special Report,** page 148; **Judaism,** page 221; **People in the news,** page 281; **Roman Catholic Church,** page 311.

IRAQ WAR

As the war in Iraq continues into a third year, the number of U.S. forces killed in the conflict surpasses 2,100 in 2005. See **Armed forces,** page 51; **Iraq,** page 211; **Italy,** page 218; **Middle East,** page 254; **United Kingdom,** page 383; **United Kingdom, Prime Minister of the,** page 387; **United States, Government of the,** page 389; **United States, President of the,** page 393.

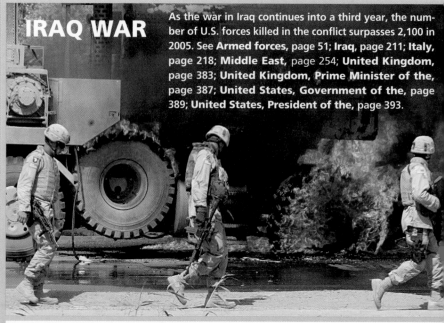

HURRICANES DEVASTATE GULF COAST

Hurricanes Katrina and Rita hit the Gulf Coast of the United States in August and September, causing one of the worst natural disasters in U.S. history. See **Year in brief,** pages 27-29; **Architecture,** page 48; **Congress, U.S.,** page 115; **Disasters: A Special Report,** page 158; **Economics, U.S.,** page 168; **Energy supply,** page 176; **Environmental pollution,** page 178; **Houston,** page 200; **International trade,** page 208; **United States, Government of the,** page 389; **United States, President of the,** page 393; **Weather,** page 409; **Zoos,** page 415.

SYRIA LEAVES LEBANON

The assassination of a former prime minister of Lebanon brings international pressure to bear on Syria to withdraw its troops from Lebanon after nearly 30 years of occupation. See **Lebanon,** page 232; **Middle East,** page 254; **Syria,** page 363.

RETREAT FROM GAZA

Israel withdraws from the Gaza Strip in 2005, and Israeli Prime Minister Ariel Sharon pulls out of the ruling Likud to establish a centrist party, developments that kindle hope for permanent settlement of the Israeli-Palestinian conflict. See **Israel,** page 216; **Judaism,** page 221; **Middle East,** page 254.

TERRORISTS STRIKE

British-born suicide bombers kill 52 civilians in a series of attacks on London's public transportation system in July. See **Terrorism,** page 371; **United Kingdom,** page 383. In Jordan in November, three suicide bombings in American-owned hotels kill nearly 60 people, including guests at a Jordanian wedding. See **Jordan,** page 221; **Middle East,** page 254; **Terrorism,** page 371; **United Kingdom,** page 383.

POSSIBLE NEW PLANET

In July, astronomers announce the discovery of what may be the solar system's 10th planet, a ball of rock and ice larger and farther away than Pluto. See **Astronomy,** page 60.

GOVERNMENT SCANDAL

A series of government scandals came to light in 2005, including the exposure of the identity of a CIA operative by a "high government official"; the indictment of the majority leader of the U.S. House of Representatives; the resignation of a California representative; and the indictment and investigation of Washington lobbyists. See **Congress, U.S.,** page 115; **Newspaper,** page 272; **United States, Government of the,** page 389.

EARTHQUAKE IN PAKISTAN AND INDIA

An earthquake in Pakistan and India in October kills more than 74,000 people. See **Asia,** page 56; **Disasters,** page 155; **Geology,** page 192; **India,** page 204; **Pakistan,** page 278.

2005

YEAR IN BRIEF

A month-by-month listing of the most significant world events that occurred during 2005.

1 Chief Justice William Rehnquist of the United States Supreme Court issues a year-end report on the federal judiciary. In the report, the chief justice criticizes politicians who threaten judicial independence, specifically pointing to conservatives who maintain that "judicial activists" should be impeached. Rehnquist notes that while judges are open to public criticism, politicians go too far when they threaten to punish or impeach judges for rulings with which they disagree.

5 A series of insurgent attacks in Iraq leaves at least 25 people dead in a fourth day of escalating violence. The Iraqi interior minister announces that 1,300 Iraqi police died in insurgent attacks during the last four months of 2004.

6 A roadside bomb attack on a U.S. convoy in Baghdad leaves seven U.S. soldiers dead. Two additional American soldiers are killed in an insurgent attack in Anbar province, west of Baghdad.

8 Severe storms across northern Europe, from the United Kingdom to Russia, leave at least 13 people dead. Winds of up to 90 miles (145 kilometers) per hour knock out electric power from Norway and Sweden to Latvia, leaving hundreds of thousands of people without light or heat.

9 Interim Palestinian leader Mahmoud Abbas is elected president of the Palestinian Authority with more than 62 percent of the vote, which political experts describe as a clear, strong mandate for forging a peaceful resolution to the Palestinian-Israeli conflict.

10 Unusually heavy rain in California triggers an enormous mudslide down a 500-foot (150-kilometer) mountain above the seaside village of La Conchita, which is approximately 70 miles (110 kilometers) northwest of Los Angeles. At least 10 people, including 3 children, are killed in the slide, which buries 15 houses under 25 feet (7 meters) of rock and debris. Five days of heavy rain have saturated the soil, turning the entire region into a flood zone. Central Los Angeles has received 22 inches (56 centimeters) of rain in the last five weeks, compared with an average of 15 inches (381 millimeters) for the entire winter season.

15 Two sections of a levee along the Wabash River at West Terre Haute, Indiana, give way as floodwaters rise to more than 14 feet (4 meters) above flood stage. The unusual January flooding of the Wabash and Ohio rivers and their smaller tributaries was triggered by melting snow and recent heavy rains.

20 George W. Bush is sworn in for a second term as the 43rd president of the United States. In his 21-minute inaugural address, the president proclaims the United States a worldwide liberator committed to aiding oppressed nations: "The survival of liberty in our land increasingly depends on the success of liberty in other lands."

24 More than 250 people are killed in a stampede at a Hindu festival at the Mandhar Devi temple in western India, approximately 150 miles (240 kilometers) southeast of Mumbai. A fire in stalls lining the path of the religious procession triggers panic among the pilgrims, who jam the narrow passage in an attempt to avoid the flames.

25 President George W. Bush asks Congress for an additional $75 billion in funding for military operations in Iraq and Afghanistan. If approved, the funding pushes the total expended on the war to more than $275 billion. A Bush administration official confirms that the additional funding is likely to boost the 2005 federal deficit to a record $425 billion.

26 Thirty U.S. Marines and Navy corpsmen are killed in a helicopter crash in Iraq near the Jordanian border. Elsewhere in Iraq, four Marines die fighting insurgents in Al Anbar province, and two other U.S. soldiers are killed in an insurgent attack on a military patrol north of

Women line up to vote in Najaf, a Shiah-dominated city in southern Iraq, on January 30 in the country's first free elections in 50 years. An estimated 60 percent of the adult population voted in the election despite the threat of violence from insurgents.

Baghdad. The loss of 37 soldiers is the highest in a single day since the war began in March 2003 and brings to 1,417 the total number of American soldiers killed in Iraq.

26 The United States Senate, in an 85 to 13 vote, confirms the nomination of Condoleezza Rice as secretary of state. She replaces retired Army General Colin Powell.

30 The U.S.-led Coalition Provisional Authority (CPA) in Iraq lost track of nearly $9 billion in funds that were transferred to Iraqi ministries between October 2003 and June 2004, reveals a U.S. inspector general for Iraq reconstruction. In a report to Congress, the inspector general notes that the CPA transferred $8.8 billion to Iraqi ministries "without assurance the moneys were accounted for."

30 Iraqis turn out in large numbers to vote in the country's first free elections in 50 years. An estimated 60 percent of the adult population vote, in defiance of insurgent death threats. The turnout is particularly heavy in the Kurdish north and Shiah-dominated cities of southern Iraq, where voters stand in long lines outside polling places despite insurgent attacks and suicide bombings that leave at least 35 people dead.

31 SBC Communications, the San Antonio, Texas, telecommunications company, announces that it has concluded a $16-billion deal to acquire AT&T. One of the most venerable of U.S. corporations, AT&T essentially will disappear within SBC, one of the so-called Baby Bells that were spun off from AT&T in 1984, when the company, then a monopoly, was broken up by the government.

A stalled storm system drops record-breaking amounts of rain on Los Angeles in February. From February 18 to 23, more than 9 inches (229 millimeters) of rain fell in Los Angeles after the region had already received in excess of 15 inches (38 centimeters) of rain in January.

1 King Gyanendra of Nepal declares a state of emergency and takes total control of the government. After dismissing the Cabinet for failing to crush a nine-year rebellion by Maoist insurgents, the king places the former prime minister and other officials under house arrest. The insurgents, who currently control much of the countryside outside the capital, Kathmandu, advocate replacing the monarchy with a Communist republic.

2 Global warming is causing the ice in Antarctica to melt faster than had previously been thought, Chris Rapley, the director of the British Antarctic Survey (BAS), tells scientists attending the Climate Change Conference in Exeter, United Kingdom. The BAS team of researchers have concluded that more than 5,000 square miles (13,000 square kilometers) of sea ice in the Antarctic Peninsula has melted in the last 50 years.

3 The inspector general of the Environmental Protection Agency (EPA) releases a report that accuses the EPA of ignoring scientific evidence and agency protocols when it set new, looser limits in 2003 on mercury pollution.

3 The U.S. Senate votes 60 to 36 to confirm Alberto Gonzales as the first Hispanic attorney general of the United States.

6 The New England Patriots win the team's second consecutive Super Bowl, its third Super Bowl title in four years, by beating the Philadelphia Eagles 24-21 in Jacksonville, Florida.

10 The government of North Korea declares that it possesses nuclear weapons. In the same announcement, the North Korean Foreign Ministry states that North Korea will boycott U.S.-sponsored regional talks designed to end the North Korean nuclear program.

15 The United Iraqi Alliance (UIA), the Shiah Muslim political party that received the most votes in Iraq's January 30 election, nominates Ibrahim al-Jafari as its candidate for prime minister. In provisional results announced on February 14, UIA took 48 percent of the vote. With less than a majority of seats, UIA is forced to form a coalition government, most likely with the Kurdistan Alliance, which took 26 percent of the vote. The *secular* (non-religious) party of the current interim prime minister, Iyad Allawi, garnered only 14 percent of the vote.

16 The National Hockey League (NHL) officially cancels the 2004/2005 season, the first time a U.S. sports league has ever called off an entire season. The cancellation stemmed from a series of disputes between players and owners over a proposed salary cap for players.

19 Eight suicide bombings leave at least 50 people dead in Baghdad and other Iraqi cities on the Shiah holy day of Ashura.

23 A series of storms has dropped 9.14 inches (232 millimeters) of rain on Los Angeles since February 18, announce officials with the National Weather Service. In the first two weeks of January, Los Angeles County received in excess of 15 inches (381 millimeters) of rain, more than the average rainfall for an entire year. Since July 1, 2004, the beginning of the official water year in California, Los Angeles has received 34 inches (864 millimeters). The torrential rains have triggered mudslides that closed 20 major highways and severely damaged or destroyed more than 100 houses. In Malibu, crews are attempting to carefully dislodge a boulder the size of a house that a mudslide left teetering over the Pacific Coast Highway.

11 A rare strain of HIV, the virus that causes AIDS, has been detected in New York City, announce city health officials. The strain is the first that has been found that is both highly resistant to multiple drug treatments and develops into full-blown AIDS very quickly.

12 Bulgarian-born artist Christo and his wife Jeanne-Claude unveil "The Gates," a $21-million art installation in New York City's Central Park. "The Gates" consists of 7,500 portals hung with saffron-colored fabric arching over 23 miles (37 kilometers) of park pathways.

14 Former Prime Minister of Lebanon Rafik Hariri is assassinated in a car bombing in Beirut, the capital. Hariri, a billionaire who spent millions of his own money rebuilding Lebanon after a long and highly destructive civil war, resigned as prime minister in October 2004 in protest of the influence neighboring Syria wields in Lebanon. Opposition leaders in Lebanon blame the murder on officials in Syria and their allies in the Lebanese government.

14 President George W. Bush asks Congress for $82 billion to support the military intervention in Afghanistan and Iraq. The requested money is in addition to the $2.57 trillion budget Bush submitted to Congress earlier in February.

28 At least 125 people are killed and 140 others are wounded in the deadliest single insurgent attack in Iraq since the fall of Saddam Hussein's regime in April 2003. A suicide bomber detonates an explosive device after slamming his car into a group of some 400 volunteers for the Iraqi National Guard and the local police force in Al Hilah, a primarily Shiah Muslim city some 60 miles (100 kilometers) south of Baghdad, the capital. The explosion sends metal shards through the crowd of job applicants, as well as into women and children shopping at a nearby produce market.

1 The United States Supreme Court abolishes the death penalty for criminals who commit a murder before the age of 18.

1 Five million German workers, 12.1 percent of the work force, were unemployed in January, announces the German Federal Labor Agency, which notes that unemployment in Germany has not been this high since the Great Depression.

2 Alan Greenspan, chairman of the Federal Reserve (the Fed), the nation's central bank, warns the House of Representatives Budget Committee that current federal deficits are "unsustainable," and he urges Congress to reexamine both spending and taxes. Greenspan notes, "Addressing the government's own imbalances will require scrutiny of both spending and taxes."

7 President Bashar al-Assad of Syria and Lebanon's Syrian-backed president, Emile Lahoud, meeting in Damascus, agree that all Syrian troops in Lebanon are to withdraw to the Bekaa Valley in eastern Lebanon by the end of March.

7 Bush administration officials issue a press pass to Garrett M. Graff, editor of the fishbowlDC Weblog. Graff is the first blogger to join the White House press corps.

9 The price of crude oil sets another new high in London, hitting $53.32 a barrel. In New York City, U.S. light crude climbs to $54.85.

10 An explosion triggered by a suicide bomber rips through a funeral tent in the courtyard of a Shiah mosque in the northern Iraqi city of Mosul, killing at least 47 people and wounding some 100 others.

11 The U.S. trade deficit climbed to $58.3 billion in January, the second highest monthly deficit on record, announce Department of Commerce officials. While exports increased by 0.4 percent, to $100.8 billion, imports rose 1.9 percent, to $159.1 billion.

14 Department of Defense auditors have found more than $100 million in questionable costs in a no-bid Halliburton Company contract for delivering fuel in Iraq, reveal members of Congress. The audit disclosed that the Halliburton subsidiary Kellogg Brown & Root Inc. (KBR) spent $27.5 million to transport liquefied gas that was purchased for $82,100. Critics in Congress claim that the Texas conglomerate, once headed by Vice President Dick Cheney, is profiteering on the war in Iraq. The Defense Contract Audit Agency reported in February that the Defense Department resumed paying Halliburton in full, plus performance bonuses, despite the fact that auditors had turned up $1.8 billion in "unsupported costs."

17 Retail gasoline prices soar to a record average of $2.05 a gallon in the United States, reports the American Automobile Association. Economists connect the high prices to high demand for oil in China and India.

18 Republican leaders in the U.S. Senate subpoena Terri Schiavo to appear before the Senate Health Committee on March 28. Schiavo is severely brain-damaged and has been in a vegetative state since 1990. Her husband, Michael Schiavo, has for years waged a court battle with his wife's parents. He contends that she would not want to be kept alive artificially. The parents insist that Schiavo might, some day, get better and should be kept alive. The Senate subpoena blocks physicians from disconnecting a feeding tube, as was ordered by a Florida court.

19 Antiwar demonstrators stage protests in cities throughout the United States and Europe on the eve of the second anniversary of the start of the war in Iraq. According to an Associated Press tally, more than 1,500 members of the U.S. military have died in Iraq since March 20, 2003.

21 President George W. Bush signs legislation that moves jurisdiction in the case of Terri Schiavo from state to federal court. The legislation allows a federal judge to reverse state court rulings.

A right-to-life advocate demonstrates outside the U.S. Supreme Court in March on behalf of Terri Schiavo, a severely brain-damaged woman who was the focus of a highly publicized seven-year legal and political battle. Schiavo died on March 31.

24 The U.S. Supreme Court refuses for the fifth time to hear appeals in the case of Terri Schiavo, the severely brain-damaged woman who on March 18 was disconnected from the feeding tube that has kept her alive. In all, 20 courts have backed the efforts of Michael Schiavo, Terri's husband, to allow his wife to die.

24 The opposition in Kyrgyzstan overruns the presidential palace and is in control of the capital, Bishkek. President Askar Akayev has fled by helicopter.

25 A series of suicide bombings and insurgent attacks leave 21 people dead in Iraq in the last 24 hours.

30 Human activity is degrading Earth at such a rate that the planet's ability to sustain future generations is threatened, report the authors of the Millennium Ecosystem Assessment, a four-year study conducted by 1,300 researchers from 95 countries. The scientists found that 60 percent of the ecosystems on Earth have been changed beyond recognition in the 60 years since the end of World War II.

31 Terri Schiavo, the severely brain-damaged woman who was the focus of a highly publicized seven-year legal and political battle, dies at a Florida hospice.

31 Spy agencies of the U.S. government were "dead wrong" in assessments of the existence of weapons of mass destruction in Iraq prior to the war in 2003, declares the Commission on the Intelligence Capabilities of the United States in its report to President George W. Bush. The authors note that the same agencies appear to know as little about current nuclear threats.

The body of the late Pope John Paul II lies in state in St. Peter's Basilica in the Vatican in Rome on April 4. The funeral on April 8, conducted by Cardinal Joseph Ratzinger, the future Pope Benedict XVI, was the largest for a pope in the nearly 2,000-year history of the Roman Catholic Church.

1 The Zimbabwe political party headed by President Robert G. Mugabe handily retains control of parliament in general elections. A number of opposition leaders and international observers condemn the results as rigged and charge Mugabe with fraud.

2 Pope John Paul II dies at the age of 84 in his apartment in the Vatican in Rome. The first non-Italian pope in more than 400 years, John Paul reigned for 26 years, the third-longest papacy in church history.

4 The University of North Carolina defeats the University of Illinois 75-70 at the Edward Jones Dome in St. Louis, Missouri, to win the 2005 National College Athletic Association basketball championship.

6 Iraq's National Assembly elects a Kurdish leader, Jalal Talabani, as the country's new president.

6 Monaco's Prince Rainier dies at the age of 81. He is succeeded by his 47-year-old son, Prince Albert.

7 Iraq's president and two deputy presidents name Ibrahim al-Jafari, the popular leader of the Daawa party, prime minister, the most powerful position in the new transitional government.

7 As many as 150 Hindu pilgrims are swept into India's Narmada River and drown when floodgates near Dharaji, about 185 miles (300 kilometers) west of Bhopal, are unexpectedly opened.

8 Pope John Paul II is buried in the Vatican Grottoes, a vast crypt below St. Peter's Basilica in Rome, after a funeral in the forecourt of the basilica that was attended by several thousand people, including representatives of all of the world's major religions.

9 Charles, Prince of Wales and heir to the British throne, marries Camilla Parker Bowles in a civil ceremony at the Windsor town Guildhall near Windsor Castle.

10 Tiger Woods takes his fourth Masters title and ninth majors championship by beating Chris DiMarco with a dramatic 15-foot birdie putt on the first playoff hole at the Augusta National Golf Club in Augusta, Georgia.

10 Thousands of Chinese demonstrators stage anti-Japanese protests in Beijing, the capital, for a second day. To the south in Guangdong province, thousands more demonstrate in the commercial city of Shenzhen and burn flags outside the Japanese consulate in Guangzhou, the provincial capital. The protests were triggered by a newly published Japanese junior high school textbook that allegedly glosses over atrocities committed during the Japanese occupation of China from 1931 to 1945.

13 The European Union (EU) parliament votes to allow Bulgaria and Romania to join the EU in 2007. The vote opens the way for an accession treaty to be signed later in April.

15 A fire sweeps through a hotel in central Paris, leaving 22 immigrants from Africa, including 10 children, dead and more than 50 others injured.

19 Cardinal Joseph Ratzinger, a native of Germany, is elected pope on the second day of the conclave of cardinals meeting at the Sistine Chapel at the Vatican in Rome. Ratzinger, who is 78 years old, takes the name Benedict XVI.

20 Prime Minister Silvio Berlusconi resigns after four years of a five-year mandate, ending Italy's longest-serving government since World War II.

20 The president of Ecuador, Lucio Gutierrez, flees the presidential palace in Quito, the capital, after the Congress votes to remove him from office. Vice President Alfredo Palacio is sworn in to replace Gutierrez.

21 Insurgents in Iraq shoot down a civilian helicopter, apparently with a missile, about 12 miles (19 kilometers) north of Baghdad. All 11 people aboard are killed.

22 The glaciers of the Antarctic peninsula are rapidly shrinking, reports a joint team from the British Antarctic Survey (BAS) and U.S. Geological Survey. According to a study published in *Science* magazine, nearly 90 percent of the glaciers moving from the mountains down to the ocean are losing mass.

25 A train carrying almost 600 commuters derails and crashes into an apartment building in Amagasaki, near Osaka, Japan, 255 miles (410 kilometers) west of Tokyo. More than 100 people are killed and at least 450 others are injured.

26 Syria withdraws all troops from Lebanon, crossing the border after a ceremony marking the end of the 29-year deployment. Lebanese troops simultaneously take up positions abandoned by the Syrians.

26 Faure Gnassingbe, candidate of Togo's ruling RPT party and son of the former leader, is declared the winner of the presidential election with 60 percent of the vote.

28 The ivory-billed woodpecker, a bird long thought extinct, has been definitely sighted in the swamp forests of eastern Arkansas, announce scientists from Cornell University. The ivory-bill was last sighted in Louisiana in 1944.

29 A wave of car and roadside bombings in and around Baghdad kills 40 people and wounds some 100 others. At least 12 separate bombs, exploding in carefully timed sequence, rock the capital, killing civilians as well as Iraqi security forces.

1 North Korea test-fires a missile into the Sea of Japan. The test is made just days after U.S. intelligence agents testified before a congressional committee that North Korea had the ability to arm a missile with a nuclear warhead.

4 Astronomers have discovered 12 new moons orbiting Saturn, bringing the total to 46, announces the codiscoverer, Dave Jewitt of the University of Hawaii.

5 The corporate credit rating of the two largest U.S. automakers, General Motors Corporation and Ford Motor Company, is cut to junk status, announces Standard & Poor's Ratings Services.

5 The discovery of fossilized bones of a dinosaur in an evolutionary transition between being carnivorous and vegetarian is announced.

6 British Prime Minister Tony Blair's Labour Party is declared the winner in the May 5 parliamentary elections. With 627 of 646 seats determined, Labour holds 324, the Conservatives have 197, and the Liberal Democrats have 62. Prime Minister Blair is the only Labour leader in British history to have won three elections in a row.

11 Angola's Ministry of Health reports to the World Health Organization that there have been 316 cases of Marburg haemorrhagic fever in Uige Province, the epicenter of the outbreak, as of May 10. The outbreak is the largest on record with a fatality rate of more than 90 percent.

13 The U.S. Department of Defense proposes shutting down 150 military installations in the United States, including 33 major bases.

14 Thousands of Uzbeks are fleeing across the border into Kyrgyzstan in the wake of two days of civil unrest. Rioters in Uzbek villages along the border set fire to the offices of police and tax collectors and take at least one local official hostage. In Andijon, the country's fourth largest city, thousands of people mass on the main square to protest the government's violent crackdown. On May 13, an estimated 500 people were killed and at least 2,000 others wounded when troops entered Andijon and put down an uprising by Islamic militants and people protesting hard economic conditions.

15 The U.S. Secretary of State, Condoleezza Rice, makes a surprise visit to Iraq. She urges the newly formed Shiah-dominated government to seek a political solution to the escalating violence by reaching out to the Sunni minority, particularly in the writing of a constitution.

16 The upsurge of violence set off by the April 28 announcement of the new government continues across Iraq. Over the last 48 hours, police in Baghdad and three other cities discovered the bodies of at least 50 murder victims at various remote sites. All were killed execution style.

19 Canadian Prime Minister Paul Martin's Liberal Party government survives a confidence crisis in the House of Commons by a single vote. An independent member of parliament (MP) votes with the government on an essential budget measure that was *tantamount* (equivalent) to a vote of confidence. The result is a 152-152 tie that is broken by the house speaker, a Liberal.

19 Uzbek government troops reclaim from rebels control of Korasuv, a city of approximately 20,000 people on the border with Kyrgyzstan. The rebels, who had announced their intention of building a strict Islamic state from Korasuv, were taken into custody without bloodshed.

21 Afleet Alex wins the 130th running of the Preakness at Baltimore's Pimlico Race Track by 4¾ lengths having been swerved into and nearly knocked off his feet by front-runner Scrappy T at the top of the stretch.

22 Seven battalions of Iraqi soldiers and police, backed by 2,500 U.S. troops, launch an offensive to clear Baghdad of insurgents.

A car bombing in Baghdad on May 7 was one of dozens of insurgent attacks that left more than 900 people dead in May 2005. Although seven battalions of Iraqi soliders, backed by 2,500 U.S. troops, launched an offensive on May 22 to clear Baghdad, the capital, of insurgents, the suicide and roadside bombing continued unabated.

23 A bipartisan group of 14 U.S. Senators joins in an agreement that allows votes on three appellate court nominees while limiting filibusters to "extraordinary circumstances."

26 President George W. Bush meets with Mahmoud Abbas, president of the Palestinian Authority, in Washington, D.C., and assures Abbas that the United States is committed to a Middle East peace plan that includes the establishment of a Palestinian nation.

28 Iran's hard-line Guardian Council approves legislation, passed by the parliament on May 15, that mandates the development of nuclear technology, including uranium enrichment. The law makes it impossible for Iran's nuclear program to be frozen as the governments of various Western countries have demanded.

30 Vice President Dick Cheney, speaking in a televised interview, declares that Iraq is in "the last throes, if you will, of the insurgency," and that he expects a substantial withdrawal of U.S. troops from Iraq before 2008.

31 President Jacques Chirac of France dismisses Prime Minister Jean-Pierre Raffarin as a result of the decisive rejection by voters on May 29 of a referendum on the constitution for Europe. Dominique de Villepin, a former career diplomat, is to replace Raffarin.

31 *The Washington Post* confirms that former FBI official W. Mark Felt was "Deep Throat," the confidential source who provided the newspaper with information regarding the Watergate scandal that led to the resignation of President Richard M. Nixon.

JUNE

2005

Rooftops in the Lebanese port of Tripoli sport posters of electoral candidates during the fourth and last stage of Lebanon's parliamentary elections on June 19. The elections gave the anti-Syrian alliance, which campaigned for an end to Syrian influence in Lebanon, a 72-seat majority in the parliament.

1 Dutch voters reject the European Union (EU) constitution by a margin of approximately 62 percent to 38 percent.

3 At least 80 U.S. soldiers died in Iraq in May 2005, reports the Associated Press based on figures supplied by the U.S. Department of Defense; 42 U.S. soldiers died in Iraq in May 2004.

3 The president of Bolivia announces a series of radical reforms, including rewriting the constitution, in an attempt to end weeks of violent protests by trade unions and the country's indigenous population.

5 A vaccine to protect monkeys against the Ebola and Marburg viruses has been successfully developed by an international team, announce team scientists. The scientists believe the vaccine could lead to a similar vaccine for human beings or even a cure.

6 The U.S. Supreme Court, in a 6-to-3 decision, determines that federal authorities may prosecute sick people whose physicians have prescribed marijuana for pain management.

9 The Israeli Supreme Court upholds Prime Minister Ariel Sharon's plan to pull out of the Gaza Strip, removing the last obstacle to the formal turnover of Gaza and four West Bank settlements to Palestinian control.

9 The president of Bolivia, Carlos Mesa, resigns with the warning that Bolivians must step back from the brink of civil war. Nevertheless, indigenous people continue to stream by the thousands out of the Andean highlands into La Paz, the capital, essentially blockading the city, where fuel and food are scarce.

10 The chief justice of Bolivia's Supreme Court, Eduardo Rodriguez, is sworn in as president.

13 The U.S. Supreme Court, in a 6-to-3 decision, overturns the Texas conviction of an African American death row inmate on the grounds that prosecutors unfairly stacked the man's jury with whites.

13 A California jury finds Michael Jackson, one of the all-time best-selling recording artists, not guilty on all charges involving child molestation. The verdict caps a highly sensational trial that lasted for more than 14 weeks.

14 Jamaican sprinter Asafa Powell runs 100 meters in 9.77 seconds at the Super Grand Prix meet in Athens, breaking the previous world record of 9.78 seconds set by Tim Montgomery in 2002.

15 Two separate attacks on security forces in and around Baghdad leave at least 33 people dead. At least 900 Iraqis have been killed in the violence that accompanied the installation of the Shiah-dominated government on April 28.

19 Lebanon's anti-Syrian alliance claims victory in the fourth and final round of parliamentary elections upon taking all 28 of the contested seats in the 128-seat parliament. The victory gives the alliance, which campaigned for an end to Syrian influence in Lebanon, a 72-seat majority in parliament.

19 Michael Campbell shoots a 69 to finish a grueling United States Open at North Carolina's Pinehurst #2 at even par, two strokes under Tiger Woods.

21 President George W. Bush meets with Vietnamese Prime Minister Phan Van Khai at the White House in Washington, D.C. The 71-year-old leader is the highest ranking Vietnamese to pay an official visit to an American president since the end of the Vietnam War in 1975.

23 A string of four simultaneously exploding car bombs along a 1-mile (1.6-kilometer) stretch of a main street in central Baghdad leaves at least 17 people dead and some 50 others wounded. A similar wave of simultaneously exploding car bombs killed more than 25 people and wounded 45 others in Baghdad's Shuala district just 12 hours earlier.

23 The United States Supreme Court, in a 5-to-4 decision, rules that local governments can, under certain circumstances, employ the constitutional power of *eminent domain* to seize private property to turn over to private developers. In a case with wide implications, the court decides against a group of homeowners who have resisted plans by city officials in New London, Connecticut, to clear working-class housing along the Thames River for commercial development.

25 Iran's interior ministry declares Mahmoud Ahmadinejad the winner in the second round of presidential elections, which took place on June 24.

27 The U.S. Supreme Court, in two 5-to-4 decisions, rules that displaying the Ten Commandments on government property can, but does not always, violate the Establishment Clause of the First Amendment to the United States Constitution.

27 The price of a barrel of oil closes above $60 on the New York Mercantile Exchange for the first time.

28 The Canadian House of Commons passes legislation legalizing same-sex marriage despite wide opposition from conservative members of Parliament.

28 Enemy fire brings down an American Chinook CH-47 helicopter in the Hindu Kush region of eastern Afghanistan. At least 16 U.S. military personnel are killed in the attack, for which the Taliban claims responsibility.

29 Jewish settlers in Gaza who oppose the Israeli pullout block the main highway into Jerusalem, disrupting traffic, as part of a planned nationwide protest. Police use water cannons to disperse the demonstrators.

1 Associate Justice Sandra Day O'Connor announces her resignation from the U.S. Supreme Court. During her 24 years on the bench, O'Connor often played a pivotal role as a moderate swinging back and forth between the court's conservatives and liberals.

3 Roger Federer of Switzerland wins his third consecutive men's singles title at Wimbledon, defeating Andy Roddick of the United States. On July 2, Venus Williams of the United States captured a third women's singles championship, beating Lindsay Davenport, also of the United States.

4 NASA's Deep Impact space probe collides with Tempel 1, a comet about half the size of Manhattan island. Launched on January 12 from Cape Canaveral, Florida, Deep Impact traveled 268 million miles (431 million kilometers) to reach Tempel 1.

4 Human settlers arrived in North America at least 25,000 to 30,000 years earlier than previously believed, announces a team of British and Mexican scientists. The archaeologists reached this conclusion after conducting carbon dating and optically stimulated luminescence dating tests on 269 human footprints preserved by volcanic ash in Mexico.

4 A powerful antenna connected to a robotic probe named Spirit, which landed on Mars on January 3, is activated and begins to beam images to Earth.

6 London is chosen to host the 2012 Olympic Games.

6 Leaders of the Group of Eight (G8) nations, including U.S. President George W. Bush and British Prime Minister Tony Blair, arrive in Scotland for three days of discussions.

6 A federal judge orders *New York Times* reporter Judith Miller jailed after she refuses to cooperate in an investigation of who leaked to the press the name of a covert official with the Central Intelligence Agency. Although Judith Miller never filed an article on the subject, she is jailed for refusing to testify before a grand jury as to who had revealed that Valerie Plame was a CIA operative.

7 Terrorists detonate four bombs in central London at the height of the morning rush hour. Three of the explosions, which occur at 50-second intervals, rip apart Underground trains crowded with commuters. The fourth bomb blows the top deck off a packed double decker bus, killing 13 people. In all, the attacks leave more than 50 people dead and at least 700 others injured, many of them seriously. A terrorist group contending to be linked to the al-Qa`ida network claims responsibility. The attacks are made on the opening morning of a Group of Eight meeting of world leaders in Scotland.

7 The al-Qa`ida terrorist network in Iraq announces on a Web site that Egypt's top envoy in Iraq has been murdered. The envoy was abducted on a Baghdad street on July 2.

7 Philippine President Gloria Macapagal-Arroyo dismisses her entire Cabinet in the midst of a scandal that has triggered widespread calls for her resignation.

10 Hurricane Dennis comes ashore near Santa Rosa Island, Florida, just east of Pensacola, with winds as high as 130 miles (210 kilometers) per hour, and heads northwest into Alabama.

13 British authorities believe the four bombings in central London on July 7 were carried out by suicide bombers, announces British Home Secretary Charles Clarke, who also reveals that police have identified all four attackers.

16 A suicide bomber detonates a body belt of explosives underneath a propane fuel tanker in the town of Mussayyib, south of Baghdad, setting off an enormous explosion that kills at least 90 people and wounds some 150 others.

17 Tiger Woods wins his second British Open at St. Andrews, Scotland.

A victim of terrorist attacks on London's Underground transportation system on July 7 is led from the Edgware Road station wearing a special dressing for burns. British police later determined that the attacks, which left more than 50 people dead, had been four suicide bombings carried out by Islamic militants who were citizens of the United Kingdom.

18 Hurricane Emily hits Mexico's Caribbean coast with winds of 130 miles (210 kilometers) per hour.

19 President George W. Bush nominates John G. Roberts, Jr., a federal appeals court judge, to fill the vacancy on the U.S. Supreme Court created by the retirement of Justice Sandra Day O'Connor.

21 Four minor explosions on three London Underground trains and on a surface bus trigger panic among commuters and force the evacuation of sections of the city's public transportation system.

24 American cyclist Lance Armstrong triumphantly enters Paris on the ceremonial final stage of his unprecedented seventh consecutive victory in the Tour de France, one of the most prestigious of international sporting events.

25 The Teamsters Union and a major service employees union pull out of the AFL-CIO at the labor federation's annual meeting being held in Chicago.

26 NASA launches its first manned space mission in more than two and one-half years. Space shuttle Discovery blasts off from the Kennedy Space Center in Cape Canaveral, Florida, for a 12-day flight to resupply the International Space Station.

29 A team of astronomers at the California Institute of Technology announces the discovery of what may be a 10th planet orbiting the sun. The unnamed object is about twice the size of Pluto.

Residents of New Orleans struggle through floodwaters in the wake of Hurricane Katrina on August 29. A storm surge, driven by the hurricane's winds, breached levees, leaving much of the low-lying city under as much as 20 feet (6.1 meters) of highly polluted floodwater.

1 King Fahd of Saudi Arabia dies at the age of 84. He became Saudi Arabia's ruler in 1982. His half-brother, Crown Prince Abdullah, is named as King Fahd's successor.

1 President George W. Bush appoints John Bolton as U.S. ambassador to the United Nations without the consent of the U.S. Senate. Under the terms of a so-called "recess appointment," Bolton will hold office until the next new session of Congress, which begins in 2007.

2 Unusually heavy monsoon rains continue to cripple Mumbai, India's financial capital. At least 1,000 people have died in the city and surrounding state of Maharashtra in the last week.

2 President George W. Bush signs the Central American Free Trade Agreement (CAFTA), a free-trade pact between the United States and six Latin American countries.

5 The U.S. economy added 207,000 jobs in July, announce officials with the U.S. Department of Labor.

6 Three U.S. soldiers are killed in Iraq, bringing to 29 the number of Americans killed in combat during the first week of August.

7 Multinational talks between North Korea, China, Japan, South Korea, Russia, and the United States collapse. North Korea's insistence that it has the right to build light-water nuclear reactors halts yet another round of discussions on eliminating nuclear weapons on the Korean Peninsula.

8 President George W. Bush signs into law an energy bill that has been long sought by his administration. Critics claim the bill provides energy companies with billions of dollars in tax subsidies while doing little to ease gas prices or to lower reliance on foreign oil. Supporters counter that the energy bill refocuses the nation's energy priorities while promoting alternative and cleaner sources of energy.

8 The biblical Pool of Siloam, a freshwater reservoir that was a major gathering place for ancient pilgrims, is found in the Old City of Jerusalem, announce archaeologists. According to the Gospel of John, the pool was the site where Jesus cured a man blind from birth.

9 The space shuttle Discovery safely returns to Earth, completing NASA's first manned shuttle flight in more than two and one-half years.

10 Oil prices climb to $65 a barrel, a rise of 14 percent in three weeks. Gasoline prices averaged $2.37 a gallon during the first week of August, up 49 cents from the same period in 2004.

11 Texas has become the fourth state of the Union to have a nonwhite majority, with 50.2 percent of the population either nonwhite Hispanic or African American, announces the U.S. Census Bureau.

14 All 121 people aboard a Helios Airways jet enroute from Larnaca, Cyprus, to Athens are killed when the plane suffers a loss of cabin pressure and slams into a mountain north of the Greek capital.

15 Members of the Israeli army distribute eviction notices to approximately 4,500 Jewish settlers in the Gaza Strip who defied a government order to leave their settlements by midnight on August 14. The evacuation notice gives the settlers an additional 48 hours to leave before they will be forcibly removed.

17 At least 43 people are killed and 88 others are injured when insurgents

detonate three car bombs in the center of Baghdad.

17 Israeli police and soldiers evict Jewish settlers who defied a government order to leave their settlements by midnight on August 14.

20 Northwest Airlines, the fourth largest U.S. carrier, replaces striking employees with approximately 1,900 contract workers and continues to maintain most scheduled flights.

27 Authorities in Austria, Bulgaria, Germany, Romania, and Switzerland report that flooding brought on by days of heavy rains has caused the deaths of more than 70 people.

28 The committee drafting Iraq's new constitution completes the charter and presents it to the National Assembly but without the endorsement of Sunni Arabs. The constitution is to be submitted to the Iraqi people in a nationwide referendum scheduled for October 15.

29 Hurricane Katrina makes landfall on the Gulf Coast and pummels Alabama, Mississippi, and southeastern Louisiana with wind gusts of 127 miles (204 kilometers) per hour.

29 Household income in the United States declined for a record fifth consecutive year in 2004, announces the U.S. Bureau of the Census.

29 The price of crude oil climbs to more than $70 a barrel on U.S. markets as Hurricane Katrina shuts down an estimated 1 million barrels per day of refining capacity in the Gulf of Mexico.

30 The governor of Louisiana, Kathleen Blanco, orders the complete evacuation of New Orleans. The failure of levees as a result of Hurricane Katrina has left at least 80 percent of the city under as much as 20 feet (6.1 meters) of water. The mayor of New Orleans, Ray Nagin, warns that it could be months before residents are allowed to return.

31 National Guard troops begin evacuating flood victims from the Superdome in New Orleans. As the first evacuees are loaded into buses for the Astrodome in Houston, 350 miles (563 kilometers) to the southwest, armed gang members roam downtown streets, looting stores.

SEPTEMBER

2005

1 The evacuation of people who had sought refuge in the Superdome in New Orleans is called off after snipers fire at a military helicopter airlifting the sick and injured to safety. Officials estimate that between 20,000 and 30,000 people may still be in the sports arena, which has not had electric power or running water for three days.

1 The mayor of New Orleans, Ray Nagin, issues a "desperate SOS" for assistance from state and federal authorities to help secure city streets, which are largely in the control of armed gangs. When a platoon of more than 85 police officers attempted to enter the New Orleans Convention Center, where thousands of evacuees are holed up, the police were forced into retreat by angry mobs outside the river front center.

2 A convoy of 1,200 National Guard troops arrives in New Orleans four days after the city was devastated by a hurricane and flooding. The troops find people freely looting businesses and houses, fires burning out of control, and corpses floating in polluted floodwaters. Officials estimate that tens of thousands of people still need to be evacuated.

4 Navy helicopters begin airlifting evacuees from the New Orleans Convention Center to the airport, from which they will be flown to Texas. While the convention center provided shelter to 15,000 evacuees, it became synonymous with squalor and violence.

5 The Army Corp of Engineers closes breaches in two New Orleans levees and begins pumping water out of the city and into Lake Pontchartrain.

5 Officials in New Orleans report that at least 300 of the city's 1,500-person police force have dropped out of the daily lineup. Two officers are known to have committed suicide.

5 The price of gasoline hits an average of $3.07 a gallon at stations across the United States.

7 The economic impact of Hurricane Katrina could exceed $100 billion and cost the U.S. economy an estimated 400,000 jobs through 2005, announces the Congressional Budget Office. Cost estimates for relief and recovery in Louisiana, Mississippi, and Alabama stand at $150 billion, which economists warn will push the federal budget deficit higher.

8 Hurricane Katrina will cost U.S. farmers an estimated $2 billion, including $500 million in higher fuel and energy prices, announces the American Farm Bureau Federation. The hurricane substantially damaged the port of New Orleans, through which the majority of U.S. grain exports flow, as well as other waterways and grain-handling facilities. Hundreds of barges carrying grain are backing up on the Mississippi River.

9 New Orleans police and federal law enforcement agents begin confiscating guns from civilians in preparation of the forced evacuation of people who have refused to leave. Officials estimate that several thousand residents may still remain. Police Superintendent P. Edwin Compass III notes that "individuals are at risk of dying" from water-borne diseases or fires. Although the Army Corps of Engineers has 37 of the city's 174 pumps up and running, neighborhoods in the northern and eastern parts of the city remain under 10 feet (3 meters) of water.

9 The U.S. Court of Appeals for the 4th Circuit rules that the president of the United States has the authority to indefinitely detain a U.S. citizen captured on U.S. soil in the absence of criminal charges. The three-judge panel declares that such authority is vital for the protection of the nation from terrorist attack. The decision is made in the case of Jose Padilla, a U.S. citizen who was arrested in Chicago in 2002 and designated an "enemy combatant" by President George W. Bush. The Bush administration claims that Padilla is an al-Qa`ida trained terrorist who planned to blow up apartment buildings in the United States.

A Bay St. Louis, Mississippi, resident points to a sign expressing local disgust with Federal Emergency Management Agency (FEMA) assistance to hurricane victims in September. Speaking on the floor of the U.S. Senate on September 8, Senator Mary Landrieu (D., Louisiana) characterized FEMA's response to the Hurricane Katrina disaster as "incompetent and insulting."

11 The government of Israel declares an end to military rule in the Gaza Strip and lowers the Israeli flag after 38 years of occupation.

12 President George W. Bush tours New Orleans two weeks after Katrina slammed into the Gulf Coast. The president, who has been the focus of criticism for the federal government's slow response to the disaster, is driven through neighborhoods still flooded with polluted water. Lieutenant General Russel Honore, head of the military recovery program in New Orleans, tells the president that while the death toll is unknown, it appears to be lower than once feared.

24 Hurricane Rita, a Category 3 storm, makes landfall along the Louisiana-Texas border. Winds of 120 miles (193 kilometers) per hour and a 15-foot (4.5-meter) storm surge level many houses and fell hundreds of trees, knocking out electric power in more than 1.5 million households.

27 Electrical power is restored to portions of New Orleans, including the French Quarter and the Central Business District. Pumps continue draining the Ninth Ward, which reflooded when heavy rain preceding Hurricane Rita fractured a patched levee along the Industrial Canal.

29 John Glover Roberts, Jr., is confirmed as chief justice of the U.S. Supreme Court, replacing William H. Rehnquist who died on Sept. 3. The Senate votes 78 to 22 in support of the 50-year-old U.S. court of appeals judge, who is sworn in at a White House ceremony.

An Indian woman turns away from the ruins of her house destroyed by an earthquake on October 8 that left nearly 75,000 people dead in Pakistan and India and the areas of Kashmir controlled by the two countries. United Nations officials estimated that the 7.6-magnitude earthquake left more than 3 million people homeless.

2 Twenty elderly sightseers drown when a small tour boat capsizes and sinks on Lake George in upstate New York.

4 Hurricane Stan slams into Mexico's Gulf Coast with winds of 80 miles (130 kilometers) per hour. Before hitting Mexico, the hurricane spawned storms that left more than 650 people dead in Guatemala.

5 The explosion of a massive bomb at the entrance of a Shiah mosque in the Iraqi city of Hillah, south of Baghdad, kills at least 35 people and leaves some 95 others wounded. The attack is made during a funeral for the victim of a separate suicide attack. Ten people were killed in a bomb attack in Hillah on September 30.

6 The flu pandemic that killed 50 million people worldwide in 1918 and 1919 has been found to be a bird flu that jumped directly to humans, announces the U.S. Centers for Disease Control and Prevention. Scientists found that the 1918 virus shares genetic mutations with the bird flu virus currently in circulation.

8 A 7.6-magnitude earthquake centered in the Hindu Kush Mountains 60 miles (95 kilometers) north of Pakistan's capital, Islamabad, causes massive damage in Indian- and Pakistan-controlled Kashmir. The death toll in India is at least 1,400. In Pakistan, more than 73,000 people are dead in what appears to be the worst natural disaster in that nation's history.

8 Nineteen U.S. soldiers were killed in Iraq during the week of October 2, announce U.S. military officials in Iraq.

11 A wave of insurgent attacks leaves dozens of civilians dead in Iraq. In the most lethal of the assaults, a suicide bomber kills at least 30 people in a market in Tall Afar, in northwest Iraq. In Baghdad, insurgents kill at least 14 people in 9 separate attacks.

14 Insurgents blow up a tower on the main power line into Baghdad from the north, cutting power in about 70 percent of the city on the eve of the constitutional referendum. The water is also off in some areas of the capital because pumps are not working.

15 Iraqis go to the polls to vote in a referendum to ratify the draft constitution. According to the head of the election commission, turnout is running at more than 60 percent of registered voters.

20 The U.S. House of Representatives passes legislation, previously passed by the Senate, that shields manufacturers and dealers of firearms from liability lawsuits. The legislation is designed to end lawsuits alleging that manufacturers and dealers are liable for negligence when guns are used in the execution of crimes. The bill has been the primary legislative priority of the National Rifle Association for several years.

21 Hurricane Wilma makes landfall on the Yucatán Peninsula after slamming into the resort island of Cozumel with sustained winds approaching 150 miles (240 kilometers) per hour.

24 Hurricane Wilma sweeps across Florida with winds of 125 miles (200 kilometers) per hour. Some 6 million households are without electricity in the largest blackout in state history. Storm damage in Ft. Lauderdale and other Atlantic Coast cities is believed to be the worst in nearly 50 years. Wilma is the 8th hurricane to strike Florida in 15 months.

24 Russia's population has declined from an estimated 149 million in 1995 to 143 million in 2005, announces the Russian federal statistics agency. The population dropped by more than 500,000 in the first eight months of 2005, during which more abortions were registered than live births. Officials blame the decline on alcoholism, poverty, and emigration.

25 The death toll of U.S. soldiers in Iraq passes 2,000. The second 1,000 U.S. troops were killed in 14 months, compared with 18 months for the first 1,000 dead. Marines account for one-third of the second 1,000 deaths, though Marines represent less than 20 percent of the total number of U.S. forces in Iraq. About 30 percent of the second 1,000 deaths were members of the National Guard and Reserve units. Iraq Body Count, a private, nonprofit organization, estimates that 26,000 to 30,000 Iraqi civilians, including police, have been killed since the war was launched in March 2003.

25 Iraqi voters, by a margin of more than 78 percent, endorsed the new constitution in the October 15 referendum, announce officials with the Independent Electoral Commission in Iraq.

26 The Chicago White Sox beat the Astros 1-0 in Houston to claim the 2005 World Series championship in a 4-game sweep. The Sox last won a World Series in 1917.

28 The U.S. gross domestic product (GDP) rose at an annual rate of 3.8 percent from July to September, compared with a 3.3-percent increase in the second quarter of 2005, reports the U.S. Department of Commerce. Personal consumption was up 3.9 percent. The GDP price index, a measure of inflation, increased 3.1 percent in the third quarter, up from 2.6 percent in the second quarter.

30 French police arrest a number of young men in a Paris suburb after a night of rioting. Throwing gasoline bombs known as Molotov cocktails, the youths set at least 15 cars on fire. The suburb, Clichy-sous-Bois, has a large population of immigrants, primarily from North Africa.

31 President George W. Bush nominates Samuel Alito, a federal appeals court judge, for the U.S. Supreme Court. The president's first choice for the vacancy, Harriet Miers, withdrew in the face of mounting criticism that she lacked the judicial and constitutional experience requisite for a position on the court.

31 Six U.S. soldiers are killed in Iraq in two attacks with improvised explosive devices on military convoys south and north of Baghdad, the capital. Their deaths bring to 92 the total number of U.S. forces killed in Iraq in October.

31

1 The government of Syria grants permission to a United Nations inquiry team to question relatives of Syria's president, Bashar al-Assad, in connection with the assassination of former Lebanese Prime Minister Rafik Hariri. An opponent of Syrian domination of Lebanon, Hariri was murdered in February in a car bombing in Lebanon's capital, Beirut.

1 Democrats in the U.S. Senate invoke a little-used procedural rule to force the Republican majority into a rare closed-door session. Infuriating the Republicans, the Democrats nevertheless extract a promise from the majority leaders to speed up an inquiry into how the administration of President George W. Bush handled Central Intelligence Agency reports in its rationale for the war in Iraq in 2003. The Democrats demand a final report on prewar intelligence from the Senate Intelligence Committee, which they claim has been purposely delayed for nearly a year.

4 Thousands of protesters chanting "Get out Bush" fill the streets of Mar del Plata, the Argentine resort where U.S. President George W. Bush is meeting with 33 Central and South American leaders to establish a free-trade zone between North and South America. Some Latin American economists believe that U.S.-backed free-market policies will push millions of people, particularly farmers, into poverty.

4 Rioting by Muslim youths in suburbs north of Paris spreads to cities around France. In the town of Trappes, near Versailles, 27 buses are destroyed when a bus depot is set on fire. In Aulnay-sous-Bois, a predominately Muslim suburb north of Paris, more than 400 cars are set on fire and a disabled person is badly burned in an attack on a city bus.

5 More than 800 cars are torched in a ninth night of violence in Arab communities in cities across France. The rioting, which began in poor Paris suburbs, has spread to Lille, Marseille, Nice, and Toulouse.

5 American forces, backed by Iraqi troops, launch a major assault along the Syrian border on the al-Qa`ida in Iraq terrorist organization. At least 2,500 U.S. Marines and 1,000 Iraqi soldiers are deployed in western Anbar province in Operation Steel Curtain. According to U.S. military intelligence, al-Qa`ida in Iraq smuggles foreign fighters, money, and equipment across the border near the town of Qaim, which is approximately 200 miles (320 kilometers), west of Baghdad.

6 A tornado cuts through parts of Evansville, Indiana, and nearby Newburgh, Indiana, killing 24 people. Most of the victims lived in a trailer park that was largely destroyed by the high winds.

21 Israel's prime minister, Ariel Sharon, quits the Likud Party, which he helped found, and forms Kadima (*forward* in Hebrew), a centrist party. Political experts note that the move may allow Sharon to escape the hard-line right-wing Likud elements that opposed his pullout of the Gaza Strip and plans for the West Bank.

22 General Motors (GM) Corporation of Detroit, Michigan, announces plans to cut 30,000 jobs in North America. Struggling to stem huge losses, GM will close nine assembly, stamping, and powertrain engine-maker plants.

22 Angela Merkel, head of the Christian Democrats, is sworn in as Germany's first woman chancellor at the Bundestag, the parliament, in Berlin. Merkel leads a grand coalition government.

25 An ice core from Antarctica, drilled to a depth of nearly 2 miles (3.2 kilometers), reveals that the greenhouse gases carbon dioxide and methane are currently at higher levels than they have been in the last 650,000 years, announces Thomas Stocker, a climatologist at the University of Bern in Switzerland. According to Stocker, carbon dioxide levels are 27 percent higher than they have been in the last 650,000 years, and methane levels are 130 percent higher.

A Jordanian soldier stands guard during an antiterrorism rally in Amman, capital of Jordan, on November 18. Tens of thousands of Jordanians demonstrated their anger at Abu Musab al-Zarqawi, leader of the so-called al-Qa`ida in Iraq terrorist group. Zarqawi, who is Jordanian, claimed responsibility for bombings in three American-owned Amman hotels on November 9 that killed at least 56 people, including guests at a Muslim wedding.

26 The Rafah border crossing between Gaza and Egypt reopens under the control of Palestinian border guards. Hundreds of Palestinians cross into Egypt through the gateway, which international affairs experts describe as vital to the economy of the Gaza Strip. Israel held the Rafah crossing for nearly 40 years.

29 Canadian Prime Minister Paul Martin announces that Canadians will go to the polls on Jan. 23, 2006, to elect a new Parliament. The announcement is made one day after his government lost a no-confidence vote in the lower house. Wounded by scandal, Martin was brought down after only 17 months in power when all three opposition parties united against his Liberal Party.

29 The price of gold surges to $500 an ounce on London markets, its highest price since 1983.

30 Former Israeli Prime Minister Shimon Peres announces that he is leaving the Labor Party to back Israeli Prime Minister Ariel Sharon's new centrist Kadima party ahead of the general election, which is scheduled for March 2006. "It matters not to whom you belong," he notes, "but where you are going. You have to lead the country to peace. On that matter, I think Sharon is taking the right step."

33

New York City commuters cross the Brooklyn Bridge on their long walks home on December 20. A strike by the city's 33,000 transit workers shut down the bus and subway systems for three days at the height of the Christmas shopping season, costing New York City businesses $1 billion in revenue.

2 The U.S. economy added 215,000 new jobs in November, announces the U.S. Department of Labor. Unemployment remained steady at 5 percent.

2 Tropical storm Epsilon strengthens into a hurricane in the Atlantic Ocean with maximum sustained winds of 75 miles (120 kilometers) per hour. A record 14th hurricane of the 2005 season, Epsilon is centered about 955 miles (1,530 kilometers) east of Bermuda. The Atlantic hurricane season, which began on June 1, officially ended on November 30. Epsilon is only the fifth December hurricane recorded in more than 120 years, according to the National Weather Service.

11 An enormous explosion sets off a massive fire and a chain reaction of secondary explosions at the Buncefield oil depot, which is one of the largest fuel depots in the United Kingdom. Smoke from the fire blackens the skies as far away as France.

14 The president of Iran, Mahmoud Ahmadinejad, declares that the Holocaust, the genocide of European Jews carried out by the Nazi Germans during World War II, is a myth. In a television address, Ahmadinejad states that the myth was created as a rationale for establishing Israel. In October, Ahmadinejad kindled international outrage by declaring that Israel should be "wiped off the map."

15 Iraqis turn out in large numbers to vote in parliamentary elections for their first full-term government since the United States deposed Saddam Hussein in 2003. Approximately 150,000 Iraqi soldiers and police officers, backed by U.S. soldiers, are on patrol across the country to maintain order and inhibit insurgent attacks. Some 6,655 candidates, representing 307 parties and 19 coalitions, registered for the ballot.

16 Allegations that President George W. Bush authorized security agents to spy on people inside the United States without obtaining a court order spark a storm of controversy in the U.S. Senate. Senator John McCain (R., Arizona) demands an explanation, and Senator Arlen Specter (R., Pennsylvania), chair of the Senate Judiciary Committee, states "there is no doubt that this is inappropriate," noting that federal law requires a secret court—the Foreign Intelligence Surveillance Court—to issue a warrant before intelligence officers can conduct surveillance on U.S. soil.

17 President George W. Bush acknowledges during a televised address that he had ordered the National Security Agency to conduct electronic surveillance of citizens within the United States without first obtaining warrants, and he vows that he will continue to do so because it is "a vital tool in our war against the terrorists." According to the president, only "people with known links to al-Qa'ida and related terrorist organizations" have been monitored.

20 More than 33,000 transit workers go on strike in New York City, shutting down the city's subway and bus services. An estimated 7 million people a day use the New York City subway system, which is the world's most extensive.

20 A federal judge in Harrisburg, Pennsylvania, rules that a public school district cannot require the inclusion of "intelligent design" in biology classes as an alternative to evolution. Proponents of intelligent design claim that biological life is so complex that it must have been created by an intelligent source. Federal District Judge John E. Jones III rules that the Dover, Pennsylvania, school board violated the U.S. Constitution when it ordered high school biology teachers to read to students a statement that cast doubt on the validity of evolution and offered "intelligent design" as an alternative explanation on the origins of life. Judge Jones notes the school board's policy order violated the establishment clause of the First Amendment of the Constitution by promoting a religious purpose in a public school.

21 Vice President Dick Cheney, as president of the Senate, breaks a 50-to-50 tie to pass a $39.7-billion, five-year budget-cutting measure, which Republicans hail as evidence of their determination to control federal spending. The legislation will allow states to impose new fees on Medicaid recipients, cut federal child-support enforcement funds, impose new work requirements on state welfare programs, fix interest rates on student loans at 6.8 percent, and cut certain agricultural crop subsidies.

22 The U.S. Congress renews for five weeks 16 controversial provisions of the USA Patriot Act, which were set to expire on December 31. A number of civil rights groups and other organizations oppose making permanent the 16 provisions, which President George W. Bush describes as essential to keeping the country safe from terrorist attack.

23 The U.S. government has secretly monitored hundreds of Muslim sites in the United States since the terrorist attacks on Sept. 11, 2001, confirms a spokesperson for the U.S. Department of Justice. Some of the mosques and private properties were checked for radiation levels, amid fears that terrorists might obtain nuclear weapons. The searches were carried out without warrants as part of a program that President George W. Bush defends as necessary to protect the country from terrorist attacks.

26 A wave of attacks in Baghdad and other Iraqi cities on security forces leaves at least 24 people, including a U.S. soldier, dead.

27 Wildfires, driven by 40-mile- (65-kilometer-) per-hour winds, race across thousands of acres of Texas and Oklahoma grasslands that are dried out by severe drought. At least 5 people are killed, and nearly 200 buildings, primarily houses, are destroyed.

29 The number of U.S. soldiers killed in Iraq since the war began in March 2003 stands at 2,175, announces the U.S. Department of Defense; 15,955 U.S. soldiers have been wounded in action.

2005 UPDATE

The major events of 2005 are summarized in more than 250 alphabetically arranged articles, from "Afghanistan" to "Zoos." Included are Special Reports that offer an in-depth look at subjects ranging from identity theft to social security. The Special Reports are found on the following pages.

SPECIAL REPORTS

126 CRIME: **Identity Theft—The New Face of Crime**
148 DEATHS: **Pope John Paul II (1920-2005)**
158 DISASTERS: **The Second Battle of New Orleans**
238 LITERATURE: **The Graphic Novel—Drawing a New Audience**
294 PHYSICS: **1905—Einstein's Miracle Year**
316 RUSSIA: **Russia in the Post-Soviet World**
334 SOCIAL SECURITY: **Benefit of Doubt—How Secure Are American Entitlements?**
394 UNITED STATES, PRESIDENT OF THE: **Preserving Legacies**

FOCUS ON

49 ARCHITECTURE: **Spectacular new museums**
68 AUTOMOBILE: **2006 Models**
194 GERMANY: **Holocaust memorial**
212 IRAQ: **The war in 2005**
216 ISRAEL: **Israel pulls out of Gaza**
260 MOTION PICTURES: **Academy Awards**
348 SPACE EXPLORATION: **New Horizons in Space**
410 WEATHER: **Natural Disasters of 2005**

PORTRAITS

202 HUMAN RIGHTS: **Rosa Parks**
236 LITERATURE: **Saul Bellow**
250 MAGAZINE: **John H. Johnson**
366 TELEVISION: **Johnny Carson**
373 THEATER: **Arthur Miller**
374 THEATER: **August Wilson**

Afghanistan, on Sept. 18, 2005, held its first parliamentary elections in more than 35 tumultuous years as it moved from war and repression toward democracy. Islamic conservatives and former warlords won a strong position in the lower house. Members were sworn in on December 19.

Parliamentary elections, postponed twice since June 2004 due to continuing conflict in many parts of the country, were a key step in organizing a popular government. Hamid Karzai had been elected president in October 2004 in the first nationwide polling since a Communist seizure of power in 1978 plunged Afghanistan into decades of warfare. The Communists lost power in 1992. Later, a fundamentalist Islamic group called the Taliban ruled the country and sheltered the al-Qa`ida terrorist movement. The Taliban was ousted in 2001 by Afghan forces with help from the United States and other Western countries.

In the parliamentary elections, some 2,800 candidates contested 249 seats in the lower house, while 3,000 others competed for 34 provincial assemblies. Political parties were effectively banned. Many of the candidates had been associated with Communist and Taliban rule, and others were local warlords. An Elections Complaints Commission barred 21 candidates still linked with armed militias.

The election campaign was violent. Taliban elements attacked voter registration centers, killing poll workers and more than 1,000 people who had registered to vote. On election day, militants attacked several of the 26,000 voting stations. Only about half of registered voters actually cast ballots. Observers from both the United Nations (UN)-affiliated Joint Election Management Board and the European Union reported significant cases of election fraud. Ballot boxes from about 1,000 voting stations came under suspicion.

Election results announced in late October showed that parliament's lower house, known as the Wolesi Jirga, would be dominated by warlords, drug lords, and conservative Muslim leaders. Female candidates were guaranteed 25 percent (about 63) of the 249 seats under new election rules; women were elected to 68 seats.

Many opponents of Karzai were elected, but some 50 educated professionals who won seats were expected to support the president. Observers estimated that the professionals, joined by others, would provide Karzai with the support of about a third of the Wolesi Jirga, while a third would oppose him, and a third would be nonaligned.

Provincial councils were also elected on September 18, but district council elections were postponed indefinitely. The Meshrano Jirga, the upper house of parliament, was supposed to draw a third of its members from provincial councils and a third from district councils, with the president appointing the final third "from among experts and experienced personalities." The Afghan Cabinet decided to appoint 34 temporary representatives to district council seats in the Meshrano Jirga.

Violence. The heaviest fighting in Afghanistan since the Taliban was defeated in 2001 occurred during 2005 in the south and east. Taliban elements seemed to have regrouped to oppose foreign, especially U.S., influence.

Guerrillas believed to be members of the Taliban attacked government outposts, aid workers, and workers trying to rebuild highways and other infrastructure destroyed in decades of warfare. Troops from the United States and European members of the North Atlantic Treaty Organization (NATO) worked with Afghan government forces to oppose the guerrillas. The United Nations Security Council on September 13 extended the NATO-led multinational force of nearly 10,000 troops in Afghanistan for another year. The United States had almost 20,000 troops stationed there.

A media report of the desecration of a Qur'an, the Islamic holy book, by U.S. troops at a military prison at Guantanamo Bay Naval Station in Cuba caused widespread anti-American demonstrations in Afghanistan in May. Several protesters died as police tried to control rioting.

American forces suffered their greatest loss since entering Afghanistan in 2001 when Afghan insurgents shot down an Army helicopter near Ghazni, 80 miles (130 kilometers) south of Kabul, the capital, on April 6, 2005, killing 18 soldiers. By late 2005, U.S. forces had suffered some 90 deaths in Afghanistan during 2005.

Opium. Afghanistan was estimated by international narcotics specialists to have produced in 2004 about 87 percent of the world's supply of opium and its derivative, heroin. A UN official announced in summer 2005 that efforts by the Afghan government, using foreign aid, to crack down on the growing of opium poppies had reduced the area under cultivation by 21 percent. However, the opium yield declined only 2 percent, due to heavy rains after years of drought.

Some poppy farmers fought government efforts to eradicate their crops. A U.S. report in May claimed that the government program was ineffective, partly because Karzai "has been unwilling to assert strong leadership." Visiting the United States, Karzai asserted that his government had worked hard on the problem. He blamed Western countries for failing to deliver economic aid to help farmers survive without poppy income.

■ Henry S. Bradsher

See also **Asia; Disasters; Islam; Terrorism.**

AFRICA

Nigerian President Olusegun Obasanjo called for massive financial aid from wealthy Western nations to alleviate African poverty in a speech he delivered to the fourth summit of the African Union (AU), convened at Syrte, Libya, in early July 2005. Olusegun's message was sharply countered by that of Libyan President Muammar Muhammad al-Qadhafi, host of the summit, who admonished the African leaders not to go "begging" to Western nations. Established in July 2002, the AU is an alliance of 53 African countries that promotes economic and political unity on the continent.

Immediately after the AU summit, G8 leaders—a group of eight countries with advanced industrialized economies—met for a summit in Gleneagles, Scotland. The leaders agreed to double aid to developing countries to $50 billion a year by 2010 and to wipe out the $40 billion owed by the world's 18 poorest nations, 14 of them in Africa. Eventually, as many as 20 other countries—the majority of them African—could qualify for similar debt cancellation, bringing the total projected debt relief to $55 billion. Analysts predicted that most eligible African nations would prove willing to accept Western aid and debt relief despite Qadhafi's warning.

The AU increased the size of its force of peacekeepers to 2,500 in the troubled Darfur region of western Sudan by August 2005. The peacekeepers were charged with protecting military observer teams monitoring an official ceasefire between the Sudanese government and Darfur rebel groups.

NEPAD. At the April summit of the New Partnership for Africa's Development (NEPAD) in Sharm el-Sheikh, Egypt, African leaders urged wealthy donor nations to double contributions to NEPAD from the 2005 level of about $20 billion. NEPAD is an agreement initiated in 2002 in which African countries promised to embrace human rights and the rule of law in return for international financial assistance. In February 2004, four African countries had been chosen for "peer reviews"—NEPAD's mechanism by which African nations monitor each other's compliance with principles of good governance. Only two of the four countries, Ghana and Rwanda, complied fully with their peer review commitments and submitted reports in 2005. Kenya and Mauritius, the other two countries, failed to meet their NEPAD commitments. International affairs and finance experts questioned whether NEPAD partners among the developed nations would continue to fund the program if African nations failed to live up to NEPAD's founding principles.

Africa's orphans. The United Nations Children's Fund (UNICEF) marked the annual Day of the African Child on June 16 by highlighting the plight of as many as 40 million orphans in Africa, a figure that could rise to 50 million by 2010, according to Douglas Webb, UNICEF's children and AIDS advisor. Webb noted that in 2005, 60 to 80 percent of parental deaths in sub-Saharan Africa were AIDS-related and observed that the growing number of orphaned children was now the major crisis affecting Africa. He called on international donors to provide the $1 billion annually needed to care for the children.

Central Africa. The Rwandan government on July 29 began releasing from jail thousands of mostly Hutu prisoners, despite the fact that many of them had confessed to participating in the 1994 ethnic genocide of as many as 1 million Rwandans, mainly of the minority Tutsi tribe. Officials announced that a total of 36,000 prisoners would be released, though they could eventually be reincarcerated depending on the outcomes of their court cases. The prisoner release policy was driven by overcrowding, officials said. Rwanda's six prisons were built to house 30,000 inmates but by mid-2005 held 82,000.

In Burundi, former rebel leader Pierre Nkurunziza, a Hutu, was sworn in as president on August 26, following his election by parliament one week earlier. The event climaxed a series of popular elections including parliamentary elections and a February referendum that ushered in a power-sharing constitution designed to implement ethnic quotas between Hutus and Tutsis. Twelve years of civil war, beginning in 1993, between the historically oppressed Hutu majority and the historically dominant Tutsi minority had claimed as many as 300,000 lives in Burundi.

General Francois Bozize of the Central African Republic (CAR), who seized power in a *coup* (takeover) in March 2003, was on May 24, 2005, declared winner in a presidential runoff election with 65 percent of votes cast. Since independence from France in 1960, the mineral-rich CAR has weathered at least eight armed revolts and uprisings against civilian and military dictatorships.

Southern Africa. On Aug. 22, 2005, President Thabo Mbeki of South Africa warned Zimbabwe President Robert Mugabe that "we sink or swim together" and that economic collapse and political repression in Zimbabwe threatened the entire southern Africa region. Diplomats contrasted Mbeki's unusual public criticism of Mugabe with the relative silence on the topic by

African leaders gathered at the AU's July summit in Libya. Zimbabwe's economy has reeled under Mugabe's policy of farm confiscations, begun in 2000, and Mugabe and his associates came under intense international criticism for a variety of alleged human rights abuses. Conditions in Zimbabwe have caused 3.5 million Zimbabweans to flee abroad since 2000.

According to the UN's World Food Program (WFP), a number of southern African countries—including Angola, Botswana, Madagascar, Malawi, Mozambique, and Zimbabwe—faced critical food shortages in 2005. On October 6, WFP executive director James Morris announced that

12 million people in the region would need food aid by early 2006, calling the unfolding problem "the most serious humanitarian crisis in the world." One of the hardest hit countries in 2005 was Malawi, where an especially lean harvest threatened 5 million people—almost half the population—with starvation. WFP officials noted that HIV/AIDS compounded chronic hunger in 2005 by killing farmers and other workers. (HIV is the virus that causes AIDS.)

Figures released in 2005 showed that Swaziland faced an AIDS epidemic on a scale unknown anywhere else in the world, with 46.2 percent of the adult population infected with HIV. For Swazis between the ages of 25 and 29, the figure was 56 percent in 2005. Demographers said that the very survival of Swaziland, with a population of just under 1 million, was at stake.

In Mozambique, Armando Guebuza was sworn in as president on February 2, succeeding Joaquim Chissano. The ruling Frelimo party, to which both Chissano and Guebuza belonged, won parliamentary majorities as well as the presidency in December 2004 elections. Frelimo had held power in Mozambique since the country gained

A mother feeds her severely malnourished child water at a relief center in Niger in July. Millions faced starvation in Niger in 2005 due to a famine caused by drought and the destruction of crops by locusts. By November, the UN World Food Program had raised only 60 percent of the $16 million needed to counteract the effects of the famine.

FACTS IN BRIEF ON AFRICAN POLITICAL UNITS

Country	Population	Government	Monetary unit*	Foreign trade (million U.S.$) Exports[†]	Imports[†]
Algeria	33,390,000	President Abdelaziz Bouteflika; Prime Minister Ahmed Ouyahia	dinar (72.25 = $1)	32,160	15,250
Angola	14,962,000	President Jose Eduardo dos Santos	new kwanza (89.20 = $1)	12,760	4,896
Benin	7,284,000	President Mathieu Kerekou	CFA franc (528.33 = $1)	721	935
Botswana	1,650,000	President Festus Mogae	pula (5.32 = $1)	2.940	2,255
Burkina Faso	14,209,000	President Blaise Compaore	CFA franc (528.33 = $1)	419	866
Burundi	7,561,000	President Pierre Nkurunziza	franc (1,035.09 = $1)	32	138
Cameroon	16,798,000	President Paul Biya	CFA franc (528.33 = $1)	2,445	1,979
Cape Verde	486,000	President Pedro Pires; Prime Minister Jose Maria Pereira Neves	escudo (89.15 = $1)	61	387
Central African Republic	4,021,000	President Francois Bozize	CFA franc (528.33 = $1)	172	136
Chad	9,382,000	President Idriss Deby	CFA franc (528.33 = $1)	365	501
Comoros	666,000	President of the Union Assoumani Azili	franc (397.75 = $1)	28	88
Congo (Brazzaville)	4,035,000	President Denis Sassou-Nguesso	CFA franc (528.33 = $1)	2,224	749
Congo (Kinshasa)	57,683,000	President Joseph Kabila	CFA franc (528.33 = $1)	1,417	933
Côte d'Ivoire (Ivory Coast)	17,428,000	President Laurent Gbagbo	CFA franc (528.3 = $1)	5,124	3,360
Djibouti	731,000	President Ismail Omar Guelleh; Prime Minister Mohamed Dileita Dileita	franc (172.80 = $1)	155	665
Egypt	76,346,000	President Hosni Mubarak; Prime Minister Ahmed Mohamed Nazif	pound (5.77 = $1)	11,000	19,210
Equatorial Guinea	534,000	President Teodoro Obiang Nguema Mbasogo; Prime Minister Miguel Abia Biteo Borico	CFA franc (528.33 = $1)	2,771	1,167
Eritrea	4,603,000	President Isaias Afworki	nafka (13.78 = $1)	64	622
Ethiopia	70,440,000	President Girma Woldegiorgis; Prime Minister Meles Zenawi	birr (8.72 = $1)	563	2,104
Gabon	1,400,000	President El Hadj Omar Bongo Odimba; Prime Minister Jean-Francois Ntoutoume-Emane	CFA franc (528.33 = $1)	3,710	1,225
Gambia	1,533,000	Head of State Yahya Jammeh	dalasi (27.85 = $1)	114	181
Ghana	21,210,000	President John Agyekum Kufuor	cedi (9,050.00 = $1)	3,010	3,699
Guinea	9,013,000	President Lansana Conte	franc (3,790.00 = $1)	709	642
Guinea-Bissau	1,629,000	President Henrique Rosa	CFA franc (528.33 = $1)	54	104
Kenya	33,260,000	President Mwai Kibaki	shilling (74.45 = $1)	2,589	4,190
Lesotho	1,868,000	King Letsie III; Prime Minister Pakalitha Mosisili	maloti (6.25 = $1)	485	731

*Exchange rates as of Sept. 9, 2005, or latest available data.   [†]Latest available data.

Country	Population	Government	Monetary unit*	Foreign trade (million U.S.$)	
				Exports[†]	Imports[†]
Liberia	3,701,000	Chairman Gyude Bryant**	dollar (1 = $1)	1,079	5,051
Libya	6,003,000	Leader Muammar Muhammad al-Qadhafi; General People's Committee Secretary (Prime Minister) Shukri Muhammad Ghanim	dinar (1.30 = $1)	18,650	7,224
Madagascar	18,910,000	President Marc Ravalomanana	ariary (2,010.90 = $1)	868	1,147
Malawi	12,806,000	President Bingu wa Mutharika	kwacha (121.50 = $1)	503	521
Mali	14,267,000	President Amadou Toumani Toure; Prime Minister Ousmane Issoufi Maiga	CFA franc (528.33 = $1)	915	927
Mauritania	3,153,000	Chairman, Military Council for Democracy and Justice Ely Ould Mohamed Vall; Prime Minister Sidi Mohamed Ould Boubakar	ouguiya (268.17 = $1)	541	860
Mauritius	1,236,000	President Sir Anerood Jugnauth; Prime Minister Navinchandra Ramgoolam	rupee (29.65 = $1)	2,012	2,245
Morocco	29,631,000	King Mohamed VI; Prime Minister Driss Jettou	dirham (8.90 = $1)	9,754	15,630
Mozambique	19,787,000	President Armando Guebuza; Prime Minister Luisa Diogo	metical (24,441.00 = $1)	689	973
Namibia	1,978,000	President Hifikepunye Pohamba; Prime Minister Nahas Angula	dollar (6.31 = $1)	1,356	1,473
Niger	13,333,000	President Mamadou Tandja; Prime Minister Hama Amadou	CFA franc (528.33 = $1)	280	400
Nigeria	133,205,000	President Olusegun Obasanjo	naira (131.50 = $1)	33,990	17,140
Rwanda	8,788,000	President Paul Kagame	franc (542.75 = $1)	70	260
Sao Tome and Príncipe	177,000	President Fradique de Menezes	dobra (7,943.00 = $1)	7	41
Senegal	10,829,000	President Abdoulaye Wade; Prime Minister Macky Sall	CFA franc (528.33 = $1)	1,374	2,128
Seychelles	83,000	President James Alix Michel	rupee (5.42 = $1)	256	393
Sierra Leone	5,439,000	President Ahmad Tejan Kabbah	leone (2,155.00 = $1)	49	264
Somalia	10,980,000	President Abdikassim Salad Hassan	shilling (2,255.00 = $1)	79	344
South Africa	48,421,000	President Thabo Mvuyelwa Mbeki	rand (6.31 = $1)	41,970	39,420
Sudan	35,667,000	President Umar Hasan Ahmad al-Bashir	dinar (250.72 = $1) pound (2,507.20 = $1)	3,395	3,496
Swaziland	977,000	King Mswati III; Prime Minister Absalom Themba Dlamini	lilangeni (6.31 = $1)	900	1,140
Tanzania	39,962,000	President Benjamin William Mkapa; Prime Minister Frederick Sumaye	shilling (1,130.50 = $1)	1,248	1,972
Togo	5,243,000	President Faure Gnassingbe	CFA franc (528.33 = $1)	663	825
Tunisia	10,147,000	President Zine El Abidine Ben Ali; Prime Minister Mohamed Ghannouchi	dinar (1.30 = $1)	9,926	11,520
Uganda	28,606,000	President Yoweri Kaguta Museveni; Prime Minister Apollo Nsibambi	shilling (1,833.50 = $1)	622	1,306
Zambia	11,183,000	President Levy Mwanawasa	kwacha (4,515.20 = $1)	1,548	1,519
Zimbabwe	12,975,000	President Robert Mugabe	dollar (24,522.00 = $1)	1,409	1,599

**Ellen Johnson-Sirleaf was elected President of Liberia on Nov. 23, 2005, and was scheduled to take office in January 2006.

independence from Portugal in 1975.

An outbreak of the deadly Marburg virus in Angola's northern Uige province in late 2004 and early 2005 killed more than 250 people. Symptoms of Marburg include fever, vomiting, diarrhea, and internal bleeding. As many as 90 percent of those who contract the virus die. Teams from the World Health Organization (WHO) assisted local health workers in attempts to contain the virus and prevent its spread southward to Luanda, Angola's capital, a city of 3.8 million people. Angola's neighbors were on high alert in 2005, as medical experts advised them to take extra precautions and seal their borders.

West Africa. Togo's President Gnassingbe Eyadema died on February 5 after 38 years of dictatorial rule. Hopes for a democratic government appeared to be dashed when the armed forces appointed the dead president's son, Faure Gnassingbe, president. The action, in effect a military *coup* (overthrow), drew protest from the AU, which suspended Togo. In an about-face, Gnassingbe turned over the presidency to an interim leader, and Togolese officials scheduled elections for April. Gnassingbe stood for election and on April 24 won the presidency.

Opposition parties alleged that the election was rigged, and their supporters took to the streets in Lome, the capital. Clashes between demonstrators and riot police left hundreds of people dead and hundreds more wounded. On June 20, Gnassingbe took office as president. The AU promptly recognized the new government.

In Mauritania, a military junta led by Ely Ould Mohamed Vall overthrew President Ould Taya in a bloodless coup in August. The new rulers promised democratic elections by 2007. Diplomats observed that the AU and the United States tacitly endorsed the coup, despite initial public objections. Taya had imposed a repressive regime on Mauritania following the 1984 coup in which he came to power.

Liberia's election commission on Nov. 23, 2005, officially certified the election of Ellen Johnson-Sirleaf as president. Sirleaf, a U.S.-educated economist, was scheduled to become Africa's first female head of state upon taking the oath of office in January 2006. In October and November 2005, Liberia held peaceful, orderly elections for parliament and the presidency under the watchful eyes of 15,000 UN peacekeepers. The newly elected government faced the task of rebuilding and unifying Liberia following 14 years of civil war that had claimed some 200,000 lives before ending in 2003.

In Niger, a plague of locusts and catastrophic drought in 2005 left at least 2.5 million people, one-fifth of the country's population, on the brink of starvation. Situated on the southern fringe of the Sahara, Niger is one of the world's poorest countries, in which 35 percent of all children die before their fifth birthday. During 2005, the UN's World Food Program appealed for $16 million to avert famine in Niger, but by November it had received only around 60 percent of that amount. Relief agencies welcomed the influx of aid but criticized the international community for responding too slowly to the crisis.

President Laurent Gbagbo of Côte d'Ivoire in September postponed elections scheduled for October 30, explaining that rebels' refusal to disarm made elections impossible to stage. The northern rebels had risen against Gbagbo's government in September 2002, taking control of northern and western regions of the country. Some 10,000 UN and French peacekeepers continued to separate the two sides in 2005. In October, the UN and the AU endorsed a plan that permitted Gbagbo to remain in office until elections rescheduled for October 2006 but assigned responsibility for disarming forces on both sides to an independent prime minister to be selected by mediators. Led by Nigerian President Obasanjo and South African President Mbeki, the mediators in early December 2005 named Charles Konan Banny prime minister. Banny, a banker, was a member of the main opposition party in Côte d'Ivoire.

Eastern Africa and the Horn. Protesters and riot police clashed in the streets of Ethiopia's capital, Addis Ababa, in June 2005 and again in early November, resulting in at least 80 deaths and hundreds of wounded. The protests were in response to May parliamentary elections, which the opposition Coalition for Unity and Democracy claimed were rigged by Prime Minister Meles Zenawi's ruling Ethiopian People's Revolutionary Democratic Front (EPRDF). The EPRDF had won a majority of parliamentary seats in those elections.

Five years after signing a peace agreement with Eritrea in 2000, Ethiopia massed thousands of troops and hundreds of tanks near the disputed border with Eritrea on Nov. 3, 2005, amid fears of a new war in the Horn of Africa. Between 1998 and 2000, the two countries had gone to war over a disputed 620-mile (1,000-kilometer) frontier, at a cost of some 100,000 lives. Kofi Annan, secretary-general of the UN, which had 3,200 peacekeepers patrolling the buffer zone between the two nations in 2005, called on both sides to show "maximum restraint" to defuse the escalating tension.

In Tanzania, protests broke out in early November on the islands of Zanzibar, a *semiautonomous* (semi-independent) region with its own president and legislature. Following elections on October 30, supporters of the main opposition party alleged that Zanzibar President Amani

Karume and his ruling Chama Cha Mapinduzi (CCM) party had rigged the voting. Karume won the presidential contest, while CCM took 30 seats in the island region's 50-member parliament.

On June 13, Somali President Abdullah Yusuf Ahmed left Nairobi, Kenya, to relocate his transitional government in Jowhar, Somalia, 50 miles (80 kilometers) north of Somalia's capital, Mogadishu. The transitional parliament and government had been operating in exile in Nairobi since convening there in October 2004. Somali officials said that Mogadishu was simply too dangerous for the government to operate safely there. According to terrorism experts, Mogadishu had become one of the world's most dangerous cities and a haven for extremists linked to the al-Qa`ida terrorist network since Somalia's civil war in the 1990's.

In 2005, naval analysts noted the increasing threat from pirates operating in waters off the Horn of Africa. The danger was highlighted in November when pirate boats fired rocket-propelled grenades at the *Seabourn Spirit,* a luxury liner, 100 miles (160 kilometers) off the Somali coast. One crew member was injured in the attack, but the pirates did not board the ship.

◼ Simon Baynham

See also **AIDS; Terrorism; United Nations;** and the various African country articles.

Agriculture.
World production of grains and cotton was plentiful in 2005 despite destructive weather in many agricultural regions. Rice production in Indonesia remained steady in spite of the tsunami that struck in late December 2004. In the United States, drought in the key Corn Belt states of Illinois, parts of Iowa, and Indiana barely put a dent in the 2005 crop. Even hurricanes Katrina, Rita, and Wilma, which decimated parts of several Gulf Coast states, did not reduce the hardy U.S. soybean crop.

World crop production. According to a U.S. Department of Agriculture (USDA) report released in December, world wheat production totaled 615 million metric tons, slightly less than the 2004 harvest. In 2005, the largest wheat producers were the 25 member nations of the European Union (EU) with 123 million metric tons; the 12 major wheat-producing countries of the former Soviet Union with 91 million metric tons; China with 76 million metric tons; and India with 72 million metric tons.

Production of coarse grains, also known as small grain production—including corn, barley, sorghum, and oats—was 6 percent less than the 1-billion-metric-ton crop reported in 2004. In 2005, larger crops in the EU, Ukraine, and Russia offset slightly smaller crops in Brazil, Romania, and Argentina.

Oilseed production—including soybeans, sunflower seeds, cottonseed, and rapeseed—was expected to reach 387 million metric tons in 2005. Soybean production, the largest component of oilseeds, held steady in all major producing countries. In other oilseed categories, Argentina's sunflower seed production was smaller, while Russia's production was expected to reach 5.8 million metric tons, a record.

The global rice harvest totaled about 406 million metric tons, the second largest crop on record. China, with an anticipated harvest of 127 million metric tons, was the largest rice producer in the world. The U.S. rice harvest was about 7 million metric tons.

World cotton production reached 112 million bales in 2005. One bale is equivalent to 480 pounds (217 kilograms) of cotton. Larger crops in Greece, Mali, the United States, and Uzbekistan more than offset reductions in Brazil and Tajikistan. China, with 24.5 million bales, was the world's largest cotton producer.

U.S. crop production. Farmers in the United States produced the second largest corn crop on record, 11 billion bushels, just 7 percent below the record 2004 crop. Soybean production totaled 3 billion bushels, also the second largest crop on record. Cotton production reached 23 million bales, with even the storm-battered states of Florida, Georgia, Louisiana, and Texas registering increased production over 2004. Among the Gulf States, only Mississippi had a reduced crop.

Administration. On Jan. 21, 2005, Mike Johanns was sworn in as the 28th secretary of the U.S. Department of Agriculture by his predecessor, Ann Veneman. Johanns, the son of Iowa dairy farmers, had pursued a career in public service in Nebraska, where he served as governor when President George W. Bush tapped him for the Cabinet position. Johanns was the fourth Nebraskan to head the USDA.

GM crops. Planting of genetically modified (GM) crops by the world's farmers increased 20 percent during 2004, the latest year for which global statistics were available. In January 2005, the International Service for the Acquisition of Agri-Biotech Applications (ISAAA)—an organization that promotes agricultural biotechnologies in developing countries—estimated that 8.25 million farmers in 17 countries planted GM crops in 2004. In the "Global Status of Commercialized Biotech/GM crops: 2004" report, ISAAA issued a ranking of countries by acreage planted in GM crops (from greater to lesser): the United States, Argentina, Canada, Brazil, China, Paraguay, India, South Africa, Uruguay, Australia, Romania, Mexico, Spain, and the Philippines. In May 2005, Pioneer Hi-Bred International of Des Moines, Iowa, announced that the billionth acre (405 millionth hectare) of GM seed had been planted somewhere in the Northern Hemisphere in 2005.

Farmers in the United States in 2005 planted 52 percent of corn acreage in GM crops, up 13 percent from 2004; they planted 87 percent of soybean acreage in GM crops, up 1 percent from 2004; and 79 percent of cotton acreage in GM crops, up 4 percent from 2004.

A study released in October 2005 by PG Economics of London considered the impact on fuel and pesticide use when GM crops are planted. The study estimated that GM crops had reduced fuel consumption by 475 million gallons (1.8 million liters) and pesticide use by 380 million pounds (172.5 million kilograms) since the crops were first introduced in 1996.

Renewable fuels. In January 2005, USDA officials launched the Biobased Products Preferred Procurement Program. The program required federal agencies to purchase approved products such as fuels, lubricants, and cleaners made from corn, soybeans, or other non-petroleum sources.

Soybean fungus. The destructive soybean rust fungus (*Phakospora pachyrhizi*), detected in Louisiana in November 2004, had by late 2005 been detected in Alabama, Arkansas, Florida, Georgia, Kentucky, Mississippi, Missouri, North Carolina, South Carolina, Tennessee, and Texas. The windborne fungus—which attacks leaves of soybean plants, weakening them and reducing crop yields—had already widely affected soybean cultivation in Brazil and other parts of South America. Timely application of specific fungicides can control the fungus.

The USDA in 2005 allocated $1.2 million of contingency funding to soybean fungus control and monitoring programs, including an Internet-based mapping tool designed to help farmers decide whether or how to respond to the threat. Officials with the USDA noted that the fungus did not reduce U.S. soybean yields in 2005.

Avian flu. In November, the U.S. government imposed a ban on poultry from British Columbia after Canadian inspectors detected *avian* (bird) flu in a duck on a British Columbia farm. Earlier, U.S. officials had banned poultry imports from nine Asian countries and five Eastern European countries. Avian flu, a virulent influenza that first appeared in birds in Asia in 2004 and later spread to Europe and other regions, could become a human epidemic if mutations in the virus made it more easily contagious to humans.

BSE. On Dec. 11, 2005, Japan opened its market to U.S. beef and beef products from cattle 20 months or younger in age. Beef trade between the United States and Japan was stopped on Dec. 23, 2003, after the discovery of a BSE-infected cow in a herd in Washington state. BSE, or bovine spongiform encephalopathy, is a degenerative disease of the nervous system popularly known as "mad cow disease." The opening of the Japanese beef market in 2005 brought the total number of countries that have resumed trade to 70. The USDA continued testing 1,000 high-risk animals over 30 months of age for BSE per day in 2005.

Trade. On March 3, the World Trade Organization (WTO) upheld a 2004 decision against the U.S. cotton subsidy program. (The WTO oversees global trade agreements and arbitrates trade disputes among member countries.) The ruling required the U.S. Congress to repeal cotton subsidies, which had helped make U.S. cotton more competitive in the global market.

On Aug. 2, 2005, President Bush signed the Central American-Dominican Republic Free Trade Agreement (CAFTA-DR) with Costa Rica, the Dominican Republic, El Salvador, Guatemala, Honduras, and Nicaragua. Trade experts predicted that U.S. farm exports to the area would grow by $1.5 billion per year in response to the trade accord.

On November 24, USDA officials projected that U.S. agricultural exports would reach $64 billion in 2005. U.S. agricultural exports in 2004 totaled $62 billion.   ■ Patricia Peak Klintberg

See also **International trade.**

AIDS. The estimated number of people in the United States infected with HIV, the virus that causes AIDS, climbed above 1 million, according to a report presented in June 2005 by researchers from the Centers for Disease Control and Prevention (CDC) in Atlanta, Georgia. The researchers calculated that by the end of 2003, the number of U.S. residents living with the virus totaled from 1,039,000 to 1,185,000, about 100,000 more than in 2000. The 2003 figure included an estimated 405,926 people with AIDS, the final, life-threatening stage of the infection. CDC officials said the effectiveness of anti-HIV medications helped explain a 30-percent jump in the number of U.S. residents living with the virus.

The number of African Americans diagnosed with HIV/AIDS fell by about 5 percent annually from 2001 to 2004, CDC researchers reported in November 2005. The researchers tied the drop, in part, to declines in positive diagnoses among intravenous drug users. Nevertheless, the number of new cases of HIV/AIDS among blacks was 8.4 times as high as that among whites in 2004.

Heroin traffic and AIDS. Major outbreaks of HIV/AIDS are occurring along the routes used by drug traffickers to transport heroin from Afghanistan, the world's biggest heroin supplier, to central Asia and Eastern Europe, according to data presented at an international AIDS conference held in Rio de Janeiro, Brazil, in July 2005. Epidemiologist Christopher Beyrer of the Johns Hopkins Bloomberg School of Public Health in Baltimore, Maryland, reported that the outbreaks were concentrated among intravenous drug users, most of whom are sexually active young men. Fueling the outbreaks, Beyrer said, were "sharply inadequate" public health responses in the affected countries.

At the conference, United Nations officials reported that central China had become an AIDS hot spot. In the 1990's, hundreds of thousands of Chinese blood donors had contracted HIV at commercial blood collection centers. The donors received transfusions of *plasma* (the liquid portion of blood), which had not been screened for HIV, so that they could give blood more frequently.

More contagious. Evidence supporting the widespread theory that people with early-stage HIV infection are more likely to pass the virus to their sexual partners than are people with long-term infections emerged from a study reported in May 2005 by researchers from Uganda and the United States. The researchers found that people in their study who had been HIV positive for fewer than five months were eight times as likely to transmit the virus as people who had been infected for longer periods. ■ Barbara A. Mayes

See also **Africa; Asia; Drugs; Public health.**

Albania.

The right-of-center Democratic Party emerged the winner of July 2005 parliamentary elections and with three allied parties controlled 80 of the 140 seats in Albania's parliament. In September, the coalition formed a government with Sali Berisha as prime minister. Berisha had served as Albania's president from 1992 to 1997. Some members of the outgoing Socialist Party charged that the elections were fraudulent. International election monitors characterized the elections as "disorganized" but stopped short of outright condemnation.

In response to concerns about conduct of the elections, the European Union (EU) postponed completing negotiations with Albania on a Stabilization and Association Agreement (SAA) until the first half of 2006. The SAA is the first step in the long process of gaining EU membership.

In November 2005, officials with Albania's state-run power utility announced that electric power to customers was to be cut on a staggered schedule due to drought, which had reduced reservoirs supplying water to hydroelectric plants. Economists predicted that because of the power cuts the country might not meet its growth target of 6 percent for 2005. ■ Sharon L. Wolchik

See also **Europe.**

Alberta. See **Canadian provinces.**

Algeria.

The release in August 2005 of more than 400 Moroccan prisoners who had been held by the Algerian-backed Polisario movement in Western Sahara led to improved relations between Algeria and Morocco. Despite ongoing territorial disputes, Algerian President Abdelaziz Bouteflika sent a message to King Mohamed VI of Morocco expressing his determination to further strengthen relations between the countries.

In January, Algerian and Iranian officials signed an agreement on economic cooperation. The agreement opened the possibility of mutual investment, cooperation in the iron and metal industries, and direct banking.

Turkey's Deputy Prime Minister and Foreign Minister Abdullah Gul visited Algiers, the capital, in April to discuss the establishment of a free-trade zone and the signing of a friendship and cooperation treaty between Algeria and Turkey.

A peace plan to grant *amnesty* (pardon) to Islamic extremists was supported by more than 95 percent of voters in a September referendum in Algeria. President Bouteflika said the amnesty would help heal the wounds from a civil war that lasted from 1992 to 2000. ■ Mary-Jane Deeb

See also **Africa; France; Iran; Terrorism.**

Andorra. See **Europe.**

Angola. See **Africa.**

Animal. See **Biology; Conservation; Zoos.**

Anthropology.

Excavations on the Indonesian island of Flores in 2005 provided additional support for the 2004 announcement that a previously unknown species of human beings had been identified. The discovery of the diminutive species, *Homo floresiensis,* was reported in October 2004 by paleoanthropologist Peter Brown of the University of New England in Armidale, Australia. At the time, Brown said that he and his colleagues had found partial skeletons of several individuals, including a complete skull that they dated to roughly 18,000 years ago. The fossil bones indicated that *H. floresiensis* had a brain capacity of 417 cubic centimeters and a stature of approximately 3.5 feet (1.1 meter). Modern humans have brain capacities of about 1,300 cubic centimeters.

Brown and his colleague, Michael Morwood, also of the University of New England, reported in October 2005 that they had uncovered several new fossils, including a lower jaw, toe and finger bones, and portions of arm and leg bones. These fossils were about 3,000 years younger than the fossils announced in 2004. The new finds, like the 2004 finds, showed that the Flores individuals lacked chins and had relatively long arms.

Brown and Morwood noted that the combination of small brain, long arms, and chinless lower jaw are reminiscent of australopithecines (so-called "ape-men"), which lived more than 3 million years ago. However, the Flores people, in spite of their australopithecine-sized brains, apparently made stone tools and hunted large animals, as evidenced by the remains of tools and animals found with the human bones.

The scientists maintained that the small size of the Flores people was due to a process called *island dwarfism,* in which smaller body size is favored in environments with limited resources because a small body requires less energy than a large body. Brown and Morwood continued to dispute the proposals of scientists who claimed that the Flores fossils were from *pathological* (diseased) or pygmy *H. sapiens* (the same species to which modern human beings belong).

Brown and Morwood said the newly recov-ered bones confirmed that the small body size of *H. floresiensis* was common on Flores for an extended period, reinforcing their designation of the finds as a distinct species. However, the researchers were not sure where *H. floresiensis* fit in the human family tree—whether it was a descendant of *Homo erectus,* a much larger species, or whether it descended directly from australopithecines.

Oldest *Homo sapiens.* Two previously known *crania* (skull bones) of *H. sapiens* from southern Ethiopia near the Omo River were redated to 195,000 years ago, scientists reported in February 2005. When the Oma fossils were initially found in 1967 by anthropologist Richard Leakey, the age of the specimens could not be determined, but they were believed to be much younger than 195,000 years.

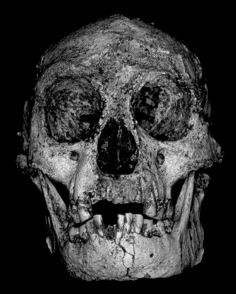

The small, 18,000-year-old skull of a human being (left, next to a modern skull) that was discovered in 2004 continued to stir debate among anthropologists in 2005. In March, researchers at Florida State University in Tallahassee reported that the interior structure of the *Homo floresiensis* skull indicated that the brain—though small—had enlarged lobes that made it capable of higher thinking and reasoning skills.

A team consisting of geologist Ian McDougall of Australian National University, geologist Frank Brown of the University of Utah in Salt Lake City, and anthropologist John Fleagle of State University of New York in Stony Brook, relocated the spot where Leakey made his finds. They dated a volcanic ash layer underlying the sediment that contained the crania at 195,000 years ago, setting that as the approximate age of the fossils. The redating made the Omo crania the oldest known evidence for anatomically modern human beings.

First fossil chimp. In September 2005, anthropologists reported the first finding of a fossil chimpanzee, providing insight into the evolution of the closest living relative of human beings. The fossils, dated to roughly 545,000 years ago, were recovered from the Tugen Hills region in central Kenya by anthropologists Sally McBrearty of the University of Connecticut in Storrs and Nina Jablonski of the California Academy of Sciences in San Francisco. The Tugen Hills fossils attested to the presence of early chimpanzees some 370 miles (600 kilometers) east of their present-day distribution.

■ Donald C. Johanson
See also **Archaeology.**

Antigua and Barbuda. See Latin America; West Indies.

Archaeology.
In September 2005, researchers from the Austrian Academy of Sciences uncovered one of the earliest-known deliberate burials. The burial site is in northern Austria near the city of Krems, on the Danube River. The archaeologists, led by Christine Neugebauer-Maresch, dated the grave to 27,000 years ago.

The grave, which was only 16 inches (40 centimeters) deep, contained the bones of two infants placed side by side facing east. The bones of each infant were the same size, indicating that they may have been twins, reported Neugebauer-Maresch.

The remains of the infants were coated in *red ocher* (an iron pigment) and covered by the large shoulder blade of a woolly mammoth, an extinct relative of elephants. Thirty-one beads made of mammoth bone were found near one of the infants.

The archaeologists noted that, throughout history, the status of newborns has been a "gray area." In some cases, infants were accepted as full members of society, but in other cases, acceptance came only after infants survived into childhood. Neugebauer-Maresch said that the elaborate burial of the Krems infants—with deliberate placement of the bodies, red ocher pigment, and mammoth bone beads and cover—indicated that these newborns were included as full members of human society 27,000 years ago.

Exquisite Egyptian mummies. Australian archaeologists reported in May that they had made a surprising find at Saqqarah, which is 15 miles (24 kilometers) south of Cairo, the Egyptian capital. The discovery came while the scientists were investigating the tomb of Meri, the tutor of Pepi II, a long-lived pharaoh of the ancient Egyptian Dynasty VI. Although the dates of the reign of Pepi II are subject to debate, like all dates in the history of ancient Egypt, a generally accepted approximation of his reign is 2290 to 2196 B.C.

A team led by archaeologist Naguib Kanawati of Macquarie University in Sydney, Australia, discovered a statue of Meri and his wife and, in a room behind the statue, three undisturbed wooden coffins. The team determined that the coffins, and mummies inside, were from Dynasty XXVI (approximately from 664 to 525 B.C.), long after the time of Meri and Pepi II.

The archaeologists concluded that the area around the tomb apparently fell into neglect until some 2,600 years after the time of Meri and Pepi II. The area then began to be used as a cemetery once again.

Two of the mummies in the tomb are decorated with elaborate nets of colorful beadwork depicting the deceased person's face, as well as protective gods and goddesses. The third mummy has similar motifs, but they are painted on the mummy's linen wrappings.

Bulgarian treasures. Archaeologists with the Bulgarian Archaeological Institute made two key discoveries in 2005. The discoveries shed light on the elite members of an ancient society in what is now Bulgaria.

In late July, the archaeologists opened the unplundered tomb of a high-status male, perhaps a governor or local ruler, near the modern village of Zlatinitsa, in southeastern Bulgaria. The researchers dated the burial in the wood-paneled pit, based on the style of Greek pottery found in the tomb, to approximately 360-370 B.C. A wreath of gold leaves, a gold finger ring engraved with a horseman being crowned by a goddess, silver *rhytons* (drinking vessels), body armor, and horse trappings were recovered from the grave. Two horses and a dog had been sacrificed and buried with the man in the tomb.

In August, another team from the Bulgarian Archaeological Institute, excavating at the village of Dabene, recovered 15,000 miniature gold rings and other ornaments. The items were found in a cremation burial site, more than 4,000 years old, of an elite male member of society. The individual's cremated remains and his golden treasures had been covered with an earthen mound.

Maya "Site Q" identified. The discovery in April 2005 of a carved stone panel at the

A newly discovered marble head depicting Constantine the Great, emperor of Rome from A.D. 308 to 337, is unveiled in Rome in July 2005. The head, 24 inches (61 centimeters) high, was found in an ancient drainage system and was originally part of a sculpture located in the Roman Forum.

Guatemalan site of La Corona solved one of the great mysteries of the Maya world. The Maya formed a civilization that peaked in Central and South America from about A.D. 250 to 900.

Hieroglyphs (picture writing) on the stone panel record a date in A.D. 677 for the founding of a shrine dedicated to the god K'uhul Winik Ub'. The carvings match—in style, size, subject, and time period—a group of previously known sculptures and inscriptions from an unknown site, usually referred to as "Site Q," according to the team of archaeologists from Yale University in New Haven, Connecticut, and Southern Methodist University in Dallas, Texas.

Some two dozen sculptures, many purchased on the antiquities market, have been identified from the mysterious Site Q since the mid-1960's. In 1997, Yale researchers found an inscription in La Corona that mentioned a king named Chak Kutz (Red Turkey), who was also mentioned in a Site Q inscription from A.D. 690 that was purchased on the antiquities market in 1965. The item purchased in 1965 suggested that La Corona was Site Q. However, Maya kings from one site often appear in inscriptions at other sites, so doubt remained. The find in 2005 eliminated any doubt that La Corona was indeed Site Q.

■ Mark Rose

See also **Anthropology.**

Architecture. The rebuilding of New Orleans after Hurricane Katrina was the biggest architectural story of 2005. In August, the storm flooded about 80 percent of the city, destroyed 200,000 residences in the New Orleans area, and left the city's infrastructure in ruins. The rebuilt city will likely be half its former size. Whether it would be similar to the old New Orleans or a strange architectural hybrid became a subject of fierce debate in autumn 2005. Preservationists pushed for a return to architecture based on durable historic models. Other urban planners called for a denser and more complicated city appropriate for more complex times. Critics noted that rebuilding decisions were likely to have a large impact on future urban American architecture.

The World Trade Center site in New York City underwent major changes in 2005. Responding to security concerns from the New York Police Department, architect David Childs in June redesigned Daniel Libeskind's twisted 1,776-foot (541-meter) Freedom Tower into an obelisk resting on a 20-story concrete base. To make it resistant to car and truck bombs, the new base had no windows at street level. One critic compared the design with a gigantic paperweight.

Due to opposition from victims' families, the Lower Manhattan Development Corporation, the organization responsible for rebuilding Ground

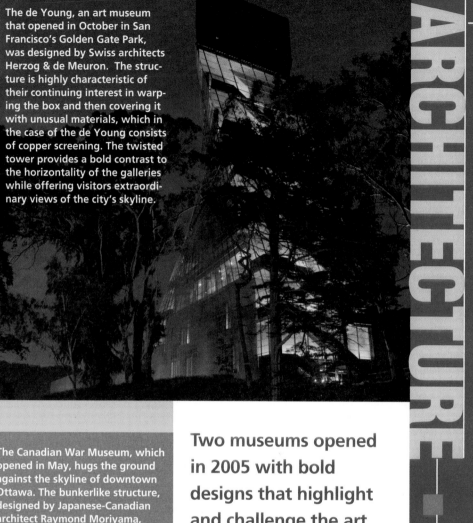

The de Young, an art museum that opened in October in San Francisco's Golden Gate Park, was designed by Swiss architects Herzog & de Meuron. The structure is highly characteristic of their continuing interest in warping the box and then covering it with unusual materials, which in the case of the de Young consists of copper screening. The twisted tower provides a bold contrast to the horizontality of the galleries while offering visitors extraordinary views of the city's skyline.

The Canadian War Museum, which opened in May, hugs the ground against the skyline of downtown Ottawa. The bunkerlike structure, designed by Japanese-Canadian architect Raymond Moriyama, houses a collection of Canadian military artifacts in galleries with slanted concrete walls, which one critic described as "giving a sensation of strain and instability" appropriate for "a museum about war and its consequences."

Two museums opened in 2005 with bold designs that highlight and challenge the art and artifacts they contain.

Zero and the surrounding area, scrapped the International Freedom Center, which was to be housed in a building designed by the Norwegian firm Snohetta. However, the memorial by Michael Arad and Peter Walker, "Reflecting Absence," and Santiago Calatrava's train station were still slated for construction.

Museums and cultural centers were big hits across the United States in 2005. Two of the most significant projects were the $70-million expansion of the Walker Art Center in Minneapolis and the new de Young Museum in San Francisco, both designed by the Swiss firm Herzog & de Meuron. The two structures displayed the firm's continued interest in warping the box and then covering it with unusual materials.

The Walker Art Center expansion is a shimmering cube that rises up beside the 1971 building designed by Edward Larrabee Barnes. While the original is clad in red brick and is nearly windowless, the additions are covered in a crimped aluminum mesh that sparkles like ice. The expansion, which opened in April 2005, doubles the museum's space and enhances its reputation as an innovative, risk-taking institution.

After years of lawsuits and public hearings, the $202-million de Young Museum opened in October in San Francisco's Golden Gate Park. The structure replaced a building severely damaged in the 1989 Loma Prieta earthquake. The new museum is a large copper box, strategically punctuated with gardens and courtyards. A 144-foot (44-meter) tower rises at the rear of the site, providing spectacular views of the city while offsetting the bold horizontality of the rest of the project.

The Memorial to the Murdered Jews of Europe, Peter Eisenman's controversial Holocaust Memorial in Berlin, opened in May 2005. The memorial consists of 2,711 blank concrete pillars arranged on an undulating 5-acre (2-hectare) site near the Brandenburg Gate. Visitors wander freely among the pillars, becoming progressively more confused and isolated from the rest of the world—a metaphor for the experience of Jews in Nazi Germany. "We wanted a silent field, a deafening silence in the age of noise," said the architect.

The Gates, a joyful, swirling installation designed by the artists Christo and Jeanne-Claude in New York City's Central Park, was the public design event of the year. For two weeks in February, the park was lined with 7,500 orange-colored arches, each 16-feet (5-meters) high, through which several million visitors streamed in amazement. The project cost $21 million, almost all of it raised from the sale of Christo's drawings. The installation helped New Yorkers and others rediscover one of America's great urban landscapes.

Philip Johnson, a patron and father figure to generations of American architects, died in June at the age of 98. In 60 years of practice, Johnson designed many notable and sometime notorious buildings, including the AT&T building in New York City, Pennzoil Place in Houston, and his famous Glass House in New Canaan, Connecticut. Yet Johnson's true legacy was his extraordinary generosity to young and emerging architects and his tireless promotion of architecture as art.

Awards. The 2005 Pritzker Prize, the "Nobel Prize" of architecture, was awarded to Thom Mayne, a Los Angeles architect known for controversial buildings that challenge conventional ideas about form, materials, and technology. Mayne's California Transportation Authority District 7 headquarters and the Science Education Resource Center/Science Center School, both in Los Angeles, are two of his most recent works.

The American Institute of Architects awarded its 2005 Gold Medal for lifetime achievement to Spanish architect Santiago Calatrava. His most recent works include the Milwaukee Art Museum, with its wing-shaped, moving sunscreen, and the design for a new train station at Ground Zero in New York City. Although Calatrava's materials are steel, glass, and concrete, his forms often derive from nature, especially birds, waves, and seashells.

◼ David Dillon

See also **Art; Building and construction; Germany; New York City; People in the news.**

Argentina. President Néstor Kirchner scored solid gains in mid-term Congressional elections on Oct. 23, 2005. Candidates of the Victory Front he had created to oppose old-line factions within his own Justicialist, or Peronist, party, increased their seats in the 257-member lower chamber from 40 to 100. (Peronist refers to Juan Perón, Argentina's president from 1946 to 1955 and again from 1973 to 1974.) The chief loser in the mid-term elections was former President Eduardo Duhalde, leader of one of the factions that Kirchner opposed.

In a high-visibility contest between the Kirchner and Duhalde factions, the wives of the two men confronted each other in an election campaign for the prestigious senate seat for Buenos Aires province, comprising the capital and environs. Cristina Fernandez de Kirchner, a lawyer and experienced politician in her own right, defeated Hilda Chiche Gonzales, Duhalde's wife, by closely identifying herself with Eva Duarte de Perón (1919–1952), or "Evita," Juan Perón's wife.

Economic rebound. Argentina, which had experienced the deepest economic depression in its history following the precipitous devaluation of its currency in 2001, was projected to finish 2005 with a robust 7.3-percent increase in its *gross domestic product* (GDP)—the value of all goods and services produced in a country in a given year. Strong demand and high global prices for Argentine exports figured significantly in the country's resurgent economy.

Another factor in Argentina's economic recovery was Kirchner's success in persuading most of Argentina's creditors to accept repayment at 30 cents on the dollar for the $103 billion in Argentine debt that had been in default since 2001. Freed of this burden, Kirchner's administration boosted wages of civil servants and members of the armed forces by 20 percent in July 2005.

Close ties. In August, Venezuelan President Hugo Chavez Frias paid an official visit to Buenos Aires, during which President Kirchner publicly thanked him for Venezuela's purchase of $500 million in Argentine bonds. The purchase helped Argentina's government avoid seeking immediate financial assistance from the International Monetary Fund (IMF). Kirchner had been at loggerheads with officials of the IMF—a United Nations-affiliated international financing body—since settling the country's defaulted debts without IMF assistance. Kirchner and Chavez launched several joint projects, including a trust fund to promote small businesses and a planned expansion of Argentine shipyards to service Venezuela's growing merchant fleet.

Utilities selloff. In June 2005, Electricité de France (EDF), a French utililty company, announced the sale of a majority share in Edenor, Argentina's biggest electrical utility, to an Argentine company, pending approval by regulators. In September, officials of another French company, Suez SA, announced their intention of selling holdings in Aguas Argentinas, the water utility serving Buenos Aires. These companies, which had bought controlling interests in the Argentine utilities when they were privatized in the 1990's, claimed they could not operate the businesses profitably owing to government rate restrictions. The action of Suez SA sent Argentine officials scrambling to find investors to keep the water utility running past the end of 2005.

Amnesty laws struck down. In June, Argentina's supreme court declared unconstitutional two amnesty laws. The laws had prevented prosecution of soldiers and police officers for human rights abuses against dissidents during the so-called "dirty war," an era of repressive government from 1976 to 1983 when Argentina was ruled by a military dictatorship. The court's ruling allowed the reinstatement of hundreds of lawsuits against individuals suspected of torturing or killing Argentines. Human rights organizations estimated that between 10,000 and 30,000 Argentines were murdered or disappeared under suspicious circumstances during the "dirty war."

■ Nathan A. Haverstock

See also **Latin America.**

Armed forces. The United States military in 2005 was dominated by the Iraq War. Two years after U.S. President George W. Bush declared that the military phase of the war was over, about 160,000 U.S. troops remained stationed in Iraq and engaged in battling an insurgency. In October 2005, U.S. deaths from the war reached 2,000, a grim milestone that touched off new waves of criticism about the conflict. Bush vowed he would not withdraw U.S troops until stability was restored to Iraq and a democratic government was installed.

Iraq War. Throughout 2005, Bush administration officials and military commanders offered upbeat appraisals of the war. Vice President Dick Cheney declared in May that the insurgency was in its "last throes." On July 27, General George W. Casey, Jr., the Iraq commander, predicted that "some fairly substantial reductions" in troop levels might begin in early 2006. In September 2005, Casey backed away from his prediction, citing "a period of a little greater uncertainty" on the ground. On September 29, military commanders told members of the U.S. Congress that the number of Iraqi army battalions capable of fighting without U.S. assistance had dropped from three to one. Officials with the U.S. Department of Defense predicted that at least 100,000 U.S. soldiers could remain in Iraq until 2009.

By the end of 2005, about 2,150 U.S. soldiers had died in Iraq and more than 15,000 soldiers had been wounded. Most of the casualties were caused by roadside bombs detonated against U.S. convoys by insurgents.

Rising casualties in 2005 triggered a definite decline in public support for the war. Public opinion polls showed for the first time that a majority of Americans believed the war in Iraq was a mistake. In late 2005, polls showed that more than 55 percent of people thought that the United States should have never invaded Iraq. These polls stood in sharp contrast to polls taken at the start of the war, when 69 percent of Americans supported the action.

The strain on U.S. combat assets prompted critics to claim that the military was stretched dangerously thin and would have difficulty responding to other threats. In a written "risk assessment" submitted to Congress in May, General Richard B. Myers, chairman of the Joint Chiefs of Staff, said the U.S. military could accomplish any mission it was assigned. However, he added that any such mission would be longer, more difficult, and "result in higher casualties and collateral damage" because so many combat units were deployed in Iraq and Afghanistan.

Congress approved an $82-billion emergency appropriations bill for Iraq in May and an additional $50 billion in the defense spending bill. By the end of 2005, war costs had exceeded $250 billion, and congressional analysts estimated that figure would reach $500 billion by 2010. The United States spent approximately $4.5 billion a month in 2005 to sustain operations in Iraq and Afghanistan.

Prison scandal. On Sept. 27, 2005, Private First Class Lynndie R. England was sentenced to three years in a military prison for her role in the abuse and torture of prisoners in 2003 at Abu Ghraib prison in Iraq. England was one of nine Army Reserve enlisted soldiers convicted in connection with the scandal. All nine soldiers received prison terms from military tribunals. A photograph of England with a naked Iraqi prisoner on a leash inflamed public opinion in the United States and abroad, particularly among Muslims. The alleged ringleader of the scandal, Corporal Charles A. Graner, Jr., received a 10-year sentence in January 2005. Brigadier General Janis Karpinski, a reserve officer, was demoted to colonel and reprimanded. Karpinski claimed that she had been made a scapegoat by the Army to protect more senior officers who had allowed the mistreatment to continue to gain intelligence from the prisoners.

Overriding objections from the Department of Defense, the U.S. Senate overwhelmingly voted to establish new restrictions on prisoner interrogations in Iraq and throughout the world. The measure was led by Senator John McCain (R., Arizona), a former prisoner of war during the Vietnam War (1957-1975).

Afghan war. The Iraq War overshadowed U.S. military operations in Afghanistan throughout 2005. Four years after a U.S. invasion toppled the radical *Taliban* (an extremist Islamic group that gained control of most of Afghanistan beginning in the mid-1990's), nearly 20,000 U.S. troops remained stationed in Afghanistan. By late 2005, more than 250 soldiers had been killed in Operation Enduring Freedom. In the single worst combat loss of the war, 16 troops died on June 28 when Afghan insurgents shot down a special forces helicopter.

Hurricane relief. The largest domestic military deployment in U.S. history was triggered by Hurricane Katrina, which ravaged the Gulf Coast on August 29 and destroyed major portions of New Orleans, Louisiana, and towns in Mississippi and Alabama. More than 70,000 soldiers were mobilized to lead relief and recovery efforts. At least 20 U.S. Navy ships were diverted to hurricane relief duties. As a result of the military's strong performance, Bush said in September that he was considering asking Congress to allow the Defense Department to have a larger role in large-scale domestic disasters. By law, active duty military troops cannot perform law enforcement duties in the United States.

Base closings. A controversial round of military base closures was approved by Congress after being endorsed by President Bush in September. In May, the Defense Department proposed closing 33 major bases and realigning operations at 29 others, with lesser reductions at 775 smaller installations. The final list prepared by the Defense Base Closure and Realignment Commission (BRAC) spared several major installations the Defense Department wanted closed, including the naval shipyard at Portsmouth, New Hampshire; the submarine base at New London, Connecticut; and Ellsworth Air Force Base in South Dakota. Prominent installations scheduled to close included Fort Monroe, Virginia; Fort McPherson, Georgia; and Walter Reed Army Medical Center in Washington, D.C.

The BRAC commission endorsed Defense Department plans to move 14,600 U.S. troops from Germany to four U.S. bases as part of the Army's modernization efforts. Defense officials estimated that the government would save $49 billion over 20 years from the closings and consolidations. The first major closings were scheduled to begin in 2007 and be completed by 2011.

On Dec. 31, 2005, the United States returned Rhein-Main Air Base in Frankfurt to Germany, ending a 60-year presence. The historic base played a prominent role in the Berlin Airlift, an effort in which France, the United Kingdom, and the United States supplied West Berlin with food and fuel entirely by air during a Soviet blockade in 1948 and 1949.

Weapons systems. In 2005, the Defense Department continued developing a variety of new weapons systems, including a joint strike fighter, new classes of nuclear aircraft carriers and destroyers, a new generation of armored fighting vehicles, an Air Force strategic bomber, and the Littoral Combat Ship, a small, mobile, shallow-draft vessel capable of close-in warfare at high speed along enemy coastlines.

After years of development and numerous safety problems, the V-22 Osprey tilt-rotor plane was approved for full production in September. The Osprey, which takes off and lands like a helicopter but flies like a conventional aircraft, will be used as a troop carrier by the Marine Corps. The military planned to purchase 400 Ospreys at an estimated cost of $19 billion.

Ships commissioned by the Navy during 2005 included the nuclear attack submarine *Jimmy Carter*, named for the 39th president, and a Burke-class guided missile destroyer. The Navy awarded a $1.7-billion contract to Lockheed Martin of Bethesda, Maryland, in January to build a new fleet of presidential helicopters.

Nuclear strategy. In 2005, the Defense

Department revised its nuclear doctrine to allow commanders to request presidential permission to use nuclear weapons to preempt an attack from other nations or terrorist groups with weapons of mass destruction. The new strategy reflected the policy change by the Bush administration after the terrorist attacks on the United States in 2001 that would allow for preemptive use of such weapons to avert a nuclear strike by a rogue regime.

The last MX "Peacekeeper" intercontinental ballistic missile was deactivated on Sept. 19, 2005, at Warren Air Force Base in Wyoming. The MX was the largest nuclear missile in the U.S. nuclear arsenal, and its deployment was a major component of the military buildup of the 1970's and 1980's. Fifty of the missiles were deployed, but with the end of the Cold War they began to be phased out in 2001. (The Cold War was a period of intense rivalry between United States allies and Communist nations that began after World War II [1939-1945] and ended with the collapse of the Soviet Union in 1991.)

Personnel developments. The war in Iraq had a negative impact on military recruiting in 2005, particularly for the Army, which for the first time since 1999 missed its target by 7,000 recruits. In July 2005, the Army significantly raised cash benefits for recruits. Army officials said that they were spending $15,000 on each new recruit, a 25-percent increase since 2003.

The war in Iraq also took a heavy toll on the Army National Guard, which had seven combat brigades deployed in the Persian Gulf region and at one point represented 40 percent of all troops in Iraq. Of the estimated 400,000 members of the National Guard, approximately 175,000 had been called to support the wars in Iraq and Afghanistan. A Government Accountability Office (GAO) report issued in 2005 concluded the Army National Guard had lost so much equipment to combat operations in Iraq and Afghanistan that its ability to respond to a domestic emergency had been significantly compromised.

In October, General Peter Pace became chairman of the Joint Chiefs of Staff, the first Marine Corps officer to hold the position.

Defense budget. In February, the Bush administration submitted a $419.3-billion defense budget for fiscal 2006, which began on Oct. 1, 2005. The request was 4.8 percent more than in fiscal 2005 but did not include funding for the wars in Iraq and Afghanistan. The additional cost of financing the military conflicts was expected to push total defense spending to $500 billion in 2006.　　■ Tom DeFrank

See also **Congress of the United States; Human rights; Iraq; United States, Government of the.**

Art. The art world in 2005 continued to grapple with the issue of art treasures plundered during World War II (1939-1945). In November 2005, a three-member panel in Austria began deliberations in a high-profile dispute over the ownership of six paintings by Austrian Art Nouveau artist Gustav Klimt. The paintings, valued at about $200 million, had been seized by Germany's Nazi government during the war. Five of the paintings have been in the collection of Austria's national gallery, housed in the Belvedere palace in Vienna, for more than 50 years.

The works belonged to Austrian industrialist Ferdinand Bloch-Bauer, who fled Vienna in 1938 as German troops seized the country. His niece and only surviving heir, Maria V. Altmann, began a lawsuit to recover the artwork in 1998. The case precipitated a landmark United States Supreme Court decision in June 2004 in which the court ruled that a foreign government could be sued in the United States over looted art. In May 2005, Altmann and the Austrian government agreed to turn the matter over for arbitration, which was to end all litigation.

Trophy art displayed. The State Pushkin Museum of Fine Arts in Moscow presented a controversial exhibit of some 550 ancient artworks in May 2005. The works, often called *trophy art,* had been seized by Soviet troops from the ruins of Berlin at the end of World War II. The works are part of a collection of tens of thousands of pieces of art that the Soviet Union claimed as compensation for the damage caused by the German invasion of Russia in 1941. None of the artworks—which include Greek bronzes, Etruscan figures, and fragments of Roman wall paintings—had been seen in public for more than 60 years. The works had been restored by Pushkin curators.

Recovered Rembrandt. In September 2005, Danish police recovered a self-portrait by Dutch master Rembrandt, nearly five years after it was stolen from the Swedish National Museum. Four men were arrested during the recovery. Dating from 1630, the painting was reportedly undamaged and in its original frame.

Silent sale. In May 2005, the New York Public Library sold a landmark painting in the Hudson River School style in a silent auction. The sale of *Kindred Spirits* (1849) by Asher B. Durand for a reported $35 million set an auction record for an American painting. The buyer, Alice L. Walton, heiress to the Wal-Mart fortune, planned to exhibit the painting in a museum being built by a Walton family foundation in Bentonville, Arkansas.

The painting depicts artist Thomas Cole, founder of the Hudson River School of painting, and New York City civic leader and poet William Cullen Bryant standing on a cliff in the Catskill

black-and-white canvas entitled *Crow Dancer* by American abstract expressionist Franz Kline sold for $6.4 million.

At Sotheby's auction house in New York City, the early photorealist painting *John* (1971-1972) by American artist Chuck Close sold for $4.8 million in May 2005. A set of five prints of *John* also sold for a record $204,000.

Met acquisition. The Metropolitan Museum of Art in New York City acquired the historic Gilman Paper Company Collection of photographs in March. The archive, which includes more than 8,500 works from photography's earliest era, is largely thought to be the most significant private photography collection in the world. Among the early masterworks are works by William Henry Fox Talbot, an inventor of the medium. The collection's notable photographs from 1900 to 2000 include images by Americans Edward Steichen and Man Ray and French photographers Eugène Atget and Henri Cartier-Bresson.

Museum expansions. The Walker Art Center in Minneapolis, Minnesota, unveiled a $70-million expansion by prize-winning Swiss architects Jacques Herzog and Pierre de Meuron in April 2005. The addition doubled the museum's size and increased its exhibition space by one-third, with 11,000 square feet (1,022 square meters) of new galleries. The renovation included a new restaurant, shop, and a 385-seat performance space for dance, music, and theater programs. The same firm, Herzog & de Meuron, also designed the new de Young Museum in San Francisco, which opened in October.

The Art Institute of Chicago also opened its expanded galleries of American art in April. The

Mountains. Many New Yorkers expressed dismay that the painting was leaving New York, with which it had long been associated. In November 2005, an additional 16 paintings and busts brought a disappointing $15.6 million at public auction.

Record prices. Sculptor Constantin Brancusi's *Bird in Space,* a previously unrecorded version of the work that had been in a private collection since 1937, sold for $27.5 million at Christie's auction house in New York City in May 2005. The sale set a record for a sculpture at auction.

The spring sales at Christie's also set auction records for other artists. *Chair Car,* a 1965 image of a rail car's interior by American realist painter Edward Hopper, sold for $14 million. A 1958

new first- and second-floor space includes a chronological sequence of 23 galleries featuring selections from the museum's eminent collection of more than 3,500 pieces dating from the Colonial period to 1950. In May 2005, the Art Institute unveiled the final design for a three-story glass, steel, and limestone addition scheduled to open in 2009. The $258-million new wing was designed by award-winning Italian architect Renzo Piano. The 264,000-square-foot (24,526-square-meter) addition will increase the size of the museum's gallery space by approximately one-third. The design includes a pedestrian bridge leading from the south end of neighboring Millennium Park to the new building's rooftop.

Exhibitions. Bohemian life in the Parisian district of Montmartre at the beginning of the 1900's is the subject of "Toulouse-Lautrec and Montmartre," which opened at the National Gallery of Art in Washington, D.C., in March 2005. On view were paintings, posters, and other works depicting dance halls, cabarets, and performers, primarily by popular French artist Henri de Toulouse-Lautrec. Also exhibited were works by Lautrec's colleagues, including Edouard Manet, Edgar Degas, Vincent van Gogh, and Pablo Picasso. The major exhibition traveled to the Art Institute of Chicago in July.

At the Metropolitan Museum, "Matisse, The Fabric of Dreams: His Art and His Textiles," which opened in June, examined how the modern French artist's vast collection of textiles and clothing inspired his art at various times during his career. "The Kingdom of Siam: The Art of Central Thailand, 1350-1800" displayed Thailand's predominantly Buddhist art, ranging from large stone temple sculptures to miniature ivory shrines, at the Asian Art Museum in San Francisco and the Peabody Essex Museum in Salem, Massachusetts. The paintings of one of the great masters of Dutch landscapes in the 1600's were featured in "Jacob van Ruisdael: Master of Landscape" at the Los Angeles County Museum of Art and the Philadelphia Museum of Art.   ■ Sally Ruth May

See also **Architecture; New York City.**

Visitors walk through one of eight twisted steel sculptures by American artist Richard Serra at the Guggenheim Bilbao Museum in Bilbao, Spain. The installation, entitled "The Matter of Time," opened in June 2005.

ASIA

A devastating earthquake shook the Himalayan region of Jammu and Kashmir, disputed by Pakistan and India, in 2005 while some coastal Asian countries were still recovering from the massive loss of life and destruction caused by an earthquake and subsequent tsunami in late 2004. The string of natural disasters killed hundreds of thousands of people and left millions of others homeless. Health officials in 2005 worried about the possibility of another disaster from the spread among humans beings of a form of flu initially found among birds in Asia.

Both earthquakes were caused by movement northward of a plate of Earth's surface, part of a continual shifting known to geologists as plate tectonics. The Indian plate, composed of both the land mass of South Asia encompassing Bangladesh, India, Nepal, Pakistan, and Sri Lanka, and the floor of the Indian Ocean, pushes against Asia at a rate of several inches a year.

The *epicenter* (the point on Earth's surface directly above the initial break) of the 7.6-magnitude earthquake on Oct. 8, 2005, in Kashmir was under the area administered by Pakistan. The quake also devastated northern areas of Pakistan itself as well as Indian-administered Kashmir. Officials working with international aid agencies estimated in November that the death toll in Pakistan was more than 73,000. India reported approximately 1,400 deaths. An estimated 3 million people lost their residences.

Relief work was slow to start, which triggered criticism of Pakistan's government. The mountainous terrain in the affected areas posed major problems. Landslides cut off many roads, isolating hard-hit villages. The only way to reach many survivors was with helicopters, which were provided by Pakistan's military as well as United States military forces stationed in Afghanistan. The United Nations (UN) and private aid groups tried to hire private helicopters, but appeals for money failed to raise the amount needed.

Officials feared that the death rate would escalate as winter in the mountainous region brought temperatures far below freezing. More than 200,000 villagers remained crowded into aid camps in late 2005, where officials warned of health problems due to inadequate clean water and sanitation.

Tsunami. Tens of thousands of people in regions around the Indian Ocean continued to live in tents and other temporary housing at the end of 2005, a year after the Dec. 26, 2004, earthquake and tsunami. The disaster killed more than 175,000 people. Almost 50,000 others remained missing and were presumed dead at the end of 2005.

The tsunami was caused by a 9.0-magnitude earthquake. A part of the Indian Ocean floor suddenly jolted near the Indonesian island of Sumatra, displacing massive amounts of water. The tsunami sent walls of water along coastlines from Sumatra around the Indian Ocean to East Africa. With little or no warning, villagers, fishermen, and tourists on tropical beaches were drowned or crushed in churning debris. The waves devastated towns, farmlands, roads, and bridges. Bodies were buried in silt or swept out to sea.

The worst-hit areas were on Sumatra, near the quake's epicenter. Indonesia counted at least 128,000 dead, mainly in Aceh province on the northwest tip of Sumatra. More than 31,000 people died in Sri Lanka, severely affecting the country's economy. Along India's eastern coast, more than 10,000 people were killed. More than 5,000 people were killed along the coast of Thailand, where many Western tourists had gathered at beach resorts during the Christmas holiday season.

United Nations aid officials estimated in 2005 that reconstruction would take from 5 to 10 years in most places. Reconstruction costs could rise as high as $10 billion. An outpouring of international aid did not reach this level, and aid was hampered by logistical and bureaucratic problems.

Border disputes flared in East Asia during 2005. Japan accused China of drawing natural gas from beneath Japan's claimed boundary in the East China Sea—a boundary that China disputed. Japan also argued with South Korea over their sea border. Malaysia and Indonesia, which both claim ownership of territory in the South China Sea near the island of Borneo, awarded oil exploration rights there to rival firms in 2005, and Indonesia sent warships into the area to support its claimed boundary. Most nations had agreed in 2002 to resolve such disputes peacefully.

Piracy. Four Southeast Asian nations increased efforts in 2005 to battle piracy at sea, a worldwide problem, in the region. Indonesia, Malaysia, Singapore, and Thailand were interested in combating pirates who regularly commandeered vessels, kidnapping or sometimes killing their crews.

Pirates were especially active in recent years

Massive economic growth in China, particularly in Shanghai, the financial capital, has triggered an unprecedented building boom that has displaced thousands of residents and reduced old neighborhoods to rubble. In 2005, 2,000 high-rise buildings were under construction in Shanghai, which began the year with 3,000 buildings over 18 stories tall.

in the Strait of Malacca between Indonesia and Malaysia. Annually, some 55,000 ships carrying between a quarter and a third of the world's seaborne commerce, including half the world's oil trade, sail through the strait. Indonesia, Malaysia, and Singapore began in July 2004 to coordinate naval patrols in the area. On Sept. 13, 2005, Indonesia, Malaysia, and Singapore, aided by Thailand, launched regular patrol flights over the waters.

Underwriters in London announced in June that they were considering raising insurance rates for ships sailing through the strait. Regional governments and shipowners protested, claiming that the number of pirate attacks had been declining and that the targets were mainly small coastal vessels.

Mongolia. Nambaryn Enkhbayar won a presidential election on May 22, 2005, with 53.4 percent of the votes. The Russian- and British-educated former prime minister represented the Mongolian People's Revolutionary Party (MPRP), the former Communist party that ruled the northeast Asian country for almost 70 years. Under Mongolia's new democratic system, par-

liament and a prime minister hold the most power. However, a disputed parliamentary election in 2004 led to the MPRP and opposition Democratic Party sharing power, which gave the president a more influential role.

Brunei. Sultan Haji Hassanal Bolkiah announced sweeping government changes on May 25, 2005. He removed four Cabinet ministers, including a conservative education minister. Political observers suggested that this may indicate a willingness to accept gradual political and economic reforms, including more religious tolerance in the Islamic state. The sultan also created a new energy ministry. Oil and gas production supplies 90 percent of Brunei's export earnings.

Maldives was among the nations devastated by the 2004 tsunami. More than 80 people died in the tiny island nation, and the economy struggled in 2005 from

FACTS IN BRIEF ON ASIAN COUNTRIES

Country	Population	Government	Monetary unit*	Foreign trade (million U.S.$)	
				Exports[†]	Imports[†]
Afghanistan	26,929,000	President Hamid Karzai	afghani (42.79 = $1)	446	3,759
Armenia	3,400,000	President Robert Kocharian; Prime Minister Andranik Markaryan	dram (463.50 = $1)	850	1,300
Azerbaijan	8,616,000	President Ilham Aliyev; Prime Minister Artur Rasizade	manat (4,593.00 = $1)	3,168	3,622
Bangladesh	134,840,000	President Iajuddin Ahmed; Prime Minister Khaleda Zia	taka (65.73 = $1)	7,478	10,030
Bhutan	814,000	King Jigme Singye Wangchuck; Prime Minister Lyonpo Yeshey Zimba	ngultrum (43.75 = $1)	154	196
Brunei	382,000	Sultan and Prime Minister Haji Hassanal Bolkiah	dollar (1.68 = $1)	7,700	5,200
Cambodia (Kampuchea)	13,698,000	King Norodom Sihamoni; Prime Minister Hun Sen	riel (4,105.00 = $1)	2,311	3,129
China	1,338,331,000	President Hu Jintao; Premier Wen Jiabao	yuan (8.09 = $1)	583,100	552,400
East Timor	964,000	President Xanana Gusmao; Prime Minister Mari Bin Amude Alkatiri	dollar (1.00 = $1)	8	167
Georgia	4,244,000	President Mikhail Saakashvili; Prime Minister Zurab Nogaideli	lari (1.80 = $1)	909	1,806
India	1,103,121,000	President Abdul Kalam; Prime Minister Manmohan Singh	rupee (43.80 = $1)	69,180	89,330
Indonesia	226,875,000	President Susilo Bambang Yudhoyono;	rupiah (10,204.00 = $1)	69,860	45,070
Iran	68,899,000	Supreme Leader Ayatollah Ali Khamenei; President Mahmoud Ahmadinejad	rial (9,015.00 = $1)	38,790	31,300
Japan	127,927,000	Emperor Akihito; Prime Minister Junichiro Koizumi	yen (109.71 = $1)	538,800	401,800
Kazakhstan	15,316,000	President Nursultan A. Nazarbayev; Prime Minister Daniyal Akhmetov	tenge (134.06 = $1)	18,470	13,070
Korea, North	22,954,000	Chairman of National Defense Commission Kim Jong-il	won (2.20 = $1)	1,200	2,100
Korea, South	48,360,000	President Roh Moo-hyun; Prime Minister Lee Hae-chan	won (1,025.50 = $1)	250,600	214,200
Kyrgyzstan	5,345,000	President Kurmanbek Bakiev	som (40.85 = $1)	647	775
Laos	6,046,000	President Khamtai Siphandon; Prime Minister Boungnang Volachit	kip (10,375.00 = $1)	366	580

the extensive destruction, especially of the vacation resorts that were vital to the economy.

In October, a Maldives court sentenced opposition activist Jennifer Latheef to 10 years in prison for reportedly inciting a riot in September 2003. The government, which had been repeatedly criticized by human rights groups for repressive measures and unfair election practices, denied that the verdict was politically motivated.

East Timor settled a dispute with Australia in 2005 over revenue from an offshore oil and gas field in the Timor Sea between the two countries. Australia, which had been getting 82 percent of revenue from early development of the field, agreed in late April that impoverished East Timor would get 90 percent of income from the Greater Sunrise field, where development would be increased. The two nations agreed to postpone final settlement of their sea border for between 50 and 60 years.

Bhutan. Jigme Singye Wangchuck, king of Bhutan, announced on Dec. 17, 2005, that he would give up the throne in 2008, and his small Himalayan country would become a multiparty parliamentary democracy under a new constitu-

Country	Population	Government	Monetary unit*	Foreign trade (million U.S.$)	
				Exports[†]	Imports[†]
Malaysia	25,745,000	Paramount Ruler Tuanku Syed Sirajuddin ibni Almarhum Tuanku Syed Putra Jamalullail, the Rajah of Perlis; Prime Minister Abdullah bin Ahmad Badawi	ringgit (3.77 = $1)	123,500	99,300
Maldives	321,000	President Maumoon Abdul Gayoom	rufiyaa (12.87 = $1)	90	392
Mongolia	2,580,000	President Nambaryn Enkhbayar; Prime Minister Tsakhiagiyn Elbegdorj	tugrik (1,193.00 = $1)	853	1,000
Myanmar (Burma)	51,223,000	Chairman of the State Peace and Development Council Than Shwe; Prime Minister Soe Win	kyat (6.42 = $1)	2,137	1,754
Nepal	25,636,000	King Gyanendra	rupee (69.75 = $1)	568	1,419
Pakistan	165,035,000	President Pervez Musharraf; Prime Minister Shaukat Aziz	rupee (59.73 = $1)	15,070	14,010
Philippines	84,093,000	President Gloria Macapagal-Arroyo	peso (56.09 = $1)	38,630	37,500
Russia	142,190,000	President Vladimir Putin; Prime Minister Mikhail Fradkov	ruble (28.27 = $1)	162,500	92,910
Singapore	4,240,000	President Sellapan Rama Nathan; Prime Minister Lee Hsien Loong	dollar (1.67 = $1)	174,000	155,200
Sri Lanka	19,500,000	President Mahinda Rajapakse	rupee (101.61 = $1)	5,306	7,265
Taiwan	22,781,000	President Chen Shui-bian; Premier (President of the Executive Yuan) Frank Hsieh	dollar (32.74 = $1)	170,500	165,400
Tajikistan	6,574,000	President Emomali Rahmonov; Prime Minister Oqil Oqilov	somoni (3.18 = $1)	1,130	1,300
Thailand	64,645,000	King Bhumibol Adulyadej (Rama IX); Prime Minister Thaksin Shinawatra	baht (40.93 = $1)	87,910	80,840
Turkmenistan	5,092,000	President Saparmurad A. Niyazov	manat (5,200.00 = $1)	4,000	2,850
Uzbekistan	27,250,000	President Islam A. Karimov; Prime Minister Shavkat Mirziyayev	som (1,141.35 = $1)	3,700	2,820
Vietnam	84,655,000	Communist Party Secretary-General Nong Duc Manh; President Tran Duc Luong; Prime Minister Phan Van Khai	dong (15,880.00 = $1)	23,720	26,310

*Exchange rates as of September 2005, or latest available data.
[†]Latest available data.

tion. His son, Jigme Khesar Namgyel Wangchuck, will become king in 2008 after assuming royal responsibilities sometime earlier.

Over a period of some 50 years, Bhutan's kings had voluntarily and gradually introduced democracy in the previously feudal country. The proposed constitution, which the king had circulated among his subjects in March 2005, emphasized preserving Buddhist customs and the environment in the mountainous, heavily forested nation.

Laos. Some 170 members of the Hmong ethnic minority surrendered to the government on June 4, 2005, after spending decades hiding in remote areas. Hmong warriors, organized by the United States Central Intelligence Agency, had fought Laotian Communists backed by North Vietnam in the 1970's. When the Communists won control of Laos in 1975, many Hmong fled to adjacent Thailand while others hid in jungled mountains. During 2005, Thailand brought pressure on the more than 5,000 Hmong living in that country to return to Laos, but they remained fearful of returning. ■ Henry S. Bradsher

See also **Disasters; Terrorism;** various Asian country articles.

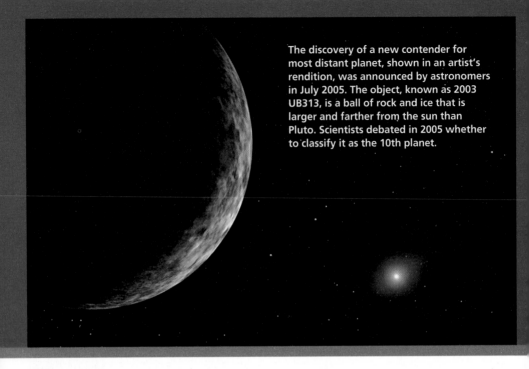

The discovery of a new contender for most distant planet, shown in an artist's rendition, was announced by astronomers in July 2005. The object, known as 2003 UB313, is a ball of rock and ice that is larger and farther from the sun than Pluto. Scientists debated in 2005 whether to classify it as the 10th planet.

Astronomy.

The European Space Agency (ESA) probe Huygens in 2005 became the first craft to land on a satellite of a planet other than Earth. Astronomers also studied the interior of a comet, discovered a new planet candidate, detected the light of a planet outside the solar system, and saw a massive explosion at the edge of the universe.

Huygens explores Titan. On January 14, the ESA's Huygens probe descended through the atmosphere of Saturn's largest moon, Titan, opened its parachute, and landed on the satellite's icy surface. Released by the United States National Aeronautics and Space Administration (NASA) Cassini spacecraft, which had been orbiting Saturn since July 2004, Huygens was the first spacecraft to penetrate the dense clouds that hide Titan's surface.

Instruments on Huygens photographed the surface of Titan as the probe descended, revealing a moon shaped by flowing liquid, with branching river channels and deltas visible from above. The rivers, however, cannot be water because the temperature of Titan, −290 °F (−143 °C), is far below water's freezing point. While much of Titan's surface is currently covered with water ice, the moon is also rich in simple hydrocarbons, especially methane (CH_4) and ethane (C_2H_6), which can exist in liquid form at very low temperatures.

Color images taken by Huygens from the surface of Titan showed a landscape bathed in a hazy orange light, tinted by the complex hydrocarbons that form a kind of smog in its atmosphere. The probe showed that while Titan is distant from the sun and shrouded in clouds, its surface is very geologically and meteorologically active.

A 10th planet and its moon? Astronomers announced in July 2005 the discovery of an object at the fringes of the solar system that is larger than Pluto. The object, officially known as 2003 UB313, was discovered by Michael E. Brown of the California Institute of Technology in Pasadena; Chadwick Trujillo of the Gemini Observatory in Mauna Kea, Hawaii; and David Rabinowitz of Yale University in New Haven, Connecticut.

The scientists first detected the object with a telescope at the Palomar Observatory in California in October 2003. They found that it was about 9 billion miles (14.5 billion kilometers) from the sun, about twice the distance of Pluto, and that it takes about 560 years to complete one orbit. Further observations with the Keck II telescope in Hawaii in September 2005 revealed a small moon orbiting 2003 UB313 about once every 14 days.

Some astronomers have argued that if Pluto is considered the 9th planet of the solar system, then 2003 UB313 must be considered the 10th planet. Other scientists contended that none of these distant objects, including Pluto itself, should be categorized as planets. They argued that these objects belong only to a class of bodies called Kuiper Belt Objects, remnants of the debris that formed the other planets about 4.6 billion years ago.

Deep Impact. The NASA spacecraft Deep Impact, while orbiting the sun about 80 million miles (130 million kilometers) from Earth, released a block of copper about the size of a washing machine into the path of Tempel 1, a comet about 6 miles (10 kilometers) in diameter, in July 2005. Minutes later, the projectile collided with the comet, smashing a crater into its surface and a cloud of debris into space. For the next several days, more than 80 telescopes in space and on the ground observed the aftermath of the collision.

Astronomers estimated that Deep Impact released about 20 million pounds (9 million kilograms) of the interior of Comet Tempel 1 into space, leaving behind a crater at least 100 feet (30 meters) deep. By observing the debris, astronomers were able to determine the chemical composition of the material inside the comet. Only inside a comet—unaltered by weather or planetary geology—can scientists find samples of the original material from which the solar system formed.

The first light from planets outside the solar system was detected in March 2005 by astronomers using NASA's Spitzer Space Telescope. Although planets had been found around other stars since 1991, their presence was inferred only from changes in the light of the stars caused by the orbiting planets.

By using the Spitzer telescope, two teams of astronomers—one led by Drake Deming of NASA's Goddard Space Flight Center and the other by David Charbonneau of the Harvard-Smithsonian Center—were able to measure the light reflected by each planet. HD209458b, observed by Deming's team, orbits a star 153 light years away, in the constellation Pegasus. (A light year is the distance light travels in one year, about 5.9 trillion miles [9.5 trillion kilometers].) Charbonneau's group studied TrES-1, which is 489 light years away, in the constellation Lyra.

Most distant explosion. NASA's Swift Satellite in September 2005 detected a burst of radiation from the farthest explosion ever studied. The explosion, named GRB 050904, occurred when a dying star many times more massive than the sun formed a black hole. Such explosions occur

almost daily, producing bursts of gamma rays that last from a few seconds to several minutes. The Swift satellite detects these bursts and relays the information to a network of telescopes on Earth. Astronomers used telescopes in Chile and Hawaii to determine that the blast was located near the edge of the universe, almost 13 billion light years from Earth, close to the distance of the farthest object ever discovered. ■ Laurence A. Marschall

See also **Space exploration.**

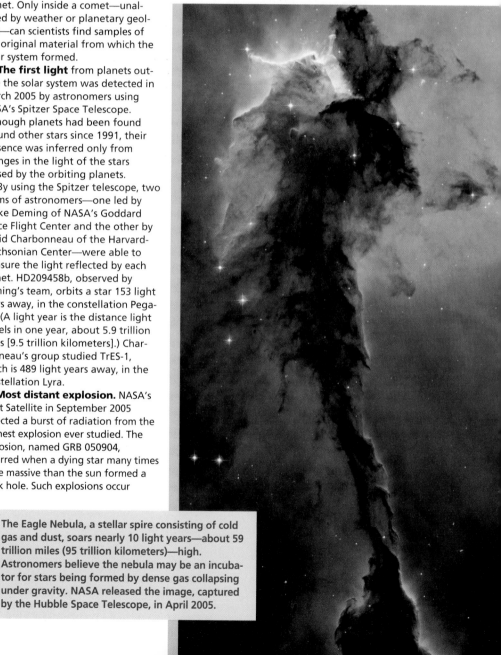

The Eagle Nebula, a stellar spire consisting of cold gas and dust, soars nearly 10 light years—about 59 trillion miles (95 trillion kilometers)—high. Astronomers believe the nebula may be an incubator for stars being formed by dense gas collapsing under gravity. NASA released the image, captured by the Hubble Space Telescope, in April 2005.

AUSTRALIA

Australia began 2005 by observing a day of national mourning on January 16. The day commemorated the thousands of people who died in the tsunami that struck many Asian countries in the wake of an undersea earthquake off the Indonesian island of Sumatra on Dec. 26, 2004. According to official figures, more than 20 Australians, mostly people vacationing in Thailand and Sri Lanka, died in the disaster.

The year was further marred by the deaths of Australians in bombings in London in July 2005 and on the Indonesian island of Bali in October. The shadow of terrorism also fell on Australia for the first time in 2005.

Sports-loving Australians will remember 2005 as the year that Makybe Diva became the first horse in the 145-year history of the Melbourne Cup to win the world-famous race for a third time.

Security. Several Australians were injured in the bombings in London on July 7. One Australian, Sam Ly from Melbourne, later died from his injuries. Surveys showed that many Australians feared that similar attacks would take place in Australia.

Prime Minister John Howard met with 13 moderate Islamic leaders in Canberra, the capital, in August to seek ways of improving relations between the general public and Australia's relatively small Muslim community. They discussed a number of ideas, including a proposal for a system of accreditation for *imams* (Muslim spiritual leaders) and the training of Australian-born Muslims to become imams.

A report by British security expert Sir John Wheeler released in September was highly critical of the government's failure to ensure safety in Australian airports. Howard announced a $200-million plan to plug gaps. (All amounts are in Australian dollars.) On September 27, Howard met with state and territory leaders in Canberra to discuss terrorism. They agreed to several strong measures, including placing suspected terrorists under house arrest for up to 12 months.

Terrorism again affected Australia on October 1, when four Australians staying on the Indonesian resort island of Bali died in bombings that killed a total of 22 people. Five of the most seriously injured Australians were flown to Singapore for treatment. The rest were evacuated to Australia. Prime Minister Howard sent a contingent of Australian Federal Police officers to the island to help with investigations. He also pledged $1 million to buy medical equipment to help blast victims. Aza-

hari bin Husin, a Malaysian-born Australian-educated terrorist alleged to have masterminded the 2005 bombings as well as a similar attack on the island in 2002, was shot by Indonesian police in November 2005.

The biggest antiterrorist operation in Australian history began on November 8 with the arrest of nine men in Melbourne and eight others in Sydney. The alleged terrorists were all either Australian-born or Australian citizens. Police stated that the Sydney arm of an alleged Islamic terrorist group had stockpiled enough chemicals to make at least 15 large bombs.

Afghanistan and Iraq. In January, Mamdouh Habib, an Australian citizen captured in Pakistan in 2001 for suspected contact with the al-Qa`ida terrorist network in Afghanistan, was released from a United States prison in Guantanamo Bay, Cuba, without ever being charged with an offense. Another Australian, David Hicks, who had been captured in Afghanistan in 2001, remained at Guantanamo Bay at the end of 2005.

In February, Prime Minister Howard announced that a new task force was to be sent to Iraq for one year. He explained that the force of 450 soldiers was needed to support Japanese troops performing humanitarian work.

In January, Flight Lieutenant Paul Pardoel of the United Kingdom's Royal Air Force became the first Australian servi die in Iraq. In June, Douglas Wood, an Aus born engineer who had been working on tion of military accommodations, was res kidnappers in Iraq. Wood had been held b gents for 47 days before his rescue by Iraq

Drugs. Relations between Australia an Asian neighbors became strained in 2005 number of Australian citizens imprisoned charges. On April 17, nine Australians were of importing heroin into Bali, a charge tha the death penalty in Indonesia. (Australia ished the death penalty in 1967.) On May Indonesian judges sentenced beautician Sc Corby to 20 years in prison for smuggling (4 kilograms) of marijuana. Corby maintai knew nothing about the drugs, which wer

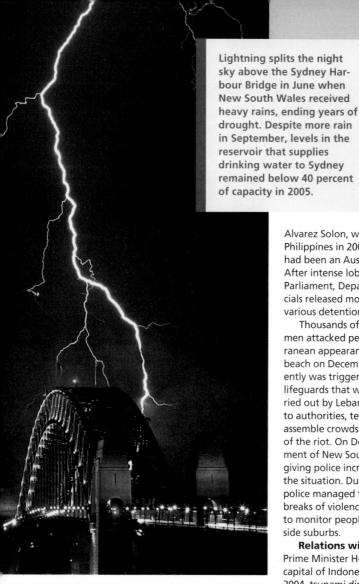

Lightning splits the night sky above the Sydney Harbour Bridge in June when New South Wales received heavy rains, ending years of drought. Despite more rain in September, levels in the reservoir that supplies drinking water to Sydney remained below 40 percent of capacity in 2005.

in Baxter Detention Center in South Australia for 10 months. Rau, who was suffering from a mental illness, was mistaken for an illegal immigrant because she spoke with a German accent. The inquiry also examined the deportation of Vivian Alvarez Solon, who had been sent to the Philippines in 2001 despite the fact that she had been an Australian citizen since 1986. After intense lobbying by some members of Parliament, Department of Immigration officials released more than 40 children held in various detention centers around Australia.

Thousands of young, white Australian men attacked people of Arabic and Mediterranean appearance on Sydney's Cronulla beach on December 11. The incident apparently was triggered by assaults on two white lifeguards that were said to have been carried out by Lebanese immigrants. According to authorities, text messages were used to assemble crowds on the beach in anticipation of the riot. On December 15, the state Parliament of New South Wales passed new laws giving police increased powers to deal with the situation. During the following week, the police managed to control any further outbreaks of violence by setting up roadblocks to monitor people entering southern beachside suburbs.

Relations with Indonesia. In January, Prime Minister Howard flew to Jakarta, the capital of Indonesia, to discuss the Dec. 26, 2004, tsunami disaster with Southeast Asian leaders. Howard later visited Aceh, on the island of Sumatra, where Australian troops and medical volunteers were helping tsunami victims. Much of Aceh was leveled by the tsunami, and as many as 125,000 people were killed in the province.

Howard pledged a total of $1 billion in aid for Indonesia. The gift more than doubled Australia's existing aid to its neighbor and was designed to cover emergency military, medical, and civilian aid. It also included hundreds of millions of dollars to be spent on reconstruction. Australia also set aside money for scholarships to train Indonesian engineers and health professionals.

Economy. Australia continued to enjoy a thriving economy during 2005. In March, the Reserve Bank of Australia raised interest rates by 0.25 percent. Unemployment continued to

in her surf board cover when she arrived in Bali from Australia. In October, her sentence was reduced to 15 years. On August 20, Michelle Leslie, an Adelaide-born model, was arrested in Bali for having two ecstasy tablets in her possession. She was convicted on November 18 and sentenced to three months in jail but was released on November 19 because she already had served her time between her arrest and sentencing.

Immigration. In July, an inquiry headed by former Federal Police Commissioner Mick Palmer recommended sweeping changes to the Department of Immigration and its system of holding illegal immigrants in detention centers. The inquiry was called following widespread outrage after it was revealed that the department had wrongfully detained Cornelia Rau, a legal Australian resident,

Population	20,324,000
Government	Governor General Michael Jeffrey; Prime Minister John Howard
Monetary unit*	dollar (1.29 = $1 U.S.)

Foreign trade (million U.S.$)
Exports[†]	86,890
Imports[†]	98,100

*Exchange rate as of Sept. 9, 2005, or latest available data.
[†]Latest available data.

fall and reached a 28-year low of 5 percent in the fall of 2005. The only negative aspects of the economy were high gasoline prices and a record high negative trade imbalance. Neither of these factors negatively affected the stock market, which continued to soar to record highs during 2005. The All Ordinaries Accumulation Index, which measures total returns on Australian shares, rose by almost 30 percent from January 1 to September 30, which was the biggest gain in 12 years. A sudden crash wiped more than $40 billion from the market value of Australian stocks in early October, but most analysts shrugged off the drop as a temporary correction in the market, which began to climb again during November.

Treasurer Peter Costello presented his 10th budget to Parliament on May 10. He announced tax cuts of nearly $22 billion. Costello predicted that 190,000 people would move off welfare by 2008 or 2009. He also announced a future fund that would be set up to cover pension payments. Costello outlined how the fund would be administered by an independent board, which would farm out investment to private sector fund managers.

Telecommunications and labor relations. On Aug. 19, 2005, the Liberal National Party coalition gained control of the Senate, Australia's upper house of Parliament, when 14 new members were sworn in. For the first time in 24 years, one party had control of both houses. Prime Minister Howard seized this opportunity to pass laws governing telecommunications and industrial relations that had previously been held up by the Senate.

In August, Howard's Cabinet proceeded with the sale of the government's remaining 51 percent share of Telstra, the country's largest telecommunications organization. To win over opponents within the Liberal's coalition partner, the National Party, the Cabinet agreed to place $3 billion from the proceeds of the sale into a fund to finance future services in rural areas. The sale, scheduled for 2006, was expected to raise more than $30 billion.

In November 2005, the government introduced legislation to replace union-based contracts with workplace agreements reached between individu-als and their employers. Government officials believed that increased job flexibility would aid the country's economy. Trade union officials argued that the change would make it easier for employers to fire workers, which would destabilize workplaces. Trade unions staged mass demonstrations around Australia to protest these controversial alterations to the nation's industrial laws.

Politics. Mark Latham, the leader of the opposition Australian Labor Party, resigned from Parliament in January, citing health reasons. In September, he published *The Latham Diaries*, in which he bitterly attacked the structure of the Labor Party and its leading members, including his successor, Kim Beazley.

Clare Martin, chief minister of Australia's Northern Territory, led Labor to a second election victory in June. Later in June, the leader of the National Party, Deputy Prime Minister John Anderson, resigned for health reasons. Mark Vaile was made National Party leader.

In August, Bob Carr, the Labor premier of New South Wales, retired from politics after a record 10 years in office. He was succeeded by Morris Iemma, who had served as state minister of health. In August, the leader of the New South Wales Opposition Liberal Party, John Brogden, resigned the leadership and later retired from Parliament for reasons of health. Peter Debnam was elected as the new party leader.

Drought. In June, New South Wales received heavy rains for the first time in many years. Further rain in September led to a drop from 77 percent to 38 percent in the area of the state that was officially drought stricken.

Despite the rain, levels in the main reservoir that supplies drinking water to Sydney remained below 40 percent of capacity. Restrictions on the use of water for gardens remained in force through 2005. In July, the New South Wales state government announced a plan to build a desalination plant. In August, the Queensland state government announced plans to build more dams, investigate desalination plants, and recycle waste water to serve the 1 million people expected to move north to Queensland by 2025.

Although the Liberal National Party coalition government had refused to sign the Kyoto Protocol on global warming, it accepted a private consulting group's 159-page report on climate change in July 2005. (The Kyoto Protocol is an international agreement to reduce the emission of greenhouse gases.) The authors of the report concluded that Australia would face some degree of increased temperatures over the next 30 to 50 years. The authors forecast that the continent would suffer from more cyclones, forest fires, droughts, and water shortages.

MEMBERS OF THE AUSTRALIAN HOUSE OF REPRESENTATIVES

The House of Representatives of the 42nd Parliament first met Nov. 28, 2005. As of Dec. 9, 2005, the House of Representatives consisted of the following members: 74 Liberal Party of Australia, 60 Australian Labor Party, 12 National Party of Australia, 3 independents, and 1 Northern Territory Country Liberal Party. This table shows each legislator and party affiliation. An asterisk (*) denotes those who served in the 41st Parliament.

Australian Capital Territory
Annette Ellis, A.L.P.*
Bob McMullan, A.L.P.*

New South Wales
Tony Abbott, L.P.*
Anthony Albanese, A.L.P.*
John Anderson, N.P.*
Peter Andren, Ind.*
Bruce Baird, L.P.*
Bob Baldwin, L.P.*
Kerry Bartlett, L.P.*
Sharon Bird, A.L.P.*
Bronwyn Bishop, L.P.*
Chris Bowen, A.L.P.*
Tony Burke, A.L.P.*
Alan Cadman, L.P.*
Ian Causley, N.P.*
John Cobb, N.P.*
Justine Elliot, A.L.P.*
Pat Farmer, L.P.*
Laurie Ferguson, A.L.P.*
Joel Fitzgibbon, A.L.P.*
Peter Garrett, A.L.P.*
Joanna Gash, L.P.*
Jennie George, A.L.P.*
Sharon Grierson, A.L.P.*
Jill Hall, A.L.P.*
Luke Hartsuyker, N.P.*
Michael Hatton, A.L.P.*
Chris Hayes, A.L.P.
Kelly Hoare, A.L.P.*
Joe Hockey, L.P.*
John Howard, L.P.*
Kay Hull, N.P.*
Julia Irwin, A.L.P.*
Jackie Kelly, L.P.*
Sussan Ley, L.P.*
Jim Lloyd, L.P.*
Louise Markus, L.P.*
Robert McClelland, A.L.P.*
Daryl Melham, A.L.P.*
John Murphy, A.L.P.*
Gary Nairn, L.P.*
Brendan Nelson, L.P.*
Julie Owens, A.L.P.
Tanya Plibersek, A.L.P.*
Roger Price, A.L.P.*
Philip Ruddock, L.P.*
Alby Schultz, L.P.*
Ken Ticehurst, L.P.*
Malcolm Turnbull, L.P.*
Mark Vaile, N.P.*
Danna Vale, L.P.*
Tony Windsor, Ind.*

Northern Territory
Warren Snowdon, A.L.P.*
David Tollner, C.L.P.*

Queensland
Arch Bevis, A.L.P.*
Mal Brough, L.P.*
Steven Ciobo, L.P.*
Peter Dutton, L.P.*
Kay Elson, L.P.*
Craig Emerson, A.L.P.*
Warren Entsch, L.P.*
Teresa Gambaro, L.P.*
Gary Hardgrave, L.P.*
Michael Johnson, L.P.*
David Jull, L.P.*
Robert Katter, Ind.*
De-Anne Kelly, N.P.*
Andrew Laming, L.P.*
Peter Lindsay, L.P.*
Kirsten Livermore, A.L.P.*
Ian Macfarlane, L.P.*
Margaret May, L.P.*
Paul Neville, N.P.*
Bernie Ripoll, A.L.P.*
Kevin Rudd, A.L.P.*
Bruce Scott, N.P.*
Peter Slipper, L.P.*
Alexander Somlyay, L.P.*
Wayne Swan, A.L.P.*
Cameron Thompson, L.P.*
Warren Truss, N.P.*
Ross Vasta, L.P.*

South Australia
Alexander Downer, L.P.*
Trish Draper, L.P.*
Kate Ellis, A.L.P.*
David Fawcett, L.P.*
Steve Georganas, A.L.P.*
Christopher Pyne, L.P.*
Kym Richardson, L.P.*
Rodney Sawford, A.L.P.*
Patrick Secker, L.P.*
Andrew Southcott, L.P.*
Barry Wakelin, L.P.*

Tasmania
Dick Adams, A.L.P.*
Mark Baker, L.P.*
Michael Ferguson, L.P.*
Duncan Kerr, A.L.P.*
Harry Quick, A.L.P.*

Victoria
Kevin Andrews, L.P.*
Fran Bailey, L.P.*
Phillip Barresi, L.P.*
Bruce Billson, L.P.*
Russell Broadbent, L.P.*
Anna Burke, A.L.P.*
Anthony Byrne, A.L.P.*
Ann Corcoran, A.L.P.*
Peter Costello, L.P.*
Simon Crean, A.L.P.*
Michael Danby, A.L.P.*
Martin Ferguson, A.L.P.*
John Forrest, N.P.*
Petro Georgiou, L.P.*
Steve Gibbons, A.L.P.*
Julia Gillard, A.L.P.*
Alan Griffin, A.L.P.*
David Hawker, L.P.*
Greg Hunt, L.P.*
Harry Jenkins, A.L.P.*
Catherine King, A.L.P.*
Jenny Macklin, A.L.P.*
Stewart McArthur, L.P.*
Peter McGauran, N.P.*
Brendan O'Connor, A.L.P.*
Gavan O'Connor, A.L.P.*
Sophie Panopoulos, L.P.*
Chris Pearce, L.P.*
Andrew Robb, L.P.*
Nicola Roxon, A.L.P.*
Bob Sercombe, A.L.P.*
Tony Smith, L.P.*
Sharman Stone, L.P.*
Lindsay Tanner, A.L.P.*
Kelvin Thomson, A.L.P.*
Maria Vamvakinou, A.L.P.*
Jason Wood, L.P.*

Western Australia
Kim Beazley, A.L.P.*
Julie Bishop, L.P.*
Graham Edwards, A.L.P.*
Barry Haase, L.P.*
Stuart Henry, L.P.*
Dennis Jensen, L.P.*
Michael Keenan, L.P.*
Carmen Lawrence, A.L.P.*
Judi Moylan, L.P.*
Geoffrey Prosser, L.P.*
Don Randall, L.P.*
Stephen Smith, A.L.P.*
Wilson Tuckey, L.P.*
Mal Washer, L.P.*
Kim Wilkie, A.L.P.*

THE CABINET OF AUSTRALIA*

John Howard—prime minister
Warren Truss—minister for transport
  and regional services
Peter Costello—treasurer
Mark Vaile—minister for trade; deputy prime
  minister
Robert Hill—minister for defence;
  leader of the government in the Senate
Helen Coonan—minister for communications,
  information technology, and the arts
Alexander Downer—minister for foreign affairs
Kevin Andrews—minister for employment and
  workplace relations
Amanda Vanstone—minister for immigration
  and multicultural and indigenous affairs
Ian Campbell—minister for the environment and
  heritage
Philip Ruddock—attorney-general
Nick Minchin—minister for finance and
  administration
Peter McGauran—minister for agriculture,
  fisheries, and forestry
Kay Patterson—minister for family and
  community services
Brendan Nelson—minister for education,
  science, and training
Tony Abbott—minister for health and ageing
Ian Macfarlane—minister for industry, tourism,
  and resources

*As of December 31, 2005.

PREMIERS OF AUSTRALIAN STATES

State	Premier
New South Wales	Morris Iemma
Queensland	Peter Beattie
South Australia	Mike Rann
Tasmania	Paul Lennon
Victoria	Steve Bracks
Western Australia	Geoff Gallop

CHIEF MINISTERS
OF AUSTRALIAN MAINLAND TERRITORIES

Australian Capital Territory	Jon Stanhope
Northern Territory	Clare Martin

Arts. In March, the Archibald Prize—Australia's most prestigious award for painting—was awarded to John Olsen for *Self Portrait Janus Faced.* In June, Andrew McGahan's novel *The White Earth* won Australia's leading book prize, the Miles Franklin Literary Award. The award is bestowed annually for a work portraying various aspects of Australian life.

Australian actor Geoffrey Rush won two prestigious awards in 2005 for his performance in the made-for-television film *The Life and Death of Peter Sellers.* Rush won a Golden Globe award in January, and at the annual Emmy Awards in September, Rush was honored as an outstanding actor in a television mini-series. In February, Australian actress Cate Blanchett won an Academy Award for best supporting actress for her work in *The Aviator.*

Science. In October, two Australian researchers, Barry Marshall and Robin Warren, were awarded the 2005 Nobel Prize in physiology or medicine. The scientists received the award for discovering in the 1980's that stomach ulcers were caused by bacteria.

Melbourne-based drug manufacturer CSL Limited announced in October 2005 positive results for an international trial of a vaccine for cervical cancer. The vaccine, known as Gardasil, had been developed by Ian Frazer of the University of Queensland and was tested on more than 12,000 women in 13 countries.

In October, the 2005 Australian Prime Minister's Prize for Science was awarded to David Boger, a chemical engineer from the University of Melbourne, whose work on fluid mechanics proved highly valuable to mining companies for controlling waste in tailings dams.

■ Brian Kennedy

See also **Australia, Prime Minister of; Indonesia; Iraq; Motion pictures; Nobel prizes; Pacific Islands; Terrorism; United Kingdom.**

Australia, Prime Minister of.

John Howard, who was 66 years old in 2005, hinted in an interview in Athens in April that he might stay on as leader of the Liberal Party beyond the elections of 2007. The deputy leader of the party, Peter Costello, refused to confirm or deny that he had told Howard that he was not prepared to wait indefinitely for his chance to become prime minister.

Howard began a busy year of international travel by flying to the Indonesian capital, Jakarta, in January to attend a summit meeting with Asian leaders to discuss plans for aid to areas hit by the tsunami that followed an undersea earthquake off the island of Sumatra on Dec. 26, 2004. On April 25, 2005, Howard appeared at Anzac Cove in Turkey to celebrate the 90th anniversary of the ill-fated landing of the Anzacs—the Australian and New Zealand Army Corps—on the Gallipoli Peninsula during World War I (1914-1918).

In November 2005, Howard attended the Commonwealth Heads of Government Meeting (CHOGM) in Malta. The CHOGM are biennial meetings between the leaders of 53 independent nations and other political units formerly governed by the United Kingdom. ■ Brian Kennedy

See also **Australia.**

Australian rules football. The Sydney Swans defeated the West Coast Eagles by four points to win their first ever Australian Football League (AFL) premiership in Melbourne on Sept. 24, 2005. The final was the closest since 1966, with the Swans reclaiming a 20-point lead at halftime and hanging on to win by 8 goals, 10 behinds (58 points) to 7 goals, 12 behinds (54 points).

The final quarter of the game was one of the most exciting in Grand Final history. The Eagles clawed back to take the lead, but the Swans scored the final goal in the 19th minute to win.

The Eagles' Ben Cousins was awarded the Brownlow Medal for being the best and fairest player during the 2005 regular season. West Coast midfielder Chris Judd won the Norm Smith Medal for the best player on the ground in the Grand Final match.

Sandringham defeated Werribee 11.17 (83) to 11.8 (74) to win the Victorian Football League Cup on September 18. In the AFL Queensland Grand Final, the Southport Sharks beat the Morningside Panthers 16.15 (111) to 6.14 (50) on September 18. In the South Australian National Football League, Central District defeated the Woodville-West Torrens Eagles 15.14 (104) to 11.10 (76) on October 1.　　▪ Brian Kennedy

Austria. The ruling center-right coalition government of Austria, made up of the People's Party and the Alliance for the Future of Austria, faced challenges in 2005 from the opposition Social Democratic Party. The Social Democrats pressured the government over its poor record in increasing economic growth. The declining popularity of the ruling coalition resulted in disappointing performances by candidates of both parties in state elections in October in Burgenland and Styria.

Immigration and asylum continued to be important issues in Austria during 2005. Both government and opposition parties agreed in June on a tough new asylum law. The law allows authorities to detain for up to 10 months asylum seekers who have been turned down and are awaiting deportation. It also allows the force-feeding of hunger-strikers awaiting deportation.

Austria's economic growth declined slightly in 2005. According to European Union (EU) economists, growth fell from 2.4 percent in 2004 to 1.7 percent in 2005. At 5.0 percent, unemployment was relatively low in 2005, compared with the EU average of 8.7 percent. However, public sector debt remained high at 64 percent of *gross domestic product* (the total output of goods and services produced in a country in a given year).

▪ Jeffrey Kopstein

See also **Europe.**

Austrian dignitaries and representatives of the Allied nations that occupied the country after World War II (1939-1945) gather at the Belvedere Palace outside Vienna on May 15, 2005, to celebrate the 50th anniversary of the signing of the treaty that restored Austria's sovereignty.

Honda Insight

Volkswagen Beetle

Toyota Prius

Skyrocketing gas prices in 2005 refocused the attention of consumers on fuel-efficient vehicles

Two hybrid cars—the Honda Insight and the Toyota Prius—average 60 miles (97 kilometers) per gallon in city driving, making them the most fuel-efficient vehicles of 2005, according to the Environmental Protection Agency. The most fuel-efficient compact car, the 2005 Volkswagen Beetle, gets 37 miles (60 kilometers) per gallon in city driving.

Automobile. The United States automobile market experienced another solid, but stormy, year in 2005 despite high gasoline prices. Through the first nine months of 2005, sales of cars and light trucks totaled 13.2 million units for a 3-percent gain over the same period in 2004. Summer sales in 2005 increased thanks to the traditional Big Three automakers—General Motors (GM) Corporation of Detroit; Ford Motor Company of Dearborn, Michigan; and the United States division of DaimlerChrysler AG of Germany—offering consumers the same discounts that automakers' employees receive. Analysts noted that the discounts lured potential buyers into showrooms in the middle of the year, but hurt sales in the final quarter. Nevertheless, an estimated 17 million units were sold in 2005, slightly ahead of the 16.9 million sold in 2004.

Even with the employee discount offers, the Big Three lost market share to their Asian rivals. Detroit's market share was 59.1 percent through September 2005, compared with 60.5 percent during the same period in 2004. Asian automakers saw their market share rise to 36.1 percent for the first nine months of 2005, up from 34.4 percent a year earlier. The market share of European carmakers dipped to 4.8 percent through September 2005, compared with 5.1 percent in the same period in 2004. In July 2005, incentives offered by Ford, Chrysler, and General Motors averaged $3,942 per vehicle, compared with $1,236 per vehicle for Japanese automakers, $1,945 for Korean companies, and $2,382 for European automakers. Industry incentives totaled a record $5.3 billion in July 2005.

The Ford F-series truck was the best-selling vehicle of the 2005 model year, with 890,790 units sold. The Toyota Camry claimed the top honor for cars with 438,015 units sold. Sales of hybrid vehicles, which combine gasoline and electric power, also grew in 2005, and 10 different models were offered, according to a study conducted by the Troy, Michigan-based research firm J.D. Power-LMC Automotive Forecasting Services. The authors of the report predicted that 44 such vehicles would be on the market by 2012.

Big Three. The year 2005 was tumultuous for the number one automaker. General Motors' domestic sales were down 1 percent to 3.5 million units through the first nine months of the year, and its market share dropped to 26.9 percent from 28 percent in 2004. Sales of the company's high-profit-margin sport utility vehicles, such as Chevrolet's Suburban and Tahoe models, fell in 2005, but the automaker achieved solid sales with its Pontiac Solstice roadster. GM lost $3.8 billion through the first nine months of 2005, compared with a net income of $2.9 billion in the same period in 2004. The automaker's struggles prompted credit rating agencies to lower GM's bond to below investment grade, or junk status.

To address GM's problems, company Chairman Rick Wagoner announced in April 2005 that he was taking responsibility for the automaker's North American operations. The automaker also sought to cut health care costs through a tentative agreement in October with the United Automobile Workers union (UAW). The company estimated that the agreement would reduce its retiree health care liability by $15 billion and save the company $1 billion a year. The UAW approved the health care agreement by a 61-percent majority in November. However, continuing problems prompted GM to announce on November 21 that it would eliminate 30,000 manufacturing jobs from 2005 to 2008. The automaker announced that it would close nine assembly, stamping, and power train plants in North America. GM said its plans would reduce costs by $7 billion at the end of 2006. GM also sold its 20-percent interest in Japan's Fuji Heavy Industries in October 2005 at an anticipated profit of $70 million. Earlier in 2005, GM paid the Italian car manufacturer Fiat SpA. $2 billion, dissolving joint ventures formed in 2000. GM retained jointly developed technical advances in developing diesel engines and transmissions. Former GM subsidiary Delphi Corporation, an automotive parts maker based in Troy, Michigan, filed for bankruptcy in October 2005. Delphi, the largest auto parts maker in the United States, spun off from GM in 1999.

Ford also had problems in 2005. Rating services lowered Ford's debt to junk status as well. The automaker's domestic sales dropped 1 percent to 2.5 million units through September 2005, and its market share fell to 18.6 percent, compared with 19.4 percent in the same period in 2004. Ford, the second largest selling automaker in the United States, reported a net income of $1.9 billion through the first nine months of 2005, compared with $3.4 billion in 2004. Ford took a series of steps throughout the year to strengthen the company, including reducing its salaried work force by 2,750 employees. In September 2005, the company announced a deal to sell its Hertz rental car subsidiary, which was expected to bring Ford $5.6 billion. Chairman Bill Ford announced in October that he would unveil a major restructuring plan in January 2006. Sales of Ford's Explorer and Expedition sport utility vehicles declined in 2005, while sales of the Ford Mustang increased. Ford also introduced its second hybrid vehicle, the Mercury Mariner sport utility vehicle, in July and announced that it would have the capacity to build 250,000 hybrids annually by 2010.

DaimlerChrysler's U.S. division was the only one of the traditional Big Three to post stronger sales and a better market share through September 2005. Chrysler's sales rose to 1.8 million units, a 7-percent increase over the same period in 2004. Its market share grew to 13.6 percent in

2005 from 13.1 percent in 2004. The division reported an operating profit of $1.3 billion for the first nine months of 2005, compared with $1.25 billion for the same period in 2004. The Chrysler group benefited from better sales of its 300 Series cars, which totaled 106,364 units through September 2005, compared with 71,903 a year earlier. Chrysler also got a new leader in September when Tom LaSorda became president and chief executive officer.

Asian manufacturers. Toyota was a big winner in sales and market share growth through September 2005. The automaker's sales rose to 1.7 million units, an 11-percent increase over the same period in 2004. Its market share rose to 13 percent in 2005, compared with 12.1 percent a year earlier. In 2005, Toyota enjoyed higher sales for its Camry, Corrolla, and Prius hybrid. The company announced in May plans to build hybrid Camrys at its Georgetown, Kentucky, plant in 2006. Through September 2005, Honda's sales grew 6 percent, to 1.1 million units. Its market share grew to 8.5 percent from 8.2 percent in 2004. Nissan's sales rose 15 percent to 836,151 units through the first nine months of 2005, and its market share edged up to 6.4 percent, compared with 5.7 percent in 2004. In May 2005, Korean-based Hyundai Motor Company formally opened its Montgomery, Alabama, assembly plant that produced Sonatas. ■ Mike Casey

Automobile racing.
Tony Stewart dueled Greg Biffle to capture the NASCAR Nextel Cup championship in 2005, but the spotlight shined brightest on Danica Patrick's quest to become the first woman to win a race on a major circuit.

Patrick, a 23-year-old racer from the United States, became one of the sport's hottest stars, accomplishing a host of firsts for female racers, including leading—and nearly winning—the Indianapolis 500 on May 29 and claiming the *pole position* (starting position earned by the racer with the fastest qualifying times) three times.

Indianapolis 500. Patrick became the fourth female driver to qualify for the Indy 500, starting the race in the fourth position, the best ever qualifying position for a woman driver. On the 56th lap, Patrick became the first woman to take the lead in an Indy 500 race, grabbing the top spot as the other leaders stopped for fuel.

The eventual winner, Dan Wheldon, retook the lead with 14 laps to go. Patrick burst past Wheldon with 10 laps to go, but because she had taken an earlier final pit stop than Wheldon, she had to use fuel-saving techniques to ensure she would finish the race. Wheldon, the first British man in 39 years to win the Indy 500, passed Patrick for good with seven laps to go.

Wheldon averaged 157.603 miles (253.633 kilometers) per hour and beat Vitor Meira by 0.13 second. Patrick led for 19 laps overall and her fourth-place finish was the best ever for a female driver.

Formula One. Seven-time champion Michael Schumacher of Germany struggled in 2005, winning just once in the first 15 races as Spain's Fernando Alonso rolled to a huge points lead, scoring six victories and 10 top-10 finishes in the first 13 races of the 19-race circuit. Alonso went on to capture the points total on September 25 with a third-place finish at the Brazilian Grand Prix in Sao Paolo.

NASCAR. Tony Stewart won the Nextel Cup championship on November 20 at Homestead-Miami Speedway with a 15th-place finish. Stewart finished 35 points ahead of Greg Biffle.

Greg Biffle won five races early in the season to jump out to a big points lead, but Jimmie Johnson's consistency helped him to take the points lead in mid-July. Tony Stewart, who won three of four races in the early summer, also surged ahead of Biffle. Under the format adopted in 2004, the point totals of the top 10 drivers with 10 races to go—and any other driver within 400 points of the leader—are adjusted to create a "Chase for the Championship" among the top drivers. Star drivers who did not have enough points to participate in 2005 included Dale Earnhardt, Jr., and Jeff Gordon.

IRL. Dan Wheldon won 4 of the first 5 races of the Indy Racing League (IRL) to take a commanding lead in the points standings ahead of Sam Hornish, Jr., and 2004 champ Tony Kanaan through 14 of the 17-race circuit. Wheldon captured the title on Oct. 16, 2005, with 628 points.

On July 2, Danica Patrick became the second woman to capture the pole position in an IRL race, joining Sarah Fisher who did so in 2002. Patrick earned two more pole positions in 2005.

Champ Car. Sebastien Bourdais of France recorded three wins and six top-five finishes early in the Champ Car World Series circuit, taking a big points lead. He captured the title on October 23, finishing with 348 points, 60 more than Oriol Servia of Spain.

Endurance. Tom Kristensen of Denmark won his record seventh 24 Hours of Le Mans on June 19 in Le Mans, France. Kristensen drove with J. J. Lehto of Finland and Marco Werner of Germany.

Max Angelelli, Wayne Taylor, and Emmanuel Collard captured the Rolex 24-hour race at Daytona Beach, Florida, on February 6, averaging 105 miles (169 kilometers) per hour.

Dragsters. Tony Schumacher won the 2005 National Hot Rod Association (NHRA) top fuel division championship; Gary Scelzi won the funny car division; and Greg Anderson won the pro stock division. ■ Michael Kates

See also **People in the News** (Danica Patrick).

Inspectors examine the wreckage of an Air France airbus A340 at Pearson International Airport in Toronto, Canada, after the aircraft on August 3 landed during a severe thunderstorm, skidded off the runway, and broke into three parts. Before the jet burst into flames, all 309 passengers and crew escaped in an evacuation that took less than two minutes.

Aviation. The economic recovery of the airline industry continued to be hampered in 2005 by increases in the cost of fuel oil. The price of crude oil reached a record high of $70.85 a barrel on August 30, after Hurricane Katrina—in one of the worst natural disasters in the history of the United States—struck the Gulf Coast, reducing oil production in the region by 92 percent. The airline industry had been in a slump since a decline in air travel following the terrorist attacks on the United States on Sept. 11, 2001.

Bankruptcies. Delta Air Lines Inc. of Atlanta, Georgia, and Northwest Airlines Corp. of Eagan, Minnesota—the second and fourth largest U.S. carriers, respectively—both filed for bankruptcy protection on Sept. 14, 2005. Industry analysts cited increased fuel costs and competition from low-cost carriers, as well as high labor costs for the so-called "legacy" airlines, as reasons for the moves. (Legacy airlines are older carriers that are bound by union contracts and bear billions of dollars in pension costs.)

On September 15, a bankruptcy court judge approved the request for a merger between US Airways Group Inc. of Arlington, Virginia—which had entered bankruptcy in 2004 for the second time in two years—and America West Airlines Inc. of Tempe, Arizona. Both airlines had experienced financial difficulties for several years and had received considerable financial support from the U.S. government in the form of loan guarantees. The new carrier, the nation's sixth largest airline, began operations under the US Airways name, but under America West's management team.

New aircraft. The world's largest passenger aircraft, the Airbus A380, made its maiden flight on April 27, 2005, at Toulouse, France. The double-deck aircraft can carry 555 passengers, dwarfing Chicago-based Boeing Company's 747, which had been the dominant large passenger aircraft for 30 years. The first commercial flight of the A380, by Singapore Airlines, was scheduled for mid-2006. Airbus is jointly owned by European Aeronautic Defense and Space Company of the Netherlands and BAE Systems of the United Kingdom.

Rather than building a new larger aircraft, Boeing in 2005 began promoting a middle-sized jet designed to serve smaller international markets with more frequent flights. The 787 Dreamliner (formerly the 7E7), which seats from 200 to 300 people, was expected to make its debut in 2008.

The development of the new aircraft revived a longstanding diplomatic dispute between the United States and the European Union (EU) concerning government subsidies to Airbus and Boeing. Both sides filed complaints with the World Trade Organization (WTO), which oversees international trade. The United States claimed that the

EU's low-cost, noncommercial loans to Airbus distorted competition. The EU claimed that Boeing received support by state grants, military contracts, and tax concessions to assist in the development of the 787. The WTO began an investigation into the claims in July 2005.

Fares. Competition from low-cost airlines prompted some of the larger, more established carriers in 2005 to simplify their fare structure and reduce the disparity between different types of fares. For many years, airlines charged higher fares for business travelers, who tend to make reservations shortly before traveling and prefer to travel on weekdays. In January, Delta announced a reduction in the maximum price for a trip to $499 each way in coach and business class. In addition, Delta dropped its requirement that passengers book a trip that extends over a Saturday night to qualify for a discounted fare. The "Saturday night stay" long had been a feature of airline pricing, designed to help airlines distinguish between business travelers and price-sensitive leisure travelers. Other airlines quickly followed Delta's lead and also dropped the requirement.

Electronic communication. In May, the Federal Aviation Administration (FAA) approved a request by United Airlines, based in Elk Grove Village, Illinois, to install wireless Internet connections on Boeing 757 aircraft. Such connections would allow passengers to surf the Internet and check their e-mail using personal laptop computers during flight. Several airlines provide such service on international flights. However, United's was to be the first application for U.S. domestic flights. The service was to begin in 2006.

A more contentious issue in 2005 was the ongoing debate among Federal Communications Commission and FAA officials over whether to permit the use of cellular telephones in flight. During Congressional hearings in July, FAA officials indicated that they would not lift the ban on cell phone use aboard aircraft until such issues as security concerns and the annoyance to fellow passengers of people talking on their cellphones during flights had been addressed.

Security. In May, the Transportation Security Administration (TSA), a division of the U.S. Department of Homeland Security, announced plans to require that airlines request the full name and birthdate of passengers who purchase tickets. The TSA was in the process of developing a computerized passenger screening program called Secure Flight that compares passengers' names with a list of terrorist suspects. The additional information, TSA officials believed, would reduce problems for some passengers who have similar names to those on the watch list and are therefore delayed whenever they board a flight. ■ Ian Savage

See also **Energy supply.**

Azerbaijan. Protests followed Azerbaijan's disputed parliamentary elections of Nov. 6, 2005. After the Central Electoral Commission announced that the ruling Yeni Azerbaijan Party of President Ilham Aliyev had won 63 of the 125 seats, opposition parties challenged the results. International observers denounced the election as flawed, citing numerous failings both before and during the election, including arbitrary detentions of opposition leaders, ballot stuffing, and intimidation at polling places. The charges echoed those from the October 2003 presidential election, which had also sparked protests and arrests. Although President Aliyev admitted only to isolated irregularities in 2005, the government annulled election results in several districts in response to criticism. Some 500 unsatisfied opposition candidates met in Baku, the capital, on Nov. 16, 2005, to denounce what was described as the "total falsification" of the results.

Azerbaijan's long-awaited Baku-Tbilisi-Ceyhan oil pipeline opened in May, carrying oil from the Caspian Sea to the Turkish port of Ceyhan. Western leaders supported the construction of the pipeline in order to reduce their dependence on Middle Eastern oil. ■ Juliet Johnson

See also **Asia; Russia: A Special Report.**

Bahamas. See **Latin America; West Indies.**

Bahrain. See **Middle East.**

Ballet. See **Dance.**

Bangladesh. More than 400 small bombs exploded in a one-hour period in 63 of Bangladesh's 64 local government districts on Aug. 17, 2005, killing 2 people and wounding approximately 150 others. Leaflets found at some bomb sites demanded the introduction of Islamic law, Shari`ah, in Bangladesh. Suicide bombers killed 11 people in the southern city of Chittagong and the central town of Gazipur in late November.

The government blamed the violence on Jamaat-ul-Mujahideen, an extremist group that had been outlawed earlier in 2005. At least 90 percent of Bangladesh's 130 million people are Muslims, but its major political parties have maintained secular traditions. The bombings came amid political violence that has continued for years. Prime Minister Khaleda Zia's Bangladesh Nationalist Party and the opposition Awami League have long blamed each other for widespread lawlessness. Control of Bangladesh has switched back and forth between Zia and Sheikh Hasina Hajed, head of the League, since the 1990's.

Some of the violence was attributed to the continuing bitter competition for political power by the two parties. The League, however, accused Zia of being under the influence of two Islamic parties in her coalition and, therefore, ignoring violence by Islamic extremists. ■ Henry S. Bradsher

See also **Asia; Disasters.**

Bank. United States President George W. Bush nominated Ben S. Bernanke to be the chairman of the powerful Federal Reserve Board on Oct. 24, 2005. The Federal Reserve System (the Fed), the central bank of the United States, also serves a critical role in the economy by adjusting interest rates that banks charge one another, which ripple out to the broader economy. The Fed typically raises interest rates to thwart *inflation* (a continual increase in prices throughout a nation's economy), when the economy is expanding too quickly. At times of slow economic growth, the Fed is likely to cut interest rates, which makes it easier for businesses to borrow and expand.

At the time of his appointment, Bernanke was serving as the chairman of the Council of Economic Advisers, a government agency whose members advise the president on economic policy. He had previously been an economic professor at Princeton University in Princeton, New Jersey, and governor of the Federal Reserve. Bernanke was expected to be confirmed by the U.S. Senate before Jan. 31, 2006, when Alan Greenspan was due to retire after 18 years as chairman of the Fed.

In Senate confirmation hearings in 2005, Bernanke generally endorsed the policies of his predecessor. Greenspan had been widely regarded as an astute observer of the economy, who engineered "soft landings" from rapid growth by gradually increasing interest rates. The policy also helped to avoid *recessions* (a decline in overall business activity) by ratcheting rates downward, particularly after a stock market crash in 1987, which occurred shortly after he became chairman of the Fed. Greenspan was credited with helping to guide the economy through its longest period of sustained growth on record.

Interest rates. The Federal Reserve continued to raise short-term interest rates in 2005 as a means to head off inflation. On November 1, the Fed raised short-term interest rates that banks charge each other for overnight loans to 4 percent from 3.75 percent. The hike marked the 12th consecutive interest-rate increase and raised interest rates to their highest level since June 2001. However, rates were still far below the most recent peak of 6.5 percent at the end of 2000.

The long stretch of low interest rates in the 2000's helped bolster the U.S. economy by reducing the costs of borrowing to buy residences, furniture, cars, and other consumer products. Economists expected the Fed to continue raising interest rates by quarter-point increments through early 2006.

Industry earnings. Banks reported strong earnings in the first half of 2005. In the first quarter, commercial banks and savings institutions insured by the Federal Deposit Insurance Corporation, a government agency that provides insurance coverage for bank deposits up to $100,000, reported net income of $34.3 billion, a record. In the second quarter of 2005, the industry reported net income of $33.1 billion.

Bankruptcy changes. The banking industry struggled to adjust to a new bankruptcy law that took effect Oct. 17, 2005. The new law was intended to steer consumers away from filing Chapter 7 bankruptcy protection, which allowed for the quick discharge of credit cards and other debts, and into Chapter 13, which required debtors to pay off at least a portion of their loans over five years. More than 500,000 Americans filed for bankruptcy protection in the final 10 days before the new law took effect, which represented about a third of the total number of bankruptcies in 2004.

Economists expected the losses in 2005 to be troubling for the nation's biggest banks, where credit cards have become an increasingly large portion of their business. New York City-based J.P. Morgan Chase & Co., the second largest credit card issuer in the country, announced it would set aside an additional $100 million in the third quarter to help absorb losses from its customers filing for bankruptcy and nulling their credit card debt. Citigroup, of New York City, the third largest credit card issuer, claimed that it would be forced for the same reason to write off an additional $200 million in pretax credit costs during the third quarter. Some analysts predicted that the rush of bankruptcies would shave $1 billion worth in earnings in 2005 from banks that issue credit cards.

Citigroup, the nation's largest bank, with $1.48 trillion in assets, was broadly criticized when its CitiFinancial subsidiary announced on June 2 that it lost financial data for 3.9 million customers. The information was held on computer tapes, which were lost by a United Parcel Service delivery truck on its way to a credit bureau. CitiFinancial officials noted that there was little risk of the information being misused, but the security breach occurred at a time of increasing concern over privacy and identity theft, in which personal information is stolen and used by others to falsely obtain credit, among other things. Citigroup announced that it would improve its security measures and would begin *encrypting,* or coding, customer information and transmitting it electronically.

WorldCom lawsuits. On March 16, J.P. Morgan Chase, the second largest U.S. bank, with assets of more than $1.2 trillion, agreed to pay $2 billion to settle lawsuits connected with its transactions with WorldCom, a telecommunications company based in Clinton, Mississippi, that filed for bankruptcy in 2002. Many investors subsequently filed suit against Morgan Chase, alleging that it did not conduct adequate investigations into the financial condition of WorldCom before selling WorldCom securities. Morgan Chase was the last of 17 banks associated with WorldCom to settle. The bank closed the suit in March, just two days after WorldCom's former chief executive, Bernard J. Ebbers, was found guilty of fraud.

Enron settlement. On June 14, J.P. Morgan Chase agreed to pay $2.2 billion to investors in Enron Corporation, an energy company based in Houston. Investors accused the bank of participating in the accounting fraud that led to Enron's collapse and bankruptcy in 2001. Citigroup also agreed to a $2-billion settlement in the case on June 10, 2005.

Mergers. In one of the biggest transactions of 2005, Bank of America Corp., based in Charlotte, North Carolina, agreed to buy MBNA Corp., of Wilmington, Delaware, the third largest U.S. credit card lender, for $35 billion on June 30. Bank of America, with $1.27 trillion in assets, also agreed to acquire a $3-billion stake in China's second largest lender, China Construction Bank.

■ Paulette Thomas

See also **Crime: A Special Report; Economics; Stocks and bonds.**

Baseball. The Chicago White Sox in 2005 ended an 88-year drought, winning the World Series in a 4-game sweep of the Houston Astros. It was the Astros' first World Series appearance since the franchise came into existence in 1962.

Both teams rode spectacular starting pitching to the 2005 World Series, particularly the White Sox. During the American League Championship Series (ALCS), White Sox starting pitchers tossed four consecutive complete games, the first time a team accomplished that feat since 1956.

World Series. In the opening game of the Series, which the White Sox won 5-3, the Sox drove Astros pitching ace Roger Clemens from the game after only two innings. Clemens strained his left hamstring in the damp, cold weather, and his team rallied to tie the game at three in the third inning, only to allow unanswered runs in the fourth and eighth.

In Game 2 the following night, Chicago's Scott Podsednik, who had not hit any home runs in the regular season, gave the White Sox a 7-6 win by belting the game-winning homer in the bottom of the ninth against Houston star reliever Brad Lidge.

Game 3 in Houston on Oct. 25, 2005, was one of the strangest in the annals of World Series history. The White Sox eventually won the game 7-5, but it was not easy. The game lasted 5 hours,

Members of the Chicago White Sox winning team (from left to right)—Aaron Rowand, Geoff Blum, and Joe Crede—wave to fans during a ticker-tape parade in downtown Chicago on October 28. The parade celebrated the Sox ending an 88-year drought by winning the 2005 World Series in a 4-game sweep of the Houston Astros.

FINAL STANDINGS IN MAJOR LEAGUE BASEBALL

AMERICAN LEAGUE

American League champions—
Chicago White Sox
(defeated Los Angeles Angels, 4 games to 1)

World Series champions—
Chicago White Sox (defeated Houston Astros, 4 games to 0)

Eastern Division	W.	L.	Pct.	G.B.
New York Yankees	95	67	.586	—
Boston Red Sox*	95	67	.586	—
Toronto Blue Jays	80	82	.494	15
Baltimore Orioles	74	88	.457	21
Tampa Bay Devil Rays	67	95	.414	28

Central Division	W.	L.	Pct.	G.B.
Chicago White Sox	99	63	.611	—
Cleveland Indians	93	69	.574	6
Minnesota Twins	83	79	.512	16
Detroit Tigers	71	91	.438	28
Kansas City Royals	56	106	.346	43

Western Division	W.	L.	Pct.	G.B.
Los Angeles Angels	95	67	.586	—
Oakland Athletics	88	74	.543	7
Texas Rangers	79	83	.488	16
Seattle Mariners	69	93	.426	26

Offensive leaders

Batting average	Michael Young, Texas	.331
Runs scored	Alex Rodriguez, New York	124
Home runs	Alex Rodriguez, New York	48
Runs batted in	David Ortiz, Boston	148
Hits	Michael Young, Texas	221
Stolen bases	Chone Figgins, L.A.	62
Slugging percentage	Alex Rodriguez, New York	.610

Leading pitchers

Games won	Bartolo Colon, L.A.	21
Earned run average (162 or more innings)—	Kevin Millwood, Cleveland	2.86
Strikeouts	Johan Santana, Minnesota	238
Saves	Francisco Rodriguez, L.A.	45
Shut-outs	Jon Garland, Chicago	3
Complete games	Roy Halladay, Toronto	5

Awards†

Most Valuable Player ....Alex Rodriguez, New York
Cy Young ....Bartolo Colon, L.A.
Rookie of the Year ....Huston Street, Oakland
Manager of the Year ....Ozzie Guillen, Chicago

NATIONAL LEAGUE

National League champions—
Houston Astros
(defeated St. Louis Cardinals, 4 games to 2)

Eastern Division	W.	L.	Pct.	G.B.
Atlanta Braves	90	72	.556	—
Philadelphia Phillies	88	74	.543	2
Florida Marlins	83	79	.512	7
New York Mets	83	79	.512	7
Washington Nationals	81	81	.500	9

Central Division	W.	L.	Pct.	G.B.
St. Louis Cardinals	100	62	.617	—
Houston Astros*	89	73	.549	11
Milwaukee Brewers	81	81	.500	19
Chicago Cubs	79	83	.488	21
Cincinnati Reds	73	89	.451	27
Pittsburgh Pirates	67	95	.414	33

Western Division	W.	L.	Pct.	G.B.
San Diego Padres	82	80	.506	—
Arizona Diamondbacks	77	85	.475	5
San Francisco Giants	75	87	.463	7
Los Angeles Dodgers	71	91	.438	11
Colorado Rockies	67	95	.414	15

Offensive leaders

Batting average	Derek Lee, Chicago	.335
Runs scored	Albert Pujols, St. Louis	129
Home runs	Andruw Jones, Atlanta	51
Runs batted in	Andruw Jones, Atlanta	128
Hits	Derek Lee, Chicago	199
Stolen bases	Jose Reyes, New York	60
Slugging percentage	Derek Lee, Chicago	.662

Leading pitchers

Games won	Dontrelle Willis, Florida	22
Earned run average (162 or more innings)—	Roger Clemens, Houston	1.87
Strikeouts	Jake Peavy, San Diego	216
Saves	Chad Cordero, Washington	47
Shut-outs	Dontrelle Willis, Florida	5
Complete games	Chris Carpenter, St. Louis	7
	Dontrelle Willis, Florida	7

Awards†

Most Valuable Player ....Albert Pujols, St. Louis
Cy Young...Chris Carpenter, St. Louis
Rookie of the Year ....Ryan Howard, Philadelphia
Manager of the Year..................................Bobby Cox, Atlanta

*Qualified for wild-card play-off spot.
†Selected by the Baseball Writers Association of America.

---

41 minutes, the longest in World Series history. The game also tied the mark for most innings (14) and broke Series records for pitchers used (17), players used (43), players left on base (30), and double plays (6). Houston had tied the game in the bottom of the eighth, but the White Sox took the lead for good on a two-out solo home run by seldom-used utility player Geoff Blum in the top of the 14th.

The White Sox won the title on October 26 with a 1-0 victory. The Sox scored the winning run when Series MVP Jermaine Dye grounded a single up the middle with two outs in the top of the eighth. Chicago's dominant post-season performance of 11 wins and 1 loss matched the 1999 Yankees for the best play-off record since play-offs were expanded in 1995.

Play-offs. The White Sox made their first World Series appearance since 1959 by beating the Los Angeles Angels of Anaheim 4 games to 1. The Sox advanced to the ALCS by sweeping the Boston Red Sox 3 games to none, while the

Professional baseball players (from left to right) Sammy Sosa, Mark McGwire, Rafael Palmeiro, and Kurt Schilling listen to testimony during a House of Representatives committee hearing in Washington, D.C., on March 17, 2005. Lawmakers demanded that professional sports leagues stiffen penalties for players who test positive for steroids.

Angels beat the New York Yankees 3 games to 2.

The Astros earned their World Series spot by defeating the St. Louis Cardinals 4 games to 2. The Astros clinched the series on Oct. 19, 2005, with a 5-1 victory in St. Louis. To reach the NLCS, the Cardinals swept the San Diego Padres 3 games to none. The Astros had beaten the Atlanta Braves 3 games to 1 in the Division Series, clinching the series by winning the longest postseason game in history, an 18-inning, 5-hour and 50 minute affair, by a score of 7-6.

Regular season. The St. Louis Cardinals rolled to the best record in baseball in 2005, winning the NL Central 100-62, 11 games better than wild-card winner Houston, which 89-73. The Astros, which lost 30 of their first 45 games, became the first team since the 1914 world champion Boston Braves to go to the Series after being 15 games below .500. The Atlanta Braves (90-72) won the NL East, while San Diego won the NL West with a record of 82-80, the worst mark for a play-off team in a non-strike year since 1969.

All three AL division races came down to the final week of the season. The Angels (95-67) secured the AL West first, followed by the White Sox (99-63), which led the AL Central by 15 games on August 1 only to see the Cleveland Indians go on an 18-5 run in September to trim the lead to 1½ games. However, the White Sox clinched the division by winning their fourth-to-last game and then sweeping the Indians in Cleveland to eliminate their rivals from the wild-card race. In the

AL East, the Yankees started the season 11-19, their worst start since 1966, and fell 9 games off the lead. The Yankees trailed Boston by 5½ games on Aug. 11, 2005, but the Yankees went 35-12 the rest of the way to win their eighth straight AL East title. Boston secured the wild card when the Indians lost their last game of the season.

Steroid controversy. On March 17, 2005, the United States House of Representatives held a hearing in which lawmakers criticized Major League Baseball's steroid policy. Prominent current and former baseball stars were called to testify, including Sammy Sosa, Mark McGwire, and Rafael Palmeiro. While Sosa did not answer many questions and McGwire refused to talk about the past, Palmeiro adamantly denied using steroids. In August, however, Palmeiro was suspended for 10 games for testing positive for steroids.

Lawmakers, angry that Palmeiro tested positive after testifying that he had never taken steroids, considered charging him with perjury. However, they later claimed that there was not enough evidence to prosecute Palmeiro.

In late 2005, Major League Baseball and the players' union bowed to congressional pressure and agreed on a tougher policy on steroid use. Under the new plan, players would be suspended for 50 games for a first offense and 100 games for a second positive test. Players testing positive a third time faced a lifetime ban.

Power outage. The average number of home runs hit per game dropped 8 percent in 2005, compared with 2004, and was the lowest since 1997. Major league sluggers hit 2.06 homers per game in 2005, according to the Elias Sports Bureau, down from 2.25 in 2004.

Milestones. On June 15, 2005, Seattle's Ichiro Suzuki became just the third player since 1900 to get 1,000 hits in fewer than 700 games. Suzuki reached the 1,000 hit mark in just 696 games.

On July 15, 2005, Rafael Palmeiro became only the fourth player in Major League Baseball history to collect 3,000 hits and hit 500 home runs in a career.

Deaths. Hall of Famer Al Lopez, who managed the 1959 White Sox during the team's last World Series appearance, died Oct. 30, 2005, at the age of 97.

Joe Bauman, who in 1954 hit a then-professional record 72 home runs in a season in the minor league Class C Longhorn League, died Sept. 20, 2005, at the age of 83.

College. The University of Texas (Austin) swept the Univeristy of Florida (Gainesville) three games to none to win the National Collegiate Athletic Association (NCAA) College World Series with a 6-2 win on June 26 in Omaha, Nebraska. It was the school's sixth national title.

Youth. A team from West Oahu, Hawaii, won the Little League World Series on August 28 in Williamsport, Pennsylvania, by defeating the defending champions from Willemstad, Curacao, 7-6 in seven innings.
■ Michael Kates

Basketball.
The San Antonio Spurs won their third National Basketball Association (NBA) title in seven years in 2005, toppling the defending champion Detroit Pistons four games to three behind a strong performance from Tim Duncan, who won his third NBA Finals Most Valuable Player (MVP) award.

In college basketball, the University of North Carolina (Raleigh) won its fourth National Collegiate Athletic Association (NCAA) title, giving coach Roy Williams his first championship. The victory denied the University of Illinois (Champaign-Urbana) a chance to break the NCAA record for most wins in a season. Baylor University (Waco, Texas) captured its first women's title, and coach Kim Mulkey-Robertson became the first woman to win a title as a player and a coach.

Professional men. Home-team blowouts were the theme of one of the most unusual NBA Finals, the first since 1994 to go seven games. The San Antonio Spurs won the first two games at home by 15 points and 21 points. The Detroit Pistons rebounded at home to win

NATIONAL BASKETBALL ASSOCIATION STANDINGS

EASTERN CONFERENCE

Atlantic Division	W.	L.	Pct.	G.B.
Boston Celtics*	45	37	.549	—
Philadelphia 76ers*	43	39	.524	2
New Jersey Nets*	42	40	.512	3
Toronto Raptors	33	49	.402	12
New York Knicks	33	49	.402	12
Central Division				
Detroit Pistons*	54	28	.659	—
Chicago Bulls*	47	35	.573	7
Indiana Pacers*	44	38	.537	10
Cleveland Cavaliers	42	40	.512	12
Milwaukee Bucks	30	52	.366	24
Southeast Division				
Miami Heat*	59	23	.720	—
Washington Wizards*	45	37	.549	14
Orlando Magic	36	46	.439	23
Charlotte Bobcats	18	64	.220	41
Atlanta Hawks	13	69	.159	46

WESTERN CONFERENCE

Northwest Division	W.	L.	Pct.	G.B.
Seattle Supersonics*	52	30	.634	—
Denver Nuggets*	49	33	.598	3
Minnesota T'wolves	44	38	.537	8
Portland Trail Blazers	27	55	.329	25
Utah Jazz	26	56	.317	26
Pacific Division				
Phoenix Suns*	62	20	.756	—
Sacramento Kings*	50	32	.610	12
Los Angeles Clippers	37	45	.451	25
Los Angeles Lakers	34	48	.415	28
Golden State Warriors	34	48	.415	28
Southwest Division				
San Antonio Spurs*	59	23	.720	—
Dallas Mavericks*	58	24	.707	1
Houston Rockets*	51	31	.622	8
Memphis Grizzlies*	45	37	.549	14
New Orleans Hornets	18	64	.220	41

INDIVIDUAL LEADERS

Scoring	G.	F.G.	F.T.M.	Pts.	Avg.
Allen Iverson, Philadelphia	75	771	656	2,302	30.7
Kobe Bryant, Los Angeles	66	573	542	1,819	27.6
LeBron James, Cleveland	80	795	477	2,175	27.2
Dirk Nowitzki, Dallas	78	663	615	2,032	26.1
Amare Stoudemire, Phoenix	80	747	583	2,080	26.0
Tracy McGrady, Houston	78	715	431	2,003	25.7
Gilbert Arenas, Washington	80	656	521	2,038	25.5
Vince Carter, New Jersey	77	696	367	1,886	24.5
Dwyane Wade, Miami	77	630	581	1,854	24.1
Ray Allen, Seattle	78	640	378	1,867	23.9
Michael Redd, Milwaukee	75	625	369	1,723	23.0

Rebounding	G.	Off.	Def.	Tot.	Avg.
Kevin Garnett, Minnesota	82	247	861	1,108	13.5
Ben Wallace, Detroit	74	292	610	902	12.2
Shawn Marion, Phoenix	81	235	680	915	11.3
Emeka Okafor, Charlotte	73	275	520	795	10.9
Troy Murphy, Golden State	70	251	505	756	10.8
Shaquille O'Neal, Miami	73	253	507	760	10.4
Kurt Thomas, New York	80	170	661	831	10.4
Dwight Howard, Orlando	82	287	536	823	10.0
Dirk Nowitzki, Dallas	78	96	661	757	9.7
Tyson Chandler, Chicago	80	261	514	775	9.7
Elton Brand, Los Angeles	81	296	474	770	9.5

NBA champions—San Antonio Spurs (defeated Detroit Pistons, 4 games to 3)

*Made play-offs.

Marvin Williams of the North Carolina Tar Heels dunks against Jack Ingram of the University of Illinois during the National Collegiate Athletic Association's men's basketball title game on April 4, 2005. North Carolina defeated Illinois 75-50 to win its fourth championship.

In the Western Conference regular season, Phoenix showed a vast improvement over the 2003-2004 season, easily winning the Pacific Division with the best record in the NBA, 62 wins and 20 losses. Steve Nash led Phoenix, which started the season 31-4. Nash, who was named league MVP, is the first Canadian and just the fourth point guard to be so honored.

San Antonio edged Dallas by one game with a 59-23 mark to win the Southwest Division, while Seattle won the Northwest Division with a record of 52-30.

game 3 by 17 points and game 4 by 31 points. The final three games proved to be much more competitive. San Antonio rallied on June 19, 2005, to win game 5 in Auburn Hills, Michigan, 96-95 in overtime on a late three-point shot by Robert Horry. Detroit then won game 6 on June 21 in San Antonio, 95-86, to set the stage for game 7.

The Spurs won the title game 81-74 on June 23 behind Duncan, who scored 25 points and grabbed 11 rebounds. Both defense-minded teams combined to score 77 points in the first half, the fewest in the first half of a game 7 in NBA history. Duncan scored 17 of his points in the second half and grabbed 6 rebounds in the third quarter. Duncan won his third finals MVP award, adding to the MVP awards he received in 1999 and 2003.

The Spurs earned the Finals berth by eliminating the top-seeded Phoenix Suns 4 games to 1, including winning three times at Phoenix. The Spurs had beaten Denver 4 games to 1 in the first round and defeated Seattle 4 games to 2 in the conference semifinals.

The Pistons gained their Finals slot by ousting the Miami Heat, the top seed in the East, 4 games to 3, taking games 1 and 7 at Miami. Detroit had beaten Philadelphia 4 games to 1 in the first round and defeated Indiana 4 games to 2 in the conference semifinals.

In the Eastern Conference, the Miami Heat, led by Shaquille O'Neal, who had been acquired from the Lakers during the off-season, posted the best record, 59-23, to finish atop the Southeast Division. Detroit won the Central Division with a record of 54-28, seven games better than the Chicago Bulls. Boston ended with a record of 45-37, edging Philadelphia for the top record in the Atlantic Division.

The Chicago Bulls joined Phoenix as one of the season's biggest surprises. The Bulls began the season 0-9, tying a team mark for worst start, but finished with 47 wins despite losing two starters to injuries.

Retirements. Two stellar players—Indiana's Reggie Miller and Utah's Karl Malone—retired in 2005. Miller, who played in the NBA for 18 years, attempted and made more three-point shots than any other player in league history. Miller's 25,279-point record ranks 12th all-time. Malone, a two-time NBA MVP, had the second-most points in league history (36,928); was a 14-time All-Star; and won two Olympic gold medals.

Icon dies. George Mikan, who led the Minneapolis Lakers to five NBA titles in six seasons in the late 1940's and early 1950's, died on June 1, 2005. Mikan, who was a tremendous scorer and

THE 2004-2005 COLLEGE BASKETBALL SEASON

COLLEGE TOURNAMENT CHAMPIONS

NCAA (Men) Division I: North Carolina
Division II: Virginia Union
Division III: Wisconsin-Stevens Point

(Women) Division I: Baylor
Division II: Washburn
Division III: Millikin

NAIA (Men) Division I: John Brown
Division II: Walsh

(Women) Division I: Union
Division II: Morningside

NIT (Men) South Carolina

Sophia Young of Baylor University (right) is defended by Kelli Roehrig of Michigan State University during the NCAA women's championship game on April 6, 2005. Baylor defeated Michigan State 84-62 to win its first NCAA title.

MEN'S COLLEGE CHAMPIONS

CONFERENCE	SCHOOL
America East	Vermont*
Atlantic 10	
East Division	Saint Joseph's
West Division	George Washington*
Atlantic Coast	North Carolina
	Duke (tournament)
Atlantic Sun	Gardner Webb–Central Florida* (tie)
Big 12	Oklahoma–Kansas (tie)
	Oklahoma State (tournament)
Big East	Boston College–Connecticut (tie)
	Syracuse (tournament)
Big Sky	Portland State
	Montana (tournament)
Big South	Winthrop*
Big Ten	Illinois*
Big West	Pacific
	Utah State (tournament)
Colonial	Old Dominion*
Conference USA	Louisville*
Horizon League	Wisconsin (Milwaukee)*
Ivy League	Pennsylvania†
Metro Atlantic	Niagara*–Rider (tie)
Mid-American	Ohio (tournament)
East Division	Miami
West Division	Western Michigan–Toledo (tie)
Mid-Continent	Oral Roberts
	Oakland (tournament)
Mid-Eastern	Delaware State*
Missouri Valley	Southern Illinois
	Creighton (tournament)
Mountain West	Utah
	New Mexico (tournament)
Northeast	Monmouth
	St. Francis (tournament)
Ohio Valley	Tennessee Tech
	Eastern Kentucky (tournament)
Pacific 10	Arizona
	Washington (tournament)
Patriot League	Holy Cross
	Bucknell (tournament)
Southeastern	Florida (tournament)
Eastern	Kentucky
Western	Alabama–Louisiana State (tie)
Southern	
North Division	Tennessee-Chattanooga*
South Division	Davidson
Southland	Southeastern Louisiana*–
	Northwestern State (tie)
Southwestern	Alabama A&M
	Alabama State (tournament)
Sun Belt	Louisiana-Lafayette (tournament)
East Division	Arkansas-Little Rock
West Division	Jackson State
West Coast	Gonzaga*
Western Athletic	Nevada
	Texas-El Paso (tournament)

*Regular season and conference tournament champion.
†No tournament played.
Sources: National Collegiate Athletic Association (NCAA); National Association of Intercollegiate Athletics (NAIA); National Invitation Tournament (NIT); Conference Web sites.

defender, was the first player to dominate professional basketball.

Professional women. The Sacramento Monarchs flew past the Connecticut Sun 3 games to 1 to claim their first Women's National Basketball Association (WNBA) crown in Sacramento, California, on September 20. The Monarchs went 7-1 in the post-season. Sacramento's Yolanda Griffith led the team in scoring in every post-season game and was voted Finals MVP.

College men. North Carolina (33-4) toppled a scrappy Illinois team 75-70 on April 4 in St. Louis, Missouri, to win the NCAA crown. The game was the first between No. 1 seeds since 1999 and the first title game between the two top-ranked teams since UCLA beat Kentucky (Lexington) in 1975. The Illini (37-2), the nation's top-ranked team for most of the season, trailed by as many as 15 points in the second half but rallied to tie the game twice late in the contest. However, Illinois's Luther Head missed a three-point shot with 17 seconds left that would have tied the game, and the Illini failed to make a basket in the last 2 ½ minutes. Sean May led North Carolina with 26 points on 10-for-11 shooting and was named most outstanding player.

Illinois reached the final by beating Louisville 33-5, the fourth seed from the Albuquerque regional on April 2 by a score of 72-57. Illinois had pulled off one of the biggest comebacks in NCAA tournament history in its regional final against Arizona (Tempe) on March 26 in Chicago. The Illini rallied from 15 points down with four minutes to play to win in overtime. Illinois's only loss before the title game was to Ohio State on a three-pointer with five seconds left on March 6 in Columbus, Ohio.

North Carolina, the top seed in the Syracuse regional, reached the title game by routing Michigan State (East Lansing) (26-7), the fifth seed in the Austin regional, 87-71.

College women. Baylor University (33-3) toppled three No. 1 seeds, including finishing off Michigan State 84-62 on April 5 in Indianapolis, to win the NCAA women's title. Sophia Young scored 26 points, leading Baylor to win by the second-largest margin in NCAA women's history. Young was named the Final Four's most outstanding player.

Michigan State (33-4) had made the biggest comeback in women's Final Four history, rallying from being down by 16 points in its semifinal victory on April 3 to beat Tennessee 68-64 and make its first finals appearance. The same day, Baylor mounted a furious comeback of its own, rallying from 15 down to beat the tournament's top seed, Louisiana State University (Baton Rouge), 68-57, and earn its first finals appearance. Baylor had beaten No. 1-seeded North Carolina in the Elite Eight to reach the Final Four.   ■ Michael Kates

See also **Sports.**

Belarus. Belarusian President Aleksandr Lukashenko started 2005 on the defensive after the Orange Revolution, in which protests forced a regime change in neighboring Ukraine. He declared in January that there would be no such revolutions in Belarus. The European Union, the United Nations, and even Russia, his closest ally, all rebuked Lukashenko in 2005 for his increasingly autocratic rule.

Belarusian officials introduced new restrictions in 2005 on opposition groups, including a requirement that they register with the government. The repression sparked widespread demonstrations, including a March 25 rally in Minsk, the capital, protesting Lukashenko's decision to seek a third presidential term, and an April 26 rally on the 19th anniversary of the Chernobyl nuclear disaster. Protest organizers and the reporters covering the rallies faced arrests and prison terms for their actions.

The Belarusian government increased pressure on independent media throughout the year. Opposition paper *Narodnaya Volya,* in the midst of a major libel suit, lost access on October 1 to a countrywide network of newsstands, over which the government had a monopoly. On October 18, Vasily Grodnikov, a journalist critical of Lukashenko who wrote for *Narodnaya Volya,* was found murdered in his apartment.   ■ Juliet Johnson

See also **Europe; Russia: A Special Report; Ukraine.**

Belgium. The coalition government of Belgium, led by Guy Verhofstadt, remained fragile in 2005. Improving economic growth, which slowed to 1.4 percent in 2005, and maintaining fiscal discipline were hampered by conflict between the Flemish and the Walloons. (The Flemish are Dutch speakers who live primarily in the north; the Walloons are French speakers who live primarily in the south.) In January, a debate erupted over the language and political rights of Walloons in Flemish areas. Walloons who had moved from Brussels, the capital, to surrounding towns and cities demanded a voice in local politics. The Flemish responded by attempting to pass a law prohibiting Walloon parties from running in local elections.

Belgium's regional governments also continued to assert their authority. In February, the media revealed that the government of the Walloon region had authorized the export of ammunition production machinery to Tanzania. The export was incompatible with Belgian peace policies in central Africa, a region with which Belgium has strong historical ties. The Belgian Foreign Ministry agreed to work more closely with regional authorities to avoid future policy conflicts.   ■ Jeffrey Kopstein

See also **Europe.**

Belize. See **Latin America.**

Benin. See **Africa.**

Bhutan. See **Asia.**

Biology. The largest freshwater fish ever recorded was caught by fishermen in Thailand's Mekong River in May 2005. Before biologists could thoroughly examine the fish, it died and was eaten by the fishermen and their friends. Fortunately, local officials and a photographer were able to measure, weigh, and photograph the fish before it became a meal. They reported that the fish was almost 9 feet (3.7 meters) long and weighed 646 pounds (293 kilograms). The WWF (formerly the World Wildlife Fund), an international conservation agency based in Geneva, Switzerland, and the National Geographic Society, a scientific and educational organization headquartered in Washington, D.C., confirmed that the fish had indeed broken the size record.

The mammoth fish was a Mekong giant catfish (*Panasius gigas*), an endangered species. Dams and other construction projects on the Mekong River have drastically reduced the population of this species.

Cloned canine questioned. Scientists at Seoul National University in South Korea announced in July that they had produced the first *clone* (genetic duplicate) of a dog. Cloning involves the replacement of the *nucleus* (central part containing genetic information) of an egg cell taken from a female animal with the nucleus of a body cell taken from another animal, known as the *donor*. The resulting embryo is then implanted into the womb of a surrogate mother, who will give birth to an animal that is genetically identical to the donor.

Late in 2005, a scientist involved in the project, Hwang Woo Suk, was accused of fabricating results of research unrelated to the dog cloning. He could present no evidence to corroborate his claim that he had cloned human embryos and extracted from them stem cells that genetically match patients. In December, Hwang requested that a U.S. scientific journal retract a paper he had written on the subject. Attacks on Hwang's credibility led many scientists to question the validity of Hwang's claim to having cloned a dog.

Chimpanzee genes. Another genetic milestone occurred in September 2005,

Hundreds of walruses sun themselves on a beach in the Walrus Islands State Game Sanctuary off Alaska's southern coast in July. Cameras installed at the sanctuary in 2005 allow scientists the chance to study the walruses, as well as sea lions, in their natural environment. Web surfers can find a live stream of the beach party on the Internet.

when a team of scientists from the United States and several other countries reported that they had *sequenced* (determined the order of) the *genome* (total amount of genetic information) of the chimpanzee. The sequencing of the 2.8 billion pairs of chemical building blocks, called *nucleotides,* that make up the chimp's genome allowed scientists to compare the chimpanzee's genome with that of human beings. Two teams of scientists announced in 2000 that they had each sequenced the human genome.

Genetic similarity between chimpanzees and humans has long led biologists to believe that chimpanzees are the closest living relatives of human beings. The scientists, led by geneticist Robert Waterston of the University of Washington School of Medicine in Seattle, reported that less than 4 percent of the chimp's 2.8 billion pairs of nucleotides differ from those in humans.

The researchers noted that the task ahead is for scientists to examine the specific genes that chimpanzees have and humans lack and vice versa. Such analyses could help answer questions about which genes were involved in the evolutionary divergence of the chimp and human species, believed to have taken place more than 5 million years ago. The scientists claimed that their research also has many implications for understanding disease. For example, a chimp gene that is not found in humans seems to protect the ape from Alzheimer's disease.

Chimpanzees, gorillas, and tools. Two reports in 2005 shed light on tool use among apes—and possibly human ancestors.

Results of a three-year study published in August indicate that, unlike humans, most wild chimpanzees are left-handed. Primate researchers Elizabeth Lonsdorf and William Hopkins of the Yerkes National Primate Research Center at Emory University in Atlanta, Georgia, observed 17 chimpanzees in Tanzania as the apes "fished" termites out of their mounds with sticks. The investigators reported that 12 of the 17 apes used their left hand for this job.

The scientists argued that their observations may shed light on how the brain evolved as early humanlike creatures developed from apelike animals. They noted that each hand is controlled by the opposite side of the brain—an important aspect of *brain lateralization* (the division of brain function into left and right sides). The scientists concluded that brain lateralization likely evolved before the chimp-human evolutionary divergence more than 5 million years ago.

Complex tool use among gorillas was described in September by keepers at a gorilla sanctuary in Goma, Congo, affiliated with the Dian Fossey Gorilla Fund International. The keep-

ers reported observing female gorillas smashing palm nuts between rocks using a "hammer-and-anvil" technique, which zoologists noted was one of the more complex kinds of tool use known among apes. Zoologists claimed that this observation supported the idea that the use of tools might have arisen among ancestors common to both apes and humans.

Dolphins teach tool use. Biologists reported in June that they had observed bottlenose dolphins in Shark Bay, Western Australia, stuffing their snouts into cone-shaped sea sponges. The aquatic mammals continued wearing the snugly fitting sponges while poking around the sea floor for food. The biologists, led by Michael Krutzen of Zurich University in Switzerland, concluded that the sponges apparently protect the dolphins against stings and bites from creatures hiding on the ocean bottom.

Krutzen's team reported that genetic analyses of several dolphins revealed that almost all the sponge-using individuals belonged to a single maternal lineage. However, the scientists determined that the behavior was not inherited— mothers passed the skill to their young through teaching.

Mice sing like birds. Male mice "sing" with high-frequency sounds that are out of the range of human hearing, according to a November report by biologists at Washington University in St. Louis, Missouri. The biologists noticed the previously unknown phenomenon by analyzing recordings of mouse vocalizations that were lowered in pitch using special computer software. The recordings revealed that the vocalizations had similar characteristics to bird song, including distinct syllables repeated in complex phrases. The researchers speculated that male mice make these sounds in the presence of females as part of a mating ritual.

Killer caterpillar. All caterpillars have glands that produce silk to build cocoons. In July, researchers from the University of Hawaii at Manda revealed that one species of caterpillar found in Hawaii also uses its silk for the same purpose spiders do—to catch prey. The caterpillar, of the *genus* (group of species) *Hyposmocoma,* is the first caterpillar known to do so, as well as the first known to eat mollusks. Its victims are tiny snails.

The researchers, led by *entomologist* (insect expert) Daniel Rubinoff, reported that the killer caterpillar, wrapped in its silk cocoon, crawls along leaves until it finds a snail. It immediately covers the snail in the silk. Held fast, the snail cannot fall to the ground or seal the opening of its shell. The caterpillar then creeps into the shell to eat the mollusk's soft body. ■ Edward Ricciuti

See also **Conservation; Ocean; Zoos.**

British sailor Ellen MacArthur guides her 75-foot (23-meter) trimaran *B & Q* into Falmouth Bay near Falmouth, England, after breaking the solo around-the-world sailing record on Feb. 7, 2005. MacArthur completed the trip in 71 days, 14 hours, 18 minutes, and 33 seconds.

Boating. British sailor Ellen MacArthur established a new solo around-the-world sailing record in 2005, while the man whose record she broke, Francis Joyon of France, set a new North Atlantic record. Another Frenchman, Vincent Riou, established a new record in the Vendee Globe solo nonstop around-the-world race.

Around-the-world records. MacArthur set the new solo around-the-world mark when she sailed her 75-foot (23-meter) trimaran *B & Q* across the finish line near Ushant, France, on February 7, finishing the 27,000-mile (43,450-kilometer) journey in 71 days, 14 hours, 18 minutes, and 33 seconds.

On February 3, Vincent Riou captured the fifth Vendee Globe race. The Vendee Globe, which is held every four years, requires sailors to go around the world solo without stopovers or assistance. The race started and finished at Les Sables d'Olonne, France, and covered 23,680 miles (38,100 kilometers). Riou completed the journey in his 60-foot (18-meter) monohull *PRB* in 87 days, 10 hours, 47 minutes, and 55 seconds.

North Atlantic record. Francis Joyon broke the speed record for sailing across the North Atlantic solo on July 6, 2005. He obliterated the world record, completing the 2,925-mile (4,700-kilometer) journey from New York City to Lizard

Point off Cornwall, England, in 6 days, 4 hours, 1 minute, and 37 seconds. During his journey, Joyon sailed his 90-foot (27-meter) trimaran *IDEC* at an average of 19.75 knots. Laurent Bourgnon of Switzerland had set the previous mark of 7 days, 2 hours, 34 minutes, and 42 seconds, in 1994.

Schooner record. In June 2005, helmsman Mike Sanderson of New Zealand broke a 100-year-old record in the Rolex Transatlantic Challenge, a race for monohulls at least 70 feet (21 meters) long with no power winches. Sanderson completed the trip aboard the 140-foot (42-meter) schooner *Mari Cha IV* in 9 days, 15 hours, 55 minutes, and 23 seconds. Sanderson smashed the previous mark, set in 1905 by Charlie Barr of the United States aboard *Atlantic*, by more than two and a half days.

America's Cup. New Zealand skipper Russell Coutts, the winner of three consecutive America's Cup campaigns, was dismissed in July 2005 by the Swiss Alinghi syndicate. Swiss Alinghi officials claimed Coutts violated his employment contract. As a result, Coutts will not seek a fourth straight title in the 2007 America's Cup.

Powerboats. On July 17, 2005, Terry Troxell piloted *Miss Al Deeby Dodge* to victory in the 101st running of the Gold Cup race for Unlimited Hydroplanes in Detroit. ■ Michael Kates

Bolivia.

Bolivia. Evo Morales, an Aymara Indian and head of the leftist Movement Toward Socialism, was elected president of Bolivia on Dec. 18, 2005. Morales was the first *indigenous* (native Indian) Bolivian ever elected to the country's presidency.

The election of Morales marked the end of a politically turbulent year in Bolivia. Street protests mounted by indigenous people in and around La Paz, the capital, had paralyzed the country and led to the resignation of President Carlos Mesa Gisbert and installation of interim president Eduardo Rodriguez Veltze in June.

Morales, leader of the Federation of Coca Farmers and a member of Bolivia's congress, had been the chief power broker in securing the resignation of Mesa and the selection of Rodriguez as his replacement. On taking office, Rodriguez set in motion a reform program that included elections for a new president, a new congress, and an overhaul of Bolivia's constitution.

International affairs experts speculated that Morales would not find a ready ally in the administration of President George W. Bush of the United States. Morales's support for the production of coca, the use of which is legal in Bolivia, put him squarely at odds with the U.S. war on drugs, which aims at eradicating the crop because it is the source of the drug cocaine.

Morales's base of support. The key to Morales's presidential victory and the overthrow of the Mesa government in June was the indigenous urban population of Bolivia, particularly the 750,000 or more Aymara and Quechua Indians living in El Alto, a new squatter city on the edge of La Paz. During the height of the antigovernment protests in May and June, El Alto activists blocked major routes leading into La Paz, causing shortages of food, fuel, and other supplies in the capital.

Unemployment and poverty have long plagued Bolivia's indigenous population. The country's native people, according to social scientists, have often been treated as second-class citizens by descendants of Europeans and *mestizos* (people of mixed Indian and European blood). William Powers, formerly an official with the U.S. foreign aid program in Bolivia, described the social and cultural situation in Bolivia as a "pigmentocracy of power" that largely excluded indigenous people from positions of importance in government and business.

Morales's constituents were also in the forefront of the antiglobalization movement. Their aim was to prevent international corporations from exploiting Bolivia's nonrenewable mineral and energy wealth and banking the profits abroad. In the face of continued agitation, foreign energy companies in 2005 curtailed their investment in Bolivia, though the country possessed natural gas reserves second in size only to Venezuela's in South America.

The autonomy movement. Politicians and business leaders in eastern Bolivia lobbied in 2005 for constitutional changes that would grant the relatively affluent, resource-rich east *autonomy* (self-rule). Most of Bolivia's natural gas reserves are located in the eastern Amazonian lowlands, where the chief city, Santa Cruz, had become by 2005 a boomtown of 1.4 million residents. Bowing to demands of eastern regional leaders, congressional leadership promised to hold a referendum on the autonomy issue in July 2006. Critics claimed that autonomy proponents were motivated by a desire to prevent the sharing of energy wealth with western regions, home to the majority of Bolivia's indigenous people.

Indictment. In February 2005, Bolivian prosecutors charged former President Gonzalo Sanchez de Lozada, living in exile in the United States, with *genocide* (systematic extermination of a racial group). The indictment alleged that Lozada was responsible for killing more than 60 people during protests that led to his own resignation in 2003. Prosecutors later added corruption charges to the indictment. ■ Nathan A. Haverstock

See also **Latin America.**

Books. See Literature; Literature for children; Poetry.

Bosnia-Herzegovina.

Bosnia-Herzegovina. Political instability in 2005 complicated efforts to establish a stable, democratic society in Bosnia-Herzegovina. However, the ethnically divided country did achieve consensus for the first time on military and police reforms urged by the European Union (EU), the United Nations (UN), and NATO.

Police reforms. In October, the parliament of the Republika Srpska (RS), one of the two main political entities of Bosnia-Herzegovina, approved reforms that would meld the country's separate police forces into a unified, ethnically integrated force. The RS had twice rejected the legislation and was the chief stumbling block in implementing the reforms.

Politically, Bosnia consists of the RS, governing an enclave of Bosnian Serbs, and the Muslim-Croat Federation (MCF), an entity consisting mainly of ethnic Croats and Muslim Bosnians. An overarching central government loosely links these entities together in one state.

EU officials insisted that Bosnia endorse police reforms before the association of 25 European countries would open the way for negotiations on a stabilization and association agreement (SAA), the first step in the long process of gaining EU membership. In September, EU officials rejected SAA negotiations with Bosnia but later agreed to reconsider the issue in December.

Empty coffins are borne through the streets of Srebrenica, Bosnia-Herzegovina, on July 11, 2005, the 10th anniversary of the Srebrenica Massacre, in memory of victims. In July 1995, Bosnian Serbs overran the region around the city, a United Nations-designated "safe zone," and killed more than 7,000 Bosnian Muslim men and boys in what has been described as the worst civilian slaughter in Europe since the end of World War II (1939-1945).

Military reforms. Bosnia's national parliament in October approved military reforms designed to combine the separate RS and MCF armed forces into a unified, ethnically diversified national army. NATO officials had identified the reforms as a precondition for Bosnia's membership in the Partnership for Peace Program, which is generally recognized as a first step toward full NATO membership.

Political instability. A new government, headed by Prime Minister Pero Bukejlovic, came to power in the RS in February 2005 following a two-month governmental crisis. On Dec. 17, 2004, Prime Minister Dragan Mikerevic had resigned to protest sanctions imposed on RS officials. Paddy Ashdown, the UN High Representative in Bosnia and chief enforcer of the 1995 Dayton Accords that ended the Bosnian war, imposed the sanctions to compel RS officials to cooperate with international authorities in hunting down war criminals.

In March, the Croatian member of Bosnia's tripartite rotating presidency, Dragan Covic, was indicted on charges of bribery and removed by UN High Representative Ashdown. The Bosnian parliament in May approved Ivo Miro Jovic as Covic's replacement.   ■ Sharon L. Wolchik

See also **Europe**.

Botswana. See Africa.

Bowling. Patrick Allen of Tarrytown, New York, enjoyed his best season as a professional bowler in 2005, earning Player of the Year honors by winning his first major title and finishing in the top five in all four major tournaments on the Professional Bowlers Association (PBA) tour.

Allen's first major victory came on April 3 when he defeated Chris Loschetter 235-210 in the World Championship in Ypsilanti, Michigan. Allen also led the PBA in points and earnings ($350,740) for the 2004-2005 season and posted the sixth-best average (223.50).

Allen had lost the first major of the season, the American Bowling Congress Masters, held in Milwaukee, Wisconsin, in October 2004, to Danny Wiseman of Baltimore by a score of 268-183.

In the second major, the U.S. Open held in February 2005 in North Brunswick, New Jersey, Allen lost by one pin, dropping the title match 213-212 to Chris Barnes of Flower Mound, Texas. It was Barnes's first career major victory.

In the season's final major, the Tournament of Champions played in Uncasville, Connecticut, in April, Steve Jaros of Yorkville, Illinois, claimed his first career major with a 248-242 victory over Norm Duke of Clermont, Florida.

Historic victory. On August 21, Liz Johnson of Cheektowaga, New York, became the first woman to win a PBA tour event by capturing the

PBA East Region Kingpin Lanes Open in Rome, New York. Johnson defeated Michael Fagan in the title match by a score of 244-171. In March, Johnson had become the first woman to advance to the nationally televised finals of a PBA Tour event, finishing second in the Banquet Open in Grand Rapids, Michigan.

Seniors. On the PBA Senior Tour, Bob Glass, Tom Baker, and Vince Mazzanti, Jr., all enjoyed strong 2005 seasons and were in the running for Player of the Year honors. Baker, of Buffalo, New York, captured the Senior U.S. Open on May 20 in Sterling Heights, Michigan. Mazzanti captured the other major, the Senior Masters, on June 16 in Las Vegas, defeating Glass 697 to 627. Glass finished the season with 183,626 points, comfortably ahead of Baker's 171,034.

Glass won only one event but had two second-place finishes. Baker had two second-place finishes to go with his major title victory. Mazzanti, of Levittown, Pennsylvania, finished in fifth place in the points race, third in earnings, and eleventh in scoring average. However, he had three second-place finishes in addition to a first-place finish on the 11-event circuit. Dale Eagle, of Tavares, Florida, finished third in points, ranked fourth in both earnings and average, and was the only bowler with two tour wins. ■ Michael Kates

See also **Deaths; Sports.**

Boxing. The deaths in 2005 of two boxers less than three months apart after bouts in Las Vegas prompted the Nevada State Athletic Commission to form a panel—composed of three former commission chairmen, a state assemblyman, and a physician—to try to make the sport safer. Six boxers have died after fights in Las Vegas since 1994.

On Sept. 22, 2005, Leavander Johnson, a 35-year-old lightweight from Atlantic City, New Jersey, died five days after suffering bleeding on the brain in a failed defense of his International Boxing Federation (IBF) title on September 17. After losing the fight, Johnson walked out of the ring but collapsed on the way to the dressing room. Surgeons tried to relieve the pressure on his brain, but he never recovered.

On July 2, Martin Sanchez, a 26-year-old boxer from Mexico City, died one day after getting knocked out by Rustam Nugaev of Russia in a super lightweight bout. Sanchez was bleeding from his nose and mouth, but two physicians examined him and determined that he was not seriously injured. When someone later noticed Sanchez walking strangely, he was rushed to the hospital.

Tyson falls. Boxing fans speculated that Mike Tyson's strange boxing career may have come to an end on June 11 in Washington, D.C., when he quit after six rounds after taking a beating from Irish heavyweight Kevin McBride. In the sixth round, Tyson appeared to try to break McBride's arm and intentionally head-butted him, causing a cut over McBride's right eye. Tyson did not return to the ring when the seventh round began.

In November, a cameraman accused Tyson of assaulting him in a nightclub in Sao Paolo, Brazil. A judge in the United States subsequently ordered Tyson to return to Brazil to face trial.

Other title fights. World Boxing Council (WBC) heavyweight champion Vitali Klitschko announced his retirement on November 9, only two days before a heavily promoted fight with Hasim Rahman. On November 10, the WBC awarded the title to Rahman.

Antonio Tarver beat former champion Roy Jones, Jr., on October 1 in Tampa, Florida, in a unanimous decision to retain his IBO light heavyweight title. Tarver had won the crown by knocking out Jones in May 2004.

Chris Byrd retained his International Boxing Federation (IBF) heavyweight title with a decision over DaVarryl Williamson in Reno, Nevada, on Oct. 1, 2005.

Floyd Mayweather, Jr., won the WBC super lightweight title on June 25 in Atlantic City, New Jersey, by battering former champion Arturo Gatti, improving his record to 34-0.

■ Michael Kates

WORLD CHAMPION BOXERS

WORLD BOXING ASSOCIATION

Division	Champion	Country	Date won
Heavyweight	Nikolay Valuev	Russia	12/05
Light heavyweight	Fabrice Tiozzo	France	3/04
Middleweight	Jermain Taylor	United States	7/05
Welterweight	Zab Judah	United States	2/05
Lightweight	Juan Diaz	United States	7/04
Featherweight	Chris John	Indonesia	9/03
Bantamweight	Wladimir Sidorenko	Ukraine	2/05
Flyweight	Lorenzo Parra	Venezuela	12/03

WORLD BOXING COUNCIL

Division	Champion	Country	Date won
Heavyweight	Hasim Rahman	United States	8/05
Light heavyweight	Tomasz Adamek	Poland	5/05
Middleweight	Jermain Taylor	United States	7/05
Welterweight	Zab Judah	United States	2/05
Lightweight	Diego Corrales	United States	5/05
Featherweight	Injin Chi	Korea	4/04
Bantamweight	Hozumi Hasegawa	Japan	4/05
Flyweight	Pongsaklek Wonjongkam	Thailand	3/01

Brazil. The administration of President Luiz Inacio Lula da Silva, brought to power by an electoral landslide in late 2002, was rocked by multiplying revelations of political corruption during 2005. By year's end, dozens of high-ranking members of the president's administration and party, the Workers Party, had resigned in disgrace. The scandals were revealed in highly publicized Congressional probes, as millions of Brazilians watched dramatic hearings on live television.

In June, President da Silva's chief of staff and confidant, Jose Dirceu de Oliveira e Silva, resigned to face allegations by members of the Brazil congress that he had masterminded a scheme whereby more than a dozen Brazilian congressmen received bribes of $12,500 a month in return for supporting administration legislation. According to further allegations, some politicians had received from Dirceu one-time payments of $400,000 to switch parties.

As the congressional investigation widened, more than 50 high-ranking politicians fell under suspicion of corruption and resigned their posts. The web of corruption eventually reached well beyond da Silva's administration and party. In September, Severino Cavalcanti, the speaker of Brazil's chamber of deputies and member of an opposition party, stepped down amid allegations that he was pocketing $4,000 a month in kickbacks from the owner of a restaurant operating in the legislative building in Brasilia, the capital.

Strong economy. Despite the uncertainty created by political scandals, Brazil's economy continued to grow in 2005. Economists projected that the nation's gross domestic product (GDP)—the value of all goods and services produced in a country in a given year—would increase by 3 to 3.5 percent in 2005. Exports remained strong, with the country posting a record trade surplus, estimated at $39 billion in 2005, compared with $33.6 billion in 2004. The volume of Brazil's trade with sub-Saharan Africa, China, India, the Middle East, and Russia expanded in 2005.

Antitrust action. In August, Brazil's Administrative Council of Economic Defense (CADE), a government antitrust enforcement agency, issued a ruling requiring Brazil's Companhia Vale do Rio Doce (CVRD), based in Rio de Janeiro, one of Latin America's most powerful corporations, to relinquish some of its mining interests. The landmark decision was made after CVRD had increased its market share of Brazilian iron ore production from 65 percent in 1999 to 92 percent in 2005, giving it control of one-third of all international iron ore trade.

New Amazon preserves. In February, President da Silva signed a decree creating two huge preserves in the Amazon basin. One is an 8.15-million-acre (3.3-million-hectare) forest preserve; the other is a 1.1-million-acre (446,000-hectare) national park. Both are in the state of Para, where illegal loggers have cut substantially into the rain forest and have routinely terrorized opponents among the local population.

Da Silva's decree was issued shortly after the February 12 assassination of Sister Dorothy Stang, a United States-born nun and environmental activist who had led opposition to activities of the loggers. Five men were subsequently arrested and charged with her murder.

Water project. In March, the Brazilian government authorized $1.7 billion to construct a canal system that would divert water from the Sao Francisco River to the semiarid *sertao*. The sertao region of northeastern Brazil is home to 50 million people, most of them living in poverty by subsistence farming. The source of the river, a vital commercial artery, is about 400 miles (645 kilometers) northwest of Rio de Janeiro. It flows north and east for 2,000 miles (3,200 kilometers) before emptying into the south Atlantic Ocean. Protests by environmentalists, including a Roman Catholic bishop who undertook a hunger strike, stalled the Sao Francisco project for most of 2005.

■ Nathan A. Haverstock

See also **Latin America.**

British Columbia. See Canadian provinces.

Brunei. See Asia.

Building and construction. The longest cable-stayed bridge in North America opened in South Carolina in July 2005, when traffic from United States Route 17 began moving over the Arthur Ravenel, Jr., Bridge. The main section of the bridge spans 1,546 feet (471 meters) across the Cooper River between Charleston and Mt. Pleasant. The $640-million structure replaced two narrow, aging bridges that were no longer able to handle the daily traffic load of 70,000 vehicles.

The tips of the new bridge's two diamond-shaped towers rise 572 feet (174 meters) above Charleston Bay, supporting a concrete deck eight lanes wide. In addition to the four vehicular lanes in each direction, the bridge's southern side includes a pedestrian and bicycle lane 12 feet (3.6 meters) wide. The deck rises 186 feet (56.7 meters) above the river. With the towers and other supporting structures, the entire bridge is 13,200 feet (4,023 meters) in length.

Charleston, throughout its history, has sustained heavy damage from a number of natural disasters, including a devastating earthquake in 1886 and Hurricane Hugo in 1989. With this in mind, engineers designed the Ravenel Bridge to structurally resist a 7.4-magnitude earthquake. The towers, which are supported by 128 steel cables, were engineered to withstand wind gusts

A construction worker puts the finishing touches on the royal entrance to the Emirates Palace in Abu Dhabi, United Arab Emirates, in March 2005. The $3-billion structure, with 400 rooms and 60 acres (24 hectares) of interior space, was the most expensive hotel ever constructed.

of up to 300 miles (480 kilometers) per hour.

German cathedral rises again. A reconstructed Lutheran cathedral, originally built in the 1700's, opened for worship in Dresden, Germany, in October 2005—more than 60 years after Allied bombers leveled the structure during World War II (1939-1945). The Dresdner Frauenkirche (Dresden's Church of Our Lady), an example of High Baroque architecture, was designed by George Bahr (1666-1738). Its distinctive domed tower is said to have withstood more than 100 direct hits from cannonballs fired by Frederick the Great's Prussian Army during the Seven Years' War (1756-1763). However, after two days and nights of heavy bombing by Allied warplanes in February 1945, the church's walls collapsed.

The ruins of the cathedral were preserved as a war memorial. Reconstruction plans gained momentum after the reunification of Germany in 1990. In 1994, molecular biologist Gunter Blobel, a U.S. citizen born in Germany, founded a non-profit organization to support the architectural restoration of Dresden. In 1999, Blobel won the Nobel Prize in physiology or medicine, and he dedicated his award money to the rebuilding of the Frauenkirche and a synagogue in Dresden.

A team of architects and engineers led by Eberhard Burger used Bahr's original drawings to plan the reconstruction. The team incorporated some 3,800 of the 8,500 original stones salvaged

from the ruins. The architects and engineers also used photographs and documents to replicate the original building as much as possible. The reconstructed Frauenkirche was to be a key component in celebrations in 2006 marking the 600th anniversary of the founding of Dresden.

Arizona Cardinals Stadium. Engineers took only seven days in February 2005 to position the massive retractable roof over the new home of the Arizona Cardinals football team in Glendale, Arizona. The 5,400-ton (4,900-metric-ton) assembly was, according to many observers, the most striking feature of the new stadium, which was scheduled to open for the 2006 National Football League season.

Architect Peter Eisenman designed the 65,000-seat stadium to resemble a barrel cactus, with cladding consisting of alternating metallic panels and recessed glass strips. The fabric-covered roof is 500,000 square feet (46,500 square meters) in area. Twin teardrop Brunel trusses, 699 feet (213 meters) long and 257 feet (78 meters) apart, create the longest clear span of any retractable roof. The eight panels of the roof ride on a cable-drive system with 32 steel crane wheels.

China's Chongzun Expressway. The southern portion of the Chongzun Expressway, the most technically challenging segment of China's National Trunk Highway System (NTHS), opened in July 2005. Similar to the U.S. Interstate Highway System, the NTHS is an interprovincial network of high-speed roadways crisscrossing China from north to south and east to west. In 2005, Chinese and multinational contractors raced to complete the system by 2010 in anticipation of a nationwide traffic boom.

The Chongzun Expressway, dubbed the "Highway in the Clouds," traverses 73 miles (118 kilometers) through the Dalhousan Mountains in northern Guizhou Province. Slopes are steep along the route, which varies greatly in elevation. Engineers excavated 17 tunnels and built 121 bridges in this seismically active zone, incorporating structural elements to help the expressway withstand earthquakes.

The road, which cost an estimated $827 million, was partially funded by the Asian Development Bank, an institution that lends money to developing countries in Asia to promote their economic growth. The Chongzun Expressway was designed as a vital link between Chengdu, the capital of Sichuan Province, and China's southeastern coastal ports.

By tunneling through the mountains and bridging the valleys, the engineers hoped to convert what had been a treacherous 12-hour journey to an easy 4-hour drive. The northern section of the road was scheduled to open in January 2006.　■ Andrew Wright

See also **Architecture.**

Bulgaria. The Bulgarian Socialist Party won parliamentary elections in June 2005, netting 82 seats in the 240-seat legislative body. The ruling National Movement Simeon II (NMSII) came in a distant second, with 53 seats. The Socialists, NMSII, and a Turkish minority party established a governing coalition in August and elected Sergei Stanishev, a Socialist, prime minister.

The new Bulgarian leader pledged to continue reforms to prepare Bulgaria to enter the European Union (EU) in 2007. In October 2005, the European Commission, the executive arm of the EU, reported that Bulgaria was on track for admission to the EU in 2007 but warned its leaders not to fall behind on necessary reforms. During 2005, Bulgaria adopted a new criminal code, one of several legal reforms urged by the EU.

In May, Bulgaria's parliament passed a resolution calling for withdrawal of Bulgarian troops from Iraq in early 2006. Bulgaria had about 400 soldiers in Iraq in 2005.　■ Sharon L. Wolchik

See also **Europe.**

Burkina Faso. See Africa.

Burma. See Myanmar.

Burundi. See Africa.

Bush, George W. See United States, President of the.

Business. See Banks; Economics, U.S.; Economics, World; International trade.

Cabinet, U.S. United States President George W. Bush appointed nine new members to his Cabinet soon after his inauguration on Jan. 20, 2005. He chose Condoleezza Rice to become secretary of the U.S. Department of State. Rice had served as national security adviser during Bush's first term and as both director and senior director of Soviet and East European affairs in the administration of President George H. W. Bush.

President George W. Bush appointed Alberto Gonzales as the U.S. attorney general. He had served as counsel to Bush since 2001. When Bush was the governor of Texas, Gonzales was Bush's general counsel and then his secretary of state.

Another Texan, Margaret Spellings, joined the Cabinet in 2005 as secretary of the Department of Education. Other newly appointed secretaries included Michael O. Leavitt at the Department of Health and Human Services; Mike Johanns at the Department of Agriculture; Michael Chertoff at the Department of Homeland Security; Carlos M. Gutierrez at the Department of Commerce; R. James Nicholson at the Department of Veterans Affairs; and Samuel W. Bodman at the Department of Energy.　■ Geoffrey A. Campbell

See also **People in the news** (Michael Chertoff; Alberto Gonzales; Carlos M. Gutierrez; Margaret Spellings).

Cambodia. The United Nations (UN)-led effort to put on trial the surviving leaders of the Khmer Rouge bogged down in 2005. The Communist Khmer Rouge, during its brutal rule between 1975 and 1979, was responsible for the deaths of more than 1.5 million Cambodians. No Khmer leader has ever been brought to justice for the atrocities.

In April 2005, the UN announced that it had raised enough money from international donors to create a special court to try Khmer Rouge leaders. The court, which would sit for three years, was expected to cost more than $50 million. Japan pledged $21 million, and Cambodia was expected to contribute $13 million. However, Cambodian Prime Minister Hun Sen announced in August that his country did not have the money.

Hun Sen, who had been a member of the Khmer Rouge but had left the party prior to the mass murders, began to use legal proceedings in 2005 to silence his critics. Before 2005, Hun Sen's critics often had been murdered. Opposition leader Sam Rainsy fled the country in February after his parliamentary immunity was lifted. A supporter of Rainsy was sentenced on August 9 to seven years in prison in what human rights monitors called a political verdict.　■ Henry S. Bradsher

See also **Asia.**

Cameroon. See Africa.

CANADA

Canadian Prime Minister Paul Martin announced on Nov. 29, 2005, that Canadians will go to the polls on Jan. 23, 2006, to elect a new Parliament. The announcement was made one day after his government lost a no-confidence vote in the lower house. Wounded by scandal, Martin was brought down after only 17 months in power when all three opposition parties united against his Liberal Party. The prime minister, who fought off a no-confidence motion in May 2005, had not been implicated in the scandal, but the opposition claimed that he had lost the moral authority necessary to govern. Canadian governments have fallen by losing votes on budget or censure motions, which are interpreted as a loss of confidence, but the vote on November 28 was the first time in Canadian history that a government has fallen on a straight no-confidence vote. Martin's government was to remain in office until the election was held.

Inquiry. During the first six months of 2005, Parliament carried out its meetings against the troubling background of a judicial enquiry set up in 2004 to investigate irregularities in the awarding of contracts to advertising firms in Quebec. The firms had been hired to promote the image of the central government in Quebec, which in 1995 had narrowly voted down a proposal to separate from Canada. Public funds were to be spent to provide federal endorsement to cultural and sporting events. Some of the funds were disbursed without due regard to government accounting procedures. Allegations were made that some of the funds had been siphoned off to support the election campaigns of Liberal Party candidates in Quebec. Ministers, civil servants, and advertising executives were all implicated in the scandal. The charges were damaging to the reputation of former Liberal Prime Minister Jean Chrétien—whose administration began the Quebec advertising campaign—and to his successor, Paul Martin, minister of finance under Chrétien.

In February 2005, Chrétien and Martin testified before the inquiry being carried out by Justice John Gomery. The occasion marked the first time since 1873 that a prime minister was questioned in an inquiry about his conduct in office. Both prime ministers claimed that they were "out of the loop" in the disbursement of the funds and blamed rogue members of their party and public servants for the lapses. In a national television address in April 2005, Martin pleaded with the Canadian people to allow Judge Gomery to complete his inquiry before they

A giant rainbow flag, standard of the gay rights movement, is raised in June on the grounds of Canada's Parliament Buildings in Ottawa, the capital, in support of legislation legalizing marriage between same-sex couples. On June 28, Canada became the third country, after Belgium and the Netherlands, to recognize the legality of marriages between persons of the same sex.

condemned the Liberal Party and his government. He promised to hold an election to decide the fate of his government within 30 days after Gomery released his report, the first part of which was issued in November.

The report exonerated Paul Martin of any part in the scandal but harshly criticized his predecessor, Jean Chrétien. Gomery found that Chrétien had devised the program and administered it from his office without regard for government accounting and contracting procedures. According to the report, a lack of oversight permitted illegal contributions to be made to the Liberal Party in Quebec.

The revelations brought out by the Gomery enquiry disturbed Canadians across the country, but especially in Quebec, where it was felt that the province had been humiliated by the corruption. The scandal also gave momentum to the separatist parties active in both provincial and federal politics. It led to a resurgence of the Quebec separatist movement. A poll in April showed that 54 percent of Quebecers favored another referendum on the establishment of a separate status for Quebec.

Budget. The Martin government, working against these difficulties, presented its budget on February 23. Finance Minister Ralph Goodale revealed a sweeping list of new expenditures that would affect nearly every part of Canadian society from fiscal year 2005 (April 1-March 31, 2006) to 2009. Martin abandoned the restraint that had marked his nine years as finance minister in the previous Chrétien administration. The new spending resulted from promises Martin had made in the parliamentary election campaign of 2004 and from an effort to win support among the opposition parties.

The budget focused on issues supported by the Conservatives, including nearly $13 billion for defense, with funding for additional troops and new equipment. (All amounts are in Canadian dollars.) The spending also provided for social programs, principally a $5-billion national child-care plan. About $5 billion went to foreign aid. The budget boosted Canada's development aid as a proportion of gross domestic product (GDP) from 0.25 percent to 0.3 percent. (GDP is the total value of goods and services produced within a country in a year.)

The budget devoted about $5 billion to environmental protection, including meeting Canada's commitments under the Kyoto Protocol to curb dangerous emissions. (The Kyoto Protocol is an international treaty that requires many industrialized nations to reduce their greenhouse gas emissions.) Cities were to be awarded a larger share of gas tax revenue to support effective public transport. Five cents a liter from the gas tax would yield $5 billion over the next five years.

Goodale promised a balanced budget, the eighth in a row. The government protected itself by ensuring that the largest proportion of the new spending would come in the later years of the five-year spending commitments. It was nevertheless apparent that the budget represented a massive increase in federal expenditures.

Out of concern for parliamentary support of his budget, Martin on April 26 entered into an agreement with Jack Layton, the leader of the New Democratic Party, which held 19 seats in the House of Commons. At Layton's demand, an additional $4.6 billion was allocated over the next two years for housing, child-care, the environment, and foreign aid. Corporate tax cuts promised by Goodale were rolled back. In return for these concessions, Layton and his party vowed to support the budget when it came before Parliament. With the agreements, the Martin government took an important step toward its survival.

A dramatic moment in the Commons occurred on May 17 when a leading member of the Conservative Party, Belinda Stronach, crossed the floor to sit with the Liberals. Stronach had been regarded as a rising star in her party. Her defection, which arose from dissatisfaction with the Conservative leader, Stephen Harper, and with some of the party's social policies, gave the Liberal Party a valuable vote in the Commons.

Two days after Stronach's move, the important vote on the Goodale budget, as amended by Jack Layton, took place. Attention was concentrated on the positions of a number of independent members in the Commons, whose crucial votes on the budget could not be determined in advance. The Commons divided equally, 152 for the budget, 152 against. In this circumstance, British parliamentary practice—the basis of Canada's system—dictates that the elected Speaker of the Commons casts a vote. To the delight of the Martin government, the Speaker voted in favor of the budget.

Gay marriage. In another historic vote, the Commons on June 28 approved a measure chang-

ing the definition of marriage to include relationships between persons of the same sex. The political parties were divided in their attitude toward the issue. Although some members of Parliament disagreed with their party's stand on the question, only the Conservatives openly opposed the measure. The NDP and the 54-member separatist Bloc Québécois (BQ) party voted with the Liberal Party. Even before the Commons vote, the new definition had been upheld by the Supreme Court of Canada as well as by senior courts in 9 of the 10 provinces. (In Canada, the definition of marriage is controlled by the federal government, though its regulation falls to the provincial governments.) With the new law, Canada became the third country, after Belgium and the Netherlands, to permit same-sex marriages. Canada's new marriage law did not require churches to change their marriage practices—the law applies only to civil marriages.

Revenue disputes. With a healthy treasury, the federal government responded to demands

FEDERAL SPENDING IN CANADA
Estimated budget for fiscal 2005-2006*

Department or agency	Millions of dollars†
Agriculture and agri-food	2,651
Atlantic Canada opportunities agency	447
Canada customs and revenue agency	3,201
Canadian heritage	2,974
Citizenship and immigration	946
Economic development agency of Canada for the regions of Quebec	444
Environment	1,337
Finance	70,058
Fisheries and oceans	1,440
Foreign affairs and international trade (foreign affairs)	4,691
Foreign affairs and international trade (international trade)	210
Governor general	19
Health	4,063
Human resources and skills development	4,429
Human resources development (social development)	29,500
Indian affairs and northern development	5,827
Industry	4,291
Justice	1,398
National defence	13,435
Natural resources	1,347
Office of infrastructure of Canada	794
Parliament	501
Privy Council	285
Public works and government services	2,484
Solicitor general	5,449
Transport	1,518
Treasury board	2,720
Veterans affairs	2,853
Western economic diversification	393
Total	**169,705**

*April 1, 2005, to March 31, 2006.
†Canadian dollars; $1 = U.S. $0.85 as of Sept. 9, 2005.

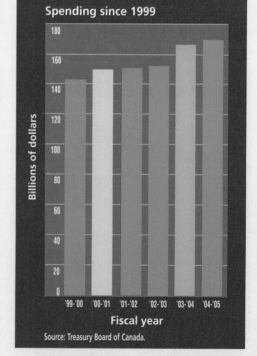

Spending since 1999

Source: Treasury Board of Canada.

from some of the provinces for a larger allocation of its revenues. Newfoundland and Nova Scotia had long claimed that they had been denied their fair share of royalties from oil and gas resources lying off their shores. The federal government had held back a portion of oil and gas revenues under a program designed to provide payments to provinces that could not meet national standards in social services. On January 28, an agreement was reached that allowed the two provinces to keep their share of offshore royalties as well as retain the equalization grants paid to the poorer provinces. Newfoundland received $2 billion in up-front payments; Nova Scotia, $830 million. Saskatchewan, which also has energy resources, made a similar claim.

The large province of Ontario also raised a financial dispute in 2005. Provincial Premier Dalton McGuinty argued that there was a fiscal imbalance between what the federal government receives in revenue from Ontario and the sums that the federal government returns to the province in federal programs. He claimed that the shortfall amounted to $5 billion a year. He also stated that federal grants to Ontario for services to immigrants were set at a lower level than those provided to Quebec. The premier and the prime minister held a long bargaining session in early May to discuss the claims. Martin agreed to pay the province $5.75 billion over the next five years. Ontario promised to use the funds for language and job training for immigrants, for apprenticeship programs, and for postsecondary education.

Environment. On April 13, the Canadian government revealed its long-awaited plan to implement the 1997 Kyoto Protocol to curb greenhouse gas emissions and limit climate change caused by global warming. Over the next seven years, the government would devote $10 billion to reduce greenhouse gases to 6 percent below 1990 levels. Reductions would be made by cutting the consumption of fossil fuels, implementing a variety of energy-saving measures, and purchasing emission credits, both in Canada and abroad. The provinces were required to share in this ambitious, long-range effort.

Health care. In a narrow decision, Canada's Supreme Court on June 9 recognized flaws in the country's prized state medical system. The court found that Quebec's public health system was unable to provide timely access to needed medical care. The delays placed the health and lives of residents at risk, which violated Quebec's charter of rights. The court ruled that a Quebec law banning private insurance for medically necessary treatment was illegal. In August, the court granted Quebec 12 months to change its legislation.

Public medical care in Canada, though substantially financed by the federal government, is pro-

2005 CANADIAN POPULATION ESTIMATES

PROVINCE AND TERRITORY POPULATIONS

Alberta	3,246,700
British Columbia	4,242,600
Manitoba	1,179,700
New Brunswick	752,200
Newfoundland and Labrador	515,400
Northwest Territories	43,400
Nova Scotia	937,900
Nunavut	30,100
Ontario	12,529,000
Prince Edward Island	138,500
Quebec	7,595,600
Saskatchewan	996,400
Yukon Territory	31,900
Canada	32,239,400

CITY AND METROPOLITAN AREA POPULATIONS

	Metropolitan area	City
Toronto, Ont.	5,292,100	2,562,400
Montreal, Que.	3,635,600	1,846,300
Vancouver, B.C.	2,179,400	573,100
Ottawa-Hull	1,154,100	
Ottawa, Ont.		820,500
Hull, Que.		*
Calgary, Alta.	1,055,800	984,800
Edmonton, Alta.	1,012,600	710,200
Hamilton, Ont.	716,000	509,400
Quebec, Que.	715,700	514,500
Winnipeg, Man.	708,000	620,400
London, Ont.	462,000	345,600
Kitchener, Ont.	455,500	200,800
St. Catharines-Niagara Falls	395,300	
St. Catharines, Ont.		127,800
Niagara Falls, Ont.		80,400
Halifax, N.S.	382,800	372,900
Oshawa, Ont.	340,300	143,000
Windsor, Ont.	333,200	217,600
Victoria, B.C.	332,200	74,600
Saskatoon, Sask.	235,400	199,400
Regina, Sask.	200,000	176,500
St. John's, Nfld. Lab.	181,200	97,100
Sherbrooke, Que.	164,100	75,200
Abbotsford, B.C.	164,100	124,500
Greater Sudbury, Ont.	161,100	147,800
Kingston, Ont.	157,300	115,900
Saguenay	153,300	
Chicoutimi, Que.		57,800
Jonquiere, Que.		53,600
Trois-Rivieres, Que.	142,000	44,600
Thunder Bay, Ont.	127,500	105,500
Saint John, N.B.	126,800	67,500

*Hull became part of the city of Gatineau in 2002. Gatineau's projected 2005 population was 238,700.

Source: World Book estimates based on data from Statistics Canada.

vided by the provinces. In 2005, some provinces allowed varying degrees of private medical care. The ruling clearly forced the provinces to reexamine health care systems at every level.

New governor general. Michaëlle Jean, a black woman of Haitian origin and a prominent television journalist in the largely French-speaking province of Quebec, assumed office as Canada's governor general in September. In a primarily sym-

MEMBERS OF THE CANADIAN HOUSE OF COMMONS

The House of Commons of the first session of the 38th Parliament convened on Oct. 5, 2004. As of Oct. 11, 2005, the House of Commons consisted of the following members: 133 Liberal Party, 54 Bloc Québécois, 98 Conservative Party of Canada, 19 New Democratic Party, and 3 Independent. This table shows each legislator and party affiliation. An asterisk (*) denotes those who served in the 37th Parliament.

Alberta
Diane Ablonczy, C.P.C.*
Rona Ambrose, C.P.C.
Rob Anders, C.P.C.*
Leon E. Benoit, C.P.C.*
Rick Casson, C.P.C.*
David Chatters, C.P.C.*
Ken Epp, C.P.C.*
Peter Goldring, C.P.C.*
Art Hanger, C.P.C.*
Stephen Harper, C.P.C.*
Rahim Jaffer, C.P.C.*
Brian Jean, C.P.C.
Dale Johnston, C.P.C.*
Jason Kenney, C.P.C.*
David Kilgour, Ind.*
Anne McLellan, Lib.*
Ted Menzies, C.P.C.
Rob Merrifield, C.P.C.*
Bob Mills, C.P.C.*
Deepak Obhrai, C.P.C.*
Charlie Penson, C.P.C.*
Jim Prentice, C.P.C.
James Rajotte, C.P.C.*
Lee Richardson, C.P.C.
Monte Solberg, C.P.C.*
Kevin Sorenson, C.P.C.*
Myron Thompson, C.P.C.*
John Williams, C.P.C.*

British Columbia
Jim Abbott, C.P.C.*
David Anderson, Lib.*
Don Bell, Lib.
Raymond Chan, Lib.
Jean Crowder, N.D.P.
Nathan Cullen, N.D.P.
John Cummins, C.P.C.*
Libby Davies, N.D.P.*
Stockwell Day, C.P.C.*
Ujjal Dosanjh, Lib.
John Duncan, C.P.C.*
David Emerson, Lib.
Paul Forseth, C.P.C.*
Hedy Fry, Lib.*
Jim Gouk, C.P.C.*
Gurmant Grewal, C.P.C.*
Nina Grewal, C.P.C.
Richard Harris, C.P.C.*
Russ Hiebert, C.P.C.
Jay Hill, C.P.C.*
Betty Hinton, C.P.C.*
Peter Julian, N.D.P.
Randy Kamp, C.P.C.
Gary Lunn, C.P.C.*
James Lunney, C.P.C.*
Keith Martin, Lib.*
James Moore, C.P.C.*
Stephen Owen, Lib.*
John Reynolds, C.P.C.*
Werner Schmidt, C.P.C.*
Bill Siksay, N.D.P.
Darrel Stinson, C.P.C.*
Chuck Strahl, C.P.C.*

Mark Warawa, C.P.C.
Randy White, C.P.C.*

Manitoba
Reg Alcock, Lib.*
James Bezan, C.P.C.
Bill Blaikie, N.D.P.*
Bev Desjarlais, N.D.P.*
Steven Fletcher, C.P.C.
Inky Mark, C.P.C.*
Pat Martin, N.D.P.*
Anita Neville, Lib.*
Brian Pallister, C.P.C.*
Raymond Simard, Lib.*
Joy Smith, C.P.C.
Vic Toews, C.P.C.*
Merv Tweed, C.P.C.
Judy Wasylycia-Leis, N.D.P.*

New Brunswick
Claudette Bradshaw, Lib.*
Jean-Claude D'Amours, Lib.
Yvon Godin, N.D.P.*
Charles Hubbard, Lib.*
Dominic LeBlanc, Lib.*
Rob Moore, C.P.C.
Andy Savoy, Lib.*
Andy Scott, Lib.*
Greg Thompson, C.P.C.*
Paul Zed, Lib.

Newfoundland and Labrador
Gerry Byrne, Lib.*
Norman Doyle, C.P.C.*
R. John Efford, Lib.*
Loyola Hearn, C.P.C.*
Bill Matthews, Lib.*
Todd Norman Russell, Lib.
Scott Simms, Lib.

Northwest Territories
Ethel Blondin-Andrew, Lib.*

Nova Scotia
Scott Brison, Lib.*
Bill Casey, C.P.C.*
Rodger Cuzner, Lib.*
Mark Eyking, Lib.*
Gerald Keddy, C.P.C.*
Peter MacKay, C.P.C.*
Alexa McDonough, N.D.P.*
Geoff Regan, Lib.*
Michael Savage, Lib.
Peter Stoffer, N.D.P.*
Robert Thibault, Lib.*

Nunavut
Nancy Karetak-Lindell, Lib.*

Ontario
Peter Adams, Lib.*
Dean Allison, C.P.C.
Charlie Angus, N.D.P.
Jean Augustine, Lib.*
Navdeep Bains, Lib.

Sue Barnes, Lib.*
Colleen Beaumier, Lib.*
Mauril Bélanger, Lib.*
Carolyn Bennett, Lib.*
Maurizio Bevilacqua, Lib.*
Ray Bonin, Lib.*
Ken Boshcoff, Lib.
Don Boudria, Lib.*
Ed Broadbent, N.D.P.
Bonnie Brown, Lib.*
Gord Brown, C.P.C.
Sarmite Bulte, Lib.*
John Cannis, Lib.*
Gary Carr, Lib.
Colin Carrie, C.P.C.
Aileen Carroll, Lib.*
Marlene Catterall, Lib.*
Brenda Chamberlain, Lib.*
Mike Chong, C.P.C.
David Christopherson, N.D.P.
Joe Comartin, N.D.P.*
Joe Comuzzi, Lib.*
Roy Cullen, Lib.*
Paul DeVillers, Lib.*
Barry Devolin, C.P.C.
Ruby Dhalla, Lib.
Ken Dryden, Lib.
Diane Finley, C.P.C.*
Joe Fontana, Lib.*
Cheryl Gallant, C.P.C.*
Roger Gallaway, Lib.*
Marc Godbout, Lib.
John Godfrey, Lib.*
Gary Goodyear, C.P.C.
Bill Graham, Lib.*
Albina Guarnieri, Lib.*
Helena Guergis, C.P.C.
Mark Holland, Lib.
Tony Ianno, Lib.*
Susan Kadis, Lib.
Jim Karygiannis, Lib.*
Wajid Khan, Lib.
Daryl Kramp, C.P.C.
Walt Lastewka, Lib.*
Guy Lauzon, C.P.C.
Jack Layton, N.D.P.
Derek Lee, Lib.*
Judi Longfield, Lib.*
Dave Mackenzie, C.P.C.
Paul H. Macklin, Lib.*
Gurbax Malhi, Lib.*
John Maloney, Lib.*
Diane Marleau, Lib.*
Tony Martin, N.D.P.
Brian Masse, N.D.P.*
John McCallum, Lib.*
David McGuinty, Lib.
John McKay, Lib.*
Dan McTeague, Lib.*
Larry Miller, C.P.C.
Peter Milliken, Lib.*
Maria Minna, Lib.*
Andy Mitchell, Lib.*
Lynn Myers, Lib.*
Rob Nicholson, C.P.C.

Pat O'Brien, Ind.*
Gordon O'Connor, C.P.C.
Bev Oda, C.P.C.
Carolyn Parrish, Ind.*
Jim Peterson, Lib.*
Beth Phinney, Lib.*
Jerry Pickard, Lib.
Pierre Poilievre, C.P.C.
Russ Powers, Lib.
Joe Preston, C.P.C.
Yasmin Ratansi, Lib.
Karen Redman, Lib.*
Scott Reid, C.P.C.*
Anthony Rota, Lib.
Gary Schellenberger, C.P.C.*
Judy Sgro, Lib.*
Mario Silva, Lib.
Lloyd St.-Amand, Lib.
Brent St. Denis, Lib.*
Paul Steckle, Lib.*
Belinda Stronach, Lib.
Paul Szabo, Lib.*
Andrew Telegdi, Lib.*
Liu Temelkovski, Lib.
David Tilson, C.P.C.
Alan Tonks, Lib.*
Paddy Torsney, Lib.*
Rose-Marie Ur, Lib.*
Tony Valeri, Lib.*
Roger Valley, Lib.
Peter Van Loan, C.P.C.
Joseph Volpe, Lib.*
Tom Wappel, Lib.*
Jeff Watson, C.P.C.
Bryon Wilfert, Lib.*
Borys Wrzesnewskyj, Lib.

Prince Edward Island
Wayne Easter, Lib.*
Lawrence MacAulay, Lib.*
Joe McGuire, Lib.*
Shawn Murphy, Lib.*

Quebec
Guy André, B.Q.
Gérard Asselin, B.Q.*
Claude Bachand, B.Q.*
Eleni Bakopanos, Lib.*
André Bellavance, B.Q.
Stéphane Bergeron, B.Q.*
Bernard Bigras, B.Q.*
Raynald Blais, B.Q.
Alain Boire, B.Q.
Francoise Boivin, Lib.
France Bonsant, B.Q.
Robert Bouchard, B.Q.
Marc Boulianne, B.Q.
Diane Bourgeois, B.Q.*
Paule Brunelle, B.Q.
Serge Cardin, B.Q.*
Robert Carrier, B.Q.
Roger Clavet, B.Q.
Bernard Cleary, B.Q.
Denis Coderre, Lib.*
Guy Coté, B.Q.
Irwin Cotler, Lib.*

THE MINISTRY OF CANADA*

bolic post, she represents Canada's head of state, Queen Elizabeth II of the United Kingdom. Jean's appointment dramatically symbolizes the multiracial and bilingual character of Canada.

Economy. The Canadian economy performed strongly in 2005, powered by substantial growth in the energy sector. Higher prices for oil and gas continued to strengthen the Canadian dollar against its U.S. counterpart. Overall growth in the GDP was estimated at 2.9 percent for 2005 by the International Monetary Fund, an organization based in Washington, D.C., that works to improve international financial relations. The inflation rate stood at 2.6 percent in October as energy prices eased. The unemployment rate in October held at 6.6 percent—the lowest rate since the 1970's. Jobs in the service sectors grew, though employment in manufacturing was somewhat weaker.

Finance Minister Ralph Goodale delivered an economic update on Nov. 14, 2005. He announced $30 billion in tax relief to individuals and businesses beginning in fiscal year 2005 and extending through the year 2010. Goodale also reported a $4.6 billion surplus in government operations.

Foreign affairs. In 2005, Canada declined for a second time to participate in an important U.S. foreign policy initiative—President George W. Bush's decision to deploy a missile defense shield over continental North America. Canada's refusal to take part in the projected shield followed a decision not to join the United States in its 2003 intervention in Iraq without United Nations (UN) authorization. The Martin government had wrestled for many months in 2005 over the question of the missile defense shield, knowing the subject had divided Canadians. Among the political parties, the Conservatives favored participation.

Foreign Minister Pierre Pettigrew announced the government's decision in the House of Commons on February 24, in a statement that led to a heated debate in Parliament. The discussion was confused because two days earlier the recently appointed Canadian ambassador to the United States, Frank McKenna, had announced that Canada was already involved in the preparations for the missile defense shield. He referred to a 2004 amendment to the treaty between the two countries defining the tasks of North American Aerospace Command (NORAD), a military alliance responsible for defending the United States and Canada against air attack. The amendment broadened NORAD procedures to allow it to communicate surveillance to the U.S. Northern Command, the military arm assigned to operate the ballistic missile defense scheme. Because of this amendment, McKenna argued that Canada was partly inside the continental defense plan.

Canada made its own contribution to the promotion of stability in the Middle East through its cooperation with the United States and North Atlantic Treaty Organization (NATO) by sending security forces to Afghanistan. Canada had assigned forces to uphold stable conditions in Kabul, the Afghan capital, since August 2003. In the summer of 2005, Canada began sending troops to Kandahar, where the ultraconservative Muslim Taliban movement remained strong. About 1,250 Canadian troops were based in Kandahar by early 2006.

Leaders of the Group of Eight (G8) industrialized nations, including Canada, met at their annual summit in Scotland in July 2005. The G8, an organization that plays a major role in raising issues in the global community, promised U.S. $25 billion of aid to Africa by 2010. Canada also participated in the summit's promise to cancel the foreign debts of 18 of the world's poorest countries.

U.S. relations. Canada and the United States settled a troublesome bilateral dispute in 2005. Since May 2003, when "mad cow disease" was discovered in a single cow in northern Alberta, the United States had banned live cattle imports from Canada. The closure brought hardship to ranching provinces such as Alberta. As a result, Canada's government provided assistance to ranchers unable to dispose of their livestock. Increased testing of animals on both sides of the border led to the decision by the U.S. government to reopen the border, which prompted Montana ranchers to secure a court order against the plan. On July 14, a U.S. appeals court set aside the order, and live cattle again moved across the border.

Another major bilateral dispute remained in stalemate in 2005. The U.S. International Trade Commission had, in 2002, imposed a 28-percent duty on construction lumber entering the United States from Canada. The U.S. lumber industry had claimed that Canadian lumber producers received unfair assistance from their government. Under the tax, over $5 billion in duties had been paid by Canadian lumber exporters. Canada had appealed the tax on three occasions to North American Free Trade Association (NAFTA) panels. On Aug. 10, 2005, a three-member special panel of NAFTA struck down the basis for the U.S. duty and called for the United States to stop taxing soft wood lumber and return the collected sum to Canada. The United States responded that it did not recognize the panel's decision and urged Canada to return to negotiations. Canada refused, arguing that the rule of commercial law, as laid down by NAFTA, should govern the settlement.

■ David M. L. Farr

See also **Canada, Prime Minister of; Canadian provinces; Canadian territories; Montreal; People in the news** (Michaëlle Jean); **Toronto.**

Canada's prime minister, Paul Martin, addresses the Liberal Party at a caucus in Ottawa, Ontario, on November 28. He attempted to rally party members for a campaign after his minority government fell in a vote of no confidence in the lower house of Parliament.

Canada, Prime Minister of.

Paul Martin's minority government fell on Nov. 28, 2005, when three opposition parties brought down the Liberal Party with a vote of no confidence in the House of Commons. Martin's 17-month tenure as prime minister was plagued by a corruption scandal he had inherited from the previous Liberal administration of Jean Chrétien. In early November, Justice John Gomery released a report on his investigation of the scandal. The report exonerated Martin but charged Chrétien and other senior Liberal Party officials with illegal campaign finance activities.

Martin's minority government maintained a tenuous hold on power during most of 2005. A healthy economy allowed Martin to create a budget that appeased the fiscal demands of other political parties and the provinces. However, the budget, and Martin's government, only narrowly passed a May 19 confidence vote.

Martin worked to improve Canada's image, which since the 1990's had been diminished by a smaller role in international diplomacy. Martin traveled to Asia in January 2005 to pledge support to countries damaged by the tsunami of 2004. In July 2005, he announced that Canada would double its annual aid to Africa to nearly $3 billion (Canadian dollars) by 2008. ■ David M. L. Farr

See also **Canada; Canadian provinces; Canadian territories.**

Canadian provinces.

Several of Canada's 10 provinces challenged the federal government in 2005 for control of revenues from their natural resources. Nova Scotia and Newfoundland and Labrador celebrated a historic agreement that permitted them to keep a greater portion of their offshore oil and natural gas revenues. Other provinces, including Ontario and Saskatchewan, sought similar fiscal deals with the national government as they battled deficits, crumbling infrastructure, and pressure for increased spending. Energy-rich Alberta, meanwhile, warned the federal government not to touch the province's skyrocketing oil and gas royalties or risk rousing separatist sentiment.

Alberta, along with Saskatchewan, celebrated the 100th anniversary of its entrance in 1905 to Confederation. (Confederation was the union of British colonies that formed the Dominion of Canada in 1867 and developed into present-day Canada.) The province, named after Princess Louise Caroline Alberta, the fourth daughter of British Queen Victoria I, held yearlong festivities that included a visit in May 2005 from Elizabeth II, Queen of Canada and the United Kingdom.

On March 3, four officers of the Royal Canadian Mounted Police were shot and killed at a marijuana operation in Mayerthorpe, Alberta, about 80 miles (130 kilometers) northwest of Edmonton, the provincial capital. Their killer died

A red tide of Royal Canadian Mounted Police (RCMP) flows down a street in Edmonton, Alberta, on March 10 during a national memorial to honor four fallen officers. More than 10,000 Canadian and U.S. officers attended the largest memorial in RCMP history.

simple majority electoral system to a form of proportional representation called the single transferable ballot. The initiative needed to receive 60 percent of the popular vote provincewide and 50 percent of the vote in at least 48 of the electoral districts to pass. The proposition failed, though it received 57.69 percent of the vote, including an outright majority in all but two constituencies.

from a self-inflicted gunshot. The incident was the single largest loss of officers for the force in Canadian history. Premier Ralph Klein urged the federal government to abandon legislation that would decriminalize possession of even small amounts of marijuana.

Alberta continued in 2005 to have the soundest finances in all of Canada. The government posted a second consecutive surplus of $5 billion on April 13. (All amounts are in Canadian dollars.) High oil and gas prices produced royalties that filled the provincial treasury. Economists predicted Alberta was headed toward its 12th consecutive balanced budget in fiscal year 2005 (April 1-March 31, 2006). Key budget planks included increases in health, social services, and education spending.

British Columbia. In an election on May 17, 2005, voters retained the provincial government in office, but with a much-reduced majority of seats in the legislature. The governing center-right Liberal Party won 46 of 79 seats with 45.8 percent of the vote. The left-wing New Democratic Party took the other 33 seats with 41.5 percent of the vote.

Residents also voted on a referendum on whether to change British Columbia's traditional

The federal government announced in March that the Ottawa-based Canadian Tourism Commission headquarters would be moved to Vancouver in a bid to boost the province's and the nation's tourism industry in the lead-up to the 2010 Winter Olympics. The city will share the games with Whistler, a British Columbia ski resort about 75 miles (120 kilometers) north of Vancouver.

The British Columbia Teachers Federation launched an illegal strike on Oct. 7, 2005, forcing about 600,000 public school students to stay home for two weeks. The province's 38,000 teachers began the protest after the government, through special legislation, imposed a two-year contract. On October 23, the federation accepted a settlement proposed by mediator Vince Ready that included $40 million to harmonize salaries throughout the province, $20 million to cut class sizes and fund programs for special needs students, and $5 million to raise salaries for substitute teachers.

The province issued a balanced budget on February 15 featuring a $1.7-billion debt reduction. A September update forecast a $1.3-billion surplus.

Manitoba. The Canadian government pressured Manitoba's lucrative Internet pharmacy industry in 2005 to stop selling prescription medications to residents of the United States. With 2,000 jobs and a billion-dollar industry at stake, the provincial government and the Canadian International Pharmacy Association, a Winnipeg-based trade group, argued that the federal government was infringing on the province's constitutional right to regulate pharmacies. Federal Health Minister Ujjal Dosanjh decided that Canada would ban bulk exports of prescription drugs but permit individual prescriptions to be filled. National price control legislation and large government orders kept Canadian prices for some medications much lower than U.S. prices in 2005.

A North Dakota water diversion project vigorously opposed by the Manitoba and Canadian governments was approved by the provincial and federal governments on August 6 after tense negotiations with the U.S. government. Environmentalists feared that the plan to divert some of the water in North Dakota's Devils Lake to the Sheyenne River, which flows into the Red River and up to Manitoba's Lake Winnipeg, would introduce invasive foreign fish and plant species and pollutants into the Canadian lake system. An 11th-hour deal ensured an advanced filtration system would be built to remove dangerous organisms.

Minister of Finance Greg Selinger presented a balanced budget on March 8 that continued to repay outstanding debt, projected a $196-million surplus, and increased funding for health, education, and transit and water systems.

New Brunswick. The province's native population was dealt a significant setback in July when the Supreme Court of Canada rejected extensive logging claims by the Mi'kmaq tribe to federally owned land in New Brunswick and Nova Scotia. The First Nation, which earlier won the right to fish their traditional waters in order to make a modest living, sought to extend the decision to logging rights and potentially to other natural resources. The justices found the group had not traditionally logged in the areas named in the suit at the time a trading treaty was signed in 1760.

The provincial government decided in September 2005 to renovate the aging Point Lepreau nuclear power plant, despite the federal government's refusal to contribute funds to the project. Premier Bernard Lord noted the decision was based on a study that determined upgrading the plant was more cost-effective than closing Lepreau and funding a new coal-fired plant. The project was expected to cost $1.4 billion and was scheduled to be completed by 2009.

Provincial Finance Minister Jeannot Volpé presented a balanced budget on March 30, 2005, that included $2.3 billion for health and senior care,

$1.2 billion in education, and an anticipated surplus of $98.9 million.

Newfoundland and Labrador. The province's major industries faced serious challenges in 2005. In July, forestry giant Abitibi Consolidated, Incorporated, announced it would close its paper mill in Stephenville. The shutdown cost the once thriving town of 8,000 people 300 high-paying jobs. Although the Montreal-based company considered the operation efficient and its work force productive, high energy and timber costs forced the closure. In October, the province agreed to give the company an energy subsidy if the mill reopened. The company offered its employees a reduced benefits plan, but the union rejected the proposal and the mill remained closed.

During the summer of 2005, dozens of people protested a fishing ban by participating in illegal cod fishing off Newfoundland and Labrador. The fishers disagreed with the Department of Fisheries and Oceans' claim that cod stocks were too weak for fishing and noted that they had found the stocks plentiful. Protesters argued that the cod was a part of the province's culture. The department charged numerous protesters with illegal fishing over several weekends in August.

After years of uncertainty and loss of wealth, Newfoundland and Labrador's fiscal picture brightened in 2005. Thanks in part to a $2-billion offshore oil and gas revenue deal with the federal government, the budget presented on March 21 slashed the deficit to $492 million. A November fiscal update projected a $1.5-million surplus.

Nova Scotia. The provincial government welcomed Rodney MacDonald as its first immigration minister in January 2005. Although immigration is primarily a federal responsibility, Nova Scotia created the position to combat such demographic trends as an aging population and people moving from rural Nova Scotia to large cities in other provinces. Nova Scotia hoped to attract 3,600 people from other countries each year by 2010.

In June 2005, crab fishers in Cape Breton and the eastern part of the province launched a series of protests in response to changes in their quotas. The fishers blocked an interprovincial ferry service, picketed national parks, and demonstrated on Parliament Hill in Ottawa, the capital, in a bid to overturn the decision. However, fisheries officials would not commit to any policy changes.

The provincial budget, presented on April 27, projected a $63.3-million surplus. Nova Scotia Premier John Hamm pledged to apply the entire amount of an $830-million offshore oil and gas revenue deal with the federal government toward the province's outstanding debt.

Ontario. Canada's first provincial ban on pit bull dogs went into effect in Ontario on August 29. After a 60-day grace period, all pit bulls born after October 28 or brought into Ontario could be confiscated and destroyed. A special clause in the ban protects dogs born before that date, but all existing pit bulls were to be spayed or neutered, leashed, and muzzled when off their owner's property. A bite or attack could result in a $10,000 fine and a six-month jail term for the owner.

Ontario's auto sector boomed in 2005. In March, Oshawa-based General Motors of Canada, Limited, announced a $2.5-billion investment in its operations in Ontario, the largest expansion in Canadian history. In July, Toronto-based Toyota Motor Corporation named Woodstock as the location of its new $800-million auto assembly plant. Although some American states offered double the tax breaks extended by the Canadian governments, Toyota chose Ontario because the public health care system and the province's low training costs provided more long-term savings.

The Northern Ontario School of Medicine opened in August to combat a chronic shortage of physicians in rural and northern Ontario. In its inaugural year, 56 positions were available—24 at Thunder Bay's Lakehead University and 32 at Sudbury's Laurentian University. In order to reflect the demography of the region, applicants who had spent 10 years or more in rural, remote, or northern urban communities, *francophone* (people whose first language is French) applicants, and native Canadian applicants were given a slight advantage during the admissions process.

The provincial budget presented on May 11 focused on investments in education and training. According to projections, post-secondary education and training will receive a $6.2-billion increase between fiscal years 2005 and 2009. The budget also promised more financial aid for 135,000 low- and middle-income students and increased apprenticeship positions to 26,000 annually by 2007-2008.

Prince Edward Island (P.E.I.). Agriculture, Fisheries, and Aquaculture Minister Kevin MacAdam intensified his battle against the federal Department of Fisheries and Oceans in 2005. In January, MacAdam charged that an administrative error had removed a herring exclusion zone near the island, allowing New Brunswick fishermen to use the area, which threatened the fishery's stock. The provincial government launched a P.E.I. Supreme Court suit in February against the department and its minister that challenged its power under the federal Fisheries Act.

Provincial Treasurer Mitch Murphy presented a budget on April 7 that cut hundreds of civil servant jobs in Canada's smallest province. The cuts affected 330 people; 280 positions were eliminated in health care alone.

Quebec. The Supreme Court of Canada ruled on the constitutionality of Bill 101 on March 31. The law, introduced by the separatist Parti Québé-cois in the 1970's to protect the French language, ensures that children who attend public schools are instructed in French if both of their parents also attended French language schools in Quebec. The court rejected the pleas of French-speaking parents who sought to send their children to English-language schools in order to give them a competitive advantage in the job market. However, the court did ask the province to revamp the law to bring it in line with Canada's Charter of Rights and Freedoms (the Canadian bill of rights). Political experts noted if the law had been struck down, separatists might have used the issue to push for another referendum on *sovereignty* (independence).

A decision by the provincial government to transform $103 million worth of grants into student loans prompted a strike among Quebec's high school and university students in 2005. At its peak, over 200,000 students had joined the protest. A proposed settlement in April revealed divisions among members of the student coalition, and by the end of the month, most students returned to classes to finish the school year. The agreement guaranteed $70 million would be returned to grant status in 2005-2006 and the full amount would be reinstated for four subsequent years. In 2005, Quebec had the lowest tuition fees in the country.

On April 21, Quebec's minister of finance, Michel Audet, forecast a balanced budget for fiscal year 2005. Highlights included free medications for severely disadvantaged seniors; $145 million to create 2,600 affordable housing spaces; and $4.9 billion to repair public infrastructure.

Saskatchewan. A provincewide smoking ban in public buildings that went into effect in January prompted discussion about whether it could be enforced on First Nations reserves, which are under federal jurisdiction. Leaders of the Federation of Saskatchewan Indian Nations stated that the province's First Nations bands were not likely to follow the law and may institute their own bylaws. Members of the province's hospitality and tourism industry launched a challenge, arguing that tourists could smoke in casinos on First Nations lands, which made the reserves' exemption an unfair economic advantage. The government defended the ban by arguing that the section of the federal Charter of Rights and Freedoms that ensures equality under the law was meant to prevent racial discrimination and not regulate economic competition.

Saskatchewan's financial situation continued to improve in 2005. High oil prices helped the province to achieve another balanced budget on March 23, but the government still had to use $145 million from its fiscal stabilization account, or "rainy day" fund, to remain solvent.

■ David M. L. Farr and William Stos

See also **Canada; Canadian Territories; Montreal; Toronto.**

Canadian territories. The importance of Canada's far North became evident in 2005, as record high oil and gasoline prices prompted different factions to exploit or protect the resource-rich Canadian territories. Native groups, large corporations, and local governments jousted for control over the natural assets of the Northwest Territories, Nunavut, and Yukon.

Northwest Territories. The development of a proposed oil pipeline in the Mackenzie Valley generated headlines in 2005 as government and industry leaders negotiated with First Nations in hopes of reaching an agreement to build the $7-billion project. (All amounts are in Canadian dollars.) Residents feared that the money that will pour into these isolated communities could lead to alcoholism and drug addictions, destroy traditional culture, and provide no lasting economic benefit. The Deh Cho First Nation was particularly vocal during negotiations. In the spring, Toronto-based Imperial Oil Limited, which heads the pipeline group, announced it had halted work on the project, blaming the slow progress of land claims negotiations and regulatory approval. In July, the First Nations dropped a lawsuit that had delayed progress and accepted a settlement worth about $31.5 million. In turn, the federal government unveiled a 10-year, $500-million plan for social spending in communities affected by the pipeline.

The territory's booming diamond mining industry expanded in 2005 as Mountain Province Diamonds, Incorporated, based in Ontario, California, and Toronto-based De Beers Canada, Incorporated announced plans to develop a new diamond deposit northeast of the city of Yellowknife. De Beers earmarked $38.5 million to conduct further drilling and sampling at the site, called Gahcho Kue. Canada's two existing diamond mines, Ekati and Diavik, produced about 20 percent of the Northwest Territories' *gross domestic product* (GDP) by 2002. (GDP is the value of all the goods and services produced in a region during a year.)

A projected $46-million operating deficit for fiscal year 2004 (April 1-March 31, 2005) became a $44-million operating surplus, according to the territorial government's Feb. 10, 2005, budget. The turnaround was due to higher transfers from the federal government and increased tax revenues.

Nunavut. During the summer of 2005, all eyes were fixed on Hans Island, a 0.8-mile (1.3-kilometer) land mass on the Arctic coast, as Canada and Denmark engaged in a war of words over its ownership. Both countries claimed the island, but neither country had expressed much interest in it until the early 2000's, when it appeared that global warming could melt enough ice to open the famed Northwest Passage as a shipping route. An unannounced visit to the island by Canada's Minister of National Defence Bill Graham on July 13, 2005, prompted an angry diplomatic response from Denmark. In September, the two sides met in New York City to debate ownership. Negotiations between the two countries in 1973 had established a border in the Kennedy Channel between Nunavut and Greenland, but the ownership of Hans Island was not decided.

The Nunavut government presented a balanced budget of $935.8 million on February 25 that increased funding for all territorial departments. Key spending initiatives included an 18-percent increase for the Department of Health and Social Services to make health care delivery simpler and more accessible for the territory's dispersed population. The Nunavut Housing Corporation received $181.2 million to build 80 affordable housing units in the 2005 construction season.

Yukon. Efforts by United States President George W. Bush to open up parts of the Arctic National Wildlife Refuge in Alaska to oil and gas exploration dominated the news in Yukon in 2005. The refuge is home to the calving grounds of the Yukon's Porcupine caribou herd, a vital part of the Vuntut Gwitchin First Nation's culture and diet. Residents in some of the territory's villages are opposed to any oil development and urged authorities to take action. Opponents won a reprieve on November 9 when the U.S. House of Representatives voted to remove provisions from a budget bill that would have allowed drilling in the refuge.

Four members of the U.S. Senate toured the territory in August to gain firsthand knowledge of how climate change is affecting the far North. Senators John McCain (R., Arizona), Susan Collins (R., Maine), Hillary Rodham Clinton (D., New York), and Lindsey Graham (R., South Carolina) took an aerial tour over the melting Friday Creek and Alligator ice patches in southwest Yukon. The senators also saw evidence of beetle infestations in the Kluane area. More than 988,000 acres (400,000 hectares) of forest have been affected by the largest single outbreak of spruce beetle in a Canadian forest, which has been blamed on warmer weather.

Yukon's capital, Whitehorse, will host the 2007 Canada Winter Games. The 2007 games will be the first held north of the 60th parallel. The premiers of all three northern territories announced in 2005 their intentions to collaborate and use the event to showcase the North's unique culture.

The Yukon government presented the largest budget in the territory's history—about $784 million—on March 24. The government reported an estimated $25-million surplus for fiscal year 2004 and predicted a $29-million surplus for fiscal year 2005.   ■ David M. L. Farr and William Stos
See also **Canada.**

Cape Verde. See Africa.

Census. The United States Census Bureau issued reports showing vast population changes in the nation in 2005. On June 9, the bureau reported that the U.S. immigrant population—particularly among Hispanics, who made up the nation's largest minority group—had grown and become markedly younger. One of every five children under the age of 18 in the United States was Hispanic in 2004, according to census figures. Hispanics made up roughly half of the nation's overall population growth of 2.9 million people from July 1, 2003, to July 1, 2004, and one of every seven people in the country was Hispanic in 2004. Half of all Hispanics in the United States in 2004 were under the age of 27, compared with half of all non-Hispanic whites who were older than 40.

"Majority-minority" states. Texas became the fourth state in the nation in which minority groups constituted a majority of the population, the bureau reported on Aug. 11, 2005. Hawaii, New Mexico, and California were the other three majority-minority states. The District of Columbia also had a majority-minority population in 2005. According to the bureau's July 1, 2004, population estimates, Texas had a minority population of 11.3 million people, making up 50.2 percent of the state's total population of 22.5 million. Hawaii's population was 77 percent minority; New Mexico's population was 57 percent minority; California's population was 56 percent minority; and the District of Columbia's was 70 percent minority.

Future population growth. The Census Bureau on April 21, 2005, issued projections that nearly half of the total U.S. population growth between 2000 and 2030 would take place in just three states—Florida, California, and Texas. The bureau projected that the three states would gain more than 12 million people between 2000 and 2030, 46 percent of the national total. Under the projections, California and Texas would remain the nation's most populous states in 2030. Florida would pass New York in total population by 2011.

Annual support payments increase. The bureau on Feb. 24, 2005, reported that alimony and child support payments increased by 18 percent between 1997 and 2002, rising from $34 billion to $40 billion. The report also revealed that 7.8 million people made support payments, an 8-percent increase. The average annual amount of financial support was $5,200, up from $4,700 paid in 1997. The findings were adjusted for inflation.

Employment. The Census Bureau on Aug. 8, 2005, revealed that businesses in New York County (Manhattan), New York, had the highest payroll in the country, at an average of $73,032, per employee. Los Angeles County, California, had the highest number of businesses—235,085.

On March 28, the bureau issued data revealing that workers with a bachelor's degree earned an average of $51,206 annually, compared with workers with a high school diploma who earned an average of $27,915 a year. Workers with advanced degrees earned an average of $74,602 annually. Those who lacked a high school diploma made an average of $18,734 annually.

Voter turnout. The bureau reported on May 26, 2005, that 64 percent of eligible U.S. citizens voted in the 2004 presidential elections, up from the 60 percent who participated in the 2000 elections. According to the bureau, 67 percent of non-Hispanic whites voted in the 2004 election, an increase of 5 percent from 2000; 60 percent of African Americans voted in 2004, up 3 percent from 2000; and Asians and Hispanics made up 45 and 47 percent of the 2004 election voters, respectively, a rate unchanged over 2000 figures. Voter turnout was highest among women and people with college degrees.

Scam shut down. The bureau shut down a bogus Web site in May 2005 that claimed to be the official Census Bureau Web site. The site's creators e-mailed individuals requesting that they click on a link to the fake site, where they were asked, with the promise of $5, to answer questions about the Iraq War and to provide bank information. ◾ Geoffrey A. Campbell

See also **City; Crime: A Special Report; State government.**

Chemistry. In April 2005, food chemist Bruce R. Hamaker and his colleagues at Purdue University in West Lafayette, Indiana, explained why some popcorn kernels pop and others remain inedible "duds." The chemists concluded that the secret is a well-ordered hull.

As a good popcorn kernel heats up in a microwave oven, the water inside expands, building the pressure up to nine times atmospheric pressure. The hull, or *pericarp,* is then ripped apart by an explosion, and the starch in the kernel expands into a fluffy treat. However, some kernels leak moisture as they heat and never pop.

To understand how unpopped kernels are different from popped kernels, the Purdue scientists investigated the hulls of 14 Indiana-grown varieties of popcorn that were heated in a microwave oven. They used *crystallography,* a technique for visualizing the arrangement of atoms, to compare the molecular structures of the hulls, which are made of long-chain molecules, mostly cellulose and hemicellulose.

The scientists found that the kernels differed in the amount and location of cellulose. With kernels that pop, there is greater alignment among the cellulose molecules and the other molecular chains as they heat, allowing to lock in moisture. The duds have weaker, less-ordered hulls that leak moisture.

By knowing the ideal molecular composition of kernels, popcorn producers now have the right target for breeding or *genetically engineering* (manipulating the genes of) improved varieties of popcorn. According to Hamaker, the research may lead to new microwave popcorn on grocery shelves by 2010.

Clearing clots. A copper-laced coating may help prevent medical implants from being fouled by blood clots, making the devices longer lasting, more accurate, and less likely to be rejected by the patient's body. The promising development was reported in March 2005 by chemistry professor Mark E. Meyerhoff of the University of Michigan at Ann Arbor.

Clotting is more likely to occur when a blood vessel is constricted than when it is relaxed. The injection of nitric oxide into the bloodstream causes the veins and arteries to ease up, which forms the basis for using nitroglycerin as a medication for *angina pectoris,* chest pain that occurs when the heart does not receive enough blood. Knowing this, scientists add nitric oxide to implants to extend their usefulness in the body. Unfortunately, this compound becomes depleted over time. Patients can take certain medicines to keep blood vessels relaxed, but these medicines produce side effects, including headache and dizziness.

Meyerhoff and his team developed a method to continually create nitric oxide in the body in the immediate vicinity of the implant. Nitrosothiols, compounds that are naturally present within the bloodstream, can be prompted to break down into nitric oxide in the presence of copper. By adding certain *polymers,* large molecules formed by chemically linking smaller molecules, to the chemical composition of the implant and "doping" the polymers with copper, the scientists encouraged the creation of nitric oxide in the bloodstream. The scientists showed that this method discourages clotting both in laboratory blood tests and in animal tests.

The researchers noted that various questions remained about which polymers are best to use and how individual variations in the levels of nitrosothiols can be controlled.

Bright, thin, and strong. *Nanotubes,* which are rolled, hexagonal sheets of carbon resembling chicken wire on an atomic scale, can light up, conduct electricity, and be formed into fabrics that are ultrathin yet as strong as steel. In 2005, these extraordinary materials could be manufactured in bulk, according to an article published in August by chemist Ray H. Baughman and his team at the University of Texas in Dallas and chemist Ken Atkinson from the Commonwealth Scientific and Industrial Research Organization in Geelong, Australia.

Scientists have known since the 1990's that nanotubes are electrically conductive, lightweight, and easy to manipulate. However, producing nanotubes in useful, bulk forms while retaining their properties has been difficult. Previously, researchers have used papermaking processes to create nanotube sheets, but none of these sheets have been shown to be transparent, strong, and highly conducting at the same time.

Baughman's group first created a "forest" of nanotubes on a glass surface by using a chemical catalyst to stimulate the growth of the tiny tubes. They then pressed an adhesive strip against the nanotubes and pulled the tubes away. These strips were rolled up as they were produced at the rate of 23 feet (7 meters) per minute—in a method similar to spinning yarn in a mill.

The scientists noted that having such materials available in bulk creates several possibilities for manufacturers, including the production of improved solar cells, ultralight airplanes, and lightweight, flexible computer screens. The materials, they added, might also bring certain imaginative science fiction ideas closer to reality, including the development of solar sails that can propel spacecraft between stars without fuel and the creation of elevators that can rise up superlong poles to carry people into space.   ■ Peter Andrews

Chess.
Veselin Topalov of Bulgaria became the 2005 world chess champion by winning the Fédération Internationale des Échecs (FIDE) title in a tournament held from September 28 to October 16 in San Luis, Argentina. FIDE is the governing body of international chess. Without losing a single game, Topalov dominated an eight-player field of the world's best, which included Judit Polgar, the highest-rated woman player in history. The championship featured a return to slower time controls, allowing the players more time to consider their moves.

Kasparov retires. Garry Kasparov of Russia announced his retirement from top-level chess after winning a highly regarded annual tournament in Linares, Spain, in March. Kasparov first won the FIDE championship in 1985, then a unified title. In 1993, he broke with FIDE after a dispute, causing a title fissure. He held his piece of the then-fractured world chess title until fellow Russian Vladimir Kramnik defeated him in 2000.

Bobby Fischer. Iceland granted citizenship to former world champion Bobby Fischer in March 2005. He had been detained in Tokyo by Japanese officials since July 13, 2004, when he was apprehended trying to travel with an expired United States passport to the Philippines. Fischer has lived outside the United States since ignoring instructions from the U.S. government not to travel to Yugoslavia to play a 1992 chess match against Boris Spassky of Russia.

U.S. events. Joel Benjamin, of Waldwick, New Jersey, and Vadim Milo of Biel, Switzerland, led 455 players to share first prize at the 106th Annual U.S. Open Championship in Phoenix, Arizona, on Aug. 14, 2005. Susan Polgar, who is Judit's sister and a former women's world champion, broke the record for the number of games played at once—326, in Palm Beach Gardens, Florida. During the session, which took more than 16 hours, Polgar walked more than 9 miles (14.5 kilometers) from board to board, losing only 3 games.

Young champions. A record 5,270 students played in the Supernational III Chess Championship in Nashville, Tennessee, from April 8 to 10. The students represented at least 1,300 schools from 48 states. Catalina Foothills High School of Tucson, Arizona, won the high school championship. Hunter College Campus School of New York City won both the junior high and elementary championships. On July 27, Alex Lenderman of Brooklyn, New York, placed first in the boys' under-16 division of the 2005 World Youth Championship in Belfort, France.

■ Al Lawrence

See also **Russia**.

Chicago. Federal authorities investigated corruption allegations in several Chicago city agencies in 2005, resulting in a major shakeup of Mayor Richard M. Daley's administration. Daley's popularity plummeted in the wake of the investigations. A *Chicago Tribune* poll in May found that only 53 percent of voters approved of Daley's job performance, his lowest approval rating since he was first elected mayor in 1989. The poll also found that 57 percent held him personally responsible for the scandals.

The investigation began in January 2004, when a bribery case involving the city's trucking contracts led authorities to expand their inquiry into a broad examination of political patronage. By 2005, allegations of hiring and contracting corruption touched several city departments, including aviation, streets and sanitation, transportation, water management, and Daley's lobbying office. In July, United States Attorney Patrick Fitzgerald claimed that Chicago government had undergone more than a decade of "massive fraud" in city hiring. Fitzgerald's office indicted two senior city administrators on charges that they rigged hiring tests to ensure jobs for campaign workers.

In August, a federal judge appointed an attorney to serve as an independent overseer of hiring at city hall. On August 26, Daley, who denied any

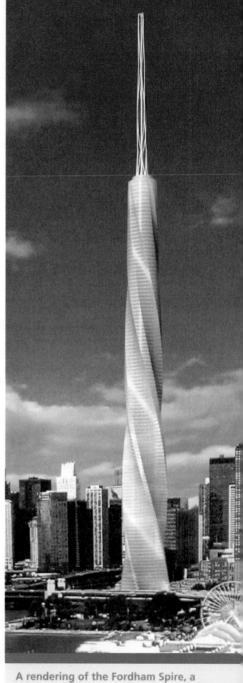

A rendering of the Fordham Spire, a 1,458-foot- (444-meter-) high residential building proposed for Chicago's lakefront, was unveiled by the developer, the Fordham Company, in July 2005. If built, the skyscraper, designed by Spanish architect Santiago Calatrava, would be the tallest building in the United States.

role in the scandals, was interrogated by federal investigators.

By late 2005, the criminal inquiry resulted in more than 23 convictions. Eight members of Daley's Cabinet and three other top officials tainted by the corruption investigation either resigned or were dismissed, and more than 40 city employees were dismissed.

Daley's troubles extended beyond the corruption investigation. His ambitious Renaissance 2010 plan to build new schools was put on hold in 2005 because of lack of funding. He also ran into resistance over his efforts to expand O'Hare International Airport. In July, a report by the U.S. Department of Transportation disputed Daley's contention that adding more runways would alleviate congestion at the airport. The report claimed that the expansion would have a "minimal impact" on the airport's traffic problems.

World Series champs. In October, the Chicago White Sox captured the team's first World Series title in 88 years, sweeping the Houston Astros in a four-game series. After clinching the title in Houston, the team returned to Chicago, where their victory was celebrated with a ticker-tape parade through the streets of downtown Chicago. The 2005 title was the third for the White Sox, who previously won the World Series in 1906 and 1917.

Millennium Park, a 24.5-acre (9.9-hectare) park in downtown Chicago that opened in 2004, continued to attract scores of tourists in 2005, but park managers were criticized for the delay in completing the park's Cloud Gate sculpture—popularly known as "the bean." The sculpture's unveiling was stalled for months because buffing the seams of the stainless steel sculpture took longer than expected. In addition, the park's underground garage brought in only $7.5 million in revenue in 2005, falling short of the $8.8 million needed to service the garage's debt.

Traffic. In January, Chicago transferred ownership of the 7.8-mile (12.5-kilometer) elevated Chicago Skyway to a private partnership for 99 years for a cash payment of $1.83 billion. In May, the Texas Transportation Institute of College Station, Texas, ranked the Chicago area second only to Los Angeles in traffic congestion.

Deaths. Chicago author Saul Bellow, recipient of the Nobel Prize in literature, died on April 5, 2005, at age 89. Publishing pioneer John Johnson, founder of *Ebony* and *Jet* magazines, died on August 8. Restaurateur Arnold "Arnie" Morton, originator of the Taste of Chicago festival, died on May 28 at age 83.   ■ Harold Henderson

See also **Baseball; Deaths; Literature: A Portrait; Magazine: A Portrait.**

Children's books. See Literature for children.

Chile. Michelle Bachelet, a Socialist and former minister in the incumbent Concertacion government, won the Dec. 11, 2005, presidential election, but failed to receive 50 percent of the vote as required by Chilean law. Her opponent, Sebastian Pinera, a wealthy businessman of the center-right National Renewal Party, trailed her by a large margin. Bachelet was heavily favored to become Chile's first woman president in runoff elections scheduled for Jan. 15, 2006.

Chile's economy grew by 6.3 percent in the first half of 2005. Economists credited record-high world prices for copper, which accounted for 45 percent of Chile's export earnings in 2005.

More than 40 Chilean army recruits perished in a May blizzard while on a training exercise near the Antuco volcano in the Andes Mountains. Several officers were dismissed following an investigation, which found them culpable for having ordered the exercise despite weather that caught the soldiers ill-equipped for conditions.

The wife and son of General Augusto Pinochet Ugarte, Chile's military dictator from 1973 to 1990, were arrested in August 2005 for income-tax evasion. Pinochet faced trial on similar charges after he was stripped in October of the immunity he had enjoyed as a former president.

■ Nathan A. Haverstock

See also **Latin America.**

China. The Chinese Communist Party (CPC), amid rising popular unrest and protests, issued a government report on Oct. 19, 2005, stating that its rule was democratic and that it "upholds and improves the people's democratic dictatorship." The report emphasized that the CPC's primary goals were economic development and social stability.

Protests. In recent years, protests have washed across the Chinese countryside, often turning violent. Farmers particularly objected to the seizure of their land to build factories or suburban housing, pollution from new factories, corruption, and other abuses. Public Security Minister Zhou Yongkang announced in July that the number of "mass incidents" had risen from 58,000 in 2003 to 74,000 in 2004, with 3.6 million people involved in the 2004 protests. He said the number and scale of protests were "constantly expanding." Reports from many sources accused Communist bosses and local bosses of using violence against people who tried to exercise an officially announced policy allowing elections or who complained about other abuses.

The state media announced on Aug. 18, 2005, that the government was setting up riot police units in 36 cities to quell any trouble. On October 11, the CPC called for "greater emphasis on social equity" and alleviating a "widening income gap between regions and parts of society."

On Dec. 6, 2005, police opened fire on protesters in Dongzhou, a village near Hong Kong, in the deadliest known use of force in China since the Tiananmen Square incident. (In 1989, soldiers fired into and killed many demonstrators at a peaceful assembly of students in Beijing's Tiananmen Square.) The Dongzhou villagers were protesting government seizure of their land. Officials said that 3 people were killed, but villagers claimed that at least 20 people were killed and 42 others remained missing days after the incident.

Social and human rights. In 2005, Chinese officials tightened rules to deny use of the Internet and other forms of communication to anyone challenging authority. In May, the government abruptly canceled an international conference on human rights, the rule of law, and democracy that was to be held in Beijing, the capital. The United Nations (UN) commissioner for human rights, Louise Arbour, noted in Beijing on September 2 that China was making progress on political and social rights, but that additional progress was needed. One of her investigators reported on December 2 that China widely used torture in law enforcement.

A committee of China's parliament, the National People's Congress (NPC), amended the Law on the Protection of Rights and Interests of Women, making sexual harassment of women unlawful. The NPC stated that equality between men and women "is one of the country's basic national principles." Critics characterized the amendment as vaguely worded, saying that it left uncertain how much help there might be for the 79 percent of women who reported sexual harassment in a national survey.

Military tensions. A United States Department of Defense report released on July 19 claimed that China was modernizing its armed forces "to fight and win short-duration, high-intensity conflicts" over Taiwan. Both China and the island of Taiwan formally agree that the two are one nation, but Taiwan had been separate since Communists came to power in China in 1949. China repeatedly warned that it would invade Taiwan if the island's government renounced the one-nation status. In March 2005, the NPC authorized the use of force if Taiwan moved too far toward independence. The U.S. report revealed that China had Russian-made weapons, including jet fighters and some 700 missiles, deployed near Taiwan.

With the United States committed to defending Taiwan against a Chinese attack, the continual military buildup in 2005 greatly concerned U.S. Defense Department officials. They claimed the build-up could reduce the effectiveness of U.S. forces in the area, especially naval forces.

China's foreign ministry denounced the report

as based on reckless accusations that ignored facts and tried to spread the idea of a China threat. China also objected to U.S. efforts to keep European Union (EU) countries from lifting an embargo on selling weapons to China.

China and Russia held their first joint military exercises in August 2005. Some 10,000 troops plus warships and military jets participated. The announced reason for the exercises was practice for fighting terrorism and separatism, but Western observers suggested the maneuvers were unrelated to such problems.

Taiwan. Chinese hostility toward the governing political party in Taiwan, the Democratic Progressive Party (DPP), led by President Chen Shui-bian, continued in 2005. Before coming to power in 2000, the DPP had advocated making Taiwan an independent nation. Once in power, however, DPP officials played down this position to avoid provoking China.

Leaders of Taiwan's main opposition party, who sought warmer relations with China than did Chen, were invited in 2005 to visit Beijing. On April 29, heads of the CPC and Taiwan's Nationalist Party (KMT)—bitter enemies through China's long civil war that ended in a 1949 Communist victory and the KMT's retreat to Taiwan—shook hands. The two leaders, President Hu Jintao of China and the KMT's Lien Chan, pledged to work together against Taiwan's independence. Taiwan's government denounced the agreement as an attempt to undermine its authority.

Education. Prime Minister Wen Jiabao announced in March 2005 the elimination of school fees for 14 million students in China's poorest counties. By 2007, all rural students will receive free primary education, he said. A report revealed that only 23 percent of the nation's education budget

2005, after being publicly criticized by President Hu. The reason Tung gave was fatigue and failing health, but the unpopular leader was widely believed to have been pushed out by China's government.

Donald Tsang, a popular civil servant who had risen to head Hong Kong's bureaucracy, was selected to succeed Tung and was sworn in on June 24. To the anger of many politically conscious Hong Kong residents, China reinterpreted Hong Kong law to limit Tsang to completing the last two years of Tung's term, rather than allowing him to begin a regular five-year term. The maneuver was seen as a way of increasing Chinese influence on Tsang. Tsang, who had been knighted by the United Kingdom for his long service, was distrusted by many Chinese loyalists in Hong Kong.

Economy. The end of international limits on textile exports brought a surge of Chinese shipments to the United States and Europe in 2005. Both the U.S. government and the EU sought to restrict them, but U.S. trade talks with Chinese officials on restrictions broke down in October. In November, they did reach an agreement in which Chinese textile exports to the United States were allowed to rise by tiered price increments from 2006 to 2008.

The United States had for several years urged China to raise the value of its currency, the yuan, as a way to reduce the enormous imbalance of trade between the two countries. On July 21, 2005, China abandoned its nine-year-old policy of fixing the yuan at 8.28 to the U.S. dollar. China raised the yuan's value by 2.1 percent, and later in the year it rose slightly higher. American officials criticized the change as insufficient, calling for a higher rate.

Explosions. A chemical factory explosion polluted northeastern China's Songhua River on November 13, forcing millions of people to stop using river water for weeks. An explosion on November 27 in a coal mine in the same area killed more than 160 workers.

Death. Zhao Ziyang died January 17. On becoming head of the Communist Party in 1987, Zhao introduced limited reforms. When student demand for further reforms led to the Tiananmen Square demonstrations in May 1989, Zhao tried to calm them. However, hard-line party elements took control, and Zhao was ousted and held under house arrest for the rest of his life. ■ Henry S. Bradsher

See also **AIDS; Asia; Disasters; Japan; People in the News** (Hu Jintao); **Public health.**

was spent in the countryside. Most of China's 1.3 billion people live in rural areas. With many families too poor to pay school fees, rural children received far fewer educational opportunities than children in cities.

Health problems. Health standards had improved in China after the Communists came to power in 1949. Using paramedics called "barefoot doctors," they spread basic medical and sanitation care into rural areas. Such endemic diseases as *tuberculosis* (an infection typically located in the lungs) and *schistosomiasis* (a blood disease caused by parasitic worms) were largely eradicated. However, by 2005 these and other diseases were resurgent after the government cut free medical care and began emphasizing user fees as part of economic changes.

A government advisory body reported in August that "Most of the medical needs of society cannot be met because of economic reasons. Poor people cannot even enjoy the most basic health care." According to the World Health Organization, a UN affiliate, China's health system was in 2005 one of the most unfair in the world.

Hong Kong. Tung Chee-hwa, a shipping magnate whom China named chief executive of Hong Kong when China took control of the former British colony in 1997, resigned on March 10,

City. Disaster planning became a more immediate concern among city officials across the United States in 2005. The devastating aftermath of Hurricane Katrina and other storms that battered the Gulf Coast and Florida prompted many city officials to reexamine local conditions that could increase their vulnerability to natural disasters and to review emergency plans. City leaders also continued to press federal and state officials for a larger role in national disaster planning and greater local control over federal funds allocated for emergency management.

Preparedness recommendations. In October, the Conference of Mayors renewed its calls for federal officials to follow "a more focused process to work directly with mayors and first responders to review and make changes to the national disaster preparedness and recovery process." The Washington, D.C.-based Conference of Mayors is a *nonpartisan* (politically unaffiliated) 1,100-member organization made up of mayors of cities with a population of at least 30,000.

The mayors' conference released its 2005 National Action Plan on Safety and Security in America's Cities after a private meeting between a special working group of the organization and Michael Chertoff, director of the U.S. Department of Homeland Security (DHS). Chertoff reportedly agreed to work with the mayors but did not promise to meet their recommendations.

The National Action Plan declared that following Hurricane Katrina "aid did not come on time" and offered a number of recommendations for improving cities' ability to respond quickly to emergencies. For example, the plan urged the U.S. Congress to provide direct aid to first responders—local police, fire, and emergency medical personnel. Currently, aid passes to cities through state agencies. The plan also proposed allowing cities to by-pass state emergency officials and request immediate assistance directly from U.S. military forces after a major natural disaster or terrorist attack.

The mayors' plan also called for increased spending on *interoperability*—the ability of emergency responders from different agencies to communicate with one another. A 2004 survey by the Conference of Mayors found that 77 percent of responding cities had interoperable communications between police and fire departments. However, 60 percent of responding cities were not interoperable with their state's emergency operations center. About 88 percent of the cities surveyed reported that they were not interoperable with the Federal Emergency Management Agency and other agencies of the DHS. Seventy-five percent of the cities blamed limited funding for their inability to establish interoperable communications systems.

Since 2001, the DHS has provided $1.5 billion to cities and states for radios and other communications equipment. However, a 2001 report by the U.S. Office of Management and Budget revealed that interoperable communications systems nationwide would cost at least $15 billion.

More disaster recommendations. Greater involvement by local officials in "key decisions affecting homeland security, disaster preparedness and response" also topped a list of eight recommendations for improving government's ability to deal with emergencies that was released in October 2005 by the National League of Cities (NLC). The NLC, based in Washington, D.C., seeks to improve the quality of life in U.S. cities. The recommendations were presented to Congress by Audwin M. Samuel, vice chair of the NLC's Public Safety and Crime Prevention Policy Committee and mayor pro tempore of Beaumont, Texas.

In testimony before the House Committee on Homeland Security, Samuel complained that the need to obtain approval from emergency management officials in Washington, D.C., prevented Beaumont officials from distributing stockpiled generators, ice, and other needed supplies for several days after Hurricane Rita struck the area in September. Samuel also asked Congress to give cities the flexibility to tailor emergency preparedness spending to meet local conditions.

The NLC recommendations also included the establishment of a national emergency warning system and increased funding for annual city hazard and risk assessments as well as public and private projects to reduce those risks. In addition, the NLC renewed calls for Congress to set aside part of the radio spectrum for emergency communications. In November, the House of Representatives and Senate passed bills setting deadlines for allocating part of the radio spectrum to public safety agencies.

Eminent domain. Cities in 2005 reacted strongly to efforts by Congress and state legislatures to restrict cities' ability to use their power of eminent domain in the wake of a controversial decision issued by the U.S. Supreme Court in June. Eminent domain is the power of a government to take private property for public use in return for a fair price. Governments often use eminent domain to acquire private property for roads, bridges, and other public works.

In a 5-4 decision, the court ruled that cities may use eminent domain to promote economic redevelopment that meets a public need. The case involved a decision by officials in New London, Connecticut, to condemn private property as part of a plan to build office, hotel, and retail space in a depressed and polluted area of the city. Some homeowners, however, refused to sell

50 LARGEST CITIES IN THE UNITED STATES

Rank	City	Population*
1.	New York, N.Y.	8,098,536
2.	Los Angeles, Calif.	3,871,848
3.	Chicago, Ill.	2,848,965
4.	Houston, Tex.	2,015,587
5.	Philadelphia, Pa.	1,463,380
6.	Phoenix, Ariz.	1,448,508
7.	San Diego, Calif.	1,264,814
8.	San Antonio, Tex.	1,258,746
9.	Dallas, Tex.	1,215,725
10.	San Jose, Calif.	911,702
11.	Detroit, Mich.	888,089
12.	Jacksonville, Fla.	786,862
13.	Indianapolis, Ind.	784,022
14.	San Francisco, Calif.	736,630
15.	Columbus, Ohio	731,453
16.	Austin, Tex.	690,294
17.	Memphis, Tenn.	670,740
18.	Baltimore, Md.	629,275
19.	Fort Worth, Tex.	621,755
20.	Charlotte, N.C.	603,557
21.	El Paso, Tex.	602,283
22.	Milwaukee, Wis.	580,065
23.	Seattle, Wash.	572,555
24.	Boston, Mass.	560,541
25.	Louisville, Kent.	557,967
26.	Denver, Colo.	557,632
27.	Las Vegas, Nev.	553,391
28.	Washington, D.C.	549,456
29.	Nashville, Tenn.	548,349
30.	Oklahoma City, Okla.	531,245
31.	Portland, Ore.	528,091
32.	Tucson, Ariz.	517,171
33.	Albuquerque, N. Mex.	495,414
34.	Long Beach, Calif.	477,878
35.	Sacramento, Calif.	464,148
36.	Fresno, Calif.	463,600
37.	New Orleans, La.	456,673
38.	Cleveland, Ohio	453,915
39.	Kansas City, Mo.	445,163
40.	Virginia Beach, Va.	444,205
41.	Mesa, Ariz.	443,737
42.	Atlanta, Ga.	418,516
43.	Omaha, Nebr.	414,788
44.	Oakland, Calif.	396,427
45.	Miami, Fla.	383,243
46.	Tulsa, Okla.	379,758
47.	Honolulu, Hawaii	378,108
48.	Minneapolis, Minn.	371,918
49.	Colorado Springs, Colo.	370,060
50.	Arlington, Tex.	364,508

*2005 World Book estimates based on data from the U.S. Census Bureau.

50 LARGEST METROPOLITAN AREAS IN THE UNITED STATES

Rank	Metropolitan area*	Population†
1.	New York–Northern New Jersey–Long Island, NY-NJ	18,833,671
2.	Los Angeles, Long Beach–Santa Ana, CA	13,126,015
3.	Chicago–Naperville–Joliet, IL–IN–WI	9,480,622
4.	Dallas–Fort Worth–Arlington, TX	5,875,405
5.	Philadelphia–Camden–Wilmington, PA-NJ-DE-MD	5,827,032
6.	Miami–Fort Lauderdale–Miami Beach, FL	5,473,006
7.	Houston–Baytown–Sugar Land, TX	5,317,228
8.	Washington–Arlington–Alexandria, DC-MD-VA-WV	5,280,976
9.	Atlanta–Sandy Springs–Marietta, GA	4,848,505
10.	Detroit–Warren–Livonia, MI	4,501,097
11.	Boston–Cambridge–Quincy, MA-NH	4,465,816
12.	San Francisco–Oakland–Fremont, CA	4,171,363
13.	Riverside–San Bernardino–Ontario, CA	3,916,564
14.	Phoenix–Mesa–Scottsdale, AZ	3,827,795
15.	Seattle–Tacoma–Bellevue, WA	3,203,659
16.	Minneapolis–St. Paul–Bloomington, MN-WI	3,154,874
17.	San Diego–Carlsbad–San Marcos, CA	3,004,523
18.	St. Louis, MO–IL	2,759,099
19.	Baltimore–Towson, MD	2,656,575
20.	Tampa–St. Petersburg–Clearwater, FL	2,622,410
21.	Pittsburgh, PA	2,397,814
22.	Denver–Aurora, CO	2,377,162
23.	Cleveland–Elyria–Mentor, OH	2,133,854
24.	Portland–Vancouver–Beaverton, OR-WA	2,114,347
25.	Sacramento–Arden-Arcade–Roseville, CA	2,097,927
26.	Cincinnati–Middletown, OH-KY-IN	2,069,712
27.	Kansas City, MO-KS	1,948,114
28.	Orlando, FL	1,910,988
29.	San Antonio, TX	1,892,949
30.	San Jose–Sunnyvale–Santa Clara, CA	1,731,000
31.	Las Vegas–Paradise, NV	1,717,914
32.	Columbus, OH	1,713,118
33.	Virginia Beach–Norfolk–Newport News, VA-NC	1,676,559
34.	Providence–New Bedford–Fall River, RI-MA	1,648,153
35.	Indianapolis, IN	1,640,587
36.	Milwaukee–Waukesha–West Allis, WI	1,522,538
37.	Charlotte–Gastonia–Concord, NC-SC	1,508,197
38.	Austin-Round Rock, TX	1,460,942
39.	Nashville–Davidson–Murfreesboro, TN	1,409,199
40.	New Orleans–Metairie–Kenner, LA	1,318,821
41.	Memphis, TN-MS-AR	1,260,707
42.	Jacksonville, FL	1,258,222
43.	Louisville, KY–IN	1,207,320
44.	Hartford–West Hartford–East Hartford, CT	1,196,474
45.	Richmond, VA	1,164,744
46.	Oklahoma City, OK	1,156,837
47.	Buffalo–Niagara Falls, NY	1,153,164
48.	Birmingham–Hoover, Al	1,085,836
49.	Rochester, NY	1,043,067
50.	Salt Lake City, UT	1,028,065

*The U.S. Census Bureau defines a metropolitan area as a large population nucleus with adjacent communities having a high degree of economic and social integration.

†2005 World Book estimates based on data from the U.S. Census Bureau.

and sued the city, arguing that public use did not include transferring property from one private owner to another. A majority of justices, however, said that creating jobs and increasing tax revenue qualifies as a public use.

The public backlash from the decision prompted about 30 state legislatures to review or announce plans to review laws on eminent domain. In November, the House of Representatives passed a bill that would transfer decisions about land use from cities and states to the federal government and freeze federal funding to local and state governments that use eminent domain for economic redevelopment.

Organizations representing cities and state governments strongly opposed legislative attempts to limit cities' ability to condemn private property. In a statement released after the Supreme Court ruling, the Conference of Mayors asserted that "without the use of eminent domain, cities cannot make the changes necessary to sustain healthy economic and demographic growth."

Urban population growth. Metropolitan (metro) areas in the United States continued to gain residents during the early 2000's, though at a slower pace than during the 1990's, according to a report released by the Census Bureau in September 2005. The report defined a metro area as composed of at least one whole county or equivalent entity with a population of at least 50,000.

All eight metro areas in the United States with a population of at least 5 million gained residents. Their total population grew by 3.8 percent from 2000 to 2003, compared with 13 percent from 1990 to 2000. The 12 U.S. metro areas with a population of from 2.5 million to 4.99 million grew the fastest during the early 2000's, by a total of 4.4 percent. The 23 metro areas with a population of from 50,000 to 99,999 continued to experience the slowest growth rate, 1.4 percent. During the 1990's, the growth rates of the latter two categories were 16.2 percent and 9 percent, respectively.

By 2003, 54 percent of the U.S. population lived in the 50 metro areas with a population of at least 1 million. About 23 percent lived in one of eight areas with a population of at least 5 million. Metro areas in the West grew the fastest (15.5 percent), followed by those in the South (12.9 percent). Metro areas in the Northeast and the Midwest grew by less than 5 percent. Near Denver, the Greeley, Colorado, metro area, whose population grew by 16.8 percent, was the fastest-growing metro area in the United States during the early 2000's.   ■ Barbara A. Mayes

See also **Chicago; Disasters: A Special Report; Houston; Los Angeles; New York City.**

50 LARGEST URBAN CENTERS IN THE WORLD

Rank	Urban center*	Population
1.	Tokyo, Japan	35,320,000
2.	Mexico City, Mexico	18,988,000
3.	New York City, U.S.	18,479,000
4.	Sao Paulo, Brazil	18,330,000
5.	Mumbai, India	18,289,000
6.	Delhi, India	15,283,000
7.	Kolkata, India	14,276,000
8.	Buenos Aires, Argentina	13,356,000
9.	Jakarta, Indonesia	13,149,000
10.	Shanghai, China	12,695,000
11.	Dhaka, Bangladesh	12,479,000
12.	Los Angeles, U.S.	12,173,000
13.	Karachi, Pakistan	11,800,000
14.	Rio de Janeiro, Brazil	11,467,000
15.	Osaka, Japan	11,277,000
16.	Cairo, Egypt	11,147,000
17.	Lagos, Nigeria	11,059,000
18.	Beijing, China	10,839,000
19.	Moscow, Russia	10,671,000
20.	Manila, Philippines	10,666,000
21.	Paris, France	9,839,000
22.	Istanbul, Turkey	9,749,000
23.	Seoul, Republic of Korea	9,575,000
24.	Tianjin, China	9,341,000
25.	Chicago, U.S.	8,715,000
26.	Lima, Peru	8,190,000
27.	London, U.K.	7,628,000
28.	Bogota, Colombia	7,586,000
29.	Tehran, Iran	7,335,000
30.	Hong Kong, China	7,190,000
31.	Chennai, India	6,912,000
32.	Taipei, Taiwan	6,603,000
33.	Bangkok, Thailand	6,589,000
34.	Essen, Germany	6,574,000
35.	Bangalore, India	6,517,000
36.	Lahore, Pakistan	6,351,000
37.	Hyderabad, India	6,131,000
38.	Wuhan, China	5,992,000
39.	Baghdad, Iraq	5,912,000
40.	Kinshasa, Congo	5,690,000
41.	Santiago, Chile	5,617,000
42.	Riyadh, Saudi Arabia	5,498,000
43.	Miami, U.S.	5,381,000
44.	St. Petersburg, Russia	5,319,000
45.	Philadelphia, U.S.	5,317,000
46.	Belo Horizonte, Brazil	5,297,000
47.	Ahmadabad, India	5,157,000
48.	Madrid, Spain	5,138,000
49.	Toronto, Canada	5,062,000
50.	Ho Chi Minh City, Vietnam	5,025,000

Source: 2005 estimates based on data from the United Nations and other official government sources.

*The United Nations defines an urban center as a city surrounded by a continuous built-up area having a high population density.

Classical music. Conductor Marin Alsop became the first female music director of a major United States orchestra in July 2005, when she was appointed to lead the Baltimore Symphony Orchestra. Alsop's appointment, which was to take effect in 2007, generated controversy among many of the orchestra's musicians, who complained that they were not consulted before Alsop was hired. In September 2005, Alsop was awarded a prestigious MacArthur Fellowship. The fellowship, often called a "genius grant," is issued by the John D. and Catherine T. MacArthur Foundation, a private grantmaking program in Chicago. The fellowships are awarded annually to talented individuals who have shown "exceptional merit and promise of continued and enhanced creative work," according to the foundation. Alsop was among 25 fellows to receive a stipend of $500,000.

Mutiny at La Scala. A dramatic power struggle that captured the attention of the classical music world came to a climax in April 2005 when Riccardo Muti, among the most eminent opera and symphony conductors in the world, resigned as music director of La Scala in Milan, Italy. The fiery maestro, who had served as music director of the legendary opera house since 1986, stepped down in 2005 after approximately 700 La Scala employees called for his resignation. Backstage tensions between Muti and the orchestra musicians, which had been simmering for years, erupted in February 2005 when La Scala's board of directors dismissed Carlo Fontana, the theater's general manager, who had a difficult relationship with Muti. The board replaced him with Mauro Meli, the former director of La Scala's theater division and an ally of Muti. For months following Fontana's dismissal, musicians and other workers staged periodic strikes that forced the cancellation of several performances. Muti cited "the vulgar hostility of colleagues" as his reason for resigning.

Beethoven and Bach discoveries. In July, a librarian discovered the manuscript of a rare piano transcription by German composer Ludwig van Beethoven at an evangelical seminary near Philadelphia. The 80-page manuscript, which was one of Beethoven's final compositions and written in his own hand, is a solo piano version of his "Grosse Fuge" ("Great Fugue"), originally written for string quartet. Never before seen by scholars, it was written a few months before the composer's death in 1827.

In June 2005, a previously unknown work by the German Baroque master Johann Sebastian Bach, hidden in an old shoebox for three centuries, was discovered by a musicologist in Weimar, Germany. The aria, for soprano, harpsichord, and strings, lasts four to five minutes and is thought to be part of a longer, lost Bach cantata. Christoph Wolff, a professor at Harvard University in Cambridge, Massachusetts, and a leading expert on Bach's life, helped authenticate the score.

New operas. The Metropolitan Opera in New York City performed the world premier of *An American Tragedy* in December 2005. The opera, by American composer Tobias Picker and set to a libretto by Gene Scheer, is based on Theodore Dreiser's novel of the same name that centers on a love triangle that ends in murder. James Conlon conducted an all-star cast headed by the singers Nathan Gunn, Patricia Racette, and Susan Graham.

Doctor Atomic, with music by John Adams and libretto by Peter Sellars (who also directed), received its world premiere by the San Francisco Opera in October. The opera, which represented the fourth stage collaboration between Adams and Sellars, is a poetic meditation on the creation of the atomic bomb. The text was drawn from a variety of sources, including memoirs, letters, declassified U.S. government documents and poetry by Charles Baudelaire and John Donne.

In May, the Michigan Opera Theatre in Detroit presented the premierproduction of *Margaret Garner,* by the U.S. composer Richard Danielpour, with a libretto by the novelist Toni Morrison. The opera, set in Kentucky in the 1850's, was inspired by the true story of an escaped slave who sacrifices her children rather than see them returned to slavery. The opera was co-commissioned by the Cincinnati Opera and the Opera Company of Philadelphia.

In March 2005, the Houston Grand Opera premiered U.S. composer Mark Adamo's second opera, *Lysistrata, or The Nude Goddess.* The opera, based on a legendary comedy by the classic Greek dramatist Aristophanes, is about the wives of warriors who, disgusted by a pointless war, withhold sexual favors from their husbands until the men declare a truce.

New orchestral works. Two major American orchestras performed world premieres of works by Elliot Carter on the same evening in October. James Levine directed the Boston Symphony Orchestra in the first performance of Carter's *Three Illusions for Orchestra,* and the Chicago Symphony Orchestra introduced Carter's *Soundings*, with Daniel Barenboim as both conductor and piano soloist. At 96 years of age, Carter was still considered one of the leading composers in the United States in 2005.

In May, Robert Spano directed the Atlanta Symphony Orchestra in the world premiere of David Del Tredici's *Paul Revere's Ride,* for soprano, chorus, and orchestra. In March, pianist Anthony de Mare premiered Del Tredici's *Gotham Glory* in New York's Zankel Hall. The DaPonte String Quartet performed the world premiere of Del Tredici's *String Quartet No. 1* in February at the University of North Texas in Denton.

Classical Album, *Adams: On the Transmigration of Souls;* Lorin Maazel, conductor; Brooklyn Youth Chorus and New York Choral Artists, John Adams, producer; New York Philharmonic, Lawrence Rock, producer.

Orchestral Performance, *Adams: On the Transmigration of Souls;* Brooklyn Youth Chorus, New York Choral Artists, New York Philharmonic, Lorin Maazel, conductor.

Opera Recording, *Mozart: Le Nozze di Figaro;* René Jacobs, conductor; Patrizia Ciofi, Véronique Gens, Simon Keenlyside, Angelika Kirchschlager, Lorenzo Regazzo, soloists; Martin Sauer, producer.

Choral Performance, *Berlioz: Requiem;* Atlanta Symphony Orchestra, Robert Spano, conductor; Frank Lopardo, tenor; Norman Mackenzie, choir director.

Instrumental Soloist with Orchestra, *Previn: Violin Concerto "Anne-Sophie" and Bernstein: Serenade;* Boston Symphony Orchesta and London Symphony Orchestra, André Previn, conductor; Anne-Sophie Mutter, violin.

Instrumental Soloist without Orchestra, *Aire Latino;* David Russell, guitar.

Chamber Music Performance, *Prokofiev (Arr. Pletnev): Cinderella—Suite for Two Pianos and Ravel: Ma Mère L'Oye;* Martha Argerich, piano; Mikhail Pletnev, piano.

Small Ensemble Performance, *Chávez: Complete Chamber Music, Vol. 2;* Southwest Chamber Music, Jeff von der Schmidt, conductor.

Classical Vocal Performance, *Ives: Songs;* Susan Graham, mezzo soprano; Pierre-Laurent Aimard, piano.

Classical Contemporary Composition, *Adams: On the Transmigration of Souls;* John Adams, composer; Lorin Maazel, conductor; Brooklyn Youth Chorus and New York Choral Artists; New York Philharmonic.

Classical Crossover Album, *LAGQ's Guitar Heroes;* Los Angeles Guitar Quartet.

Ford Made in America, a 13-minute piece by U.S. composer Joan Tower, was among the more unusual orchestral premieres of 2005. Sixty-five community orchestras from across the United States received a grant from the Ford Motor Company Foundation of Detroit to commission a new work from Tower. The work, which premiered in October in Glens Falls, New York, was scheduled to be performed by small orchestras in all 50 of the United States in 2005 and 2006. The project was the largest consortium commission ever planned by U.S. orchestras.

Pulitzer Prize. In April 2005, U.S. composer Steven Stucky won the Pulitzer Prize for Music for his *Second Concerto for Orchestra.*

Notable deaths. Carlo Maria Giulini, the charismatic Italian symphonic and operatic conductor, died in June at age 91. David Diamond, one of the most gifted and prolific U.S. composers, died at age 89 in June. George Rochberg, the U.S. composer who was credited with some of the most emotionally gripping works of the late 1900's, died in May at age 86. Russian pianist Lazar Berman died in February at age 74. ■ John von Rhein

See also **Deaths; People in the news** (Marin Alsop); **Popular music.**

Clothing. See Fashion.

Coal. See Energy supply.

A new staging of Franz Schreker's *Die Gezeichneten (The Branded)* is performed in July at the Salzburg Festival in Salzburg, Austria. The story of a utopia that mutates into a nightmare capped the festival's series of operas by composers repressed during Germany's Nazi era.

Colombia. The Constitutional Court of Colombia in November 2005 approved a constitutional amendment that permits presidents consecutive terms of office. The decision enables incumbent President Alvaro Uribe Velez to run for reelection in 2006. In late 2005, Uribe had an approval rating of nearly 80 percent and seemed poised to win reelection. Political analysts noted that Colombians credited Uribe with restoring a measure of tranquility to the country with massive military aid from the United States.

In rural areas of Colombia, however, intermittent fighting between government forces and Marxist rebels belonging to the Revolutionary Armed Forces of Colombia (FARC) continued in 2005. In June, 20 Colombian soldiers were killed in a FARC attack on a remote army outpost near the border with Ecuador. With casualties mounting, Defense Minister Jorge Alberto Uribe resigned in July after only 20 months on the job, a period during which 700 government troops were killed in battles with FARC forces at scattered locations.

Controversial amnesty law. Colombia's Congress passed the Justice and Peace Law in June 2005, which prescribed conditions under which armed insurgents—either leftist guerrillas or rightist paramilitary units, which began forming in the 1980's to fight the guerrillas—could disarm and receive amnesty or reduced sentences for their offenses. However, the bill was crafted primarily for the benefit of paramilitary fighters collectively known as the United Self-Defense Forces of Colombia (AUC), who were willing to accept an amnesty from the government.

The law drew sharp criticism from human rights groups. They alleged that paramilitary fighters who had committed atrocities would not be held accountable for their deeds. Human Rights Watch, a New York City-based human rights advocacy group, issued a report in July alleging that Colombia's Peace and Justice law trampled on victims' rights and conferred legitimacy on perpetrators of human rights abuses. Colombian officials defended the law, claiming that it was the best way to disarm the right-wing paramilitaries and protect civilian populations.

The Colombian government estimated that the amnesty program, which provided payments to demobilized insurgents and vocational programs to retrain them for peaceful occupations, would cost $160 million, and made known its expectation that the U.S. government would defray this cost with aid. However, members of the U.S. Senate appropriations committee balked when the issue first came under consideration in mid-2005, with some legislators noting that the United States had officially labeled AUC a terrorist group. American officials also expressed concern that the amnesty law would prevent extradition of some Colombians to the United States to face drug trafficking charges. Under pressure from the administration of President George W. Bush, Congress did provide $20 million for the amnesty program in an appropriations bill passed in November.

Atrocity revealed. In August, forensic experts unearthed the remains of 72 people who had been brutally murdered—some hacked to death—at El Palmar, a farm in northern Colombia. All evidence pointed to AUC fighters as the perpetrators, and the farm was known to have served as an AUC base. Officials with the Association of Families of the Detained-Disappeared, based in Colombia's capital, Bogota, estimated that more than 3,000 Colombians had vanished since 2000. Many of them were feared dead.

Colombian heads regional bank. In late July 2005, the governors of the Inter-American Development Bank (IDB), a financial institution that provides loans and other forms of assistance to member nations in the Caribbean and Latin America, elected Luis Alberto Moreno, Colombia's ambassador to the United States, to a five-year term as IDB president. In a rare show of defiance, eight member nations voted against the U.S.-backed Moreno.   ■ Nathan A. Haverstock

See also **Latin America.**

Commonwealth of Independent States. See Asia; Azerbaijan; Belarus; Georgia; Kazakhstan; Russia: A Special Report; Ukraine.

Comoros. See Africa.

Computer. Two major incidents of identity theft in 2005 revealed the vulnerability of some of the financial industry's largest computer databases to electronic crime. Identity theft is the stealing of personal or financial information for fraudulent purposes.

In February, ChoicePoint, Incorporated, of Alpharetta, Georgia—a company that collects personal and financial data—revealed that more than 110,000 of their records had been released to individuals posing as financial professionals. Authorities said that about 700 victims had their mailing addresses changed by the identity thieves, perhaps in an effort to redirect mailed credit card offers.

MasterCard International, based in Purchase, New York, announced in June an electronic intrusion into the computer files of CardSystems, Incorporated, of Atlanta, Georgia, a processor of credit card transactions. The incident put more than 40 million records at risk. According to industry officials, the intrusion was particularly worrisome because CardSystems annually processes more than 120,000 transactions in the United States.

Mac Mini. Apple Computer, Inc., debuted a radically redesigned Macintosh computer in January. The Cupertino, California-based company introduced the Mac Mini—a 6.5-inch (16.5-cen-

Television shows, music videos, and family photographs flash across the screens of the latest iPods unveiled by Apple Computer, Inc., in October 2005. The Cupertino, California-based company integrated video downloads into its iTunes software and online store for easy access to visual content.

timeter) wide and 2-inch (5-centimeter) thick Mac that included a combination DVD/CD-ROM drive, hard disk, and devices that allowed the computer to connect to television and sound systems.

With its small size and a low-end price of $499, Apple hoped the Mac Mini would attract a mass-market audience with the same success as its iPod music player. The computer proved so popular—some consumers reported waiting weeks for their orders—that Apple was forced in April to substantially increase production of the new product.

Google and Sun. Google expanded its corporate horizons in October, when the Mountain View, California-based company announced a partnership with Sun Microsystems, Inc., also of Mountain View. Sun is a software developer and major manufacturer of networked computers for business and science.

As part of the new relationship, Google tools will be included in Sun products, including Sun's OpenOffice collection of word processing, financial, and other software. Some industry analysts

The iPod Nano, a digital music player smaller than a credit card and thinner than a No. 2 pencil, was introduced by Apple in September 2005. The high-end Nano model is capable of storing more than 1,000 songs and displaying 25,000 digital photos on its tiny color screen.

viewed the move as an attempt by both companies to compete with Microsoft Corporation of Redmond, Washington, and its Microsoft Office, the leading suite of office tools. Sun's OpenOffice is based on the Linux operating system, which is freely distributed—unlike Windows, which must be licensed from Microsoft. ■ Keith Ferrell

See also **Crime: A Special Report; Electronics; Internet; Telecommunications.**

Congo (Brazzaville). See Africa.

Congo (Kinshasa). The Democratic Republic of Congo continued to struggle in 2005 to recover from the effects of a civil war (1998-2002), which at various times had involved as many as six neighboring countries. Regional experts estimated that more than 3 million people died during the conflict, mainly from war-related disease and famine. In 2005, ongoing clashes in the Ituri region in the northeastern part of the country threatened a fragile peace agreement concluded in 2003. According to that agreement, the former rebels shared power in a transitional government headed by President Joseph Kabila.

UN role. On Feb. 25, 2005, nine United Nations (UN) peacekeepers, all Bangladeshis, were killed when their patrol was ambushed 20 miles (32 kilometers) east of Bunia, the chief city in Ituri, by a Congolese militia associated with the Lendu ethnic group. Various tribal-based rival guerrilla factions controlled much of Ituri's territory in 2005. The ambush represented the deadliest attack against the 16,700-strong UN mission in Congo (Kinshasa) since the first UN peacekeepers arrived in 1999.

On March 1, 2005, UN commanders launched a counterattack on the Ituri rebels, deploying helicopters and killing about 60 enemy combatants. The battle was the biggest undertaken by a UN force since 1994, when

U.S. troops operating under a UN mandate in Somalia had killed up to 1,000 Somali fighters during the so-called "Black Hawk Down Battle."

Controversy dogged the UN's Congo mission in 2005 as allegations surfaced that some of the UN peacekeepers had sexually exploited and abused local women and girls. In response, UN Secretary-General Kofi Annan announced in February a "nonfraternization" policy that prohibited UN peacekeepers in Congo (Kinshasa) from having sex with the local people.

Elections postponed. On May 13, the Congo (Kinshasa) National Assembly approved a draft constitution, which prescribed a checks-and-balances system of government, guaranteed minority rights, and limited presidential tenure to two five-year terms. Progress towards ratifying the constitution was set back in June when Kabila's power-sharing administration postponed elections due to have been held on June 30 for at least six months. (The 2003 peace accord specifies that a newly elected government must be in place by June 30, 2006.) Announcement of the election postponement was greeted by protests as thousands of opposition demonstrators marched in Kinshasa, the capital. Riot police deployed by the Kabila government killed at least 10 protesters. ■ Simon Baynham
See also **Africa**.

Congress of the United States.

Lawmakers in 2005 tackled a range of issues, from reform of class-action lawsuits to dealing with the aftermath of natural disasters. In the face of multiple hurricanes and the resulting disasters, Congress approved a number of emergency measures. The indictment of a powerful member of the House of Representatives forced a change in leadership in 2005.

Hurricane disaster relief. Days after Hurricane Katrina struck the Gulf Coast on August 29, Congress passed legislation appropriating funds to help the victims in Alabama, Mississippi, and Louisiana recover from one of the worst disasters in U.S. history. The bill provided $10 billion to the Department of Homeland Security and $500 million to the Department of Defense for relief efforts. The legislation was introduced, passed by both houses of Congress, and signed by President George W. Bush in one day, September 2.

On September 8, Congress approved a second appropriations bill for Katrina-related expenses. The legislation provided the Department of Defense with an additional $1.4 billion for hurricane relief efforts. The bill earmarked $400 million for the Army Corps of Engineers to repair levees and other flood control infrastructure and to drain floodwater from the city of New Orleans. The supplemental emergency legislation also provided Homeland Security with another $50 billion for disaster relief. In addition, the legislation authorized the government to forego certain federal procurement rules. It allowed executive agencies to purchase goods and services for hurricane rescue and relief operations without seeking competitive bids, provided an agency employee determined that a purchase price was reasonable.

In an attempt to ensure that the legal system in the Hurricane Katrina disaster area continued to function, Congress approved legislation, which was signed into law on September 9, that enabled federal district courts, circuit courts of appeal, bankruptcy courts, and magistrate judges to hold special sessions outside normal jurisdictions. However, the legislation prohibited criminal trials from being conducted in special sessions outside the state in which the alleged crime had been committed unless the defendant agreed to an out-of-state trial. The legislation also required that criminal jury pools be made up of people from the court's normal district unless the defendant agreed to be tried by jurors from the district in which the special session was held.

On September 21, President George W. Bush signed into law a measure accelerating grants to states under the Temporary Assistance for Needy Families (TANF) program. The measure directed the Department of Health and Human Services to pay each state its family assistance grant for the first quarter of 2006 as soon as possible after passage of the law. The accelerated payments were designed to provide assistance to low-income families hurt by Katrina.

Congress approved legislation on Sept. 21, 2005, amending tax law to allow individuals who have incurred losses in a federally declared natural disaster to withdraw tax-free up to $100,000 from retirement accounts. The measure was designed to help hurricane victims cover living and rebuilding expenses. The legislation temporarily removed limitations on the tax deductions for cash contributions to charitable organizations made from August 28 to Dec. 31, 2005. In addition, the legislation provided a new personal tax exemption for individuals who provided free housing to people displaced by Hurricane Katrina. Under the measure, signed into law on September 23, any person who provided such housing for 60 consecutive days was eligible for a personal tax exemption of $500 for each sheltered person, up to a maximum exemption of $2,000.

Congress also approved legislation to provide national emergency grant funds to states to be used to provide disaster relief employment in federally declared disaster areas. The funds could be used to provide disaster relief employment to people who have relocated from the disaster area.

Firearms liability. Wading into the politically contentious realm of gun legislation, Congress approved a measure in 2005 that insulates gun makers and gun sellers from civil suits arising from the misuse of their products. Titled the Protection of Lawful Commerce in Arms Act, the law prohibits state and federal courts from accepting civil liability suits against manufacturers or sellers of guns, gun components, or ammunition that arise from the criminal use of firearms. The law also prohibits civil suits against trade groups representing gun manufacturers and sellers. The legislation, which was signed into law October 26, required that any such actions pending in state or federal court be dismissed. The new law provides for some exceptions. A harmed party may bring a civil suit against a person who transferred a gun with the knowledge that it would be used to commit a violent crime or a crime involving drug trafficking. The measure still allows suits against gun manufacturers in cases alleging injuries resulting from defects in the design or manufacture of a weapon. The Senate passed the legislation in a 65-31 vote on July 29; the House passed the bill in a 283-144 vote on October 20.

Budget measure. On December 21, Vice President Dick Cheney broke a 50-to-50 tie to pass a $39.7-billion, five-year budget-cutting measure, already passed by the House, which Republicans hailed as evidence of their determination to control federal spending. The legislation, among other provisions, allowed states to impose new fees on Medicaid recipients; cut federal child-support enforcement funds; imposed new work requirements on state welfare programs; fixed interest rates on student loans at 6.8 percent; and cut certain agricultural crop and soil conservation subsidies by $2.7 billion.

Torture. On December 22, Congress approved a military spending bill that included $50 billion for the wars in Iraq and Afghanistan and a provision, sponsored by Senator John McCain (R., Arizona) that bans cruel, inhumane, and degrading treatment of prisoners in U.S. custody.

USA Patriot Act. Congress on December 22 agreed to extend for five weeks 16 major provisions of the USA Patriot Act that were set to expire on December 31. The act, passed in the wake of the terrorist attacks on the United States on Sept. 11, 2001, greatly expanded government power to conduct surveillance and covert investigations. The Act also touched off intense debate among civil and human rights advocates over how to balance national security and civil liberties. On December 16, Majority Leader Bill Frist (R., Tennessee) had failed to muster the 60 votes necessary to end debate on the Patriot Act, essentially shelving its permanent reauthorization, which the House had passed earlier.

Class action lawsuits. President Bush signed legislation into law on February 18 that was designed to curtail multimillion-dollar class action lawsuits against corporations by moving such suits from state to federal courts. Under the new law, class action suits involving $5 million or more in damages will be heard in state court only if the primary defendant and more than one-third of the plaintiffs are from the same state. Federal courts are expected to permit far fewer large class action suits than state courts. Many political leaders and business executives have characterized class action suits—suits in which a single person or a small group can represent the interests of thousands of individuals in court—as frivolous litigation that enable lawyers to reap huge profits at the expense of businesses.

Energy bill. Congress in late July approved a vast energy policy bill, which critics claimed did little to reduce pollution or the nation's dependence on foreign oil. Under the legislation, which was signed into law on August 8, oil, gas, coal, nuclear, and electric utility companies received some $13 billion in tax breaks and direct subsidies. Congress did, however, approve $1.3 billion in tax credits for individuals who purchase fuel-efficient cars and home appliances. The law provided incentives, through federal loan guarantees, for construction of new nuclear power plants, and it gave the Federal Energy Regulatory Commission power to determine placement of natural gas pipelines and related facilities—powers that previously had been left to the states. The measure repealed the Public Utility Holding Company Act. The repeal allows independent regional utilities to be purchased by unrelated companies, such as oil corporations or banks.

Pork-barrel spending. In August, the House and Senate passed a $286-billion highway transportation bill, which critics complained included more than 6,000 so-called "pork-barrel" projects—projects designed to be politically advantageous to individual legislators. One of these projects, $315 million in funding to build a bridge in Alaska, became known as the "bridge to nowhere" when the media revealed that it was to connect the mainland with an island that had only 50 residents. In the aftermath of the emergency disaster relief spending, some of the "pork-barrel" projects were cancelled, including the Alaska bridge, which Senator John Cornyn (R., Texas) described as "a symbol of federal spending that's out of control." However, under a compromise, Alaska still received the same funding, but its purpose was no longer specifically earmarked.

Scandals. In February, Republican leaders in the House stripped Joel Hefley (R., Colorado) of the chairmanship of the House ethics committee and removed him from the committee. He was replaced by Richard Hastings (R., Washington), whom political experts described as a "close ally" of Tom DeLay (R., Texas), the House majority leader, whom political experts described as one of the most powerful members of Congress. Under Hefley's leadership in 2004, the Committee on Standards of Official Conduct had admonished DeLay three times for various ethical lapses.

A Texas grand jury on Sept. 28, 2005, indicted DeLay on charges of criminal conspiracy in a campaign finance scheme. (A Texas judge threw out the charge on December 6.) Under congressional rules, the indictment forced DeLay to step down as majority leader. House Majority Whip Roy Blunt (R., Missouri) temporarily filled the post. On October 3, a Texas grand jury indicted DeLay on charges of money laundering in a transaction involving the movement of some $190,000 in corporate donations from a Texas political action committee to the Republican National Committee.

According to the indictment, the money was used to fund Texans for a Republican Majority, which DeLay organized to orchestrate a Republican takeover of the Texas House of Representatives. (Using corporate money to finance election campaigns is illegal in Texas.) The takeover, successfully accomplished in 2002, allowed Texas House Republicans to reapportion congressional districts in Texas. According to political experts, the redistricting cemented Republican control of the U.S. House of Representatives in 2004.

DeLay also was the center of an inquiry in 2005 into whether lobbyist Jack Abramoff paid DeLay's expenses for travel abroad, including a golf outing in Scotland. On November 18, Jack Abramoff's business partner, Michael Scanlon, a former aide to Tom DeLay, was charged with conspiring to defraud Indian tribe clients of millions of dollars. The indictment alleged that Scanlon recruited a member of Congress with campaign contributions, entertainment,

gifts, meals, and trips to affect the passage of legislation. The Senate Indian Affairs Committee also investigated Scanlon and Abramoff, whom six Indian tribes with casinos paid more than $80 million between 2001 and 2004.

Representative Randy "Duke" Cunningham (R., California) resigned from the House on Nov. 28, 2005, after publicly confessing that he had evaded paying incomes taxes and pocketed some $2.4 million in bribes. According to prosecutors, Cunningham "demanded, sought, and received" cash, cars, home furnishings, house payments, and vacations from various defense contractors.

■ Geoffrey A. Campbell

See also **Courts; Democratic Party; Republican Party; United States, Government of the.**

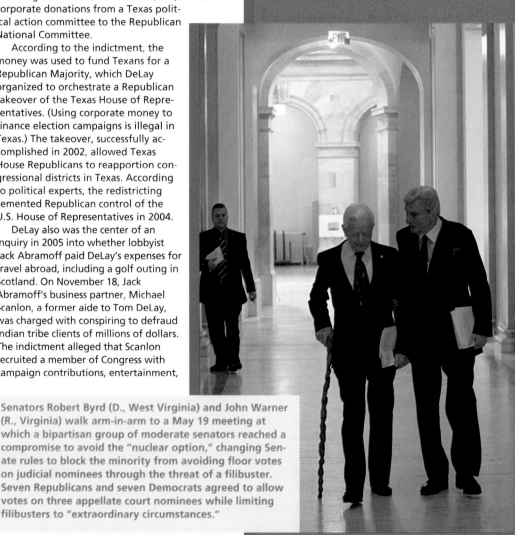

Senators Robert Byrd (D., West Virginia) and John Warner (R., Virginia) walk arm-in-arm to a May 19 meeting at which a bipartisan group of moderate senators reached a compromise to avoid the "nuclear option," changing Senate rules to block the minority from avoiding floor votes on judicial nominees through the threat of a filibuster. Seven Republicans and seven Democrats agreed to allow votes on three appellate court nominees while limiting filibusters to "extraordinary circumstances."

The House of Representatives of the second session of the 109th Congress consisted of 202 Democrats, 231 Republicans, and 1 Independent (not including representatives from American Samoa, the District of Columbia, Guam, Puerto Rico, and the Virgin Islands) when it convened on Jan. 6, 2006. This table shows congressional district, legislator, and party affiliation. Asterisk (*) denote those who served in the 108th Congress; dagger (†) denotes "at large"; double dagger (‡) denotes vacant seat to be filled in 2006.

Alabama
1. Jo Bonner, R.*
2. Terry Everett, R.*
3. Mike Rogers, R.*
4. Robert Aderholt, R.*
5. Bud Cramer, D.*
6. Spencer Bachus, R.*
7. Artur Davis, D.*

Alaska
†Donald E. Young, R.*

Arizona
1. Rick Renzi, R.*
2. Trent Franks, R.*
3. John Shadegg, R.*
4. Ed Pastor, D.*
5. J. D. Hayworth, R.*
6. Jeff Flake, R.*
7. Raul Grijalva, D.*
8. Jim Kolbe, R.*

Arkansas
1. Marion Berry, D.*
2. Vic Snyder, D.*
3. John Boozman, R.*
4. Mike Ross, D.*

California
1. Mike Thompson, D.*
2. Wally Herger, R.*
3. Dan Lungren, R.*
4. John Doolittle, R.*
5. Doris O. Matsui, D.
6. Lynn Woolsey, D.*
7. George E. Miller, D.*
8. Nancy Pelosi, D.*
9. Barbara Lee, D.*
10. Ellen Tauscher, D.*
11. Richard Pombo, R.*
12. Tom Lantos, D.*
13. Pete Stark, D.*
14. Anna Eshoo, D.*
15. Mike Honda, D.*
16. Zoe Lofgren, D.*
17. Sam Farr, D.*
18. Dennis Cardoza, D.*
19. George Radanovich, R.*
20. Jim Costa, D.
21. Devin Nunes, R.*
22. Bill Thomas, R.*
23. Lois Capps, D.*
24. Elton Gallegly, R.*
25. Howard McKeon, R.*
26. David Dreier, R.*
27. Brad Sherman, D.*
28. Howard Berman, D.*
29. Adam Schiff, D.*
30. Henry Waxman, D.*
31. Xavier Becerra, D.*
32. Hilda Solis, D.*
33. Diane Watson, D.*
34. Lucille Roybal-Allard, D.*
35. Maxine Waters, D.*
36. Jane Harman, D.*
37. Juanita Millender-McDonald, D.*
38. Grace Napolitano, D.*
39. Linda Sanchez, D.*
40. Ed Royce, R.*
41. Jerry Lewis, R.*
42. Gary Miller, R.*
43. Joe Baca, D.*
44. Ken Calvert, R.*
45. Mary Bono, R.*
46. Dana Rohrabacher, R.*
47. Loretta Sanchez, D.*
48. John Campbell, R.
49. Darrell Issa, R.*
50. ‡
51. Bob Filner, D.*
52. Duncan Hunter, R.*
53. Susan Davis, D.*

Colorado
1. Diana DeGette, D.*
2. Mark Udall, D.*
3. John Salazar, D.
4. Marilyn Musgrave, R.*
5. Joel Hefley, R.*
6. Tom Tancredo, R.*
7. Bob Beauprez, R.*

Connecticut
1. John Larson, D.*
2. Rob Simmons, R.*
3. Rosa DeLauro, D.*
4. Christopher Shays, R.*
5. Nancy L. Johnson, R.*

Delaware
†Michael Castle, R.*

Florida
1. Jeff Miller, R.*
2. Allen Boyd, D.*
3. Corrine Brown, D.*
4. Ander Crenshaw, R.*
5. Virginia Brown-Waite, R.*
6. Clifford B. Stearns, R.*
7. John Mica, R.*
8. Ric Keller, R.*
9. Michael Bilirakis, R.*
10. C. W. Bill Young, R.*
11. Jim Davis, D.*
12. Adam Putnam, R.*
13. Katherine Harris, R.*
14. Connie Mack, R.
15. Dave Weldon, R.*
16. Mark Foley, R.*
17. Kendrick Meek, D.*
18. Ileana Ros-Lehtinen, R.*
19. Robert Wexler, D.*
20. Debbie Wasserman Schultz, D.
21. Lincoln Diaz-Balart, R.*
22. E. Clay Shaw, Jr., R.*
23. Alcee Hastings, D.*
24. Tom Feeney, R.*
25. Mario Diaz-Balart, R.*

Georgia
1. Jack Kingston, R.*
2. Sanford Bishop, Jr., D.*
3. Jim Marshall, D.*
4. Cynthia McKinney, D.
5. John Lewis, D.*
6. Tom Price, R.
7. John Linder, R.*
8. Lynn Westmoreland, R.
9. Charles Norwood, R.*
10. Nathan Deal, R.*
11. Phil Gingrey, R.*
12. John Barrow, D.
13. David Scott, D.*

Hawaii
1. Neil Abercrombie, D.*
2. Ed Case, D.*

Idaho
1. C. L. Otter, R.*
2. Mike Simpson, R.*

Illinois
1. Bobby Rush, D.*
2. Jesse L. Jackson, Jr., D.*
3. Daniel Lipinski, D.
4. Luis Gutierrez, D.*
5. Rahm Emanuel, D.*
6. Henry J. Hyde, R.*
7. Danny Davis, D.*
8. Melissa Bean, D.
9. Janice Schakowsky, D.*
10. Mark Kirk, R.*
11. Gerald Weller, R.*
12. Jerry F. Costello, D.*
13. Judy Biggert, R.*
14. J. Dennis Hastert, R.*
15. Timothy Johnson, R.*
16. Donald Manzullo, R.*
17. Lane A. Evans, D.*
18. Ray LaHood, R.*
19. John Shimkus, R.*

Indiana
1. Peter J. Visclosky, D.*
2. Chris Chocola, R.*
3. Mark Souder, R.*
4. Steve Buyer, R.*
5. Dan Burton, R.*
6. Mike Pence, R.*
7. Julia Carson, D.*
8. John Hostettler, R.*
9. Mike Sodrel, R.

Iowa
1. Jim Nussle, R.*
2. Jim Leach, R.*
3. Leonard Boswell, D.*
4. Thomas Latham, R.*
5. Steve King, R.*

Kansas
1. Jerry Moran, R.*
2. Jim Ryun, R.*
3. Dennis Moore, D.*
4. Todd Tiahrt, R.*

Kentucky
1. Edward Whitfield, R.*
2. Ron Lewis, R.*
3. Anne Northup, R.*
4. Geoff Davis, R.
5. Harold (Hal) Rogers, R.*
6. Ben Chandler, D.*

Louisiana
1. Bobby Jindal, R.
2. William J. Jefferson, D.*
3. Charles Melancon, D.
4. Jim McCrery, R.*
5. Rodney Alexander, R.*
6. Richard Hugh Baker, R.*
7. Charles Boustany, Jr., R.

Maine
1. Thomas Allen, D.*
2. Michael Michaud, D.*

Maryland
1. Wayne T. Gilchrest, R.*
2. C. A. Ruppersberger, D.*
3. Benjamin L. Cardin, D.*
4. Albert Wynn, D.*
5. Steny H. Hoyer, D.*
6. Roscoe Bartlett, R.*
7. Elijah Cummings, D.*
8. Chris Van Hollen, D.*

Massachusetts
1. John W. Olver, D.*
2. Richard E. Neal, D.*
3. James McGovern, D.*
4. Barney Frank, D.*
5. Martin Meehan, D.*
6. John Tierney, D.*
7. Edward J. Markey, D.*
8. Michael Capuano, D.*
9. Stephen F. Lynch, D.*
10. William Delahunt, D.*

Michigan
1. Bart Stupak, D.*
2. Peter Hoekstra, R.*
3. Vernon Ehlers, R.*
4. Dave Camp, R.*
5. Dale Kildee, D.*
6. Frederick S. Upton, R.*
7. Joe Schwarz, R.
8. Mike Rogers, R.*
9. Joseph Knollenberg, R.*
10. Candice Miller, R.*
11. Thaddeus McCotter, R.*
12. Sander M. Levin, D.*
13. Carolyn Kilpatrick, D.*
14. John Conyers, Jr., D.*
15. John Dingell, D.*

Minnesota
1. Gil Gutknecht, R.*
2. John Kline, R.*

3. Jim Ramstad, R.*
4. Betty McCollum, D.*
5. Martin O. Sabo, D.*
6. Mark Kennedy, R.*
7. Collin C. Peterson, D.*
8. James L. Oberstar, D.*

Mississippi
1. Roger Wicker, R.*
2. Bennie Thompson, D.*
3. Charles Pickering, R.*
4. Gene Taylor, D.*

Missouri
1. William Clay, D.*
2. Todd Akin, R.*
3. Russ Carnahan, D.
4. Ike Skelton, D.*
5. Emanuel Cleaver II, D.
6. Samuel Graves, R.*
7. Roy Blunt, R.*
8. Jo Ann Emerson, R.*
9. Kenny Hulshof, R.*

Montana
†Dennis Rehberg, R.*

Nebraska
1. Jeff Fortenberry, R.
2. Lee Terry, R.*
3. Tom Osborne, R.*

Nevada
1. Shelley Berkley, D.*
2. Jim Gibbons, R.*
3. Jon Porter, Sr., R.*

New Hampshire
1. Jeb Bradley, R.*
2. Charles Bass, R.*

New Jersey
1. Robert E. Andrews, D.*
2. Frank LoBiondo, R.*
3. H. James Saxton, R.*
4. Christopher H. Smith, R.*
5. Scott Garrett, R.*
6. Frank Pallone, Jr., D.*
7. Mike Ferguson, R.*
8. William Pascrell, Jr., D.*
9. Steven Rothman, D.*
10. Donald M. Payne, D.*
11. Rodney Frelinghuysen, R.*
12. Rush Holt, D.*
13. Robert Menendez, D.*

New Mexico
1. Heather Wilson, R.*
2. Steve Pearce, R.*
3. Thomas Udall, D.*

New York
1. Tim Bishop, D.*
2. Steve Israel, D.*
3. Peter King, R.*
4. Carolyn McCarthy, D.*
5. Gary L. Ackerman, D.*
6. Gregory Meeks, D.*
7. Joseph Crowley, D.*
8. Jerrold Nadler, D.*
9. Anthony Weiner, D.*
10. Edolphus Towns, D.*
11. Major R. Owens, D.*

12. Nydia Velazquez, D.*
13. Vito J. Fossella, R.*
14. Carolyn Maloney, D.*
15. Charles B. Rangel, D.*
16. Jose E. Serrano, D.*
17. Eliot L. Engel, D.*
18. Nita M. Lowey, D.*
19. Sue Kelly, R.*
20. John Sweeney, R.*
21. Michael R. McNulty, D.*
22. Maurice Hinchey, D.*
23. John McHugh, R.*
24. Sherwood Boehlert, R.*
25. James Walsh, R.*
26. Thomas Reynolds, R.*
27. Brian Higgins, D.
28. Louise M. Slaughter, D.*
29. Randy Kuhl, R.

North Carolina
1. G. K. Butterfield, D.*
2. Bob Etheridge, D.*
3. Walter Jones, Jr., R.*
4. David Price, D.*
5. Virginia Foxx, R.
6. Howard Coble, R.*
7. Mike McIntyre, D.*
8. Robin Hayes, R.*
9. Sue Myrick, R.*
10. Patrick McHenry, R.
11. Charles H. Taylor, R.*
12. Melvin Watt, D.*
13. Brad Miller, D.*

North Dakota
†Earl Pomeroy, D.*

Ohio
1. Steve Chabot, R.*
2. Jean Schmidt, R.
3. Michael Turner, R.*
4. Michael G. Oxley, R.*
5. Paul E. Gillmor, R.*
6. Ted Strickland, D.*
7. David L. Hobson, R.*
8. John A. Boehner, R.*
9. Marcy Kaptur, D.*
10. Dennis Kucinich, D.*
11. Stephanie Tubbs Jones, D.*
12. Pat Tiberi, R.*
13. Sherrod Brown, D.*
14. Steven LaTourette, R.*
15. Deborah Pryce, R.*
16. Ralph Regula, R.*
17. Timothy Ryan, D.*
18. Bob Ney, R.*

Oklahoma
1. John Sullivan, R.*
2. Dan Boren, D.
3. Frank Lucas, R.*
4. Tom Cole, R.*
5. Ernest Jim Istook, R.*

Oregon
1. David Wu, D.*
2. Greg Walden, R.*
3. Earl Blumenauer, D.*
4. Peter A. DeFazio, D.*
5. Darlene Hooley, D.*

Pennsylvania
1. Robert Brady, D.*
2. Chaka Fattah, D.*
3. Philip English, R.*
4. Melissa Hart, R.*
5. John Peterson, R.*
6. Jim Gerlach, R.*
7. W. Curtis Weldon, R.*
8. Michael Fitzpatrick, R.
9. Bill Shuster, R.*
10. Donald Sherwood, R.*
11. Paul E. Kanjorski, D.*
12. John P. Murtha, D.*
13. Allyson Schwartz, D.
14. Michael Doyle, D.*
15. Charles Dent, R.
16. Joseph Pitts, R.*
17. Tim Holden, D.*
18. Tim Murphy, R.*
19. Todd Platts, R.*

Rhode Island
1. Patrick Kennedy, D.*
2. James Langevin, D.*

South Carolina
1. Henry Brown, Jr., R.*
2. Joe Wilson, R.*
3. J. Gresham Barrett, R.*
4. Bob Inglis, R.
5. John M. Spratt, Jr., D.*
6. James Clyburn, D.*

South Dakota
†Stephanie Herseth, D.*

Tennessee
1. William Jenkins, R.*
2. John J. Duncan, Jr., R.*
3. Zach Wamp, R.*
4. Lincoln Davis, D.*
5. Jim Cooper, D.*
6. Bart Gordon, D.*
7. Marsha Blackburn, R.*
8. John S. Tanner, D.*
9. Harold E. Ford, Jr., D.*

Texas
1. Louis Gohmert, R.
2. Ted Poe, R.
3. Sam Johnson, R.*
4. Ralph M. Hall, R.*
5. Jeb Hensarling, R.*
6. Joe Barton, R.*
7. John Culberson, R.*
8. Kevin Brady, R.*
9. Al Green, D.
10. Michael McCaul, R.
11. Mike Conaway, R.
12. Kay Granger, R.*
13. Mac Thornberry, R.*
14. Ron Paul, R.*
15. Ruben Hinojosa, D.*
16. Silvestre Reyes, D.*
17. Chet Edwards, D.*
18. Sheila Jackson Lee, D.*
19. Randy Neugebauer, R.*
20. Charlie Gonzalez, D.*
21. Lamar S. Smith, R.*
22. Tom DeLay, R.*
23. Henry Bonilla, R.*

24. Kenny Marchant, R.
25. Lloyd Doggett, D.*
26. Michael Burgess, R.*
27. Solomon P. Ortiz, D.*
28. Henry Cuellar, D.
29. Gene Green, D.*
30. Eddie Bernice Johnson, D.*
31. John Carter, R.*
32. Pete Sessions, R.*

Utah
1. Rob Bishop, R.*
2. Jim Matheson, D.*
3. Christopher Cannon, R.*

Vermont
†Bernard Sanders, Ind.*

Virginia
1. Jo Ann Davis, R.*
2. Thelma Drake, R.
3. Robert Scott, D.*
4. J. Randy Forbes, R.*
5. Virgil Goode, Jr., R.*
6. Robert Goodlatte, R.*
7. Eric Cantor, R.*
8. James P. Moran, Jr., D.*
9. Rick C. Boucher, D.*
10. Frank R. Wolf, R.*
11. Tom Davis, R.*

Washington
1. Jay Inslee, D.*
2. Rick Larsen, D.*
3. Brian Baird, D.*
4. Doc Hastings, R.*
5. Cathy McMorris, R.
6. Norman D. Dicks, D.*
7. Jim McDermott, D.*
8. Dave Reichert, R.
9. Adam Smith, D.*

West Virginia
1. Alan B. Mollohan, D.*
2. Shelley Moore Capito, R.*
3. Nick J. Rahall II, D.*

Wisconsin
1. Paul Ryan, R.*
2. Tammy Baldwin, D.*
3. Ron Kind, D.*
4. Gwen Moore, D.
5. James Sensenbrenner, Jr., R.*
6. Thomas E. Petri, R.*
7. David R. Obey, D.*
8. Mark Green, R.*

Wyoming
†Barbara Cubin, R.*

Nonvoting representatives
American Samoa
Eni F. H. Faleomavaega, D.*

District of Columbia
Eleanor Holmes Norton, D.*

Guam
Madeleine Bordallo, D.*

Puerto Rico
Luis Fortuno, R.

Virgin Islands
Donna M. Christensen, D.*

MEMBERS OF THE UNITED STATES SENATE

The Senate of the second session of the 109th Congress consisted of 43 Democrats, 55 Republicans, and 1 Independent when it convened on Jan. 18, 2006. The first date in each listing shows when the senator's term began. The second date in each listing shows when the senator's term expires.

STATE	TERM	STATE	TERM	STATE	TERM
Alabama		**Louisiana**		**Ohio**	
Richard C. Shelby, R.	1987-2011	Mary L. Landrieu, D.	1997-2009	Mike DeWine, R.	1995-2007
Jeff Sessions, R.	1997-2009	David Vitter, R.	2005-2011	George V. Voinovich, R.	1999-2011
Alaska		**Maine**		**Oklahoma**	
Theodore F. Stevens, R.	1968-2009	Olympia Snowe, R.	1995-2007	James M. Inhofe, R.	1994-2009
Lisa Murkowski, R.	2003-2011	Susan M. Collins, R.	1997-2009	Tom Coburn, R.	2005-2011
Arizona		**Maryland**		**Oregon**	
John McCain III, R.	1987-2011	Paul S. Sarbanes, D.	1977-2007	Ron Wyden, D.	1996-2011
Jon Kyl, R.	1995-2007	Barbara A. Mikulski, D.	1987-2011	Gordon Smith, R.	1997-2009
Arkansas		**Massachusetts**		**Pennsylvania**	
Blanche Lambert Lincoln, D.	1999-2011	Edward M. Kennedy, D.	1962-2007	Arlen Specter, R.	1981-2011
Mark Pryor, D.	2003-2009	John F. Kerry, D.	1985-2009	Rick Santorum, R.	1995-2007
California		**Michigan**		**Rhode Island**	
Dianne Feinstein, D.	1992-2007	Carl Levin, D.	1979-2009	Jack Reed, D.	1997-2009
Barbara Boxer, D.	1993-2011	Debbie Stabenow, D.	2001-2007	Lincoln D. Chafee, R.	1999-2007
Colorado		**Minnesota**		**South Carolina**	
Wayne Allard, R.	1997-2009	Mark Dayton, D.	2001-2007	Lindsey Graham, R.	2003-2009
Ken Salazar, D.	2005-2011	Norm Coleman, R.	2003-2009	Jim DeMint, R.	2005-2011
Connecticut		**Mississippi**		**South Dakota**	
Christopher J. Dodd, D.	1981-2011	Thad Cochran, R.	1978-2009	Tim Johnson, D.	1997-2009
Joseph I. Lieberman, D.	1989-2007	Trent Lott, R.	1989-2007	John Thune, R.	2005-2011
Delaware		**Missouri**		**Tennessee**	
Joseph R. Biden, Jr., D.	1973-2009	Christopher S. (Kit) Bond, R.	1987-2011	Bill Frist, R.	1995-2007
Thomas Carper, D.	2001-2007	Jim Talent, R.	2003-2009	Lamar Alexander, R.	2003-2009
Florida		**Montana**		**Texas**	
Bill Nelson, D.	2001-2007	Max Baucus, D.	1978-2009	Kay Bailey Hutchison, R.	1993-2007
Mel Martinez, R.	2005-2011	Conrad Burns, R.	1989-2007	John Cornyn, R.	2003-2009
Georgia		**Nebraska**		**Utah**	
Saxby Chambliss, R.	2003-2009	Chuck Hagel, R.	1997-2009	Orrin G. Hatch, R.	1977-2007
Johnny Isakson, R.	2005-2011	Ben Nelson, D.	2001-2007	Robert F. Bennett, R.	1993-2011
Hawaii		**Nevada**		**Vermont**	
Daniel K. Inouye, D.	1963-2011	Harry M. Reid, D.	1987-2011	Patrick J. Leahy, D.	1975-2011
Daniel K. Akaka, D.	1990-2007	John Ensign, R.	2001-2007	James M. Jeffords, I.	1989-2007
Idaho		**New Hampshire**		**Virginia**	
Larry E. Craig, R.	1991-2009	Judd Gregg, R.	1993-2011	John W. Warner, R.	1979-2009
Mike Crapo, R.	1999-2011	John E. Sununu, R.	2003-2009	George F. Allen, R.	2001-2007
Illinois		**New Jersey**		**Washington**	
Richard J. Durbin, D.	1997-2009	Robert Menendez, D.	2006	Patty Murray, D.	1993-2011
Barack Obama, D.	2005-2011	Frank R. Lautenberg, D.	2003-2009	Maria Cantwell, D.	2001-2007
Indiana		**New Mexico**		**West Virginia**	
Richard G. Lugar, R.	1977-2007	Pete V. Domenici, R.	1973-2009	Robert C. Byrd, D.	1959-2007
Evan Bayh, D.	1999-2011	Jeff Bingaman, D.	1983-2007	John D. Rockefeller IV, D.	1985-2009
Iowa		**New York**		**Wisconsin**	
Charles E. Grassley, R.	1981-2011	Charles E. Schumer, D.	1999-2011	Herbert Kohl, D.	1989-2007
Tom Harkin, D.	1985-2009	Hillary Rodham Clinton, D.	2001-2007	Russell D. Feingold, D.	1993-2011
Kansas		**North Carolina**		**Wyoming**	
Sam Brownback, R.	1996-2011	Elizabeth Dole, R.	2003-2009	Craig Thomas, R.	1995-2007
Pat Roberts, R.	1997-2009	Richard Burr, R.	2005-2011	Mike Enzi, R.	1997-2009
Kentucky		**North Dakota**			
Mitch McConnell, R.	1985-2009	Kent Conrad, D.	1987-2007		
Jim Bunning, R.	1999-2011	Byron L. Dorgan, D.	1992-2011		

Conservation. Revelations early in 2005 that the government of India had failed to control *poaching* (illegal hunting) of endangered tigers caused a national scandal. In January, wildlife conservation officials announced that they had found no sign of tiger movement in Sariska National Park during the previous six months, indicating that all of the approximately 15 tigers in this important habitat had been killed by poachers.

In 2005, India was home to, at most, 3,500 tigers—about half the world's remaining wild population. In the early 1900's, there were an estimated 50,000 tigers in India. The destruction of their forest habitat eliminated many of these big cats. Poachers, who can sell tiger parts used in Asian folk medicine for thousands of dollars, thinned out the survivors.

After the Sariska disclosure, the government admitted that at least 122 Indian tigers had been killed between 1999 and 2003. In March 2005, Indian Prime Minister Manmohan Singh ordered police to investigate poaching rings. He also established a National Wildlife Crime Prevention Bureau and created a task force to examine the tiger problem. In August, the task force recommended that some communities living in areas adjoining tiger habitat be relocated—a highly controversial idea.

The government promised increased law enforcement and improved assistance to local authorities to protect tigers and their habitat. The government also called upon international conservation experts to help conduct a comprehensive survey to better determine the numbers and locations of tigers in India. In addition, scientists began using satellite imagery to map tiger habitat in India.

Planet of the apes. Representatives of countries where *great apes* live, along with a host of scientists, met in Kinshasa, capital of the Democratic Republic of the Congo, in September 2005 to launch new plans for protecting these imperiled creatures. Great apes include bonobos, chimpanzees, gorillas, and orangutans. The countries participating in the conference belonged to the United Nations (UN)-backed Great Apes Survival Project. Nineteen of the countries, including Cameroon, Congo (Kinshasa), Rwanda, and Uganda, are in Africa, where gorillas, chimpanzees, and bonobos are found. Orangutans, the only Asian great apes, inhabit Malaysia and Indonesia.

Scientists believe that fewer than 500,000 great apes remain in the wild. Furthermore, scientists warn that without an international mobilization to protect these animals, the great apes may become extinct by 2050. According to the Great Apes Survival Project, there were approximately 100 great ape habitats remaining in 2005, and most of these had been severely damaged by human activities. Threats to great apes include deforestation, poaching for food, the illegal wildlife trade, wars, and disease.

Scientists at the Kinshasa conference noted that Ebola hemorrhagic fever, a disease that has caused many deaths of people in Africa, has also killed hundreds, perhaps even thousands, of gorillas in central Africa. The scientists found that influenza and other respiratory diseases contracted from human beings also have killed many gorillas in Rwanda and Uganda. Armed rebels in the conflict-ridden eastern Congo (Kinshasa) have been yet another serious threat to gorilla populations, killing large percentages of the apes in parts of the country, scientists with the project reported.

The Kinshasa conference concluded with a call for conservation organizations and governments, particularly those of industrial nations, to focus on aiding the conservation of great apes. The declaration stressed that help was needed in two main areas—control of poaching and development of ecologically sustainable livelihoods for people in areas inhabited by apes.

Forum on forests. A 10-percent reduction in worldwide deforestation by 2010 was targeted by delegates at the May 2005 meeting of the UN Forum on Forests in New York City. The goal was set by the WWF (formerly the World Wildlife Fund), an international conservation organization based in Geneva, Switzerland, and the World Bank, an international lending organization headquartered in Washington, D.C. The two groups began cooperating on forest conservation in 1998. Globally, about 47 million jobs depended on forests in 2005, according to the WWF, which stressed that forests must be utilized by both people and wildlife.

Tropical rain forests. With scientific and financial support from the WWF and World Bank, the government of Brazil in February 2005 declared 9.4 million acres (3.8 million hectares) of Amazon tropical rain forest a protected area. The move was meant to counter illegal logging and clearing of forests, which has long been rampant in the Amazon Basin. Calling the protected area a "giant step" in conserving the Amazon ecosystem, the WWF noted that the area contains many rare species, including jaguars, harpy eagles, and a variety of macaws.

A report issued by the WWF in April revealed that, from 1994 to 2004, at least 361 new plant and animal species had been discovered in Borneo's rain forests. The new species included many insects, crabs, fish, frogs, toads, lizards, snakes, and plants. The report was part of a

The report in April 2005 that the ivory-billed woodpecker (female at top left, male at bottom), long believed extinct, had been spotted in a cypress woods in Arkansas in 2004 electrified the birding world. In August 2005, ornithologists from Cornell University in Ithaca, New York, released a recording of the bird's distinctive call and drumming on trees to provide proof of their find.

WWF effort to work with Brunei, Indonesia, and Malaysia to conserve the forests of Borneo.

Court battle over forests. During the late summer of 2005, the governments of California, New Mexico, and Oregon sued the administration of U.S. President George W. Bush in federal appeals court. The states opposed the administration's plans, announced in May, to open more than 90,000 square miles (233,100 square kilometers) of undeveloped national forest lands to new roads, logging, and other commercial enterprises. The new directives overturned a ban on such activities enacted by the administration of former President Bill Clinton in 2001.

Almost all of the land involved in the dispute was in western states and Alaska. Environmentalists claimed that the Bush administration's move threatened the nation's last pristine forests, a claim that the administration denied.

Comeback kid. Excitement swept through the birding world in April 2005 when *ornithologists* (scientists who study birds) from Cornell University in Ithaca, New York, reported sighting an ivory-billed woodpecker, last seen in 1944 and believed to be extinct. The large bird was spotted in the deep woods of the Cache River National Wildlife Refuge in Arkansas. To back up the reported sighting, the researchers produced a fuzzy photograph of the woodpecker. Some scientists, however, remained skeptical. By August, these skeptics had changed their minds when the Cornell team provided a tape recording of the bird's distinctive call and double-rap drumming on trees.

■ Edward R. Ricciuti

See also **Biology; Zoos.**
Costa Rica. See **Latin America.**
Cote d'Ivoire. See **Africa.**

Courts in the United States in 2005 ruled on major cases involving pollution, terrorist attacks, and cigarette companies. In May, moderates in the U.S. Senate averted a crisis involving the confirmation of controversial judicial nominees.

Judicial nominees. On May 23, a *bipartisan* (supported by two political parties) group of 14 senators reached a compromise that allowed several controversial judicial nominees to receive a yes-or-no confirmation vote in the Senate. Democrats had blocked the nominations with a threat of staging a *filibuster*. (A filibuster is the practice by which a minority in the Senate uses extended debate to block or delay action.)

Prior to the announcement of the compromise—which guaranteed a vote on the nominations of Janice Rogers Brown, William Pryor, and Priscilla R. Owen—the Senate was poised to debate a procedural change that would have eliminated the filibuster on future judicial nominations. The Democrats involved in the compromise maintained that they would filibuster future judicial nominee votes only under extraordinary circumstances. The seven Republicans promised not to seek changes to the filibuster rule.

Intelligent design. A federal judge in Harrisburg, Pennsylvania, ruled on December 20 that a school district cannot require the introduction of "intelligent design" in biology classes as an alternative to the theory of evolution. Intelligent design proponents claim that biological life is so complex that it must have been originated by an intelligent source. Federal District Judge John E. Jones III ruled that the Dover, Pennsylvania, school board violated the U.S. Constitution when it ordered high school biology teachers to read to students a statement that cast doubt on the validity of evolution and offered intelligent design as an alternative explanation on the origins of life. Judge Jones noted the school board's policy order violated the establishment clause of the First Amendment of the U.S. Constitution by promoting a religious purpose in a public school.

The "20th hijacker." Zacarias Moussaoui pleaded guilty on April 22 to being part of a conspiracy planned and carried out by the al-Qa`ida terrorist network to crash jets into buildings in U.S. cities on Sept. 11, 2001. Moussaoui—the only person tried in the United States for involvement in the 2001 terrorist attacks—told U.S. District Court Judge Leonie M. Brinkema that he understood that his plea might lead to his execution. Moussaoui, however, denied that he was involved in the attacks successfully carried out and asserted that his intention had been to fly a plane into the White House. Attorney General Alberto R. Gonzales instructed federal prosecutors to seek the death penalty in the sentencing phase of Moussaoui's trial, scheduled for 2006.

Enemy combatants. The U.S. Department of Justice charged Jose Padilla on Nov. 22, 2005, with aiding terrorists and conspiracy to murder. A U.S. citizen, Padilla had been held under military arrest as an enemy combatant for three years without being charged with a crime. He had been arrested on the accusation that he planned to explode a radioactive "dirty bomb." The federal indictment, however, did not deal with that allegation, but rather accused him of conspiring to murder U.S. nationals outside the United States. In October 2005, Padilla's lawyers filed an appeal before the U.S. Supreme Court, asking "Does the president have the power to seize American citizens in civilian settings on American soil and subject them to indefinite military detention without criminal charge or trial?" According to legal experts, removing Padilla from military custody and charging him in a civilian court averted a court decision that might have resulted in a constitutional showdown over the president's authority to detain U.S. citizens as enemy combatants without bringing charges against them.

Cigarette manufacturers. In June, the Justice Department asked for $14 billion in damages for racketeering from U.S. cigarette makers and sought to prevent the companies from marketing cigarettes to people under age 21. The government initially had asked for $280 billion in damages, but a federal appeals court in February rejected the demand, saying court-imposed sanctions needed to discourage future misconduct rather than penalize past behavior. The government lowered its monetary demands after a government witness testified that a 25-year antismoking campaign would cost $130 billion. However, Justice Department lawyers asked for only $10 billion to fund a five-year antismoking program. The reduction stunned some judicial experts who speculated whether it had been ordered by Justice Department officials for political reasons or as a reflection of a legal reality; that is, whether judges can order the funding of any antismoking program at all. At year's end, Federal District Judge Gladys Kessler had yet to decide the case.

Eric Rudolph pleaded guilty in April to four bombings carried out in the 1990's. He received two life sentences for a 1998 bombing of an abortion clinic in Birmingham, Alabama, and two additional life sentences for three bombings in Atlanta, Georgia—at the Olympic Summer Games in 1996 and at an abortion clinic and a gay club in 1997. Rudolph was spared the death penalty by agreeing to help authorities locate more than 250 pounds (110 kilograms) of explosives he had hidden in North Carolina. ■ Geoffrey A. Campbell

See also **Congress of the United States; Supreme Court of the United States; Terrorism.**

Cricket. In February 2005, former Zimbabwe captain Heath Streak and player Andy Blignaut agreed to rejoin the Zimbabwe cricket squad, ending a dispute between the players and the Zimbabwe Cricket Council dating back to 2004. Streak and Blignaut—along with 13 others—were dismissed in 2004 after alleging that Zimbabwe officials chose players because of their race.

While one dispute was resolved, another took its place as the West Indies Cricket Board (WICB) feuded with its leading players over sponsorships. The problem arose when the WICB signed an agreement with one company while several players, including West Indies captain Brian Lara, signed a deal with another company. The two sides finally reached an agreement in October.

The Ashes. The traditional battle for the Ashes between England and Australia in 2005 will be remembered as one of the greatest ever. After several tense matches between what many fans believe to be the best sides in the world, England outdueled Australia to take the Ashes contest for the first time since 1987.

In the first test on July 21, 2005, Australia defeated England by 239 runs in an exciting match. England roared back, however, to win a closely fought second test by the extremely narrow margin of two runs. In the third test—held in Manchester, England—both teams fought to a draw in a nail-biting match that ended with Australia needing only one wicket with one wicket remaining, only to come up short. England then won the fourth test by three wickets, putting the team 2-1 ahead in the series. In the fifth and final test held September 8-12 in London, Australia needed a victory, but the match ended in a draw with England taking the competition.

During the Ashes matches, many players distinguished themselves with their fine play. Australian leg-spinner Shane Warne bowled superbly, taking 40 wickets in the five tests, and opening bowler Glenn McGrath was outstanding. England's Andrew Flintoff emerged as a major international all-rounder, while newcomer Kevin Pietersen impressed fans with his batting.

Super Series Test. Despite their loss to England in the Ashes, Australia remained atop the rankings of the International Cricket Council (ICC) as the world's top test side.

In October, a six-day test match was staged in Sydney between Australia and a Rest of the World XI side selected by the ICC. Despite great players, the Rest of the World side failed as a team and Australia beat them by 210 runs over four days, a satisfying result after the loss of the Ashes. The Super Series included three one-day internationals, all of which Australia won easily. In November, Australia also beat West Indies 3-0. During the series, Brian Lara overtook Australian

Alan Bordera's world record run aggregate of 11,174 runs in test cricket, while Shane Warne took his total number of test wickets to 645.

Other test series. In January, Bangladesh won its first test match in 35 attempts, defeating a weakened Zimbabwe team. Bangladesh also won the series 1-0 because the other test was drawn. Also in January, Australia took its series against Pakistan 3-0, while England defeated South Africa 2-1, with two matches drawn. In March, Australia also beat New Zealand 2-0, with one match drawn. New Zealand later won series against Sri Lanka and Zimbabwe.

Pakistan visited India in March, and the two sides split an exciting series 1-1, with one match drawn. In March-April, South Africa defeated a weakened West Indies team 2-0, with two matches drawn. In May, Pakistan visited the West Indies and the series ended 1-1.

In December, India beat Sri Lanka 2-0 with one match drawn and moved to second place in test rankings, overtaking England. During the series, Sachin Tendulkar scored a 35th test century, a new record.

One-Day Internationals (ODIs). Australia beat Pakistan in the final matches of the Victoria Bitters series, in which the West Indies also participated. Australia, Bangladesh, and England played a triangular ODI series in June, with Bangladesh handing Australia a surprising defeat in one of the matches. England and Australia fought to a draw in the final, sharing the trophy.

In March and April, eight countries took part in the one-day Women's World Cup in South Africa. Australia (215-4) defeated India (117) by 98 runs in the final on April 10. In July, Scotland defeated Ireland to take the ICC Trophy in another one-day competition held in Ireland. The matches featured emerging cricket countries. Because of their success, Ireland, Scotland, Bermuda, Canada, and Holland all became eligible to play in the 2007 ICC Cricket World Cup.

Twenty20. Many cricket observers believe that Twenty20, a shortened version of cricket developed in England in 2003, may soon become a regular feature of international cricket. The first international Twenty20 match of 2005 took place in Auckland, New Zealand, on February 17. Australia made 214-5 in their 20 overs, while New Zealand only mustered 170. In another international Twenty20 in June, England (179-8) comfortably defeated Australia (79) by 100 runs.

Rules and administration. The ICC in 2005 tried to end decades of disputes by relaxing its rule on how players bowl. Under the new rule, bowlers can bend their arms up to 15 degrees. Also in 2005, the ICC moved its headquarters from Lord's Cricket Ground in London to Dubai, United Arab Emirates.   ■ Keith Lye

Crime. The rate of violent crime in the United States declined for the 13th consecutive year in 2004, the Federal Bureau of Investigation (FBI) announced in October 2005. In its annual report, the FBI's Uniform Crime Reporting (UCR) Program revealed that forcible rape was the only category of violent crime that increased in 2004. The number of property crimes fell by 1.1 percent over 2003 levels. The UCR program collects data from about 17,000 U.S. law enforcement agencies on four types of violent crime—murder and nonnegligent homicide, forcible rape, robbery, and aggravated assault—and three types of property crime—burglary, larceny-theft, and motor vehicle theft.

The UCR program estimated that the rate of violent crime in 2004 dropped to 465.5 per 100,000 U.S. inhabitants, down from 475.8 in 2003 and 758.2 in 1991. The 2004 rate was the lowest since 1974. The total number of violent crimes also dropped, to 1.37 million in 2004 from an estimated 1.38 million in 2003. The South, the most populous region in the United States, accounted for 41.9 percent of all violent crime, a slight decrease over the percentage in 2003. Among all regions, the Northeast had the largest decrease in violent crime, a 2.5-percent drop over 2003.

According to the report, the number of murders reported to police in 2004 fell for the first time since 2000, to 16,137. The figure represented a 2.4-percent drop over the number in 2003 and a 33.2-percent drop from 1995. The number of robberies dropped by 3.1 percent, while aggravated assaults fell by 0.5 percent. However, the estimated number of forcible rapes in 2004 rose by 0.8 percent to 94,635.

Hate crimes. The number of hate crimes in the United States in 2004 increased by about 2 percent over 2003 levels, to 7,649, with the number of race-based incidents rising by 5 percent. Incidents motivated by bias against sexual orientation and ethnicity fell slightly. California led the nation in hate offenses against both people and property, followed by New Jersey.

Mental illness and crime. People with severe mental illness (SMI) living in U.S. communities are about 11 times as likely to become victims of violent crime as people in the general population, according to an August 2005 study by researchers at the Feinberg School of Medicine at Northwestern University in Evanston, Illinois. The researchers found that about 25 percent of people with SMI living in the community became victims of violent crime in 2004. People with SMI were 15 times as likely to be assaulted or raped and 140 times as likely to be victims of theft. Lead researcher Linda Teplin theorized that disorganized thought processes, impulsivity, and other symptoms associated with SMI reduce the ability to perceive risks and take protective action.

White-collar crime. Judges in 2005 handed down sentences in a number of high-profile cases involving white-collar crime. John J. Rigas, founder of Adelphia Communications Corporation, a cable company based in Greenwood Village, Colorado, received a 15-year prison term in June for stealing millions from his now-bankrupt company and concealing $2.3 billion in debt from investors. His son, Timothy J. Rigas, Adelphia's former chief financial officer, received a 20-year sentence in the case.

In July, Bernard Ebbers, former chief executive officer (CEO) of WorldCom Inc. received a 25-year prison term for organizing the largest accounting fraud in U.S. history. The $11-billion fraud forced WorldCom (now MCI) into a $107-billion bankruptcy in 2002—also the largest in U.S. history—and left 17,000 company employees jobless.

In September 2005, a New York judge sentenced Dennis Kozlowski and Mark Swartz to 8 to 25 years in prison for looting millions from Tyco International Ltd. The two former executives used the money to support a lavish lifestyle, notoriously symbolized by a $6,000 shower curtain. Kozlowski and Swartz were also ordered to pay nearly $240 million in fines and restitution.

Scrushy acquitted. A jury in Birmingham, Alabama, in June brought in a not-guilty verdict against Richard Scrushy, former CEO of HealthSouth Corporation of Birmingham. Scrushy denied any knowledge of a six-year, $2.7-billion fraud at the company. Fifteen Health-South employees had earlier pleaded guilty to participating in the fraud.

BTK killer. Serial killer Dennis Rader, who called himself "BTK," was sentenced in June to 10 consecutive life terms in prison for murders he committed in Kansas from 1974 to 1991. Rader called himself "bind, torture, and kill" in reference to his method of murdering his victims. Police arrested Rader in February 2005, 11 months after he resumed communications with police following a 25-year silence. A former church leader and Boy Scout leader, Radar pleaded guilty to murdering 10 men, women, and children in Wichita and nearby Park City.

Jackson not guilty. In a trial marked by nearly continous coverage by cable news channels, pop singer Michael Jackson in June was acquitted on charges of child molestation, conspiracy, and false imprisonment. A jury in Santa Maria, California, ruled that the prosecution had failed to prove that Jackson had sexually abused a 13-year-old cancer patient from Los Angeles in 2003 or had conspired to abduct and imprison the accuser and other members of his family.

■ Barbara A. Mayes

See also **Bank; Civil rights; Courts; Immigration; Prison; Terrorism.**

Identity Theft

The New Face of Crime

By Kevin J. Delaney

A company that collects credit information about consumers and sells it to businesses revealed in February 2005 that thieves posing as customers had obtained sensitive information about 145,000 people. In March, computer tapes containing personal information about some 600,000 past and present employees of a major media conglomerate disappeared while en route to a secure storage facility. A shoe chain announced in March that thieves had stolen information about roughly 1.4 million credit card and check transactions.

A publishing company announced in April that thieves had accessed personal data on 310,000 United States citizens through its computer systems. In May, computer hackers stole data from a company that does behind-the-scenes processing of credit card transactions. (The word *hacker* is used in this article to refer to a computer programmer who engages in criminal activity.) The digital break-in exposed credit card data and other information about 40 million cardholders. The list of thefts of sensitive data, such as individuals' Social Security numbers, credit card numbers, and birth dates, goes on. In the hands of savvy thieves, who use it run up charges, set up credit cards, borrow money, and assume false identities, that information is as good as gold.

> **Identity theft is one of the fastest growing crimes in the United States. Are you protected?**

While identity theft is not new, the public has learned more about it thanks to a 2003 California law that requires businesses to disclose data breaches that affect residents of the state. Before the California law, many people were unaware that whole groups of businesses hold sensitive personal data in databases, often with insufficient protection against thieves. During this same period, criminals have become increasingly savvy, thanks in large part to the Internet. Internet Web sites offered a whole new way to trade and sell credit card numbers, Social Security numbers, and other sensitive information. In some instances, professional criminals already implicated in drug trafficking and other illegal activities turned to identity theft as a lucrative new operation. Unfortunately for their victims, this new criminal class proved to be extremely successful. The Federal Trade Commission (FTC), an independent U.S. government agency that, among other things, protects consumers against unfair practices, estimates that identity thieves annually run up approximately $50 billion in fraudulent charges to U.S. businesses and individuals.

Identity theft takes several forms, but in all of them criminals use personal information to impersonate an individual in one fashion or another—whether to buy merchandise using the individual's credit card; to take out a mortgage in the victim's name; or to assume an individual's identity when dealing with law enforcement or a potential employer. Identity thieves use techniques as simple as rifling through an individual's household garbage and as complex as breaking into his or her computer.

Financial identity theft

The most common type of identity theft is financial. Banks, credit card companies, and other financial institutions rely on some basic information about individuals before establishing accounts for them. Identity thieves capitalize on this, stealing that information from individuals to run up charges and drain their accounts or set up additional accounts they can draw on without the victims' knowledge. The FTC estimates that thieves have fraudulently opened such accounts in the names of 10 million U.S. citizens over the past five years.

With an individual's Social Security number and other basic information, a criminal can easily impersonate that person and establish credit cards and even take out mortgages in that person's name. The thief can have the statements for those accounts delivered to another address, sometimes a vacant building where he or she can retrieve any mail without it being traced. Under these circumstances, the victim is not immediately aware that his or her identity is being used.

Identity thieves employ various methods for extracting data. One common method involves stealing credit card applications mailed to individuals from their mailboxes or garbage bins. The thief then applies for credit cards and has them sent to a fraudulent address. Another tactic is called phishing. In a phishing scam, hackers, posing as a bank or other trusted institution, send e-mails to consumers. The e-mails often direct individuals to a Web site where they are requested to enter account information or other personal data. The original e-mail and Web site often include company logos and appear legitimate. Criminals also get personal information by stealing it from companies that hold it or by trading for those data online.

A victim is not responsible for most of the financial damage that an identity thief causes, once the victim proves that he or she has been victimized. Financial institutions and other businesses generally have rules limiting most consumer liability. However, consumers can spend years cleaning up their financial reputation once they have been victimized. Victims must convince a broad list of companies that someone else has been borrowing money or running up bills. Until victims have done this, they can find it difficult or impossible to borrow money or be issued credit cards. Financial institutions look at an individual's credit history, kept with three main private U.S. credit rating agencies, before deciding whether to do business with that person. If a person's record shows a history of unpaid loans and bills, many creditors will not lend that person money.

Criminal identity theft

Criminal identity theft involves giving a victim's personal information to police or other law enforcement officials in place of the criminal's own information. In some cases, criminals have secured

The author:
Kevin J. Delaney is a Staff Reporter for *The Wall Street Journal.*

WHAT INFORMATION ARE IDENTITY THIEVES LOOKING FOR?

- ■ Social Security number
- ■ Credit card / debit card / ATM card number
- ■ Credit card security number (on back of card)
- ■ Home address
- ■ Phone number
- ■ Birth date
- ■ Identification numbers
- ■ Driver's license number
- ■ Credit reports

fraudulent drivers' licenses or other counterfeit identity cards to pose as their victims. Stopped by police for a traffic violation or shoplifting, the criminal gives a victim's identifying information instead of his or her own. In such cases, the police generally release the criminal. They might notify the criminal that he or she will have to appear in court at a later date because of the current infraction. Of course, the criminal does not show up in court. When the police go after the lawbreaker, they go after the wrong person.

As a result of this identity theft, it is the victim whom the police believe to be the criminal. When the police apprehend a criminal, the police generally enter an individual's identifying information into law enforcement databases. A victim of criminal identity theft might find his or her information entered into one of those databases as a result of the thief's actions and end up with a criminal record.

Employers can access information obtained from those databases when doing background checks of potential hires. In some cases, innocent individuals have been denied jobs because their records have been tarnished by criminal identity thieves.

Identity cloning

Another kind of identity theft, identity cloning, often includes elements of financial and criminal identity theft. With identity cloning, a thief impersonates an individual in an array of ways. The thief might apply for jobs using a victim's identity, for example, pretending to possess the victim's educational background and work experience.

Illegal aliens and criminals looking to start over with a clean slate are the most common perpetrators of identity cloning. In one type of scam, the perpetrator assumes the identity of a person who has died. Death certificates in many places include sensitive information about the deceased, including birth dates and Social Security numbers. A criminal can use this information to pretend to be the deceased person, since there is often a lag between a person's death and updates of databases. In some cases, the dead person's heirs can find their inheritances endangered by mortgages or other loans that an identity thief has taken out in the name of the deceased.

HOW INFORMATION IS STOLEN

■ **Dumpster Diving:** Thieves in search of personal data steal bills and other documents from household trash, the trash of businesses, and landfills.

■ **Phishing:** Thieves send fraudulent e-mail messages posing as legitimate institutions to trick consumers into providing them with bank account or credit card information.

■ **Business Record Theft:** Thieves steal files (both physical and digital) from businesses or other institutions, such as banks, hospitals, and schools. Some thieves hack into computer systems for this information; others acquire it from their places of employment.

■ **"Shoulder Surfing":** Thieves watch as victims enter personal information into an ATM, watch as people write checks at a grocery store, or listen as victims provide information such as credit card numbers, addresses, or bank account numbers over the telephone.

■ **Under the Color of Authority:** Thieves can obtain credit reports by posing as people who may have a legitimate right to that information, such as landlords and employers.

■ **Skimming:** Thieves can use a special data collection and storage device known as a "skimmer" to steal credit and debit card account numbers as cards are processed at restaurants, stores, or other businesses.

Business or commercial identity theft

Businesses also are greatly affected by identity theft. Criminals pretending to be a company official can run up charges or take out loans in the name of a business. Impersonating the business owner or an executive, the criminal can often acquire credit cards or even checkbooks. Officials from the company often do not realize what has happened until they receive notices from collection agencies or get turned down for credit.

In one case, criminals impersonated the lending arm of Omega Financial, a company based in Manchester, New Hampshire. The criminals ran ads in newspapers across the United States offering loans. When prospective customers called the toll-free number given in the ad, they were asked for personal information, such as their Social Security and bank account numbers. When the customers were contacted several days later and told that they had been approved for a loan, they were asked to send a "commitment fee" to hold the loan. Omega Financial, which had closed its lending arm in December 2001, learned of the scam in late 2002. Victims began contacting Omega wondering about the status of their loans. Newspapers also began trying to collect fees for the advertisements the criminals had placed.

How to protect oneself

Some aspects of identity theft are largely outside of the control of consumers. One can do little about the security of personal data stored with financial institutions, employers, data brokerage firms, physicians, and businesses. There are, however, numerous precautions a consumer can take to make himself or herself less vulnerable.

Security experts warn people to be cautious about providing personal information. In general, consumers should not give out sensitive data, such as birth dates or Social Security numbers, in response to unsolicited requests by phone, the Internet, or mail. Identity thieves can easily impersonate legitimate institutions. If a consumer is unsure whether a message purporting to be from an institution is legitimate, the consumer should call the institution using the phone number given out by the company.

Security experts also advise that people be selective when providing companies with personal data and warn against giving out a Social Security number unless absolutely necessary, such as for some tax, employment, or banking transactions. A person's Social Security number is a primary key to his or her credit. It needs to be guarded carefully.

Many criminals continue to obtain sensitive information about individuals through offline methods. Experts advise that consumers take extra precautions in storing, mailing, and disposing of papers that contain personal data. They recommend storing sensitive documents in a locked cabinet, especially when people have roommates or have workers coming in and out of their residences.

Security experts also suggest mailing sensitive information—such as loan applications—from a post office rather than leaving it in a mailbox for the postal service to pick up. In addition, they recommend shredding documents containing personal information. Shredding makes it nearly impossible for criminals to steal an entire document from the trash. Finally, experts recommend logging on to the Consumer Credit Reporting Industry's Opt-Out Web site or calling its office. Consumers can contact the Consumer Credit Reporting Industry to stop receiving applications for preapproved credit cards and insurance policies that thieves can steal from unlocked mailboxes.

The records maintained by the national credit agencies also play a role in efforts to combat identity theft. These companies hold extensive dossiers with the credit history of nearly all U.S. consumers. Consumers can order copies of these reports from the credit agencies and should carefully examine the reports to make sure that no unauthorized loans or credit card accounts are listed under their name.

As of Sept. 1, 2005, all U.S. citizens became eligible to receive annually a free report from each of the three national credit agencies. The individual credit agencies and others also offer fee-based monitoring services that alert people when credit has been applied for in their name. In addition, some consumers, depending on the state where they live, have the option of blocking businesses from access to their credit reports.

Computer security

Many identity thieves carry out their illegal activities over the Internet. Therefore, practicing safe computing techniques are an important step toward preventing identity theft. Computer security experts recommend installing antivirus and antispyware programs onto home computers. These programs prevent hackers from tracking users' activity online and stealing account numbers and passwords without their knowledge. These programs do not protect against phishing or other scams in which a victim is tricked into providing information. For online banking, for example, computer security experts recommend typing in the financial institution's Web address directly, rather than clicking on a Web link in an e-mail. Special encrypted Web sites increase the security of users' Internet activities. Those sites are usually indicated by the appearance of a padlock icon in Web browser software and "https" rather than "http" at the start of a Web address. Experts recommend carefully guarding passwords for banking and other accounts. They also suggest asking an institution how personal information is used and protected.

How to reclaim a lost identity

Many victims of identity theft spend thousands of hours trying to clear their names and records, according to a 2003 study by the Identity Theft Resource Center, a nonprofit organization based in San Diego. The increasing number of criminals that have become more effective at trading stolen personal data and exploiting it is the primary reason it takes so long to clear one's name. Many thieves are able to and do use a person's stolen information in a relatively short time.

Consumer liability for financial misdeeds committed in a victim's name is usually limited. Credit card companies generally hold a victim liable for a maximum of only $50 on compromised accounts that he or she has opened. A consumer is not held responsible for loans or charges criminals have made once it has been proved that identity theft has taken place. However, a victim needs to repair his or her tarnished credit history. One key to doing so quickly is trying to limit the damage.

Experts recommend that victims of identity theft put an alert on their files with the credit agencies indicating that they have been victimized. Through the agencies, victims can request that creditors telephone them before extending any credit. Identity theft victims in some states can also request a freeze to prevent creditors from accessing their credit information from the credit agencies. Identity theft victims have to notify the institutions handling compromised or fraudulently established accounts to have them shut down or configured with new passwords.

Victims should file reports with their local police and obtain a copy of the police report. Such a report is an important document for persuading financial institutions to close accounts and not to hold victims liable for any debts. Victims might also file reports with the U.S. postal inspector and their state department of motor vehicles, if the fraud involved mail or a driver's license number. Victims should also report the identity theft to the FTC.

In the case of criminal identity theft, where a criminal has posed as someone else after being caught engaging in criminal activity, the victim needs to contact the police department or court agency initiating or handling the case. He or she should make sure that criminal records and law enforcement databases are updated fully after his or her name is cleared.

Experts emphasize that victims need to be vigilant in monitoring their credit records and other financial accounts to make sure no new instances of fraud have occurred. In addition, they should keep detailed records of their efforts to recover from identity theft, as such documentation can be important in clearing their credit records and avoiding financial liability.

Protection for consumers

As of 2005, laws providing for consumer protection and disclosure related to identity theft continued to vary widely from state to state. California enforces some of the most extensive protections, including laws providing for consumer notification in the case of data theft. California, Louisiana, Texas, and Vermont all allowed consumers to put "security freezes" on their records with the credit agencies, largely shutting off access to the records. Such a move, while sometimes incurring cost and inconvenience for consumers, is a particularly potent weapon against financial identity theft, since few companies will extend credit without access to a credit history. By late 2005, several other states were considering similar "security freeze" laws.

The publicity surrounding large-scale personal data theft in 2005 provided momentum for prospective federal laws to increase consumer protections. Under consideration was legislation that would give the FTC authority to regulate organizations that handle sensitive personal information. If enacted, the law would limit the use of Social Security numbers, require notification to consumers of data theft, and allow for easier freezes on credit reports. Another piece of legislation under consideration would increase the penalties for unauthorized use of personal information. A third proposed law would impose fines on companies that lose individuals' sensitive data.

Although identity theft is a large problem that shows no signs of shrinking, awareness of the problem and of the thieves' techniques is increasing. By being careful about giving out personal information, diligently checking credit reports, not falling for phishing schemes, and reducing unsolicited credit card and loan offers, consumers can greatly reduce the likelihood that they will become victims of identity theft. By contacting the proper authorities if they think they have been the victims of identity theft, consumers can greatly reduce the damage and expedite the process of getting their lives back on track.

HOW TO PROTECT AGAINST IDENTITY THEFT

- Do not give out Social Security numbers unless absolutely necessary.
- Shred documents that contain a Social Security number, credit card number, or password.
- Do not fall for phishing schemes; never respond to spam e-mail.
- Request credit reports and make sure there have not been unauthorized transactions or accounts made in your name.
- Store sensitive documents, such as those containing Social Security numbers or credit card numbers, in locked cabinets.
- Keep your computer clean of spyware and viruses.
- Pick complex passwords—do not use birth dates or a mother's maiden name, for example; do not share passwords with anyone.

FOR ADDITIONAL INFORMATION

Web sites

Consumer Credit Reporting Industry Opt-Out Prescreening—
    http://www.optoutprescreen.com
Annual Credit Report—http://www.annualcreditreport.com
Consumer information from the federal government—http://www.consumer.gov/
Federal Trade Commission—http://www.ftc.gov

Croatia. Olli Rehn, the enlargement commissioner of the European Union (EU), announced on Oct. 3, 2005, that the association of European nations was prepared to start accession talks with Croatia without further delay. *Accession,* or admission, to the EU is a complicated process requiring several years of negotiations between applicant nations and EU representatives. Earlier plans to start accession talks had been derailed in March by EU dissatisfaction over Croatia's lack of cooperation with the International War Crimes Tribunal in arresting individuals indicted for alleged war crimes during Croatia's war (1991–1995) with the former Yugoslavia.

Rehn's October 2005 announcement followed on the heels of a statement by Carla da Ponte, chief prosecutor for the War Crimes Tribunal, that Croatia was now deemed to be cooperating fully with the tribunal. Political analysts noted, however, that the breakthrough actually was the result of a political deal in which EU member nation Austria demanded Croatia's EU candidacy in return for shelving its veto on accession talks for Turkey.

President Stipe Mesic won reelection to a second five-year term in January. Mesic pledged to continue economic reforms that would position Croatia to gain EU membership at the earliest possible date.

Economy. Officials of the International Monetary Fund (IMF)—a United Nations-affiliated international financing body—reported in September that Croatia's economic policies were beginning to deliver results, including a relatively high rate of growth and low inflation. They noted, however, that Croatia's foreign debt as a share of *gross domestic product* (GDP)—the value of all goods and services produced in a country in a given year—was more than double the average in other emerging economies.

In the first quarter of 2005, the Croatian economy registered only 1.8 percent growth in GDP. However, GDP growth accelerated to 4 percent in the second quarter, and IMF officials forecast that it would average 3.4 percent for all of 2005, compared with 3.8 percent in 2004.

Relations between Croatia and Serbia showed clear signs of improvement in 2005. In October, Croatia and Serbia reopened Danube River ferry traffic between the two countries for the first time in 15 years. In November, Serbian Prime Minister Vojislav Kostunica met with Croatian Prime Minsiter Ivo Sanader in Zagreb, Croatia's capital. The visit was the first from a Serbian head of state since hostilities broke out in the early 1990's between Serbia, then still a part of Yugoslavia, and Croatia, which had seceded from Yugoslavia. ■ Sharon L. Wolchik

See also **Europe.**

Cuba. The sugar industry, long the mainstay of Cuba's economy, continued a steep decline in 2005, which President Fidel Castro blamed on a two-year drought and the high cost of fuel to process the crop. The 2005 harvest, officials confirmed in September, was just 1.3 million tons (1.18 million metric tons), the smallest since 1908.

Cuban officials sought to cushion the blow of the impending shutdown of 50 of the island's remaining sugar refineries by pledging to retrain tens of thousands of laid-off workers for other jobs in agriculture. The abandoned sugar infrastructure would be used, officials said, to process replacement crops such as cacao (the source of chocolate), soybeans, and sunflower seeds. Officials also promised fresh investments in nickel and cobalt mining, which together brought in annual revenues of $100 million.

Cuba's tourism industry continued to experience modest growth during 2005. Despite a United States ban on travel to Cuba, the island country reported an estimated 2.3 million visitors during 2005. Hotels once frequented by U.S. citizens were now crowded with European and Chinese tourists, reported travel industry experts.

Venezuelan oil. Under an agreement made in 2000, Venezuela continued in 2005 to supply Cuba with approximately 75,000 barrels of oil per day on highly favorable terms. Cuba paid for much of the cost of the fuel by stationing in Venezuela 20,000 Cuban physicians, nurses, and dentists who provided health care in poor Venezuelan communities.

Offshore oil discovery. Two Canadian energy companies, Perbercan and Sherritt International, confirmed in early 2005 that they had discovered sizable oil deposits in Cuban waters. Oil from these reserves, estimated at 100 million barrels, was expected to begin flowing in 2006.

Cuban entertainers defect. In July 2005, U.S. authorities granted asylum to 50 Cuban performers, comprising one of the largest en masse Cuban defections under Communist rule. The performers, appearing nightly at resorts in Las Vegas, Nevada, had requested asylum in November 2004.

Preparedness pays off. Cuba sustained substantial storm damage during the unusually active 2005 hurricane season. In July, Hurricane Dennis struck the island's south coast with winds of 145 miles per hour (233 kilometer per hour) and heavy rains, inflicting $1.4 billion in damage and leaving 17 dead. Analysts attributed the relatively small number of hurricane-related fatalities to preparedness measures, which included the evacuation of more than 1 million Cubans in Dennis's path. ■ Nathan A. Haverstock

See also **Latin America; Venezuela; Weather.**

Cyprus. See Middle East.

Czech Republic. Prime Minister Stanislav Gross resigned on April 25, 2005, ending a months-long political crisis triggered by a personal scandal. In January, the Czech media broke a story that Gross in 1999 had bought a luxury apartment beyond his means. Gross attempted to explain how he obtained the money to buy the apartment, but his explanations failed to convince many of his associates in the government or Transparency International, a Berlin-based organization devoted to combatting governmental and institutional corruption. Upon receiving Gross's resignation, Czech President Vaclav Klaus named Jiri Paroubek prime minister. Paroubek, a minister in Gross's Cabinet and member of the Social Democrats, held Gross's three-party ruling coalition together through 2005.

Analysts questioned whether Paroubek's government would be able to complete reforms designed to bring the Czech Republic in line with economic targets set by the European Union (EU), which the country had joined in 2004. An ongoing disagreement between President Klaus and Paroubek's ruling coalition over the proper role of the EU complicated the Czech Republic's position within the European association. Klaus, a member of the opposition Civic Democratic Party and an acknowledged "Euroskeptic," frequently criticized the EU.

In June 2005, debate over the EU heated up when voters in France and the Netherlands, two of the organization's founding member nations, rejected the proposed EU constitution in referendums. President Klaus then advocated abandoning the EU draft constitution, while Paroubek proposed postponing the issue until 2007.

Pension reform. The Czech parliament in September 2005 raised the retirement age from 55 to 65, to go into effect in 2027. Other reforms were considered, including creation of a reserve fund to handle future payouts. Analysts predicted that the pension system would be swamped in about 20 years by a high ratio of retirees to working-age people.

Economic growth in the Czech Republic continued at a rate of better than 4 percent during 2005, economists reported, comparing favorably to the 4.4-percent rate registered in 2004. Unemployment continued to decline from a February 2004 high of 10.9 percent to 8.8 percent in September 2005.

Foreign policy. In 2005, the Czech Republic maintained troops in NATO peacekeeping missions in Afghanistan and Kosovo and in United States-led peacekeeping operations in Iraq. In August, Czech troops took over command of the center multinational brigade in Kosovo for one year.   ■ Sharon L. Wolchik

See also **Europe.**

Dallas voters overwhelmingly rejected a proposal on May 7, 2005, that would have greatly increased the governing powers of the city's mayor. The proposal—called the strong mayor proposition—would have changed the structure of Dallas's city-manager form of government. Under that system, the mayor has relatively few powers and the day-to-day running of the government is delegated to a professional city manager hired by the city council.

Dallas Mayor Laura Miller endorsed the proposal, arguing that an expansion of mayoral powers would reduce government inefficiency. The measure drew strong opposition from city council members, who feared it would strip the council of much of its governing powers, and from African American leaders, who were angered when Miller referred to the city's first black police chief as "an idiot" during a debate on the proposition. In November, voters defeated a modified version of the proposition.

Bribery probe. The Federal Bureau of Investigation (FBI) launched a corruption probe in August that focused on several Dallas City Council members and a member of the Dallas City Plan Commission. FBI agents investigated whether city officials accepted bribes from real estate developers in return for support for construction projects and tax incentives.

Downtown development. In August, the Dallas City Council unanimously approved a plan to redevelop nine vacant downtown office towers, including the Mercantile Bank complex. The City Council agreed to subsidize the project by providing $70 million in incentives to Forest City Enterprises, a Cleveland-based company that will develop the property into residential high-rises with retail space on the lower floors. The dilapidated bank complex, which was built in the early 1940's and had been vacant since the late 1980's and had become a symbol of the economic decline of downtown Dallas.

Love Field battle. Dallas-based Southwest Airlines intensified its efforts in 2005 to urge the United States Congress to repeal the Wright Amendment, which restricts airlines serving Dallas Love Field to routes within Texas and adjacent states. The law was enacted in 1979 to protect the just completed Dallas-Fort Worth International Airport from competition from the older but more convenient Love Field. In May 2005, Southwest launched an advertising campaign blasting the amendment. In September, proponents of the amendment countered with advertisements calling for Southwest Airlines to begin service at Dallas-Fort Worth International, where there are no flight restrictions.

Performing arts center. The Dallas Center for the Performing Arts Foundation broke ground in November on a new arts complex in the downtown Dallas Arts District. Plans for the new center included an opera house, a theater, a performance hall for dance, and an outdoor stage. The foundation planned to raise more than 90 percent of the cost of the $275-million project from private donors. In September, the Dallas City Council agreed to pay $2.5 million annually to maintain the center, which is scheduled for completion in 2009.

Hurricane Katrina. Dallas provided shelter to more than 25,000 people displaced by Hurricane Katrina, which struck Alabama, Louisiana, and Mississippi in August 2005. Tens of thousands of evacuees were sheltered in the Dallas Convention Center and Reunion Arena, the former home of the Dallas Mavericks basketball team, while relief agencies sought temporary housing for the storm victims. The Dallas Independent School District registered approximately 1,900 students from areas devastated by the hurricane.

Homeless Center. Voters approved a proposal in November authorizing $23.8 million in bonds to fund a homeless assistance center in downtown Dallas. The center will provide mental health and substance abuse counseling, medical treatment, and job training to more than 6,000 homeless people.   ■ Henry Tatum

See also **City; Disasters: A Special Report.**

Dance. Revivals of some of the masterpieces of the last century highlighted the world of dance in 2005. New York City-based American Ballet Theater (ABT) mounted a celebration of Michel Fokine, a choreographer whose ballets are rarely performed even though he was the major choreographer for Serge Diaghilev's legendary Ballets Russes in the early 1900's. Fokine composed more than 60 one-act ballets between 1905 and 1942. The dance and scenery in his ballets merge with the mood and drama of the music to create a powerful theater event.

ABT, which staged Fokine's *Les Sylphides* and *Specter de la Rose* in 2004, made a full-evening tribute to Fokine when it added *Petrouchka* and *Polovtsian Dances* to its repertory on Feb. 4, 2005, at the Kennedy Center for the Performing Arts in Washington, D.C. The remarkably varied program —ranging from the lyricism of *Les Sylphides* (music by Chopin) to the powerful dramatic impact of *Petrouchka* (to a commissioned score by Igor Stravinsky)—was a success, though many critics complained that *Polovtsian Dances,* with its faux-barbaric style, was a bit dated.

In performances at New York's City Center in October and November, ABT rolled out even more great works from the past—including Agnes de Mille's iconic piece of Americana, *Rodeo* (1942); Kurt Jooss's *The Green Table* (1932), a famous anti-

war ballet; and Twyla Tharp's *In the Upper Room* (1986), a galvanic spectacle driven by a score by Philip Glass.

A revival of Frederick Ashton's full-length *Sylvia,* to the score by Leo Delibes, was a centerpiece of ABT's 2005 summer season at the Metropolitan Opera House at Lincoln Center in New York City. Ashton created *Sylvia* in 1952 for the Royal Ballet in London, when the great British ballerina Margot Fonteyn, who danced the heroine, was at her peak. The ballet was dropped from the repertory in the 1960's. Christopher Newton staged the revival in 2005 for the Royal Ballet, as well as for ABT. The ballet is a meeting of the minds between Ashton's delicate footwork and the refinement of the French music.

The Martha Graham Company brought back Graham's *Deaths and Entrances* (1943) during its two-week run in April 2005 at the New York City Center. Graham, who pioneered the modern dance movement in the 20th century, often used dance to interpret the feelings of women. *Deaths and Entrances,* considered one of Graham's most mysterious works, is ostensibly about the Brontë sisters (three British novelists who lived in the 1800's), but it is actually about the relationships between three women as they remember their past, memories triggered by ordinary objects such as a sea shell or a vase.

Don Quixote, a full-length ballet by legendary choreographer George Balanchine, was revived by Suzanne Farrell for a week in June 2005 at the Kennedy Center. Farrell created the central dance role of Dulcinea at its premiere by the New York City Ballet in 1965, with Balanchine himself playing the Don. That Balanchine should make a very rare appearance as a performer was seen at the time as a measure of his love for Farrell, who some consider to be Balanchine's ideal ballerina. Her revival of the ballet in 2005 was a sentimental as well as an artistic occasion. Working largely from memory, Farrell staged the ballet using dancers from her own Suzanne Farrell Ballet and from the Toronto-based National Ballet of Canada, which will dance *Don Quixote* on its own in 2006.

Critics have long considered *Don Quixote* to be one of Balanchine's more unusual works. It has as much mime as dancing and is an explicitly personal statement about man's need for an ideal love.

The Kirov Ballet from St. Petersburg, Russia, in October 2005 brought Konstantin Sergeyev's 1962 production of *Sleeping Beauty* to the Dorothy Chandler Pavilion in Los Angeles; Zellerbach Auditorium in Berkeley, California; and the Detroit Opera House. Diana Vishneva, a soloist ballerina with Kirov since 1996 who created a sensation when she danced with ABT as the principal ballerina in the summer of 2005, danced in the role of Princess Aurora.

Moscow's Bolshoi Ballet toured the United States in 2005, performing rechoreographed versions of old ballets. Pierre Lacotte modeled his *The Pharaoh's Daughter* on Marius Petipa's masterpiece of 1862, while artistic director Alexei Ratmansky transformed *The Bright Stream* from a heavy-handed hymn to farm laborers, reflecting the era of Soviet Realism in which the ballet was made, into a sparkling farce about mixed-up pairs of lovers. The Bolshoi also performed *Don Quixote* and Yuri Grigorovich's 1968 *Spartacus,* a quintessentially Soviet work celebrating the gladiator-turned-revolutionary in Imperial Rome. After a two-week season in July 2005 at the Metropolitan Opera in New York City, the Bolshoi traveled to the Mann Center for the Performing Arts in Philadelphia; Wolf Trap in Vienna, Virginia; and the Orange County Performing Arts Center in Costa Mesa, California.

The San Francisco Ballet inaugurated a new dance festival in Paris, called Paris Summer Dance. The festival took place in July outdoors in the courtyard of an imposing building from the 1700's, with seating capacity of 2,000. Helgi Tomasson, artistic director of the troupe, marked the occasion in high style by commissioning three new works. Paul Taylor made *Spring Rounds*. Lar Lubovitch composed a jazzy piece to music by Dave Brubeck. Using composers ranging from Bach to John Cage, Christopher Wheeldon made *Quaternary,* depicting the four seasons. Wheeldon's ballet received the most praise, and he also won top honors for a ballet he premiered in January for the New York City Ballet during its winter season at the New York State Theater in New York City.

Masters of African-American Choreography premiered at the Kennedy Center for a week in April. A total of 17 companies performed 24 works that spanned 63 years of dance. Among the highlights was Katherine Dunham's *Choros,* from 1944, danced by the Cleo Parker Robinson Dance Ensemble of Denver, Colorado. *Choros* knits together primary elements of ceremonial African dance with techniques of modern dance. Michael Kaiser, president of the Kennedy Center, called the festival the "most important modern dance project in the history of the Kennedy Center."

Dudley Williams, the long-standing star of the Alvin Ailey American Dance Theater of New York City, gave his farewell performance on May 8, 2005, at the New Jersey Performing Arts Center in Newark. At 66, he was one of the oldest dancers to still be working with a major company.

Karen Kain, former ballerina of the National Ballet of Canada, was named its new artistic director in June, replacing James Kudelka.

■ Nancy Goldner

DEATHS

in 2005 included those listed below, who were Americans unless otherwise indicated.

Adams, Don (Donald James Yarmy) (1926–September 25), comedian who played Maxwell Smart on "Get Smart," the 1960's TV James Bond spoof.

Adams, Mason (Mason Abrams) (1919–April 26), character actor who was best known as the managing editor on the TV series "Lou Grant."

Albert, Eddie (1906–May 26), actor who appeared in more than 100 films, including *Roman Holiday* (1953) and *Oklahoma!* (1955), but was best known as a befuddled big city lawyer-turned-farmer in the TV situation comedy "Green Acres."

Alderson, Samuel W. (1914–February 11), inventor of crash test dummies, which helped revolutionize automobile safety.

Alexander, Shana (1925–June 23), columnist who was teamed with James Kilpatrick on the Point/Counterpoint segment of "60 Minutes," a political exchange mercilessly spoofed on "Saturday Night Live."

Anderson, Alfred (1896–November 21), British World War I veteran who was the last survivor of the "Christmas Truce" of 1914, when British and German troops spontaneously laid down their arms and together celebrated the holiday.

Anderson, Jack (1922–December 17), investigative columnist who topped President Richard Nixon's enemies list and broke the Iran-Contra story.

Atkinson, Ted (1916–May 5), Canadian-born Hall of Fame jockey who in 1945 became the first rider to win more than $1 million in a single season.

Bahcall, John N. (1934–August 17), astrophysicist and father of neutrino astronomy. Bahcall calculated the expected neutrino output from the sun, which led to new insights into astrophysics and the most basic forces of nature.

Ba Jin (Li Yaotang) (1904–October 17), Chinese author whose novels, including the classic *Family* (1931), explore the evils of pre-Revolutionary China. Ba survived the Cultural Revolution to be hailed as a great literary icon.

Baldry, "Long" John (1941–July 21), influential British-born blues-rock singer who helped start the careers of Rod Stewart, Mick Jagger, Charlie Watts, Elton John, Jimmy Paige of the Yardbirds and Led Zeppelin, and Jack Bruce and Ginger Baker of Cream.

Bancroft, Anne (1931–June 6), versatile actress who won Tony and Academy awards for her interpretation of Annie Sullivan in the stage and film productions of *The Miracle Worker* and who garnered even greater fame as the predatory Mrs. Robinson in *The Graduate*.

Barker, Ronnie (1929–October 3), English actor who was half of the comedic team the Two Ronnies, on the long-running British variety program.

Bel Geddes, Barbara (1922–August 10), actress who achieved her greatest fame as Miss Ellie on the TV series "Dallas" but enjoyed a distinguished film career and originated the role of Maggie the Cat in Tennessee Williams's *Cat on a Hot Tin Roof.*

Bellow, Saul (1915–April 5), Canadian-born novelist who was awarded the 1977 Nobel Prize for redefining the scope of the American novel. See Portrait at Literature.

Anne Bancroft, actress

Benenson, Peter (1921–February 25), British lawyer who, in 1961, founded Amnesty International, launching a worldwide citizen's movement to expose and confront government injustice.

Benson, Renaldo "Obie" (1936–July 1), singer and songwriter who provided the bass and much of the choreography for The Four Tops.

Berenstain, Stan (1923–November 26), author and artist who, with his wife Jan Berenstain, created the highly popular Berenstain Bears books.

Best, George (1946–November 25), Northern Ireland soccer player who was the sport's first iconic star and who in 1968 was named British Footballer of the Year and European Player of the Year.

Bethe, Hans Albrecht (1906–March 6), German-born physicist and prominent champion of nuclear disarmament who received the 1967 Nobel Prize for his discovery of how some stars fuse hydrogen into helium, releasing nuclear energy that becomes heat and light.

Bochner, Lloyd (1924–October 29), suave, Canadian-born character actor who made hundreds of film and television appearances, most notably as Chambers in the famous "Twilight Zone" episode *To Serve Man* (1962).

Bond, Ruth Clement (1904–October 24), educator and civic leader whose designs for what came to be called the "TVA quilts" transformed the utilitarian bed cover into avant-garde art.

Bond, Tommy (1926–September 24), child actor who played Butch the bully in the 1930's movie serial "Our Gang," later rechristened "The Little Rascals" for television.

Sandra Dee, actress

Booth, Wayne (1921–October 9), scholar and author whose 1961 textbook *The Rhetoric of Fiction* and 1974 textbook *The Rhetoric of Irony* remain standards of literary criticism.

Brown, Clarence "Gatemouth" (1924–September 10), guitarist, fiddler, and singer who synthesized blues, Cajun, country, jazz, and R&B in what he called "American music, Texas-style."

Brown, Oscar, Jr. (1926–May 29), singer, actor, and playwright whose blend of entertainment and social consciousness celebrated African American life.

Cabrera Infante, Guillermo (1929–February 21), Cuban poet and novelist who was one of the most influential literary figures of Latin America.

Callaghan, James (1912– March 26), British prime minister whose Labour government (1976–1979) was beset by strikes that nearly shut down the country during the winter of 1978–1979.

Cappuccilli, Piero (1929–July 12), Italian "Prince of Baritones" who was notable for his bel canto repertory and world famous for mastering 17 Verdi baritone roles during a 36-year career.

Carson, Johnny (1925–January 23), droll, amiable comedian who dominated late-night television for 30 years. See Portrait at Television.

Charles, Dame Eugenia (1919–September 6), "Iron Lady" of Dominica who spearheaded that country's independence from the United Kingdom and served as prime minister from 1980 to 1985.

Chibitty, Charles (1921–July 20), the last of the Comanche "code talkers" who like the Navajo code talkers used their native language to transmit messages for the Allies during World War II.

Chisholm, Shirley (1924–January 1), educator turned politician who was the first African American woman elected to the U.S. House of Representatives and the first to wage a serious presidential campaign.

George Best, soccer player

Clements, Vassar (1928–August 16), fiddler of stylistic virtuosity whose range extended from bluegrass and country to jazz and classical.

Cochran, Johnnie L., Jr. (1937–March 29), flamboyant and charismatic attorney who became famous in 1995 for defending O. J. Simpson.

Conroy, Frank (1936–April 6), author of the classic memoir *Stop-Time* (1967) who influenced a generation of writers as head of the Writers' Workshop at the University of Iowa.

Cook, Robin (1946–August 6), British foreign secretary who resigned from Tony Blair's Cabinet in 2003 to protest the U.S.-led war in Iraq.

Creeley, Robert (1926–March 30), influential poet who was one of the founders of the Black Mountain movement of the 1950's and played a major roll in the American literary avant-garde.

Crist, Ray (1900–July 25), chemist who contributed to the creation of the first atomic bomb and who later did research on how toxic metals could be extracted from the environment.

Cummings, Constance (1910–November 23), actress whose long, varied career stretched from playing opposite Harold Lloyd in *Movie Crazy* (1932) to portraying Martha in a 1964 London production of *Who's Afraid of Virginia Woolf?*

Cutler, Lloyd N. (1917–May 8), lawyer and Washington, D.C., insider who served as counsel to Presidents Jimmy Carter and Bill Clinton.

Dancer, Stanley (1927–September 8), harness racing's most successful trainer and breeder who was the sport's only driver to ever win three triple crowns for 3 year olds.

Dantzig, George Bernard (1914–May 13), mathematician and "father of linear programming" who created an algorithm that revolutionized complex business and military planning, scheduling, and network design.

Davenport, Guy (1927–January 4), author, poet, and scholar who was renowned for his prose style and literary criticism, particularly *The Geography of the Imagination* (1981).

Davis, Ossie (Raiford Chatman Davis) (1917–February 4), actor, director, producer, and writer who, with wife Ruby Dee, was a social advocate and voice for racial justice and equality.

Dee, Sandra (Alexandra Zuck) (1942–February 19), film actress who is best remembered for her portrayals of teen-agers dealing with the

James Doohan, actor

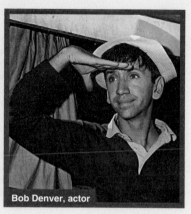

Bob Denver, actor

frustrations of adolescent romance in three 1959 movies—*Gidget, A Summer Place*, and *Imitation of Life*.

Delli Colli, Tonino (1923–August 17), Italian cinematographer whose masterful use of light made him a favorite of film directors.

Delorean, John (1925–March 20), controversial General Motors executive who developed the Delorean sports car, now a collector's item.

Deloria, Vine, Jr. (1933–November 13), author whose books on the Native American experience, including *Custer Died for Your Sins* (1969), demythologized American Indian culture.

De los Angeles, Victoria (Victoria Gomez Cima) (1923–January 14), Spanish soprano whose lyrical, expressive voice in such roles as Mimi in *La Boheme*, Violetta in *La Traviata*, and the title role in *Carmen* made her a mainstay of opera houses in the 1950's and 1960's.

Denker, Arnold (1914–January 2), "Dean of American Chess" who was U.S. champion in 1944, 1945, and 1946 and who competed until 2002.

Dennis, Clarence (1909–July 11), physician who developed the heart-lung bypass machine as well as other mechanical heart devices that extended the life spans of millions of people.

Denver, Bob (1935–September 2), actor who found fame as Maynard G. Krebs on the TV sitcom "The Many Loves of Dobie Gillis" and rerun immortality as the hapless Gilligan on "Gilligan's Island."

Diamond, David (1915–June 13), symphonic composer whose expressive, lyrical music underwent a renaissance late in the 20th century.

Doll, Sir Richard (1912–July 24), British physician whose studies linked smoking to lung cancer, emphysema, heart disease, and other disorders.

Doohan, James (1920–July 20), Canadian-born actor who played Scotty on the original "Star Trek" television series and inspired the catch-phrase "Beam me up, Scotty."

Dos Santos, Lucia de Jesus (Lucia Abobora) (1907–February 13), Portuguese Roman Catholic nun who was one of the three children who told of seeing the Virgin Mary in 1917 in Fatima.

Drucker, Peter (1909–November 11), pioneering business consultant whose emphasis on training and development influenced generations of corporate managers.

Duisenberg, Willem (1935–July 31), Dutch banker who was called the "father of the euro" for presiding over the European currency's introduction in 2002.

Dworkin, Andrea (1946–April 9), radical feminist whose scathing writings and tireless campaign against sexual violence and pornography cast her as a provocateur of the women's movement.

Eberhart, Richard (1904–June 9), Pulitzer Prize-winning poet who was critically acclaimed for his lyric verse.

Edwards, Ralph (1913–November 16), radio and early television host who created "Truth or Consequences" and "This Is Your Life."

Eisner, Will (1917–January 3), comic-book artist who created the Spirit, a hero without superpowers, and produced the first graphic novel, *A Contract with God*.

Eyadema, Gnassingbe (1935–February 5), president of Togo and Africa's longest serving head of state who kept an iron grip on power after engineering a coup in 1967.

Fahd of Saudi Arabia (1923–August 1), king who modernized Saudi Arabia while guiding it through economic, political, and religious upheavals.

Fiedler, John (1925–June 25), character actor whose high-pitched voice made him a standout as Piglet in Walt Disney's Winnie-the-Pooh films.

Fitzgerald, Geraldine (1913–July 17), Irish actress whose long film career included *Dark Victory* (1939), *Wuthering Heights* (1939), and *Arthur* (1981).

Fletcher, Arthur (1924–July 12), civil rights advocate and "father of affirmative action" who served as an adviser to Presidents Richard Nixon, Gerald Ford, and Ronald Reagan.

Floren, Myron (1919–July 23), accordion virtuoso whom Lawrence Welk featured weekly on the folksy bandleader's long-running television show.

Foote, Shelby (1916–June 27), novelist, historian, and author of the critically acclaimed, three-volume *The Civil War: A Narrative*. His appearance in Ken Burns's Civil War documentary left

Foote a highly reluctant celebrity.

Forman, James (1928–January 10), civil rights pioneer who helped coordinate demonstrations in Selma and Birmingham, Alabama, and the 1963 march on Washington, D.C.

Fowles, John (1926–November 5), British novelist whose wide-ranging works, including *The Magus* (1965) and *The French Lieutenant's Woman* (1969), achieved both critical and popular success.

Franklin, Gretchen (1911–July 11), British character actress who found fame as the dog-loving busybody Ethel Skinner on the BBC soap opera "EastEnders."

Freas, F. K. (1922–January 2), artist who created myriad images of aliens for science-fiction magazines and books; the Alfred E. Neuman face for *Mad* magazine; and the shoulder patch for Skylab 1 astronauts.

Fry, Christopher (Christopher Fry Harris) (1907–June 30), English playwright who crafted highly successful verse plays for John Gielgud, Laurence Oliver, and Vivien Leigh and whose best-known

Geraldine Fitzgerald, actress

Percy Heath, musician

work, *The Lady's Not for Burning* (1948), endures.

Giulini, Carlo Maria (1914–June 14), Italian conductor who led Milan's LaScala opera company during the 1950's and later inspired audiences with his performances with the London, Chicago, Vienna, and Los Angeles symphony orchestras.

Gorshin, Frank (1933–May 17), master impressionist and character actor who played the Riddler on "Batman," the campy 1960's television series.

Grant, Joe (1908–May 6), Walt Disney studio artist and writer who designed the queen-witch in *Snow White and the Seven Dwarfs* (1937), co-authored *Dumbo* (1941), and created the storyline for *Lady and the Tramp* (1955).

Gray, L. Patrick, III (1916–July 6), FBI director whose allegiance to President Richard Nixon during Watergate investigations resulted ultimately in Gray's resignation.

Griffin, Jimmy (1943–January 11), a founding member of the soft-rock group Bread who helped write the Academy Award-winning song "For All We Know" and 10 other Top 20 hits.

Grunwald, Henry A. (1922–February 26), refugee from Nazi-controlled Austria who upon arriving in New York City rose from copy boy at *Time* magazine to managing editor and finally editor in chief of all Time Inc. publications.

Guerrero, Lalo (Edwardo Guerrero, Jr.) (1916–March 16), barrio singer and composer whose wide-ranging, bilingual songs of the bicultural experience earned him the title "father of Chicano music."

Haas, Karl (1913–February 6), German-born concert pianist whose long-running "Adventures in Good Music" (1959-2003) was once the most listened to classical music radio program.

Hackworth, David (1931–May 4), retired U.S. Army colonel and most highly decorated veteran of the Vietnam War who later became an outspoken critic of the war.

Hagedorn, Horace (1915–January 31), advertising executive who built a major corporation through the development and promotion of Miracle-Gro.

Hagen, Kevin (1928–July 9), character actor who capped a career playing villains with the role of kindly Doc Baker on "Little House on the Prairie."

Hallaren, Mary A. (1907–February 13), colonel who led the first battalion of the Women's Army Corps to serve in Europe and commanded the corps during its integration into the regular Army in 1948.

Hariri, Rafik (1944–February 14), former prime minister of Lebanon who helped rebuild the country after a devastating civil war.

Haver, June (June Stovenour) (1926–July 4), blond star of 1940's movie musicals who gave up her career to enter a convent only later to marry actor Fred MacMurray.

Heath, Sir Edward (1916–July 17), British prime minister (1970-1974) who led the United Kingdom into what is now the European Union.

Heath, Percy (1923–April 28), bassist who was the last surviving member of the legendary Modern Jazz Quartet.

Helms, Chet (1942–June 25), rock promoter and "father of the Summer of Love" who founded Big Brother and the Holding Company and promoted Janis Joplin, the Grateful Dead, and Jefferson Airplane.

Philip Johnson, architect

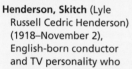

Hildegarde, nightclub chanteuse

George Kennan, diplomat

Henderson, Skitch (Lyle Russell Cedric Henderson) (1918–November 2), English-born conductor and TV personality who led the "Tonight" show house band in the 1950's and 1960's and founded the New York Pops orchestra.

Herman, George (1920–February 8), CBS news correspondent who was the first reporter to file sound-and-film reports from abroad and who moderated "Face the Nation."

Hildegarde (Hildegarde Sell) (1906–July 29), chanteuse whom Walter Winchell dubbed "the incomparable" and whom cabaret star Bobby Short described as having "the slickest night-club act of all time."

Hilleman, Maurice (1919–April 11), microbiologist who is credited with saving millions of lives through the vaccines he developed for chicken-pox, Haemophilus influenzae, hepatitis A, hepatitis B, measles, meningitis, mumps, and pneumonia.

Holmes, Ray (1914–June 27), British World War II fighter pilot who, in one of the most celebrated episodes during the Battle of Britain, prevented a direct hit on Buckingham Palace by ramming a German bomber, slicing off its tail.

Horn, Shirley (1934–October 20), pianist and singer, known for her cool, unhurried style, whom critics ranked as one of the greatest jazz singers.

Hunter, Bob (1941–May 2), Canadian journalist who was a founder and president of Greenpeace, the international environmental group that initially challenged nuclear testing.

Hunter, Evan (Salvatore Lombino) (1926–July 6), novelist—*The Blackboard Jungle* (1954)—and screenwriter—*The Birds* (1963)—who is credited with inventing the police procedural in his 87th Street Precinct novels written under the name Ed McBain.

Hussey, Ruth (1911–April 19), film actress of the 1940's who is best remembered as the photographer in *The Philadelphia Story* (1940), for which she was nominated for an Academy Award.

Iakovos, Geron (Demetruis A. Coucouzis) (1911–April 10), Turkish born clergyman who served as archbishop of the Greek Orthodox Archdiocese in North and South America from 1959 to 1996 and is credited with leading the church into mainstream American religious life.

Janeway, Elizabeth (1913–January 15), best-selling novelist of the 1940's whose later sociological and feminist writings included *Man's World, Woman's Place* (1971).

Jennings, Peter (1938–August 7), Canadian-born television journalist who capped a distinguished career as a foreign correspondent with a 27-year stint as ABC's chief news anchor.

John Paul II (Karol Wojtyla) (1920–April 2), pope who reshaped the Roman Catholic Church during a 26-year reign that was the third longest papacy in history. See Deaths: A Special Report.

Johnson, John H. (1918–August 8), magazine publisher and entrepreneur who became one of the nation's most influential and wealthy African Americans. See Portrait at Magazine.

Johnson, Philip (1906–January 25), architect whose advocacy of new styles—from "glass box" Modernism to Postmodernism to Deconstructivism—made him a highly influential tastemaker.

Keeling, Charles D. (1928–June 20), Scripps Institution of Oceanography scientist whose highly precise measurements showing steadily rising amounts of carbon dioxide in the air set off concerns of global warming.

Kempner, Nan (1930–July 3), socialite and clotheshorse who was famous for her wit, self-deprecating humor, and charm as a hostess.

Kennan, George F. (1904–March 17), academic and diplomat who was the intellectual force behind the U.S. Cold War policy of containment of the Soviet Union.

Kennedy, Rosemary (1918–January 7), oldest sister of President John F. Kennedy and the inspiration for the Special Olympics.

Khachiyan, Leonid (1952–April 29), Russian-born mathematician whose groundbreaking 1979 theorem greatly advanced linear programming, a mathematical approach to resource allocation.

Kilby, Jack (1923–June 23), electrical engineer who was awarded a Nobel Prize for his invention of the integrated circuit, which provided the technical foundation for microchip cell phones, computers, DVD players, and most modern appliances.

Langford, Francis (1913–July 11), singer who popularized "I'm in the Mood for Love," appeared in movie musicals—including *Yankee Doodle Dandy* (1942)—and traveled widely with Bob Hope entertaining troops during World War II.

LeDoux, Chris (1948–March 9), rodeo champion who achieved his greatest fame as a singer and composer of songs about life on the rodeo circuit.

Lee, Eugene (Eurgene Less) (1933–October 16), child actor who played Porky in the 1930's movie serial "Our Gang," later rechristened "The Little Rascals" for television.

Lehman, Ernest (1915–July 2), novelist and screenwriter who wrote such classic films as *Sabrina* (1954), *Sweet Smell of Success* (1957), *North by Northwest* (1959), and *The Sound of Music* (1965).

Lester, William (1908–March 12), mechanical engineer who invented an automatic molding machine that launched the plastics industry.

MacLane, Saunders (1909–April 14), mathematician who was the cocreator of category theory, an abstract branch of algebra that has applications in computer science.

Martin, Barney (1923–March 21), New York City police detective turned actor who most famously played Jerry Seinfeld's father on "Seinfeld."

Martin, Jimmy (1927–May 14), virtuoso guitarist who was known as the "king of bluegrass."

Mayo, Virginia (Virginia Clara Jones) (1920–January 17), film actress who most memorably played erring wives in *The Best Years of Our Lives* (1946) and *White Heat* (1949).

McCarthy, Eugene (1916–December 10), Minnesota senator whose opposition to the Vietnam War led him to run for the Democratic nomination for president in 1968, upending incumbent Lyndon Johnson's plans for reelection.

McCormick, Pat (1927–July 30), veteran comedian and comedy writer who was Johnny Carson's frequent guest on "The Tonight Show."

McKibbon, Al (1919–August 5), bassist who played with Dizzy Gillespie's big band, pianist George Shearing, Thelonious Monk, and Miles Davis and later backed Ella Fitzgerald and Frank Sinatra.

Merchant, Ismail (Ismail Noormohamed Abdul Rehman) (1936–May 25), Indian-born filmmaker who with director James Ivory produced sumptuously staged and highly successful period pictures, including *A Room with a View* (1985), *Howard's End* (1992), and *The Remains of the Day* (1993).

Messick, Dale (Dalia Messick) (1906–April 5), cartoonist whose spunky "Brenda Starr, Reporter," launched in 1940, gained its female creator entry into the all-male world of newspaper comic strips.

Mikan, George (1924–June 2), Minneapolis Lakers center who was the first real star of professional basketball and led the Lakers to seven championships from 1946 to 1956.

Miller, Arthur (1915–February 10), playwright whose *All My Sons* (1947), *Death of a Salesman* (1949), and *The Crucible* (1953) place him in the first rank of American dramatists. See Portrait at Theater.

George Mikan, basketball star

John Mills, actor

Prince Rainier of Monaco

Mills, Sir John (1908–April 23), British actor who portrayed an extraordinary range of roles in a career that spanned more than 75 years of stage, screen, and television appearances. Mills was the father of actresses Juliet and Hayley Mills.

Montana, Allison "Tootie" (1922–June 27), New Orleans Mardi Gras Indian tribe big chief whose elaborate, handmade costumes were displayed in museums and whose life was documented on film.

Moog, Robert (1934–August 21), engineer who invented the Moog Synthesizer, an instrument that transformed electric currents into sound and changed popular music.

Moore, Constance (1920–September 16), singer-actress who is best remembered for playing opposite Buster Crabbe in the "Buck Rogers" serial.

Morita, Pat (Noriyuki Morita) (1932–November 24), actor who played Arnold on the TV show "Happy Days" and taught a boy martial arts through household chores in *The Karate Kid* (1984).

Morris, Howie (1919–May 21), raspy-voiced comedian who appeared on Sid Caesar's "Your Show of Shows" and "The Andy Griffith Show."

Morrison, Philip (1915–April 22), physicist who helped assemble the first atomic bomb and who subsequently spent the rest of his life campaigning against such weapons.

Motley, Constance Baker (1921–September 28), lawyer who was involved in nearly every important civil rights case of the 1950's and 1960's, including desegregation of schools, buses, and lunch counters, and who was the first African American woman to serve as a federal judge.

Mowlam, Marjorie "Mo" (1949–August 19), British politician who while serving as the Northern Ireland minister helped negotiate the Good Friday peace agreement of 1998.

Narayanan, Kocheril Raman (1920–November 9), former Indian president who overcame centuries of prejudice to become the first Dalit, or "untouchable," to occupy high office in India.

Nelson, Gaylord (1916–July 3), senator (D., Wisconsin) and Earth Day founder who made air and water quality a national issue.

Nichols, Jack (1938–May 2), pioneer gay rights activist who cofounded the Mattachine Society, published the first gay newspaper in the United States, and successfully challenged the American Psychiatric Association to stop defining homosexuality as a mental illness.

North, Sheree (Dawn Bethel) (1933–November 4), actress whose early career as a blond sex symbol was eclipsed by years of excellent performances as a character actress in films and on television.

Nowak-Jezioranski, Jan (Zdislaw Jezioranski) (1913–January 27), World War II Polish underground fighter—the "Courier from Warsaw"—whose life-long struggle for a democratic Poland made him a national symbol of Polish patriotism.

Nye, Louis (1913–October 9), comedian and TV veteran whose "Hi-ho, Steverino" greeting for late-night television host Steve Allen became a catchphrase of the 1950's.

O'Brien, George H., Jr. (1926–March 11), U.S. Marine lieutenant who was awarded the Medal of Honor in 1952 for spearheading, while wounded, the capture of an enemy-held hill, which halted a North Korean drive for Seoul.

Owen, Mickey (1916–July 13), Brooklyn Dodgers catcher whose infamous dropped third strike helped cost the Dodgers the 1941 World Series against the Yankees.

Parks, Rosa (1913–October 24), African American activist whose refusal to give up her bus seat to a white man sparked the modern civil rights movement. See Portrait at Human rights.

Patten, Edward (1939–February 25), singer who sang both tenor and bass with Gladys Knight & the Pips.

Peck, M. Scott (1936–September 25), psychiatrist who helped launch the "self-help" book genre with *The Road Less Traveled* (1978), which sold some 10 million copies.

Perdue, Frank (1920–March 31), entrepreneur who transformed his father's backyard egg business into one of the world's largest chicken processing companies.

Perry, Elwood L. "Buck" (1915–August 12), angler who invented the Spoonplug lure and who is regarded as the father of structure fishing.

Proxmire, William (1915–December 15), former Wisconsin senator who crusaded against big

Richard Pryor, comedian

spending and government waste.

Pryor, Richard (1940–December 10), stand-up comedian and actor who mined his many personal demons to forge a unique brand of comedy that influenced a generation of comics.

Radcliffe, Ted (1902–August 11), Negro League baseball star whom Damon Runyon nicknamed "Double Duty" after seeing Radcliffe catch in the first game of a double header and pitch in the second.

Rainier III (1923–April 6), prince of Monaco who married an American movie star, Grace Kelly. Together they transformed a fading casino town into a modern steel-and-glass resort and attractive tax haven.

Raitt, John (1917–February 20), baritone who originated the roles of Billy Bigelow in *Carousel* and Sid Sorokin in the Broadway and film productions of *The Pajama Game*. Raitt was the father of blues singer Bonnie Raitt.

Ravenscroft, Thurl (1914–May 22), actor and singer with the Mellowmen, Norman Luboff Choir, and Johnny Mann singers who gave voice to Tony the Tiger's booming "They're Great" endorsement of Kellogg Frosted Flakes cereal.

Rehnquist, William H. (1924– September 3), chief justice of the United States Supreme Court who led a conservative judicial revolution during his 33-year tenure, a period that spanned the Watergate Scandal, the Clinton impeachment trial, and the contested 2000 presidential election.

Ricoeur, Paul (1913–May 20), French philosopher whose study of phenomenology—how a reality is shaped by personal perception of world events—reflected his own experiences in World War II German prison camps.

Rodino, Peter W. (1909–May 7), former congressman representing New Jersey who chaired the House Judiciary Committee hearings in 1974 that led to the resignation of President Richard M. Nixon.

Rossi, Jim (1936–September 3), hall of fame cyclist who won the U.S. national championship six times and competed in the 1956 and 1960 Olympics.

Rossner, Judith (1935–August 9), author of 10 novels, including the best-sellers *Looking for Mr. Goodbar* (1975) and *August* (1983).

Rotblat, Joseph (1908–August 31), Polish-born British physicist who was the only scientist to resign from the Manhattan Project on moral grounds and received the Nobel Peace Prize for his efforts to eliminate atomic weapons.

Rothschild, Dame Miriam (1908–January 20), self-taught British naturalist who was the world expert on fleas and promulgated the widespread planting of wildflowers across open spaces in England.

Russell, Nipsey (1924–October 2), comedian whose impromptu rhymes and topical one-liners made him a popular guest on TV talk and game shows in the 1970's.

Saikley, Charlie (1936–June 17), "Godfather of beach volleyball" who is credited with transforming a California pastime into an Olympic sport.

Sample, Johnny (1938?–April 25), former defensive back whose interception in Super Bowl III led to the New York Jets beating the Baltimore Colts in a stunning upset.

Saunders, Dame Cicely (1918–July 14), British medical social worker who founded the hospice movement, transforming the care and treatment of the terminally ill.

Schell, Maria (1926–April 26), Austrian-born actress who made more than 200 film and television appearances, in Europe and America, and was the sister of actor Maximilian Schell.

Schenkel, Chris (1923–September 11), television sportscaster in the 1950's, 1960's, and 1970's who was the voice of the Professional Bowlers Association tour until it was dropped by ABC in 1997.

Schiavo, Terri (1963–March 31), woman who was at the center of a years-long "right-to-die" court battle that divided a family and a nation.

William H. Rehnquist, chief justice of the U.S. Supreme Court

Joseph Rotblat, physicist

Max Schmeling, boxer

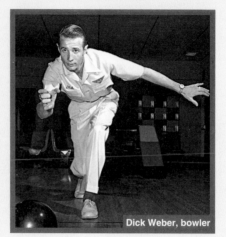

Dick Weber, bowler

Schmeling, Max (1905–February 2), German heavyweight boxing champion who unwittingly became a Nazi symbol of "Aryan supremacy" upon knocking out Joe Louis in 1936. In 1938, Louis knocked out Schmeling in what may be history's most famous bout.

Settle, Mary Lee (1918–September 27), novelist and travel book writer who was best known for the "Beulah Quintet," which began with the best-selling *O Beulah Land* (1956).

Sheard, Michael (1938–August 31), British character actor who portrayed Bronson on the British TV series "Grange Hill" and as Admiral Ozzel in *The Empire Strikes Back*.

Shibicky, Alex (1914–July 9), Canadian hockey player who was on the New York Rangers team that won the 1940 Stanley Cup and who is credited with using the first slap shot.

Short, Bobby (1924–March 21), premier cabaret singer and pianist whose pared renditions of standards, particularly by Cole Porter, epitomized urban sophistication and glamour.

Simon, Claude (1913–July 6), Madagascar-born French writer who received the Nobel Prize in literature in 1985 for a "deepened awareness of time in the depiction of the human condition" in his "nouveau roman" novels.

Simon, Danny (1918–July 26), television comedy writer—"Your Show of Shows," "Make Room for Daddy," "Diff'rent Strokes"—who claimed his greatest accomplishment was launching the careers of his brother, Neil Simon, and of Woody Allen.

Simon, Simone (1911–February 22), French film actress who was described as one of the great beauties of the French film industry in the 1930's and who became internationally known for her lead role in the 1942 thriller *Cat People*.

Sin, Cardinal Jaime (1928–June 21), former head of the Philippine Roman Catholic Church who was called the nation's "moral compass" and credited with playing a key role in the toppling of Presidents Ferdinand Marcos in 1986 and Joseph Estrada in 2001.

Smiley, Richard (1943–October 28), chemist who was awarded a Nobel Prize in 1996 for his role in the discovery of a new form of carbon, which he and colleagues named buckminsterfullerene, or buckyballs.

Smith, Jimmy (1928–February 8), musician known as "emperor of the Hammond organ" who reinvented the electric organ as a modern jazz instrument.

Spencer, John (1946–December 16), actor who played Leo McGarry on "The West Wing" series.

Stockdale, James B. (1923–July 5), vice admiral of the Navy and Medal of Honor recipient who was H. Ross Perot's running mate in the presidential election of 1992.

Stram, Hank (1923–July 4), National Football League coach who led the Kansas City Chiefs into a Super Bowl victory in 1970 and was inducted in the Hall of Fame in 2003 for such innovations as the "moving pocket," the "stack defense," and the "two tight-end offense."

Tange, Kenzo (1913–March 22), Japanese architect whose twin sports arenas for the 1964 Olympics in Tokyo placed Japanese culture back onto the world's stage; his boldly articulated reinforced concrete structures are credited with spawning "Brutalism."

Tantaquidgeon, Gladys (1899–November 1), venerable Mohegan medicine woman who was a 10th-generation descendant of Uncas, the famed Mohegan chief of the Pequot War (1636-1637).

Thompson, Hunter S. (1937–February 20), counterculture author who pioneered gonzo journalism in such works as *Hell's Angels: A Strange and Terrible Saga* (1966) and *Fear and Loathing in Las Vegas* (1972).

Toti, Andrew (1915–March 20), prolific inventor of an automated feather plucker that revolutionized the poultry industry; of vertical window blinds; of the "Mae West" flotation vest, which has saved an untold number of lives; and, with a partner, of the EndoFlex endotracheal tube to limit abrasive injury during surgery.

Vandross, Luther (1951–July 1), Grammy Award-winning R&B singer whose smooth, heartfelt style on 14 best-selling albums moved soul music into a more lush, romantic direction.

Vernon, John (1932–February 1), Canadian-born character actor who found fame as the humorless Dean Vernon Wormer attempting to impose order on chaos in *Animal House* (1976).

Voris, Roy "Butch" (1919–August 10), World War II ace who was the first squadron leader of the Blue Angels precision flying team.

Walsh, Kay (1911–April 16), English character actress who appeared in more than 50 films, including *In Which We Serve* (1942), *This Happy Breed* (1944), and *Oliver Twist* (1948)—all directed by her then-husband David Lean.

Warrick, Ruth (1916–January 15), actress who played Emily Norton Kane in Orson Welles's film *Citizen Kane* (1945) and Phoebe Tyler Wallingford on the soap opera "All My Children" for nearly 35 years.

Weber, Dick (1929–February 14), Professional Bowlers Association charter member who was named the best bowler of the 20th century.

Weizman, Ezer (1924–April 24), Israeli military leader and politician who built up the air force, helped arrange the country's first peace treaty with an Arab nation, and served as president from 1993 to 2000.

Westmoreland, William C. (1914–July 18), Army general and Vietnam veteran advocate who led U.S. forces in Vietnam from 1964 to 1968 and served as chief of staff from 1968 to 1972.

Wiesenthal, Simon (1908–September 20), Austrian Holocaust survivor who devoted his life to bringing more than 1,000 Nazi war ciminals, including Adolf Eichmann, to justice.

Wilson, August (1945–October 2), playwright who chronicled African American life in the 20th century in a 10-play cycle of enormous ambition. See Portrait at Theater.

Wilson, Earl (1934–April 23), baseball player who pitched for the Boston Red Sox and for the Detroit Tigers in the 1968 World Series.

Winchell, Paul (1922– June 24), ventriloquist, inventor, and children's TV show host ("The Paul Winchell-Jerry Mahoney Show") who later supplied voices for a number of animated features, including Tigger in Walt Disney's Winnie-the-Pooh series.

Wind, Herbert Warren (1916–May 30), dean of golf sportswriters who coined the term "Amen Corner" at the Augusta National.

Wise, Robert (1914–September 14), versatile film director who won Academy Awards for *West Side Story* (1961) and *The Sound of Music* (1965) and who edited the Orson Welles's classic *Citizen Kane* (1941).

Woode, Jimmy (1926–April 30), bassist who spent five years with the Duke Ellington band before immigrating to Europe, where he was a leading figure on the jazz scene for 40 years.

Woods, Rose Mary (1917–January 22), Richard M. Nixon's long-time secretary whose explanation for how 18½ minutes of a tape was accidentally erased placed her at the center of one of the great Watergate mysteries.

Woolley, Catherine (1904–July 23), author of 87 children's books, including the "Ginnie and Geneva" series, who also wrote under the pen name Jane Thayer.

Wright, Robert (1914–July 27), composer and lyricist who, with George Forest, transformed music by Edvard Grieg and Alexander Borodin into the Broadway hits *Song of Norway* (1944) and *Kismet* (1953).

Wright, Teresa (1918–March 6), only actress who was nominated for Academy Awards for each of her first three films—*The Little Foxes* (1941), *The Pride of the Yankees* (1942), and *Mrs. Miniver* (1942), for which she won the award for best supporting actress.

Wriston, Walter (1919–January 19), banker who transformed Citicorp into the world's largest bank and revolutionized how people handle money through the use of automatic teller machines.

Zhao Ziyang (1919–January 17), former general secretary of China's Communist Party who was stripped of power for supporting students protesting in Beijing's Tiananmen Square in 1989.

Bobby Short, cabaret performer

Robert Wise, film director

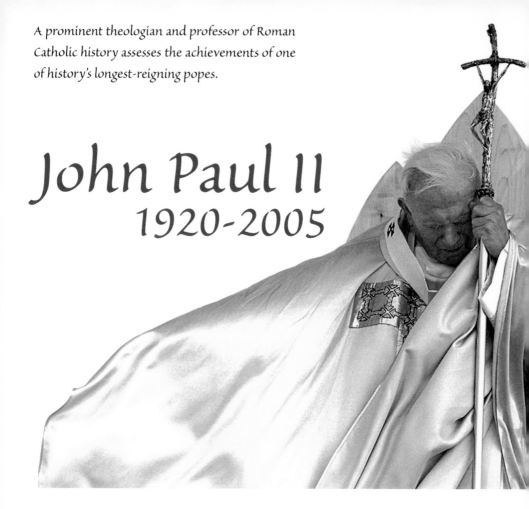

A prominent theologian and professor of Roman Catholic history assesses the achievements of one of history's longest-reigning popes.

John Paul II
1920-2005

By R. Scott Appleby

Pope John Paul II, who died on April 2, 2005, after enduring the most highly publicized protracted illness in history, will be remembered as one of the greatest popes of all time. Elected by the College of Cardinals on Oct. 16, 1978, as the 264th pope, successor to St. Peter (the first Bishop of Rome and the apostle Jesus chose to lead his church), John Paul II reigned for more than 26 years, longer than all but two previous popes. More importantly, he served as the supreme *pontiff* during a time of crisis in both the Roman Catholic Church and the world, and his leadership forever changed both. (*Pontiff* comes from the Latin word *pontifex,* which means *bridge;* for Catholics, the pope is a bridge between God and humanity.)

John Paul II personified Catholicism's renewed commitment, proclaimed by the Second Vatican Council, to share "the joys and the hopes, the griefs and the anxieties" of all people. Also known as Vatican II, the *ecumenical* (worldwide) council consisted of more than 2,500 church fathers, including some 225 bishops, among whom was the future Pope John Paul II.

From 1962 to 1965, the bishops and other leaders of the church met annually in Rome under the direction of Pope John XXIII and his successor, Pope Paul VI, to discuss and *promulgate* (solemnly publish) a total of 16 decrees designed to renew the pastoral life of the church. The major teachings and aspirations of Vatican II are reflected in any list of John Paul's achievements as pope, including his pivotal role in the fall of Communism in Eastern Europe; his demand for universal human rights; his massive popularity; his renewal of the pride and piety of millions of Catholics through his intellectual attainments and personal example; and his innovative teaching.

Achievements as pope

Political role. What some have called the *nonviolent revolution* against atheistic Communism was sparked by a Polish labor movement—Solidarity—which was inspired by John Paul's historic return to his homeland on June 2, 1979. On that occasion, the pope addressed the largest gathering in Polish history, urging workers and students to cast off fear, place their faith in Christ and the church, and stand resolute against oppression. On subsequent visits to Poland, he bolstered Solidarity by using his moral authority to undermine the regime. In 1989, during the first and only meeting between a pope and a secretary general of the Communist Party of the Soviet Union, John Paul commended Mikhail Gorbachev for his policy of reform, a policy that contributed to the collapse of the Soviet Union in 1991.

In other parts of the world, including Paraguay, Chile, and the Philippines, John Paul II urged such dictators as Alfred Stroessner, Augusto Pinochet, and Ferdinand Marcos, respectively, to honor the human rights of their citizens. Opposition movements in the three countries eventually ousted these rulers. In a move that stirred controversy, John Paul chastised Catholic *liberation theologians* for their Marxist inclinations and warned bishops and priests about using the Gospel to advance a particular political ideology. (Liberation theology, which originated in Latin America in the 1960's, combined aspects of Catholic theology with socialist principles to justify forms of rebellion.) At the same time, several of John Paul's *encyclicals* (letters to the entire church) lamented the empty materialism of the West and challenged the leaders of free-market economies to narrow the gap between rich and poor.

Widespread appeal. During his reign, John Paul II developed a massive following among Catholics and non-Catholics alike. He visited more than 125 countries and traveled over 750,000 miles (1.2 million kilometers)—more miles than all previous popes combined. He was particularly beloved by young people, who responded enthusiastically to the ability of the one-time actor and poet to use signs and gestures to convey his humanity and love.

Intellectual attainments and personal example. John Paul II authored more than 50 major church documents—encyclicals, apostolic constitutions, formal letters, and treatises—and several best-selling books, including the autobiography *Pope John Paul II: In My Own Words.* He promulgated two new codes of *canon* (church) law and the landmark *Catechism of the Catholic Church.* As part of his campaign to demonstrate the possibility of attaining holiness, even in a world of materialism and violence, John Paul *beatified* (formally recognized as "blessed," the first step toward sainthood) more than 1,300 men and women. He *canonized*

The author:
R. Scott Appleby is a professor of history and director of The Joan B. Kroc Institute for International Peace Studies at the University of Notre Dame in Indiana.

(elevated to sainthood) more than 480 men and women, including lay people from various walks of life.

The pope's own heroic and holy acts proved equally important. On Dec. 27, 1983, he visited the prison cell of Mehmet Ali Agca to forgive and be reconciled with the Turkish terrorist. Ali Agca had attempted to assassinate John Paul on May 13, 1981, as the pope was riding in his jeep in St. Peter's Square.

Innovative teachings. John Paul condemned what he called "a culture of death" while championing the "gospel of life"; he unstintingly defended religious freedom for all peoples, not only for Catholics; he pushed the Catholic social tradition closer toward an ethic of nonviolence, as exemplified in his condemnation of the war in Iraq in 2003 and in his virtual outlawing of capital punishment; and he developed a theology of apology, forgiveness, and reconciliation.

Indeed, John Paul II made history by apologizing on repeated occasions for the historic sins of Catholics, including the crime of *anti-Semitism* (prejudice against Jews). He called on the world to adopt a similar attitude of repentance. Decrying what he saw as a careless or ruthless attitude toward life at its most vulnerable, John Paul repeatedly urged bishops and lay Catholics to fight abortion and *euthanasia* (helping or allowing people to die), declaring that the "slaughter of the innocents" must be stopped. He argued that moral justification for the death penalty is practically nonexistent in the modern age, and his interventions sometimes saved the lives of death-row inmates. On the international level, the pope raised the bar considerably on the use of lethal force, refusing to endorse United States and European bombing campaigns in Iraq and the former Yugoslavia.

Each of these achievements embodies one or another dimension of Vatican II. Indeed, without the Council's decision to open the Church to the world, it is unlikely that the Cardinals in 1978 would have elected an archbishop from Krakow, Poland, to become the first non-Italian pope in 455 years and the first Slavic pope ever.

Early life and priesthood

John Paul II was born Karol Józef Wojtyla on May 18, 1920, in the small town of Wadowice, near Kraków. Karol's mother, Emilia, died just before his ninth birthday, an event, some scholars suggest, that may have led to the devotion that he showed throughout his life for the Virgin Mary. In 1932, his only brother, Edmund, a physician, died of scarlet fever. At age 20, Karol lost his father, also named Karol, an army officer.

These personal tragedies framed Wojtyla's coming of age. In 1938, he began working toward a philosophy degree at the Jagiellonian University in Kraków, joined the university's speech and drama clubs, wrote poetry, and played soccer. As a teen-ager, Wojtyla already displayed a remarkable talent for languages.

When Germany invaded Poland on Sept. 1, 1939, the life of 19-year-old Wojtyla changed forever. He embarked on a lifelong show of resistance to tyranny. Germany's Nazi government closed the university and began to deport able-bodied men to Germany. Wojtyla avoided deportation by finding work in a quarry and a chemical factory, jobs that

Father Wojtyla pauses on a ski slope as a young priest in 1955. Wojtyla was known for his athleticism throughout his life and enjoyed camping, hiking, and kayaking.

were considered a vital part of the war effort. He continued his studies in an underground university and helped to establish the *clandestine* (secret) "Rhapsodic Theater," which performed in private apartments. "Any day I could have been picked up on the street, at the factory or at the stone quarry and sent to a concentration camp. Sometimes I asked myself: 'So many people at my age were losing their lives, why not me?'" he wrote on the 50th anniversary of his ordination to the priesthood.

Pope John Paul II greets well-wishers outside a cathedral in Kielce, Poland, during a visit in 1991. During his 26-year reign, the pope traveled more than 750,000 miles (1.2 million kilometers)—more miles than all other popes combined.

The young Wojtyla answered this question with action. In 1942, he entered an underground theological seminary in Kraków, a step that entailed great risk because the Gestapo (Nazi secret police) kept a close watch on anyone involved in religious activities. As the Nazi occupation of Poland gave way to the subtler horrors of a Communist regime in 1946, Wojtyla was ordained a priest. Father Wojtyla was sent to Rome, where he studied ethics at Angelicum University. For his thesis, he chose to write about Saint John of the Cross, a mystic of the 1500's.

In 1948, Father Wojtyla was assigned to work as an assistant to the pastor in the village of Niegowic, 20 miles (30 kilometers) outside of Kraków. A year later, he became pastor at Saint Florian Parish in Kraków, where he also served as a university chaplain. With a passion for athletics and the outdoors, Wojtyla enjoyed taking groups of students hiking, cycling, skiing, camping, and kayaking.

At the direction of the archbishop of Kraków, Wojtyla earned a second doctorate, in moral theology. In 1953, he joined the faculty of a university in Lublin, Poland, about 100 miles (160 kilometers) southeast of Kraków. Although only in his mid-30's, Father Wojtyla had already published many articles and several books on ethics, as well as poems and plays.

The pope meets with Soviet President Mikhail Gorbachev in 1990, one year after their first, historic meeting. John Paul's support of Gorbachev's reform policy and his encouragement of the Polish people to withstand oppression were considered pivotal steps in the collapse of Communism in Eastern Europe.

In 1958, Wojtyla was named an auxiliary bishop of Kraków, the youngest bishop in Polish history. He was appointed archbishop of Kraków in 1964. Three years later, at age 47, he became one of the youngest cardinals in the church. Cardinal Wojtyla immediately began to attend the final session of the Second Vatican Council, during which he helped compose the landmark document *Gaudium et Spes (The Church in the Modern World)*.

Progressive on social and economic matters, Cardinal Wojtyla remained highly traditional on matters of personal and sexual morality.

In the 1960's, he was influential in shaping the controversial encyclical *Humanae Vitae (On Human Life)*, which reiterated the church's condemnation of birth control, abortion, and euthanasia.

After being elected pope in 1978, John Paul II began a whirlwind of activity, including trips around the world, press conferences, meetings with world leaders, and writings on the role of Jesus Christ in the modern world. He began a dialogue with members of other faiths, as he traveled to Orthodox Christian countries that no pope had ever visited before. From 1999 to 2002, the pope visited Bulgaria, Georgia, Greece, Romania, and Ukraine. He became the first pontiff ever to enter a Lutheran church, a Jewish synagogue, or a Muslim mosque. He convened unprecedented "prayer summits," during which hundreds of religious leaders met in the Italian hill town of Assisi. At one such summit after the terrorist attacks upon the United States on Sept. 11, 2001, the leaders condemned the use of violence in the name of religion.

Pope John Paul II, during a visit to Jerusalem in March 2000, prays before the Western Wall (part of of the Second Temple destroyed by the Romans in A.D. 70). The pope placed a note in a crack between the stones, apologizing to the Jewish people in the name of all Catholics for the historic sin of anti-Semitism.

Defender of religious freedom, apostle of human rights

John Paul II was a pope of many surprises. "Who could have predicted," exclaimed Samuel Huntington, a political scientist from Harvard University in Cambridge, Massachusetts, "that the world's leading advocate of religious freedom in the final decades of the 20th century would be the pope?" Yet defending the inalienable right to choose one's own beliefs and religious practices—or none at all—is the centerpiece of John Paul's formidable legacy. No government or society can abolish this right by coercing people to join a particular church or other religious body or by penalizing them if they do, he insisted. Indeed, no church—including the "one, true church" (the Roman Catholic Church, according to John Paul and all other Catholic bishops)—can justly collaborate with a government or other civil authority to compel religious belief and practice. That this teaching was proclaimed by the successor of medieval and modern popes who had preached the opposite made it all the more astonishing. Several popes in the history of the church had ordered or approved the persecution of heretics and insisted that religious freedom is a form of "madness."

No one who had paid attention to Archbishop Wojtyla's interventions in the Second Vatican Council was surprised, however, by Pope John Paul's ringing support of the council's historic Declaration on Religious Freedom. The document's Latin title—*Dignitatis Humanae (On Human Dignity)*—became the clarion call for John Paul's papacy. Dignity, the quality of spirit that emanates from our share in God's perfect goodness and eternal life, the council proclaimed, is the defining characteristic of humanity. Possessing dignity is not dependent on one's race, religion, income, family background, or any other quality; life alone provides it. Depriving individuals of basic human rights on such grounds is, therefore, always unjust. The ability to find one's way to God, the fundamental expression of the freedom that accompanies human dignity, is *the* basic human right.

John Paul II himself lived and expanded upon this teaching of Vatican II, which reversed centuries of Roman Catholic policy. (Such policy included the doctrine that a rightly ordered nation must be Roman Catholic, with non-Catholics enjoying rights—or being deprived of them—at the whim of Catholic authorities.) Religious freedom, he explained, is the path to true peace because it is the path to God. Peace and human flourishing are inseparable, according to Catholic theology, and both require the freedom of the human person, which finds its fulfillment in striving toward ultimate meaning, toward God. The evils of the 20th century were rooted in the attempt to replace God with the totalitarian state. The pope had personally encountered the most destructive of these evils in Nazism and the socialism of the Soviet state. The result was carnage, the violation of human dignity, and the reduction of human beings to objects. Today, the rivals to God are more subtle, John Paul warned. They include the love of material goods, wealth, and personal power.

How did the pope recommend fending off these "pseudo-religions" of totalitarianism, consumerism, and materialism? By nudging the world and its governments toward policies and laws that promote—or at least do not inhibit—the quest for the true God. In a religious competition for souls, the pope believed, Catholicism must take its chances; the church need not be supported by government, but it must not be restricted or persecuted by governments.

Not everyone warmed to the pope's message. During a papal visit to India in 1999, some Hindu leaders accused him of using "religious freedom" as a justification for attempting to convert Indians to Roman Catholicism. Despite John Paul's pathbreaking dialogues with other religions, he never wavered on Catholicism's claim that Christ alone is the sole redeemer of humankind.

In countless ways, John Paul II left a lasting imprint on his church and his world—through learned treatises, dramatic gestures, impassioned preaching, tireless travel, doctrinal firmness, heartfelt prayer, and canny leadership designed to extend his influence. (John Paul appointed virtually all the cardinals who chose his successor.) Millions of Catholics who grew to maturity during his pontificate call themselves part of the "John Paul II generation." It is a fitting tribute to one of history's great popes.

Some 300,000 mourners fill St. Peter's Square in Rome on April 8, 2005, during the funeral Mass for Pope John Paul II. During the preceding week, nearly 1.4 million people had filed by his casket as the pope, who had been loved by Catholics and non-Catholics alike, lay in state in St. Peter's Basilica.

Democratic Party.

Democratic candidates fared well in off-year elections in 2005, after suffering widespread defeats in the 2004 general election. In 2005, Republicans controlled the presidency, both houses of Congress, and a majority of state governorships. In November, however, Democrats handily won two governor's races and spearheaded a campaign in California to defeat a series of ballot initiatives backed by Republican Governor Arnold Schwarzenegger.

Dean tapped for DNC post. Democrats in 2005 selected former Vermont governor and presidential candidate Howard Dean to chair the Democratic National Committee, or DNC. The 447-member committee elected Dean chairman by a voice vote on February 12. He succeeded Terence R. McAuliffe.

Dean had been a front-runner for his party's nomination for president early on during the 2004 primaries. However, his campaign lost steam after he was defeated in the New Hampshire primary and gave an over-the-top speech that left voters with the impression that he may have been somewhat out of control. Accepting the chairmanship of the Democratic Party in 2005, Dean outlined an ambitious agenda for rebuilding party strength, vowing, "Today will be the beginning of the reemergence of the Democratic Party."

Howard Dean was selected in part because of the fund-raising prowess that he exhibited in seeking the Democratic presidential nomination in 2004. During the campaign, Dean demonstrated the power of the Internet as a tool in political fund-raising. Nevertheless, fund-raising efforts by the Democratic Party in 2005 proved slow compared with those of the Republican Party. From January through September, the DNC raised $42 million and had $6.8 million in the bank, according to the Federal Election Commission. During the same period, the Republican National Committee raised $81.5 million, with $34 million in the bank.

Corzine victorious. On November 8, United States Senator Jon Stevens Corzine, a Democrat, defeated Republican businessman Douglas Forrester for the governorship of New Jersey. The previous governor, Richard J. Codey, took office in late 2004 after Governor James E. McGreevey resigned after admitting that he had been involved in an extramarital relationship with a man. Corzine and Forrester ran on a platform of reducing the state's property tax rate and restoring integrity to state government, but their highly negative campaigns appeared to turn off many voters, according to political experts.

Virginia governor's race. Lieutenant Governor Timothy M. Kaine of Virginia was elected governor on Nov. 8, 2005, defeating the state's former attorney general, Jerry Kilgore, a Republican. Kaine succeeded Democrat Mark R. Warner, who under the state constitution was barred from succeeding himself. At the beginning of the race, Kilgore led Kaine in the polls. However, Kaine's campaign steadily picked up momentum. In an attempt to boost Kilgore's campaign, President George W. Bush campaigned for Kilgore the day before the gubernatorial election. Democrats later asserted that Bush's very public endorsement of Kilgore backfired, causing Democrats and independents to turn out in large numbers in support of Kaine. Political experts suggested that the response to the president may have reflected the unpopularity of the war in Iraq. Kaine's election was particularly satisfying for Democrats because he opposed the death penalty and refused to rule out the possibility of new taxes but was still elected in a Southern state that in 2005 was regarded as a Republican stronghold.

Washington state election challenge. In 2005, Democrats successfully beat back Republican efforts to overturn the 2004 gubernatorial election of Christine Gregoire as Washington's governor. On June 6, 2005, state Judge John Bridges rejected Republican claims that Gregoire benefited from fraud in her victory over Republican Dino Rossi. The decision made Washington the first state to simultaneously have a female governor and two female U.S. senators, Patty Murray and Maria Cantwell.

Rossi was the apparent winner by 261 votes in the November 2004 election. However, a subsequent machine recount reduced Rossi's lead to 42 votes. Democrats in December 2004 successfully petitioned for a hand recount. On December 23, the recount put Gregoire ahead by 130 votes. The election was made official on December 30, when the Republican secretary of state, Sam Reed, certified Gregoire as the winner.

Democrats organized in California. Californians overwhelmingly rejected ballot initiatives that Governor Schwarzenegger had proposed to overhaul and reform state government. Public employee unions as well as Democrats spent millions of dollars campaigning against Schwarzenegger's proposals to require teachers to work longer before achieving tenure; to limit political spending by unions; to slow the growth of state spending; and to reform the way states draw congressional districts, removing the process entirely from the purview of elected officials.

■ Geoffrey A. Campbell

See also **Congress of the United States; Elections; Republican Party; State government; United States, Government of the; United States, President of the.**

Denmark. Prime Minister Anders Fogh Rasmussen's right-of-center Liberal Party won 52 seats—the largest number—in Denmark's parliamentary elections held in February 2005. The result enabled the right to win two consecutive elections for the first time since World War II (1939-1945). Rasmussen formed a minority coalition with the Conservative People's Party and retained the support of the Danish People's Party, a far-right, anti-immigration political organization.

The platform of the new government supported continuation of a generally popular tax freeze. (Danish taxes are among the highest in Europe.) The government also remained committed to maintaining the tight immigration requirements passed in 2002, which are among the most restrictive in the European Union. Debate in 2005 centered on such immigration policies as permitting police to detain foreign nationals in prison while they await deportation. (The international norm is for illegal aliens awaiting deportation to remain free but to report to the police every two weeks.) The Danish law enjoyed broad popular support.

Although the Rasmussen government continued in 2005 to support the United States in the war in Iraq, the policy remained unpopular among Danes.   ■ Jeffrey Kopstein

See also **Canadian territories; Europe.**

Dinosaur. See Paleontology.

Disability. Passengers with disabilities who sail on cruise ships that visit ports in the United States are protected, to a degree, under the Americans with Disabilities Act (ADA) even if the ships are registered in a foreign country. The U.S. Supreme Court issued the ruling in June 2005.

The case was brought by a group of passengers with disabilities who claimed that they had been charged higher prices for accommodations aboard the *Norwegian Sea* and *Norwegian Star.* The passengers reported that they did not have access to such public areas as restrooms, elevators, and certain recreational facilities, or to life preservers.

A lower court had ruled that the ADA does not apply to foreign ships. However, the Supreme Court determined that the ADA's requirement of "readily achievable" modifications does apply. Cruise ships that dock in the United States, therefore, will be required to make such modifications, including the installation of grab bars and the lowering of water fountains. Ships docking at U.S. ports must also eliminate higher charges for people with disabilities. However, they will not be required to perform such structural modifications as widening doorways or installing elevators.

Access to public transportation. According to the National Council on Disability, a federal agency with headquarters in Washington, D.C., progress has been made since the passage of the ADA in 1990 to provide people with disabilities access to public transportation. At least 90 percent of buses and 65 percent of key rail stations have become accessible. However, according to "The Current State of Transportation for People with Disabilities in the United States," a report published by the council in June 2005, public transportation is still inaccessible or inadequate for a significant number of people with disabilities.

The council reported that a U.S. Bureau of Transportation Statistics study conducted in 2002 revealed that 6 million disabled people still had problems accessing the transportation services they need. In rural areas, they lack bus routes; in cities, they lack taxi cabs that are accessible to service animals and wheelchairs, as well as reliable access to train platforms. The authors of the report concluded that increased funding of public transportation would greatly improve the ability of the system to serve disabled riders.

Special education. The parents of disabled children were disappointed in November 2005 with a Supreme Court ruling regarding special education plans. In cases where parents disagree with a school district's plan for their special needs child, the Supreme Court ruled, parents bear the burden of proving that the plan is inadequate.
                                                  ■ Kristina Vaicikonis

See also **Supreme Court of the United States.**

Disasters. The deadliest disaster of 2005 was an earthquake that struck Pakistan and India on October 8, killing more than 74,000 people. Disasters that resulted in 20 or more deaths include the following:

Aircraft crashes

February 3—Afghanistan. A Kam Air Boeing 737 traveling from Herat to Kabul, the capital, crashes in a snowstorm 22 miles (35 kilometers) northeast of Kabul, killing all 104 passengers and crew members.

August 14—Greece. A Helios Airways 737 en route from Larnaca, in Cyprus, to Athens loses cabin pressure and crashes into a mountain near Grammatiko, a village 25 miles (40 kilometers) north of Athens. All 121 people aboard the plane are killed in Greece's worst aviation disaster.

August 16—Venezuela. All 160 people are killed when a West Caribbean Airways plane crashes in Venezuela's western state of Zulia after reporting engine trouble. The plane was carrying tourists returning from Panama to Martinique.

August 23—Peru. A TANS airline Boeing 737 jet crashes during an emergency landing near the Amazonian town of Pucallpa, about 520 miles (840 kilometers) northeast of Lima, the capital. Forty of about 100 passengers and crew members, traveling from Lima to Pucallpa, are killed.

September 5—Sumatra. An Indonesian airliner, flying from the Sumatran port of Medan to the capital, Jakarta, crashes moments after take-off. About 100 passengers and crew members, as well as 49 people on the ground, are killed.

October 23—Nigeria. All 117 people aboard a Belleview Airlines craft that crashed just after take-off from Lagos, Nigeria, on October 22 were killed, confirms an official with the Nigerian government. Several high-level Nigerian officials, on their way to the city of Abuja for a meeting, and a United States consular official were also aboard the twin-engine plane.

December 6—Iran. A military transport plane experiences engine trouble after take-off from a Tehran airport and crashes into an apartment building. About 108 people—including all passengers and crew as well as people in the building—are killed.

December 10—Nigeria. A Sosoliso Airlines jet crashes in the southern Nigerian city of Port Harcourt, killing 103 people on board, the majority of them children from a school in Abuja, the capital.

Earthquakes

February 22—Iran. About 600 people are killed when a 6.4-magnitude earthquake occurs near Zarand, about 460 miles (740 kilometers) southeast of Tehran, the capital. An additional 30,000 people in surrounding villages are left homeless.

March 28—Indonesia. An 8.7-magnitude earthquake near the island of Nias causes the deaths of more than 900 people. The earthquake occurred in the same area as the quake and tsunami of December 2004.

October 8—Pakistan and India. A 7.6-magnitude earthquake strikes Pakistan's North-West Frontier province and Kashmir, an area governed partly by Pakistan and partly by India. More than 73,000 people are killed in Pakistan and at least 1,400 in India. Millions of people are left homeless.

Explosions and fires

February 14—Iran. A fire during evening prayers in a mosque in central Tehran kills 67 worshipers and injures some 300 others.

March 7—Dominican Republic. A fire in an overcrowded prison in the eastern town of Higuey causes the deaths of 136 inmates. Authorities say the fire was set by rival gangs in a fight over control of the prison drug trade.

September 23—Texas. Twenty-three elderly patients of a Bellaire nursing home are killed when the bus in which they are fleeing Hurricane Rita bursts into flames near Dallas. Witnesses report that the fire, which seemed to begin in one of the vehicle's wheel wells, ignited oxygen tanks in use by some of the passengers.

Mine disasters

February 14—China. A coal mine explosion in the northeastern city of Fuxin kills 214 miners in the country's worst mining disaster since 1949.

March 19—China. Seventy-two miners are killed when an explosion tears through an illegally operated coal mine in Shuozhou, in China's northern Shanxi province.

July 11—China. A gas explosion in a coal mine in the western Xinjiang region operating without a safety permit leaves 83 miners dead. Observers suggest that the demand for coal by China's industries is pressuring mine operators to ignore safety in favor of higher production.

November 27—China. At least 171 miners are killed when coal dust explodes in a mine in China's northeastern Heilongjiang province.

December 7—China. More than 90 miners are killed when gas explodes in a coal mine in Hebei province in northern China.

Shipwrecks

February 19—Bangladesh. An overcrowded ferry in the Buriganga River near Dhaka, the capital, capsizes after being struck by a tornado. Some 120 of the estimated 260 people aboard are killed.

May 22—Bangladesh. Local officials report that three boat accidents during the past week have caused the deaths of at least 150 people. On May 15, an overcrowded ferry in the southern district of Patuakhali sank during a storm; on May 17, a ferry in central Manikganj district capsized; and on May 19, a fishing trawler sank in stormy weather in the southern Bhola district.

July 7—Indonesia. As many as 200 people are drowned when a ferry in eastern Indonesia sinks amid heavy rains and 13-foot (4-meter) waves. The ferry was traveling from the port town of Merauke to Tanah Merah, about 125 miles (201 kilometers) to the north.

August 12—Colombia. About 100 people are drowned when an Ecuadorean vessel carrying illegal immigrants to the United States capsizes 100 miles (160 kilometers) off the coast of Colombia.

August 15—Nigeria. As many as 90 people are killed when an overcrowded ferry crossing the flooded Lamurde River capsizes near Jalingo, 250 miles (400 kilometers) east of Abuja, the capital.

October 2—New York. Twenty elderly passengers are killed when a Lake George excursion boat capsizes.

Storms and floods

February 25—India, Pakistan, Afghanistan. Authorities report that at least 850 people were killed during a week of torrential rain and snow, the heaviest in more than 10 years. The rain caused a dam to burst near Pasni, in southwestern Pakistan, killing at least 135 people.

March 20—Afghanistan. Government officials report that more than 200 people in central Uruzgan province and in the western province of Farah have been killed in recent weeks by floods caused by torrential rains and melting snow.

April 7—India. As many as 150 Hindu pilgrims are drowned when flood gates on the Narmada River near Dharaji, about 185 miles (300 kilometers) west of Bhopal, are unexpectedly opened.

May 1—Ethiopia. Government officials report that torrential rains that began on April 21 in the eastern Somali region have caused major flooding that resulted in the deaths of about 170 people. More than 250,000 others have been displaced.

June 10—China. Flooding from torrential rains in Heilongjiang province in northeastern China inundates a school in the village of Shalan, killing more than 100 children. Local officials, who were warned of the impending flood, claimed to be too busy to evacuate the school.

June 28—China. Officials with the Ministry of Civil Affairs report that more than 770 people died in June as a result of heavy flooding throughout southern China. At least 2.9 million people have been left homeless.

July 26—India. During one 24-hour period, monsoon rains inundate the capital, Mumbai (formerly Bombay), with 37.1 inches (944.2 millimeters) of rain, the heaviest rainfall ever recorded in a single day in India. Officials estimate that more than 1,000 people in Mumbai and other parts of Maharashtra state died from storm-related causes.

August 27—Central and Eastern Europe. Authorities in Austria, Bulgaria, Germany, Romania, and Switzerland report that week-long flooding brought on by heavy rains has caused the deaths of more than 70 people. Hardest hit was Romania's central Harghita region, where 33 people died as floodwaters inundated their houses.

August 29—Southeastern United States. Hurricane Katrina slams into the Gulf Coast at the Mississippi-Louisiana border. More than 1,200 people are killed as floodwaters submerge 80 percent of New Orleans and parts of other towns and cities in Louisiana, Mississippi, Alabama, and Georgia. Katrina initially made landfall on Florida's east coast on August 25, killing 14 people.

September 6—China. Government officials report that Typhoon Talim, which made landfall in China's eastern Fujian province on September 1, caused the deaths of at least 100 people. Nearly 500,000 people had to be evacuated.

October 17—Latin America. Relief officials report that at least 650 people were killed in Guatemala, some 800 remain missing, and 280,000 were left homeless in flooding and mudslides triggered by torrential rains from Hurricane Stan. The hurricane struck Central America October 4, bringing 10 days of rain—and causing an additional estimated 130 deaths—to Costa Rica, El Salvador, Guatemala, Honduras, Nicaragua, and Mexico.

Train wrecks

April 25—Japan. A train carrying nearly 600 commuters derails and crashes into an apartment building at Amagasaki, near Osaka, 255 miles (410 kilometers) west of Tokyo. More than 100 people are killed, and at least 450 others are injured.

July 13—Pakistan. About 130 people are killed and more than 100 others are injured when three passenger trains collide in Pakistan's Sindh province near the town of Ghotki, about 370 miles (600 kilometers) northeast of Karachi.

October 29—India. A train derails after flash floods wash away part of the track, killing 114 of 1,000 people aboard. The accident occurs south of Hyderabad as passengers were traveling to celebrate Diwali, the festival of lights, on November 1.

Other disasters

January 3—China. At leat 54 Tibetan Buddhists are killed and more than 40 others are injured when the truck in which they were riding overturns on a mountain road. The pilgrims were returning from Lhasa, the Tibetan capital and home of the Dalai Lama, Tibetan Buddhism's leader, to Sichuan province in southwest China.

January 24—India. More than 250 pilgrims are killed during a stampede near the village of Wai, about 150 miles (250 kilometers) southeast of Mumbai in western India. The pilgrims were attending a Hindu festival.

April 21—Vietnam. Thirty passengers and their driver are killed when a bus in which Vietnamese veterans of the Vietnam War are traveling plunges off a mountain about 100 miles (160 kilometers) southeast of Danang. The group was en route to Ho Chi Minh City for a commemoration of the end of the war.

June 23—India and Pakistan. Officials report that a heat wave that began in May has caused the deaths of nearly 400 people. Temperatures in central Pakistan rose to 120 °F (49 °C), while those in southern India reached 122 °F (50 °C).

August 31—Iraq. Nearly 1,000 Shiah Muslim pilgrims are killed and more than 800 others are injured in a stampede on a Baghdad bridge during a religious procession. The stampede began after rumors of a suicide bomber spread through the crowd of 1 million people.

September 20—India and Nepal. Health officials report that more than 1,000 people across northern India and Nepal have died in a post-monsoon outbreak of *Japanese encephalitis* (a mosquito-borne disease). ■ Kristina Vaicikonis

See also **Disasters: A Special Report; Guatemala; India; Indonesia; Iraq; Pakistan; Weather.**

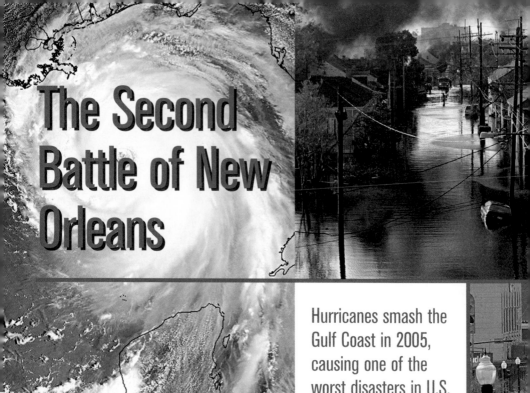

The Second Battle of New Orleans

Hurricanes smash the Gulf Coast in 2005, causing one of the worst disasters in U.S. history.

New Orleans in 2005 joined the ranks of such American cities as Chicago and San Francisco whose histories are forever divided by the before and after of disaster. Fate finally caught up with historic, exotic New Orleans, a city largely below sea level, which always existed precariously behind walls, surrounded by water. On the morning of August 29, Hurricane Katrina made landfall east of the city. At first, the storm's path appeared to spare New Orleans from the worst effects of one of the strongest hurricanes on record.

The full wrath of Katrina hit the Gulf Coast of Mississippi, which was slammed by wind gusts of 127 miles (204 kilometers) per hour. The wind drove a giant rush of seawater called a *storm surge* as high as 29 feet (8.8 meters) into Pass Christian, Gulfport, Biloxi, and Pascagoula. Whole areas were leveled, including waterfront *antebellum* (pre-Civil War) houses and ancient live oaks that had survived countless other storms.

In New Orleans, winds of nearly 100 miles (160 kilometer) per hour shattered windows in downtown high-rises and peeled the outer layer from the roof of the city's vast Superdome, allowing rain into the interior where more than 20,000 people had taken shelter. The real disaster, however, came in with the sea. The winds drove a storm surge up the

Flooding (above, center) prevents New Orleans firefighters from reaching a house fire sparked by a gas leak on September 5. Evacuees wait for buses (above) on September 1 outside the Louisiana Superdome, where thousands of people were forced to live for days in squalid and dangerous conditions. Floodwaters fill New Orleans's famed Canal Street (left) on August 31, two days after Hurricane Katrina had devastated the city.

Gulf Intracoastal Waterway into the Inner Harbor Navigation Canal. The force of the surge both overtopped and breached the levee, flooding the Lower 9th Ward and Desire neighborhoods. Similar breaches in the 17th Street and London Avenue canals allowed Lake Pontchartrain to flow into the city, which behind its levees filled like a bathtub. By the time the depth of the lake and the water in New Orleans equalized, 80 percent of the city was flooded. In some areas, a vile stew of salt water, chemicals, gasoline, dead snakes and rats, mud, and debris stood 20 feet (6 meters) high, over the roofs of many single-story houses.

The flood stranded as many as 100,000 people, primarily the poor and elderly, who lacked the resources to evacuate. To escape rising water,

Volunteers with the Bay St. Louis, Mississippi, Emergency Management Agency rescue a family trapped on their vehicle by massive flooding during Hurricane Katrina on August 29. A storm surge as high as 29 feet (8.8 meters) driven by wind gusts of 127 miles (204 kilometers) per hour leveled whole neighborhoods in such Gulf Coast cities as Pass Christian and Biloxi, Mississippi.

people climbed into attics. Many who lacked the strength or tools to hack their way through roofs drowned. The Katrina death toll at the end of 2005 stood at more than 1,300 people. At least 1,075 people died in the New Orleans metropolitan area. Most were old or very young.

The people who had fled to the Superdome and the New Orleans Convention Center were trapped for days without water and electric power, living in squalor and in real danger from roving street gangs. With little assistance arriving from federal or state authorities, first responders—police and firefighters—became desperate. Some police officers committed suicide. Others walked off the job in the face of a situation that had deteriorated into chaos.

The Louisiana Hospital Association reported on August 31 that thousands of patients and health care workers were stranded in hospitals without electric power, running water, or ventilation. Physicians and nurses operated ventilators by hand to keep people alive. Patients at a nursing home in St. Bernard Parish were less lucky. At least 32 elderly men and women died after being abandoned by the staff.

The blame game

On September 1, Michael Brown, director of the Federal Emergency Management Agency (FEMA), revealed to a newscaster that he was unaware that thousands of evacuees were marooned at the Convention Center. His gaffe directed media attention onto the federal relief effort and into a power

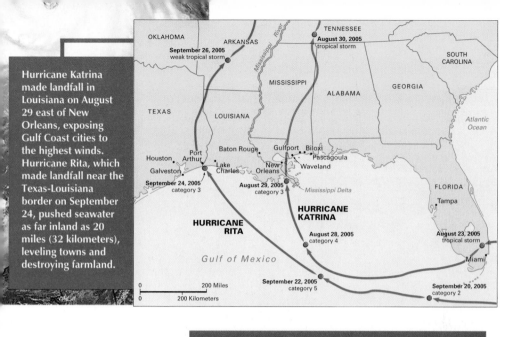

Hurricane Katrina made landfall in Louisiana on August 29 east of New Orleans, exposing Gulf Coast cities to the highest winds. Hurricane Rita, which made landfall near the Texas-Louisiana border on September 24, pushed seawater as far inland as 20 miles (32 kilometers), leveling towns and destroying farmland.

The only recognizable feature of a Long Beach, Mississippi, apartment complex, obliterated by Hurricane Katrina on August 29, is a swimming pool into which a car was blown.

Backed by winds of nearly 100 miles (160 kilometers) per hour, Katrina's storm surge drove up the Gulf Intracoastal Waterway into the Inner Harbor Navigation Canal (see map below). The force of the water both overtopped and breached the levee (above), flooding New Orleans's Lower 9th Ward and Desire neighborhoods. Similar breaches in the 17th Street and London Avenue canals allowed water from Lake Pontchartrain to flow into other areas of the city that are below sea level.

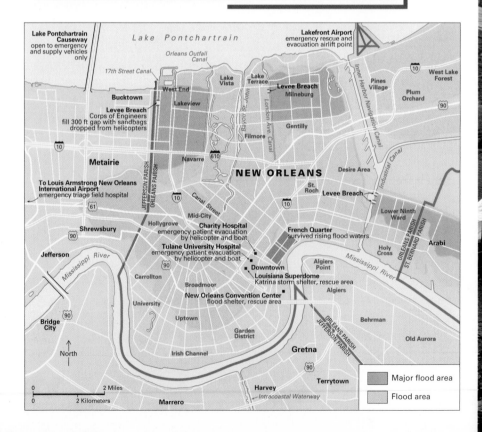

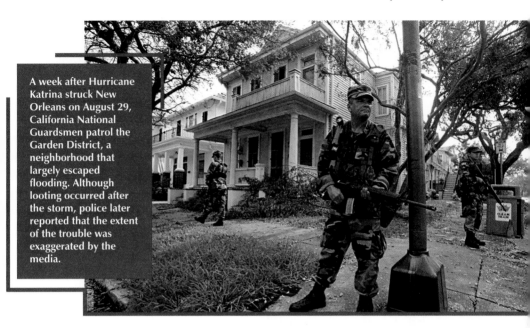

A week after Hurricane Katrina struck New Orleans on August 29, California National Guardsmen patrol the Garden District, a neighborhood that largely escaped flooding. Although looting occurred after the storm, police later reported that the extent of the trouble was exaggerated by the media.

A U.S. Coast Guard helicopter crew rescues people trapped by floodwater on a roof in New Orleans on September 1. In the aftermath of Hurricanes Katrina and Rita, the Coast Guard rescued more than 22,000 people in the Gulf Coast region, 11,000 by air, and evacuated another 9,400 patients from hospitals.

struggle between Louisiana Governor Kathleen Blanco and President George W. Bush over who would control National Guard troops sent into the beleaguered city. Brown's lack of experience in the management of emergencies became the subject of intense scrutiny, and he was eventually replaced. Although President Bush repeatedly visited New Orleans and the Gulf Coast in the wake of the storm, the disaster ultimately proved politically costly, with critics claiming that his administration had taken days to mobilize aid while thousands languished without food and water.

Independent of FEMA, the U.S. Coast Guard started rooftop rescues in New Orleans within hours after the storm ended. In the aftermath of Katrina and Hurricane Rita—which made landfall at the Louisiana-Texas border on September 24—the Coast Guard rescued or evacuated some 30,000 people. Tens of thousands of residents also were evacuated by National Guard units or by such private aid organizations as the American Red Cross.

The price of evacuation

By the time the Army Corps of Engineers had plugged breaches in the levees and pumped out the floodwater, New Orleans was essentially deserted, and much of the city lay in ruins. The French Quarter and Garden District survived relatively undamaged, but many neighborhoods emerged from water choked in mud and debris and alive only with mold.

The disaster drove out some 500,000 people in a migration that may prove as calamitous as the flood for a city that already was losing population and economic muscle. Too many may never return.

In New Orleans, a husband's makeshift grave for his lost wife, marked "Here Lies Vera, God Help Us!" offers a rare bit of civility at a time when dozens of bodies lay unattended in streets and floodwater. A National Guardsman (right) wades through muck during a house-to-house search for victims in New Orleans.

The threat of Hurricane Rita, then a Category 4 storm with sustained winds of 150 miles (240 kilometers) per hour, triggers a vast exodus, and a vast traffic jam, out of Houston and other cities in south Texas on September 22. Rita largely missed Houston, but a 15-foot (4.5-meter) storm surge caused serious damage in Beaumont and Port Arthur, Texas; Lake Charles, Louisiana; and other smaller communities.

Oil spills into Sabine Lake from a wrecked fishing boat at Port Arthur, Texas, after Hurricane Rita pounded the city on September 24. The two powerful storms, hitting the Gulf Coast less than a month apart, crippled the region's important fishing and seafood industry.

Drug abuse. In 2004, 121 million Americans—more than half of the U.S. population age 12 or older—were current drinkers, 70.3 million were current smokers of cigarettes, and 19.1 million were illegal drug users, according to the National Survey on Drug Use and Health (NSDUH), released in September 2005. The figures were based on past-month use of the substances, according to the Substance Abuse and Mental Health Services Administration (SAMHSA), which conducts the survey annually.

Alcohol and youth. The 2004 NSDUH found that the highest rates of alcohol abuse were among youth. About 41 percent of young adults age 18 to 25 years were current binge drinkers, and about 15 percent reported heavy alcohol use. According to the American Academy of Pediatrics (AAP), an organization of pediatricians based in Elk Grove Village, Illinois, alcohol abuse is a major factor in the three most common causes of teenage death: car accidents, homicide, and suicide. Research by the AAP also revealed that alcohol abuse in youth greatly increases a person's chances of becoming an alcoholic as an adult.

Tobacco. The Monitoring the Future Survey, an annual survey of 8th-, 10th-, and 12th-graders conducted by researchers at the University of Michigan in Ann Arbor, found in 2004 that more than half of Americans had tried smoking by the 12th grade and 25 percent of 12th-graders were current smokers. The 2004 NSDUH found that cigarette use by youths age 12 to 17 decreased from 13 percent in 2002 to about 12 percent in 2004.

Illegal drugs. According to the NSDUH, about 8 percent of Americans age 12 or older used illicit drugs—such as marijuana, ecstasy, heroin, or cocaine—in 2004. About half of all Americans had used an illicit substance, usually marijuana, at least once in their lifetime.

Methamphetamines became the nation's leading drug problem in 2005, according to a survey of sheriffs conducted by the National Association of Counties, a research organization based in Washington, D.C. Methamphetamines are a class of addictive stimulants that trigger increased energy levels and a feeling of well-being. However, they may also cause feelings of depression and anxiety. Methamphetamine use can also lead to fatal cardiovascular problems. The 2004 NSDUH found that 11.7 million Americans (4 percent) had used the drugs in their lifetime.

In the early 2000's, authorities focused on the widespread usage and manufacturing of methamphetamines in rural areas. According to the U.S. Drug Enforcement Agency, based in Washington, D.C., authorities in 2004 seized nearly 16,000 methamphetamine labs, many of which were in the Midwest.   ■ David C. Lewis

See also **Drugs.**

A pharmacist in Omaha, Nebraska, stocks cold medicine containing the chemical pseudoephedrine on a shelf behind the pharmacy counter. In 2005, many states restricted the over-the-counter sale of drugs containing pseudoephedrine and ephedrine, key ingredients used to manufacture a class of addictive drugs called methamphetamines.

Drugs. Women with an aggressive form of early-stage breast cancer can halve their risk of a relapse by taking a drug already approved for patients with advanced breast cancer, according to three clinical studies (studies with living people) published in October 2005. Many breast cancer specialists hailed the findings as a breakthrough in the treatment of patients with HER2-positive breast cancer, which affects about 20 percent of all breast cancer patients. The drug, trastuzumab, is sold under the brand name Herceptin.

Unlike most anticancer drugs, trastuzumab targets only cancerous cells, sparing healthy cells. In particular, it attacks tumor cells producing large amounts of a protein called human epidermal growth factor receptor 2 (HER2). The studies evaluated a total of 6,500 women with early-stage breast cancer who took trastuzumab while also undergoing surgery and chemotherapy.

Race-specific drug. BiDil, the first drug intended for a specific racial group, won approval from the Food and Drug Administration (FDA) on June 23. A 2004 clinical study found that self-described African American participants taking BiDil along with drugs commonly prescribed for heart failure were 43 percent less likely to die of heart failure than participants who took the standard drugs alone. In heart failure, the heart does not pump efficiently because of any of a number of diseases. African Americans are more likely than whites to develop this condition; they are less likely to benefit from ACE inhibitors, the drugs commonly used to treat heart failure; and they are more likely to die of the condition. In general, the medical community praised the idea of tailoring drug treatments to specific groups most likely to benefit from them. Some critics, however, expressed concern that such treatments could promote the scientifically discredited idea that race has a genetic basis.

Vioxx developments. In 2005, juries in two trials disagreed over whether Merck & Co., Inc., should be held liable for heart problems in two men who had taken the company's popular arthritis drug Vioxx. New Jersey-based Merck pulled Vioxx from the market in 2004 after a study found a doubled risk of heart attack and stroke in long-term users. The company faced charges that it had covered up evidence about Vioxx's risks. In August 2005, a Texas jury decided in favor of a woman whose husband died while taking the drug. In November, however, a jury in New Jersey determined that Vioxx had played no role in causing a postal worker's nonfatal heart attack. At year's end, the company still faced thousands of Vioxx-related lawsuits.

"Morning-after" pill. Congressional investigators reported in November that FDA officials had decided to reject an application for over-the-counter (OTC) sales of an emergency contraceptive months before an agency advisory panel completed its review of the application. The drug, sold under the brand name Plan B, generally prevents pregnancy if taken within 72 hours of unprotected sex. Opponents of abortion have argued against the use of the drug.

The FDA panel approved OTC sales for Plan B in 2003. In May 2004, however, FDA officials rejected the application, saying more study was needed to determine if teen-agers younger than age 14 might be more likely to engage in risky sex if the drug was available. The congressional report noted that FDA officials had never before raised the issue of age when reviewing an application for OTC sales of a contraceptive.

NSAID warning. In April 2005, the FDA ordered the makers of all prescription non-steroidal anti-inflammatory drugs (NSAID's) to include on their packages a "black box" warning about the risks of cardiovascular problems and gastrointestinal bleeding associated with these painkillers. A black box warning is the strongest the FDA may require. Prescription NSAID's include Vioxx, Celebrex, and Bextra (withdrawn from the market in April) as well as larger dosages of such older pain relievers as ibuprofen and naproxen. The FDA also required stronger warnings for NSAID's sold over the counter.

Schizophrenia drug study. Newer drugs for treating people with schizophrenia are generally no more effective than an older drug that is available at one-tenth the cost, according to an unusual study reported in September by the National Institute of Mental Health (NIMH) in Bethesda, Maryland. Nearly all clinical drug trials compare the effectiveness and side effects of the drug under study with those of a *placebo* (inactive element). The NIMH study, however, compared the older drug perphenazine (sold under the brand name Trilafon) with four newer drugs promoted for their ability to reduce the symptoms of schizophrenia while causing fewer or less serious side effects. Annual U.S. sales of the newer drugs total about $10 billion.

The NIMH researchers found that 74 percent of the study's participants quit taking their medication within one year, usually because the drug was not working or produced severe side effects. In general, however, the newer drugs worked no better than perphenazine in controlling the symptoms of schizophrenia. In addition, the newer drugs caused side effects that, though different, were equally serious. The results of the study renewed calls for the FDA to require drug companies to test new drugs against the drugs they are intended to replace as well as against placebos.   ■ Barbara A. Mayes

See also **AIDS; Health care issues; Medicine.**

Eastern Orthodox Churches. The

Greek Orthodox Church of Jerusalem dismissed its Patriarch, Eirenaios I, in 2005 after his Patriarchate made a controversial land deal in Jerusalem's politically charged Old City. The Church of Jerusalem, which has about 100,000 members, is one of the most ancient of Orthodox churches; the custodian of many sacred sites; and the owner of vast amounts of land and buildings in Jerusalem.

On March 18, the Israeli newspaper *Maariv* reported that the church in August 2004 had sold land to Jewish buyers within traditionally Palestinian areas of the Old City. Some Palestinian authorities viewed the sale as an attempt to change the population in the area so that Israel could refuse the right of the Palestinians to claim the Old City as their future capital. Arab Orthodox Christians and church leaders held Patriarch Eirenaios I responsible and demanded his resignation.

Leaders of 12 major Orthodox Churches from around the world met in Istanbul, Turkey, on May 24 under Ecumenical Patriarch Bartholomew, the spiritual head of Orthodox Christians. The patriarchs voted to withdraw recognition of Eirenaios as Patriarch of Jerusalem. On August 22, the Church of Jerusalem elected Theophilos III, a former archbishop in the Czech Republic, as the 140th Patriarch of Jerusalem. Despite protests from the Israeli government, Theophilos was enthroned in late November.

Greece. A series of corruption and sex scandals left the Church of Greece in turmoil in 2005. A senior metropolitan bishop, Panteleimon of Attica, was suspended amid charges of money laundering and embezzlement from a monastery near Athens. Other Greek priests were suspended after accusations of sexual impropriety. Archbishop Christodoulos of Athens launched a program for greater financial accountability and called for a moral cleanup.

Romania. In a bizarre event, a Romanian Orthodox monk crucified a trainee nun during an exorcism ritual in June. The Romanian Orthodox Church defrocked the monk, closed the nunnery, and condemned what it called a "deviant act."

United States. Archbishop Demetrios of the Greek Orthodox Archdiocese of America, who is also the *Exarch* (Representative) of the Ecumenical Patriarchate in America, gave testimony on March 16 before the U.S. Commission on Security and Cooperation in Europe and for the Congressional Working Group on Religious Freedom. The archbishop's presentation, called "The Unfair Treatment of the Ecumenical Patriarchate by the Turkish Government," highlighted numerous actions taken by the Turkish government that denied freedom to the Ecumenical Patriarchate to exercise its worldwide religious responsibilities. ■ Stanley S. Harakas

Economics, United States. Commer-

cial activity in the United States remained generally strong in 2005 even as energy prices soared, interest rates moved sharply higher, and a series of powerful hurricanes inflicted heavy regional damage that echoed throughout the national economy. Consumer spending slowed, especially as summer gave way to autumn, and manufacturing cooled from 2004 levels. Nevertheless, the U.S. *gross domestic product* (GDP)—the total output of all goods and services in a year—expanded by 3 percent or greater, even registering 4.1 percent growth in the hurricane-beset third quarter.

Gulf Coast destruction. On August 29, Hurricane Katrina, the most destructive storm in U.S. history, came ashore along the Gulf Coast, ravaging parts of Alabama, Louisiana, and Mississippi. The storm claimed more than 1,200 lives and caused massive damage. The failure of multiple levees left much of New Orleans flooded and uninhabitable.

Months after Hurricane Katrina struck, the magnitude of the storm's immense impact on the economy of the central Gulf Coast—particularly metropolitan New Orleans—was still undetermined. Katrina's winds and the flooding damaged as many as 500,000 houses in the metropolitan area and destroyed perhaps 200,000 others, according to the estimates of various state and federal agencies. Katrina inflicted extensive damage to the region's infrastructure, including $1 billion in damage to the Port of New Orleans.

The Port of New Orleans, the nation's fifth largest seaport, in 2004 handled $37 billion in cargo, generated $2.8 billion in federal tax revenue, and directly or indirectly supported 380,000 U.S. jobs. Two months after Katrina, the port was operating at only 40-percent capacity, according to port officials.

The extent of the U.S. government's response to the disaster also remained unclear in late 2005. President George W. Bush pledged billions in aid to the region in the storm's aftermath, but payouts by the Federal Emergency Management Agency (FEMA) were repeatedly delayed, and the Small Business Administration had a backlog of almost 25,000 loan applications in November. According to officials with the Louisiana Small Business Development Center, the New Orleans metropolitan area had lost at least 40 percent of its small businesses in the wake of Katrina.

Local governments, sustaining huge losses of tax bases, struggled to pay for repairs and services. Louisiana staggered under debt and laid off state employees in the wake of the storm. Analysts predicted that at least 500,000 Louisiana residents who had left either as evacuees or storm refugees would not return, further eroding the state's tax base.

The economic turmoil wrought by Hurricane Katrina was amplified by two subsequent hurricanes—Rita, which struck near the Louisiana-Texas border in late September, and Wilma, which struck south Florida in October. According to insurance industry experts, the total cost of these three 2005 hurricanes to the international insurance industry would amount to $60 billion.

Fuel prices. Katrina's impact on oil facilities put further pressure on already tight fuel supplies, pushing pump prices yet higher and forcing consumers and businesses to cut fuel usage. The average U.S. price for regular gasoline, which began the year at $1.78 a gallon, hit $2.61 by August 22 and surged to $3.07 on September 5. In Katrina's wake, President Bush ordered releases of crude oil from the U.S. Petroleum Reserve to refineries. Pump prices were slow to fall, however, and consumer spending tightened, economists observed. According to the U.S. Department of Commerce, consumer spending, adjusted for inflation, declined 1 percent in August and 0.4 percent in September, the first back-to-back declines recorded in 15 years.

The impact of soaring fuel costs was felt throughout the industrial and transportation sectors. Costlier jet fuel helped drive two major U.S. airlines into Chapter 11 bankruptcy in 2005—Atlanta-based Delta Airlines and Eagon, Minnesota-based Northwest Airlines. United Airlines of Elk Grove Village, Illinois, and U.S. Airways of Pittsburgh, Pennsylvania, were already in bankruptcy. High fuel prices also cut profits for trucking firms, railroads, and shipping firms.

The Fed's push. Throughout 2005, the Federal Reserve System (the Fed), the nation's central bank, continued raising short-term interest rates in quarter-point hikes. In December, the Fed pushed its key overnight lending rate to 4.25 percent, up sharply from the 1-percent rate in June 2004.

Consumer prices in September 2005 rose by 1.2 percent, spurred by energy costs, pushing nominal annual inflation to 4.7 percent. By November, with energy costs finally receding, consumer prices fell by 0.6 percent. Economists noted that core inflation—a measure of inflation minus volatile food and energy prices—had risen only 2.1 percent in 2005.

Housing and the mortgage market. By early 2005, many analysts were warning that feverish home buying had bid up prices into a speculative bubble, as borrowers took advantage of financing rates still near historic lows and as more buyers bought houses as investments rather than as their own residences. Fed data revealed that in 2005 the population was carrying more mortgage debt relative to disposable income

SELECTED KEY U.S. ECONOMIC INDICATORS

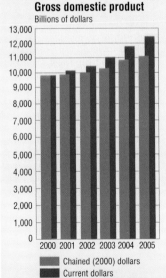

Gross domestic product
Billions of dollars

Chained (2000) dollars
Current dollars

Sources: U.S. Department of Commerce and U.S. Department of Labor, except 2005 figures, which are estimates from The Conference Board.

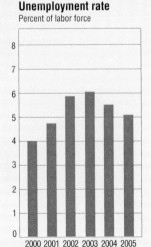

Unemployment rate
Percent of labor force

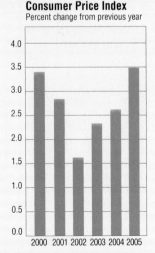

Consumer Price Index
Percent change from previous year

The gross domestic product (GDP) measures the value in current prices of all goods and services produced within a country in a year. Many economists believe the GDP is an accurate measure of the nation's total economic performance. Chained dollars show the amount adjusted for inflation. The unemployment rate is the percentage of the total labor force that is unemployed and actively seeking work. The Consumer Price Index measures inflation by showing the change in prices of selected goods and services consumed by urban families and individuals.

than at any time in the past 25 years. Fed officials noted that some mortgage lenders were offering riskier financing methods, such as interest-only loans, to attract buyers who might not otherwise qualify for mortgages. Such practices, they warned, posed a threat to the nation's financial stability.

Unemployment. The U.S. jobless rate hovered near 5 percent for much of 2005. Despite worries that the Gulf Coast hurricanes would drive up the national unemployment rate, the U.S. Department of Commerce reported an even 5-percent unemployment rate for November and the addition of 215,000 jobs to the nation's economy. Economists noted that unemployment in the central Gulf Coast region was much higher, particularly among nonwhites.

Manufacturing in the United States presented an uneven profile in 2005. The Institute for Supply Management (ISM)—a professional organization based in Tempe, Arizona, of U.S. purchasing managers—reported in May that its index of overall factory activity declined to 51.4 that month from 56.4 in January. The gauge indicates economic contraction below 50 and expansion above that level. The ISM index later indicated recovery from the spring slump, registering 59.4 in September and 58.1 in November. The U.S. Bureau of Labor Statistics reported that manufacturers added 15,000 jobs in October and 11,000 in November—the first back-to-back monthly gain in over a year.

Troubled auto industry. On October 8, auto parts maker Delphi Corporation of Troy, Michigan, filed for bankruptcy protection in federal court. Chief executive officer Robert S. Miller, Jr., said that Delphi, the largest company in the auto industry ever to seek Chapter 11 protection, had been unable to compete successfully with overseas parts makers. The Delphi filing prompted executives of General Motors (GM) Corporation of Detroit, Delphi's largest creditor, to deny that GM was also considering filing for bankruptcy. Amidst slumping demand for GM products, however, the company in 2005 announced future plant closings and employee layoffs, as did rival Ford Motor Company of Dearborn, Michigan.

Bernanke to the Fed. President Bush on October 24 announced his nomination of Ben Bernanke, head of the Council of Economic Advisors (CEA), to replace Alan Greenspan as chairman of the Fed. Greenspan, who took the powerful Fed post in 1987, was due to leave early in 2006. Bernanke had served three years on the Fed board under Greenspan before taking the CEA chair in June and was widely expected to maintain Greenspan's policies.   ■ John D. Boyd

See also **Automobile; Disasters: A Special Report; Economics, world; Energy supply.**

Economics, world. Global economic output continued to expand during 2005, though at a slower pace than in 2004. Natural disasters, soaring energy prices, and significant weakening of economic strength in Europe did not appear to seriously hinder global economic growth, at least in the short term.

Most economists agreed, however, that sharply rising energy costs in 2005 posed the most serious long-term threat to the global economy. During 2005, the price of a barrel of oil traded on the New York Mercantile Exchange topped $54 in March, $65 in August, and $70 in the wake of hurricanes Katrina and Rita in the U.S. Gulf Coast region in September. Later in 2005, oil prices drifted downward for a time, but analysts expected heating oil demand in the winter months to halt price declines and possibly send prices back up.

Some economists suggested that rising energy prices might spur a more general inflation. However, several key central banks that set interest rate policies for their nations—including the Federal Reserve System in the United States—reported that inflation outside the energy sector was still restrained in 2005. Nonetheless, the concern remained that rising energy costs might sufficiently drain consumer finances and cause a significant global slowdown in 2006.

Sluggishness. The International Monetary Fund (IMF)—a United Nations-affiliated organization that provides short-term credit to member nations—reported in its 2005 World Economic Outlook, issued in September, that in the second quarter of the year there was a slight weakening of leading economic indicators and business confidence. IMF economists lowered their forecast for world economic growth from the 4.4 percent projected earlier in 2005 to 4.3 percent, compared with 5.1 percent in 2004.

Regional trends. As in previous years, the economies of the United States and China in 2005 functioned as engines for global economic growth. In the United States, the *gross domestic product* (GDP)—the value of all goods and services produced in a country in a given year—grew by 4.1 percent in the third quarter of the year. China's economic momentum remained "robust," according to IMF economists, who forecast a 9-percent increase in GDP in 2005 and 8.2 percent for 2006. Other economies in Asia showed strength as well. For 2005, IMF economists forecast 7.1-percent GDP growth in India and 2-percent growth in Japan—which only a few years earlier had been in recession.

The European economy faltered, however, as the region struggled with uncertain policy direction in the wake of voter rejection in France and the Netherlands of a proposed European Union

(EU) constitution. For most of 2005, the European Central Bank (ECB) held interest rates steady in the Eurozone—the group of 12 EU member nations using the euro as their common currency. Despite some calls to lower the rate to boost lagging economic growth, the ECB on December 1 raised its key lending rate a quarter-point to 2.25 percent. Late in the year, analysts projected GDP growth within the Eurozone of just 1.2 percent for 2005, down from 2 percent in 2004. GDP growth in the United Kingdom—an EU nation not participating in the Eurozone—slowed to 1.75 percent in 2005 from 3.2 percent in 2004.

Elsewhere, oil revenues helped the Middle East maintain steady growth. Many parts of sub-Saharan Africa sustained economic growth in 2005, but an economic recession in Zimbabwe deepened and began to adversely affect neighboring economies, including South Africa's. Otherwise, the promise of aid and debt relief by the G8 group of wealthy industrial nations in July helped improve Africa's economic prospects.

Economic growth in Russia remained steady as it did in other nations of the former Soviet Union and in the emerging economies of Eastern Europe. In Latin America, most economies also continued to grow steadily. However, after a strong rebound in 2004, the largest Latin American economies, those of Mexico and Brazil, slowed to a 3-percent growth rate in 2005.

Oil and international politics. China, with strong manufacturing growth, had by 2005 become a major oil importer, and Chinese industrialists attempted to gain control over energy sources. In June, the China National Offshore Oil Corporation (CNOOC) attempted to buy Unocal, a Los Angeles-based energy company, and the extensive oil and natural gas reserves it owned. Alarmed by the prospect of Chinese control of U.S.-based energy resources, a *bipartisan* (including multiple parties) group of legislators in the U.S. Congress threatened to block the deal. Faced with the prospect of U.S. governmental intervention, CNOOC withdrew its bid.

Currency imbalance. China was also under pressure from the United States in 2005 to allow its currency, the yuan, to rise in value in foreign exchange markets. Economists said that because the value of the yuan was tied to that of the U.S. dollar, the yuan did not reflect China's actual economic strength, which gave China an unfair pricing advantage in international trade. A more appropriately valued yuan would be worth more, making Chinese goods more expensive on the international market and thereby restraining Chinese trade volume. The United States incurred record-high trade deficits in 2005, due in part to the enormous volume of Chinese imports flowing into the United States.

In July, the Chinese government briefly let the yuan float against other currencies. As a result, the value of the yuan rose about 2 percent. Many currency experts claimed, however, that the yuan remained undervalued by as much as 40 percent in late 2005.

Restructuring in Japan. Led by Prime Minister Junichiro Koizumi, Japan's ruling Liberal Democratic Party (LDP) won a wide majority in parliament in September 2005 elections, virtually guaranteeing that Koizumi's government would proceed with a broad program of structural economic reforms. In October, Japan's parliament approved Koizumi's reform of Japan's massive postal system. Extending far beyond mail delivery, the Japanese postal system included a state-owned bank and life insurance company. In 2005, it held $3 trillion in assets and employed 280,000 workers. The reform legislation set timetables for selling off the various units of the agency to private companies. Economists predicted that shifting the agency's swollen assets into the private sector would spur a wide range of economic activity. Political analysts predicted that Koizumi's administration would soon turn to other structural reforms, such as overhauling Japan's medical and banking systems. ■ John D. Boyd

See also **Bank; Economics, United States; Energy supply; International trade; Japan.**

Ecuador. Vice President Alfredo Palacio assumed the presidency of Ecuador on April 20, 2005, following the ouster of President Lucio Edwin Gutiérrez by the Ecuadoran Congress. The presidential shakeup capped a week of street protests against Gutiérrez, whom opponents accused of packing the nation's supreme court to obtain a dismissal of corruption charges against former president Abdalá Bucaram Ortiz (1996-1998). President Palacio pledged to call a constitutional referendum on government reform.

In mid-August, protesters in Ecuador's Amazonian lowlands dynamited an oil pipeline, cut power lines, and blocked access to oil wells operated by Petroecuador, the state oil company, and several foreign companies. The violence curtailed Ecuador's oil production by an estimated 1.5 million barrels and caused $400 million of damage.

The protesters, residents of the oil-rich but impoverished provinces of Sucumbíos and Orellana, demanded that the oil companies do more to improve the local infrastructure and economy. Protest leaders and oil company representatives on August 25 endorsed an agreement in which oil companies pledged to pave roads in the region and the government promised to allocate more of the tax revenues from oil companies to local projects. ■ Nathan A. Haverstock

See also **Latin America.**

Education. An estimated 54.7 million youngsters enrolled in prekindergarten, elementary, and high schools in the United States in fall 2005, according to the U.S. Department of Education. About 11 percent of students were enrolled in private schools, a percentage that has remained virtually unchanged since 1995.

Undergraduate college enrollment hit an estimated 14.8 million in 2005, an increase of about 2.5 million since the 2005 college freshmen began first grade. About 80 percent of undergraduates attended publicly funded colleges, and nearly 58 percent of them were women.

Costs. Public elementary and high schools spent $406 billion in 2005—about $8,412 per student—in local, state, and federal funds. Based on 2002 Department of Education figures (the latest available), New Jersey spent the most per student —$12,568. Utah, at $4,838, spent the least.

The price of attending a public, four-year university in 2005 rose 6.6 percent to $12,127, the College Board reported. The average price of attending a private university also rose, to $29,026, or 5.7 percent. Policy experts continued to warn that the price of college is beyond the reach of an increasing number of students. According to the Pell Institute for the Study of Opportunity in Higher Education in Oskaloosa, Iowa, the cost of one year of college is equal to 53 percent of a family's annual income when the family makes less than $34,300 a year but only 12.5 percent of income in households where parents earn more than $95,000.

The Nation's Report Card. The education department released its National Assessment of Educational Progress test results, which are required every two years by the No Child Left Behind law, in October. (The assessment is also known as The Nation's Report Card.) The results showed that average reading scores for fourth- and eighth-graders were essentially the same as in 2003, but that math scores had edged up among fourth-graders. About 80 percent of fourth-graders have at least a basic command of math, up from 77 percent. However, only about one in three students is reading and working on math at a "proficient" level, or with a strong command of the subject.

SAT's and ACT's. In March 2005, the College Board introduced a new version of its SAT college-entrance exam. The new test required students to write an essay for the first time and included more advanced math questions and critical-reading passages. For the most part, only students who were juniors in spring 2005 took the new exam. Compared with juniors who took the old SAT in 2004, the 2005 test takers earned higher math scores and lower reading scores. They scored an average 516 out of a possible 800 points on the writing exam. The College Board cautioned colleges not to use the essay as an admissions factor until the company had collected its own data about applicants' performance on the exam.

Seniors in 2005 generally took the old SAT and scored an average 520 on math—a 2-point increase from 2004—and 508 in reading, the same as in 2004. Scores were also flat on the ACT, the admissions test owned by ACT Inc. The average score on the four-subject ACT was 20.9 out of 35.

No Child Left Behind (NCLB) faced new problems in 2005, even as Washington lawmakers continued to support the law that is the cornerstone of President George W. Bush's education program. In April, the Utah legislature ordered Utah schools to ignore parts of NCLB that conflict with state education goals or require the schools to spend state or local money to meet its terms. Meanwhile, the National Education Association, the union that represents mainly suburban teachers, sued the Department of Education to force it to pay the full cost of testing and improvement requirements in the law. In November, a federal judge dismissed the suit.

Bills and resolutions opposing the law circulated in two dozen other state legislatures, but without action. States can opt out of the law's requirements. However, doing so means forfeiting federal education funds, which account for about 8 percent of most state education spending.

To defuse some of the criticism, Education Secretary Margaret Spellings made a regulation change to NCLB. The change was designed to ensure that fewer schools fail annual progress goals because of the test scores of their special education students. Spellings assumed the position of education secretary in January. She previously helped develop the NCLB plan as President Bush's domestic policy adviser during his first term.

In November, Spellings took a further step to halt criticism by announcing she would allow up to 10 states to change the way they measure student progress. Currently, test scores of students in, for example, fourth grade, are measured against scores of the previous year's fourth-graders. Critics of that system point out that it attempts to compare different groups of children. Spellings said she will allow states, on an experimental basis, to track individual students' growth over the years. Critics noted that few states are likely to benefit from the new flexibility because it requires records systems that most states lack. Among the states that have those systems, Florida tracks student test scores and their growth from year to year, even as students move to new schools or cities within the state.

Evolution and intelligent design. Controversy erupted in several states in 2005 over the teaching of students in science classes about the origins of life. Most public school standards specify the teaching of evolution. According to this scientific theory, intelligent life evolved over time through a process called natural selection.

In September 2005, a school district in Dover, Pennsylvania, went to court to defend its policy of telling students that a higher power may have created life. Eleven parents had challenged the policy, which sought to inform students about *intelligent design,* the idea that intelligent life is so complex that it must have been created by an unidentified force, rather than evolving. Opponents of the school district's policy charged that intelligent design is really *creationism*—a literal reading of the Bible's story of creation—and violates the Constitution's guaranteed separation of church and state. The U.S. Supreme Court in 1987 ruled that schools could not be required to teach creationism along with evolution. In November 2005, eight of nine members of the Dover school board who were up for reelection were voted off the board and replaced with candidates who opposed the teaching of intelligent design. In December, a U.S. District Court judge ruled that intelligent design cannot be taught in Pennsylvania public school science classes.

In Kansas, the State Board of Education voted in November to adopt new standards for the teaching of science. The new standards require that public schools teach that the theory of evolution is flawed. They also redefined science to eliminate references to it as a discipline that seeks "natural explanations" for questions about the world.

◼ June Kronholz

Egypt. Political opposition in Egypt to President Hosni Mubarak, who had assumed power in 1981, increased during 2005. The main challenge to the Mubarak regime came from the al-Ghad (Future) Party. Al-Ghad was formed in October 2004 by liberals who left the New Wafd party after that party had been taken over by Islamic extremists. The rising popularity of Ayman Nour, the leader of the al-Ghad Party, prompted Egyptian authorities to arrest him in January 2005 and jail him for six weeks.

The Egyptian Movement for Change, better known as the Kefaya (Enough) Movement, also attracted adherents in 2005. Kefaya was composed of liberals and *secularists* (individuals who believe that religion should not control government). On February 21, the Kefaya Movement demonstrated outside Cairo University, in the Egyptian capital, where the participants chanted anti-Mubarak

The face of 19-year-old Tutankhamun, king of Egypt, who died nearly 3,300 years ago, is revealed in a reconstruction based on computed tomography (CT) scans, made in January 2005, of Tutankhamun's mummy. The image is the first facial reconstruction created by a team of artists and scientists using CT technology.

slogans. On April 27, Kefaya organized demonstrations in 13 Egyptian cities under the slogan "No Constitution Without Freedom."

Elections. On May 10, the Egyptian parliament passed a constitutional amendment allowing multicandidate presidential elections for the first time. However, the amendment did not put an end to protests by opposition groups. During a peaceful demonstration on May 25, Kefaya protesters were beaten by supporters of President Mubarak.

Presidential elections were held on September 7. As most political analysts expected, President Mubarak won, with 88.5 percent of the cast ballots. His main challenger, Ayman Nour, received just 7.1 percent of the vote. Turnout was lower than 20 percent.

November parliamentary elections were marred by clashes between police and supporters of the Muslim Brotherhood, an opposition organization (which had been allowed to operate freely but had lacked recognition) calling for the nationwide implementation of Islamic law. Many political analysts said that the Mubarak regime allowed the Muslim Brotherhood to increase its seats in these elections as a way to crush the regime's secular opposition.

Terrorist bombings. On July 23, three coordinated terrorist car bombings targeted the Sharm el-Sheik resort area on the Red Sea. Experts on terrorism noted that the attacks, which resulted in the deaths of more than 90 people, occurred on the 53rd anniversary of the 1952 revolution that brought down the Egyptian monarchy and gave legitimacy to the *incumbent* (ruling) regime. The Abdullah Azzam Brigades, a group linked to the al-Qa`ida terrorist network, claimed responsibility for the Sharm el-Sheik attacks. The attacks were condemned by Egypt's highest-ranking Islamic cleric, Muhammad Sayid Tanatawi, grand imam of al-Azhar. ■ Marius Deeb

See also **Middle East; Terrorism.**

Elections.

Voters in the United States cast ballots in 2005 in gubernatorial and mayoral races. They also voted on a number of significant social issues raised by ballot initiatives in a variety of locales.

Gubernatorial races. On Nov. 8, 2005, U.S. Senator Jon Stevens Corzine, a Democrat, won his bid to become New Jersey's governor, beating Republican businessman Douglas Forrester. Many voters considered the gubernatorial campaign highly negative, with adverse accusations from both candidates. Forrester supporters even ran a negative advertisement featuring Corzine's former wife. Corzine assumed the office in January 2006 from acting Governor Richard J. Codey, who had replaced James E. McGreevey.

McGreevey had resigned in late 2004 after admitting to an extramarital affair with a man.

In another November 2005 race, Lieutenant Governor Timothy M. Kaine, a Democrat, defeated former Virginia Attorney General Jerry W. Kilgore, a Republican, for the Virginia governorship. President George W. Bush campaigned for Kilgore, which Kilgore aides claimed helped to increase Republican turnout. However, Kaine supporters believed voter disenchantment with the Iraq War and the U.S. economy spurred state Democrats and independents to turn out for Kaine.

Mayoral races. Democrat Antonio Villaraigosa became the mayor of Los Angeles when he defeated incumbent James K. Hahn, also a Democrat, in a landslide election on May 17. Villaraigosa was the city's first Hispanic mayor since 1872.

Mayor Michael R. Bloomberg, a Republican, won a landslide victory on November 8 to secure a second term as mayor of New York City. Bloomberg defeated Democrat Fernando Ferrer, a former president of the Bronx Borough.

In Detroit, Mayor Kwame Kilpatrick, a Democrat, secured his second term in November. However, the Federal Bureau of Investigation (FBI) announced that it was investigating the manner in which absentee ballots in the election were handled. The FBI confirmed that it would also investigate allegations that ballots had been cast in the names of people who were deceased. Kilpatrick endured a scandal-plagued first term, during which it was revealed that he had used city credit cards to finance lavish out-of-town travel. Kilpatrick defeated Democrat Freman Hendrix, a former deputy mayor.

In November, Cincinnati voters elected Senator Mark Mallory, a Democrat, as the city's first elected black mayor. Mallory defeated city Councilman David Pepper, also a Democrat.

California initiatives. California voters on November 8 rejected a ballot initiative that would have required that parents be notified when minors seek abortions. California voters also rejected initiatives supported by Governor Arnold Schwarzenegger to overhaul state government, specifically to slow the growth of state spending; to change how congressional districts are redrawn; to require teachers to work a longer period before achieving tenure; and to limit political spending by public employee unions.

Gay marriage. In April, Kansas citizens voted overwhelmingly to adopt a measure defining marriage as solely between one man and one woman. In Texas, voters on November 8 approved a constitutional amendment banning same-sex marriages by defining marriage as being between a man and a woman. However, the implications of the vote were unclear because state law already banned gay marriage. Eighteen other states have adopted similar bans. Voters in Maine retained a law passed by the state legislature that prohibits discrimination based on sexual orientation.

Marijuana possession. Voters in Denver on Nov. 1, 2005, approved a measure that made it legal for adults to possess up to 1 ounce (0.028 kilogram) of marijuana. However, possession of marijuana remains illegal under both Colorado state and federal law. Voters in the ski community of Telluride, Colorado, defeated a measure on November 1 that would have made marijuana possession the lowest law enforcement priority.

Other measures. Voters in White Settlement, Texas, a town near Fort Worth, on November 8 rejected a proposal to rename the city West Settlement. The city's settlers had named the city based on the fact that the area was heavily populated by Native Americans.

Oklahoma voters on September 13 rejected an initiative that would have forced the state government to establish minimum support levels for highway and bridge maintenance and to create a fund to pay for it. The measure also would have raised state taxes by 5 cents a gallon for unleaded fuel and 8 cents a gallon for diesel fuel.

Wisconsinites on April 5 voted to establish four-year term limits for some county offices. Colorado voters on November 1 approved a ballot measure that temporarily removed state spending limits and allowed Colorado to retain nearly $4 billion that otherwise would have been refunded to taxpayers.

■ Geoffrey A. Campbell

See also **Congress of the United States; Democratic Party; People in the news** (Antonio Villaraigosa); **Republican Party; State government; United States, Government of the; United States, President of the.**

Electronics.
The iPod line of digital music players from Apple Computer, Inc. of Cupertino, California, continued to generate excitement among electronics buyers in 2005. In September, Apple introduced the iPod Nano, its smallest iPod yet. About as thick as a pencil and as small as a business card, the $199 Nano model could hold 500 songs; a $249 model held 1,000 songs. The Nano's small size resulted from its use of electronic memory rather than hard disks to store music.

While initial response to the Nano was strong, some consumers reported a problem with the music player's screen, which cracked in less than 1 percent of the devices. Apple promised to replace any Nanos with defective screens.

Apple unveiled a video-capable iPod in October that included a 2.5-inch (6.4-centimeter) screen and sold for $299 or $399, depending upon its storage capacity. The larger-capacity model could hold 150 hours of video programming, 25,000 digital photographs, or 15,000 songs. The $299 model offered half that amount of storage.

Users could transfer home video to their players or purchase video content through Apple's iTunes online store. In 2005, Apple offered music videos; short films from Pixar, a motion picture company owned by Apple chief executive officer Steve Jobs; and television programs by the Walt Disney Company of Burbank, California.

Cell phones, like many other consumer electronics, became increasingly computerlike in 2005, making them vulnerable to the same problems that plague desktop computers. In January, a software *virus* (program that spreads itself from one system to another by copying itself within another computer program) infected phones running the Symbian operating system. The virus, called Commwarrior, spread through messages received by the phones. While the initial infection did little damage, the virus could erase phone numbers and other data stored in the phones.

The virus initially targeted phones manufactured by Finland-based Nokia Corp. Commwarrior was followed by more advanced versions of the original virus, as well as by new viruses that targeted phones from other manufacturers.

Antivirus software makers, including Symantec Corp. of Cupertino, California, released protective products in May. The antivirus software was itself designed to be sent wirelessly to cell phones. By June, virus programmers had designed yet a new virus, which was passed off as an antivirus product.

Digital cameras that store images and films as computer files continued to spur the electronics industry in 2005. While sales growth slowed for digital still-photography cameras, a new generation of low-priced, feature-loaded digital video cameras generated large sales.

Typical of the new cameras, known as mini-DV's, for miniature Digital Video, was the JVC GR-D250, manufactured by JVC Corporation of Yokohama, Japan. The JVC mini-DV weighed less than a pound. Another camera, the Canon ZR100, released in March by Canon Inc. of Tokyo, Japan, included a wide-screen recording mode. Both cameras had manufacturer prices of over $400 but were widely available at retail prices near $300.

Robots on the road. The United States Defense Advanced Research Projects Agency (DARPA), a U.S. Department of Defense agency located in Arlington, Virginia, funded a $2-million contest in October to encourage robot technology development. The agency's goal was to fully automate one-third of U.S. military land vehicles by 2015.

The contest challenged entrants to build a vehicle capable of driving a 132-mile (212-kilometer) course without human assistance through rugged desert terrain in Nevada. The 23 entries combined artificial intelligence, lasers, and radar to navigate. Three vehicles completed the route, with a car designed by a team from Stanford University of Stanford, California, reaching the finish line first. ■ Keith Ferrell

See also **Computer; Telecommunications.**

Employment. See **Economics, U.S.; Labor.**

Endangered species. See **Conservation.**

El Salvador. In July 2005, President Elias Antonio (Tony) Saca appointed a panel of advisors to suggest ways of coping with rising crime in El Salvador. In August, Saca's administration reassigned 1,000 soldiers to El Salvador's National Civilian Police force to assist in the war on crime. The measures were in response to a surge in violence that resulted in at least 1,750 murders of Salvadorans during the first six months of 2005. Authorities attributed 60 percent of the killings to gangs, which participated in drug trafficking and the smuggling of illegal immigrants into the United States. Particularly notorious was the gang known as Mara Salvatrucha, which had originated among Central American immigrants in Los Angeles in the mid-1980's. In 2005, the gang had an estimated 10,000 members in El Salvador, Guatemala, Honduras, and Mexico.

In May, the government of Israel temporarily recalled its ambassador to El Salvador to protest the dedication of a plaza in San Salvador, El Salvador's capital, to the memory of Yasir Arafat. Arafat, the late leader of the Palestinian Authority, died in 2004. El Salvador has a large community of people descended from Palestinian immigrants, among them President Saca. The country has historically maintained close ties with Israel. ■ Nathan Haverstock

See also **Latin America.**

Energy supply. The world's supply of energy failed to keep pace with demand in 2005. The deficit resulted in record prices of crude oil, gasoline, and other fuels. Although the world's use of petroleum and other energy sources continued to rise throughout the year, higher prices slowed the growth of demand. However, two late-summer hurricanes caused supply disruptions that more than offset this effect. In the Middle East, home to many of the world's oil reserves, the Iraq War and other political tensions added to oil-supply problems.

Hurricanes Katrina and Rita halted oil and natural gas output in the Gulf of Mexico, an important production region, when the storms struck in August and September 2005. Offshore, the storms damaged, sunk, or set adrift 192 oil and gas drilling rigs and production platforms, according to the United States Energy Information Administration (EIA) in Washington, D.C. Onshore, along the U.S. Gulf Coast, many major petroleum refineries and other oil and gas facilities, including pipelines, were disabled, some for months.

World oil demand rose in 2005 due in part to thriving global economies and rising oil use by fast-developing China and India. According to the International Energy Agency, an energy policy organization based in Paris, world oil consumption rose by more than 1 million barrels a day, approaching an average of 85 million barrels a day in late 2005.

The United States was still the world's largest user of petroleum in 2005, consuming around 20.6 million barrels a day, or nearly one-fourth of the world's supply. Gasoline, the most-used fuel, accounted for an average of more than 9 million barrels a day. The United States imported more than one-half of all the oil it consumed in 2005. The imported oil, much of it from the volatile Middle East, was a major contributor to the growing U.S. trade deficit.

Record prices. Crude oil reached a peak price of more than $70 a barrel in 2005, a significant rise from the $41.44 a barrel average of 2004. A barrel contains 42 gallons (159 liters), and the per-gallon prices of fuels—such as gasoline—processed from crude oil made similar jumps. After averaging less than $2 a gallon for 2004, prices of gasoline rose to more than $3 a gallon by September 2005.

Gasoline prices fell back in late 2005 after Europe shipped surplus gasoline to the United States, but prices still remained higher than they had been before Hurricane Katrina hit in August. Diesel, jet fuels, and home heating oil also were much more expensive in 2005. For the 2005-2006 winter, U.S. residents were expected to pay about 32 percent more to heat their residences with fuel oil and about 48 percent more to heat their houses with gas.

According to the EIA, the average residential price of gas rose by 20 percent during 2005. In states where gas was widely used to generate electric power, such as Texas, costs went up sharply. The cost of coal, which is used to generate more than one-half of the electric power used in the United States, also rose. However, it was the skyrocketing price of petroleum that angered many consumers and prompted members of Congress to consider tax penalties for prospering oil companies. Oil executives contended they had little control over prices.

OPEC. Oil ministers of the Organization of the Petroleum Exporting Countries (OPEC), an association of 11 nations that depend heavily on oil exports for their incomes, claimed in 2005 that they were doing all they could to keep petroleum prices stable. Most of the OPEC nations pumped flat out through 2005, at an average rate of nearly 31 million barrels a day. The high output left OPEC little leverage to restrain price hikes. For much of 2005, OPEC's spare capacity was at historic low levels estimated at from 1 million to 1.5 million barrels a day.

Most energy analysts expected crude oil prices to hover in a range of $50 to $60 a barrel through 2006, well above the $20 to $30 range of the early 2000's. Some industry experts claimed that the governments of the OPEC countries would reduce production if necessary to keep crude costs relatively high. Others contended that global demand was forcing higher prices.

Energy efficiency. High oil and gas prices in 2005 called attention to energy efficiency in the United States. Sales of gas-guzzling sport utility vehicles plunged in 2005. Hybrid cars, which are powered by both gasoline and electricity for better gas mileage, grew in popularity.

A new focus on alternate fuels was another positive development. However, so-called renewable energy accounted for only 6.3 percent of U.S. energy needs in 2005. Many energy analysts encouraged wider use of natural gas, which is less polluting than petroleum or coal. Although there is a surplus of natural gas worldwide, the gas is difficult to transport over long distances.

Liquefied Natural Gas (LNG) represented one way to bring more gas to the United States. Companies sought to import natural gas from major supply regions, such as the Middle East, by turning the gas into a liquid and shipping it in special tankers. Several new facilities to process

An oil rig, torn free from its moorings when Hurricane Katrina struck the U.S. Gulf Coast in August, drifted down the Mobile River and slammed into a suspension bridge in Mobile, Alabama. The hurricane damaged or destroyed 192 oil and gas rigs and production platforms.

shipments of LNG were being built in 2005. As a result, gas imports were expected to increase, possibly resulting in lower prices. ■ James Tanner

See also **Disasters: A Special Report; Latin America; Venezuela.**

Engineering. See **Building and construction.**
England. See **United Kingdom.**

Environmental pollution. The Kyoto Protocol, an international treaty requiring developed countries to substantially cut their emissions of greenhouse gases, went into force on Feb. 16, 2005. The accord required industrialized nations to reduce their emissions by an average of 5.2 percent below 1990 levels by 2012.

Under the agreement, the treaty could not go into effect until it was ratified by countries representing at least 55 percent of worldwide emissions. The milestone was reached in October 2004, when Russia added its name to the treaty. By February 2005, 141 nations had ratified the agreement. The United States—the largest emitter of greenhouse gases—and Australia did not sign the treaty. The administration of U.S. President George W. Bush cited a lack of involvement of developing countries and the expected high cost of compliance as its reasons for not joining the agreement.

Climate dialogue heats up. In 2005, the U.S. Senate signaled a possible shift in the U.S. policy of resisting efforts to reduce greenhouse gas emissions. The Senate passed a nonbinding resolution in June that acknowledged the dangers posed by climate change and called for mandatory limits on emissions. President Bush, while on his way to the Group of Eight (G8) summit of industrialized nations in Scotland, stated in July that, "I recognize that the surface of the Earth is warmer and that an increase in greenhouse gases caused by humans is contributing to the problem."

However, other actions by the administration suggested continued resistance. *The New York Times* reported in June that Philip Cooney, chief of staff for the White House Council on Environmental Quality (CEQ), downplayed the effects of greenhouse gas emissions on global warming when he edited a report on climate change written by government scientists.

States take action. In June, California Governor Arnold Schwarzenegger announced that the state would take steps to reduce its greenhouse gas emissions to 2000 levels by 2010 and to 1990 levels by 2020. California joined nearly a dozen other states and more than 130 cities that have set their own greenhouse gas controls. California was the first state to limit greenhouse gas emissions from automobiles, an action challenged in court by several automakers and the Bush administration.

Millennium Ecosystem Assessment. A landmark study of the environment, conducted by several agencies of the United Nations, was completed in March 2005. The investigation, known as the Millennium Ecosystem Assessment (MEA),

Fishermen employed by the Mexican national oil company PEMEX clean an oil spill in January 2005 in the Coatzacoalcos River, near its entry to the southern edge of the Gulf of Mexico. An explosion in a PEMEX pumping station in December 2004 ruptured an oil pipeline, killing six workers and emptying 5,000 barrels of crude oil into the river.

studied Earth's natural *ecosystems* (the biological and physical environment of an area) and the effect that human activities are having on them. Nearly 1,400 experts from 95 countries synthesized information from scientific literature, private sector sources, local communities, and indigenous peoples during the course of the four-year project.

According to the assessment, "over the past 50 years, humans have changed ecosystems more rapidly and extensively than in any comparable period of time in human history, largely to meet rapidly growing demands for food, fresh water, timber, fiber, and fuel." For example, in 2005, humans used from 40 to 50 percent of all yearly accessible fresh water, double the amount used from 1960 to 2000.

The MEA reported that almost two-thirds of Earth's natural ecosystems were being degraded by human activities. Since 1980, 20 percent of the world's coral reefs had been destroyed and another 20 percent badly damaged. At least 25 percent of all fish stocks were overharvested. An estimated 90 percent of the total weight of the fish targeted by industrial fisheries—such as tuna and swordfish—had disappeared. About 12 percent of bird species, 23 percent of mammals, and 32 percent of all amphibians were threatened with extinction. However, the report concluded that humans could reverse the degradation over the next 50 years if substantial changes in policy and practice were initiated.

Global warming. Scientists studying global warming had long puzzled over data that had shown temperatures in the atmosphere's lowest level, the troposphere, had not warmed over the last two decades and had actually cooled in the tropics. Skeptics of climate science had long pointed to these data as evidence against the theory that Earth is warming due to human activity.

However, in August 2005, two independent studies found errors in the methods used to create historic temperature records. The studies were done by researchers at Yale University in New Haven, Connecticut, and at Remote Sensing Systems, a satellite technology company in Santa Rosa, California. A third study by scientists at Lawrence Livermore National Laboratory in Livermore, California, found that when the errors were taken into account, weather records showed that the troposphere actually became warmer.

Ice continues to recede. Glaciers around the world continued their retreat in 2005, a fact cited by some scientists as a visible sign of the effects of global warming. The Pasterze, Austria's biggest glacier, was measured as decreasing in height by 13 to 26 feet (4 to 8 meters) per year. The glacier had been steadily declining since its peak in the middle of the 1800's. The sea-level edge of the Exit Glacier, near Seward, Alaska, was found to have receded nearly 1,000 feet (300 meters) over the past 10 years. Alaska's Portage Glacier, located 50 miles (80 kilometers) south of Anchorage, was retreating 165 feet (50 meters) per year.

The Swiss ski resort of Andermatt embraced an unusual solution to its own receding glacier problem in 2005. At a cost of $83,000, the ski area wrapped about 4,000 square yards (3,300 square meters) of the shrinking Gurschen glacier with insulating fabric to retard the decline and maintain natural access to ski runs on the glacier.

Climate change and oceans. The relationship between climate change and ocean warming was linked to disasters on two fronts in 2005. In July, the Royal Society, the United Kingdom's leading scientific organization, warned of a new and dangerous threat to marine life. Using basic chemistry models of carbon dioxide and seawater, the society showed that increasing carbon dioxide concentrations in ocean water, caused by the burning of fossil fuels, will make the water more acidic by 2100 than it had been in the last 420,000 years. The increased acidity could slow the growth rate of coral reefs, reduce populations of sea life with calcium carbonate shells, and disrupt the food chain.

The link between warm ocean waters and hurricanes led many climatologists to speculate in August and September 2005 whether global warming was in part to blame for the devastating hurricanes Katrina and Rita. Both hurricanes grew in intensity as they passed over the abnormally warm Gulf of Mexico. Many scientists were cautious to make the connection, pointing out that cyclical fluctuations in storm activity could be responsible. However, some environmentalists pointed to the unusually large sizes of these storms as evidence for the link to climate change.

Chemical spill in China. An explosion at a chemical plant in Jilin, in northeast China, released a toxic slick of benzene into the Songhua River in November 2005. The benzene slick was 50 miles (80 kilometers) long as it flowed through the city of Harbin, located 120 miles (195 kilometers) northwest of Jilin. Officials shut down Harbin's water system, and none of the city's 3.8 million people were sickened. However, the Chinese government did not confirm that the river had been polluted with benzene until 10 days after the explosion. Environmentalists charged that the incident underscored the environmental harm caused by China's growing economy and poorly enforced public safety standards.   ■ Andrew Hoffman

See also **Conservation; Disasters: A Special Report; Global warming.**

Equatorial Guinea. See Africa.

Eritrea. See Africa.

Estonia. See Europe.

Ethiopia. See Africa.

EUROPE

The European Union (EU), Europe's main political and economic bloc, confronted serious challenges in 2005. After engaging in an unprecedented enlargement of its membership from 15 to 25 countries in 2004, the governments and people of Europe needed time to integrate the new nations into the EU and its institutions. The agenda for 2005, however, included ratification of a new constitution by the member states and starting membership negotiations with Turkey. Neither proved popular with many Europeans.

In the end, the constitution failed to win a majority in France and the Netherlands, which effectively put off into the future the adoption of any new constitution. Membership talks did begin with Turkey in October, but only after difficult backroom deals brokered by the leadership of British Prime Minister Tony Blair helped overcome the opposition of several key member states. (The United Kingdom held the rotating presidency of the EU from July to December 2005.) The EU economies grew slowly in 2005, and this slow growth was expected to continue in 2006.

Rejection of the EU constitution. The purpose of the Constitutional Treaty, which had been signed by government leaders in Rome in October 2004, was to systematize all of the older treaties that had given rise to the EU. The new constitution was to streamline decision-making processes within the EU and enhance the EU's role in foreign policy making. In many policy areas, under the rules in effect in 2005, unanimity among the member states was required to pass legislation, making it difficult to pass laws. By permitting more laws to be adopted by majority vote, the constitution was to enable more efficient decision making.

The constitution was also to enhance the EU's role as a foreign policy actor by creating the positions of EU president (who would serve for a 30-month term) and a single EU foreign minister. Finally, the constitutional treaty was to entrench civil, political, and social rights in a Charter of Fundamental Rights, bringing the EU a step closer to U.S.-style judicial review.

The constitution required ratification by all 25 member states. Some states, such as Germany and Hungary, ratified the document by parliamentary vote. Others, such as France and the Netherlands, held a referendum. After a tightly fought campaign, 55 percent of French citizens and 62 percent of Dutch voters rejected the constitution in May and June, respectively.

Public opinion polls suggested that the constitution had been turned down for a number of reasons. Some Europeans feared that it would erode national cultures and undermine employment security and the welfare state. Others feared that it would create a large bureaucracy. Many voters felt that the recent enlargement had made the EU too large too quickly and feared that the constitution would pave the way for Turkey's too-rapid admission to the bloc.

Although some EU leaders spoke of revising the treaty and putting it before the electorate again, the consensus of most was that the new constitution was dead. Nevertheless, the rejection of the constitution did not throw the EU into crisis. The treaties that created the EU and the legislation by which it operates remained in force. The problems that the constitution was designed to resolve—slow decision making in a new and enlarged union and the weakness of the EU as a foreign policy actor—remained as well.

Turkey's accession. Turkey was scheduled to begin negotiations for entering the EU on October 3. Having taken over the EU's rotating six-month presidency after the failure of the constitution referenda in France and the Netherlands, Blair's first task was to shepherd the process of Turkey's accession to its first stage: negotiations. Many European leaders and a large majority of the European public opposed Turkish accession. The first concern was economic. As a large and comparatively poor country, Turkey

would be entitled to transfer payments and agricultural subsidies from the EU that currently go to other regions of Europe. In addition—and perhaps more important—because the citizens of Turkey would be entitled to live and work anywhere in Europe, they could, in effect, compete for jobs in countries that already have high levels of unemployment.

The issue of Islam also came into play, as more than 98 percent of the people of Turkey are Muslims. Not only did many Europeans worry about competition from Turkish workers, they also expressed concern about Turkey's commitment to democracy and the rule of law. Some European leaders identify the borders of Europe with Christianity. Others, including the German and Austrian right-of-center parties, opposed Turkey's accession but favored a "privileged partnership."

French President Jacques Chirac and German Chancellor Gerhard Schröder favored Turkey's membership. They argued that not only had Turkey been assured previously that membership talks would begin, but that excluding Turkey from the EU would send the wrong signal to the Muslim world and destabilize an important country on Europe's borders. Chirac assured French citizens that negotiations did not automatically mean accession and that any enlargement would be subject to ratification in France by a referendum.

It was ultimately Austria, however, that threatened to block the start of negotiations. Austria refused to sign off on Turkey unless Croa-

tia was allowed to begin negotiations with the EU at the same time. Croatia's membership had long been dependent on increased cooperation with the International Criminal Court in the Hague, set up to prosecute crimes committed during the war in the former Yugoslavia. Nevertheless, Austria pushed for Croatian membership because of its historical ties with the country and to secure its own western and southern borders.

After a marathon negotiation session that continued into the night on October 2, the British presidency secured Austria's assent. Both Turkey and Croatia formally began negotiations for EU membership. Turkey, however, was not expected to join the EU for at least a decade. On April 25, 2005, Bulgaria and Romania signed accession treaties with the EU, paving the way for their membership in either 2007 or 2008.

Foreign policy. The EU played an active role in foreign policy in 2005. In February, U.S. President George W. Bush paid a two-day visit to Brussels, where he met with the leaders of the North Atlantic Treaty Organization (NATO, the military alliance between Europe and the United States) and the European Union. The discussions between the leaders centered on the Middle East, climate change, poverty, and terrorism. President Bush's visit was seen as a triumph for EU foreign policy because it represented the first time that a U.S. president had devoted so much attention to Europe as a coherent entity.

The EU continued in 2005 to be a large source of foreign aid to Africa, Asia, and the Middle East. At the June meeting of the European Council in Brussels, European leaders agreed to boost EU aid to 90 billion euros ($108 billion) by 2015.

On Sept. 5, 2005, the EU and China held their eighth annual summit, during which they signed a number of "strategic partnership" agreements. The agenda included discussions on trade, transportation, space exploration, and environmental issues. In 2004, the EU became China's largest trading partner.

The EU did not fully engage in the recon-

FACTS IN BRIEF ON EUROPEAN COUNTRIES

Country	Population	Government	Monetary unit*	Foreign trade (million U.S.$) Exports[†]	Imports[†]
Albania	3,243,000	President Alfred Moisiu; Prime Minister Sali Berisha	lek (100.15 = $1)	552	2,076
Andorra	77,000	Co-sovereigns bishop of Urgel, Spain, and the president of France; Head of Government Albert Pintat	euro (0.82 = $1)	58	1,077
Austria	8,143,000	President Heinz Fischer; Chancellor Wolfgang Schuessel	euro (0.82 = $1)	102,700	101,200
Belarus	9,769,000	President Aleksandr Lukashenko; Prime Minister Sergei Sidorsky	ruble (2,153.50 = $1)	11,470	13,570
Belgium	10,372,000	King Albert II; Prime Minister Guy Verhofstadt	euro (0.82 = $1)	255,700	235,000
Bosnia-Herzegovina	4,221,000	Chairman of the collective presidency Ivo Miro Jovic	marka (1.57 = $1)	1,700	5,200
Bulgaria	7,702,000	President Georgi Parvanov; Prime Minister Sergei Stanishev	lev (1.58 = $1)	9,134	12,230
Croatia	4,380,000	President Stjepan Mesic; Prime Minister Ivo Sanader	kuna (5.98 = $1)	7,845	16,700
Czech Republic	10,236,000	President Vaclav Klaus; Prime Minister Jiri Paroubek	koruna (23.52 = $1)	66,510	68,190
Denmark	5,408,000	Queen Margrethe II; Prime Minister Anders Fogh Rasmussen	krone (6.01 = $1)	73,060	63,450
Estonia	1,283,000	President Arnold Ruutel; Prime Minister Andrus Ansip	kroon (12.60 = $1)	5,701	7,318
Finland	5,231,000	President Tarja Halonen; Prime Minister Matti Taneli Vanhanen	euro (0.82 = $1)	61,040	45,170
France	60,093,000	President Jacques Chirac; Prime Minister Dominique de Villepin	euro (0.82 = $1)	419,000	419,700
Germany	82,636,000	President Horst Koehler; Chancellor Angela Merkel	euro (0.82 = $1)	893,300	716,700
Greece	10,981,000	President Karolos Papoulias; Prime Minister Costas Karamanlis	euro (0.82 = $1)	15,500	54,280
Hungary	9,956,000	President Laszlo Solyom; Prime Minister Ferenc Gyurcsany	forint (196.89 = $1)	54,620	58,680
Iceland	296,000	President Olafur Grimsson; Prime Minister Halldor Asgrimsson	krona (62.53 = $1)	2,902	3,307
Ireland	4,076,000	President Mary McAleese; Prime Minister Bertie Ahern	euro (0.82 = $1)	103,800	60,650
Italy	58,029,000	President Carlo Azeglio Ciampi; Prime Minister Silvio Berlusconi	euro (0.82 = $1)	336,400	329,300 (includes San Marino)
Latvia	2,244,000	President Vaira Vike-Freiberga; Prime Minister Aigars Kalvitis	lat (0.56 = $1)	3,569	5,970
Liechtenstein	34,000	Prince Hans Adam II; Prime Minister Otmar Hasler	Swiss franc (1.24 = $1)	2,470	917

struction of Iraq in 2005. However, it did sign a joint political declaration with the government of Iraq in September. The purpose of the document was to lay a framework for future cooperation. By 2005, the EU had contributed 518 million euros ($607 million) to Iraq's reconstruction.

Under British, French, and German leadership, the EU continued negotiations in 2005 with the government of Iran in an attempt to persuade the Iranians to abandon the goal of building nuclear weapons. Iran had suspended nuclear development activities in November 2004 but resumed them in August 2005. On September 24, the board of governors of the International Atomic Energy Agency, an organization that promotes safe and peaceful uses of nuclear energy throughout the world, adopted a resolution drafted by the EU. According to the terms of the resolution, if Iran does not suspend its nuclear development activities, the case would be referred to the United Nations Security Council.

Country	Population	Government	Monetary unit*	Foreign trade (million U.S.$)	
				Exports[†]	Imports[†]
Lithuania	3,391,000	President Valdas Adamkus; Prime Minister Algirdas Mykolas Brazauskas	litas (2.78 = $1)	8,880	11,020
Luxembourg	467,000	Grand Duke Henri; Prime Minister Jean-Claude Juncker	euro (0.82 = $1)	13,400	16,300
Macedonia	2,085,000	President Branko Crvenkovski; Prime Minister Vlado Buckovski	denar (47.85 = $1)	1,629	2,677
Malta	398,000	President Edward Fenech Adami; Prime Minister Lawrence Gonzi	lira (0.35 = $1)	2,625	3,407
Moldova	3,598,000	President Vladimir Voronin; Prime Minister Vasile Tarlev	leu (12.49 = $1)	1,030	1,830
Monaco	34,000	Prince Albert II; Minister of State Jean-Paul Proust	euro (0.82 = $1)	no statistics available	
Netherlands	16,357,000	Queen Beatrix; Prime Minister Jan Peter Balkenende	euro (0.82 = $1)	293,100	252,700
Norway	4,586,000	King Harald V; Prime Minister Jens Stoltenberg	krone (6.28 = $1)	76,640	45,960
Poland	38,485,000	President Lech Kaczynski; Prime Minister Kazimierz Marcinkiewicz	zloty (3.16 = $1)	75,980	81,610
Portugal	10,777,000	President Jorge Sampaio; Prime Minister José Sócrates	euro (0.82 = $1)	37,680	52,100
Romania	21,422,000	President Traian Basescu; Prime Minister Calin Popescu-Tariceanu	new leu (2.79 = $1)	23,540	28,430
Russia	142,190,000	President Vladimir Putin; Prime Minister Mikhail Fradkov	ruble (28.27 = $1)	162,500	92,910
San Marino	30,000	2 captains regent appointed by Grand Council every 6 months	euro (0.82 = $1)	336,400	329,300 (includes Italy)
Serbia and Montenegro	10,510,000	President Svetozar Marovic	euro (0.82 = $1) new dinar (70.51 = $1)	3,245	9,538
Slovakia	5,415,000	President Ivan Gasparovic; Prime Minister Mikulas Dzurinda	koruna (30.72 = $1)	29,240	29,670
Slovenia	1,975,000	President Janez Drnovsek; Prime Minister Janez Jansa	tolar (192.77 = $1)	14,970	16,070
Spain	41,205,000	King Juan Carlos I; Prime Minister José Luis Rodríguez Zapatero	euro (0.82 = $1)	172,500	222,000
Sweden	9,003,000	King Carl XVI Gustaf; Prime Minister Goran Persson	krona (7.50 = $1)	121,700	97,970
Switzerland	7,298,000	President Samuel Schmid	franc (1.24 = $1)	130,700	121,100
Turkey	74,204,000	President Ahmet Necdet Sezer; Prime Minister Recep Tayyip Erdogan	new lira (1.34 = $1)	69,460	94,500
Ukraine	46,691,000	President Viktor Yushchenko; Prime Minister Yuri Yekhanurov	hryvnia (5.02 = $1)	32,910	31,450
United Kingdom	60,715,000	Queen Elizabeth II; Prime Minister Tony Blair	pound (0.54 = $1)	347,200	439,400

*Exchange rates as of September 2005, or latest available data. [†]Latest available data.

Trade dispute. A trade dispute between the United States and the EU heated up in 2005, when the EU retaliated against the Byrd amendment. The amendment, formally known as the Continued Dumping and Subsidy Offset Act (CDSOA), was passed by the U.S. Congress in 2000. The law allows U.S. firms that successfully demonstrate that European competitors have sold goods in the United States at unfairly low prices to collect the duties and tariffs imposed on the European firms. The World Trade Organization (WTO) ruled in 2003 that the amendment violates international trade agreements. (The WTO is an international organization that promotes trade among nations.) However, the United States did not withdraw the legislation. As a result, in November 2004, the WTO allowed the EU and several individual nations—including Brazil, Canada, Chile, India, Japan, Mexico, and South Korea—to impose economic sanctions on the United States.

On May 1, 2005, the EU placed an additional 15-percent duty on certain U.S. agricultural, textile, machinery, and paper products. At the same time, Canada imposed a 15-percent tariff on cigarettes, oysters, live hogs, and various types of fish. In September, Japan followed with a 15-percent duty on steel imports. By the end of 2005, legislation had been introduced in the U.S. Congress to repeal the CDSOA. In addition, the Bush administration filed an amendment to the CDSOA in October, prohibiting the distribution of duties and tariffs collected from European competitors that contradict WTO policies.

Transparency. During 2005, the EU sought to make its financial and policy-making processes more transparent to the public. Many of Europe's citizens had expressed in polls concerns about such matters as whether funds transferred from the member states to the EU bureaucracy in Brussels are wasted. In March, EU Administrative Affairs and Anti-Fraud Commissioner Siim Kallas proposed a European Transparency Initiative. The initiative would increase the financial accountability of EU funding; strengthen the integrity and independence of EU institutions; and impose stricter controls on lobbyists. The proposal was adopted by the entire EU Commission in November, and a "Green Paper" was to be published in early 2006 to launch a debate on how to improve transparency.

Economic malaise. In 2005, the countries of the EU disagreed on a budget and on the best way out of the continent's general economic malaise. Although the EU had agreed at a meeting in Lisbon, Portugal, in 2000 to make the EU "the most competitive and dynamic knowledge-driven economy by 2010," the "Lisbon agenda" remained mostly a series of declarations.

In October 2005, the leaders of the EU gathered for a summit in the United Kingdom. However, the leaders of the bloc could not agree on how to reduce the agricultural subsidies that dominated the EU's budget and created tensions within the WTO. They also disagreed on the best way of increasing economic competitiveness without sacrificing the security of the welfare state.

In 2005, unemployment remained high among the 25 EU economies, at 8.7 percent. Nevertheless, it had fallen from 9.0 percent in 2004, and EU economists forecast that it would continue to drop, to 8.5 percent in 2006. The economy grew by 1.5 percent in the EU in 2005, a slowdown from 2.4 percent in 2004. EU economists forecast that it would rise to 2.1 percent in 2006 and reach 2.4 percent again in 2007. ■ Jeffrey Kopstein

See also various European country articles.

European Union. See Europe.
Explosion. See Disasters.
Farm and farming. See Agriculture.

Fashion, in 2005, was, more than ever, a potpourri of colors, especially bright ones; shapes, from pencil-slim to bouffant; lengths, from mini to maxi; and fabrics, ranging from shiny to nubby. Still, there were some fashion constants in 2005: from jeans to skirts, dresses, and jackets, denim remained the all-around favorite.

Designers. Predictably, 2005 had no single design leader, no designer with the influence of, for example, Christian Dior, who single-handedly revived French couture after World War II (1939-1945); or Karl Lagerfeld, who led the house of Chanel to success beginning in the early 1980's. Nevertheless, some of the younger designers taking over at famous houses attracted favorable attention in 2005—Francisco Costa at Calvin Klein; Nicolas Ghesquiere at Balenciaga; and Olivier Theyskens at Rochas. However, many houses continued in 2005 to change designers each season, hoping to find the right chemistry.

Not only did the year produce no preeminent design leader, but it also became apparent in 2005 that one nation could no longer dominate the fashion industry, as France did through much of the 1800's and 1900's. National borders became insignificant in the fashion world with the advent of instant communication. Women in Tokyo, Shanghai, London, and Beverly Hills showed ever-more similar tastes, and the next hot clothing designer might hail from nearly anywhere.

The number of successful designers creating clothing aimed at mass markets continued to grow in 2005. In the fall, the Swedish retailer Hennes & Mauritz (H & M) featured a low-priced collection designed by Stella McCartney, a follow-up to the 2004 collection for H & M designed by Karl Lagerfeld. Lagerfeld's designs had sold out very quickly—at some stores, within hours of being released. McCartney's designs also sold very well. Some items from the collection were even being offered, at a substantial mark-up, by enterprising customers on an online auction site hours after the collection was available. Earlier, the collection had run into unexpected difficulties not related to the garments. Supermodel Kate Moss was contracted to be the "face" of McCartney's line until a British tabloid published photographs of her allegedly taking illegal drugs. H & M pulled the entire ad campaign and used a different model.

Fur and glitter. Fur underwent a small revival in 2005, with designers refashioning it in an attempt to appeal to younger customers. The mink coat that once was considered essential by some fashion followers no longer appealed to middle-aged and younger women. Fur was now being used in such items as little boleros, big collars on fitted jackets, and fringed scarves. The new furs were less expensive. In many instances, attractive synthetics were substituted for animal fur.

Flip flops were worn *everywhere* during the summer of 2005. Some members of Northwestern University's champion lacrosse team caused a flip flop flap when they appeared at the White House in July shod in what an earlier generation considered appropriate only for the beach or a shower stall.

Some sort of sparkle often appeared in dresses for day as well as in evening wear. Sequins and paillettes glistened on patterned cotton skirts, and wide belts were frequently covered in glitter. Metallics were used for fall, especially in shoes and handbags.

Shoes, boots, and bags. In 2005, for a second year, flip flops, once considered beach shoes, were more prominent than conventional sandals, and even sneakers, on city streets. Until recently, flip flops could be found in drugstores for 99 cents. Popularity caused a considerable rise in price.

Boots were a fashion item for fall. The many different styles—boots with high stiletto heels, riding boots with flat heels, boots with pointy toes, boots that laced—reflected just how varied trends were in 2005.

Handbags became a must-have item in the luxury market. While designer handbags had been popular since the 1970's, fashion-conscious women in 2005 paid $1,000 or more for certain status bags from such lines as Prada, Marc Jacobs, and Jimmy Choo. For some, a bag had become more important to their look than clothing. Large, colorful handbags became popular in 2005. The trend was so pronounced that New York City street vendors, who once focused on large black tote bags, began stocking these decorative bags. ■ Bernadine Morris

Finland. Finland's coalition government, made up of the Center Party, the Social Democratic Party (SDP), and the Swedish People's Party, remained stable in 2005 and was expected to remain in office until the next scheduled elections in 2007. In March 2005, Paavo Lipponen, chairman of the SDP, resigned. Lipponen, a former prime minister, had shepherded Finland into the European Union in 1995. He was replaced by Eero Heinäluoma, who had been SDP secretary.

The race for president of Finland began in 2005. The current president, Tarja Halonen, announced in May that she would seek a second term. Halonen remained the favorite in a three-way race against the National Coalition Party's Sauli Niinistö and the Center Party's Matti Vanhanen, the current prime minister. The race was to be decided in January 2006.

Finland's economy grew at a slower rate in 2005, by 1.9 percent, down from 3.6 percent in 2004. The increase in the value of the euro against the United States dollar slowed export growth in Finland's strong technology sector. Finland continued to suffer moderately high levels of unemployment—over 8 percent throughout 2005. Nevertheless, the country's traditionally generous social benefits helped mitigate the risks of unemployment for most workers. ■ Jeffrey Kopstein

See also **Europe.**

MyPyramid
STEPS TO A HEALTHIER YOU
MyPyramid.gov

| GRAINS | VEGETABLES | FRUITS | MILK | MEAT & BEANS |

The United States Food and Drug Administration released MyPyramid in April 2005, a new food pyramid that uses colored bands to help consumers choose healthy amounts of food from various food groups. The figure at the side emphasizes the importance of exercise.

Food. New *Dietary Guidelines for Americans* were released by the United States departments of Health and Human Services (HHS) and Agriculture (USDA) on Jan. 12, 2005. The guidelines, which are updated every five years, represent the most current science-based dietary advice for Americans.

According to the new guidelines, people without special dietary needs should eat a variety of nutritious foods and beverages from the basic food groups daily. They should limit saturated and trans fats, cholesterol, added sugars, salt, and alcohol. For the first time, the guidelines emphasized the importance of exercise. To maintain a healthy weight and reduce the risk of chronic disease, people should balance calorie intake with regular physical activity, exercising for at least 30 minutes beyond their usual activity most days of the week.

In April, the USDA released MyPyramid, a new symbol and interactive food guidance system that replaced the Food Guide Pyramid introduced in 1992. MyPyramid is a visual representation of the food guidelines, with colored bands corresponding to the food groups. A new government Web site (www.mypyramid.gov) allows visitors to personalize the guidelines by entering their age, gender, and activity levels to receive specific diet recommendations. In September 2005, the USDA unveiled MyPyramid for Kids, nutrition information targeting children 6 to 11 years of age.

On September 30, the USDA Economic Research Service released a study of consumer behavior and retail food market conditions that resulted from the new guidelines. The authors of the study reported a decline in low carbohydrate diets, lower meat sales, and increased sales of whole-grain foods, a key recommendation of the guidelines. As sales of whole grain pasta and bread increased, many food companies shifted focus from low-carb products to healthier products for a balanced diet. Companies such as Campbell Soup Co. of Camden, New Jersey, and Sara Lee Corp. of Chicago launched new products or revised old ones to include whole grain, fiber, and folic acid while eliminating or reducing trans fat, saturated fat, and sugar. Atkins Nutritionals Inc. of Ronkonkoma, New York, which heavily promoted the low-carb diet that was very popular in the early 2000's, filed for bankruptcy in August 2005.

Childhood obesity. The Centers for Disease Control and Prevention (CDC) in Atlanta, Georgia, reported in October that the percentage of overweight American youths aged 12 to 19 increased from 5 percent in the late 1970's to 16 percent in the early 2000's. Because most youths are in school for a significant part of each day, CDC researchers conducted a survey in 2004 to learn what types of foods are available to them. Although most schools have a USDA meals program, they also sell what the USDA calls "competitive foods" through vending machines, school stores, and snack bars. The survey revealed that more than 80 percent of secondary schools allowed students to purchase less nutritious snacks at school. The CDC urged schools to reconsider the types of snacks available to students. In August 2005, the USDA Food and Nutrition Service reported that more than half of the states had already either restricted, or were in the process of restricting, the sale on school grounds of less nutritious snacks and beverages.

Chocolate. In April, the USDA's Agricultural Research Service reported that the more cocoa powder chocolate contains, the more *antioxidant* properties it has. Antioxidants protect against high blood pressure and unhealthy blood clotting and help reduce levels of "bad" LDL cholesterol while boosting "good" HDL cholesterol. Natural cocoa powder has the highest level of antioxidants, followed by unsweetened baking chocolate, "Dutch" cocoa powder, dark chocolate, semisweet chocolate baking chips, and milk chocolate.

Retail food prices rose slightly in 2005, according to a report issued by USDA economists in September. Prices were expected to continue to rise because of an increase in oil prices after Hurricane Katrina struck the Gulf Coast on August 29. Prices in 2005 rose 3.5 percent from 2004, with fresh fruit and vegetable prices increasing by 6 percent. ■ Robert C. Gatty

Football.

The University of Texas (Austin) pulled off a stunning come-from-behind upset over the University of Southern California (USC) 41-38 in the Rose Bowl on Jan. 4, 2006, to win its first national championship since 1969. Texas quarterback Vince Young put on a dazzling and memorable performance, throwing and scrambling for 467 yards and 3 touchdowns.

In the National Football League (NFL), the New England Patriots became just the second team in history to win three Super Bowls in four seasons by defeating the Philadelphia Eagles 24-21 in Super Bowl XXXIX on Feb. 6, 2005, in Jacksonville, Florida. The Super Bowl victory was the Patriots's second in a row.

In the 2005-2006 NFL season, the Indianapolis Colts won their first 13 games but failed in their attempt to become the first team to go unbeaten in the regular season since the schedule was expanded to 16 games in 1978. The Colts were hoping to join the 1972 Miami Dolphins (17-0 overall), the only team to go unbeaten in the regular season and win the Super Bowl.

College. On Jan. 4, 2006, second-ranked Texas stunned top-ranked USC 41-38 in a high-scoring championship game that fans had been expecting from the two top offenses in the country. Texas quarterback Vince Young overwhelmed

USC's defense, rushing for 200 yards and throwing for 267 more. Young's 8-yard touchdown run—his third in the game—on fourth down with 19 seconds left, finished off USC and ended its bid to become the first school to take three consecutive national football titles.

In other major bowls, Ohio State University (Columbus) defeated the University of Notre Dame 34-20 in the Fiesta Bowl; Penn State University (State College) defeated Florida State (Tallahassee) 26-23 in the Orange Bowl; and the University of West Virginia (Morgantown) defeated the heavily favored University of Georgia (Athens) 38-35 in the Sugar Bowl.

BCS changes. After several seasons of controversy in crowning a national football champion, the Associated Press (AP) in late 2004 told officials of the Bowl Championship Series (BCS), the body that determines which teams play for the championship, to stop using the AP poll in its standings. AP officials said they had never sanctioned the use of the poll, and they feared that the poll was losing its credibility. Instead, BCS officials selected Harris Interactive to operate a poll to select the top 25 teams. The BCS also used another poll and six computer rankings to determine the top teams in the country.

In 2005, for the first time in three seasons, the BCS avoided controversy because the two teams set to compete for the title were the only teams who went undefeated.

Beginning in the 2006 season, the BCS will add a fifth BCS bowl to the four existing bowls (Orange, Fiesta, Rose, and Sugar). The new system allows two more schools to qualify for a BCS contest. The first title game was scheduled for Jan. 8, 2007.

Back on top. The Penn State and Notre Dame football teams returned to national prominence after struggling in recent years. Notre Dame hired Charlie Weis, the offensive coordinator for the NFL's New England Patriots during the team's three Super Bowl wins, and the new coach's impact was substantial and immediate.

Sporting a more dynamic attack, Notre Dame rolled to a 9-2 regular season record, a No. 6 ranking, and its first BCS bowl appearance since the 2001 Fiesta Bowl.

In 2004, many Penn State fans called for coach Joe Paterno to step aside in response to the team's 4-7 season. The 78-year-old Paterno nevertheless stayed for the 2005 season, and the team collected its first Big Ten title in 11 years and its first BCS bowl appearance. Penn State went 7-1 in the Big Ten and rose to No. 3 in the final BCS standings.

Heisman Trophy. USC running back Reggie Bush won the Heisman Trophy on December 10 in New York City. Bush won handily with 784 first-place votes, the most since O. J. Simpson received 855 in 1968. Bush beat out University of Texas (Austin) quarterback Vince Young, who had 79 votes, and USC teammate, quarterback Matt Leinart, who received 18 votes.

NFL. On Feb. 6, 2005, the New England Patriots matched the Dallas Cowboys (Super Bowls XXVII, XXVIII, and XXX) as the only teams to win three Super Bowls in four seasons. In 2005, the Patriots won on defensive strength, unlike their previous triumphs, which were won on last-second field goals,

The Patriots scored 10 unanswered points to build up a 24-14 lead to start the fourth quarter. However, the Eagles connected on a 30-yard touchdown pass with 1:48 left to play. The Eagles then forced the Patriots to punt, taking possession of the ball at their own 4-yard line with 46 seconds to play. However, New England intercepted Eagles quarterback Donovan McNabb three plays later to seal the victory.

Patriots receiver Deion Branch caught a Super Bowl record-tying 11 passes and was named the Most Valuable Player award. Branch's performance overshadowed the return of Eagles receiver Terrell Owens, who returned for the Super Bowl after missing seven weeks with a broken leg. Owens caught 9 passes for 122 yards. New England quarterback Tom Brady, a two-time Super Bowl MVP, completed 23 of 33 passes for 236 yards and two touchdowns.

Play-offs. In the American Football Conference (AFC) wild-card play-offs, the New York Jets defeated the San Diego Chargers 20-17 in overtime on January 8, while the Indianapolis Colts used their high-flying attack to throttle the Denver Broncos 49-24 on January 9. In that game, Colts quarterback Peyton Manning passed for 457 yards, the second most in postseason history, behind only Bernie Kosar's 489 yards in 1986. The following weekend, the Patriots's defense held Manning to no touchdowns in a 20-3 win in a chilling sleet storm at Foxborough, Massachusetts, while the Pittsburgh Steelers took advantage of two missed field goals by the Jets to advance with a 20-17 victory in overtime. In the AFC title game on Jan. 23, 2005, in Pittsburgh, New England handed Steelers rookie quarterback Ben Roethlisberger his first loss as a professional with a 41-27 pounding.

In the National Football Conference (NFC) wild-card play-offs, the St. Louis Rams defeated the Seattle Seahawks 27-20 on January 8, and the Minnesota Vikings overpowered the Green Bay Packers 31-17 on January 9 in Green Bay, Wisconsin. The following week, Philadelphia toppled Minnesota 27-14, while the Atlanta Falcons

trounced St. Louis 47-17. In the NFC title game, host Philadelphia never trailed in a 27-10 victory over Atlanta on January 23.

Rice retires. Star wide receiver Jerry Rice, 42, announced his retirement on September 5. During his 20-year NFL career, Rice collected 38 NFL records, including most yards receiving (22,895), most touchdowns receiving (197), and most receptions (1,549). He retired when it appeared he would not be a starting receiver for the Denver Broncos.

2005 season milestones. On September 18, San Diego running back LaDainian Tomlinson set an NFL record by rushing for a touchdown in 14 consecutive games. Tomlinson's record score came against the Denver Broncos. On October 23, the Philadelphia Eagles snapped Tomlinson's record-tying streak of 18 straight games with a rushing or receiving touchdown. In that game, the Eagles held Tomlinson to a career low 7 yards rushing. Baltimore's Lenny Moore scored touchdowns in 18 straight games from 1963 to 1965.

THE 2005 COLLEGE FOOTBAL

NATIONAL CHAMPIONS

NCAA Div. I-A	Texas	41	Southern California	38
NCAA Div. I-AA	Appalachian State	21	Northern Iowa	16
NCAA Div. II	Grand Valley State	21	N.W. Missouri State	17
NCAA Div. III	Mount Union	35	Wisc.-Whitewater	28
NAIA	Carroll College	27	St. Francis (Ind.)	10

BOWL CHAMPIONSHIP SERIES GAMES

BOWL	RESULT			
Rose	Texas	41	Southern California	38
Orange	Penn State	26	Florida State	23
Fiesta	Ohio State	34	Notre Dame	20
Sugar	West Virginia	38	Georgia	35

OTHER BOWL GAMES

BOWL	RESULT			
Alamo	Nebraska	32	Michigan	28
Capital One	Wisconsin	24	Auburn	10
Car Care	N.C. State	14	S. Florida	0
Champs Sports	Clemson	19	Colorado	10
Cotton	Alabama	13	Texas Tech	10
Ft. Worth	Kansas	42	Houston	13
Emerald	Utah	38	Georgia Tech	10
GMAC	Toledo	45	UTEP	13
Gator	Virginia Tech	35	Louisville	24
Hawaii	Nevada	49	UCF	48
Holiday	Oklahoma	17	Oregon	14
Houston	TCU	27	Iowa State	24
Independence	Missouri	38	South Carolina	31
Insight	Arizona State	45	Rutgers	40
Las Vegas	California	35	BYU	28
Liberty	Tulsa	31	Fresno State	24
MPC Computers	Boston College	27	Boise State	21
Motor City	Memphis	38	Akron	31
Music City	Virginia	34	Minnesota	31
New Orleans	S. Mississippi	31	Arkansas State	19
Outback	Florida	31	Iowa	24
Peach	LSU	40	Miami	3
Poinsettia	Navy	51	Colorado State	30
Sun	UCLA	50	Northwestern	38

CONFERENCE CHAMPIONS

NCAA DIVISION I-A

CONFERENCE	SCHOOL
Atlantic Coast	Florida State
Big 12	Texas
Big East	West Virginia
Big Ten	Penn State—Ohio State (tie)
Conference USA	Tulsa
Mid-American	Akron
Mountain West	Texas Christian
Pacific 10	Southern California
Southeastern	Georgia
Sun Belt	Arkansas State—Louisiana-Lafayette—Louisiana-Monroe (tie)
Western Athletic	Boise State—Nevada (tie)

NCAA DIVISION I-AA

CONFERENCE	SCHOOL
Atlantic 10	Richmond—New Hampshire (tie)
Big Sky	Montana—Eastern Washington—Montana State (tie)
Big South	Coastal Carolina—Charleston Southern (tie)
Gateway	Northern Iowa—Youngstown State—Southern Illinois (tie)
Great West	U.C. Davis—California Polytechnic (tie)
Ivy League	Brown
Metro Atlantic	Duquesne
Mid-Eastern	Hampton
Northeast	Stony Brook—Central Connecticut State (tie)
Ohio Valley	Eastern Illinois
Patriot	Colgate—Lafayette (tie)
Pioneer	San Diego
Southern	Appalachian State
Southland	Texas State—Nicholls State (tie)
Southwestern	Grambling State

ALL-AMERICA TEAM

(as chosen by the Associated Press)

OFFENSE

Quarterback—Vince Young, Texas
Running backs—Reggie Bush, USC; Jerome Harrison, Washington State
Wide receivers—Dwayne Jarrett, USC; Mike Hass, Oregon State
Tight end—Vernon Davis, Maryland
Center—Greg Eslinger, Minnesota
Other linemen—Jonathan Scott, Texas; Marcus McNeill, Auburn; Max Jean-Gilles, Georgia; D'Brickashaw Ferguson, Virginia
All-purpose player—Maurice Drew, UCLA
Place-kicker—Mason Crosby, Colorado

DEFENSE

Linemen—Tamba Hali, Penn State; Haloti Ngata, Oregon; Elvis Dumervil, Louisville; Rodrique Wright, Texas
Linebackers—A. J. Hawk, Ohio State; Paul Posluszny, Penn State; DeMeco Ryans, Alabama
Backs—Jimmy Williams, Virginia Tech; Darnell Bing, USC; Michael Huff, Texas; Greg Blue, Georgia
Punter—Ryan Plackemeier, Wake Forest

PLAYER AWARDS

Heisman Trophy (best player)—Reggie Bush, USC
Bednarik Trophy (best defensive player)—Paul Posluszny, Penn State

University of Southern California running back Reggie Bush jumps high to avoid being tackled by UCLA corner back Marcus Cassel for a fourth down at a December 3 game between the hometown rivals at The Los Angeles Memorial Coliseum. Bush handily won the Heisman Trophy on December 10 with 784 first-place votes, the most since O. J. Simpson received 855 in 1968.

Chicago Bears defensive back Nathan Vasher scored the longest touchdown in NFL history on Nov. 13, 2005, returning a missed field goal 108 yards against San Francisco. On the same day, the Minnesota Vikings became the first team to score touchdowns on an interception, a kickoff return, and a punt return in the same game in their victory over the New York Giants.

Canadian Football League. The Edmonton Eskimos won their second Grey Cup in three years on November 27 in Vancouver, defeating Montreal 38-35 on a field goal in overtime. Edmonton quarterback Ricky Ray put on a show, throwing for two touchdowns and rushing for a third. ■ Michael Kates

2005-2006 NATIONAL FOOTBALL LEAGUE FINAL STANDINGS

AMERICAN CONFERENCE

North Division	W.	L.	T.	Pct.
Cincinnati Bengals*	11	5	0	.688
Pittsburgh Steelers*	11	5	0	.688
Baltimore Ravens	6	10	0	.375
Cleveland Browns	6	10	0	.375

East Division	W.	L.	T.	Pct.
New England Patriots*	10	6	0	.625
Miami Dolphins	9	7	0	.563
Buffalo Bills	5	11	0	.313
N.Y. Jets	4	12	0	.250

South Division	W.	L.	T.	Pct.
Indianapolis Colts*	14	2	0	.875
Jacksonville Jaguars*	12	4	0	.750
Tennessee Titans	4	12	0	.250
Houston Texans	2	14	0	.125

West Division	W.	L.	T.	Pct.
Denver Broncos*	13	3	0	.813
Kansas City Chiefs	10	6	0	.625
San Diego Chargers	9	7	0	.563
Oakland Raiders	4	12	0	.250

*Made play-offs

NATIONAL CONFERENCE

North Division	W.	L.	T.	Pct.
Chicago Bears*	11	5	0	.688
Minnesota Vikings	9	7	0	.563
Detroit Lions	5	11	0	.313
Green Bay Packers	4	12	0	.250

East Division	W.	L.	T.	Pct.
New York Giants*	11	5	0	.688
Washington Redskins*	10	6	0	.625
Dallas Cowboys	9	7	0	.563
Philadelphia Eagles	6	10	0	.375

South Division	W.	L.	T.	Pct.
Tampa Bay Buccaneers*	11	5	0	.688
Carolina Panthers*	11	5	0	.688
Atlanta Falcons	8	8	0	.500
New Orleans Saints	3	13	0	.188

West Division	W.	L.	T.	Pct.
Seattle Seahawks*	13	3	0	.813
St. Louis Rams	6	10	0	.375
Arizona Cardinals	5	11	0	.313
San Francisco 49ers	4	12	0	.250

*Made play-offs

TEAM STATISTICS

Leading offenses	Plays	Yards per game
Kansas City	1,059	387.0
Indianapolis	1,001	362.4
Denver	1,030	360.4
Cincinnati	1,018	358.1
New England	1,031	352.0

Leading defenses	Avg. points against	Yards per game
Pittsburgh	16.1	284.0
Baltimore	18.7	284.7
Jacksonville	16.8	290.9
Indianapolis	15.4	307.1
New York	22.2	308.8

TEAM STATISTICS

Leading offenses	Plays	Yards per game
Seattle	1,020	369.7
New York	1,055	361.7
Arizona	1,075	348.4
St. Louis	1,025	348.2
Washington	1,037	330.6

Leading defenses	Avg. points against	Yards per game
Tampa Bay	17.1	277.8
Chicago	12.6	281.8
Carolina	16.2	282.6
Green Bay	21.5	293.1
Arizona	24.2	295.6

INDIVIDUAL STATISTICS

Leading scorers, touchdowns	TD's	Rush	Rec.	Ret.
Larry Johnson, Kansas City	21	20	1	0
LaDainian Tomlinson, San Diego	20	18	2	0
Edgerrin James, Indianapolis	14	13	1	0
Corey Dillon, New England	13	12	1	0

Leading kickers	PAT made/att.	FG made/att.	Longest FG	Pts.
Graham, Cincinnati	47/47	28/32	49	131
Tynes, Kansas City	44/45	27/33	52	125
Vanderjagt, Indiana	52/52	23/25	48	121
Reed, Pittsburgh	45/45	24/29	44	117

Leading quarterbacks	Att.	Comp.	Yds.	TD's	Ints.
Tom Brady, New England	530	334	4,110	26	14
Trent Green, Kansas City	507	317	4,014	17	10
Carson Palmer, Cincinnati	509	345	3,836	32	12
Kerry Collins, Oakland	565	302	3,759	20	12
Peyton Manning, Indianapolis	453	305	3,747	28	10

Leading receivers	Passes caught	Rec. yards	Avg. gain	TD's
Chad Johnson, Cincinnati	97	1,432	14.8	9
Marvin Harrison, Indianapolis	82	1,146	14.0	12
Chris Chambers, Miami	82	1,118	13.6	11
Rod Smith, Denver	85	1,105	13.0	6

Leading rushers	Rushes	Yards	Avg.	TD's
Larry Johnson, Kansas City	336	1,750	5.2	20
Edgerrin James, Indianapolis	360	1,506	4.2	13
LaDainian Tomlinson, San Diego	339	1,462	4.3	18
Rudi Johnson, Cincinnati	337	1,458	4.3	12

Leading punters	Punts	Yards	Avg.	Longest
Brian Moorman, Buffalo	71	3,242	45.7	68
Shane Lechler, Oakland	82	3,744	45.7	64
Josh Miller, New England	76	3,431	45.1	59
Hunter Smith, Indianapolis	52	2,301	44.3	58

INDIVIDUAL STATISTICS

Leading scorers, touchdowns	TD's	Rush	Rec.	Ret.
Shaun Alexander, Seattle	28	27	1	0
Steve Smith, Carolina	13	1	12	0
Stephen Davis, Carolina	12	12	0	0
Tiki Barber, New York	11	9	2	0

Leading kickers	PAT made/att.	FG made/att.	Longest FG	Pts.
Feely, New York	43/43	35/42	52	148
Rackers, Arizona	20/20	40/42	54	140
Kasay, Carolina	43/44	26/34	52	121
Wilkins, St. Louis	36/36	27/31	53	117

Leading quarterbacks	Att.	Comp.	Yds.	TD's	Ints.
Brett Favre, Green Bay	607	372	3,881	20	29
Eli Manning, New York	557	294	3,762	24	17
Drew Bledsoe, Dallas	499	300	3,639	23	17
Matt Hasselbeck, Seattle	449	294	3,459	24	9
Jake Delhomme, Carolina	435	262	3,421	24	16

Leading receivers	Passes caught	Rec. yards	Avg. gain	TD's
Steve Smith, Carolina	103	1,563	15.2	12
Santana Moss, Washington	84	1,483	17.7	9
Larry Fitzgerald, Arizona	103	1,409	13.7	10
Anquan Boldin, Arizona	102	1,402	13.7	7

Leading rushers	Rushes	Yards	Avg.	TD's
Shaun Alexander, Seattle	370	1,880	5.1	27
Tiki Barber, New York	357	1,860	5.2	9
Clinton Portis, Washington	352	1,516	4.3	11
Warrick Dunn, Atlanta	280	1,416	5.1	3

Leading punters	Punts	Yards	Avg.	Longest
Josh Bidwell, Tampa Bay	90	4,101	45.6	61
Chris Kluwe, Minnesota	71	3,130	44.1	62
Scott Player, Arizona	73	3,206	43.9	60
Nick Harris, Detroit	84	3,656	43.5	60

Protesters set vehicles afire on November 2, during a seventh night of rioting by primarily Muslim youth of African or Arab descent in the suburbs north of Paris. The violence, which erupted on October 27 after the accidental deaths of two youths, was aggravated by frustration over discrimination, housing, and unemployment issues.

France. In October and November 2005, France experienced its most serious bouts of civil unrest since the student riots of 1968. Groups of young people—mostly the children and grandchildren of Muslim immigrants from North Africa—burned cars and destroyed public property. At the height of the rioting, more than 1,400 vehicles were set afire in a single night.

The catalyst for the unrest was the death of two teen-agers, one of North African descent and the other from Mali, in a suburb of Paris on Oct. 27, 2005. The youths, believing themselves to be pursued by the police, were accidentally electrocuted while hiding at an electric substation. The riots began almost immediately in the suburban housing developments that had become a primary place of settlement for immigrant families. The violence quickly spread to about 300 cities and suburbs throughout France.

French authorities generally blamed the unrest on high levels of unemployment. However, they also believed that the French model of integrating newcomers—which ignores cultural differences and relies on teaching children to speak French and share the values of the republic—was partially to blame. Although most of the rioters spoke excellent French, they did not feel included in the promise of liberty, equality, and fraternity that lies at the core of modern French politics. Instead, immigrant youths claimed that they continually faced discrimination in housing, education, and employment opportunities.

The official response to the unrest was almost as controversial as the unrest itself. Interior Minis-

ter Nicolas Sarkozy referred to the rioters as "scum" and called for mass arrests. Politicians on the left criticized Sarkozy for his failure to see the deeper roots of the problem and his insensitive characterization of French citizens. In fact, for days the government's response to the riots was remarkably muted, with President Jacques Chirac making few statements on the subject. When the riots spread to other cities, an emergency meeting of the French Cabinet under Prime Minister Dominique de Villepin invoked a 1955 law permitting the declaration of a state of emergency. The law allowed local authorities in affected areas to impose curfews on young people. After two weeks, the parliament voted to extend the state of emergency until February 2006.

EU constitution. On May 29, 2005, 55 percent of French voters rejected the European Union (EU) constitution in a referendum, despite the strong urging of French leaders—including Chirac—to approve it. The purpose of the constitution was to streamline decision-making processes within the EU, Europe's main political and economic trading bloc, and to give the organization a unified voice in foreign affairs.

Many French voters, however, believed that the EU no longer represented the interests of France. Rather, they claimed that the organization had become a vehicle for imposing free-market policies that would ultimately lead to longer working hours and reduced social protections.

In addition to dissatisfaction with the EU itself, many French voters rejected the constitution simply because it was supported by Chirac. By 2005,

Chirac was often perceived as ineffectual, corrupt, and distant, and his economic policies were considered ill-equipped to reduce high levels of unemployment and unacceptable levels of public debt. Many policy analysts considered the French rejection of the constitution to mark the end of efforts to revise the document for the next several years. (In order to be adopted, the constitution required ratification by all 25 EU nations.)

New prime minister. Following the failure of the referendum, Chirac dismissed Prime Minister Jean-Pierre Raffarin and replaced him on May 31 with Interior Minister Dominique de Villepin. While serving as foreign minister from 2002 to 2004, de Villepin led the opposition to the United States-led war in Iraq. De Villepin promised to implement economic reforms to reduce unemployment, but he was hemmed in by powerful public sector unions on one side and hard-driving U.S.-style economic reformers on the other. Nicolas Sarkozy replaced de Villepin as interior minister.

Economy. According to EU analysts, economic growth in France slowed from 2.3 percent in 2004 to 1.5 percent in 2005. The economy was expected to grow only slightly in 2006, to 1.8 percent. The country's budget deficit, at 3.2 percent, exceeded the EU mandated limit of 3 percent of *gross domestic product* (GDP, the total value of goods and services produced in a country in a year) for the fourth year in a row. Unemployment remained at 9.6 percent for the second straight year and was expected to fall only slightly, to 9.3 percent, in 2006.

In February 2005, Thierry Breton became the ninth finance minister to be appointed in the last 10 years, the fourth minister to hold the position in 1 year. Financial analysts blamed the lack of continuity in financial leadership, in part, for the inability to bring the budget deficit under control and to curb unemployment.   ■ Jeffrey Kopstein

See also **Europe.**

Gabon. See Africa.

Gambia. See Africa.

Gas and gasoline. See Energy supply.

Genetic engineering. See Biology; Medicine.

Geology. Teams of geologists in 2005 analyzed the two largest earthquakes to occur in the past 40 years. These events were the first "great" earthquakes ever to be recorded by modern technology. (A great earthquake is an event with a moment magnitude of at least 8.) Both earthquakes occurred on the floor of the Indian Ocean, along the boundary of the Indian-Australian and Eurasian tectonic plates.

The first quake was the Sumatra-Andaman earthquake of Dec. 26, 2004, that produced a devastating tsunami. Three teams of geologists published their analyses of the quake in the May 2005 issue of *Science*. The researchers estimated that the earthquake had a moment magnitude of at least 9.1, making it the largest seismic event in 40 years. The quake ruptured about 960 miles (1,545 kilometers) of the plate boundary, lifting sections of the Burma plate by as much as 50 feet (15 meters). Seismic waves from the earthquake propagated to the north at speeds of up to 1.7 miles per second (2.8 kilometers per second), setting off other seismic events up to 2,700 miles (4,300 kilometers) away.

The second earthquake, which had a moment magnitude of at least 8.6, occurred along a neighboring fault on March 28, 2005. This event took place near the Indonesian islands of Simeulue and Nias, about 100 miles (160 kilometers) southeast of the December 26 event. The March 28 earthquake caused extensive damage, killing more than 900 people, but did not produce a tsunami.

Forecasting earthquakes. Scientists worked in 2005 not only to model earthquakes, but also to project or "forecast" events. Earthquake prediction technology would be particularly useful for heavily populated areas, such as California, where the Pacific and North American plates are actively sliding past each other. Geologists were not able in 2005 to predict the time, location, and magnitude of an earthquake. Once a quake occurred, however, scientists could use computer models to forecast the probability and number of aftershocks likely to follow the event.

A group of geologists led by Matthew C. Gerstenberger of the United States Geological Survey in Pasadena, California, published promising results on earthquake forecasting in the May issue of *Nature*. The scientists developed computer models that analyze the probability and magnitude of ground shaking anywhere in California for 24 hours after a major earthquake. The models display this information as real-time maps—similar to weather forecast maps—which the researchers planned to put on the Internet to give the public a live view of earthquake risks.

One major limitation of earthquake forecasting science is the short time span of historical seismology records—about 100 years—compared with the interval between great earthquakes, which can occur hundreds of years apart. In May, geologists led by Ray J. Weldon of the University of Oregon at Eugene called for more data on prehistoric earthquakes—a field known as paleoseismology.

Scientists gather such data by determining the date and amount of ground displacement at sites of prehistoric earthquakes. The San Andreas Fault in California is one of the most dangerous plate boundaries in the world, due to the large human population in the region. In 2005, Weldon and his colleagues analyzed 56 dates from 12 sites of prehistoric earthquakes along the southern San Andreas Fault. Based on this information, the researchers constructed "rupture scenarios" for areas such as Los Angeles.

Weldon's team noted that there had not been a great earthquake along the southern San Andreas Fault since 1857. However, paleoseismic data indicated that there had not been a lull in great earthquakes over the past 1,600 years that lasted longer than about 200 years. The geologists concluded that the latest quiet period is likely to end with a substantial earthquake, possibly within the next 50 years.

Medical geology. A new subdiscipline of the geosciences emerged in 2005. Medical geology is based on the collaboration of health care workers and geologists seeking to improve our understanding of the relationship between the environment and human health.

In January 2005, geologist Gabriel M. Filippelli and his colleagues at Indiana University-Purdue University in Indianapolis conducted a study of lead poisoning, a major issue for medical geology. The researchers pointed out that, in 2005, about 2 percent of U.S. children were affected by lead poisoning and that this number rises dramatically to 15 percent of urban children of low socioeconomic status. Filippelli found that lead contamination in soil near urban roadways, produced by past combustion of leaded gasoline, was causing lead poisoning in urban children. The researchers argued that, by conducting further studies on the relationship, geologists could inform the medical community and improve the health of urban youth.

Geologists in 2005 also identified a relationship between soil erosion and food production. Bruce H. Wilkinson of the University of Michigan in Ann Arbor announced in March that humans are responsible for moving 10 times more soil than the combined effects of all natural processes. Wilkinson warned that the rate of soil loss to U.S. farmlands in 2005 due to human activities exceeded the rate of soil formation, which could eventually lead to an agricultural crisis. ■ Henry T. Mullins

See also **Disasters; Physics.**

Georgia. Georgian President Mikhail Saakashvili, the leader of the 2003 "Rose Revolution" that swept former president Eduard Shevardnadze from power, suffered several political setbacks in 2005. Turmoil and corruption charges dogged Saakashvili's government, while stubborn separatist conflicts in the breakaway regions of Abkhazia and South Ossetia remained unresolved despite Saakashvili's efforts to break the stalemates.

On February 3, influential Prime Minister Zurab Zhvania and an aide were found dead of carbon monoxide poisoning. On June 29, Saakashvili fired Finance Minister Valeri Chechelashvili in the wake

of bribery charges against the state tax department. Koba Bekauri, the deputy chairman of the ruling National Movement parliamentary group, resigned on September 14 following an extortion scandal. On October 19, the prime minister fired popular Foreign Minister Salome Zourabichvili, who accused the government of betraying the principles of the Rose Revolution.

In early 2005, Saakashvili offered South Ossetia directly elected local self-governance, significant *autonomy* (independence) over social and economic policies, protection for the Ossetian language, and financial compensation for Ossetians harmed during the conflict that raged from 1990 to 1992. South Ossetia rejected the offer. On Sept. 19, 2005, South Ossetian President Eduard Kokoity and Abkhazian President Sergei Bagapsh signed a treaty promising mutual aid in the event of "extreme situations." ■ Juliet Johnson

See also **Asia; Russia; Russia: A Special Report.**

Germany. Angela Merkel became the first female chancellor of Germany in November 2005, after two months of negotiations. Merkel was also the first chancellor to be elected from the former East Germany.

Former Chancellor Gerhard Schröder had called for an early election during the spring session of Germany's parliament, the Bundestag, after it became clear that his own party, the center-left Social Democratic Party (SPD), no longer backed his economic reforms. In addition, the SPD had lost several state elections to the opposition Christian Democratic Union (CDU), and the upper house of the German parliament (the Bundesrat) blocked much of Schröder's legislation. Schröder gambled that the voters would prefer his coalition government with the Green Party to an uncertain future under an untested CDU leader, Angela Merkel.

Schröder's gamble turned out badly. From the outset of the campaign, public opinion polls gave Merkel's CDU a large lead and indicated that the new government would be a coalition of the CDU with the smaller free market-oriented Free Democratic Party (FDP). Merkel, however, ran a lackluster campaign and drew fire when one of her closest advisers proposed a flat income tax. Schröder took advantage of public distrust of the tax and campaigned tirelessly, closing the gap toward the end of the race.

The election, which took place on September 18, turned out badly for both the SPD, which received 34.3 percent of the vote, and the CDU, which garnered only 35.2 percent. The Greens, with 8.1 percent, retained roughly the same share of the vote as they had in 2002. The big winners were the other smaller parties, the FDP (9.8 percent) and especially the new Left Party (Linkspartei), a merger of disaffected Social Democrats

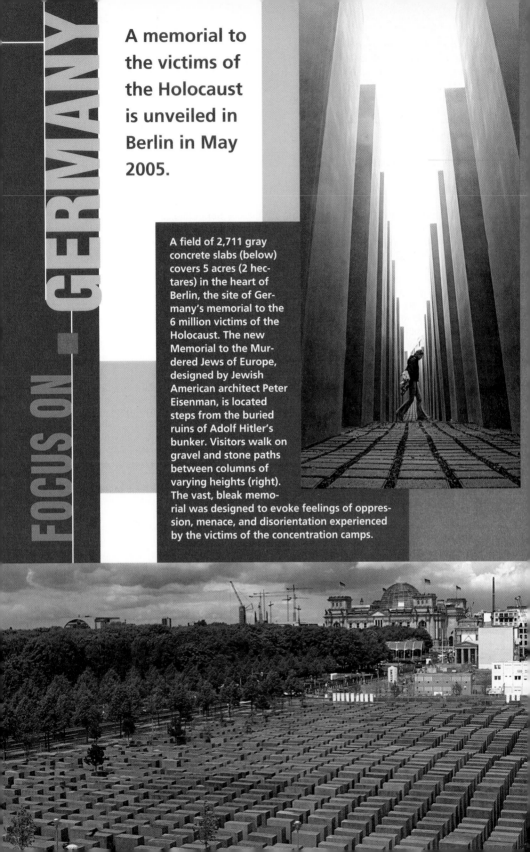

A memorial to the victims of the Holocaust is unveiled in Berlin in May 2005.

A field of 2,711 gray concrete slabs (below) covers 5 acres (2 hectares) in the heart of Berlin, the site of Germany's memorial to the 6 million victims of the Holocaust. The new Memorial to the Murdered Jews of Europe, designed by Jewish American architect Peter Eisenman, is located steps from the buried ruins of Adolf Hitler's bunker. Visitors walk on gravel and stone paths between columns of varying heights (right). The vast, bleak memorial was designed to evoke feelings of oppression, menace, and disorientation experienced by the victims of the concentration camps.

and former East German Communists. The Left Party received 8.7 percent of the vote.

After some initial confusion following the election, the parties agreed that the slim plurality won by the CDU gave it the right to form a government. To form a parliamentary majority, however, the CDU needed partners. An alliance with its traditional partners, the FDP, would not create a majority. The Greens and the FDP refused to cooperate with each other, and no party would collaborate with the Left Party. The only choice that remained was a "grand coalition" with the SPD.

Merkel had campaigned with promises of change, but the power of her own regional CDU leaders and the coalition agreement she made with the SPD ensured that her government would enact a mix of policies. To deal with the budget deficit, the coalition agreement called for raising the *value added tax* (a tax on consumer goods) and an increase in the tax rate for the highest income bracket. The retirement age was to gradually be increased from 65 to 67, in line with Schröder's modest labor market reforms to make it easier for businesses to hire and fire employees.

The German economy—Europe's largest—grew at a rate of only 0.8 percent in 2005, barely half the 1.5 percent average of the 25 EU nations, according to European Union (EU) economists. Although Germany remained the world's largest exporter of goods and services, the country continued to suffer from serious budget deficits. The forecasted deficit for 2005 was 3.9 percent, well above the eurozone benchmark of 3 percent of *gross domestic product* (GDP, the total value of goods and services produced in a year).

Economists noted that the grand coalition's plans to rein in the deficit by raising the value-added tax may slow already sluggish consumer spending—and the economy—even further. Especially serious was the problem of the labor market, which analysts considered too rigid and unable to generate a sufficient number of new jobs for young people and people living in the former East Germany. By January, unemployment in Germany had reached 5.2 million, the highest level since the Great Depression, the worldwide economic turndown of 1930's.

Eastern Germany. The five states that constituted the former East Germany continued to be a challenge for the German government in 2005. Each year since unification in 1990, the West has diverted some 90 billion euros ($106 billion) to the East, a level of subsidy that politicians maintained cannot be sustained. Unemployment in the former East Germany has remained high. Although wages in 2005 remained at approximately 65 percent of the rate in the western states, hoped-for levels of investment have never materialized because of even lower wages in the new EU member nations, such as Poland and the Czech Republic. By 2005, East Germans had become increasingly alienated from the mainstream political parties—the SPD and the CDU—and voted in increasing numbers for the Left Party.

Foreign policy. Gerhard Schröder had maintained a policy of close relations with France, Russia, and China at the expense of Poland, the United Kingdom (U.K.), and the traditional transatlantic alliance with the United States. Schröder's criticism of the U.S.-led war in Iraq and of American unilateralism remained his most popular policy. Chancellor Angela Merkel was expected to improve relations with the U.K., Poland, and especially the United States. However, her efforts were seen as likely to be constrained by the CDU's coalition partners and by public opinion, which was much friendlier to France than to the transatlantic alliance.   ■ Jeffrey Kopstein

Ghana. See Africa.

Global warming. News reports indicated and scientific data confirmed that the most recent surge in global temperature that began in the 1970's continued in 2005. Most scientists agreed that global warming was at least partly responsible for the melting of Arctic sea ice, which in 2005 shrank to its lowest levels since 1978, the year when satellites began measuring the ice. Scientists also investigated whether the rise in temperature had contributed to severe weather in 2005. Fed by energy from unusually warm water, an unprecedented number of hurricanes churned through the Atlantic Ocean. Among them was Hurricane Wilma, the most intense storm ever observed in the Western Hemisphere. Delayed monsoon rains in Pakistan and Bangladesh led to a punishing heat wave in May and June that sent temperatures as high as 122 °F (50 °C). Frequent sunny, hot spring and summer days contributed to the worst drought in Spain and Portugal since the 1940's.

Global average temperatures. Researchers at the United States National Aeronautics and Space Administration's (NASA) Goddard Institute for Space Studies in New York City announced in October 2005 that preliminary data showed that the global average temperature near the surface of Earth in 2005 was the highest since 1880, when the agency began keeping records. Temperature in 2005 eclipsed the previous mark set in 1998 by about 0.2 °F (0.1 °C). However, two other widely used global temperature histories, one compiled by the National Climactic Data Center in Asheville, North Carolina, and another by the Climate Research Unit at the University of East Anglia in England, continued to list 1998 as the warmest year on record. The research groups used many of the same temperature data but employed different methods to statistically combine the data, which resulted in slight differences in the final values of annual global average temperature. A report examining the different methods to track temperature trends published in the August 2005 edition of *Science* noted the great challenges scientists face in attempting to measure very small year-to-year temperature differences.

Arctic ice. In 2005, many scientists believed that the build-up of carbon dioxide and other greenhouse gases in the atmosphere, brought about by industry, was causing global warming. They theorized that the accelerated breakup of polar ice was an important indicator of climate change.

In September, scientists at the University of Colorado at Boulder announced that coverage of Arctic ice, which reaches an annual minimum each September, had shrunk to a record 200 million square miles (51.8 billion hectares), 500 thousand square miles (130 million hectares) less than its average since the first satellite recordings of the ice in 1978. Scientists in 2005 calculated the rate of shrinkage at 8 percent per decade and predicted extremely low ice coverage for summer 2006.

A report published in 2004 revealed that the Arctic is warming twice as fast as the rest of the planet. The Arctic Climate Impact Assessment, a four-year study involving hundreds of scientists, projected an additional temperature rise of about 7 to 12.5 °F (4 to 7 °C) by 2100. According to meteorological data compiled by NASA, the average Arctic temperatures in the late 1960's were at their lowest levels since the 1920's. By 2005, Arctic temperatures had risen by about 3.5 °F (2 °C). Arctic temperatures also surged by about 4.5 °F (2.5 °C) between the late 1910's and the late 1930's before falling in the late 1960's.

A large sample of ice taken from Antarctica showed that the levels of carbon dioxide and methane were considerably higher in 2005 than at any other time in the last 650,000 years, scientists for the European Project for Ice Coring in Antarctica reported in the November 2005 issue of *Science*. Carbon dioxide and methane are atmospheric gases that absorb energy emitted by Earth, called greenhouse gases, that have greatly increased since the mid-1800's, when modern industry became widespread. The thousands of layers of snow and compressed air bubbles that compose the Antarctic ice capture the atmosphere that existed hundreds of thousands of years ago, which allows scientists to study ancient climates. The ice core research supports the widely held theory that human activity in the second half of the 1800's, 1900's, and the 2000's has significantly altered the planet's climate.

Tropical cyclones. A record 26 named tropical storms and hurricanes formed in the Atlantic Ocean in 2005, including three of the six most-intense storms on record in the Atlantic basin,

surpassing the previous record of 21 set in 1933. The normal yearly average is 10 named storms.

In September 2005, researchers from the Georgia Institute of Technology in Atlanta reported that while the North Atlantic had shown a statistically significant increase in storm activity, there was no global trend in the number of tropical storms and hurricanes. The researchers found an increase in the number of intense hurricanes across the world during the period of their analysis, which began in 1970, the year when satellites were first used to monitor tropical storm development. The researchers concluded, however, that a longer data record and a deeper understanding of the role of hurricanes in global weather patterns was required to relate hurricane activity to the recent warming near the surface of the Earth.   ■ Fred Gadomski

See also **Disasters; Disasters: A Special Report; Environmental pollution; Weather.**

Golf. Eldrick "Tiger" Woods roared back to peak form in 2005, bouncing back from a nearly three-year drought to capture two Professional Golfers' Association (PGA) major championships. However, on May 13, Woods saw his record streak of *making the cut* (qualifying for the final two rounds) in 142 consecutive tournaments come to an end. He missed the cut at the Byron Nelson Classic in Irving, Texas, by one stroke.

Golf said farewell to one of its greatest champions. Jack Nicklaus played in his final major, the British Open, at St. Andrews, Scotland, in July.

Annika Sorenstam won the first two majors of the season and tied a Ladies Professional Golf Association (LPGA) record by winning five consecutive tournaments.

PGA. On April 10, Woods became only the third man to win four Masters titles when he edged out Chris DiMarco with a 15-foot (4.6-meter) birdie putt on the first play-off hole at Augusta, Georgia. DiMarco gave Woods a spirited fight, capitalizing on Woods's bogeys on the final two holes to force a tie, but Woods overpowered him in the play-off. With his fourth Masters victory, Woods tied Arnold Palmer and trails only Jack Nicklaus, who won the Masters six times.

Michael Campbell of New Zealand won the U.S. Open at Pinehurst, N.J., on June 19. Woods made a strong charge, but Campbell survived, beating Woods by two strokes.

Woods cruised to a five-shot victory over Colin Montgomerie at the British Open on July 17 in St. Andrews, Scotland. During the tournament, golf legend Jack Nicklaus made an emotional exit from competitive golf, playing in his last major tournament. Nicklaus is widely regarded as the greatest golf champion of all time, having won 18 majors, including the British Open three times.

Phil Mickelson won his second career major

Annika Sorenstam of Sweden watches as her chip shot flies toward the 15th green during the first round of the Ladies Professional Golf Association (LPGA) championship on June 9 in Havre de Grace, Maryland. Sorenstam went on to win the tournament, her ninth major LPGA win and record fifth consecutive tournament victory.

Jang led after each round and fired a 16-under for her first win on the LPGA tour in her six-year career.

Champions Tour. On the tour for men older than 50, Mike Reid won the Senior PGA Championship on May 29 in Ligonier, Pennsylvania. Reid eagled the final hole of regulation play, forcing a play-off with Jerry Pate and Dana Quigley. Reid then won with a birdie on the first play-off hole.

Peter Jacobsen shot 15-under to edge Hale Irwin by one shot to win the Senior Players Championship on July 10 in Dearborn, Michigan. It was Jacobsen's second major title in less than a year.

Tom Watson won the Senior British Open for the second time in three years, topping Des Smyth of Ireland on July 24 in Aberdeen, Scotland. Watson and Smyth finished tied at 4-under in regulation, but Watson won the play-off.

Allen Doyle shot a tournament final-round record 8-under 63 to finish at 10-under-par and win the U.S. Senior Open on July 31 in Kettering, Ohio.

Loren Roberts won the final major, The Tradition, on August 28 in Aloha, Oregon. Roberts and Dana Quigley were tied at 15-under after regulation play. On the second hole of the play-off, Roberts bogeyed but Quigley double-bogeyed, giving Roberts the win. ■ Michael Kates

Great Britain. See **United Kingdom.**

Greece. The center-right government of Prime Minister Costas Karamanlis's New Democracy Party focused in 2005 on fighting corruption. Upon coming to power in 2004, Karamanlis denounced five firms that obtained insider contracts worth billions of euros for construction related to the Olympic Games held in Athens in 2004. In addition, the previous Socialist government had repeatedly misrepresented Greece's budget deficit so that Greece would qualify for admission to the European Union (EU). The Karamanlis government conducted an audit to gauge the extent of corruption and proposed solutions.

Conflict between Greece and Turkey centered in 2005 on Turkey's accession to the EU in light of Turkish refusal to endorse the internationally recognized Republic of Cyprus. In October, Greece agreed to allow accession negotiations to begin in return for Turkey's eventual acceptance of the Greek Cypriot government.

The Greek economy grew by a healthy 3.5 percent in 2005. Nevertheless, the budget deficit—at 3.7 percent of *gross domestic product* (GDP, the value of all goods and services produced in a country in a year)—remained above the 3 percent limit permitted for countries using the euro.

■ Jeffrey Kopstein

See also **Europe.**

Grenada. See **Latin America.**

title on August 15 with a one-shot victory in the PGA Championship in Springfield, New Jersey. Mickelson pitched out of deep rough and drained the two-foot birdie putt on the final hole, giving him the win over Steve Elkington of Australia and Thomas Bjorn of Denmark.

LPGA. Sorenstam dominated the Kraft Nabisco Championship in Rancho Mirage, California, on March 27, shooting 15-under-par to win by eight strokes. She followed that performance with her ninth major victory, winning the LPGA Championship on June 12 in Havre de Grace, Maryland, shooting an 11-under to beat amateur Michelle Wie by three strokes.

Birdie Kim of South Korea stopped Sorenstam's run at the U.S. Women's Open on June 26 in Cherry Hills Village, Colorado. Kim holed a bunker shot for birdie on the 18th hole to win with a final score of 3-over-par.

Jeong Jang of South Korea won the Women's British Open on July 31 in Merseyside, England.

Guatemala. Torrential rains associated with Hurricane Stan lashed Guatemala in early October 2005, unleashing mudslides that buried villages and washed out roads and bridges. Authorities reported 1,500 people dead or missing, tens of thousands homeless, and crop devastation on 1.7 million acres (688,000 hectares) of land. International aid organizations, warning that hundreds of thousands of Guatemalans were in danger of starvation, issued pleas for donations.

President Oscar Berger Perdomo identified fighting crime as his administration's number-one priority in a June speech in which he announced the purchase of 200 patrol cars for Guatemala's national police force. Berger attributed Guatemala's crime wave to the activities of street gangs involved in drug trafficking. In 2005, Guatemala's defense ministry began a four-year, $212-million plan to modernize the country's armed forces.

In November, a judge in Mexico City granted Alfonso Portillo Cabrera a hearing pending his extradition to Guatemala to stand trial on corruption charges. Portillo, Guatemala's president from 2000 to 2004, fled to Mexico shortly after leaving office. ■ Nathan A. Haverstock

See also **Latin America**.

Guinea. See Africa.
Guinea-Bissau. See Africa.
Guyana. See Latin America.

Haiti. Government officials repeatedly postponed elections that were to have taken place in Haiti in November 2005. Late in the year, officials rescheduled the anticipated two-round elections for January and February 2006, abandoning hope of meeting a February 7 constitutional deadline for the inauguration of a new government.

In 2005, Haitians prepared for the pending elections with help from a 7,300-member United Nations (UN) peacekeeping mission and representatives of the Washington, D.C.-based Organization of American States (OAS). The UN peacekeepers sought to quell sporadic violence, while the OAS officials assisted Haiti's interim government in registering voters.

Gangs challenged the interim government's authority in 2005 as they had in 2004. In July 2005, 400 armed UN peacekeepers made an incursion into Cite Soleil, a slum in Port-au-Prince, the capital, seeking out armed gang members. A five-hour gun battle ensued, which left five suspected gang members dead. Critics noted that control of Cite Soleil reverted to the gangs as soon as the UN force withdrew.

In early July, Hurricane Dennis dealt Haiti a glancing blow. At least 10 Haitians died in storm-caused flooding. ■ Nathan A. Haverstock

See also **Latin America**.

Harness racing. See Horse racing.

Health care issues. Hurricanes that hit the Gulf Coast of the United States in 2005 greatly affected the nation's health care system. The worst damage took place in New Orleans, where 13 of 16 area hospitals were forced to close and were unable to reopen for several weeks or even months. Charity and University hospitals sustained damage so severe that they were declared "unsalvageable" by the Louisiana State University Health Care Services Division, which oversees the facilities. The two hospitals treated 500,000 patients annually. Charity was the city's primary public health facility.

Medicaid and Medicare. In 2005, several states and the federal government cut funding for Medicaid, the primary health care provider for many low income, disabled, and elderly people. Tennessee dropped more than 300,000 beneficiaries from TennCare, its Medicaid program. Missouri shed nearly 90,000 beneficiaries in 2005. The federal government granted Florida permission to transfer administration of much of its Medicaid program to private insurers. South Carolina sought a similar arrangement in 2005.

In December, the U.S. Congress passed a five-year budget program that increased out-of-pocket costs for Medicaid recipients through higher co-pays and premiums; allowed states to scale back benefits; tightened eligibility for nursing home benefits; and changed how Medicaid prescription drug benefits were to be paid.

The program cut $6.4 billion from Medicare, the federal health insurance program that covers nearly all people age 65 or older. The bill reduced some payments to private health plans and for certain medical procedures, and it froze home health care payments at current rates.

In 2005, Medicare launched a prescription drug program, which allowed beneficiaries to buy prescription drug coverage through private insurers. When enrollment in the program began on October 1, many beneficiaries complained that it was confusing and complicated and that the marketing practices of the private insurers seemed overly aggressive. In 2005, the Congressional Budget Office estimated that the program would cost $849 billion over 10 years, more than twice what Congress had budgeted.

Terri Schiavo. An important right-to-die legal case ended in 2005 amidst major controversy. On March 21, President George W. Bush signed legislation, passed by Congress the same day, that moved jurisdiction in the case of Terri Schiavo from state courts to federal court. Terri Schiavo was a severely brain-damaged woman who had been in a vegetative state since 1990. Her husband, Michael Schiavo, had waged a court battle for years with his wife's parents. He contended that his wife would not want to be kept alive artificially. The parents insisted that Terri might, some day, get better and should, therefore, be kept alive.

Schiavo's feeding tube was removed by order of a Florida court on March 18, 2005, one day after the U.S. Supreme Court had declined to hear the case. After the case was transferred to the federal judiciary, two separate panels of judges refused to reverse state court rulings. Terri Schiavo died on March 31.

Health and Human Services. In late 2004, President Bush nominated former Utah Governor Mike Leavitt to replace Tommy Thompson as Secretary of the Department of Health and Human Services (HHS). Leavitt was confirmed on Jan. 26, 2005. On July 19, the Senate confirmed Lester Crawford as commissioner of the Food and Drug Administration (FDA), an HHS agency. At the time, the FDA had been without a permanent commissioner for more than half of Bush's presidency, and the agency remained embroiled in controversy involving FDA approval of drugs later discovered to have dangerous side effects, such as the arthritis pain reliever Vioxx. Crawford resigned abruptly and without explanation on September 23. He was replaced by Andrew von Eschenbach, then director of the National Cancer Institute. ■ Emily Friedman

See also **Social Security: A Special Report.**

Hockey. The National Hockey League (NHL) in 2005 became the first North American professional sports league to cancel an entire season. The season was officially canceled on February 16, when a labor agreement was not reached.

The NHL "locked out" its players—not allowing them to practice or play—on Sept. 16, 2004, upon the expiration of their labor agreement. The player's union refused to consider a salary cap, despite the NHL's claim that teams had lost $1.8 billion over the last decade. The owners and players finally reached an agreement in July 2005, and the 2005-2006 season began on time.

World championships. The Czech Republic captured its first men's world championship since 2001 with a 3-0 rout of two-time defending champion Canada on May 16, 2005, in Vienna, Austria. Russia took the bronze. In the women's world championship, the United States won its first world gold with a 1-0 shootout victory over Canada on April 9 in Linkoping, Sweden.

College. The University of Denver (Boulder) won its second straight men's National Collegiate Athletic Association Division I title with a 4-1 victory over North Dakota on April 9. In the women's final, the University of Minnesota (Minneapolis-St. Paul) took the title with a 4-3 victory over Harvard on March 28. ■ Michael Kates

Honduras. See **Latin America.**

Horse racing. A pair of longshots surging down the stretch of a crowded 2005 Kentucky Derby prevented a horse named Afleet Alex from becoming the first Triple Crown winner since Affirmed in 1978.

Afleet Alex finished third in the Derby, behind Giacomo and Closing Argument. However,

MAJOR HORSE RACES OF 2005

THOROUGHBRED RACING

Race	Winner	Value to Winner
Atto Mile (Canada)	Leroidesanimaux	$600,000
Belmont Stakes	Afleet Alex	$600,000
Blue Grass Stakes	Bandini	$465,000
Breeders' Cup Classic	St. Liam	$2,433,600
Breeders' Cup Distaff	Pleasant Home	$1,040,000
Breeders' Cup Filly & Mare Turf	Intercontinental	$551,200
Breeders' Cup Juvenile	Stevie Wonderboy	$826,800
Breeders' Cup Juvenile Fillies	Folklore	$520,000
Breeders' Cup Mile	Artie Schiller	$1,053,000
Breeders' Cup Sprint	Silver Train	$520,000
Breeders' Cup Turf	Shirocco	$1,185,600
Canadian International Stakes	Relaxed Gesture	$1,009,920
Dubai World Cup (United Arab Emirates)	Roses in May	$3,600,000
Haskell Invitational	Roman Ruler	$600,000
Hollywood Gold Cup	Lava Man	$450,000
Irish Derby (Ireland)	Hurricane Run	745,100 euros
Jockey Club Gold Cup	Borrego	$600,000
Kentucky Derby	Giacomo	$1,639,600
Kentucky Oaks	Summerly	$343,728
King George VI and Queen Elizabeth Diamond Stakes (United Kingdom)	Azamour	£408,030
Lane's End Stakes	Flower Alley	$300,000
Oaklawn Handicap	Grand Reward	$300,000
Pacific Classic	Borrego	$600,000
Preakness Stakes	Afleet Alex	$600,000
Prix de l'Arc de Triomphe (France)	Hurricane Run	1,028,000 euros
Santa Anita Derby	Buzzards Bay	$450,000
Santa Anita Handicap	Rock Hard Ten	$600,000
Stephen H. Foster Handicap	Saint Liam	$496,800
Travers Stakes	Flower Alley	$600,000
Vodafone Derby (U.K.)	Motivator	£725,000

HARNESS RACING

Race	Winner	Value to Winner
Cane Pace	Royal Flush Shark	$173,000
Hambletonian	Vivid Photo	$750,000
Kentucky Futurity	Strong Yankee	$305,000
Little Brown Jug	P Forty Seven	$195,177
Meadowlands Pace	Rocknroll Hanover	$500,000
Messenger Stakes	Gryffindor	$136,400
Woodrow Wilson	Western Ace	$187,500
Yonkers Trot	Strong Yankee	$148,908

Sources: *The Blood Horse Magazine* and U.S. Trotting Association.

he rebounded dramatically in the Preakness Stakes and staged a rout in the Belmont Stakes to win two of the three Triple Crown races.

In August, Hall of Fame jockey Pat Day, one of the greatest jockeys of all time, retired after 32 years of racing. During his career, Day's horses earned some $297 million, more than any other jockey in racing history. Day won five Preakness Stakes, three Belmont Stakes, and the 1992 Kentucky Derby.

Three-year-olds. On May 7, 2005, in Louisville, Kentucky, in front of the second largest crowd in Kentucky Derby history, Giacomo, a 50-1 longshot, became the second biggest longshot in Derby history to win. Giacomo surged from 11th place on the turn for home and flew past the field to beat Closing Argument by half a length. People who bet $2 on Giacomo to win and Closing Argument to take second won $9,814.80.

On May 21, Afleet Alex and jockey Jeremy Rose overcame a near-fall to win the Preakness Stakes at Baltimore's Pimlico Race Course. At the top of the home stretch, front-runner Scrappy T veered in front of Afleet Alex, clipping his heel. Rose was able to keep Afleet Alex upright to take the win by 4¾ lengths.

Afleet Alex found a higher gear two weeks later in the Belmont Stakes, held June 11 in Elmont, New York. Afleet Alex took control late in the race and rolled to a decisive seven-length victory over Andromeda's Hero.

International. Roses in May captured the $6-million Dubai World Cup, held March 26 in Dubai, United Arab Emirates, defeating Dynever by three lengths for the $3.6-million top prize.

In European racing, Motivator won the Vodafone Derby on June 4. Hurricane Run captured the Irish Derby on June 26 and the Prix de l'Arc de Triomphe on October 2.

Harness. In the trotting triple crown, Vivid Photo captured the $1.5-million Hambletonian on August 6, while Strong Yankee won both the Yonkers Trot on August 20 and the Kentucky Futurity on October 1.

In the pacing triple crown, 16-1 longshot Royal Flush Shark won the Cane Pace on September 5; P Forty Seven captured the Little Brown Jug on September 22; and Gryffindor won the Messenger Stakes on October 17.

Record sale. On September 14, Sheik Mohammed, crown prince of Dubai, paid $9.7 million for a colt sired by the stallion Storm Cat, the highest price ever paid for a race horse. ■ Michael Kates

Hospital. See Health care issues.

Housing. See Building & construction.

Houston. Two hurricanes—Katrina and Rita—left an indelible mark on Houston in 2005. After striking the Louisiana and Mississippi coasts on August 29, Katrina flooded New Orleans and sent tens of thousands of people to Houston in the greatest migration in the United States since the Dust Bowl of the 1930's.

Estimated numbers of evacuees who fled New Orleans for Houston ranged from 150,000 to 250,000 people. Nearly 30,000 people stayed for up to three weeks in city and county shelters at large public buildings, including the Astrodome south of downtown Houston. Harris County officials scrambled to open additional buildings after initially being told to expect just 2,000 evacuees.

By December 2005, about 150,000 evacuees remained in Houston, many of whom had found housing, jobs, and schools for their children. Vacancy rates in Houston's housing and office space rental markets were halved in the month following Hurricane Katrina.

Just as the last evacuees were being relocated from Houston's public shelters to apartments and houses, Hurricane Rita formed southeast of Florida in late September. Rita, one of the most intense storms ever measured in the Gulf of Mexico, appeared poised to make a direct hit on Houston, which lies only about 50 miles (80 kilometers) inland. Just weeks after the largest migration into Houston, Rita spurred the largest evacuation out of the area.

Between 2.5 million and 3 million people fled the city in advance of Rita, to Dallas, San Antonio, Austin, and other Texas cities, where hotel rooms were already filled by Katrina evacuees. The exodus caused gridlocked traffic on freeways within Houston and on interstates leading to other cities. The prolonged waits caused many drivers to run out of gas, and with most service stations closed, their vehicles were stranded until officials trucked in fuel supplies.

Shortly before landfall, Rita veered east, slamming into east Texas and western Louisiana on September 24. The move spared most of greater Houston hurricane-force winds. Nevertheless, nearly 1 million people lost power, a major problem as Houston weathered its warmest September since record keeping began in 1882. The average high for the month was 93.2 °F (34 °C).

The Houston Astros in 2005 became the first baseball team from Texas to go to the World Series. Although the team lost the series in four straight games to the Chicago White Sox, the loss did little to dampen Houston's baseball fever. Standing-room-only tickets for games three and four of the series in Houston, with a face value of $45, sold for over $700. Houston fans also celebrated hometown heroes Andy Pettitte and Roger Clemens, who had returned to the city from New

York City, where they had played for the Yankees in 2003.

Texas City. An explosion at a petroleum refinery near Houston in March 2005 killed 15 people and injured 170 others in one of the nation's most deadly workplace disasters in the last two decades. London-based British Petroleum, the operator of the plant in Texas City, agreed to pay a record $21.3-million fine as part of a settlement with the U.S. Occupational Safety and Health Administration, which found 300 safety and health violations at the plant. The energy company also agreed to pay millions of dollars to several of the families of employees who died in the blast.

Safe Clear. To alleviate traffic on Houston's freeways, Mayor Bill White initiated a controversial program called Safe Clear on January 1. Designed to quickly move stalled vehicles and those involved in accidents, Safe Clear declared all freeways immediate tow zones. The program angered many freeway users because the minimum $75 towing fee was mandatory, even if a driver was simply changing a flat tire. Under public pressure and threat of action by state legislators, White revised the plan. The city paid tow drivers to move vehicles just off the highway, and drivers had the option of calling their own towing firm for a tow home or to a mechanic. ■ Eric Berger

See also **Disasters: A Special Report.**

Human rights. In 2005, prisoner abuse by United States troops at the Abu Ghraib prison in Iraq during 2003 and 2004 led to a number of legal proceedings. Most of the allegations centered around nine soldiers from two units, a military police unit sent to guard prisoners at Abu Ghraib and a military intelligence unit responsible for interrogating the prisoners. Among the enlisted soldiers brought up on charges, four accepted plea bargains in 2004 and were sentenced to prison terms ranging from no prison time to 8 years in prison. In 2005, two additional soldiers accepted plea bargains and received terms of 6 months and 10 months in prison.

The trials of three other soldiers took place in 2005. Specialist Charles A. Graner, Jr., considered the ringleader among the military police unit suspects, was found guilty on January 14 of conspiring to mistreat prisoners, maltreatment, and dereliction of duty. In addition, he was found guilty of assault, battery, and indecent acts. Graner was sentenced to 10 years in federal prison. Specialist Sabrina Harman was sentenced on May 17 to 6 months in prison for prisoner abuse. Private Lynndie R. England, who was photographed holding a naked Iraqi prisoner on a leash, was sentenced on September 27 to 3 years in prison for conspiracy, maltreating prisoners, and committing an indecent act.

Two commanding officers were also sentenced in May. Brigadier General Janis Karpinski, who had been commanding officer of the military police unit at the prison, was demoted to the rank of colonel. Colonel Thomas M. Pappas, commander of the military intelligence unit in charge of interrogation, was fined $8,000 and reprimanded.

Four top Army officers who had oversight of prison operations in Iraq were cleared by Army investigators on April 22. Among those absolved were Lieutenant General Ricardo S. Sanchez, the top military commander in Iraq at the time of the scandal; Major General Walter Wojdakowski, deputy commander of U.S. forces in Iraq; Major General Barbara G. Fast, Sanchez's intelligence head in Iraq; and Colonel Marc Warren, Sanchez's top legal adviser. The decisions were met with widespread accusations by human rights groups that low-ranking soldiers had been used as scapegoats by military authorities.

Guantanamo Bay prison. On May 26, Brigadier General Jay W. Hood announced the results of a military inquiry into whether guards or interrogators at the U.S. Guantanamo Bay naval base in Cuba had mishandled the Qur'an, the Muslim holy book. Since 2001, the naval base had served as a prison for hundreds of foreign detainees taken into custody during fighting in Afghanistan. Hood said that military personnel had mishandled the book in five cases. In three cases, the mishandling was deliberate, while in two others it was inadvertent.

Hood also reported that there was "no credible evidence" that a Qur'an was ever flushed down a toilet. A *Newsweek* magazine article had reported such an assertion on May 9, 2005, which sparked widespread violent protests in the Muslim world. *Newsweek* later retracted the story.

Amnesty International rebuke. The human rights group Amnesty International, in its annual report on May 25, criticized the United States for condoning human rights violations. In releasing the document, the group's secretary general, Irene Khan, cited the Abu Ghraib prison scandal and mistreatment of prisoners at Guantanamo Bay as proof that the United States "thumbs its nose at the rule of law and human rights."

New NAACP head. The National Association for the Advancement of Colored People (NAACP) on June 25 selected Bruce Gordon as its president and chief executive officer. Gordon was a former executive at New York City-based Verizon Communications Inc. and is the first nonminister or nonpolitician chosen to lead the group since 1966. Gordon replaced Kweisi Mfume, who resigned in November 2004. The NAACP is the largest and oldest civil rights group in the United States.

Same-sex marriage. Canada became the third nation to approve same-sex marriages on

Rosa Parks
Civil Rights Pioneer

The remains of Rosa Parks lay in repose on Oct. 30 and 31, 2005, in the Rotunda of the United States Capitol, where more than 30,000 people came to pay their respects. She was the first woman in U.S. history to be thus honored. Parks, an international symbol of the worldwide movement for civil and human rights, died on October 24 at age 92.

Parks was a 42-year-old tailor's assistant when, on Dec. 1, 1955, she refused to give up her seat on a Montgomery, Alabama, bus to a white man. Her refusal was a conscious act of civil disobedience for which she was arrested, jailed, and fined $14. She had violated a city law that mandated that black passengers give up their seats to white passengers and move to the segregated rear of the bus. Her act moved thousands of the city's black residents to *boycott* (refuse to use) the municipal bus system for 382 straight days—from Dec. 5, 1955, to Dec. 20, 1956. Martin Luther King, Jr., a Baptist minister from Atlanta, Georgia, led the protest. The boycott ended only after the U.S. Supreme Court had declared Montgomery's segregation law unconstitutional. Historians point to her act of defiance as one of the formative events sparking the civil rights movement.

Rosa Louise McCauley was born on Feb. 4, 1913. She attended various rural schools as well as high school at Alabama State Teacher's College in Montgomery. In 1932, she married Raymond Parks. Her act of defiance cost Parks and her husband their jobs and exposed them to harassment and death threats. In 1957, they moved to Detroit, where Representative John Conyers, Jr. (D., Michigan), eventually hired her to work in his Detroit office.

Rosa Parks's fight against racial inequality began before the boycott and continued long after. She served as secretary of the Montgomery chapter of the National Association for the Advancement of Colored People from 1943 to 1956. In 1987, she and her husband opened the Rosa and Raymond Parks Institute for Self Development, a Detroit-based mentoring organization for young people.

Parks's legacy of quiet courage in the face of injustice earned her numerous honors. The Rosa Parks Museum and Library and the Civil Rights Memorial Center, both in Montgomery, recognize her contribution to the movement. She received the Presidential Medal of Freedom in 1996 and the Congressional Gold Medal in 1999. On her death, African American leader Jesse Jackson, Jr., noted, "[Rosa Parks] sat down and inspired a modern civil rights movement to stand up."

■ Heather McShane

The remains of Rosa Parks lie in repose in the Rotunda of the U.S. Capitol on October 30. She was the first woman in U.S. history to be granted this honor.

July 20, 2005, when Governor General Adrienne Clarkson signed a bill allowing gay and lesbian couples to marry. The Netherlands and Belgium had previously adopted such a policy. On June 30, the Spanish Parliament legalized gay marriage.

In the United States, Massachusetts Governor Mitt Romney vowed to support efforts to make same-sex marriage illegal in his state. The effort came more than a year after Massachusetts became the first state to legalize such unions. The California legislature passed a bill allowing same-sex marriages in September. However, Governor Arnold Schwarzenegger vetoed the legislation.

Former Klansman convicted. Former Ku Klux Klan member Edgar Ray Killen was sentenced on June 23 to 60 years in prison for his role in the 1964 deaths of three civil rights workers. Killen, now 80 years old, was convicted of manslaughter in the deaths of James Chaney, Andrew Goodman, and Michael Schwerner. The three had been murdered by a group directed by Killen.

Lynching apology. The U.S. Senate on June 13, 2005, apologized for never having outlawed *lynching* (mob killing). The practice is believed to have taken the lives of at least 5,000 people, mostly southern blacks, between 1882 and 1968. ▪ Geoffrey Campbell

See also **Armed forces; Iraq; United States, Government of the.**

Hungary. Laszlo Solyom, formerly the chief judge of Hungary's Constitutional Court, was elected president of Hungary on June 7, 2005. In Hungary, the president, who is the ceremonial head of state, is elected by the parliament. The ruling Socialist Party, headed by Prime Minister Ferenc Gyurcsany, had attempted to elect a Socialist candidate, but the Socialists' junior partner in the ruling coalition, the Free Democrats, abstained in the balloting, guaranteeing the election of the opposition candidate. The Socialists and Free Democrats later healed their breach.

Hungary's finance minister confirmed in September that the country's budget deficit would reach 6.1 percent of *gross domestic product* (GDP) in 2005 instead of 3.6 percent as forecast. (GDP is the value of all goods and services produced in a country in a given year.) In November, officials of Hungary's central bank warned that the budget deficit could reach 10 percent of GDP by 2008. The ballooning budget deficit dimmed prospects that Hungary could meet a European Union deficit target of 3 percent of GDP by 2008 and qualify for entry by 2010 into the Eurozone, a group of countries using the euro currency. Analysts said that the ruling coalition was unlikely to endorse austerity measures prior to elections in 2006. ▪ Sharon L. Wolchik

See also **Europe.**

Ice skating. Russian skaters dominated the 2005 world championships, winning three of four disciplines. Switzerland's Stephane Lambiel became the first Swiss to win gold at the world championships since 1947.

U.S. championships. Michelle Kwan of the United States won a record-tying ninth U.S. title, her eighth in a row, on Jan. 15, 2005, in Portland, Oregon. With the victory, Kwan tied Maribel Vinson, who won nine titles from 1928 to 1937. Sasha Cohen finished second, and Kimmie Meissner took the bronze.

Johnny Weir took the men's title, Timothy Goebel won the silver, and Evan Lysacek claimed the bronze medal. Garrett Lucash and Kathryn Orscher captured their first pairs title, and ice dancers Tanith Belbin and Benjamin Agosto repeated as gold medalists.

European championships. Russian skaters won all four disciplines at the European championships in Turin, Italy, in January 2005. Eugeni Plushenko won his fourth title, with Brian Joubert of France finishing second and Stefan Lindemann of Germany taking the bronze.

Irina Slutskaya won her sixth women's title, tying Sonja Henie and Katarina Witt for the record. Susanna Poykio of Finland won the silver, and Ukraine's Elena Liashenko took the bronze. Tatiana Totmianina and Maxim Marinin captured the pairs gold, while Tatiana Navka and Roman Kostomarov won the ice dancing title.

World championships. Stephane Lambiel won the men's gold in Moscow in March. Lambiel took the title after Evgeni Plushenko withdrew because of an injury. Lambiel edged out Jeffrey Buttle of Canada, who claimed the silver. Evan Lysacek of the United States won the bronze.

Irina Slutskaya landed seven triple jumps in front of her home crowd on March 19 to beat out Sasha Cohen of the United States, who settled for silver. Carolina Kostner of Italy won the bronze. Kwan finished fourth after a disappointing qualifying program, failing to medal for the first time since 1996.

Totmianina and Marinin of Russia captured the pairs title on March 16, less than five months after Totmianina suffered cuts and a mild concussion after a head-first fall. Fellow Russians Maria Petrova and Alexei Tikhonov won silver, and Chinese skaters Dan Zhang and Hao Zhang took the bronze.

Navka and Kostomarov of Russia successfully defended their ice-dancing gold on March 18. Americans Tanith Belbin and Benjamin Agosto took the silver, and Elena Grushina and Ruslin Goncharov of Ukraine won the bronze.

▪ Michael Kates

Iceland. See Europe.

Immigration. United States Customs and Border Protection (CBP) published the Advanced Passenger Information System Final Rule in the Federal Register on April 7, 2005. The rule requires commercial air and sea carriers to provide information on all passengers and crew members prior to entry in, or departure from, the United States. The rule is billed as an antiterrorism tool. An interim rule, in place since Dec. 31, 2001, required commercial airlines to submit passenger data prior to arrival in the United States.

Tsunami aftermath. United States Citizenship and Immigration Services (USCIS), part of the Department of Homeland Security, announced on Jan. 10, 2005, that it was speeding up processing of extended-stay requests from people unable to return to their home countries because of the devastation wrought by an earthquake and tsunami in Southeast Asia on Dec. 26, 2004.

On Jan. 5, 2005, the USCIS issued a statement regarding the adoption of orphans from countries affected by the disaster. While recognizing the willingness of U.S. citizens to adopt the orphans, the agency advised that children be kept close to their families and communities.

Special naturalization ceremony. Army Specialist Victor Alfonso Rojas was sworn in as a U.S. citizen on March 8 in a naturalization ceremony conducted by USCIS Director Eduardo Aguirre. The ceremony was held at Walter Reed Army Medical Center in Washington, D.C., where Rojas was taken in November 2004, for treatment of injuries he suffered in combat in Iraq. Rojas had emigrated from Mexico in 1997.

Arizona border effort. On March 30, 2005, CBP officials announced Phase II of the Department of Homeland Security's Arizona Border Control Initiative. The program is a large-scale federal law enforcement initiative designed to improve control of the Arizona border with Mexico. More than 35,000 illegal aliens were stopped from entering the United States through this border in 2004. According to the CBP, the program also supports antiterrorism efforts by making entry more difficult.

Under the plan, an additional 534 permanent and 200 temporary border patrol agents were assigned to monitor the border. A number of sophisticated aircraft also were assigned, including "A-Star" and UH-60 Black Hawk helicopters.

Increased illegal immigration. In September, the Washington, D.C.-based Pew Hispanic Center, a nonpartisan research group, reported that more illegal immigrants than legal immigrants had moved to the United States from 2001 through 2004. People from Mexico accounted for around a third of the illegal immigrants. The report noted that as the U.S. economy improved, immigration increased. It stated that 1.5 million

people immigrated in the economic boom years of 1999 and 2000, compared with 1.1 million in 2003 and 1.2 million in 2004. The report also noted that the decline could have resulted from security developments instituted after the terrorist attacks on the United States on Sept. 11, 2001.

Illegal migrants rescued. CBP border patrol agents, assisted by security officers from the Union Pacific Railroad of Omaha, Nebraska, helped rescue and return a group of undocumented migrants to Mexico who had been discovered in an abandoned railroad car. Railroad security guards found the migrants on Jan. 17, 2005, in El Paso, Texas. The guards notified border patrol agents, who took the 29 migrants into custody. The train had originated in Dallas and was en route to Long Beach, California.

Immigration reform. In November, President George W. Bush announced a strategy for securing the border with Mexico. The plan called for tighter border security, larger detention centers, tougher workplace enforcement, and the return to Mexico of all illegal aliens caught crossing the southwest U.S. border. Bush also outlined a "temporary worker" program to encourage illegal immigrants to register to work legally. He noted that the "American people should not have to choose between a welcoming society and a lawful society. We can have both at the same time." ■ Geoffrey A. Campbell

India in 2005 improved relations with neighboring Pakistan after the two nations suffered a major earthquake in the Himalaya. The two countries also made new efforts toward resolving longstanding tensions over the disputed Kashmir region.

India and Pakistan have been in conflict over control of the state of Jammu and Kashmir since 1947, when the two countries gained independence. In April 2005, Pakistan's president, General Pervez Musharraf, met for three days in New Delhi, India's capital, with Prime Minister Manmohan Singh. In a joint press conference, the leaders announced that a peace process between the two countries was "now irreversible."

Singh's predecessor, Atal Bihari Vajpayee, began expanding contacts between the two countries in 2003, which led to the opening of a bus route on April 7, 2005, between the capitals of divided Jammu and Kashmir, a state whose status remained the most explosive issue between India and Pakistan. The route began reuniting families divided since 1949 by a cease-fire line supervised by the United Nations. The line has been the frequent scene of armed clashes.

Musharraf and Singh promised to take steps to turn the line into a "soft border" with greater transit and trade. However, they did not directly tackle the state's disputed status. India, which is predominantly Hindu, holds the central area around Srinagar where Muslims constitute a large majority. India rejects calls from Pakistan, a primarily Muslim nation, for Kashmiris to be allowed to determine their future status by a public referendum.

Upon leaving India, Musharraf warned that, "unless we can resolve the core issue" of Kashmir, hostile relations could erupt again. India continued to accuse the government of Pakistan of supporting a 16-year-old guerrilla fight against India in Kashmir, where violence continued through 2005.

The earthquake on October 8 killed some 1,400 people in the India-controlled area of Kashmir. With relief work on both sides of the cease-fire line going slowly, India and Pakistan agreed to a limited opening of crossing points in order to expedite aid to victims.

The two governments agreed on August 6 to set up a telephone hotline to prevent misunderstandings that could accidentally spark conflict, and to notify each other before conducting nuclear missile tests. In recent years, unannounced missile tests by both countries increased tensions between them. The agreement followed an exchange of barbed remarks on whether each country's nuclear weapons were under secure control.

Relations with the United States improved in 2005. United States and Indian defense ministers signed a 10-year agreement for enhanced military cooperation, including joint weapons pro-

People struggle to hang on to a rope stretched across a flooded street in Mumbai, India, on July 27, 2005, one day after the heaviest rainfall ever recorded in India on a single day—more than 37 inches (94 centimeters)—left one-third of Mumbai, a city of 18.2 million people, underwater. The ensuing flooding left more than 1,000 people dead.

duction and collaboration on missile defense. Visiting Washington, D.C., in July, Prime Minister Singh was promised that U.S. restrictions on receiving help for civilian nuclear reactors—subject to approval by the U.S. Congress and other nuclear-armed nations—would be lifted.

Politics. The coalition government led by Singh and his Congress Party was widely criticized during 2005 for moving slowly on improving India's economy. However, the Congress Party had far fewer problems in 2005 than the opposition Bharatiya Janata Party (BJP), which had lost power to Congress in 2004. In the election campaign, the BJP had softened its strident emphasis of Hindu traditions in seeking votes, alienating some Hindu fundamentalists. Factional tensions led to Indian media speculation that the BJP could split.

Party tensions intensified in June when BJP President Lal Krishna Advani visited Pakistan and made complimentary remarks about Mohammad Ali Jinnah. Jinnah's advocacy of a separate Muslim state led to the partition of India in 1947. Advani's remarks outraged BJP stalwarts who wanted an undivided, Hindu-controlled nation. Advani announced on Sept. 18, 2005, that he would resign as party presidency in December but would continue to lead the BJP in Parliament. On December 29, former Indian Prime Minister Vajpayee stunned BJP party members by announcing his retirement from "power politics."

The BJP boycotted spring sessions of the lower house of Parliament to protest a minister charged with corruption who retained his position in Singh's coalition government. The minister, Lalu Prasad Yadav, from corruption-ridden Bihar state, headed a small party whose support was critical to Singh's coalition. The coalition also depended on Communist votes. However, Communist labor unions limited Singh's ability to introduce economic reforms.

Terrorism. On May 22, bombs in two movie theaters in New Delhi killed 1 person and wounded 48 others during the screening of a film considered to be offensive by some members of the Sikh religion.Three bombings on October 29 in New Delhi killed more than 60 shoppers.

Floods engulfed Maharashtra state after a record 37 inches (94 centimeters) of rain fell in 24 hours on July 26, followed by more heavy rain a few days later. Almost one-third of the city of Mumbai, formerly Bombay, which is the state's capital as well as India's financial center, was submerged and shut down. More than 1,000 people died across the region, and more than 5,000 people suffered from water-borne diseases, such as cholera, after floodwaters receded. Further flooding on October 29 washed out a bridge in southern India, causing train cars to fall into a river. The accident left 114 passengers dead.   ■ Henry S. Bradsher

See also **Asia; Disasters; Pakistan; Terrorism.**

Indian, American. Tribal leaders in June 2005 proposed a $27.4-billion settlement of the largest lawsuit ever brought against the United States government. The suit had been filed in 1996 by Elouise Cobell, a member of the Montana Blackfeet tribe, on behalf of some 500,000 Indians. Cobell's lawsuit demanded that the U.S. Department of the Interior account for as much as $176 billion in trust funds collected and managed for Indians by the government since the late 1800's. The suit also called for establishing a more accurate accounting system to monitor the funds.

The trust funds had been established in 1887, after the U.S. government divided reservations into parcels and allotted the land to individual Indians and tribes. Proceeds from mining, oil and gas extraction, timber, and grazing were to be held in trust for the individual owners.

During the trial, Interior Department officials acknowledged some mismanagement of the accounts but said the loss had been overstated. By 2005, the department had completed a review of more than 47,500 trust fund accounts at a cost of $100 million and claimed to have found "no evidence" that the funds had been systematically or deliberately mismanaged. Nevertheless, in 2002, Secretary of the Interior Gale Norton admitted that a thorough accounting was impossible because many documents had been destroyed.

Tribal leaders in 2005 expressed concern that because of the lengthy litigation process, many elderly Native Americans who have a right to the funds may not live long enough to receive them. Although the proposed settlement figure is lower than the estimated loss, even the smaller amount would ease the living conditions of the many Native Americans who live in poverty, according to Cobell. The settlement, proposed by a working group of tribal representatives, called for a lump sum payment to be distributed by the court hearing the lawsuit to the trust account owners.

In July, Senator John McCain (R., Arizona), chairman of the Senate Indian Affairs Committee, introduced a bill to settle the lawsuit. However, the document did not specify a compensation amount. In August, Interior Department officials asked that U.S. District Court Judge Royce Lamberth be removed from the case. During the nine years that Lamberth presided over the lawsuit, he had accused Interior Department officials of racism and found two Interior secretaries in contempt of court for failing to correct the mismanagement. The request was pending at the end of 2005.

In November, a federal appeals court ruled that requiring the Interior Department to provide a complete accounting of the trust funds is unreasonable, a decision with which both the government and the Indian plaintiffs agreed. Judge Lamberth ordered the government in December to pay the Indians $7 million in legal fees and expenses, a decision the government opposed.

Land ownership. Legislation governing ownership of Indian land went into effect in late 2005. The law, called the American Indian Probate Reform Act of 2004, was passed to consolidate the ownership of Indian lands, which had become increasingly fragmented. The rights to individual parcels had been passed down over the decades to, in some cases, hundreds of heirs. According to the Interior Department, by 2004, 400,000 individuals held 4 million ownership interests in 10 million acres (4 million hectares) of land on reservations. The multiple ownerships, according to the department, contributed to the difficulty of managing individual trust fund accounts.

Under the new legislation, Indian land ownership will be governed by a uniform federal law, rather than multiple state laws. In addition, individuals and tribes will be able to force the sale of highly divided pieces of land to a single owner, a right that previously applied only to non-Indians.

Apology. A resolution that the government formally apologize for the impact that past government misdeeds and policies have had on Native Americans was introduced in Congress in 2005. By the end of the year, however, Congress had not passed the measure. ■ Kristina Vaicikonis

See also **Congress of the United States.**

Indonesia signed a peace agreement on Aug. 15, 2005, with rebels from Aceh province, on the northern tip of Sumatra island, ending three decades of secessionist struggle. The civil war was estimated to have resulted in the loss of some 15,000 lives.

Aceh had sought independence and control over its considerable oil and gas resources. In the agreement, the government promised autonomy for the province, amnesty to rebels, and permission for creation of Aceh political parties. Only multiprovincial parties had been legal because the government feared separatist tendencies in several parts of the country. The rebel Free Aceh Movement dropped its demand for independence, though some rebels hoped that elections would allow them to call a referendum on autonomy.

Under the agreement, the government in late 2005 reduced its troops and police in Aceh from 50,000 to about 23,000, while rebels surrendered some weapons. Small clashes were reported after the agreement, and the Association of Southeast Asian Nations and the European Union responded by sending cease-fire monitors to Aceh.

A cease-fire in 2003 had lasted only six months before the Indonesian army launched an offensive against the rebels that left 3,000 people dead. The cease-fire talks that led to the Aug. 15, 2005, agreement resumed in Helsinki, Finland, after a

A forest ministry employee uses an elephant to remove debris in Banda Aceh, Indonesia, in January 2005. A tsunami left an estimated 130,000 people dead in Aceh province, one of the areas worst hit in the December 2004 disaster.

tsunami ravaged Aceh and other Indian Ocean areas on Dec. 26, 2004.

Tsunami. The government of Indonesia began rebuilding efforts in Aceh province early in 2005 but was accused of failing to provide sufficient aid to the battered area. The tsunami killed an estimated 130,000 of Aceh's 4 million people and left about 600,000 homeless. Much of the province's infrastructure was also destroyed. Aid supplies to the survivors were held up in some Indonesian ports due to bureaucratic and logistical problems.

Terrorism plagued Indonesia again in 2005. On the resort island of Bali, 3 suicide bombers killed 19 people in three restaurants on October 1. In October 2002, 202 people were killed in bombings of bars catering to Westerners on Bali. Police said the 2005 bombings were more sophisticated than the 2002 attacks, suggesting that terrorist groups may have become harder to detect and catch.

An Indonesian man was sentenced to death on Sept. 13, 2005, for his role in the 2004 bombing in Jakarta, the capital, of the Australian embassy, which killed 11 people, including the bomber. On Nov. 9, 2005, an elite counterterrorism unit surrounded a house 430 miles (692 kilometers) east of Jakarta. The subsequent firefight killed Azahari bin Husin, a former professor who police alleged was the terrorists' main bomb maker.

In eastern Indonesia, where some 2,000 people had died from 1999 to 2001 in clashes between Muslims and Christians prior to the signing of a peace treaty, new violence erupted in 2005. Two bombs exploded in a predominantly Christian market area on the island of Sulawesi, killing 21 people on May 28.

Polio. Indonesia's largest outbreak of polio occurred in 2005, after nearly a decade without reported cases. Medical experts suggested that the disease may have been brought to Indonesia by migrant workers returning from Africa, where the disease exists despite a worldwide eradication effort. The government mobilized 750,000 workers to immunize 24 million children under the age of 5.

Economy. Indonesia's government raised fuel prices twice in 2005. Government officials announced an almost 30-percent rise on February 28. On October 1, prices were raised by an average of 126 percent. Government fuel subsidies had kept prices low but cost the government a crippling $11 billion a year, more than 3 percent of the nation's *gross domestic product* (GDP). (GDP is the total output of goods and services produced in a country in a year.) The October hike touched off nationwide demonstrations, despite the government's providing temporary payments to 15.5 million poor households to soften the impact of the higher prices.   ■ Henry S. Bradsher

See also **Asia; Australia; Disasters; Public health; Terrorism.**

International trade. The flow of goods and services between nations shifted markedly during 2005. Sharply higher energy costs hit oil importers hard and strained trading capacity in some countries. However, booming economies in some regions—notably China and India—spurred trade expansion. China continued to export a huge volume of goods, and its growing demand for raw materials, such as oil, minerals, and soybeans, put upward pressure on prices for these and other commodities.

United States-China trade. Economists predicted that the U.S. trade deficit in 2005 would climb to between $700 billion and $800 billion. A trade deficit occurs when a country imports goods worth more than the goods it sells abroad. In 2004, the U.S. trade deficit was $618 billion.

Economists identified uneven bilateral trade between the United States and China as a major factor in the ballooning U.S. trade deficit. Late in 2005, economists predicted a U.S. trade deficit with China of $200 billion for the year.

Officials in the United States became particularly concerned during 2005 about imports of textiles and clothing from China. China's trade of these goods with the United States increased by almost 50 percent in the first three quarters of 2005. Nearly 400,000 U.S. jobs were lost in the clothing and textile industries from 2000 to 2005, and many economists identified competition from Chinese imports as a major cause.

In November, Chinese and U.S. officials announced a trade agreement designed to limit the growth of Chinese clothing and textile imports to the United States in 2006, 2007, and 2008. Trade representatives of the two countries described the pact as a "win-win" agreement.

American officials also put pressure on China in 2005 to let its currency, the yuan, float against the dollar. Critics said that the Chinese policy of pegging the yuan to the dollar's value resulted in undervaluation of the yuan, which gave China a huge pricing edge in international trade. (When a country's currency is undervalued, its goods are cheaply priced abroad.) In July, the Chinese government briefly let the yuan float against other currencies. As a result, the value of the yuan rose about 2 percent. Many currency experts claimed, however, that the yuan was still undervalued by as much as 40 percent in late 2005. In response to U.S. perceptions of unfair trading practices by China, several members of the U.S. Congress threatened to introduce legislation in 2005 to impose steep tariffs on some Chinese imports.

Oil prices. During 2005, oil prices repeatedly spiked to record highs, raising concerns that energy costs might become a drag on economic growth and trade. The price of a barrel of oil traded on the New York Mercantile Exchange topped $54 in March, rising to $65 in August. Hurricanes Katrina and Rita then hit the Gulf of Mexico and the U.S. Gulf Coast, wreaking havoc on oil drilling and refining facilities. Oil prices topped $70 per barrel in September before drifting downward due, in part, to releases of oil from U.S. and European reserve stocks. Although the impact of the hurricanes was temporary, upward pressure on oil prices exerted by burgeoning demand from China and India was likely to intensify, energy experts predicted.

Trading blocs. United States President George W. Bush on August 2 signed into law the Central American-Dominican Republic Free Trade Agreement (CAFTA-DR) after the U.S. House of Representatives passed the treaty by a razor-thin vote of 217 to 215. The agreement was designed to lower trade barriers among the United States and six Central American and Caribbean countries: Costa Rica, the Dominican Republic, El Salvador, Guatemala, Honduras, and Nicaragua.

President Bush had little success, however, moving plans forward for the Free Trade Area of the Americas (FTAA). The U.S. president tried to engage Latin American leaders on the proposal for a hemispherewide trading zone at the summit of Western Hemisphere leaders at Mar del Plata, Argentina, in November. However, leaders of nations with South America's three largest economies—Argentina, Brazil, and Venezuela—declined to negotiate on the FTAA plan.

Doha round. Trade ministers of nations within the World Trade Organization (WTO)—a Geneva, Switzerland-based group that oversees global trade agreements and arbitrates trade disputes—continued their so-called "Doha round" of negotiations in 2005. Named for a 2001 meeting of the WTO in Doha, capital of Qatar, the Doha round was a forum for negotiating a global trade accord. The negotiations stumbled in late 2005 over the issue of eliminating farm subsidies, which tend to favor farmers in wealthy countries over those in poorer, developing countries. Representatives of the European Union (EU) balked at cutting the subsidies, and negotiators worked hard to resolve the impasse before the convening of a WTO summit in Hong Kong in December.

Trade outlook. The International Monetary Fund (IMF) in its September 2005 "World Economic Outlook" projected that the volume of global trade would grow by 7 percent in 2005 after expanding by 10.3 percent in 2004. The IMF is a United Nations-affiliated organization based in Washington, D.C., that provides short-term credit to member nations and performs analyses of world economies. ■ John D. Boyd

See also **Bank; Economics, U.S.; Economics, World; Energy supply.**

Internet. Two out of every three people in the United States over the age of 18 used the Internet in 2005, according to the Pew Internet & American Life Project, a research center in Washington, D.C. In 2005, residents of the United States were twice as likely to use the Internet at home as they were at work, according to Mediamark Research Inc., a media research organization based in New York City. The company found that nearly 136 million people had Internet access at home, while only 75 million had access at work.

Media. A majority of U.S. Internet users had high-speed connections, known as broadband, in 2005, giving them the ability to rapidly download extremely large files, such as films. Fast downloads meant Internet users were more likely to listen to music, watch movies, and play games using their computers than ever before.

With increasing amounts of programming available through the Internet, distinctions between traditional media, such as radio and television, became less important. For example, in 2005, thousands of radio stations around the world transmitted their on-air broadcasts simultaneously on the Internet, typically in a process called "streaming." The technology does not require a user to download a file but instead sends the file to the user in a continuous stream. Internet broadcasts meant the station's audience was no longer limited to the reach of radio waves.

Media conglomerate Time Warner Inc. of New York City announced in November that it would offer streaming television programming from the 1970's for free online. The service, called In2TV, was scheduled to start in January 2006 with an initial offering of six channels.

Podcasts. A new kind of recorded radio broadcast, known as a podcast, gained in popularity in 2005. Podcasts began as individuals posting their commentaries and music as digital audio files on the Internet. Listeners could download these files and play them on digital music players. Podcasts are named for the iPod player made by Apple Computer, Inc., of Cupertino, California. While the iPod was the most popular device on the market in 2005, there were many competing products that also played such audio files. By mid-2005, such businesses as radio stations and newspapers had embraced the podcast format.

Piracy. While a few companies, such as Los Angeles-based MovieFlix.com, allowed Internet users to download films for a fee in 2005, the vast majority of Internet movie downloads were pirated. By using special computer programs distributed by companies like Grokster, Ltd., which is based in Nevis, West Indies, Internet users created "peer-to-peer" networks for sharing music or video stored on their personal computers with other Internet users running the programs.

According to a study by the Pew Internet & American Life Project, about 33 percent of Internet users admitted that they have shared music or video files using such networks. Nevertheless, commercial services, such as Apple Computer, Inc.'s iTunes Music Store, which allowed people to purchase a song for 99 cents, gained enormously in popularity in 2005. The Pew study found that 34 percent of people downloading music from the Internet used a paid service in 2005. When Apple debuted its iTunes service in Japan in August, users downloaded more than 1 million songs in the first four days of the store's operation.

The U.S. Supreme Court ruled in June that companies like Grokster could be held legally responsible for the theft of music or movies by Grokster users. The decision, plus lawsuits that forced dozens of peer-to-peer network users to pay thousands of dollars in fines for sharing copyrighted music with other users, encouraged Internet users to make more use of pay services such as iTunes.

Blogging. Personal journals posted on Web pages, known as "blogs" (for Web logs), also became increasingly popular in 2005. By some measures, the number of blogs was in the millions by the end of the year. Blogs are typically connected to each other over the Internet by Web links between different sites.

Some observers credited blogging with an increasing influence on the U.S. political environment. When CBS News, a division of the New York City-based television network, presented documents in 2004 supposedly demonstrating that President George W. Bush had received preferential treatment during his service in the U.S. National Guard, bloggers quickly responded. They presented arguments that the documents could not have been created on a typewriter as the source that provided the documentation to CBS had claimed. A subsequent investigation by CBS found that the source had lied about how the documents were obtained, and CBS reporters could neither confirm nor disprove the authenticity of the documents. Even so, bloggers took credit when Dan Rather stepped down after 24 years as anchor of the CBS Evening News on March 9, 2005, as a direct result of the controversy.

Many blogging enthusiasts argued that blogs were an alternative to mainstream media, such as newspapers, and would even replace them someday. Critics responded that blogs could not exist without traditional journalism, as many blogs consisted of commentary on stories from traditional news outlets. In addition, critics pointed out that the vast majority of blogs were no longer updated because the bloggers who created them apparently had nothing more to say.   ■ Dave Wilson

See also **Computer; Electronics; Popular music; Telecommunications; Television.**

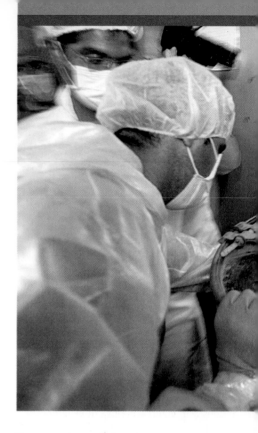

Iran. Mahmoud Ahmadinejad, the mayor of Iran's capital, Tehran, was elected president of Iran in a runoff election against former Iranian President Ali Akbar Hashemi Rafsanjani on June 24, 2005. Ahmadinejad, a hardline conservative, won 61.7 percent of the vote, compared with 35.9 percent for Rafsanjani. According to government estimates, 60 percent of eligible voters participated in the election. Ahmadinejad had appealed in his campaign to lower- and middle-class voters by using economically populist, anticorruption themes. The new president took office on August 3, succeeding Mohammad Khatami-Ardakani, who had been largely unsuccessful in attempts at reform during his two terms.

Nuclear program. In August 2005, the 35-member Board of Governors of the International Atomic Energy Agency (IAEA), a Vienna, Austria-based organization that promotes the peaceful use of nuclear energy, adopted a resolution critical of Iran's nuclear program. The resolution expressed concern that Iran had decided to resume uranium enrichment activities, which could produce fuel for either civilian nuclear reactors or nuclear bombs. The IAEA urged Iran to suspend all such activities.

When President Ahmadinejad appeared before the UN General Assembly in September, he maintained that Iran had an "inalienable right" to pro-

Iranian technicians move a barrel of yellowcake, a uranium salt used in the enrichment of uranium, at Iran's Uranium Conversion Facility in Isfahan in August. Iranian authorities announced in 2005 that they had ended Iran's freeze on uranium enrichment activities, which could produce fuel for either civilian nuclear reactors or nuclear bombs.

duce nuclear fuel to generate energy. A few days later, the IAEA adopted a European Union proposal threatening to refer Iran's violations of the Nuclear Nonproliferation Treaty to the UN Security Council.

Human rights. Akbar Ganji, an Iranian journalist imprisoned in 2000 for advocating democracy and freedom of speech, began a hunger strike in May 2005. By July, the international attention on Iran's human rights record generated by the ailing Ganji led to the acknowledgment by Iranian authorities of widespread human rights violations in prisons, including the use of torture and solitary confinement for prolonged periods. In November, both the European community and the United States called for the immediate and unconditional release of Ganji.

Remarks on Israel. On October 26, on what is known as Jerusalem Day in parts of the Muslim world, President Ahmadinejad called for Israel to be "wiped off the map." The inflammatory speech was followed by numerous anti-Israeli demonstrations throughout Tehran and other Iranian cities. World leaders condemned President Ahmadinejad's remarks, and Israel's prime minister, Ariel Sharon, called for Iran to be expelled from the United Nations. ■ Mary-Jane Deeb

See also **Israel; Middle East; People in the News** (Mahmoud Ahmadinejad); **United Nations.**

Iraq. On Jan. 30, 2005, Iraq held its first free elections in several decades. More than 8.5 million Iraqis participated, a figure that represented a voter turnout of 58 percent. However, the turnout was highly uneven. In some Kurdish areas in northern Iraq, such as Dahuk, as much as 85 percent of eligible adults turned out to vote; in Sunni-dominated areas, such as Anbar province west and northwest of Baghdad, the capital, as little as 2 percent of the population voted. The Independent Electoral Commission of Iraq (IECI) certified the results in February.

The Transitional National Assembly. Iraqis elected a Transitional National Assembly and cast ballots for governing councils in each of Iraq's 18 provinces. Twelve parties out of 111 political entities were allocated seats, including the predominantly Shiah United Iraqi Alliance (UIA), which was the big winner with 140 seats, giving it an absolute majority in the 275-member Assembly; the Kurdistan Alliance List, which brought together the 2 main Kurdish parties and won 75 seats; and the Iraqi List, headed by the former Iraqi prime minister, Ayad Allawi, which won 40 seats. The 20 other Assembly seats were distributed among 9 parties and groups, including the Iraqi Turkmen Front; the People's Union; the Islamic Group of Kurdistan; and the National Rafidain List. Most Sunni political parties boycotted the elections.

A new constitution. The primary task of the newly elected Transitional National Assembly was to draft a new constitution. Members of the Assembly formed a constitutional committee made up of 55 members, which was later expanded to 69 members. The committee split into six subcommittees to tackle various aspects of the constitution, including separation of powers and *federalism* (a political unity created by separate states or districts, each of which retains control of its own internal affairs). The deadline for completing a draft of the new constitution was extended four times because of the lack of consensus among members of the committee on a number of issues, particularly the existence of an *autonomous* (independent; self-governing) region for Kurds in the north; and *de-Baathification* (how to deal with Baath Party members of the previous government of deposed President Saddam Hussein). When the constitution was finally submitted to the Transitional National Assembly in late August, none of the Sunni members of the constitutional committee signed the completed document.

Referendum. On October 15, a national referendum on the constitution took place. Voter turnout was high with some 63 percent of the electorate participating. As many as 78 percent of the voters backed the new constitution; 21 per-

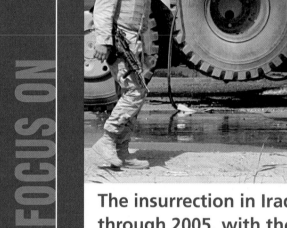

American soldiers patrol on foot as an Army truck burns in the aftermath of a roadside bombing in Baghdad in June. The death toll of U.S. soldiers in Iraq reached 2,000 on October 25 and stood at 2,175 on December 29.

The insurrection in Iraq continued unabated through 2005, with thousands of guerrilla attacks launched against U.S.-led coalition soldiers, Iraq security forces, and Iraqi civilians.

Funeral tents line a Baghdad street on July 14 in the wake of a suicide car bomb attack on U.S. soldiers handing out candy to Iraqi children. The explosion killed 28 people, including 18 children and teen-agers.

cent opposed it. Only 2 of Iraq's 18 provinces rejected the charter, which was neither enough to restart the process of drafting a new constitution nor enough to dissolve the Transitional National Assembly. Approved by a ratification of the vote, the constitution replaced the existing Law of Administration for the State of Iraq, which had been put in force by the United States-led Coalition Provisional Authority in March 2004.

United Nations (UN) Security Council. In November, the UN Security Council extended the mandate of the Iraq Multinational Forces until December 2006 and supported the continued depositing of proceeds from export sales of natural gas, petroleum, and petroleum products into the Development Fund for Iraq. The decision to extend that mandate was requested by Iraqi Prime Minister Ibrahim Aleshaiker al-Jafari in a letter dated Oct. 27, 2005, to the president of the UN Security Council. Al-Jafari stated that until Iraqi forces could assume full responsibility for the security of the Iraqi people, the multinational forces would be needed "to establish lasting peace and security" in Iraq. United States Secretary of State Condoleezza Rice responded by sending a letter on October 29 to the UN Security Council stating that the multinational force under a unified command would continue efforts to maintain security and provide humanitarian and reconstruction assistance to Iraq.

Parliamentary elections. On December 15, Iraqis again turned out in large numbers to vote for a new parliament. In late 2005, preliminary results suggested that the main Shiah coalition party, UIA, had won a majority but would need to form a coalition government. However, Sunni leaders claimed that there had been vote fraud and contested the results. Asking that the Sunni leaders end demands for a rerun of the polling, UIA leaders announced that they were willing to negotiate with Sunnis about participating in the new government. On December 30, an international team agreed to assess whether the election had been compromised by fraud.

War and casualties. The insurgency in Iraq continued through 2005 with daily attacks that left thousands of people dead

Iraqi women register to vote at a mosque in Baghdad in 2005. Voter turnout for parliamentary elections in January and December and for a constitutional referendum in October was high, particularly in the Kurdish dominated north and the Shiah Arab dominated south.

and injured. By Dec. 29, 2005, 2,175 U.S. soldiers had been killed and at least 15,955 others had been wounded in action since the war began in March 2003. No accurate figures existed for the number of Iraqis who were killed during the same period, but estimates ranged from 15,000 to 48,000. Most of the casualties, including U.S. troops, Iraqi security forces, and Iraqi civilians, died in terrorist attacks involving suicide and roadside bombings, which increased in number and intensity through 2005.   ■ Mary-Jane Deeb

See also **Armed forces; Middle East; Year in brief.**

Ireland. In 2005, *Taoiseach* (Prime Minister) Bertie Ahern's Fianna Fail party remained in power as part of a coalition with the Progressive Democrats led by Mary Harney. The Fianna Fail government had been elected in 1997 and re-elected in 2002. Although the Irish economy remained strong, critics accused Ahern's government of incompetent management of public funds. According to an *Irish Times* poll in September 2005, 58 percent of the Irish people disapproved of the government. Ahern insisted no election would be held until 2007.

Irish President Mary McAleese was forced to apologize in January 2005, after she compared the way Protestant children in Northern Ireland were taught to hate Roman Catholics with the way Nazis in the 1930's taught German children to hate Jews. David Trimble, leader of the Ulster Unionist Party in Northern Ireland, accused McAleese of trivializing the Holocaust, the systematic killing of Jews and other groups by the Nazis.

Abortion. In August 2005, three Irish women who had been forced to go to the United Kingdom for abortions because the procedure is illegal in Ireland brought a case against the Irish government before the European Court of Human Rights in Strasbourg, France. The women claimed that the country's ban on abortion violated four articles of the European Convention on Human Rights. Supporters of abortion complained that more than 6,000 Irish women annually are forced to go abroad to terminate pregnancies.

Economy. In 2005, Ireland enjoyed one of the lowest unemployment rates in Europe—4.3 percent, compared with 8.7 percent for the 25-nation European Union (EU). EU economists projected that the Irish economy would grow by 4.4 percent in 2005, more than double the 1.5 percent average rate of the other EU nations. Ireland's strong economy made it a top destination for Eastern European migrants from the new EU member nations. By November, more than 150,000 Eastern Europeans had applied for work permits in Ireland.

Easter parade. In October, Ahern announced that the government would reinstate a military parade to commemorate the Easter Rising of 1916 that led to the eventual founding of the Republic of Ireland. (The rising was a rebellion against British rule that erupted in Dublin.) The march, which traditionally processed past Dublin's General Post Office on O'Connell Street, had been abandoned in 1970 following the outbreak of violence in Northern Ireland. Political analysts claimed that the move was Ahern's attempt to separate the tradition of Irish republicanism from the nationalist party, Sinn Fein, which had ties with the Irish Republican Army and violence in Northern Ireland. ■ Rohan McWilliam

See also **Europe; Northern Ireland.**

Islam. A strong Muslim feminist movement began in 2005 in North America and Europe. In March, Amina Wadud—a professor of Islamic Studies at Virginia Commonwealth University in Richmond—led a gathering in New York City of 125 men and women in a Muslim prayer service. Although the Qur'an, the sacred book of Islam, does not discuss gender in regard to leadership of congregational prayer, it had been a custom in Islamic law that only men could lead a mixed congregation and that the sexes should be separated when praying in the same place. Wadud and former *Wall Street Journal* reporter Asra Nomani organized the gathering to call attention to what they claimed is un-Islamic gender discrimination in Muslim practice.

The event provoked extensive discussion in the Muslim world. Many Arab legal scholars and Muslims in Europe and the United States encouraged Muslims to adapt to local customs and noted that there was no reason that women could not lead a mixed congregation. Other Muslims, including Malaysian clerics and Islamic scholars in Qatar, condemned the service. They emphasized the perspective that men and women might distract each other in prayer services.

The Islamic Society of North America, a major North American Muslim organization based in Plainfield, Indiana, issued a report in July titled "Women Friendly Mosques and Community Centers: Working Together to Reclaim Our Heritage." The report called for strong reforms including an affirmative action program to place women on mosque boards and other efforts to challenge the ways in which ultraconservative Islamic rulings have denied rights to women.

In October, the first International Congress on Islamic Feminism was held in Barcelona, Spain, on "Gender Jihad," a campaign to attain—or recover, its supporters argued—full rights for Muslim women faithful to Islamic practice. (Jihad is an Arabic word for religious struggle.) According to the meeting's organizers, Islamic sacred texts have historically been read from an almost exclusively male perspective. The conference participants suggested that the feminist perspective of equality could also be found in such books as the Qur'an.

The Turkish Directorate of Religious Affairs in September appointed two female graduates of the Imam-Hatip (prayer leader-sermonizer) professional schools to serve as the first female deputy muftis in regional districts. Muftis provide religious guidance to less-religiously educated Muslims when a matter of religious concern arises. The Director of Religious Affairs, Ali Bardakoglu, stated that the directorate planned to increase the number of women deputy muftis, beginning with appointments in Turkey's major provinces.

A Muslim demonstrator displays an open Qur'an outside the U.S. embassy in Jakarta, Indonesia, in May in protest of reported U.S. Army desecration of the Islamic holy book. A false report that the Qur'an was defaced at a prisoner-of-war camp in Guantanamo Bay, Cuba, sparked the protest.

Iraq. Muslim resistance to the U.S.-led occupation of Iraq continued in 2005, some of it led by the al-Qa`ida terrorist network. In March, the head of al-Qa`ida in Iraq, Abu Musab al-Zarqawi, declared war on Shiah Muslims just days before bombings were carried out at prominent Shiah pilgrimage sites in Baghdad and Karbala, a city 50 miles (80 kilometers) south of Baghdad. American observers reported in November that some Shiite militias engaged in retaliatory killings of Sunni Muslims. As the post-Saddam Hussein government of Iraq gradually developed, both Ayatollah Ali al-Sistani—the senior Shiah cleric in Iraq—and Moqtada al-Sadr, a militia leader representing the mostly Shiah poor, grew more powerful.

Europe. Four suicide bombers affiliated with The Secret Organization of al-Qa`ida in Europe attacked London's public transportation system on July 7, killing 56 people. Britons were shocked to discover that the perpetrators were seemingly well-integrated British Muslims of Pakistani and, in one case, Jamaican descent. Several of the victims were Muslims, and the incident prompted Muslims throughout the United Kingdom and Europe to reflect upon the culture of European Islam.

The London bombings were carried out by Muslims acting in support of the global jihad movement and al-Qa`ida terrorist organizations. While the overwhelming majority of European Muslims are unsympathetic to terrorism, the attacks proved that terror was no longer a foreign phenomenon but also one arising in Europe. Muslim leaders in Europe condemned the bombings and called for Muslims to embrace the democratic, nonviolent politics of their adopted countries. The leaders also urged renewed efforts to receive Muslims into European societies.

North America. Muslims in Ontario, Canada, in 2005 asked for the right long held by some Christian and Jewish Canadians to religious arbitration in marital disputes and other family cases. The province had allowed for arbitration conducted by priests and rabbis. Muslims requested arbitration under *Shari`a* (Islamic law), conducted by Muslim experts. After considerable controversy, Premier Dalton McGuinty decided in September to abolish all religious arbitration rather than allow arbitration under Shari`a.

Muslim concerns about anti-Muslim hostility led many groups, such as the Council on American-Islamic Relations, a Washington, D.C.-based Islamic civil rights organization, to observe in 2005 that U.S. films and television programs tended to feature Muslims as the typical villains. Muslim groups objected that such stereotyping could have a negative effect on relations between non-Muslim and Muslim Americans.   ■ A. Kevin Reinhart

See also **Iraq; Terrorism; United Kingdom.**

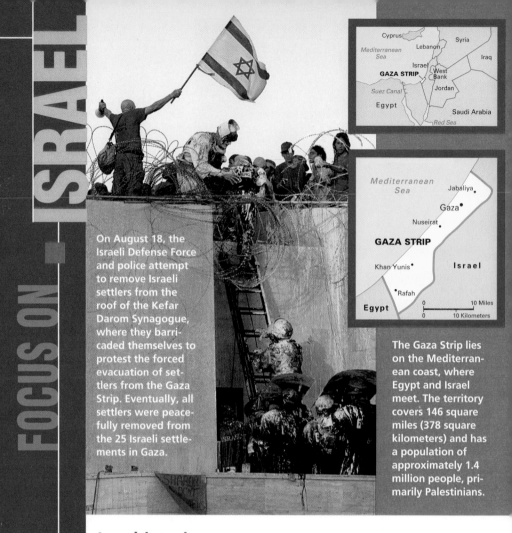

On August 18, the Israeli Defense Force and police attempt to remove Israeli settlers from the roof of the Kefar Darom Synagogue, where they barricaded themselves to protest the forced evacuation of settlers from the Gaza Strip. Eventually, all settlers were peacefully removed from the 25 Israeli settlements in Gaza.

The Gaza Strip lies on the Mediterranean coast, where Egypt and Israel meet. The territory covers 146 square miles (378 square kilometers) and has a population of approximately 1.4 million people, primarily Palestinians.

In a historic move, Israel in 2005 dismantled its settlements in the Gaza Strip and withdrew all forces after 38 years.

Israel. On Feb. 8, 2005, Prime Minister Ariel Sharon and Palestinian President Mahmoud Abbas agreed at a summit in Sharm el-Sheikh, Egypt, to "cease all acts of violence against Israelis and Palestinians everywhere." Their declaration virtually ended the Palestinian *Intifadah* (uprising) that began in September 2000. However, sporadic clashes between Palestinian militants and Israeli forces continued throughout the year.

Gaza withdrawal. Prime Minister Sharon's plan to "unilaterally disengage" from the Gaza Strip was implemented in August 2005 with the dismantling of all 25 Israeli settlements in the Palestinian-claimed area. Another four Israeli settlements were dismantled in the West Bank. The last Israeli soldier pulled out of the Gaza Strip in September.

The withdrawal was followed by intensive negotiations in which United States Secretary of State Condoleezza Rice helped Israeli and

A family of Israeli settlers confronts an Israeli soldier in the Gaza Strip in August during the forced evacuation of settlers. The settlers received compensation from the Israeli government for leaving the Gaza settlements.

Palestinian officials resolve differences regarding the opening of four routes: three connecting Gaza with Israel and one connecting Gaza with Egypt. Secretary of State Rice announced in November that agreement had been reached on opening these routes.

Improved international relations. Israel's pullout from the Gaza Strip quickly resulted in improved relations between Israel and the Islamic and Arab countries. On September 1, Israeli Foreign Minister Silvan Shalom met with Pakistani Foreign Minister Khurshid Mahmud Kasuri in Istanbul, Turkey's capital. Shalom described the meeting as "a huge breakthrough." On September 15, Shalom met with Qatari Foreign Minister Sheik Hamad bin Jassem al-Thani, who praised Israel for its withdrawal from Gaza.

Political shake-ups. Former Prime Minister Shimon Peres unexpectedly lost the leadership primary of the Labor Party to challenger Amir Peretz on November 9. Peretz, who as a child had

immigrated to Israel from Morocco, was the leader of Histadrut, the major federation of Israeli trade unions. As a union leader, Peretz had opposed the conservative economic policies pursued by Finance Minister (and former prime minister) Benjamin Netanyahu. Peretz also had long argued that the Likud government's focus on Israeli settlers in the Gaza Strip and West Bank "came at the expense of the poor in Israel proper."

After being elected Labor Party leader, Peretz pulled his party out of the national unity Cabinet, arguing that such cabinets "are anathema to democracy." By doing so, he created a political dilemma for Prime Minister Sharon, who also faced a rebellion in his own Likud Party from hard-liners who had strongly opposed the Gaza pullout.

On November 21, Prime Minister Sharon announced that he was leaving Likud, which he had cofounded in 1973, to form a new centrist party, called *Kadima* (Forward), dedicated to working toward a lasting peace with the Palestinians. Ousted Labor leader Peres later announced his support for Kadima.

In late December, Prime Minister Sharon suffered a mild stroke. On Jan. 4, 2006, he suffered a second, far more serious stroke and underwent a series of operations. His deputy, Ehud Olmert, took over as caretaker prime minister.

Rabin commemoration. On Nov. 14, 2005, Israel commemorated the 10th anniversary of the assassination of Prime Minister Yitzhak Rabin. Thousands of people, including about 30 foreign dignitaries, attended the commemoration in Tel Aviv. Among those in attendance was former U.S. president Bill Clinton, who had worked closely with Rabin for peace in the Middle East.

Earliest church. Israeli Antiquities Authority archaeologists announced in November that they had discovered what appeared to be the oldest Christian church in the Holy Land, dating back to the 200's or 300's. Excavating on the grounds of a prison at Megiddo (the biblical site of Armageddon), the archaeologists uncovered a well-preserved mosaic bearing the name of Jesus Christ in ancient Greek, as well as images of fish (a Christian symbol) and an altar. ■ Marius Deeb

See also **Judaism; Middle East; Terrorism; Turkey.**

Italy. In April 2005, Prime Minister Silvio Berlusconi, Italy's longest-serving prime minister since 1945, survived a vote of confidence in parliament. Berlusconi had been elected in 2001. He resigned on April 20, 2005, because of conflict among the parties in his Casa delle Liberta ruling coalition in the wake of a rout by the center-left opposition in regional elections. The center right had lost 12 out of 14 regions. Italian President Carlo Azeglio Ciampo asked Berlusconi to form a new government, and on April 27 and April 28, both houses of parliament approved the new Cabinet.

Romano Prodi, the leader of the center left and a former prime minister, remained more popular than Berlusconi. Nevertheless, Berlusconi's policies, which included regional business tax cuts and reducing the tax burden on low-income families, enjoyed support among a majority of Italians. In October, the left held a "primary" to choose a single candidate around whom all parties—which traditionally have been deeply divided—could unify. Prodi emerged as the victor, but it remained unclear whether he would be able to impose his authority on others within the left. The next national election was scheduled for April 2006.

Economy. Italy's *gross domestic product* (GDP, the total output of goods and services produced in a country in a year) grew by only 0.2 percent in 2005, and European Union (EU) economists pro-

jected that it would increase only by 1.5 percent in 2006. Italy's budget deficit exceeded 3 percent in 2005 and was expected to do so again in 2006. The 3-percent figure represents a benchmark of budgetary discipline for all EU member nations that share a common currency, the euro.

Although Italy was not the only country in Europe to exceed the limits of the EU's Stability and Growth Pact, it came under further pressure from the EU in 2005 over its economic statistics. In late 2004, Eurostat (the EU's statistical service) accused Italy of keeping unreliable statistics.

The resignation of Italy's economy minister, Domenico Siniscalco, in September 2005 left his successor, Giulio Tremonti, little time to draft a budget for 2006. The new budget called for 20 billion euros ($24.13 billion) in cuts and revenue-raising measures. Critics expressed doubt that the move was sufficient to eliminate the deficit.

Alliance with the United States. Italy officially continued to back the U.S.-led coalition in Iraq during 2005, despite the unpopularity of the war among most Italians. Italians were appalled in March when U.S. soldiers shot and killed a senior Italian intelligence officer, Nicola Calipari, who was traveling to the Baghdad airport with a freed Italian hostage. Immediately after the incident, Berlusconi announced that Italy would begin withdrawing its 3,000 soldiers in September. He later backtracked on the pledge. However, the opposition vowed to begin troop withdrawals immediately if elected in April 2006.

Antiterrorism. In the wake of the bombing of three subway trains and a bus in London by Islamic radicals on July 7, 2005, Italy adopted a new and extensive antiterrorist law on July 31. The law increased transportation security; banned the public wearing of *burkas* and *chadors* (traditional garments worn by Muslim women that cover the face); permitted the collection of DNA samples from suspects; and doubled the length of time suspects can be detained by police to 24 hours. The legislation followed heated public debate, frequently with racist overtones emerging from anti-immigrant members of parliament and especially from the Northern League, a right-wing political party. Italy had been the subject of several threats issued by Islamic extremist groups because of its support of U.S. troops in Iraq.

After the new law was passed, authorities ordered managers of public communication services to require passport copies of every customer using fax, telephone, and Internet services. Many Italians considered the law, especially the close monitoring of Internet cafes, to be heavy-handed, but no major opposition to it emerged. According to the Interior Ministry, more than 25 Islamic extremists were arrested on Italian soil in 2005, including one of the London subway bombers.

Mourners climb the steps of Rome's Victor Emmanuel monument in March to pay their respects to a slain Italian intelligence officer lying in state in Italy's Unknown Soldier memorial. American soldiers in Baghdad accidentally shot and killed the officer, Nicola Calipari, while he was protecting an Italian journalist, Guiliana Sgrena. The incident took place just minutes after Calipari had rescued Sgrena from kidnappers.

Scandals. Antonio Fazio, the governor of Italy's central bank (the Bank of Italy), was discovered in July 2005 to have helped Italy's 10th-largest bank, the Banca Popolare Italiana (BPI) in its bid to take over Banca Antoniana Popolare Veneta. A telephone call Fazio made to the chief executive of BPI, Gianpiero Fiorani, was recorded by Italian police who were investigating his bank for market rigging and false accounting. Italian politicians were embarrassed by the incident, and Berlusconi sought Fazio's resignation. However, in November, the European Central Bank concluded that Fazio had broken no laws.

The trial of Calisto Tanzi, the former chief executive of Parmalat, the Italian dairy conglomorate that declared bankruptcy in 2003, began in September 2005. Tanzi and his firm were charged with misleading markets and investors and with falsifying accounting records. Over the course of a decade, Parmalat reported large profits when in fact it suffered losses of over 15 billion euros ($18 billion). The firm continued to operate in 2005 and, under new leadership, sued its U.S. accountants for failing to spot the fraudulent behavior of the former management. ■ Jeffrey Kopstein

See also **Europe; Iraq; United Kingdom.**

Ivory Coast. See Cote d'Ivoire in **Africa.**

Jamaica. See West Indies.

Japan. Prime Minister Junichiro Koizumi led his Liberal Democratic Party (LDP) to a strong victory in early elections to the lower house of parliament on Sept. 11, 2005, which upset Japan's political status quo. The LDP had ruled Japan almost continuously for 50 years as an alliance of over-represented rural voters and of urban political bosses who catered to big businesses. By calling elections ahead of schedule, Koizumi challenged the LDP's vested interests and succeeded in limiting them.

Koizumi focused the election campaign on Japan's post office. With more than 24,000 branches and more than 280,000 full-time employees in 2005, Japan Post not only delivered mail but also was the world's largest savings bank and an insurance company providing life insurance to 68 million people. According to political experts, much of the money held by Japan Post was used in the past to support politically favored projects of little economic value. These projects were backed by conservative bosses of LDP factions whom Koizumi had fought since he became prime minister in 2001, against the bosses' wishes. The bosses rewarded supporters with jobs on such unproductive projects as building little-used highways, bridges, and other unnecessary infrastructure.

Koizumi argued that the post office contributed to Japan's economic stagnation. He sought to make the banking and insurance functions into private businesses that would use their money in more dynamic ways of greater benefit to the country. The LDP old guard feared a change would threaten their political power.

Showdown. Koizumi called a vote on post office reform in parliament's lower house on July 4, 2005, forcing a showdown with his LDP opponents. The bill passed by a narrow margin, but LDP rebels kept the bill from passing in the upper house on August 8. After this defeat, Koizumi immediately dissolved the lower house and called an election in order to seek public support for his postal reform plan. Koizumi, whose unusual political dynamism and flamboyant hairstyle caused him to be compared with rock stars, used his popularity to run an unconventional election campaign. He purged 37 antireform members of the lower house and recruited new faces to replace them, including television celebrities and a former model. Japanese media labeled the newcomers "assassins" trying to eliminate the LDP rebels.

Results. The LDP won 296 of the 480 elected seats in the lower house, a gain of 84 seats from its previous strength and one of the party's best showings ever. The "assassins" took 19 seats from the 32 rebels who sought reelection.

The LDP's coalition partner, New Komeito, fell from 34 seats to 31. Despite this, the two parties' combined strength of more than two-thirds of the lower house gave Koizumi the ability not only to get legislation through that house but also to override any veto by the upper house. Both houses passed Koizumi's postal reform bill in mid-October, with changes in the postal system scheduled to begin in 2007 and be completed by 2017.

Under LDP rules, Koizumi's term as prime minister was scheduled to end in September 2006. His election triumph stirred talk of changing the rules, but he said he would step down as scheduled. On Oct. 31, 2005, Koizumi named Shinzo Abe as chief Cabinet minister, making him a leading candidate to succeed to the prime minister's job. Another candidate, Taro Aso, was named foreign minister.

The opposition Democratic Party had in recent years begun to look like a credible alternative to the LDP. While Koizumi focused on the post office issue and talked only vaguely about other reforms, the Democrats campaigned for a wide range of reforms to deal with looming pension problems, issues arising from Japan's rapidly aging population, and other public questions. Democratic candidates promised to shrink the government's size, shake up the bureaucracy, and withdraw Japanese troops from Iraq, where they filled noncombat roles.

The election dropped the Democrats sharply from 175 seats to 113 in the new lower house. The setback made the development of a two-party system look more distant and left political observers worried about the lack of strong checks and balances. Katsuya Okada resigned as party leader, and 43-year-old Seiji Maehara replaced him.

The economy. The Tokyo stock market, which had been rising in anticipation of Koizumi's victory, afterward rose to the highest level since 2001. Other indicators hinted that Japan might break out of 15 years of economic drift, during which its gross public debts topped 150 percent of annual output, one of the world's highest ratios. However, a survey by the official Bank of Japan found 73 percent of the population remained skeptical of an economic recovery.

Relations with China, Japan's biggest trading partner, were troubled in 2005. New Japanese school textbooks were criticized in China as glossing over atrocities during Japan's occupation of parts of China from 1931 to 1945. With apparent Chinese government approval, demonstrators in several Chinese cities attacked Japanese diplomatic offices during April 2005. Nobutaka Machimura, then Japan's foreign minister, said China's own textbooks distorted its Communist history by omitting policy failures.

In an apparent effort to repair relations, Koizumi on April 22 expressed "deep remorse" for the "tremendous damage and suffering" inflicted on Asian neighbors during World War II (1939-1945). Chinese Vice Premier Wu Yi requested a meeting with Koizumi during a visit to Japan to ease relations. However, she abruptly canceled the meeting on May 23, 2005, angering Japanese officials. On October 17, Koizumi visited a shrine to Japan's war dead, which honors, among others, people who were found guilty of war crimes after World War II. Koizumi's visit angered neighboring countries. China postponed a planned visit by Machimura.

Japan and China also argued over territorial claims in the East China Sea. Japan announced on April 13 that it would allow oil and gas drilling inside its claimed territory, provoking Chinese protests. Japan accused China on September 20 of extracting natural gas from beneath its waters. With relations tense, China joined South Korea on opposing Japan's aspirations to win a permanent seat on the United Nations Security Council.

Holiday. In May 2005, Hirohito, who was Japan's emperor from 1926 until his death in 1989, was honored by parliament. April 29, formerly celebrated as Greenery Day, was renamed Showa Day after the official name for Hirohito's era. Parliament had earlier backed away from honoring the man associated by many Asian nations with World War II atrocities. However, supporters said that the holiday would encourage remembrance of Japan's difficult growth during Hirohito's reign, rather than glorify the man himself. ■ Henry S. Bradsher

See also **Asia; China; Disasters.**

Jordan. Three nearly simultaneous suicide bombings in hotels owned by United States corporations in Amman, the capital of Jordan, killed 58 people and injured nearly 100 others on Nov. 9, 2005. The most lethal of the attacks was carried out in a ballroom during a wedding reception attended primarily by Jordanians. The Iraqi branch of the al-Qa`ida terrorist network, led by Jordanian-born militant Abu Musab al-Zarqawi, claimed responsibility for the attacks. Jordanian officials arrested an Iraqi woman who confessed to being part of the plot.

In the days following the bombings, some 100,000 Jordanians marched through Amman to demonstrate their anger at al-Zarqawi. In response to these protests, al-Zarqawi issued a statement claiming that the bomb that killed the wedding guests had been meant to kill U.S. and Israeli intelligence agents who were allegedly staying at the hotel. Al-Zarqawi went on to threaten to kill Jordan's leader, King Abdullah II.

As a result of the attacks, Abdullah replaced his Cabinet and asked his former security chief, Major General Marouf al-Bakhit, to be the new prime minister. The 24-member Cabinet, made up mostly of technocrats, was formed on November 27. The king also called for a renewed effort to combat global terrorism. ■ Marius Deeb

See also **Iraq; Middle East; Terrorism.**

Judaism. Hurricane Katrina, which struck the Gulf Coast of the United States on Aug. 29, 2005, displaced thousands of Jews from their residences in Louisiana and Mississippi and damaged or destroyed synagogues and Jewish community centers. Jews mobilized rapidly, setting up evacuee accommodations and social services in Houston; Birmingham, Alabama; Atlanta, Georgia; and other cities. Hurricane Wilma, which struck Florida in October, affected larger numbers of Jews but displaced far fewer people.

United States. The nationwide celebration of the 350th anniversary of American Jewish life—marked by educational and cultural events—concluded on September 14 with a Washington, D.C., gala dinner where guests were addressed by President George W. Bush. In his speech, the president alluded to his program of "faith-based initiatives," which provide government funds to religious organizations. The program aroused considerable debate within the Jewish community.

Jews in the United States had several other concerns in 2005 about the role of religion in American life. In May, cadets at the U.S. Air Force Academy in Colorado Springs, Colorado, charged that evangelical chaplains had attempted to convert Jews to Christianity. Throughout 2005, court battles raged over the teaching of intelligent design, a Christian creationist view of the origin

Pope Benedict XVI (left) visits a synagogue in Cologne, Germany, in August on his first foreign trip after being elevated to the papacy. The pope condemned the Holocaust and called for sincere dialogue between Jews and Christians.

of life, in public schools. Abraham Foxman, national director of the Anti-Defamation League, a civil rights organization based in Washington, D.C., warned in November of a growing campaign to "Christianize America."

Many American Jews took offense to what some regarded as unfair treatment of Israel by churches, universities, and the U.S. media. In 2005, leaders of the Presbyterian Church (PCUSA) debated whether to "initiate a process of phased, selective divestment in multinational corporations operating in Israel." Some Jewish leaders called for renewed dialogue with the church. At Columbia University in New York City, Jewish activists challenged administrators in 2005 to discipline faculty whom, they alleged, demonized Israel and created a hostile environment for Jewish students. Jews also renewed charges of bias against such media organizations as National Public Radio for allegedly treating Israel in a one-sided manner.

Among themselves, American Jews disagreed strongly over Israeli policies. However, a majority supported Israel's peace overtures and withdrawal from Gaza, according to polls conducted in 2005.

World. The United Nations (UN) held a special session in January 2005 to mark the 60th anniversary of the liberation of the Nazi death camps. In November, the UN passed a resolution establishing January 27 as an official day of Holocaust commemoration. (The Holocaust was the systematic, state-sponsored murder of Jews and others by the Nazis during World War II [1939-1945].)

Jews mourned the death in April 2005 of John Paul II, a champion of Jewish-Catholic dialogue. His successor, Pope Benedict XVI, reaffirmed his commitment to improving relations with Jews and visited a synagogue in Cologne, Germany, in August. However, some Jews expressed concern about the pope's association, as a teen-ager, with the Nazi youth movement. In July, Israeli officials criticized the Vatican for condemning terrorism in other countries while excluding Israel.

Israel. Israeli politicians resumed the long-stalled peace process following the death of Palestinian Authority Chairman Yasir Arafat in November 2004. Israeli Prime Minister Ariel Sharon formed a new political party in November 2005 with moderate Likud and Labor members dedicated to a final peace settlement with Palestinians.

In August, Israel overcame internal opposition from right-wing and religious elements in the country and withdrew its settlers from the Gaza Strip. Some Jews feared that the withdrawal would spark civil strife within Israel, but it largely proceeded peacefully due to careful planning by the government and Israeli armed forces.

■ Jonathan D. Sarna and Jonathan J. Golden
See also **Israel; Protestantism; Terrorism.**

Kampuchea. See Cambodia.

Kazakhstan. Kazakh President Nursultan Nazarbayev won a third consecutive term on Dec. 4, 2005, taking 91 percent of the vote in an election that failed to meet international standards. Nazarbayev, who came to power in 1989, had cracked down on opposition parties and newspapers prior to the 2005 election in response to regime changes in Georgia (2003), Ukraine (2004), and Kyrgyzstan (2005). On January 6, a court ordered the opposition party, Democratic Choice of Kazakhstan, dissolved; libel judgments suspended publication of opposition newspaper *Soz* in February; and amendments to Kazakhstan's election law passed in April banned political demonstrations between election day and the official announcement of the results.

Opposition leaders, who were regularly harassed, arrested, and beaten, remained determined to contest the election. More than 500 members of the Kazakh opposition met in the southern city of Almaty on March 20 to create the new democratic bloc, which they named "For a Fair Kazakhstan." They selected former Speaker of Parliament Zharmakhan Tuyakbay as the consensus candidate to run in the December presidential election. Tuyakbay took only 6.64 percent of the vote in the December election, which international observers decried as unfair, citing instances of ballot box stuffing and media bias. ■ Juliet Johnson
See also **Asia; Russia: A Special Report.**

Kenya moved closer to international isolation in February 2005 when the United States, the United Kingdom (U.K.), and Germany suspended aid in protest of mounting corruption under President Mwai Kibaki's ruling National Rainbow Coalition (NARC). The suspensions followed the resignation of John Githongo, Kenya's anticorruption chief. Githongo gave no explanation for his resignation, but his exit from Kenya to the U.K. raised speculation that he had been purged by the Kibaki government. According to Western diplomats, more than $1 billion in Kenyan government funds had been lost due to corruption since Kibaki's election to the presidency in 2002. International organizations in 2005 ranked Kenya, East Africa's largest national economy, among the most corrupt countries in the world.

Ethnic clashes claimed the lives of scores of Kenyans in 2005. Many of the incidents involved access or ownership rights to scarce water resources. In January, armed Maasai herders attacked Kikuyu farms in southwestern Kenya and drove at least 1,500 Kikuyu off their land. In July, at the village of Turbi near the Ethiopian border, Borana tribesmen armed with automatic rifles and machetes massacred some 75 Gabra tribespeople, mostly women and children. The attackers' objective, according to news sources, was the capture of Turbi's productive wells.

Constitution rejected. President Kibaki sustained a major political defeat on Nov. 22, 2005, when 58 percent of Kenyan voters rejected a draft constitution endorsed by the president but faulted by critics for not adequately curbing presidential powers. Kibaki fired all his Cabinet members the next day, November 23, and appointed a new Cabinet on December 7. Critics speculated that Kibaki's motive was to dismiss appointees who had opposed the draft constitution.

Judicial controversy. On May 17, Thomas Cholmondeley, descendant and sole heir of the Delamere family, white landowners with huge holdings in Kenya's Rift Valley, was cleared of charges that he shot and killed an armed undercover game warden on April 19. Kenya's attorney general dismissed the charges and ordered an inquest into the death of the warden, an ethnic Maasai. Cholmondeley claimed he had shot the warden, who was investigating allegations of illegal trade in bushmeat, in self-defense. Cholmondeley's release from jail provoked widespread protest in Kenya, and Maasai leaders threatened to invade Delamere properties. According to the Maasai, the Delamere family had confiscated huge tracts of Maasai land when Kenya was a British colony. ■ Simon Baynham

See also **Africa**.

Kiribatia. See Pacific Islands.

Korea, North. Efforts led by the United States to persuade North Korea to dismantle its nuclear weapons program followed a tumultuous path in 2005 without changing a situation laden with hostility and apprehension. During four rounds of talks in 2003 and 2004, China, Japan, Russia, South Korea, and the United States had attempted to convince North Korea's Communist government to give up its weapons program in return for security guarantees and economic aid. However, in August 2004, North Korea announced that it would no longer attend negotiations.

A North Korean official claimed on Feb. 10, 2005, that the country possessed nuclear weapons. A U.S. official revealed on May 15 that "some evidence" suggested North Korea was preparing its first nuclear test explosion. The evidence was later revealed to be fragmentary, and no test occurred.

After secret talks between U.S. and North Korean representatives in New York City on May 13, North Korean leader Kim Jong-Il suggested in June that six-nation talks might resume. Later, North Korea reiterated its desire for normal relations with the United States, replacing the cease-fire that had ended the Korean War (1950-1953) with a peace treaty. A South Korean offer in June 2005 of more food aid and electric power paved the way for talks to resume in China's capital, Beijing, on July 26.

Finally, on September 19, the six nations signed a statement of principles. According to the document, North Korea would give up "all nuclear weapons and existing nuclear programs," and the United States would discuss "at an appropriate time" providing the North with a civilian nuclear power plant. However, within 24 hours of the agreement, North Korean officials announced that they would not dismantle their nuclear program until they were given the reactor, a demand rejected by both the United States and Japan.

Hunger. The United Nations World Food Program (WFP)—which, with other international aid agencies, had provided food to some 6 million of North Korea's poorest residents was told by the government in September that emergency food aid was no longer needed. The North Koreans noted that the WFP should shift its aid to development projects. Other aid groups responded that suspending food aid would lead to increased starvation in a nation where an estimated 7 percent of the population was already starving and 37 percent was chronically malnourished. Despite its differences with the North Korean government, the United States contributed 55,000 tons (50,000 metric tons) of food for the WFP to distribute in North Korea. ■ Henry S. Bradsher

See also **Asia; Korea, South**.

Korea, South. Differences between South Korea and its key ally, the United States, persisted in 2005 over how to negotiate with North Korea regarding its nuclear weapons program. South Korea sought to engage the Communist North in closer relations that might woo it away from hostility. The policy of U.S. President George W. Bush required the North to abandon nuclear ambitions or face international sanctions.

South Korean President Roh Moo-hyun discussed these differences with President Bush in Washington, D.C., on June 10. Afterward, Roh admitted that he and President Bush still disagreed on how to deal with North Korea but seemed confident that a resolution could be reached.

South Korea had tried to use increased trade as a way of winning cooperation with the North. In March, however, the South banned imports of poultry from the North after the North confirmed an outbreak of the deadly avian flu.

Military developments. South Korea and the United States in August held one of South Korea's periodic military exercises to test reactions against a possible North Korean attack. American officials called the computer-simulated drills routine, but the North repeated its usual denunciations of the exercises as preparations for an invasion of the North. Some 32,000 U.S. troops were stationed in South Korea in 2005.

South Korea's 650,000-person armed forces were caught up in controversy in 2005. On June 19, an army conscript guarding the frontier with the North killed eight fellow soldiers in a rampage reportedly triggered by taunts from an officer. The head of a South Korean advocacy group representing parents whose sons died during their military service said that more than 60 conscripts killed themselves every year, in most cases because of savage bullying. The defense ministry admitted that a culture of harassment permeated the military, in which all South Korean men are required to serve for two years. Bullying and abysmal living conditions had long been reported. The government proposed to raise conscripts' pay and improve living quarters. Military experts noted, however, that changing the attitudes that led to abuse of conscripts would prove to be difficult.

Politics. President Roh's Uri political party failed to regain a parliamentary majority when elections were held on April 30. Five of the available six seats were won by the opposition Grand National Party.

Women's rights were expanded when the Supreme Court ruled on July 21 that an ancient rule denying women the same property rights as men was outdated. The court granted a married woman the same rights as an adult male to claim equal shares in property of her father's ancestral line. ■ Henry S. Bradsher

See also **Asia; Biology; Korea, North.**

Kuwait. See **Middle East.**

Kyrgyzstan. Disputed parliamentary elections in Kyrgyzstan led to countrywide demonstrations and the eventual resignation of President Askar Akayev in 2005. Observers dubbed the Kyrgyz events the "Tulip Revolution" after the tulips carried by protesters. The successful protests after tainted elections in Georgia (the "Rose Revolution" of 2002) and Ukraine (the "Orange Revolution" of 2004) inspired the Kyrgyz demonstrators.

The troubled elections took place in two rounds, on February 27 and March 13, 2005. The Organisation for Security and Co-operation in Europe (OSCE) noted significant problems with both rounds of the election. (The OSCE is an international association of more than 50 Eastern and Western countries dedicated to enhancing the security of member nations.) Public demonstrations began soon after the March election in southern Kyrgyzstan. The largest demonstrations occurred in the cities of Osh and Jalal-Abad.

The demonstrations spread to the capital, Bishkek, on March 23, where police broke up a rally and detained journalists, students, and leaders of political organizations. The protests in Bishkek then grew more widespread and violent as demonstrators looted shops and occupied government offices. President Akayev fled to Kazakhstan on March 24 and shortly thereafter to Moscow. He officially resigned on April 4.

Police officers confront protesters in Bishkek, Kyrgyzstan, on March 25, in the wake of tainted parliamentary elections. The uprising, known as the "Tulip Revolution," forced President Askar Akayev to flee the country.

Both the newly elected parliament and the previous parliament initially claimed the right to govern. After negotiations, the old parliament dissolved itself on March 29. The new parliament named Kurmanbek Bakiev, a popular leader from southern Kyrgyzstan, acting president and prime minister. In presidential elections held on July 10, Bakiev won in a landslide with 89 percent of the vote. He selected Felix Kulov, who had been jailed under Akayev, to serve as prime minister.

Further conflict continued to plague Kyrgyzstan throughout 2005. Supporters of several losing parliamentary candidates occupied the Kyrgyz Supreme Court in late April and demanded the resignation of Chairman Kurmanbek Osmonov. The standoff continued until June 1, when armed counter-protesters retook the building.

Three members of parliament were murdered in separate incidents in 2005. One of the men, Tynchbek Akmatbaev, was killed along with two of his assistants during a visit to a prison on October 20. Akmatbaev's brother, Ryspek Akmatbaev, led several days of demonstrations in Bishkek to protest the killing. Ryspek Akmatbaev accused jailed criminal leader Aziz Batukaev of the murder and called for the resignation of Prime Minister Feliks Kulov, alleged to have ties with Batukaev. Kulov denied the charges. ■ Juliet Johnson

See also **Asia; Russia; Russia: A Special Report.**

Labor and employment. In 2005,

employment in the United States continued the expansion that began in 2004. However, monthly job growth varied, increasing by 265,000 in July 2005, for example, but only by 44,000 in October. For the year, employment grew by about 2 million jobs, according to the U.S. Bureau of Labor Statistics (BLS). In January, just over 7.7 million workers were looking for jobs. By November, about 7.6 million were unemployed but actively searching. The unemployment rate declined from 5.2 percent to 5.1 percent.

The BLS released data in November on employment by race and ethnicity, which showed that the seasonally adjusted unemployment rate for white workers was 4.3 percent in late 2005; the rate for African American workers was 10.6 percent; for Hispanic or Latino workers, 6.0 percent; and for Asian workers, 3.6 percent. BLS data on employment by gender and age showed that the jobless rate for men 20 years and over was 4.3 percent, while for women workers in the same age group it was 4.6 percent. Male and female teen-age workers were unemployed at 17.2 percent.

Compensation (wages, salaries, and benefits) of civilian workers in industries other than farming rose 3.1 percent in the 12 months ending in September 2005, according to the BLS Employment Cost Index. Wages and salaries alone rose 2.3 percent; benefits rose 5.1 percent. In current (2005) dollars, workers' average weekly earnings increased 2.3 percent in the year ending in September 2005; in constant (1982) dollars, earnings actually fell by 2.7 percent. Productivity (output per hour) of workers in industries other than farming increased 4.7 percent (annual rate) in the third quarter.

Collective bargaining. Despite the improving economy, bargaining between employees and unions was difficult in 2005. Employers tried hard to reduce employee benefit costs while unions—equally strongly—resisted.

Airline industry. United States airlines have struggled to stay aloft since the terrorist attacks on the United States on Sept. 11, 2001. Airlines already under bankruptcy protection (United Airlines of Chicago and US Airways Group Inc. of Arlington, Virginia), as well as those that entered bankruptcy in 2005 (Northwest Airlines Corp. of Eagan, Minnesota, and Delta Airlines of Atlanta), bargained with their workers for pay and benefit reductions ("give-backs"). The airlines also reduced the number of scheduled flights, canceled new equipment orders, and cut back on passenger amenities.

On January 31, members of the Air Line Pilots Association, International (ALPA) and the Association of Flight Attendants (AFA) ratified separate agreements with United Airlines, reducing wages and making other contractual changes intended to save the bankrupt airline $311 million annually. However, United indicated that it needed $725 million in annual savings to emerge from bankruptcy. At the end of January, members of the Aircraft Mechanics Fraternal Association (AMFA) rejected an agreement with United on give-backs. However, the bankruptcy judge granted the airline permission to cut the mechanics' wages by the amounts called for in the rejected agreement.

Also in January, members of the AFA ratified a contract with US Airways that cut wages by 9 percent (saving an estimated $94 million annually), reduced employees' holidays and vacation days, revised retiree health care benefits, and froze pensions. In July, members of the International Association of Machinists and Aerospace Workers (IAM) approved a contract with US Airways that cut wages and reduced benefits to save the airline $175 million annually.

On September 14, Northwest Airlines filed for bankruptcy. The company blamed its financial situation on escalating fuel costs and its inability to achieve the necessary cost savings from renegotiated labor agreements and other cost reductions. The airline had reached an agreement with its 5,400 pilots on a 15-percent pay cut over 2 years (anticipated annual savings, $265 million). Nevertheless, the airline argued that, in the face of losses of $2.3 billion since 2001, it needed $1.4 billion in annual savings from workers and other sources to avoid bankruptcy. The crisis came to a head on Aug. 20, 2005, when members of the AMFA struck Northwest Airlines. The airline immediately replaced the custodial members of the union with third-party vendors but did not begin hiring replacement mechanics until the strike lasted 25 days. (Other unions at the airline, such as the ALPA and the AFA, did not honor the striking union's picket lines.)

Hotel and restaurant industry. In January, members of UNITE HERE (the Union of Needletrades, Industrial and Textile Employees, and Hotel Employees and Restaurant Employees) approved a contract with the Hotel Association of Washington, D.C., covering 5,000 workers. The contract provided wage increases and pension plan improvements. Employers would continue to pay full health care premiums.

Retail trade. In mid-February, members of the United Food and Commercial Workers International Union (UFCW) ratified a three-year contract with three large supermarket chains in the San Francisco Bay area. The contract, covering 20,000 workers, provided lump-sum payments in 2005 and a 25-cent hourly pay increase in 2006. The employer contribution to the pension fund was increased, but future retiree benefits were to be decreased. Full payment of health care premiums was to continue.

In March 2005, UFCW members ratified a 3-year agreement with St. Paul, Minnesota, area supermarkets covering 5,000 workers. The pact provided wage increases of 2 percent in the second and third year and preserved health care coverage. In Colorado and Wyoming, UFCW members ratified a 4-year contract covering 7,000 workers with Safeway Inc. of Pleasanton, California. The agreement provided a lump-sum payment in lieu of pay increases in the first year. Workers would pay a portion of health care premiums.

In October, UFCW members approved a 3-year contract with Kroger Co. of Cincinnati, Ohio, covering 3,500 workers in 45 stores in Tennessee, Virginia, and West Virginia. The agreement included general wage increases, lump-sum payments, and employee contributions to health care premiums. In November, members approved a 3-year agreement

A member of the aircraft mechanics union mans a picket line outside a Northwest Airlines hangar at the Minneapolis-St. Paul International Airport in August, protesting proposed wage cuts. Northwest declared bankruptcy in September, citing escalating fuel costs and failure to achieve sufficient cost-saving measures.

with Kroger covering 10,000 workers in 82 stores in central Ohio and a 52-month agreement for 16,000 workers in 175 stores in Georgia.

Communications industry. In March, members of the Communication Workers of America (CWA) verified a contract with Verizon North Inc. of Marion, Ohio, covering 2,000 workers in the Midwest. The contract provided a lump-sum bonus upon ratification and general wage increases totaling 10.5 percent over the 5-year term. In October, members of the CWA ratified a 3-year agreement with Qwest Communications of Denver covering 25,000 workers in 13 states. Wages were to increase 7.5 percent over the life of the contract.

Entertainment and sports. In early March, members of the Screen Actors Guild and the American Federation of Television and Radio Artists approved a pact with the Alliance of Motion Picture and Television Producers. Under the agreement, which covered 119,000 union members, wages would increase 9 percent over the 3-year term. The producers also agreed to provide $200 million in wage and benefit improvements and new jobs.

On July 22, the National Hockey League's Board of Governors ratified the terms of a collective bargaining agreement with the NHL Players' Association. The agreement ended a 310-day work stop-page that had cost the league the 2004-2005 season. In the 2005-2006 season, no club payroll could exceed $39 million. Under the agreement, each individual player's contract was to include a 24-percent reduction of salary for every year of the contract's term. No individual player's salary can exceed 20 percent of the club's limit on payroll.

On July 30, 2005, the National Basketball Association and the National Basketball Players' Association ratified a new 6-year agreement. The salary "cap"—the maximum amount that any team can pay all its players in a year—was set at $49.5 million for the 2005-2006 season. The maximum length of individual players' contracts was reduced from 7 to 6 years. The minimum age for players being drafted into the league was increased from 18 to 19 years, and U.S. players were required to have been out of high school for at least one year.

Automobile industry. In June 2005, the United Automobile Workers (UAW) union agreed to the transfer of 17,400 workers represented by the union from the financially troubled Visteon Corporation of Van Buren Township, Michigan, to management by Ford Motor Company of Dearborn, Michigan. (Ford had spun off Visteon as a separate parts supplier in 2000.) Later in the year, Ford announced losses of $1.2 billion in the third quarter in its North American division and stated that it would have to cut jobs and close plants. In December, UAW members agreed to health care concessions designed to save Ford about $650 million annually.

Although the contract between General Motors (GM) Corporation of Detroit and the UAW was not to expire until 2007, the company and union began collective bargaining talks in 2005 because of mounting financial losses in the company's key North American division ($3.81 billion in 2005). The parties agreed in November to changes in the contract intended to save the company $1 billion a year. The changes included retirees making co-payments on health services and active workers foregoing a scheduled pay increase in 2006 and deferring quarterly cost-of-living adjustments.

Aerospace industry. In September 2005, IAM members ended a four-week strike against Chicago-based Boeing Company, ratifying a three-year contract covering 18,000 workers. Employees would receive cash payouts totaling $11,000 over three years and pension increases of about 17 percent, with no changes in health care coverage.

Unions. The proportion of U.S. workers in labor unions continued to decline in 2004 (most recent data available), falling to 12.5 percent from 12.9 percent in 2003. Membership averaged just under 13 million members, a decline of almost 168,000.

During 2005, four unions—the Service Employees International Union, the International Brotherhood of Teamsters, UNITE HERE, and the United

CHANGES IN THE UNITED STATES LABOR FORCE

	2004	2005*
Civilian labor force	147,368,000	148,976,000
Total employment	139,248,000	141,339,000
Unemployment	8,143,000	7,636,000
Unemployment rate	5.5%	5.1%
Change in weekly earnings of production and nonsupervisory workers (nonfarm business sector)		
Current dollars	2.9%	2.3%
Constant (1982) dollars	-0.5%	-2.7%
Change in output per employee hour (nonfarm business sector)	3.4%	4.1%

*All 2005 data are through the third quarter of 2005 (preliminary data).
Source: *World Book* estimates based on data from the U.S. Bureau of Labor Statistics.

Food and Commercial Workers Union—disaffiliated from the American Federation of Labor-Congress of Industrial Workers (AFL-CIO). The unions represented about one-third of the AFL-CIO membership. The breakaway unions wanted to see greater emphasis on organizing workers, rather than on political action, which they believed the AFL-CIO leadership favored. The unions began to disaffiliate just before the July AFL-CIO convention. Nonetheless, convention delegates reelected the current federation officers led by President John Sweeney.

Federal government. At the beginning of 2005, President George W. Bush reintroduced his 2004 legislative proposal to create a temporary worker program for foreign nationals in the United States. Once again, Congress did not enact the program. On Aug. 2, 2005, President Bush signed into law the Central American-Dominican Republic Free Trade Agreement (CAFTA-DR). The act provided for lower trade barriers between Costa Rica, the Dominican Republic, El Salvador, Guatemala, Honduras, Nicaragua, and the United States. Union leaders and several members of Congress opposed CAFTA-DR and the "guest worker" program, claiming that both would negatively impact U.S. workers.

International unemployment stood at 6.5 percent in September, compared with 6.8 percent in 2004, in the 27 reporting nations of the Organization for Economic Cooperation and Development (OECD). Among the major OECD nations, rates were lowest in Japan (4.2 percent) and the United States (5.1 percent) and highest in France (9.4 percent) and Germany (8.7 percent).

■ Robert W. Fisher

See also **Automobile; Aviation; Basketball; Economics; Hockey; Telecommunications; Transportation.**

Labrador. See Canadian provinces.

Laos. See Asia.

LATIN AMERICA

The people of South America's Andean nations demonstrated forcibly in 2005 that they were no longer content to be mere bystanders as foreign and domestic companies, per their claims, exploited their region's extensive energy and mineral resources. Residents of these Andean regions claimed that they bore many ill effects of environmental pollution associated with energy and mining companies' activities while receiving few benefits. Long-smoldering discontent over this issue led to the toppling of the governments of Bolivia and Ecuador in 2005 and violent protests in Colombia and Peru. Protesters throughout the region demanded a larger share of profits from local mines and oil fields in a year when global prices for energy products were at or near record highs.

Related to the rising flow of wealth in the trading of energy and other commodities, people in one Latin American nation after another demanded in 2005 a calling to account of corrupt politicians, and indictments of high-ranking officials multiplied. Ironically, some of the accused politicians had themselves come to power on promises to end corruption.

In Venezuela and other countries with left-of-center governments, leaders launched programs to wrest control of energy resources from international corporations or to force them to pay higher shares of their profits in taxes. Whether these moves would succeed—and whether they would substantially raise standards of living among Latin America's poor—were questions that remained unanswered in 2005.

Energy initiatives. In May, cabinet-level ministers of Argentina, Brazil, and Venezuela inaugurated Petrosur, a cartel-like association to coordinate their nations' petroleum policies. (A *cartel* is an association designed to control production and prices.) The Petrosur initiative, the brainchild of Venezuelan President Hugo Chavez Frias, linked Venezuela, Latin America's largest oil producer, with South America's two biggest economies, Argentina and Brazil.

On June 30, President Chavez launched another energy initiative, PetroCaribe, in which Venezuela offered to supply 190,000 barrels of oil per day in 2005 to 13 energy-poor Caribbean nations at heavily discounted prices. According to terms of the PetroCaribe program, participating nations were to export food commodities to Venezuela in partial repayment for the energy subsidy and to finance the balance over 25 years at 1 percent annual interest rate.

Building on the popularity of these energy initiatives, Venezuela's Chavez in mid-2005 proposed the formation of *Gas del Sur* (Gas of the South), a consultative body that would coordinate trade in natural gas among South American nations. Under this initiative, the region's major gas producers—including first-ranked Venezuela and second-ranked Bolivia—would coordinate development and construction of a continent-wide gas pipeline network. Chavez and other regional leaders embraced Gas del Sur as an alternative to the existing globalized arrangement of natural gas production and export, which according to polls, many Latin Americans viewed as exploitative.

Arab-South American summit. In May, 12 South American leaders met with the heads of 7 Middle East governments in Brasilia for the first Arab-South American summit, hosted by Brazilian President Luiz Inacio Lula da Silva. The participants included Jalal Talabani, the newly elected president of Iraq, and Mahmoud Abbas, president of the Palestinian Authority. The presence of these two leaders, from highly volatile areas of the Middle East, prompted extraordinary security at the two-day meeting. More than 1,000 business leaders representing the two world regions also attended the meeting. The leaders agreed to establish new airline routes linking South American and Middle Eastern countries and to create a joint committee to study proposals for a new Arab-South American bank.

Latin American television. In 2005, several Latin American nations jointly launched a new television network, *Nueva Television del Sur* (New Television of the South), or Telesur, which began broadcasting from Caracas, Venezuela, in July. The Venezuelan government defrayed 70 percent of the network's $2.5-million startup costs, with Argentina, Brazil, and Uruguay contributing the balance and cash-strapped Cuba providing technical support. Advertising was projected to finance ongoing operations through the rest of 2005.

In its first months of operation, Telesur's programming included coverage of *indigenous* (native Indian) movements and documentaries presenting grievances of landless peasants and detailing conditions of poverty in urban slums. Critics, especially in the United States, complained that the network coverage reflected the left-leaning political bias of Venezuela's current government and the governments of the other sponsoring nations.

A protester, surrounded by riot police officers, shouts slogans in the streets of La Paz, the Bolivian capital, in May 2005. Thousands of indigenous Bolivians, people of native Indian descent, massed in the streets in mid-2005 to demand equitable distribution of Bolivia's energy wealth and fair representation in government. The protests prompted Bolivian President Carlos Mesa Gisbert to resign in June.

The government of Brazil started a new network, TV Brazil, which began broadcasting in late 2005. Like Telesur, TV Brazil offered coverage of regional topics, which many Brazilians and other Latin Americans alleged were neglected by the existing international media.

Popular uprisings. During 2005, public protests toppled unpopular governments in two Andean countries. In Ecuador, protests against alleged government corruption led to the overthrow of President Lucio Edwin Gutierrez in April, marking the third time since 1997 that an elected Ecuadorean government had been removed by popular protests. Vice President Alfredo Palacio assumed Ecuador's presidency.

In Bolivia, protesters demanding equitable management of Bolivia's energy resources and political empowerment of the indigenous population pressured President Carlos Mesa Gisbert to resign in June 2005. Mesa had succeeded Gonzalo Sanchez de Lozada, who was similarly forced out of office by political protests in 2003.

The Bolivian Congress on June 9, 2005, named Supreme Court Chief Judge Eduardo Rodríguez Veltzé as the interim president. In December elections, Bolivians elected Evo Morales, an Aymara Indian, to the presidency. Upon taking office in January 2006, Morales became the country's first indigenous president.

In neighboring Paraguay, hundreds of residents of Puerto Casado, a town in the semiarid Chaco region, marched on Asuncion, the capital, in July 2005 to demand that the Paraguayan government seize 128,500 acres (52,000 hectares) of local land held by South Korea-based Reverend Sun Myung Moon's Unification Church. In recent years, the church had bought 1.48 million acres (600,000 hectares) of land in Paraguay. Despite promises by Moon's agents, little was done to develop the land and provide jobs to local people.

FACTS IN BRIEF ON LATIN AMERICA

Country	Population	Government	Monetary unit*	Foreign trade (million U.S.$) Exports†	Imports†
Antigua and Barbuda	79,000	Governor General James B. Carlisle; Prime Minister Baldwin Spencer	dollar (2.67 = $1)	689	692
Argentina	38,223,000	President Nestor Kirchner	peso (2.91 = $1)	33,780	22,060
Bahamas	325,000	Governor General Dame Ivy Dumont; Prime Minister Perry Christie	dollar (1.00 = $1)	636	1,630
Barbados	273,000	Governor General Sir Clifford Husbands; Prime Minister Owen Arthur	dollar (1.99 = $1)	206	1,039
Belize	267,000	Governor General Sir Colville Young; Prime Minister Said Wilbert Musa	dollar (1.97 = $1)	401	580
Bolivia	9,301,000	President Evo Morales	boliviano (8.04 = $1)	1,986	1,595
Brazil	180,996,000	President Luiz Inacio Lula da Silva	real (2.31 = $1)	95,000	61,000
Chile	16,366,000	President Ricardo Lagos Escobar	peso (534.19= $1)	29,200	22,530
Colombia	46,248,000	President Alvaro Uribe Vélez	peso (2,304.7 = $1)	15,500	15,340
Costa Rica	4,399,000	President Abel Pacheco de la Espriella	colon (485.35 = $1)	6,184	7,842
Cuba	11,373,000	President Fidel Castro	peso (1.00 = $1)	2,104	5,296
Dominica	79,000	President Nicholas J. O. Liverpool; Prime Minister Roosevelt Skerrit	dollar (2.67 = $1)	39	98
Dominican Republic	8,660,000	President Leonel Fernandez Reyna	peso (31.10 = $1)	5,446	8,093
Ecuador	13,553,000	President Alfredo Palacio	U.S. dollar	7,560	7,650
El Salvador	6,795,000	President Elias Antonio Saca	colon (8.75 = $1)	3,249	5,968
Grenada	102,000	Governor General Daniel Williams; Prime Minister Keith Mitchell	dollar (2.67 = $1)	46	208
Guatemala	13,280,000	President Oscar Berger	quetzal (7.61 = $1)	2,911	7,770
Guyana	768,000	President Bharrat Jagdeo	dollar (190.00 = $1)	570	650
Haiti	8,662,000	Interim President Boniface Alexandre; Interim Prime Minister Gerard Latortue	gourde (41.40 = $1)	338	1,085
Honduras	6,970,000	President Ricardo Maduro	lempira (18.86 = $1)	1,457	3,332
Jamaica	2,725,000	Governor General Sir Howard Cooke; Prime Minister P. J. Patterson	dollar (62.53= $1)	1,679	3,624
Mexico	107,725,000	President Vicente Fox Quesada	new peso (10.69 = $1)	182,400	190,800
Nicaragua	5,850,000	President Enrique Bolaños Geyer	gold cordoba (16.37 = $1)	750	2,020
Panama	3,140,000	President Martin Torrijos Espino	balboa (1.00 = $1)	5,699	7,164
Paraguay	5,747,000	President Nicanor Duarte Frutos	guarani (6,130.00 = $1)	2,936	3,330
Peru	28,360,000	President Alejandro Toledo; Prime Minister Pedro Pablo Kuczynski Godard	new sol (3.29 = $1)	12,300	9,600
Puerto Rico	3,930,000	Governor Anibal Acevedo Vila	U.S. dollar	46,900	29,100
St. Kitts and Nevis	45,000	Governor General Cuthbert Montraville Sebastian; Prime Minister Denzil Douglas	dollar (2.67 = $1)	70	195
St. Lucia	168,000	Governor General Pearlette Louisy; Prime Minister Kenny Anthony	dollar (2.67 = $1)	66	267
St. Vincent and the Grenadines	122,000	Governor General Sir Frederick Nathaniel Ballantyne; Prime Minister Ralph Gonsalves	dollar (2.67 = $1)	38	174
Suriname	445,000	President Runaldo Ronald Venetiaan	guilder (2,515.00 = $1)	495	604
Trinidad and Tobago	1,315,000	President George Maxwell Richards; Prime Minister Patrick Manning	dollar (6.27 = $1)	6,671	4,650
Uruguay	3,486,000	President Tabaré Vázquez	peso (24.15 = $1)	2,200	2,071
Venezuela	25,045,000	President Hugo Chavez Frias	bolivar (2,145.90 = $1)	35,840	14,980

*Exchange rates as of Sept. 9, 2005, or latest available data.   †Latest available data.

In August, the Paraguayan Congress approved legislation to seize about one-tenth of Moon's holdings in Paraguay. Although the bill advocated compensation for the Unification Church, no specific appropriations were included. South Korean diplomats responded to the confiscation by warning Paraguay's government that the land seizure would discourage future foreign investment in Paraguay.

Corruption. Courts in a number of Latin American countries indicted high-ranking officials for corruption in 2005. In Brazil, South America's most populous nation, the unraveling of a massive scandal threatened to engulf the leftist government of President da Silva. Similarly, the centrist government of Peru's president, Alejandro Toledo, was under pressure from critics throughout the year due to allegations of corruption touching Toledo family members and close associates.

In Nicaragua, public protests prompted the Congress to start impeachment proceedings against incumbent President Enrique Bolaños Geyer in July for corruption in office. Bolaños decried the move as political revenge for his own role in obtaining a 2003 conviction on corruption charges against his predecessor, former president Arnoldo Aleman Lacayo. In October 2005, U.S. Deputy Secretary of State Robert Zoellick asserted that the United States would withhold $175 million in promised aid if Bolaños were impeached. Bolaños and his chief congressional opponent, former president Daniel Ortega, subsequently struck a political deal that suspended the impeachment proceedings.

Bolivian prosecutors in February charged former President Gonzalo Sanchez de Lozada with genocide in connection with a 2003 police crackdown on protesters, who ultimately succeeded in driving him from office. In June 2005, the prosecutors added corruption charges to the indictment. In Guatemala, a judge issued an arrest warrant in July for former president Alfonso Portillo Cabrera, then living in exile in Mexico, to be tried on charges of corruption.

Political shift in Uruguay. On March 1, Tabaré Vázquez was sworn in as the first Socialist president in Uruguay's history. Vázquez had won election as the head of a leftist coalition in an October 2004 presidential election. Vázquez's new government launched a $100-million initiative to provide health care, housing, and jobs for hundreds of thousands of poor Uruguayans. He also resumed diplomatic relations with Cuba, which had been suspended by previous rightist governments. Analysts noted that Vázquez was aligning his country politically with Argentina, Brazil, and Venezuela, all nations led by politicians of South America's resurgent political left.

International Criminal Court. The administration of U.S. President George W. Bush continued in 2005 a policy of suspending military aid to Latin American nations that refused to sign a treaty exempting U.S. policymakers and armed service members from future prosecution at the International Criminal Court in The Hague, Netherlands. In June, the new Ecuadorian president, Alfredo Palacio, refused to sign the immunity treaty, declaring, "absolutely no one is going to make me cower." As a result, Ecuador, which had already forfeited $15 million in U.S. aid over this matter, lost another $7 million in 2005.

Organization of American States member nations elected Jose Miguel Insulza, a Chilean Socialist, as secretary general of the association of 35 American nations in May 2005, after rejecting the candidate supported by the Bush administration. The election was the first in the organization's nearly 60-year history in which the U.S.-backed candidate had failed to win the post.

Trade agreements. By a narrow margin of only two votes, the U.S. House of Representatives in July ratified the Central American-Dominican Republic Free Trade Agreement (CAFTA-DR). The agreement was designed to ease restrictions on annual trade amounting to $32 billion between the United States and six small Latin American nations: Costa Rica, the Dominican Republic, El Salvador, Guatemala, Honduras, and Nicaragua.

Protesters had mounted demonstrations against the pact in several Central American cities in late 2004 and early 2005. Opponents of CAFTA-DR predicted that the trade deal would flood their markets with cheap goods and heavily subsidized U.S. agricultural commodities.

In November, President Bush attended a two-day summit of leaders of 34 Western Hemisphere nations at Mar del Plata, Argentina. Foremost among the president's priorities was promotion of the Free Trade Agreement of the Americas (FTAA), a proposal for a hemisphere-wide free trading zone. Many of the leaders expressed reservations about FTAA, and some were openly hostile to the project. The summit ended without progress on FTAA as tens of thousands of demonstrators staged anti-Bush protests in the streets of Mar del Plata.

On December 9, Venezuela officially became a member of the South American Common Market, or Mercosur, which included Argentina, Brazil, Paraguay, and Uruguay. The expansion was the first in the trading bloc since its founding in 1991.
■ Nathan A. Haverstock

See also the various Latin American countries; **International trade.**

Latvia. See **Europe.**

Law. See **Courts; Supreme Court of the United States: United States, Government of the.**

Massive anti-Syria demonstrations are staged in Beirut, the Lebanese capital, in the wake of the February 14 assassination of former Lebanese Prime Minister Rafik Hariri. The protests culminated in the withdrawal on April 26 of all Syrian troops after 29 years of occupation.

Lebanon, in a series of historic events, liberated itself from Syrian occupation in 2005 and began the gradual transformation into a free and democratic nation. The dramatic changes grew out of the passage of United Nations (UN) Security Council Resolution 1559 in September 2004. The resolution, which called for free elections, the withdrawal of all foreign troops, and the disarming of militias in Lebanon, was a strong indication that the Lebanese opposition had the support of the West, particularly the United States. The emboldened opposition then increased its efforts to force the withdrawal of the Syrian army of occupation. (Syrian forces first entered Lebanon in 1976 in an effort to restore order during the Lebanese Civil War.)

On Feb. 14, 2005, former Lebanese Prime Minister Rafik Hariri, a major figure in the opposition movement, was assassinated in a car bombing, which UN investigators later tied to Syrian government officials. The assassination led to peaceful demonstrations by the opposition. The demonstrations culminated in a March 14 rally in Beirut, Lebanon's capital, in which 1.5 million people—almost 40 percent of the entire Lebanese population—participated. The demonstrators carried placards calling for the immediate withdrawal of Syrian troops and the Syrian intelligence services. The demonstrators also demanded to know the truth about Hariri's assas-

sination and the assassinations of other political and religious leaders allegedly ordered by Syrian officials.

The demonstrators achieved their goal on April 26, when Syria withdrew its troops and intelligence services. Political commentators dubbed the popular movement that forced the withdrawal "the Cedar Revolution," in reference to Lebanon's national symbol, the cedar of Lebanon referred to in the Bible.

Parliamentary elections. Despite the withdrawal of Syrian troops, parliamentary elections in May and June were conducted under a law devised by Syria. The law favored Lebanese allies of Syria, such as Speaker of the House Nabih Birri, who blocked the convening of a parliamentary session for changing the electoral law.

Although Speaker Birri's pro-Syria Amal and Hezbollah parties gained a significant number of seats in the new parliament, parties associated with the Lebanese opposition won a majority. In the new Cabinet, formed in July and headed by Prime Minister Fouad Siniora, anti-Syria members had control of 15 of the 24 positions. Despite their pro-Syria stand, Amal and Hezbollah were represented in Prime Minister Siniora's Cabinet.

Political analysts noted that having Cabinet members representing Hezbollah, which has both a political and military wing, might not bode well for the full implementation of UN Security Council Resolution 1559, particularly the call for disarming militias that had been drafted specifically to disarm Hezbollah.

UN investigation. After interrogating a large number of suspects and witnesses, the UN commission in charge of investigating the assassination of former Prime Minister Hariri called for the arrests of four Lebanese security chiefs who worked closely with the Syrian Intelligence Services. The Lebanese public prosecutor carried out the arrests in September 2005.

In October, the commission's preliminary report, issued by Chief Investigator Detlev Mehlis, documented Syrian threats against Hariri going back to Hariri's meeting with Syrian President Bashar al-Assad in August 2004. The Mehlis Report also described a meeting that was convened in Damascus, the Syrian capital, by Syrian security officials in which the plot for Hariri's assassination was hatched.

Journalist killed. On Dec. 12, 2005, a car bomb detonated by remote control killed Jubran Tueni and three other people in Beirut. Tueni was a member of the parliament, the publisher of Lebanon's most prestigious newspaper, and a leader of the Cedar Revolution. Syrian authorities revealed that evidence suggested that Syrian officials may have been responsible for the assassination.   ■ Marius Deeb

See also **Israel**; **Middle East**; **Syria**.

Lesotho. See Africa.
Liberia. See Africa.

Library. Natural disasters in late 2004 and 2005 caused catastrophic damage to libraries worldwide. Indonesian officials announced in early 2005 that the library system of the province of Aceh, which had been inundated by the tsunami that followed a magnitude 9.0 earthquake off the island of Sumatra on Dec. 26, 2004, was a total loss. Officials in Bangladesh, Sri Lanka, and Thailand also reported that the tsunami had left libraries heavily damaged.

In the United States, Hurricane Katrina caused massive destruction to libraries when the storm hit the Gulf Coast on Aug. 29, 2005. In New Orleans, 8 of the city's 12 branch libraries were flooded when parts of the levee system broke, leaving areas of the city under as much as 20 feet (6 meters) of water. The main library, which held most of the city archives, was spared major damage. However, New Orleans Mayor Ray Nagin, faced with disaster-related budget constraints, laid off 3,000 city workers in October, including 197 staff members of the public library system. The layoffs effectively shut down most library services. Hurricane Katrina left at least six libraries in the Louisiana parishes of Jefferson, Plaquemines, and St. Bernard totally destroyed.

Financial problems continued to plague U.S. city library systems in 2005. Threats made by city officials in Salinas, California, and Buffalo, New York, to close entire library systems prompted the American Library Association (ALA) to issue a closure alert. In December 2004, the ALA estimated that libraries across the country had lost $82 million in funding and 2,100 jobs in the previous 18 months. The closing of the Salinas libraries in late 2004 prompted public protests, and all three reopened on March 1, 2005, but on a reduced schedule. A plan to close Buffalo's entire system by September was scaled back to keeping the central library open and closing only 16 of the 52 branches.

USA Patriot Act. The ALA continued in 2005 to spar with the Department of Justice over the use of the USA Patriot Act to gain access to library records. Section 215 of the act allows government agents to inspect library patron records and bars librarians from revealing such inspections to the public. In late 2004, then Attorney General John Ashcroft denied that Section 215 had ever been employed. However, in January 2005, he admitted that Justice Department officials had used Internet records at an undisclosed New York City library to track the activities of a suspected terrorist. The ALA continued through 2005 to call for the elimination of Section 215. On December 22, Congress temporarily renewed the provision for five weeks. In August, an unnamed Connecticut library organization filed a lawsuit challenging the constitutionality of a gag order it had received following a probe of its records by the Federal Bureau of Investigation.

Google. In 2005, various organizations tried to stop Google, Inc., an Internet search service in Mountain View, California, from digitizing 15 million books from the University of Michigan in Ann Arbor; New York Public Library; Stanford University in Stanford, California; Harvard University in Cambridge, Massachusetts; and the University of Oxford in the United Kingdom. Librarians decried the effect of such huge electronic collections on the future of libraries, and publishers and writers called for the end of the project until questions of copyright could be answered. In response, Google temporarily halted the project in August until a system could be developed to allow publishers to designate which titles they did not want digitized. Those talks broke down, however, and the Association of American Publishers based in New York City and Washington, D.C., filed suit on October 19 to stop Google's project .

Map thievery. The arrest of map collector and dealer E. Forbes Smiley III at Yale University in New Haven, Connecticut, prompted U.S. libraries with significant map collections to launch searches through their collections. Smiley was arrested as he exited a Yale library, allegedly with maps excised from the library's collections in his possession.   ■ Rob Carlson

Libya. Major improvements in relations between Libya and the United States were reported in March 2005 by U.S. Assistant Secretary of State William J. Burns before the U.S. House of Representatives Committee on International Relations. Burns noted that in response to actions taken by Libyan authorities to dismantle Libya's weapons of mass destruction programs, the administration of U.S. President George W. Bush had lifted the travel ban and trade and investment sanctions against Libya; unblocked Libya's frozen assets; and reestablished direct diplomatic relations. Burns stated that the Bush administration also encouraged people-to-people exchanges in education and health between the United States and Libya and welcomed Libya's application for membership in the World Trade Organization, which oversees global trade agreements.

Following Burns's testimony, Representative Tom Lantos (D., California) introduced in Congress the United States-Libya Relations Act to "reinforce U.S. and Libyan commitments to one another, strengthen bilateral relations, facilitate the integration of Libya into the international community, and encourage positive change in Libyan society."

Oil and gas. Royal Dutch/Shell Group, the Anglo-Dutch energy giant, announced in May 2005 that the corporation had reached an agreement with the National Oil Corporation of Libya to rejuvenate and upgrade the Liquefied Natural Gas Plant at Marsa Brega, on the Libyan coast, as well as to explore for natural gas in Libya's Sirte Basin region. Royal Dutch/Shell Group planned to invest $637 million in these projects.

In July, Occidental Petroleum Corporation of Los Angeles became the first U.S. oil company to announce that it was going to resume operations in Libya after a 20-year break. Libya's licensing administration awarded Occidental 9 of 15 exploration blocks.

Illegal immigration. In April, a report by a European Union (EU) commission revealed that between 750,000 and 1.2 million illegal immigrants resided in Libya in 2005. Many of these immigrants used Libya as a transit country to reach Europe with falsified documents, according to the report.

In June, EU Justice and Home Affairs Commissioner Franco Frattini announced that he had received a formal commitment from Libyan authorities to stem the flow of migrants to Europe. Frattini said that an initial 2 million euros would be set aside to support EU-Libyan joint patrols aimed at helping Libya police its borders and coastline. ■ Mary-Jane Deeb

See also **Middle East.**

Liechtenstein. See Europe.

Literature. The year 2005 might be considered the year of the Nobel laureate. Several major Nobel laureates published well-received novels in 2005. Saul Bellow, who won the Nobel Prize in literature in 1976, died on April 5, 2005. In addition, internationally renowned playwright and poet Harold Pinter was awarded the Nobel Prize in literature in October.

Nobel laureates. If, as Bellow once wrote, "novelists who take the bitterest view of our modern condition make the most of the art of the novel," then *Slow Man* by South African novelist J. M. Coetzee, who won the Nobel Prize in literature in 2003, qualifies as an artistic achievement. The novel tells the story of a photographer both physically and psychologically incapacitated after a bicycle accident and the subsequent partial amputation of his leg. John Lanchester of *The New York Review of Books* commented that Coetzee's recent novels, *Disgrace* and *Elizabeth Costello,* as well as *Slow Man,* "are about the primacy, the all-consuming importance of suffering, and what we should learn from it."

Nadine Gordimer, who won the Nobel Prize in literature in 1991, explores similar themes in *Get a Life,* the South African writer's 14th novel. The protagonist, 35-year-old ecologist Paul Bannerman, attempts to recover from a serious battle with thyroid cancer by retiring to his parents' house and returning to a somewhat quieter life of the mind. The novel is a comment on conservation itself as radiation treatments for the cancer turn the ecologist into a radioactive threat to his own family, and he begins to reflect on questions of global importance.

Colombian writer Gabriel García Márquez, who won the Nobel Prize in literature in 1982, is concerned with the idea of love as suffering transcended in *Memories of My Melancholy Whores.* This novella, his first piece of fiction to be published in 10 years, chronicles the imagined, and chaste, love relationship between a 90-year-old professor and a 14-year-old girl. The story suggests that while love cannot save the individual from the inevitable arrival of death, it certainly serves as the most effective distraction.

Several former Man Booker Prize winners published novels in 2005. Indian-born writer Salman Rushdie, whose novel *Midnight's Children* won the "Booker of Bookers" in 1993—as the best novel to be awarded the Man Booker Prize in the prize's first 25 years—used his new novel, *Shalimar the Clown,* to critique religious fanaticism and extreme nationalism. Rushdie is no stranger to the intrusion of zealotry into everyday life. The Ayatollah Ruhullah Khomeini of Iran issued a *fatwa* (religious edict, in this case a death sentence) against Rushdie after he published *The Satanic Verses* in 1988. Rushdie's new novel is set in the Kashmir region of the Himalaya. Kashmir is claimed by both predominantly Muslim Pakistan and predominantly Hindu India. The novel examines the relationships between a Jewish American diplomat, his Hindu mistress, and her jilted Muslim husband.

Japanese-born British novelist Kazuo Ishiguro, who won the Man Booker Prize in 1989 for *The Remains of the Day*, produced *Never Let Me Go* in 2005. The novel, which *Publishers Weekly* described as an "epic ethical horror story," is set at an isolated English school and orphanage that is the home to a group of children who are sheltered from the fact that they are clones bred to provide healthy organs for the purpose of eradicating disease. *Never Let Me Go* was praised for its depiction of people who focus on miniscule details without being able to comprehend the larger picture around them.

Ian McEwan, who won the Man Booker Prize in 1998 for his novel *Amsterdam*, published in 2005 *Saturday*, which, like James Joyce's groundbreaking *Ulysses*, is a novel that takes place in the course of a single day. McEwan depicts the reactions of the individual when confronted by a world beyond his or her own sphere of control and comfort. McEwan's protagonist, neurosurgeon Henry Perowne, experiences many simple pleasures through the course of a Saturday off from work. He plays squash, visits his mother, prepares dinner—and yet the reader is constantly being reminded of the disarray and the danger of the world around Perowne. When he awakens before dawn and looks out the window, he sees a plane on fire. Later on, when he is driving in his Mercedes, he is detoured by an antiwar demonstration and gets into a traffic accident. The confrontation that arises will not be forgotten, and in the end, even Perowne and his family, despite many layers of insulation, are not spared from a violent encounter. As McEwan makes clear, and as Zoe Heller wrote in *The New York Times*, "Perowne's right to forget is constantly being assailed by the prompting of his own ethical imagination.... He cannot help seeing things from the viewpoints of others."

Other notable novels. In Zadie Smith's *On Beauty*, the author updates E. M. Forster's classic *Howards End*, which was published in 1910. According to Michiko Kakutani of *The New York Times*, Smith uses Forster "as a launching pad for a thoroughly original tale about families and generational change, about race and multiculturalism in millennial America, about love and identity and the ways they are affected by the passage of time."

Bret Easton Ellis, author of such controversial and violent novels as *American Psycho* and

Glamorama, continued to perplex readers in 2005 with *Lunar Park*. The novel seamlessly blends fact and fiction as it depicts a writer named Bret Easton Ellis who struggles under the weight of his own fame and notoriety as he is haunted by the ghost of his father.

Cormac McCarthy's *No Country for Old Men* divided readers and critics, much as his earlier novels had done. The novel follows Llewellyn Moss, a Vietnam veteran who finds a briefcase full of cash among the remains of a drug deal gone wrong. He takes the briefcase, realizing that he will be hunted down, but believing that he can outwit the drug cartel that chases him. Jeffrey Lent, in *The Washington Post*, noted that though McCarthy's dialogue and wordplay are consistent with his earlier work, *No Country for Old Men* is a minor addition to McCarthy's catalogue. Kakutani, in *The New York Times*, commented that although the novel is a "riveting ... hard-boiled Western," the passages of monologue from the small-town sheriff investigating the drug-related massacre "gradually weigh down the quicksilver suspense of the larger story."

Pulitzer Prizes. Marilynne Robinson won the Pulitzer Prize for fiction for *Gilead*, her novel of a preacher whose letter to his 7-year-old son becomes a meditation on the relationship between parents and children.

Steve Coll's *Ghost Wars: The Secret History of the CIA, Afghanistan, and Bin Laden, from the Soviet Invasion to September 10, 2001*, was awarded the Pulitzer Prize for nonfiction. Using formerly classified material, Coll traces the involvement of the United States Central Intelligence Agency (CIA) in the development of Afghanistan's militant Islamic Taliban political group as well as the al-Qa`ida terrorist organization.

Man Booker Prizes. The Man Booker Prize, sponsored until 2007 by the Man Group, a British securities fund, is the United Kingdom's most prestigious literary award. The prize competition is restricted to books published by writers from member nations of the Commonwealth of Nations and from the Republic of Ireland. (The Commonwealth of Nations is an association of about 50 independent countries and other political units that have lived under British law and government.) Irish novelist John Banville was awarded the 2005 Man Booker Prize in October 2005 for *The Sea*. The novel follows Max Morden, an Irish art historian who, after the death of his wife, returns to the place where he vacationed as a child. As he remembers both his childhood and his wife and reevaluates his life, he finds that "the past beats inside me like a second heart." *Publishers Weekly* applauded the novel for depicting "the unpredictability of life and the incomprehensibility of death."

Saul Bellow
The Impossible Idealist

Saul Bellow, praised by critics as one of the great novelists of the latter half of the 20th century, died on April 5, 2005, at the age of 89. Bellow wrote intensely personal tales of urban Americans in pursuit of professional as well as personal fulfillment. His stories, which ranged from the *Great Depression* (the worldwide economic slump of the 1930's) through the last year of the century, captured the feelings of a generation that came of age in economic depression and war.

Solomon Bellow was born on July 10, 1915, in Lachine, Canada, near Montreal, to Russian Jewish immigrant parents. When Bellow was 9 years old, his family moved to Chicago, a city that became an important element of his fictional world. As a young man, Bellow educated himself in the traditions of Western, Russian, and Jewish literature. From these influences, Bellow created a unique literary voice that blended elements of high culture, street slang, and the Yiddish spoken by his parents.

The *protagonists* (main characters) of Bellow's novels, much like their creator, grow up in the poor immigrant neighborhoods of Chicago. Unlike the more refined heroes of earlier American literature, Bellow's protagonists—endlessly scheming for money and women—revel in lives spent in a great and gritty American city. At the same time, Bellow's heroes probe the hearts of their fellow Americans—street people, social climbers, and business executives—in a quest to understand modern American society and their place in it.

While training in the United States Merchant Marine during World War II (1939-1945), Bellow published his first novel, *Dangling Man* (1944), the fictional journal of a thoughtful, young Chicago man torn between the security of home and his sense of duty to go to war.

Bellow initially found his true voice as a novelist with *The Adventures of Augie March* (1953), a rollicking coming-of-age story set during the Depression. The book vaulted Bellow to fame and won him his first National Book Award in 1954.

Many critics consider *Herzog* (1964), which also won a National Book Award, Bellow's masterpiece—a book that fused the painful reflection of the author's early work with the comedy of *Augie March*. Herzog, a Jewish professor betrayed by his wife and friends, explores his grief by writing frantic letters to the living and the dead. He resolves his confusion by accepting an impossibly idealistic view of life. While some literary figures charged that Bellow's work reflected the author's self-absorption, most critics applauded his talent

In 2005, Ismail Kadare, an Albanian living in Paris, received the inaugural Man Booker International Prize, which recognizes the entire body of work of a living author, regardless of the language in which he or she writes. An English translation of Kadare's *The Successor* was published in 2005 to positive reviews. The novel was described by Lorraine Adams in *The New York Times* as "a whodunit tragicomedy about a Communist loyalist's death before his ascension to power." Kadare's work has been compared with that of Franz Kafka, George Orwell, and Milan Kundera. Kadare's novels were banned in his native Albania, and he had to smuggle them to France to get them published.

National Book Awards. William T. Vollmann was awarded the 2005 National Book Award in the fiction category for his novel *Europe Central.* In his laudatory review of Salman Rushdie's *Shalimar the Clown* for *Publishers Weekly,* Vollmann remarked that "hatred takes on especially horrific manifestations when neighbors turn against each other." In *Europe Central,* Vollmann, like Rushdie, excels at examining the consequences of history. The 36 interrelated stories in *Europe Central* vividly portray the inhabitants of Russia and Germany during World War II (1939-1945).

Vollmann, who spent years traveling through and reporting on the war-torn and dispossessed,

for dramatizing the struggles of the ordinary, flawed human being.

In the latter half of his career, Bellow focused on the relationship between mature intellectuals and a society that is forever changing. *Mr. Sammler's Planet* (1970), which won Bellow his third National Book Award, is the tale of an educated Holocaust survivor living in New York City during the tumultuous decade of the 1960's. (The Holocaust was the systematic, state-sponsored murder of Jews and others by the Nazis during World War II.) During this period of social upheaval, Bellow grew more conservative, and his outspoken opinions stirred conflicts with feminist critics, African American writers, and a younger, more liberal generation. The conflicts prompted Bellow to closely examine the American literary establishment, including his own place in it. *Humboldt's Gift* (1975) chronicles the last days of a talented American poet brought down by the pressures of his own success. Bellow is said to have based the character on his late mentor, the poet Delmore Schwartz. In 1976, Bellow won the Pulitzer Prize for *Humboldt's Gift* and the Nobel Prize in literature for his "human understanding and subtle analysis of contemporary culture."

Bellow's habit of creating characters with qualities similar to those of his prominent friends often resulted in controversy. His final novel, *Ravelstein* (2000), tells the story of a renowned intellectual with a large conservative following who also happens to be a homosexual dying of AIDS. Critics suggested that the character was based on author and University of Chicago professor Allan Bloom, Bellow's late friend. While many readers accused Bellow of violating Bloom's privacy by disclosing his sexual orientation, others praised the book as a tender portrait of a dying friend.

The life of Saul Bellow reads much like the stories of his exuberant yet troubled heroes—great successes and outrageous scandals. Bellow lived by the anthem of his character Augie March, to "make the record in my own way." However, he also spoke for a generation of immigrant Americans making their way in a new land. As Bellow wrote tales of Americans struggling for fulfillment and identity, he established his own identity as one of the great novelists of the 20th century.

■ Marty Zwikel

is the author of eight novels; three books of short stories; a memoir; and *Rising Up and Rising Down,* a 3,000-page treatise on the relationship between ethics and violence. He noted that his goal in *Europe Central* was to "write a series of parables about famous, infamous, and anonymous European moral actors at moments of decision." Vollmann was also represented in 2005 in the collection *Expelled from Eden: A William T. Vollmann Reader.* Edited by Larry McCaffery and Michael Hemmingson, *Expelled from Eden* contains short stories, novel excerpts, and unpublished nonfiction.

Novelist and essayist Joan Didion was awarded the 2005 National Book Award in the nonfiction category for *The Year of Magical Thinking.* The book relates Didion's feelings following the sudden death of her husband, writer John Gregory Dunne, and the terminal illness of their only daughter, Quintana Roo, who died on August 26. Didion, perhaps best known for her 1968 book of essays *Slouching Towards Bethlehem,* was praised for her clarity and insight into the human condition—"confronted with sudden disaster we all focus on how unremarkable the circumstances were in which the unthinkable occurred."

■ Bernard Schwartz

See also **Deaths; Literature for children; Poetry; Pulitzer Prizes; Theater.**

THE Graphic NOVEL

Drawing a NEW AUDIENCE

by DAVID YEZZI

WHAT IS A GRAPHIC NOVEL?

In 2005, the continued rise in popularity of the graphic novel, accompanied by growing critical acclaim for the form, meant one thing for certain: comic books are not just kids' stuff anymore. The visual storytelling of comics, which typically incorporates text into a series of drawn panels, now commands a broader audience than its onetime mainstay of youngsters at the drugstore or comic book shop. Grown beyond episodic tales of superheroes in form-fitting costumes, the subject matter of graphic novels typically includes complex considerations of ordinary life, personal memoir, satire, and journalism. Many graphic novels contain adult content that includes violence and sexual references. Graphic novels are often bound in heavy paper covers like trade-paperback books and have secured a large readership as well as shelf space in mainstream bookstores.

Increasingly, the people following the latest trends in the graphic novel are not only teen-agers in tank tops but also business people in suits and ties, including publishing executives and movie producers. The reason for their interest, not surprisingly, is sales. Graphic novel sales consistently outpaced a comparatively sluggish book market with impressive growth from 2002 through 2004. According to the industry trade journal *Publishers Weekly,* the graphic novel's total estimated sales in the United States in 2004 were between $205 million and $210 million, an increase of roughly 35 percent over the previous year. General adult

A relatively new form of literature—
THE GRAPHIC NOVEL
—has rapidly gained in popularity among readers.

Graphic novels range from contemporary fiction to works of classical literature. One of the newest forms, *manga,* consists of translations of Japanese graphic novels.

trade paperback sales rose only 2.8 percent overall during the same period, according to an industry statistics report by the Association of American Publishers, headquartered in New York City. In 2003, sales of graphic novels rose nearly 50 percent above the sales of the year before, a further indication of the great strides the form has made in the market. Such mainstream publishers as W. W. Norton & Company, Random House, Inc., and Scholastic Corporation—all of which are headquartered in New York City—have added graphic novels to their rosters of published titles in the hope of capitalizing on this explosion in popularity.

Not only are graphic novels generating revenue in bookstores and comic shops, they also are proving profitable at movie box offices. In 2005, Dimension Films' *Sin City,* a film adaptation of Frank Miller's graphic novels of the same name, grossed $74 million. *The Road to Perdition,* a 2002 film version of the book by Max Allan Collins about a murderous 1930's Chicago mobster and his son, generated $104 million. A 2003 film, *American Splendor,* based on the graphic novels of Harvey Pekar, generated critical acclaim. The film featured Pekar as a character, played both by himself and by the actor Paul Giamatti. *A History of Violence*, a film based on the graphic novel by John Wagner and Vince Locke (1997), was also well received upon its release in 2005. Films, because of their wide-reaching, popular appeal, are often an excellent indicator of trends in popular culture, and the film industry has clearly embraced graphic novels.

The author:
David Yezzi is executive editor of *The New Criterion,* a journal of the arts and intellectual life.

Will Eisner is generally credited with popularizing the term *graphic novel*. His *A Contract with God* (inset), published in 1978, was the first book-length graphic story to carry the term on its cover.

Art Spiegelman's *Maus* (1986), an account of the author's father's experiences during the Holocaust, was the first graphic novel to gain widespread acceptance.

History of the graphic novel

Although the graphic novel's popularity skyrocketed in the early 2000's, its more modest origins go further back to the underground comics of the 1960's and 1970's, which were known as *comix*. The origin of the term *graphic novel* remains unclear, though the graphic novelist Will Eisner generally receives credit for popularizing the term. Eisner's series of four linked stories—*A Contract with God*—appeared in 1978 with the subtitle *A Graphic Novel* included on the paperback edition. As Andrew D. Arnold reported in *Time* magazine in 2003, "it was not actually the first long-form graphic story nor the first use of the phrase. It was, however, the first marriage of the term, which appeared on the cover, and the intent of 'serious' comix in book form." Eisner, who died in early 2005, told Arnold that the book "was intended as a departure from the standard, what we call 'comic book format.'" He explained, "I sat down and tried to do a book that would physically look like a 'legitimate' book and at the same time write about a subject matter that would never have been addressed in comic form." *A Contract with God* is a semi-autobiographical series of vignettes about life in a Bronx, New York, housing tenement in the 1930's.

The graphic novel achieved true mainstream acceptance with the publication in 1986 of Art Spiegelman's *Maus,* which recounts the experience of the author's father during the Holocaust, the systematic killing of Jews and other groups by the Nazis. The two-volume work, begun in 1978, received a special Pulitzer Prize in 1992, the only graphic novel to be so honored. In the wake of Spiegelman's landmark achievement, graphic novels began to generate serious critical attention in the literary world from such journals as *Granta* and *The Guardian* in the United Kingdom and *The New York Review of Books* and *The New York Times Book Review* in the United States. Spiegelman's graphic novel *In the Shadow of No Towers* (2004), a reaction to the terrorist attacks on the World Trade Center in New York City on Sept. 11, 2001, initially appeared in serial form in the intellectual journal the *London Review of Books* and elsewhere. Critical attention of this kind went a long way toward legitimizing the graphic novel as a serious art form.

So what is a graphic novel?

Literary critics generally tend to define the graphic novel in a broad and inclusive way, primarily because of the great variety of work published under the name and the evolving nature of the form. Essentially, a graphic novel is a book-length visual narrative. Not all graphic novels incorporate text, though most include both narrative and dialogue. The book-length graphic narrative has traditionally taken several forms. The first, like Eisner's *Contract,* is published in book form without prior serialization. Other graphic novels appear in installments in anthology comics and are later collected into individual volumes. Certain books considered graphic novels are simply collections of monthly serial comic books bound together four or five issues at a time.

As its name suggests, the graphic novel draws on the strengths of both the comic book and the prose novel in ways that distinguish it from both. The graphic novel uses the drawn panels of the comic book form to tell its story in a dynamic way, deftly creating through the impact of its imagery an emotional tone and sense of pace. The author may pare away long verbal descriptions of setting and character, replacing them with an artist's visual rendering of the same material, creating a verbal economy that can intensify the reader's experience of the narrative. Graphic novels then employ the techniques of visual storytelling, in which action is seen rather than described, to work out elaborate and extended narratives traditionally associated with the novel form. At its best, the graphic novel does something that neither the prose novel nor the comic book can manage on its own. It offers an aesthetic experience that combines the immediacy and impact of the visual arts with a prose narrative's capacity to explore complicated subjects with thoughtfulness and subtlety.

What makes **IT** Graphic?

Both graphic novels and comic books use a series of drawn panels to help tell a story. However, comic books, such as *The Batman Strikes,* published in 2004, are pamphlet-sized (fewer than 32 pages) and generally do not tell a complete story in a single issue. Comic books tend to focus on simple plots, such as superhero fantasies.

Graphic novels are longer than comic books. They either contain an entire work or, as in *Batman: The Dark Knight Returns* (1997), a series of previously published short pieces in a single bound volume. The subject matter of graphic novels is also usually more complex than that of comic books. Graphic novels explore such themes as oppression, alienation, and terrorism and may include adult content.

COMIC book

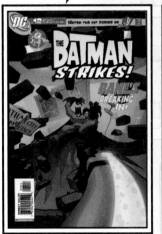

Graphic NOVEL

THIS IS DEFINITELY *NOT* A COMIC BOOK

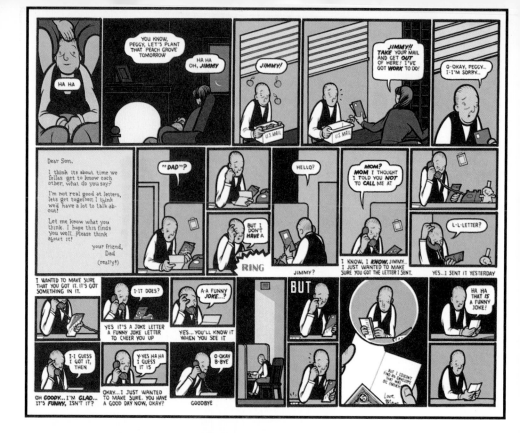

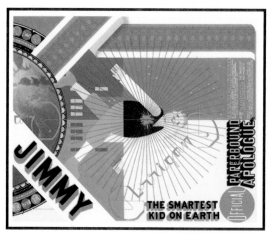

Chris Ware's *Jimmy Corrigan, The Smartest Kid on Earth* (2000), traces the melancholy lives of four generations of Corrigan men in Chicago. Ware's spare, meticulously drawn panels evoke the loneliness and despair of urban life in the modern age.

Marjane Satrapi, an Iranian woman who lives in Paris, exemplifies the graphic novelist working in a concertedly literary way. *Persepolis* (2003), the first installment of her memoir of Iranian life before, during, and after the 1979 revolution that overthrew the shah of Iran, is drawn in bold black-and-white panels and tells the story of her life from ages 10 to 14. The book, first published to critical acclaim in France, was followed by *Persepolis 2* (2004), in which Satrapi furthers her critique of religious fundamentalism and its human consequences. In *Embroideries,* published in 2005, Satrapi abandons the panel format. The work revolves around a gathering of the author's mother, grandmother, and other relatives, neighbors, and friends for an afternoon tea party in which the conversation turns to questions of marriage and sex in Iranian life.

Satrapi's mixture of historical narrative and cultural criticism has drawn comparisons with the work of Spiegelman. However, their work is by no means the only—or even the dominant—form of the graphic novel. Frank Miller's *Dark Knight* series, which confers a gritty

realism on the superhero character Batman, inspired several movies, including *Batman Begins* (2005). Superheroes, however, while commercially successful, are generally of more interest to readers in the comics world than in the book world. Miller also co-wrote and co-directed *Sin City* (2005), which was widely praised for its faithful visual re-creation of Miller's original books and their *noir* style, featuring corrupt characters, gritty urban settings, and a brooding atmosphere. Other graphic novels, beyond those by Satrapi and Spiegelman, that have crossed over to a literary audience include Chris Ware's *Jimmy Corrigan, The Smartest Kid on Earth* (2000) and Daniel Clowes's *Ghost World* (1997), which inspired the film of that name directed by Terry Zwigoff in 2001. The novels of Ware and Clowes consider modern life and human relationships with wit and pathos.

Manga

The Japanese version of the graphic novel, manga, is another strain of the genre that has found a healthy niche in mainstream bookstores. *Manga,* the Japanese word for comic book, refers to random or fanciful pictures. The form takes its name from a sketchbook known as the Hokusai Manga, created by Hokusai, a famous Japanese painter of the 1800's. Manga graphic novels are frequently presented in anthologies containing numerous series in installments of 30 or more pages. Unlike the majority of superhero comics, the form proved to be extremely popular with women in the United States and helped to bring the

Paul Giamatti plays the role of graphic novel author Harvey Pekar, while Hope Davis appears as his wife in a scene from the 2003 film *American Splendor*. Pekar later described his experiences in making a movie of his original comic series in a graphic novel called *American Splendor: Our Movie Year* (2004).

comics market to mainstream bookstores.

Manga has also been widely influential in artistic terms. Max Allan Collins, the author of *Road to Perdition,* revealed in an interview with the British Broadcasting Corporation (BBC) that his story of a rogue mobster in the 1930's is "an unabashed homage" to *Lone Wolf and Cub* (1970), a manga graphic novel by Kazuo Koike and Goseki Kojima. *Lone Wolf* tells the story of a samurai executioner who is wronged by his shogun master and travels across Japan with his young son taking jobs as a paid assassin. Unlike Western graphic novels, manga is a more fluid form, in which characters and situations change from installment to installment. A relationship that develops between people in one episode, for example, may not carry over to future episodes. The artwork of manga is always visually striking and has influenced such U.S. graphic novelists as Frank Miller and Scott McCloud.

The author as artist

The artwork of the graphic novel, like the content, may vary widely, from brilliantly colored cinematic montages to highly stylized, pared-down figures rendered in black and white. Satrapi, for example, draws the facial expressions of her characters with simple lines that nevertheless convey their emotional life with striking power and nuance. Miller's renderings of Batman, on the other hand, rely on elaborate, blood-spattered compositions for their force. Will Eisner spoke of his preference in an interview published in the Italian magazine *Famiglia Cristiana* in 2001: "I prefer black-and-white line because it is closer to the reader's mind. That is, color has an interrupting effect in that it complicates the visual." For Eisner, "Black-and-white is a more direct communicant." Many graphic novels proceed in regular panels; others break up this rhythm with full-page or double-page compositions that overlay elements of the narrative.

Not all graphic novelists illustrate their own work. Max Allan Collins collaborated with British artist Richard Piers Rayner on *Road to Perdition*. Similarly, Harvey Pekar relies on artist Robert Crumb (R. Crumb) and others to provide the visual component of his biographical and autobiographical novels. Regardless of whether the graphic novelist both writes and illustrates the work, the key to any successful visual narrative is finding the appropriate images to express the story. The artwork, even if pared down and stylized, constitutes at least half of the graphic novel's ability to convey the elements of a story and often much more than half. As a result, graphic novelists are frequently referred to as artists, a description that underscores the visual nature of the medium.

As graphic novels grow ever more prominent in bookstores and cinemas, the question remains: Will they continue to find an audience apart from the comic book crowd? Roger Sabin, the author of *Adult Comics: An Introduction* (1993), believes that graphic novels are here to stay, yet he is realistic: "We know now that adult comics are not the inexorable future of literature. They may not even be the future of comics."

The large number of emerging talents who are finding outlets at major publishing houses is, nonetheless, encouraging. An article in the April 18, 2005, issue of *Publishers Weekly* identifies several up-and-coming graphic novelists who might well be the Art Spiegelmans and Marjane Satrapis of the future. As Heidi MacDonald writes, artists Lauren Weinstein (*Inside Vineyland*, 2005), Jeffrey Brown (*Unlikely*, 2003), Raina Telgemeier (*The Baby-sitters Club*, 2006), and Bryan Lee O'Malley (*Scott Pilgrim's Precious Little Life*, 2004) are "four of the most exciting and most praised members of this new generation, turning out work that ranges from satirical fantasy to keenly observed memoir. . . . Freed from the constraints of working within the rigid guidelines of the comic book industry (i.e., bulging muscles, spandex outfits, intergalactic villains), they're turning out boundary-busting work that isn't afraid to connect with the reality of their readers' lives."

Perhaps it was Art Spiegelman himself who best summed up the future of the art form in Arnold's article for *Time* magazine in 2003: "Ultimately the future of the graphic novel is dependent on how much great work gets produced against all odds. I'm much more optimistic than I was that there's room for something and I know that right now there's more genuinely interesting comic art than there's been for decades and decades." With filmmakers and booksellers taking note and heightened public interest continuing to generate both serious critical attention and sales, there is every reason to share his optimism.

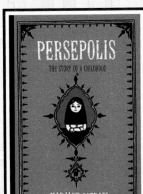

Manga

Types of Graphic NOVELS

Graphic novels vary widely in both content and artistic style. Children's stories based on Japanese manga, such as volumes in the *Fruits Basket* series, became extremely popular in the early 2000's. Nonfiction works may be autobiographical, as is *Persepolis*, Marjane Satrapi's account of growing up in Iran. The graphic novel form also brings literary classics, such as William Shakespeare's *Macbeth*, alive for young audiences.

NON-FICTION

Classic LITERATURE

Literature for children.
Fantasy, fiction, and informational books were among the strongest genres of the year. Some of the outstanding books of 2005 included the following:

Picture books. *Sleepy Cadillac: A Bedtime Drive* by Thacher Hurd (HarperCollins). A comforting fantasy about a big blue Cadillac that flies up to a little boy's window to take him for a drive in the summer twilight, gettting the boy—and readers—ready for "Pajama Land." Ages 3 to 5.

Traction Man Is Here! (Knopf) by Mini Grey. A Christmas-present action figure becomes a superhero with the help of a child's imagination. He's fierce—even if he is only fighting in the kitchen—and dignified enough to survive Granny's knitting him a cutesy green outfit. Ages 3 to 5.

Meet Wild Boars by Meg Rosoff, illustrated by Sophie Blackall (Henry Holt). Boris, Morris, and Horace are "dirty and smelly, bad-tempered and rude." That's bad enough, but then there is Doris, "bossier than a Bossysaurus." These porcine visitors will charm readers with their over-the-top antics. Ages 3 to 5.

That New Animal by Emily Jenkins, illustrated by Pierre Pratt (Farrar Straus and Giroux). Marshmallow and FudgeFudge, a couple of coddled doggies, get used to a new baby, learning how "that new animal" smells and sounds and finally accepting him. Ages 3 to 5.

The Hello, Goodbye Window by Norton Juster, illustrated by Chris Raschka (Hyperion). At Nanna and Poppy's house, there's a perfect window for playing tricks, imagining, looking out, and for remembering the inside fun as well. Ages 3 to 7.

Leonardo, the Terrible Monster by Mo Willems (Hyperion). Leonardo is a flop at being a monster, so he looks for someone to scare who's already a scaredy-cat. That's Sam. Both Sam and Leonardo are small and round in a big, wide world, and they end up becoming friends. Ages 3 to 5.

Little Rabbit Runaway by Harry Horse (Peachtree). No one's ever going to tell Little Rabbit what to do again. Until, that is, his runaway journey leads him to Molly Mouse, who can be just as bossy as his parents. Ages 4 to 7.

Show Way by Jacqueline Woodson, illustrated by Hudson Talbott (Putnam). Woodson recalls her family's history through a "Show Way," a quilt whose patches hide secret meanings. Woodson celebrates the women of her family—from a great-grandma sold as a slave in Virginia to her own daughter—for their ability to see beauty and to sew or say the truth. Ages 5 to 8.

Encyclopedia Prehistorica: Dinosaurs by Robert Sabuda and Matthew Reinhart (Candlewick). Intricate pop-ups and informational text introduce dinosaurs of the Mesozoic Era. Ages 6 and up.

Poetry. *Runny Babbit: A Billy Sook* by Shel Silverstein (HarperCollins). The late Silverstein, author of such classics as *The Giving Tree (1964)*, *Where the Sidewalk Ends (1974)*, and *A Light in the Attic (1981)*, knew how to have fun with words. His poems, composed over 20 years, will have readers calling this collection a "tun fime" as well. Ages 8 and up.

Fantasy. *Harry Potter and the Half-Blood Prince* (Scholastic) by J. K. Rowling. In Rowling's sixth volume in the series, the characters are more developed; the descriptions are more humorous; and the plot tension about an important death seems very real. Ages 10 and up.

Eldest by Christopher Paolini (Knopf). In the second volume of the Inheritance trilogy by now-19-year-old Paolini, Eragon and his dragon travel to the valley of the elves for further training, and his cousin Roran fights to save the people of the village. Ages 11 and up.

The Scarecrow and His Servant by Philip Pullman (Knopf). An orphan named Jack becomes the servant of a talking scarecrow with a turnip for a head. They try to save Scarecrow's polluted valley from the villainous Buffaloni family. Ages 9 to 14.

Inkspell by Cornelia Funke (Chicken House). Meggie has the power to bring fictional characters to life and to send them back into the books from which they came. In the second volume of Funke's trilogy, *Inkheart,* Meggie tries to help young apprentice Farid, whose master, Dustfinger, has found another reader to take him back to Inkworld. Meggie and Farid follow, but the world there is not so tidily cleaned up as either they or its author thought. Ages 10 to 14.

47 by Walter Mosley (Little, Brown). Mosley, who writes adult detective fiction, blends fantasy elements with the history of slavery. A slave named only "47" is inspired by a runaway from "beyond Africa" to free himself from a brutal master. Ages 10 to 14.

Maximum Ride: The Angel Experiment by James Patterson (Little, Brown). A popular adult author writes of a band of children, genetically bred to have wings, who escape from their laboratory. When the youngest, Angel, is caught, group leader Max organizes a rescue. Ages 11 to 14.

Publishers in 2005 also released many fantasy-fiction sequels. Some of the new titles included Books 4, 5, and 6 of *The Edge Chronicles* by Paul Stewart and Chris Riddell (David Fickling Books); Book 3 of the *Underland* series by Suzanne Collins (Scholastic); and Book 3 of the *Lion Boy* series by Zizou Corder (Dial). All, ages 11 and up.

Fiction. *Criss Cross* by Lynne Rae Perkins (Greenwillow). The lives of six teens in a small town sometimes criss-cross, but the childhood friends are all on separate wavelengths. One long, sometimes hilarious, summer highlights the small changes as they discover who they are and choose the paths they will take. Ages 11 to 14.

The Penderwicks: A Summer Tale of Four Sisters, Two Rabbits, and a Very Interesting Boy by Jeanne Birdsall (Knopf). The Penderwick sisters, ages 4 through 12, and their widowed father rent a cottage for the summer on a large estate in the Berkshire Mountains. They befriend the owner's lonely son, experience a first crush, and generally have adventures. Ages 10 to 14.

Replay by Sharon Creech (Joana Cotler Books/HarperCollins). Leo's brothers and sister call him "Fog Boy" because he's a quiet dreamer. A part in the school play and the discovery of his father's boyhood diary help Leo find a niche in his loud, friendly Italian family. Ages 10 to 14.

Informational Books. *Let Me Play: The Story of Title IX* by Karen Blumenthal (Atheneum). Photographs and political cartoons give historical depth to the story of a movement many young

(Atheneum). Using a scrapbook format, Fleming collects points of view from friends, family, and outside observers on the stages of Eleanor Roosevelt's life—her lonely childhood; ups and downs of her emotional relationship with husband President Franklin Roosevelt; her parenting; her advocacy for social causes; and her ability to recover from adversities. Ages 11 to 15.

John Lennon: All I Want Is the Truth by Elizabeth Partridge (Viking). Using Lennon's own writings and interviews, Partridge provides a careful study of Lennon's psychological and artistic development, from his childhood through the Beatles days and into the Yoko Ono years. Ages 12 to 16.

Awards. The 2005 Newbery Medal was awarded to Cynthia Kadohata for *Kira-Kira*. The award is given by the American Library Association (ALA) for "the most distinguished contribu-

A young fan begins the sixth volume of the Harry Potter series, *Harry Potter and the Half-Blood Prince,* just after its release at midnight on July 16. The book sold 6.9 million copies in the first 24 hours of its release, breaking the record of 5 million copies set by the previous volume in the series, published in 2003.

women are unfamiliar with—the struggle for equal opportunity for women in sports, education, and the workplace. Ages 11 to 14.

10,000 Days of Thunder: A History of the Vietnam War by Philip Caputo (Atheneum). Caputo, a Vietnam veteran and Pulitzer Prize-winning journalist, provides a historical perspective on that war. Personal stories, photographs, battlefield maps, and references for further reading enrich the text. Ages 9 to 14.

Our Eleanor: A Scrapbook Look at Eleanor Roosevelt's Remarkable Life by Candace Fleming

tion to children's literature" published the previous year. The ALA's Caldecott Medal for "the most distinguished American picture book" was awarded to Kevin Henkes for *Kitten's First Full Moon.* The Michael L. Printz Award for excellence in literature for young adults, sponsored by the ALA's Young Adult Library Services Association, went to Meg Rosoff for *How I Live Now.*

■ Mary Harris Russell

See also **Literature; Literature: A Special Report.**

Lithuania. See Europe.

Los Angeles.

Los Angeles. Democrat Antonio Villaraigosa was sworn in as Los Angeles's first Hispanic American mayor in 133 years on July 1, 2005, after achieving a landslide runoff victory over Mayor James K. Hahn in the May 17 primary. In the 2001 mayoral election, Hahn had defeated Villaraigosa.

The win for Villaraigosa, a former state assembly speaker, was seen as the start of an era for Hispanic Americans who historically have been underrepresented in politics in the United States. "I love being mayor of the city that I was born in, raised in, that my grandpa came [from Mexico] to 100 years ago," Villaraigosa told reporters. *Time* magazine listed the new mayor among the 25 most influential Hispanics in the United States, and *Newsweek* magazine featured him on its May 30, 2005, cover.

Villaraigosa promised that he would try to decrease city traffic problems, give tax credits to film companies to keep jobs in Los Angeles, and make the city safer. Police Chief William J. Bratton, hired by Hahn from New York City, said he would remain on the job at Villaraigosa's request. Bratton's first term expires in 2007.

The Getty. A former curator at the J. Paul Getty Museum was charged in 2005 with acquiring art through questionable means. Italian government officials alleged that former curator Marion True purchased artworks from looters. Italian authorities cited 42 potentially stolen artifacts that were at some time in the Getty Museum. Her trial in Italy began in November.

The Greek government asked the Getty Museum for the return of four allegedly looted artifacts. Greek authorities launched legal action against the museum in November.

Housing. While Los Angeles County remained the state's—and the nation's—most populous county with nearly 10 million people, the U.S. Census Bureau reported that Riverside and San Bernardino counties had become the destinations of choice for new residents seeking housing. The two counties to the east, known locally as the Inland Empire, were among the top five U.S. counties in population growth from 2003 to 2004, trailing only Maricopa County, Arizona. Despite rising housing prices, the Inland Empire remained more

Mayor Antonio Villaraigosa poses in the Los Angeles City Hall after taking office in July as the city's first Hispanic American mayor in 133 years. *Time* **magazine listed Villaraigosa among the 25 most influential Hispanics in the United States.**

affordable than Los Angeles, where the median home price was $439,000 in mid-2005. The median price for condominium resales rose to $403,000 in southern California in 2005, according to Data-Quick Information Systems, a real estate information company based in San Diego. Apartment rentals in the region increased by an average of 5.2 percent in 2005. In Los Angeles and Orange counties, the average monthly rental rate was $1,397, compared with $1,138 a month in 2004, according to RealFacts, a Novato, California-based research firm.

Police. By April 2005, the city of Los Angeles had settled approximately 200 civil lawsuits involving nearly $70 million in damages. The suits had been filed by alleged drug dealers, gang members, and others who claimed that they had been mistreated by city police. The so-called Rampart Division police scandal involved corrupt police officers who allegedly framed, beat, and shot suspected criminals. The scandal resulted in the overturning of more than 100 criminal convictions and the dismissal of more than a dozen police officers.

Ports. In 2005, the ports of Los Angeles and Long Beach remained the largest container shipping ports in the United States and the third largest port district in the world, behind Hong Kong and Singapore. The authors of a report by the Los Angeles County Economic Development Corp., a business leadership organization, predicted that the total value of two-way trade through the port district would increase 14.3 percent to a record $302.1 billion in 2005. The report also revealed that emissions from giant container ships and the hundreds of diesel-powered trains and trucks that haul cargo to and from the port are the largest source of air pollution in southern California. ■ Margaret A. Kilgore

See also **Census; City.**

Luxembourg. See Europe.

Macedonia. The government of Prime Minister Vlado Buckovski continued to pursue two major policy goals in 2005—eventual admission of the former Yugoslav republic into NATO and into the European Union (EU). Buckovski became prime minister after the resignation of former prime minister Hari Kostov in November 2004. Buckovski's government in 2005 retained the same six-party ruling coalition as that of Kostov.

Municipal elections. In March and April, Macedonia held nationwide local elections, the first since redistricting in 2004 gave Albanian Muslim minority communities greater autonomy. Albanian militants fought a rebellion in 2001 to obtain full rights in Macedonia's government, which they alleged was unfairly dominated by the majority Slavic Christian population. The Ohrid agreement of August 2001, which ended the rebellion, created multiethnic political institutions and mandated local redistricting.

The 2005 local elections took place in several rounds in March and April. Reports of procedural irregularities and voter intimidation prompted NATO and EU officials to admonish Macedonian officials that they would be held accountable for the nation's conduct of future elections.

Washington meeting. In October, Prime Minister Buckovski met with United States President George W. Bush and Secretary of Defense

Donald Rumsfeld in Washington, D.C. Secretary Rumsfeld commended the Macedonian prime minister for his country's progress on military reform and suggested that Macedonia was on track for admission to NATO in 2008.

EU candidacy. On Nov. 9, 2005, the European Commission, the executive arm of the EU, recommended that the 25 EU member nations accept Macedonia as a candidate for EU membership. However, the commission refrained from setting a date for accession talks with Macedonian officials. (Accession, or admission, to the EU is a complex process requiring several years of negotiations between applicant nations and EU officials.) Macedonian officials signed an association and stabilization agreement with the EU, the first step toward EU membership, in 2001.

Macedonia's economy grew in the second quarter of 2005 by an annual rate of 4.7 percent, putting the country on track to meet or surpass the government's target of 3.8-percent growth for calendar 2005. Macedonia's unemployment rate hovered around 37 percent in mid-2005. At an international aid donors' meeting in New York City in October, Prime Minister Buckovski identified joblessness as Macedonia's "biggest and hardest problem." ■ Sharon L. Wolchik

See also **Europe.**

Madagascar. See Africa.

Magazine publishing generally enjoyed a rebound in advertising in 2005. Between January and August, consumer magazines had a combined revenue of nearly $13.8 billion, an increase of 8.5 percent compared with the same period in 2004, according to Publishers Information Bureau (PIB), an association in New York City that measures magazine advertising spending and ad pages. During the first eight months of 2005, the number of ad pages in consumer magazines totaled 145,823, an increase of 1.9 percent over 2004, PIB reported on Sept. 12, 2005.

News weeklies, by contrast, lost advertising pages, revenues, and newsstand sales in 2005. The Audit Bureau of Circulations, an industry trade group based in Schaumburg, Illinois, reported that from January to July 1, newsstand sales of *Time* magazine declined 3.4 percent; *Newsweek* dropped 14 percent; and *U.S. News & World Report* fell 16.6 percent, compared with the same period in 2004. Ad pages declined 21.1 percent at *Time,* 18.6 percent at *Newsweek,* and 3.5 percent at *U.S. News & World Report* in the first eight months of 2005, compared with 2004, noted *Mediaweek* trade magazine based in North Hollywood, California.

TV Guide, the weekly created in 1953 as a program guide for the then-new phenomenon of television, introduced radical changes with its

John H. Johnson
Succeeding Against the Odds

John H. Johnson, the trailblazing publishing magnate whose *Ebony* and *Jet* magazines inspired generations of African Americans, died of heart failure in Chicago on Aug. 8, 2005, at the age of 87. A native of Arkansas City, Arkansas, Johnson rose from poverty to create a publishing and cosmetics empire that brought him wealth and fame and changed the face of media in the United States.

His enterprises are credited with opening the eyes of the U.S. corporate world to the power of the black consumer market and paving the way for the legions of African American business executives and media stars who followed in his path. His glossy magazines—among the first to regularly feature black actors, athletes, entrepreneurs, and other groundbreaking black achievers—served as a blueprint for success. "We wanted to give blacks a new sense of somebody-ness, a new sense of self-respect," Johnson wrote in his 1989 autobiography *Succeeding Against the Odds*.

From his gleaming 11-story headquarters, the first office tower built by an African American in downtown Chicago, Johnson wielded unprecedented influence on both black and white America. Although not the first magazines published for a black audience in the United States, Johnson's publications were the most successful and remained so for more than 60 years.

Johnson was born on Jan. 19, 1918. His father, Leroy Johnson, was killed in a sawmill accident when John was 8 years old. His mother, Gertrude Jenkins Johnson, doted on her only son and was determined to provide him with the educational opportunities she knew were not available in their impoverished, segregated town, which had no high school for blacks. In 1933, at the height of the Great Depression, she moved with her son to Chicago. In Chicago, Johnson not only finished high school, he began studying part-time at the University of Chicago while working at the Supreme Life Insurance Co., the largest black company in the North.

While working as an assistant for Harry H. Pace, president of Supreme Life, Johnson was inspired to create his first magazine. His duties included clipping articles about blacks from a variety of newspapers and periodicals and presenting them to Pace. Johnson believed a magazine providing the same service for a mass black audience had tremendous business potential. Financial institutions failed to see the wisdom of his concept, however, and he was denied a start-up loan at every turn. Undeterred, he pressed on. Using his mother's furniture as collateral, he borrowed $500 and launched *Negro Digest*—and the Johnson Publishing Co.—in 1942. *Ebony* debuted in 1945 and almost immediately became the largest-circulated black magazine in the world. In 1951, Johnson started *Jet*, a pocket-sized newsweekly.

Johnson's keen eye for recognizing entrepreneurial opportunities led him to create his company's cosmetics division in 1973. Noting the dearth of beauty products for African American women, he introduced Fashion Fair Cosmetics, one of the first lines of high-end cosmetics developed exclusively for the wide variety of black skin tones.

Johnson's enterprises not only made him wealthy, they extended his influence well beyond the black community. He had the ear of presidents, ranging from Richard Nixon to Bill Clinton. Johnson was among the first African Americans listed on *Forbes* magazine's register of the 400 richest Americans. He also was among the first blacks selected to serve on the board of directors of several major U.S. corporations. His numerous honors included the Spingarn Medal, the highest award issued by the National Association for the Advancement of Colored People, and the Presidential Medal of Freedom, presented by Clinton. In a career that spanned seven decades, the fiercely determined Johnson never allowed obstacles like racism or poverty to deter him. "Failure," he said, "is a word I don't accept." ■ Charles Whitaker

Oct. 17, 2005, issue. *TV Guide* expanded from its square digest format to a standard magazine size and cut back some of its TV listings. The circulation of the magazine, which peaked at 20 million in the late 1970's, had declined to some 4.5 million readers in 2005. Analysts said the rapid expansion of channels available on cable TV, and the popularity of online and on-screen listings, made *TV Guide*'s print listings unwieldy and obsolete.

Gruner+Jahr. In May, publishing company Gruner+Jahr (G+J) of Hamburg, Germany, announced that it was selling all of its magazines published in the United States. Meredith Corporation of Des Moines, Iowa, acquired for $350 million four of G+J titles: *Child, Family Circle, Fitness,* and *Parents.* In January, G+J had disclosed that the number of paid subscribers to several of its magazines mistakenly had been overstated by as much as 165,000. G+J filed a lawsuit against Publishers Communications Systems of Margate, Florida, alleging the independent subscription-selling company was responsible for the error.

Chicken Soup for the Soul. In July, Modern Media of Memphis, Tennessee, launched *Chicken Soup for the Soul.* The magazine was based on popular inspirational books that generated sales of $1.3 billion since 1993. ■ Mark Fitzgerald

Malawi. See Africa.

Malaysia suffered in 2005 from choking air pollution from smoke caused by jungle fires in nearby Indonesia. Malaysia's government declared a state of emergency on August 11 in areas around the capital, Kuala Lumpur, due to health dangers caused by the worsening haze. Rains cleared the air by late August. The problem occurs annually as farmers and commercial plantations on the Indonesian island of Sumatra, west of Malaysia, burn vegetation to clear land for crops. The Indonesian government promised to investigate companies that violate rules limiting burning.

Malaysia's economy started 2005 with rapid growth, continuing a trend of decreasing dependence on agriculture. Prime Minister Abdullah bin Ahmad Badawi announced on August 16 that Malaysia was developing a strategy to become fully developed economically by 2020, enabling it to compete with larger Asian countries such as China and India. The strategy focused on training a work force in fields such as bio-technology and information technology. ■ Henry S. Bradsher

See also **Asia.**

Maldives. See Asia.
Mali. See Africa.
Malta. See Europe.
Manitoba. See Canadian Provinces.
Marshall Islands. See Pacific Islands.
Mauritania. See Africa.

Mauritius. Prime Minister Paul Berenger's ruling coalition government was defeated in parliamentary elections on July 3, 2005, after five years in office. The opposition Social Alliance (SA) coalition headed by former premier and Labor Party leader Navin Ramgoolam won 38 of the 62 directly elected seats in the 70-member National Assembly. Berenger's coalition, consisting of his Militant Mauritian Movement and Deputy Prime Minister Pravind Jugnauth's Militant Socialist Movement, won just 22 seats. (According to Mauritian electoral law, eight members of parliament are chosen by an independent electoral board to ensure ethnic minority representation.) SA leader Ramgoolam, son of the nation's first postindependence leader, Sir Seewoosagur Ramgoolam, became the nation's new prime minister.

The new SA administration promised to promote broad economic growth that would benefit Mauritius's unemployed poor. Analysts concluded, however, that the government's top priority in 2005 was to negotiate better trade deals for the country's key sugar and textile industries. Better trade relations had become imperative in the face of proposed deep cuts in European Union sugar subsidies and fierce international competition from China's textile manufacturers.
■ Simon Baynham

See also **Africa.**

Medicine. A French woman who was severely disfigured by her dog received the world's first partial face transplant in November 2005. French surgeons led by Jean-Michel Dubernard of Lyon grafted a nose, lips, and chin from a brain-dead donor onto the patient. The surgeons also injected stem cells from the donor's bone marrow into the patient in an effort to prevent her immune system from rejecting the new tissue.

Many surgeons and scientists expressed alarm over the French surgeons' decision to perform what they consider a highly experimental procedure before attempting to repair the patient's face using more conventional forms of reconstructive surgery. They also expressed concerns about the novel use of stem cells as well as the long-term use of powerful drugs to suppress the patient's immune system in a case that was not life threatening. The French surgeons defended their medical preparations for the procedure and insisted that reports about the emotional instability of the patient were unfounded.

Battling lung cancer. Research published in 2005 provided strong support for an emerging new standard of care for people with the most common form of lung cancer in the United States. The study found that the use of chemotherapy after tumor surgery significantly improved the five-year survival rate of people with non-small cell lung cancer (NSCLC) that had not spread beyond the lungs. NSCLC accounts for at least 80 percent of all lung cancers. *Oncologists* (cancer specialists) considered the findings significant because about 85 percent of all lung cancer patients die within five years of their diagnosis.

The 10-year study of 482 patients with early-stage NSCLC was led by oncologist Timothy Winton of the University of Alberta in Edmonton, Canada. The researchers found that 69 percent of the participants who received chemotherapy following the surgical removal of a lung tumor were alive five years later, compared with 54 percent of those who underwent surgery alone. The patients received one of a family of drugs that interfere with cancer cells' ability to reproduce. Those who received chemotherapy lived an average of 94 months after surgery, compared with 73 months for those who had only surgery.

Revised obesity rates. Obesity remained one of the chief causes of death in the United States in 2005. However, the estimated number of deaths occurring annually because of poor diet and lack of exercise—two major causes of obesity—is about 70 percent lower than a highly publicized figure reported in 2004 by researchers at the Centers for Disease Control and Prevention (CDC) in Atlanta, Georgia.

In 2004, the CDC reported that in 2000 (the last year for which data were available) obesity annually caused about 365,000 deaths in the United States, making it the second leading cause of death, after tobacco use. However, in April 2005, other CDC researchers used a different statistical method to analyze data from three national health surveys. They found that obesity kills about 112,000 U.S. citizens annually. Despite the lower number, medical experts continued to warn of the serious health threats, including heart disease and diabetes, linked to obesity.

Breast cancer and diet. Women who have been successfully treated for early-stage breast cancer may reduce the risk that their cancer will recur by following a low-fat diet, according to a May 2005 study. The research was the first large-scale, controlled study to offer evidence for a link between lifestyle and cancer recurrence rates. Researchers led by oncologist Rowan T. Chlebowski of the Los Angeles Biomedical Research Institute in Torrance, California, followed 2,437 women with early-stage breast cancer for five years. They found that the cancer reappeared in 9.8 percent of the women following a low-fat diet, compared with 12.4 percent of those following a standard diet. Some researchers, however, argued that the women's weight loss—not the diet itself—had reduced the risk of recurrence.

■ Barbara A. Mayes

See also **Health care issues; Public health.**

Mental health. The United States Department of Health and Human Services in September 2005 announced the availability of $600,000 in mental health grants to four states with large numbers of people suffering from emotional and psychological problems resulting from the Hurricane Katrina and Rita disasters in August and September. Alabama, Louisiana, Mississippi, and Texas became eligible to receive funds for psychiatric treatment, crisis and medication management, counseling for disaster workers, and other services.

An estimated 45 percent of people in the New Orleans area surveyed in October needed some form of counseling, the director of the Louisiana Office of Mental Health reported in November. The survey, conducted by workers from the Centers for Disease Control and Prevention in Atlanta, Georgia, also found that nearly 25 percent of those surveyed were suffering from serious psychological problems.

In September, a committee of the American Academy of Pediatrics (AAP) warned health professionals of the long-term psychosocial consequences that may affect young victims of hurricanes and other traumatic events. The AAP, based in Elk Grove Village, Illinois, commissioned the report in response to the terrorist attacks on the United States on Sept. 11, 2001. However, the committee noted, its findings also apply to children affected by natural disasters.

According to the report, the damaging effects of traumatic events include anxiety, depression, and post-traumatic stress disorder (PTSD). PTSD is a psychological illness in which people repeatedly remember, relive, or dream about a terrible experience. Children who experience traumatic events may also have bereavement issues resulting from the loss of relatives or of their residences and pets. Symptoms of these conditions may include aggressive behavior, hostility toward others, anxiety, sleep disturbances, and depression.

Mental health of troops. A significant improvement in morale and a lower suicide rate were among the findings of a mental health advisory team report on U.S. soldiers serving in Iraq issued by the U.S. Army in July 2005. According to the report, the number of soldiers rating their unit's morale as "low" dropped from 72 percent in 2003 to 54 percent in 2004. In addition, the number of soldiers committing suicide during that same period fell from 24 to 9. Army officials credited the improvements, in part, to better living conditions for the troops, including improved communications facilities. In addition, the Army significantly increased the number of mental health professionals in Iraq and Kuwait and improved efforts to identify and treat front-line soldiers suffering from early PTSD symptoms.

The authors of the report also noted that about 30 percent of the combat veterans surveyed revealed that they had developed stress-related psychological problems about three to four months after leaving a combat zone. These problems included anxiety, depression, anger, and difficulty concentrating. The problems were worst among truckdrivers and convoy guards, who frequently come under attack in Iraq.

Light therapy and depression. Light therapy is about as effective as medication for treating people with seasonal affective disorder (SAD), according to an April 2005 review of 173 published studies on light treatment commissioned by the American Psychiatric Association in Washington, D.C. SAD is a disturbance of mood caused by the shortening of the period of daylight that occurs during fall and winter. Standard treatments include exposure to high-intensity, bright artificial light for a short period each day and the use of antidepressant drugs. The studies indicated that light therapy "markedly eased" SAD symptoms. The reviewers also reported that the therapy provided people with mild to moderate depression unrelated to SAD with "substantial relief" from their symptoms and appeared to magnify the therapeutic effects of their antidepressant medication.   ■ Barbara A. Mayes

See also **Drugs; Medicine.**

Mexico. President Vicente Fox Quesada of Mexico defended his presidency in his final state of the union address on Sept. 1, 2005, and in a series of radio and television commercials funded by his National Action Party (PAN). Constitutionally limited to one presidential term, Fox anticipated being replaced by the winner of a presidential election scheduled for July 2006.

In his speech, Fox emphasized his role in democratizing Mexico's government, noting that he had in 2000 defeated the presidential candidate of the entrenched Institutional Revolutionary Party (PRI) and achieved a political change of administration for the first time in 71 years. Fox went on to blame the PRI-controlled Congress for his failure to obtain passage of key legislation, including a measure to open Mexico's petroleum industry to foreign investment and reforms of the nation's tax code and energy systems.

Polls in 2005 gave Fox a 60-percent approval rating, despite what some critics regarded as his failure to win passage of his legislative program. Other analysts attributed some of the disappointments of Fox's presidency to United States President George W. Bush, who, they claimed, had failed to fulfill his promise to obtain changes in U.S. immigration policy that would have benefited Mexicans living illegally in the United States and others desiring to enter legally.

Presidential campaign. Many Mexicans in 2005 had already turned their attention from Fox toward the political campaign leading up to the 2006 presidential election. The early front-runner, according to polls, was Andres Manuel Lopez Obrador, or "AMLO" as he was dubbed by the press, mayor of Mexico City and candidate of the Party of Democratic Revolution (PRD). Lopez Obrador, who had become mayor of Mexico's immense capital in 2000, built a reputation as a reformer by cleaning up corruption, cracking down on crime, and improving services for Mexico City's millions of slum dwellers.

AMLO's political prospects became somewhat clouded in 2005 when Mexico's attorney general, a Fox appointee, ordered a judge to begin legal proceedings against Lopez Obrador. At issue was the mayor's alleged disregard in 2001 of a court order concerning a construction project.

According to pollsters, AMLO supporters and many independents viewed the court case as a ploy by political opponents to render Lopez Obrador ineligible to run for president. On April 24, 2005, at least 1 million Mexicans thronged the streets of Mexico City to demonstrate support for Lopez Obrador. In response to the massive demonstration, President Fox's administration dropped criminal charges against AMLO. The Mexico City mayor resigned his post in July to campaign full-time for the presidency.

Voting privileges. In June, Mexico's Congress granted Mexicans living abroad the right to vote in the 2006 presidential election. As a result, an estimated 10 million Mexicans living in the United States became eligible to vote by mail.

Troubled border. Rival drug gangs armed with automatic weapons, grenades, and bazookas engaged in an open battle on the streets of Nuevo Laredo in late July 2005. Nuevo Laredo, directly across the Rio Grande River from Laredo, Texas, lies astride major commercial routes between Mexico and the United States. The violence prompted U.S. officials to shut down the U.S. consulate in Nuevo Laredo for a week until the security situation improved. In August, the Mexican government sent a battalion of federal police officers to assist the local police force in regaining control of the border city's streets.

A record number of migrants, mostly Mexicans, died trying to cross illegally into the United States from Mexico in the first nine months of 2005, reported the U.S. Customs and Border Protection Agency. Most of the 464 deaths were attributed to the effects of extreme heat on those attempting to cross desert terrain on foot or in sealed vehicles.   ■ Nathan A. Haverstock

See also **Immigration; Latin America.**

Micronesia, Federated States of.

See **Pacific Islands.**

MIDDLE EAST

A number of positive developments led to improvements in the Israeli-Palestinian conflict in 2005. At a summit held on February 8 in Egypt, Israeli Prime Minister Ariel Sharon and Palestinian Authority President Mahmoud Abbas agreed to cease all hostilities—a step that officially ended the second Palestinian *Intifada* (uprising), which began in September 2000. An even more dramatic development came in August 2005 with the dismantling of all 25 Israeli settlements in the Gaza Strip, followed by the withdrawal from Gaza of Israeli troops in September. In November, the mediation of United States Secretary of State Condoleezza Rice led to the opening of three routes between Israel and Gaza and one route between Egypt and Gaza.

Several political developments related to the peace process occurred in Israel in 2005. In November, Amir Peretz, the dovish member of the Labor Party, ousted former Prime Minister Shimon Peres as leader of the party. Peres then announced his support for Kadima (*Forward*), a new centrist political party formed by Prime Minister Sharon, who quit his own Likud Party.

Lebanon's Cedar Revolution. The so-called "Cedar Revolution" was sparked in early 2005 after the Syrian government became concerned about the growing power of Lebanese forces in opposition to the Syrian occupation of Lebanon. On February 14, a car bombing killed Rafik Hariri, a prominent leader of the Lebanese opposition. The assassination, which was later tied to Syrian officials, led to anti-Syria demonstrations that culminated in a peaceful rally by 1.5 million Lebanese in the capital, Beirut, on March 14. The demonstrators demanded the immediate withdrawal of Syrian troops.

International pressure provided by the United Nations (UN) Security Council, led by the United States and France, helped persuade the Syrian government to agree to a withdrawal from Lebanon. On April 26, a major goal of the Cedar Revolution was achieved with the evacuation of all Syrian troops and intelligence services from Lebanon.

Candidates associated with the Lebanese opposition won the majority of parliamentary seats in May and June 2005. A new Cabinet headed by Prime Minister Fouad Siniora was formed in July. The Cabinet had at least two members representing Hezbollah, a pro-Syria organization with both a political and militia wing. The disarmament of militias remained another goal of Cedar Revolution leaders.

Revolutionary ripples. The ripples of the Cedar Revolution spread in 2005 to other countries in the Middle East, noted many experts in international affairs. In Syria, hundreds of intellectuals, human rights activists, and other opposition leaders called for freedom and democracy in their own country.

In Egypt, Ayman Nour, the leader of the liberal al-Ghad (*Future*) Party, contested the result of the September presidential elections, which were won by President Hosni Mubarak. The Egyptian Movement for Change, also known as Kefaya (*Enough*), held several peaceful demonstrations calling for the end of President Mubarak's 24-year reign.

Terrorist attacks by al-Qaʿida. Attacks by the Islamic terrorist network al-Qaʿida continued in 2005. The deadliest of the attacks were carried out in Egypt and Jordan.

In Egypt, three coordinated car bombings on July 23 targeted the Red Sea resort of Sharm el-Sheikh, resulting in the deaths of more than 90 people. The Abdullah Azzam Brigades, a group linked to al-Qaʿida, claimed responsibility for the attacks.

In Jordan, three suicide bombings on November 9 at American-owned hotels in the capital, Amman, caused the deaths of at least 58 people. Abu Musab al-Zarqawi, the Jordanian-born head of the Iraqi branch of al-Qaʿida, claimed responsibility for the bombings.

Moves for peace in Sudan. On January 9, a historic peace agreement was signed between officials of the Sudanese government and the chairman of the Sudan People's Liberation Movement, John Garang de Mabior. The agreement ended the 21-year civil war between the two sides, which accepted the "one-country, two-systems model" recognizing limited *autonomy* (self-rule) for the southern part of Sudan. The agreement also granted the southern Sudanese the option to renegotiate the treaty after six years, at which time they could choose to either remain part of Sudan or secede and form an independent nation.

In March, the UN Security Council adopted a series of resolutions for ending the conflict in Darfur, a western region in Sudan where violence between rebels and government forces began in 2003. Resolution 1590 established the UN mission in Sudan for a renewable six-month period. The mission consisted of 10,000 military personnel and 715 civilian police personnel, who were charged with fostering peace in Darfur in cooperation with the African Union Mission in Sudan. Resolution 1593 referred the Darfur conflict to the prosecutor of the International Criminal Court (ICC) in The Hague, Netherlands. The prosecutor began his investigation in June 2005 by collecting over 3,000 documents related to the killing of thousands of civilians and the displacement of 1.9 million people in Darfur.

Political and military developments in Iraq. On January 30, 8.5 million Iraqi voters, or 58 percent of the electorate, voted for representatives in the new Transitional National Assembly. Shiah and Kurdish parties won most of the seats in the 275-member assembly. The Shiah United Iraqi Alliance won an absolute majority of 140 seats, while the two main Kurdish parties won a total of 75 seats.

One of the main tasks of the Transitional National Assembly was the formation of a committee to draft a new constitution for Iraq. Although the 69-member committee drafted a charter, the members failed to reach a consensus on such key issues as the existence of autonomous regions for Kurds and the development of strategies for dealing with former Baathists, who had wielded power in the ousted regime of Saddam Hussein. None of the Sunni members of the committee signed the draft.

In a national referendum in October, 78 percent of the Iraqi voters approved the constitution while 21 percent rejected it. The vast majority of Iraq's Sunni Arabs opposed the new constitution.

In November, the UN Security Council extended the mandate of the Multinational Forces in Iraq until December 2006. The extension came in response to a request from Iraqi Prime Minister Ibrahim al-Jafari. In an October letter to the Security Council, Prime Minister al-Jafari wrote that until Iraqi forces could assume full responsibility for the nation's security, the Multinational Forces would be needed "to establish lasting peace and security" in Iraq.

The insurgency against U.S. forces and the newly formed Iraqi army and police forces continued unabated in 2005. From the time of the war's launch in

Syrian troops pull out of Lebanon on April 26 after occupying the country for 29 years. The Syrian army initially moved into neighboring Lebanon in 1976 during the Lebanese civil war, effectively making Syria Lebanon's political master.

FACTS IN BRIEF ON MIDDLE EASTERN COUNTRIES

Country	Population	Government	Monetary unit*	Foreign trade (million U.S.$) Exports[†]	Imports[†]
Bahrain	714,000	King Hamad bin Isa Al-Khalifa; Prime Minister Khalifa bin Salman Al-Khalifa	dinar (0.38 = $1)	8,205	5,870
Cyprus	806,000	President Tassos Papadopoulos; (Turkish Republic of Northern Cyprus: President Mehmet Ali Talat)	pound (0.46 = $1)	1,143	5,673
Egypt	76,346,000	President Mohammed Hosni Mubarak; Prime Minister Ahmed Nazif	pound (5.77 = $1)	11,000	19,210
Iran	68,899,000	Supreme Leader Ayatollah Ali Khamenei; President Mahmud Ahmadinejad	rial (9,015.00 = $1)	38,790	31,300
Iraq	27,253,000	President Jalal Talabani; Prime Minister Ibrahim al-Jafari	new dinar (1,474.63 = $1)	10,100	9,900
Israel	6,797,000	President Moshe Katzav; Prime Minister Ariel Sharon	shekel (4.50 = $1)	34,410	36,840
Jordan	5,870,000	King Abdullah II; Prime Minister Marouf al-Bakhit	dinar (0.71 = $1)	3,200	7,600
Kuwait	2,740,000	Emir Jabir al-Ahmad al-Jabir al-Sabah; Prime Minister Sabah al-Ahmad al-Jabir al-Sabah	dinar (0.29 = $1)	27,420	11,120
Lebanon	3,808,000	President Emile Lahoud; Prime Minister Fouad Siniora	pound (1,507.40 = $1)	1,783	8,162
Oman	2,826,000	Sultan and Prime Minister Qaboos bin Said	rial (0.39 = $1)	13,140	6,373
Qatar	636,000	Emir Hamad bin Khalifa al-Thani; Prime Minister Abdallah bin Khalifa al-Thani	riyal (3.64 = $1)	15,000	6,150
Saudi Arabia	26,292,000	King & Prime Minister Abdallah ibn Abd al-Aziz Al Saud	riyal (3.75 = $1)	113,000	36,210
Sudan	35,667,000	President Umar Hasan Ahmad al-Bashir	dinar (250.72 = $1) pound (2,507.20 = $1)	3,395	3,496
Syria	19,064,000	President Bashar al-Assad; Prime Minister Mohammed al-Otari	pound (52.21 = $1)	6,086	5,042
Turkey	74,204,000	President Ahmet Necdet Sezer; Prime Minister Recep Tayyip Erdogan	new lira (1.34 = $1)	69,460	94,500
United Arab Emirates	4,318,000	President Khalifa bin Zayed al-Nahyan; Prime Minister Maktum bin Rashid al-Maktum	dirham (3.67 = $1)	69,480	45,600
Yemen	21,426,000	President Ali Abdullah Saleh; Prime Minister Abd al-Qadir Ba Jamal	rial (183.10 = $1)	4,468	3,734

*Exchange rates as of Sept. 9, 2005, or latest available data.
[†]Latest available data.

March 2003 to mid-December 2005, more than 2,100 U.S. soldiers have died and 15,900 others have been wounded. More than 800 U.S. troops died in Iraq in 2005. The estimated number of Iraqis killed during the war ranged from 29,000 to 48,000.

Iran's new hardline president. On June 24, Mahmoud Ahmadinejad was elected president of Iran with 61.7 percent of the vote. The new administration replaced thousands of officials at all levels of government with hardline supporters.

In a September address to the UN General Assembly, President Ahmadinejad stated categorically that Iran had an "inalienable right" to produce nuclear fuel for the generation of energy. In October, President Ahmadinejad called for Israel to be "wiped off the map," and in December he denied the existence of the *Holocaust,* the systematic murder of millions of Jews and others by the Nazis during World War II (1939-1945). ■ Marius Deeb

See also **Iraq; People in the news** (Mahmoud Ahmadinejad); **Terrorism;** the various Middle East country articles.

Mining. See **Energy Supply.**

Moldova. Tensions over Moldova's breakaway Trans-Dniester region continued throughout 2005, with parliamentary elections on March 6 reflecting the ongoing conflict. Russia's support for Trans-Dniesterian independence led the ruling Moldovan Communist Party (PCM) and its leader, President Vladimir Voronin, to adopt an anti-Russian, pro-Western platform.

The PCM retained a majority with 46.1 percent of the popular vote, taking 56 of the 101 parliamentary seats. The pro-Russian Democratic Bloc of Moldova (BMD) took 34 seats, while the Christian Democratic People's Party (PPCD) won 11 seats. Twelve parties did not reach the required 6 percent threshold for representation.

Observers from the United States and from the Organization for Security and Cooperation in Europe (OSCE), a Vienna-based regional security organization with 55 participating nations, judged the election to be free from serious abuses but expressed concern over media bias favoring the PCM during the campaign. Eight BMD members split off to form the Democratic Party on March 24, prior to the presidential election. Voronin won the presidency again on April 4, receiving 75 of the 101 parliamentary votes.   ■ Juliet Johnson

See also **Europe; Russia: A Special Report.**

Monaco. See Europe.

Mongolia. See Asia.

Montreal. Mayor Gérald Tremblay easily won a second term as mayor of Montreal on Nov. 6, 2005. His main rival was Pierre Bourque, the former two-term head of the city council whom Tremblay defeated in the 2001 municipal elections. Bourque unsuccessfully sought a full judicial recount after claiming the new electronic vote-counting system rejected as many as 45,000 ballots. (He received slightly more than 152,500 votes, compared with Tremblay's more than 227,000.)

Olympic Games. City officials in 2005 discussed the possibility of bidding to once again host the Olympic Games. Buoyed by the success of the World swimming Championships, which took place in the city in July, Tremblay suggested that Montreal enter the competition—along with some 20 other cities around the globe—for the right to hold the 2016 Summer Games. The city had previously hosted the 1976 Summer Games.

Detractors pointed out that Montreal had taken 30 years to pay off what amounted to $2.6 billion in capital and interest for the 1976 games. (All amounts are in Canadian dollars.) The original price tag to stage the event had been $922 million. Another $462 million subsequently was spent in capital expenditures on the Olympic Stadium and surrounding installations.

The swimming championships were not without controversy. Montreal won the rights to the competition in 2001. However, in January 2005, the world aquatics governing body, Fédération Internationale de Natation (FINA), stripped the city of the privilege because local organizers failed to guarantee sufficient funding. Tremblay flew to a special FINA meeting in Frankfurt, Germany, and resecured the competition. Canada won a record 10 medals at the championships, including 2 gold medals for local diver Alexandre Despatie.

The fates of several Montreal hospitals were decided in 2005. On March 24, Quebec Premier Jean Charest ended decades of debate when he revealed that a new $1.1-billion French-language superhospital will be built on the site of the existing downtown Montreal St. Luc Hospital. The teaching hospital was to be known as the Centre Hospitalier de l'Université de Montréal (CHUM). Construction was to begin in 2006, and CHUM was scheduled to be completed in 2011.

Work was also scheduled to begin in mid-2006 on the McGill University Health Centre (MUHC), the $1.1-billion English-language counterpart to the CHUM. MUHC, which will be built in western Montreal, will replace five current downtown hospitals: Montreal Chest, Montreal Children's, Montreal General, Montreal Neurological, and Royal Victoria. Both superhospitals were to feature state-of-the-art research facilities.

On July 5, 2005, North American delegates to a Shriners annual convention in Baltimore voted by the slimmest margin—50.1 percent—to allow their 80-year-old children's hospital to remain in Montreal. (The Shrine of North America is a fraternal organization based in Tampa, Florida.) A lobbying effort had been underway for the past five years to move the Shriner's Hospital for Children to southwestern Ontario, where the city of London was being considered as a possible location.

New casino complex. Loto-Québec, the provincial government agency responsible for lotteries and gaming, announced on June 22 plans for a proposed new $1.2-billion waterfront casino and entertainment complex in Montreal. The project called for a 20-story building housing a casino, concert hall, and hotel. A monorail was to link the sprawling site with the downtown. The facility was to replace the current Montreal Casino, located on an island in the middle of the St. Lawrence River.

Presidents Cup. Canadian golfer Mike Weir, the 2003 Masters champion, announced on Aug. 15, 2005, that the coveted Presidents Cup matches will be played for the first time at the Royal Montreal Golf Club in 2007. The Presidents Cup, which is held every other year, between Ryder Cup years, is played by United States golfers against international, non-European players.   ■ Mike King

See also **Canada; City.**

Motion pictures in 2005 proved to be far less controversial than the films of 2004. No release in 2005 stirred public debate like *The Passion of the Christ* or Michael Moore's *Fahrenheit 9/11,* a 2004 documentary that was highly critical of the administration of United States President George W. Bush. By contrast, the top documentary of 2005, Luc Jacquet's *March of the Penguins,* was a heart-warming study of the migration of emperor penguins, and their mating and chick-rearing rituals.

Summer box office receipts—covering the period from Memorial Day to Labor Day—grossed $3.6 billion in 2005, down 8.5 percent from the same period in 2004. Reasons for the decline included the high price of tickets and concessions as well as poor critical reception of many films. Still, some summer entertainments proved buoyant. The strong worldwide gross of *Mr. and Mrs. Smith* was deemed a reflection of tabloid interest in its stars, Brad Pitt and Angelina Jolie. Critics were favorably disposed to Steven Spielberg's remake of *War of the Worlds,* but its popularity was also thought to reflect a media blitz prompted by the controversial public outbursts of its star, Tom Cruise. *Star Wars: Episode III—Revenge of the Sith,* the final entry in George Lucas's popular series of science-fiction epics, proved to be the summer's biggest hit.

Fall and winter releases showed a definite upswing in quality and moviegoing interest. Among the most eagerly awaited year-end films was Peter Jackson's remake of *King Kong.* High expectations were met by the giant ape saga starring Adrien Brody, Naomi Watts, and Jack Black in roles originated in 1933 by Bruce Cabot, Fay Wray, and Robert Armstrong. Expectations were equally high for an adaptation of C. S. Lewis's *The Chronicles of Narnia: The Lion, The Witch, and The Wardrobe,* which drew large family audiences when it opened in December.

Ang Lee's *Brokeback Mountain* garned high critical praise when it opened in December. The film starred Heath Ledger and Jake Gyllenhaal as two cowboys whose love for each other endures through several decades. *Brokeback Mountain* expanded director Lee's broad range, which had included such disparate films as *Crouching Tiger, Hidden Dragon; The Ice Storm; The Hulk;* and *Sense and Sensibility.*

Terry Gilliam's *The Brothers Grimm* starred Heath Ledger and Matt Damon as Jacob and Wilhelm Grimm. In Gilliam's film, instead of being famed folklorists, the brothers are con men who fool innocent villagers into believing they are being cursed, only to be recruited to break an actual curse.

Woody Allen's *Match Point* brought the idiosyncratic director his best reviews in years. Allen changed from his usual Manhattan locale, placing this story of complicated man/woman relationships in London. Scarlett Johansson, Jonathan Rhys-Meyers, and Emily Mortimer won praise for their performances. Niki Caro's *North Country* featured Charlize Theron as a female miner making a stand against sexual harrassment.

Thomas Bezucha's *The Family Stone,* a family-reunion comedy-drama with an ensemble cast

ACADEMY AWARD WINNERS IN 2005

The following winners of the 2004 Academy Awards were announced in February 2005:

Best Picture, *Million Dollar Baby*

Best Actor, Jamie Foxx, *Ray*

Best Actress, Hilary Swank, *Million Dollar Baby*

Best Supporting Actor, Morgan Freeman, *Million Dollar Baby*

Best Supporting Actress, Cate Blanchett, *The Aviator*

Best Director, Clint Eastwood, *Million Dollar Baby*

Best Original Screenplay, Charlie Kaufman, Michel Gondry, and Pierre Bismuth, *Eternal Sunshine of the Spotless Mind*

Best Screenplay Adaptation, Alexander Payne and Jim Taylor, *Sideways*

Best Animated Feature, Brad Bird, *The Incredibles*

Best Cinematography, Robert Richardson, *The Aviator*

Best Film Editing, Thelma Schoonmaker, *The Aviator*

Best Original Score, Jan A. P. Kaczmarek, *Finding Neverland*

Best Original Song, Jorge Drexler, "Al Otro Lado Del Río" from *The Motorcycle Diaries*

Best Foreign-Language Film, *The Sea Inside* (Spain)

Best Art Direction, Dante Ferretti and Francesca Lo Schiavo, *The Aviator*

Best Costume Design, Sandy Powell, *The Aviator*

Best Sound Mixing, Scott Millan, Greg Orloff, Bob Beemer, and Steve Cantamessa, *Ray*

Best Sound Editing, Michael Silvers and Randy Thorn, *The Incredibles*

Best Makeup, Valli O'Reilly and Bill Corso, *Lemony Snicket's A Series of Unfortunate Events*

Best Visual Effects, *Spider-Man 2*

Best Animated Short Film, *Ryan*

Best Live-Action Short Film, *Wasp*

Best Feature Documentary, *Born Into Brothels*

Best Short Subject Documentary, *Mighty Times: The Children's March*

including Luke Wilson, Rachel McAdams, Diane Keaton, and Sarah Jessica Parker created an enthusiastic buzz. A new version of Jane Austen's *Pride & Prejudice,* directed by Joe Wright and starring Keira Knightley as Elizabeth Bennett, was well received.

Sam Mendes, whose previous films included *American Beauty* and *Road to Perdition,* offered *Jarhead* in fall 2005. The film featured Jake Gyllenhaal as a young man who joins the U.S. Marines and is sent to Kuwait during the Persian Gulf War of 1991. Stephen Gaghan's *Syriana,* starring George Clooney as a CIA agent who uncovers an international web of intrigue centering around the oil industry, received some of the highest critical reviews of the year.

Steven Spielberg's taut thriller *Munich,* released in late December, told the story of 11 Israeli atheletes who were kidnapped and murdered by Palestinian militants during the 1972 Olympic Games. Director Rob Marshall's adaptation of Arthur Golden's novel *Memoirs of a Geisha* featured an international cast and starred Chinese actress Ziyi Zhang as a young woman who becomes one of Japan's most famous *geisha* (a Japanese woman trained to entertain men).

Graphic novels served as source material for several notable motion pictures in 2005. Robert Rodriguez and graphic novelist Frank Miller teamed up for *Sin City,* an adaptation of several of Miller's graphic novels of the same name. The film, which featured a sequence guest-directed by Quentin Tarantino, boasted an all-star cast including Bruce Willis, Jessica Alba, Clive Owen, Rosario Dawson, Benicio Del Toro, Brittany Murphy, and Mickey Rourke. The film, shot entirely on digital sets, received praise for its dark noir feel and intense visual imagery.

Iconoclastic director David Cronenberg had one of his most successful and accessible films with his adaptation of John Wagner and Vince Locke's graphic novel *A History of Violence.* The film starred Viggo Mortensen as a man working in a small-town diner who commits murder in self-defense. With strong performances from Maria Bello, William Hurt, and Ed Harris, the film explored the links between sex and violence and the deception of appearances.

Film biographies, which enjoyed a renaissance in 2004 with *Ray* and *The Aviator,* remained in vogue in 2005. Philip Seymour Hoffman gave what was arguably the most talked-about performance of 2005 as author Truman Capote in Bennett Miller's *Capote.* The film traced Capote's research and writing of the true-crime classic *In Cold Blood,* as well as his relationship with one of the condemned killers. Critics noted that Hoffman captured Capote's physical presence as well as his personal demons of neediness and narcissism.

Good Night, and Good Luck, directed by George Clooney and starring David Strathairn as legendary newscaster Edward R. Murrow, drew kudos from critics and audiences. The film concentrated on Murrow's confrontations with Senator Joseph McCarthy, whose political extremism ruined the careers of many left-of-center entertainers during the 1950's. Joaquin Phoenix and Reese Witherspoon portrayed Johnny and June Carter Cash in James Mangold's *Walk the Line.* Although the plot follows an outline similar to *Ray,* the two stars' performances received accolades.

Several smaller-profile films were well received by critics in 2005. In Jim Jarmusch's *Broken Flowers,* Bill Murray portrayed a middle-aged man who learns that he may have a son about whom he had never known. He embarks on a journey to visit his ex-girlfriends and discover the truth. Performance artist and author Miranda July directed *Me and You and Everyone We Know,* about a single father, trying to raise two sons, who meets a video artist who runs a shuttle service for the elderly. In Gus Van Sant's *Last Days,* Michael Pitt played a Kurt Cobain-like rock star enduring a complete mental and emotional collapse.

A new Bond. Among the most publicized pop-culture stories of 2005 was the naming of British actor Daniel Craig as successor to the role of globe-trotting playboy superspy James Bond. Craig will follow in the footsteps of Sean Connery, George Lazenby, Roger Moore, Timothy Dalton, and Pierce Brosnan in playing Agent 007. Craig will be seen in 2006 in *Casino Royale,* an earlier version of which, released in 1967 and starring David Niven as Bond, was a spoof of the spy film genre. Craig is best remembered for the well-received 2004 gangster film *Layer Cake.*

Documentaries. Aside from *March of the Penguins,* a number of other documentaries were well received by critics in 2005. German director Werner Herzog showed a darker side of nature in *Grizzly Man* than that depicted in *March of the Penguins. Grizzly Man* chronicled the life of Timothy Treadwell, an amateur naturalist who moved to Alaska to study grizzly bears, only to be eaten alive by his subjects.

Murderball followed the fast-paced and violent world of wheelchair rugby. *Occupation: Dreamland* profiled the U.S. Army's 82nd Airborne as it occupied the Iraqi city of Fallujah during 2004.

Several music documentaries received positive reviews in 2005. *Touch the Sound* profiled Evelyn Glennie, a Scottish percussionist who lost most of her hearing in her early teen-age years, while *dErailRoaDed* described the career of schizophrenic outsider musician Larry "Wild

Jamie Foxx won the Academy Award for best actor for his portrayal of singer Ray Charles in *Ray.* The film detailed Charles's rise to fame against such odds as his loss of eyesight at an early age and his addiction to drugs.

The 2005 Academy Awards recognized two biographical films as well as an emotionally charged boxing drama.

Leonardo DiCaprio (above left) portrays eccentric millionaire Howard Hughes in Martin Scorsese's *The Aviator.* Cate Blanchett (above right) won an Academy Award for best supporting actress for her portrayal of actress Katharine Hepburn. The film received a total of five Academy Awards.

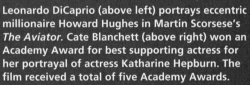

Hilary Swank portrays boxer Maggie Fitzgerald in *Million Dollar Baby*, for which she won the Academy Award for best actress. Morgan Freeman (center) won the Academy Award for best supporting actor, and Clint Eastwood (far left), who both acted in and directed the film, won the Academy Award for best director. The film won a total of four Academy Awards.

Man" Fischer. *Rock School* followed Paul Green, a music teacher who, instead of trying to connect with children through classical music, teaches his pupils classic rock. The film followed Green's students as they prepared to participate in a Frank Zappa music festival in Germany.

Foreign films. By mid-September 2005, Australian box-office revenues were down 14 percent from 2004's figures. Yet Irish moviegoing was on the rise, with the average citizen attending movies more than four times a year. One well-received Irish film in 2005 was Neil Jordan's *Breakfast on Pluto*. The film related the saga of a small-town Irish youth, played by Cillian Murphy, who becomes a popular transvestite entertainer in London.

German audiences showed enthusiasm for Marc Rothemund's *Sophie Scholl—The Final Days,* in which Julia Jentsch received praise as a young anti-Nazi dissident. *Go for Zucker!,* about a pool shark and his estranged brother trying to sort out their mother's will, was also popular.

Korean films that drew large homeland audiences included *Running Boy* (also called *Marathon*), about an autistic youth who develops running skills; Chu Chang-min's *Mapado,* a comedy about two men who track a thief to an island populated by elderly women; Park Chan-Wook's offbeat action drama *Sympathy for Lady Vengeance;* and the murder mystery *The Big Scene.*

Russia saw increased moviegoing revenues, with Alexei Sidorov's fight film *Shadow Boxing* among the champions. Dzhanik Faiziyev's *Turkish Gambit,* a detective story set in the 1877 Russian-Turkish war, was hugely successful, as was Fyodor Bondarchuk's *Company 9,* about Russian soldiers fighting in the Russian war with Afghanistan in the late 1980's.

In Colombia, Emilio Maille's directorial debut *Rosario Tijeras* created a sensation with its story of two teens and a female assassin who become involved in the underground of the city of Medellin. In Peru, Eduardo Schuldt's animated *Pirates in Callao* (also known as *Pirates of the Pacific*), based on a schoolroom classic about a young boy who travels back in time to the 1600's, was South America's first 3-D feature.

Young Spanish directors won acclaim from critics and moviegoers. Roberto Santiago's *The Longest Penalty in the World,* Benito Zambrano's *Habana Blues,* Jesus Ponce's *15 Days with You,* Vicente Penarrocha's *Body Confusion,* and Santi Amodeo's *Astronauts* were among the youth-oriented fare favorably received. ■ Philip Wuntch

See also **Literature: A Special Report; People in the News** (Jamie Foxx).

Mozambique. See Africa.

Music. See Classical music; Popular music.

Myanmar. The government of Myanmar began on Nov. 6, 2005, to move several key ministries to Pyinmana, an isolated location north of the long-time capital, Yangon. Government officials described Pyinmana as a "strategic location."

Under pressure from other members of the Association of Southeast Asian Nations (ASEAN), Myanmar agreed on July 26 to pass up in 2006 its turn to serve as chair of the 10-nation organization. The European Union (EU) and the United States had informed ASEAN that they would not attend its meetings, in which the EU and United States have cooperative roles, while Myanmar headed it. The EU and the United States condemned human rights abuses in Myanmar; its military rulers' refusal to honor election results; and many other policies.

Three bombs exploded in Yangon on May 7, 2005, killing 19 people and leaving some 160 others wounded. The blasts, which occurred within 10 minutes of each other, took place at two shopping malls and in a convention center. Myanmar's government implied that the U.S. government ordered the bombings. International affairs experts speculated that the bombings were a result of conflicts within the ruling military forces.

■ Henry S. Bradsher

See also **Asia.**

Namibia. See Africa.

Nauru. See Pacific Islands.

Nepal. King Gyanendra Bir Bikram Shah Dev, who had suspended constitutional government in 2002, tightened his control over Nepal by declaring a state of emergency on Feb. 1, 2005. He dismissed the ruling coalition government and suspended certain constitutionally guaranteed civil liberties, including free expression and assembly. The ousted prime minister, Sher Bahadur Deuba, whom Gyanendra had appointed in 2004, was later sentenced to two years in jail on a corruption charge.

Gyanendra complained that the government had made no progress toward opening peace talks with Maoist rebels, whose guerrilla war had cost some 12,000 lives since 1996. The rebels refused, however, to negotiate with the royal government that they were trying to destroy.

Demonstrations in Kathmandu, the capital, against Gyanendra's rule in September 2005 led to violence by police. Facing such protests as well as international criticism, the king promised he would hold parliamentary elections before April 2007. Nepal's major political parties forged an alliance with the Maoists on Nov. 22, 2005, to boycott any elections conducted by the royal government.

Maoist rebels announced a three-month ceasefire on September 3. However, occasional skirmishes continued. ■ Henry S. Bradsher

See also **Asia; Disasters.**

Netherlands. The centrist government of Jan Peter Balkenende confronted two major challenges to its policies in 2005. The Dutch electorate rejected a constitution for the European Union (EU), and the people began to rethink the traditional Dutch model for integrating a sizable immigrant and minority population.

The referendum on the EU constitution, held on June 1, was rejected by 62 percent of voters. Because most mainstream politicians had supported the constitution, policy analysts interpreted the "no" vote as a reflection of a general European distrust of the current political establishment. According to political analysts, "no" voters also worried about the rapid expansion of the bloc in 2004 and the prospect of beginning accession negotiations with Turkey, a poor, predominantly Muslim nation.

Political experts suggested that the primary reasons for the rejection of the constitution were a general fear that a stronger EU would increase inflation (the introduction of the euro is largely seen to have increased prices) and would interfere with socially liberal Dutch policies, such as gay marriage, a relaxed attitude toward drug use, and *euthanasia* (helping or allowing people to die).

Immigration. Experts noted that another reason for the rejection was a general fear that the Netherlands would lose control over its immigration policy. After decades of official multiculturalism, the murder of filmmaker Theo van Gogh by a native-born Islamic extremist in 2004 and the trial of members of a terrorist cell in Rotterdam in 2005 had begun to change the political landscape in the Netherlands. Both events caused many mainstream politicians and even academics to rethink their country's commitment to tolerance and multiculturalism. A 2005 report from a Dutch intelligence agency that as many as 50,000 of the country's nearly 1 million Muslims could be classified as extremist also affected attitudes.

Ballot commission members count votes in a Dutch referendum on a constitution for the European Union at the Duifkerk, a historical landmark in Amsterdam, on June 1, 2005. Dutch voters rejected the constitution, as French voters had before them, effectively tabling the charter.

Past policies sought to preseve minority identities and cultures were celebrated as recognizing differences. By 2005, the same policies were frequently characterized as a form of neglect and acceptance of unemployment and poverty among Muslim immigrants. In 2005, the Dutch parliament adopted antiterrorism laws that were widely considered to be the strictest in Europe.

The Dutch economy grew by only 0.5 percent in 2005, down from 1.7 percent in 2004. In September 2005, the government presented its 2006 budget, which called for 2 billion euros ($2.33 billion) in tax cuts in an attempt to increase private consumption and speed up the economy. ■ Jeffrey Kopstein

See also **Europe.**

New Brunswick. See **Canadian provinces.**

New York City Mayor Michael R. Bloomberg won reelection to a second term on Nov. 8, 2005, by a wide margin over his underfunded Democratic foe, former Bronx Borough President Fernando Ferrer. The billionaire mayor, who once described himself as a "wealthy Democrat," became a Republican shortly before the 2001 election, which he won narrowly. Before the 2005 election, he spent more than $70 million of his own money on the campaign.

Bloomberg's overwhelming victory, coupled with the two terms of his predecessor, Rudolph W. Giuliani, gave Republicans four consecutive mayoral wins for the first time in city history. During this period, more registered Democrats than Republicans lived in the city.

Bloomberg ran on a campaign of declining crime rates and educational reform. In 2002, he had replaced the Board of Education with what he called a Department of Education. He had installed as its chancellor Joel I. Klein, a former official with the United States Department of Justice who had attended school in New York City.

On June 1, 2005, Bloomberg announced that more than 50 percent of students in the third, fifth, sixth, and seventh grades had passed key reading and math exams, compared with 40 percent in reading and 35 percent in math in 2002. "We're on the right track," Bloomberg declared.

District attorney race. Manhattan District Attorney Robert M. Morgenthau, an iconic figure in law enforcement for more than three decades, overcame his first serious opposition in at least 20 years in the Democratic primary election on Sept. 13, 2005. The 86-year-old Morgenthau—son of former President Franklin D. Roosevelt's Treasury Secretary Henry Morgenthau, Jr., childhood friend of former President John F. Kennedy, and model for fictional District Attorney Adam Schiff on TV's "Law and Order"—defeated former New

York Supreme Court Judge Leslie Crocker Snyder. Morgenthau was known for strenuously opposing the death penalty and prosecuting such business associates as Bermuda-based Tyco International Ltd.'s chief executive L. Dennis Kozlowski.

Subway terror hoax. A terror plot that federal officials suspected was planned in Iraq caused New York City police to increase security on the city's vast transit system on October 6. Police officers even searched the bags of some of the system's 4 million daily riders.

On October 10, investigators questioned the reliability of the Iraq intelligence and rescinded the alert. Tension mounted after U.S. Department of Homeland Security employees suggested that New York officials had overreacted.

Christo and Jeanne-Claude's "The Gates: A Project for New York" brings color to the city's famed Central Park in late February. The art project involved hanging saffron-colored banners from 7,500 "gates" along 23 miles (37 kilometers) of the park's pedestrian pathways. The biggest art project in New York history, "The Gates" drew thousands of art lovers to the city during the 16-day run.

Proposed Olympics stadiums. New York City's 11-year quest for the 2012 Summer Olympics Games ended in July 2005, when the International Olympic Committee meeting in Singapore awarded the games to London. Problems arose a month earlier when the New York state financing board members defeated a bid for a new, $2-billion Olympic stadium on Manhattan's West Side, amid concerns that its construction would hamper efforts to redevelop lower Manhattan in the wake of the terrorist attack on Sept. 11, 2001. The stadium would have been the permanent home for the New York Jets. Instead, the Jets and their rivals, the Giants, decided to fund the building of a new, jointly owned stadium in New Jersey.

In a last-minute scramble for a substitute Olympics venue, the mayor and the New York Mets agreed on the construction of a new, $600-million stadium in Queens that would have been converted for the Olympics. The Mets had long sought financial support for a new ballpark next to Shea Stadium, the team's home for 41 years.

Public transportation. The Metropolitan Transportation Authority approved in November 2005 almost $3 billion for the construction of a Second Avenue subway line. The idea for the line was conceived in 1920 but, over the years, had been abandoned and revisited numerous times.

On Dec. 20, some 33,000 transit workers went on strike, completely shutting down the city's public transportation system.　■ Owen Moritz

See **Elections; People in the News** (Christo).

New Zealand. Prime Minister Helen Clark secured a record third term in September 2005 after her Labour Party edged out the rival National Party in a parliamentary election. Clark's Labour-Progressive coalition took 51 seats in the 121-seat Parliament against National's 48 seats. Labour was forced into a coalition agreement with two minor parties, New Zealand First (seven seats) and United Future (three seats), to control the voting majority in Parliament. The resurgent National Party nearly doubled its share of the vote since the last parliamentary election in 2002.

As part of the coalition agreement in 2005, the New Zealand First and United Future parties demanded appointments to ministerial posts. Peter Dunne, who led United Future, was appointed revenue minister, and the leader of the populist New Zealand First, Winston Peters, was appointed minister of foreign affairs. Peters's opposition to New Zealand's immigration policy, particularly his views against Asian migration, provoked controversy within New Zealand and abroad. Clark reassured foreign governments in November that Peters would follow foreign policies set by the government.

The election was a triumph for the newly formed Maori Party, which won four of the seven seats reserved for people of Maori descent. All four seats were previously held by Labour. The Maori Party emerged following the passage of the Foreshore and Seabed Act in 2004, which granted ownership of the country's shorelines and seabeds to the government. The law incensed Maori activists, who said it violated the Treaty of Waitangi, the 1840 document affirming Maori land rights and giving the United Kingdom sovereignty over New Zealand.

Race relations. Rudolfo Stavenhagen, a representative of the United Nations (UN) Human Rights Commission, investigated the Foreshore and Seabed Act in 2005 after the UN's Committee on the Elimination of Racial Discrimination ruled the act discriminatory. Stavenhagen described race relations in New Zealand as "unequal" but "favorable."

Economy. The amount of consumer debt rose to unprecedented levels in 2005, primarily due to increased demand for residential mortgages. In an effort to slow the housing boom, New Zealand's principal economic regulatory organization, the Reserve Bank, raised interest rates to 7 percent.

Deaths. Former Prime Minister David Lange died in August at age 63. Rod Donald, coleader of the Green Party, died in November at age 48.

■ Gavin Ellis

See also **Pacific Islands.**

Newfoundland. See Canadian provinces.

NEWS BYTES

Selected news from 2005:

Explosive anniversary. A reenactment on June 28 of the Battle of Trafalgar celebrated the 200th anniversary of the definitive victory of the British Royal Navy over a joint French and Spanish fleet. In the original battle, which took place on Oct. 21, 1805, the Royal Navy, commanded by Horatio Nelson, defeated French and Spanish ships under the control of French Emperor Napoleon Bonaparte. The victory gave the United Kingdom (then Great Britain) undisputed control of the seas for more than 100 years.

For the reenactment, which took place off the coast of Portsmouth, England, 17 tall ships from 5 countries held a mock battle, demonstrating how a sea battle would have been fought in 1805. Instead of an exact historical reenactment, the battle featured two unnamed navies, one red and one blue. The replica 1700's frigate *Grand Turk* played the part of Nelson's ship, HMS *Victory*.

In addition to watching the reenactment, Queen Elizabeth II inspected a visiting fleet of some 170 ships from 36 countries, including France, India, Nigeria, Pakistan, South Africa, Spain, and the United States. The celebration ended with a massive display of fireworks.

A record meltdown. Officials from New York City's Snapple Beverage Corporation attempted in June 2005 to break the Guinness record for the world's largest popsicle to coincide with the launch of its new kiwi-strawberry flavored drink. Using a freezer truck, Snapple shipped a 35,000-pound (15,875-kilogram) popsicle from a facility in Edison, New Jersey, to Manhattan. Officials used a giant crane to lift the popsicle into an upright position, but they quickly noticed that it had begun to melt. The giant treat covered 17th Street with pink goo, at which point Snapple officials decided to forego their attempt for the record. A crew of firefighters hosed down the streets to wash away the slippery residue before any serious injuries could take place.

Axum obelisk returned. In late April, an ancient Ethiopian artifact known as the Axum obelisk returned home after nearly 70

suffered in a lightning strike.

When the obelisk was removed from its original location in Ethiopia in 1937, it was transported by road to the seaport at Massawa. In order to be returned, the monument was cut into three 60-ton (54-metric ton) pieces and transported by plane. Axum's airstrip had to be upgraded in order to accommodate the Antonov 124 airplane, which is one of only two types of aircraft large enough to carry the sections.

Scopes Trial photos uncovered. A volunteer at the Smithsonian Institution in Washington, D.C., discovered 66 previously unpublished negatives from the famed Scopes Monkey Trial. John Scopes, a teacher in Dayton, Tennessee, was prosecuted in 1925 for violating a state law that forbade teaching the theory of evolution. The trial drew two high-profile figures: famed defense attorney Clarence Darrow and orator and three-time presidential candidate William Jennings Bryan, who argued for a literal interpretation of the Bible in his prosecution of the case. The fame of the two men brought the trial international attention. The Tennessee Supreme Court found Scopes not guilty on a technicality, avoiding issuing a ruling

years in captivity. The 1,700-year-old, 78-foot (24-meter) monument commemorates Ethiopia's adoption of Christianity in the mid-300's under the Emperor Ezana and is viewed as a symbol of national identity by most Ethiopians.

Italian troops, then occupying Ethiopia, shipped the obelisk to Rome in 1937 to celebrate dictator Benito Mussolini's 15th year in power. Despite a 1947 United Nations agreement that Italy would return the obelisk, it remained near Rome's Circus Maximus until it was dismantled in 2003 due to damage it had

Clarence Darrow (standing at right) interrogates William Jennings Bryan (seated) during the famed Scopes trial on July 20, 1925. A volunteer at the Smithsonian Institution in Washington, D.C., in 2005 discovered previously unknown photographs of the two famed orators.

on evolution. The Scopes trial was later dramatized in the play and film *Inherit the Wind*.

The newly discovered negatives include shots of Scopes, as well as one of Darrow questioning Bryan. The Smithsonian posted several of the photographs on its Web site, and officials discussed the possibility of creating a small exhibit based on the negatives.

Lost waterfall rediscovered. Rangers at Whiskeytown National Recreation Area in northern California announced in August 2005 the discovery of a waterfall along Crystal Creek that had been previously unknown to Park Service rangers and staff. Wildlife biologist and park ranger Russ Weatherbee is credited with the find.

Weatherbee originally began looking for the falls when he discovered a logging map from the 1960's that gave a location for Whiskeytown Falls, a feature absent from more recent maps. Weatherbee went looking for the falls but found nothing. In 2003, he was examining an aerial photograph of the area and noticed a section of the creek that featured a rapid drop in elevation. Using those photos, he located the 300-foot (91-meter)

A ranger at Whiskeytown National Recreation Area in northern California stands at the base of a waterfall that was rediscovered in August. Park officials were unsure how a 300-foot (91-meter) waterfall that once appeared on maps could have been lost for decades.

In July, the granite face of Thomas Jefferson at Mount Rushmore National Memorial in South Dakota gets its very first bath. A German cleaning company used hot water to clean grime and lichens from the presidential faces to prevent future cracking.

waterfall, which turned out to be more than 1 mile (1.6 kilometers) away from the spot noted on the logging map.

The Park Service completed a trail to the lower section of the falls in September 2005 and expected to have a trail to the upper portion completed by late summer 2006.

Presidential facelift. Mount Rushmore National Memorial got its very first bath in July 2005. The memorial, which is located in the Black Hills National Forest in South Dakota, features giant carvings of the faces of George Washington, Thomas Jefferson, Abraham Lincoln, and Theodore Roosevelt. The 608-foot- (185-meter-) tall sculptures are carved from the granite mountainside.

The memorial was unveiled in 1941. Although the sculpture is checked every year for cracks, it had never been cleaned. Park officials were concerned that *lichens* (plantlike organisms) could cause irreparable damage to the sculptures. Lichens anchor themselves with fun-

gal strands that burrow into rock. Moisture becomes trapped in the tiny holes left when the lichens die. During the winter months, this moisture freezes and expands, causing cracking. Some experts feared that these holes could, over long periods of time, lead to features breaking off of the sculptures.

No chemicals were used to clean the dirt, grime, and lichens from the presidential faces. Instead, the cleaning crew used highly pressurized hot water. Park rangers assisted a German cleaning company that has cleaned other major monuments around the world, including the Statue of Liberty in New York City.

Around the world in 2¾ days. Millionaire adventurer Steve Fossett in March 2005 became the first person to fly an airplane around the globe solo nonstop, without refueling. His specially designed airplane, the Virgin GlobalFlyer, had a 114-foot (35-meter) wingspan. Fossett took off from Salina, Kansas, on March 1. He flew east, crossing the Atlantic Ocean, North Africa, Asia, and the Pacific Ocean during the trip. Fossett subsisted on protein milk shakes.

The journey was not without its problems. Shortly after takeoff, the plane's navigation system partially broke down, leaving Fossett effectively flying blind and relying on directions from mission control. Later, as he began to cross the

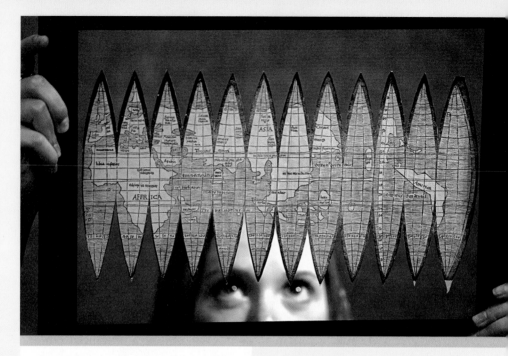

An employee at famed London auction house Christie's holds the first printed map to show America as well as the first to depict Earth as a globe. The map, printed in 1507, was sold for more than $940,000 on June 8.

Pacific, gauges revealed that the craft had unexpectedly lost 2,600 pounds (1,200 kilograms) of fuel. However, favorable tailwinds convinced Fossett to continue his journey, and he landed safely back in Salina on March 3.

Fossett has broken dozens of other aviation records. In June, he and a copilot re-created the first transatlantic airplane crossing, which took place in 1919. The duo flew from Newfoundland to Ireland in under 19 hours.

Sweet ride. In August 2005, a former Hollywood stuntman put the finishing touches on a replica Viking longship made from 15 million ice cream sticks and launched it in Amsterdam harbor. The 50-foot (15-meter) long ship took Robert McDonald and two friends two years to build. The project was sponsored by OLA/Unilever Ice Cream, which donated imperfect and recycled ice cream sticks for the project. Children around the world also collected and donated discarded sticks. McDonald, who runs the Sea Heart Foundation children's charity, ultimately hopes to sail the ship, which supports a crew of 25, across the Atlantic in the style of the Vikings.

Neither Ringo's home nor Strawberry Fields are forever. The children's home where future Beatle John Lennon played and that inspired him to write the song "Strawberry Fields Forever" closed in May. Strawberry Field, located in Lennon's hometown of Liverpool, England, was operated by The Salvation Army, an international Christian religious and charitable organization. A spokesperson for the Salvation Army said the center was closing because of the trend of placing children in foster care rather than in institutions.

The birthplace of Beatle Ringo Starr (born Richard Starkey) fared no better than Strawberry Field. The Victorian terrace house was among 460 houses the Liverpool City Council had marked for demolition. A campaign by Liverpool residents in July appeared to save many of the houses, including the former Beatle's birthplace, from the wrecking ball. In September, however, the council announced that, although the birthplaces of former Beatles John Lennon and Paul McCartney had earlier been preserved "because they spent a significant part of their lives in them," Starr's house was slated for demolition because he had only lived in it for three months.

Jazz auction. The first auction to feature only items relating to jazz music took place in February 2005 at Guernsey's in New York City. The auction featured 450 items from some of the giants of jazz, including an alto saxophone specially modified for Charlie Parker, as well as several of Parker's pocket watches, a Benny Goodman clarinet, a vibraphone owned by Lionel Hampton, one of Dizzy Gillespie's famous bent trumpets, a handwritten score for John Coltrane's classic "A Love Supreme," and the player piano from Coltrane's childhood home on which he first learned to play. Some less music-related items included one of Thelonious Monk's high school notebooks, which featured a book report on *A Tale of Two Cities*, as well as handwritten letters from a variety of artists.　■ S. Thomas Richardson

Osaka University's Hiroshi Ishiguro (right) stands beside a humanoid robot that he designed and exhibited at the Prototype Robot Exhibition in Nagakute, Japan, in June. The robot, which is covered in a skinlike substance and appears to breathe, served as a tour guide for expo visitors. Ishiguro noted that human beings found it easier to interact with a humanoid robot than a robot that looks too mechanical.

Newspaper. Two prestigious newspapers in the United States became embroiled in controversy in 2005 when it became known that two reporters had withheld from their editors information regarding issues of national security that had been leaked to them. Judith Miller, a reporter for *The New York Times,* was jailed on July 6 after she refused a federal judge's order to testify before a grand jury about the identity of a news source to whom she promised anonymity. She was released September 29 after agreeing to testify. According to Miller, she was then willing to testify because her source, I. Lewis Libby, chief of staff to U.S. Vice President Dick Cheney, offered her a personal waiver of her pledge of confidentiality. Libby had revealed to Miller the identity of Central Intelligence Agency (CIA) agent Valerie Plame, possibly violating a federal law against identifying government employees working undercover. Libby, who had previously testified to a grand jury that he had no role in leaking Plame's identity and had, in fact, learned her identity from a reporter, was indicted on charges of perjury on October 28.

Plame is the wife of diplomat Joseph C. Wilson IV, who had criticized the administration of President George W. Bush for manipulating intelligence reports to justify going to war in Iraq. The CIA sent Wilson to Niger in 2002 to investigate reports that yellowcake uranium was being sold to Saddam Hussein to build a nuclear weapon. Wilson found no evidence of such an operation and so informed the CIA, which relayed Wilson's findings to the Bush administration. Nevertheless, the administration continued to claim that Hussein was buying uranium from Niger. *The New York Times* on July 6, 2003, published a commentary written by Wilson stating these allegations. Soon after, Plame's identity as a CIA operative was leaked to the press. This series of events remained under investigation through 2005 by special prosecutor Patrick J. Fitzgerald.

On November 14, Bob Woodward, a prominent journalist with *The Washington Post,* testified before a grand jury in Washington, D.C., that a current or former member of the Bush administration, though not Libby, had informed Woodward of Plame's identity in 2003. He noted that he had received this information prior to the publication of a column by Robert D. Novak in the *Chicago Sun-Times* in which Plame's identity was made public. Woodward's testimony made it apparent that he was one of several journalists whom Bush administration officials had informed about Plame's role at the CIA. Like Miller, Woodward neither wrote about the revelation nor informed his editors at the newspaper of his knowledge, though he repeatedly denigrated Fitzgerald's investigation on television talk shows. Earlier in the year, Woodward had been in the news after the most famous confidential source in newspaper history, whom Woodward and fellow *Washington Post* reporter Carl Bernstein called "Deep Throat" during their reporting on the Watergate scandal of 1972 to 1974, was revealed in May 2005. W. Mark Felt, a retired FBI official, identified himself as the anonymous tipster.

Newspaper circulation underwent its biggest decline in nearly a decade in 2005. According to the Audit Bureau of Circulations, a trade group located in Schaumburg, Illinois, the combined sales of 814 daily newspapers in the United States decreased by 2.6 percent during the six-month period that ended September 30, compared with the same period in 2004.

New Orleans. On Aug. 30, 2005, flooding from Hurricane Katrina forced about 240 employees of the New Orleans *Times-Picayune,* the 35th largest daily newspaper in the United States, to abandon its office building and printing plant. The newspaper, which had a circulation of about 270,000 copies, updated its Web site from temporary offices to report the news of its stricken hometown. The paper resumed publishing on September 2 with 50,000 copies printed at *The Courier* in Houma, Louisiana. The *Times-Picayune's* printing presses were not damaged, and the paper resumed publishing from New Orleans on October 11.

Shuffling ownership. McLean, Virginia-based Gannett Company, Inc., the largest U.S. newspaper chain, sold *The Detroit News* to Denver, Colorado's MediaNews Group Inc. and bought the *Detroit Free Press* from San Jose-based communications company Knight Ridder Inc., in an unusual three-way deal on August 3. Gannett traded *The Idaho Statesman* in Boise, *The Bellingham* (Washington) *Herald*, and *The Olympian* in Olympia, Washington, to Knight Ridder in exchange for the *Tallahassee* (Florida) *Democrat*. The Detroit dailies continued to be published under a joint operating agreement, allowing rival newspapers to share costs and revenues while competing for news. Lee Enterprises of Davenport, Iowa, became the seventh largest U.S. newspaper chain in terms of circulation with the purchase, announced January 30, of Pulitzer, Inc., for $1.46 billion. Pulitzer consisted of the *St. Louis Post-Dispatch* and 13 other dailies. Executives at Knight Ridder announced on November 14 that they were considering selling the company's 32 daily newspapers after a major investor threatened to replace the Knight Ridder board.

Conrad Black, former chief executive of Hollinger International Inc., owner of the *Chicago Sun-Times* and other newspapers, appeared in federal court in Chicago on December 1 to face criminal charges of fraud. Black was accused of "looting" Hollinger of $400 million from 1997 to 2003. ■ Mark Fitzgerald

See also **People in the News** (Patrick Fitzgerald, I. Lewis Libby); **United States, Government of the.**

Nicaragua. An embattled President Enrique Bolaños Geyer overcame the threat of impeachment in 2005 with the help of the Organization of American States (OAS) and the United States government. During 2005, Bolaños's chief opponents in the Nicaraguan Congress—former President Daniel Ortega and allies of former President Arnoldo Aleman Lacayo—stripped the presidency of powers and initiated impeachment proceedings. Bolaños alleged that his political foes sought revenge for his role in obtaining a corruption conviction against Aleman in 2003.

The impasse was broken, analysts reported, when U.S. Deputy Secretary of State Robert Zoellick visited Managua, the capital, in October 2005 and threatened to withhold U.S. aid should Bolaños be impeached. Zoellick's visit followed an OAS mission to Nicaragua, which had laid the groundwork for a political settlement.

The Congress subsequently terminated impeachment proceedings and restored full presidential powers to Bolaños. Among those powers was control over armaments, a key concern of U.S. officials, who urged Bolaños to destroy thousands of Russian-made shoulder-launched missiles that could, if acquired by terrorists, be used against aircraft. ■ Nathan A. Haverstock

See also **Latin America.**

Niger. See Africa.

Nigeria. Figures released by Nigeria's Economic and Financial Crimes Commission (EFCC) on June 24, 2005, revealed that from independence from the United Kingdom in 1960 to restoration of civilian government in 1999, Nigeria's rulers embezzled or squandered $500 billion. The amount approximately matched the sum of all Western aid given to Africa between 1960 and 1997, international affairs experts noted.

In 2002, President Olusegun Obasanjo signed into law legislation creating the EFCC, which was designed to investigate corruption. International investors applauded the Obasanjo government's anticorruption efforts but noted that the EFCC and related legislation represented only a first step in rooting out corruption.

Constitutional conference. On Feb. 21, 2005, President Obasanjo launched a national conference to consider political reforms. The reforms included changes to the constitution, drafted under military rule and implemented when civilian government returned to the country in 1999. Political leaders in Nigeria had criticized the 1999 charter as undemocratic.

The conference, called the National Political Reform Conference, convened in multiple sessions between February and July 2005. Disagreements among the delegates led to bitter divisions, mainly along regional and ethnic lines.

One controversial proposal outlined a rotational presidency, intended to disperse presidential power among sections of the country. The most divisive issue, however, was how to allocate Nigeria's oil revenues. Under the existing system, states in the Niger Delta, where most of the oil currently is drilled, received 13 percent of oil revenues with the balance going to the federal government and other state governments. Delta state governors at the conference demanded up to 50 percent of revenues. The conference ended when they refused to lower their demands.

In July, President Obasanjo submitted to parliament recommendations endorsed by the conference delegates. Critics claimed that he was using the reform measures to change existing presidential term limits, allowing him to run for reelection in 2007.

Terror alert. Several Western diplomatic missions in Nigeria's chief city, Lagos, were closed for several days in June 2005 due to a terrorist threat described by the U.S. Department of State as "specific and credible." Terrorist experts said that non-Nigerian Islamic militants were responsible, noting that al-Qa`ida leader Osama bin Laden had previously cited Nigeria—home to about 60 million Muslims—as a target for "liberation" from Western domination. ■ Simon Baynham

See also **Africa; Terrorism.**

Nobel prizes in literature, peace, the sciences, and economics were awarded in October 2005 by the Norwegian Storting (parliament) in Oslo and by the Royal Swedish Academy of Sciences, the Karolinska Institute, and the Swedish Academy of Literature, all in Stockholm. Each prize was worth about $1.3 million.

The 2005 Nobel Prize in literature went to English playwright Harold Pinter, known for his masterful use of silence to communicate tension and misunderstandings. The Swedish Academy praised Pinter as "the foremost representative of British drama in the second half of the 20th century." He was also honored for restoring theater to "its basic elements: an enclosed space and unpredictable dialogue, where people are at the mercy of each other and pretense crumbles."

Pinter made his playwriting debut with *The Room* (1957). Some of his dramas, including *The Caretaker* (1960) and *The Homecoming* (1965), explore the power struggles in human relationships. Still others, such as *No Man's Land* (1975) and *Betrayal* (1978), examine the elusive and conflicting nature of memory.

Pinter has also used drama to attack human rights abuses and other repressive government actions. His plays on this theme include *One for the Road* (1984), *Mountain Language* (1988), and *The New World Order* (1991). In March 2005, Pinter announced his retirement from playwriting to concentrate on writing poetry and speaking out on political issues.

The 2005 Nobel Peace Prize went to the International Atomic Energy Agency (IAEA) and its director general, Mohamed ElBaradei. The IAEA is a United Nations organization that promotes the safe, secure, and peaceful uses of nuclear technologies. In its announcement, the Norwegian Nobel Committee praised the IAEA for work of "incalculable importance" at a time "when disarmament efforts appear deadlocked, when there is a danger that nuclear arms will spread both to states and to terrorist groups...."

ElBaradei, an Egyptian lawyer, was appointed to his first term as director general of the IAEA in 1997. He won a third appointment in September 2005, despite opposition by the administration of United States President George W. Bush. The administration and ElBaradei had clashed over ElBaradei's policy of relying on diplomacy to halt the spread of nuclear weapons.

The 2005 Nobel Prize in physiology or medicine was awarded to Australians Barry J. Marshall, a gastroenterologist at the University of Western Australia in Nedlands, and J. Robin Warren, a retired pathologist from the Royal Perth Hospital in Perth. The two scientists were honored for their discovery in the 1980's that a bacterium, *Helicobacter pylori*, causes stomach ulcers and *gastritis* (inflammation of the stomach lining). Their finding disproved a long-standing medical belief that ulcers resulted from an overproduction of stomach acid triggered by stress and spicy foods. Their research also has led to new discoveries about the role inflammation plays in many diseases.

The 2005 Nobel Prize in economic sciences was awarded to Thomas C. Schelling of the University of Maryland in College Park and to German-born mathematician Robert J. Aumann of the Hebrew University of Jerusalem in Israel. The two were recognized for "enhancing our understanding of conflict and cooperation" using *game theory*, a method of studying decision-making situations in which the choices of two or more individuals or groups influence one another. Schelling's classic book, *The Strategy of Conflict* (1960), for example, applied game theory to global security and the arms race. Aumann was recognized for helping develop *the theory of repeated games with incomplete information*. This theory explores long-term interactions in which one party knows more about some aspect of the game than another party.

The 2005 Nobel Prize in chemistry was awarded to U.S. chemists Robert H. Grubbs of the Massachusetts Institute of Technology in Cambridge and Richard R. Schrock of the California

Institute of Technology in Pasadena and to French chemist Yves Chauvin of the French Petroleum Institute in Rueil-Malmaison. The three scientists developed a simplified version of *organic synthesis*, a method of rearranging groups of atoms within molecules. Their reaction, called *the metathesis method*, provides a more efficient method of creating drugs and plastic products while reducing the production of hazardous by-products.

The 2005 Nobel Prize in physics went to Roy J. Glauber of Harvard University in Cambridge, Massachuetts; John L. Hall of JILA, a research institute in Boulder, Colorado; and Theodor W. Hänsch of the Max Planck Institute for Quantum Optics in Garching, Germany. Glauber won half of the prize for his work on applying quantum physics, the study of atoms and subatomic particles, to optics, the branch of physics that deals with the properties of light. Hall and Hänsch shared half the prize for contributing to the development of optical-frequency-comb technology, a highly precise method of measuring light. The applications of the three scientists' work include improvements in laser technology, Global Positioning System (GPS) technology, and long-distance communication. ■ Barbara A. Mayes

See also **Literature**.

Northern Ireland. Major breakthroughs in the stalled Northern Ireland peace process occurred in July 2005. The Irish Republican Army (IRA) declared a formal end to its 36-year armed campaign against the United Kingdom's (U.K.) presence in Northern Ireland and announced plans to *decommission* (dismantle) all of its weapons.

Violence between the Protestant and Roman Catholic communities in Northern Ireland, a province of the U.K., had erupted in 1969. Protestants tended to support Unionist or Loyalist parties that wanted Northern Ireland to remain part of the U.K., while Catholics favored republican or nationalist parties that wanted the province to join the Republic of Ireland. The Good Friday Agreement of 1998 had produced a cease-fire and an assembly through which the province largely governed itself. However, distrust and allegations about the IRA's continued retention of weapons and illegal methods had led to the suspension of the assembly in 2002 and the revival of direct rule from London. In the 2003 election, moderate parties had been eclipsed by the more extreme unionist and republican parties.

The IRA, the military wing of the republican party, Sinn Fein, was linked with a 2004 armed robbery of Belfast's Northern Bank. Although the IRA denied the allegation, the incident threatened the Good Friday Agreement as it suggested the IRA had not abandoned violence. In February 2005, the IRA threatened to withdraw from the peace process, angered by criticism from both the U.K. and Irish governments.

The McCartney murder. On January 31, a 33-year-old Catholic, Robert McCartney, died after being stabbed during a fight at a Belfast pub. IRA members were believed to have been involved, but witnesses were unwilling to report what they had seen. McCartney's family charged that the IRA had destroyed crucial evidence and intimidated witnesses to protect its members. The family launched a campaign to demand justice, receiving widespread support—including that of United States President George W. Bush and Senator Edward Kennedy (D., Massachusetts)—that embarrassed the IRA. The IRA expelled three men in February and offered to shoot the killers, a proposal that was met with international condemnation. In June, the police charged IRA member Terence Davison with the murder.

Election. In the U.K. general election in May, the moderate Ulster Unionist Party lost four of its five seats, including that of its leader, Nobel Peace Prize laureate David Trimble. Protestant voters were impatient with Trimble's strategy, which included sharing power with Sinn Fein in the Northern Ireland Assembly before its dissolution. The more extreme unionist party, the Democratic Unionist Party (DUP) led by Reverend Ian Paisley, went from four to nine seats (half of Northern Ireland's seats). Sinn Fein got five seats while the more moderate republican party, the Social Democratic and Labour Party led by Mark Durkan, retained three seats. David Trimble resigned as leader of the Ulster Unionists and was replaced by Sir Reg Empey in June. As part of a British Cabinet reshuffle in May, the Northern Ireland minister, Paul Murphy, was replaced by Peter Hain.

IRA. On July 28, the IRA announced a formal end to its armed campaign and declared that it would decommission all of its remaining weapons. Adams hailed the event, while Paisley expressed skepticism. Hain promised to continue reducing the British army's presence in Northern Ireland and called for talks to restore the assembly. In September, the International Independent Commission on Decommissioning reported that all IRA weapons had been placed beyond use.

U.K. loyalists sparked violence in July when they engaged in a traditonal march through the Catholic areas of Belfast. Riots also occurred in August and September (following a rerouting of a parade by the Orange Order, the leading Protestant movement). The violence was the worst in Belfast in many years. ■ Rohan McWilliam

See also **Ireland; United Kingdom**.

Northwest Territories. See **Canadian territories**.

Norway. Norwegians elected a new government in 2005. In elections for the parliament, the Storting, held on September 12, the ruling center-right coalition lost to a center-left coalition led by the Labor Party. Labor Party leader Jens Stoltenberg formed Norway's first majority government in 20 years.

The results of the election surprised some observers because the country's 2005 unemployment rate was low—3.4 percent in September—and wages were high. A large portion of the profits from the country's large North Sea oil reserves was saved in a Petroleum Fund that in 2005 contained more than $190 billion. The presence of such huge reserves, however, made it difficult for many Norwegians to accept shortages of teachers, waiting lists at hospitals, and high taxes and gasoline prices. Stoltenberg promised to improve education, the public health care system, and care for the elderly, though not to lower taxes.

Norway's economy grew by 3.6 percent in 2005, according to the finance ministry. The growth was supported by a strong demand for North Sea oil from China. ■ Jeffrey Kopstein

See also **Europe.**

Nova Scotia. See **Canadian provinces.**

Nuclear energy. See **Energy supply.**

Nunavut. See **Canadian territories.**

Nutrition. See **Food.**

Ocean. The first well-documented example of culture in marine animals was announced in June 2005. A team of scientists found a group of bottlenose dolphins that use sponges as tools. The team, led by biologist Michael Krützen of the University of Zurich in Switzerland, showed that dolphin mothers teach their daughters to wear sponges on their snouts while foraging for food. The scientists speculated that sponges protect dolphins from sharp coral or stinging fish.

Many animals use tools. Crows, for example, select twigs to help with extracting food. Most animal behavior, however, is instinctual, inherited through genes. Culture, in contrast, refers to the transmission of behavior or information in a population by members interacting with one another.

The researchers studied more than 850 bottlenose dolphins in Shark Bay, Western Australia, and found that 15 dolphins put sponges on their snouts. Genetic tests showed that almost all of these "spongers" were closely related females. However, an analysis of genetic data from sponging and nonsponging dolphins provided strong evidence that sponging was not inherited; female dolphins were learning from their mothers.

The discovery of dolphin culture, the scientists said, illustrates the complex social structure of these intelligent animals and blurs distinctions often made between humans and other animals.

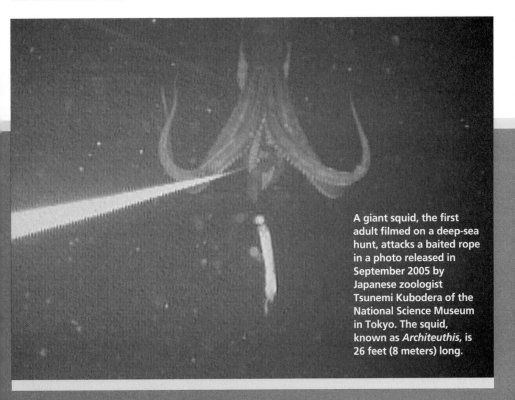

A giant squid, the first adult filmed on a deep-sea hunt, attacks a baited rope in a photo released in September 2005 by Japanese zoologist Tsunemi Kubodera of the National Science Museum in Tokyo. The squid, known as *Architeuthis*, is 26 feet (8 meters) long.

Oceanography from space. A team of scientists, including researchers from the National Aeronautics and Space Administration (NASA), led by biologist Michael Behrenfeld of Oregon State University in Corvalis, used satellite images to analyze marine *ecosystems* (the biological and physical environment of an area) in January. The team used the Sea-viewing Wide Field-of-view Sensor (SeaWiFS), an optical-scanning device carried by NASA's SeaStar satellite, to produce the images.

Behrenfeld's team calculated subtle changes in the hue and brightness of green shades of seawater from the SeaWiFS data. Knowledge of such changes allowed investigators to study *ocean productivity*—a marine ecosystem's capacity to support fish and other animal life—at a level of detail never before possible. The scientists said their new technique may help with predictions of fish stock population sizes and evaluations of the effects of pollution on marine ecosystems.

In July, NASA officials announced that they were able for the first time to pinpoint the rate at which sea level is changing by using satellite observations. Sea level was estimated to be rising at a rate of about 0.08 inches (2 millimeters) per year during the 1900's. Waleed Abdalati, head of the Cryospheric Sciences Branch at NASA's Goddard Space Flight Center in Greenbelt, Maryland, said that more than 100 million people could be affected by a 3-foot (1-meter) increase in sea level. The main cause of sea level rise is the melting of ice covering land.

Oceans warming. Sea level rise studies were consistent with evidence that human activities are warming the world's oceans. In February 2005, climate researchers Tim Barnett and David Pierce, both at Scripps Institution of Oceanography in La Jolla, California, and their colleagues reported that human-produced climate warming had penetrated into the world's oceans in the past 40 years.

Using computer models, the researchers were able to reproduce the warming only by including the effects of man-made *greenhouse gases* (heat-trapping atmospheric gases). The finding supports widespread belief among scientists that human activities are altering global climate. Barnett claimed that the ocean warming could lead to summertime water shortages for millions of people in regions of South America and Asia.

Iceberg blocks penguins. In January 2005, a huge chunk of a massive iceberg ran aground in Antarctica's McMurdo Sound in the Ross Sea, devastating Adélie penguin colonies. The iceberg, named B-15A, prevented adult Adélie penguins from feeding in normally open waters. Many penguin chicks died of starvation while their parents trudged across the vast ice sheet in search of food.   ■ Christina S. Johnson

See also **Biology; Global warming.**

Olympic Games. The International Olympic Committee (IOC) in 2005 surprised the world by awarding the 2012 Summer Olympic Games to London and not Paris, which many observers considered an overwhelming favorite. The competition also included Madrid, New York City, and Moscow.

The IOC members made their decision on July 6, 2005, in Singapore. London topped Paris 54 votes to 50 on the fourth ballot, making it the first city to host the Games three times. Paris, which never led in any round of the voting, failed for the third time in 20 years to land the Games.

Each of the 28 existing Olympic sports was put to a secret vote by the IOC on July 8, and members chose to drop baseball and softball, beginning with the 2012 Games. Neither sport received the simple majority required to stay on the program.

Ethics scandal. In July 2005, the IOC expelled Ivan Slavkov of Bulgaria, an IOC member since 1987, for alleged ethical misconduct. In 2004, an undercover British television documentary crew had filmed Slavkov while he discussed how votes could be bought in the bidding for the 2012 Games.   ■ Michael Kates

Oman. See **Middle East.**
Ontario. See **Canadian provinces.**
Opera. See **Classical music.**

Pacific Islands. Prospects for short-term economic growth in the Pacific Island nations were at best marginal in 2005, reported the Asian Development Bank (ADB) in a study released in April. The Manila, Philippines-based ADB promotes economic development of multiple nations in Asia and the Pacific. ADB economists predicted a growth rate of approximately 2 percent for the Pacific Island nations for 2005 through 2007, based on current *gross domestic products* (GDP). GDP is the total value of goods and services produced in a country during a given year. Growth in the GDP of Papua New Guinea, the region's largest economy, was expected to be 2.4 percent from 2005 to 2007. By contrast, the ADB estimated that the GDP's of the Asian member nations would grow by more than 6 percent during the same period. In 2005, the rate of employment on the islands grew at a much slower pace than in Asian nations, and tourism remained the largest single industry.

Tonga. Around 3,000 public service workers in Tonga went on strike on July 19 to protest their low pay, which for many averaged $25 per week. They had been offered pay raises of 30 percent, while senior government officials were to receive increases of up to 80 percent. An agreement was reached in September that provided workers with a 60 to 80 percent raise over the next two years.

In the strike's aftermath, more than 10,000 Ton-

FACTS IN BRIEF ON PACIFIC ISLAND COUNTRIES

Country	Population	Government	Monetary unit*	Foreign trade (million U.S.$) Exports[†]	Imports[†]
Fiji	866,000	President Rata Josefa Iloilovatu Uluivuda; Prime Minister Laisenia Qarase	dollar (1.68 = $1)	609	835
Kiribati	91,000	President Anote Tong	Australian dollar (1.29 = $1)	35	83
Marshall Islands	60,000	President Kessai Hesa Note	U.S. dollar	9	54
Micronesia, Federated States of	112,000	President Joseph J. Urusemal	U.S. dollar	22	149
Nauru	13,000	President Ludwig Scotty	Australian dollar (1.29 = $1)	1	20
New Zealand	4,087,000	Governor General Dame Silvia Cartwright; Prime Minister Helen Clark	dollar (1.41 = $1)	19,850	19,770
Palau	21,000	President Tommy Esang Remengesau, Jr.	U.S. dollar	18	99
Papua New Guinea	5,757,000	Governor General Sir Paulius Matane; Prime Minister Sir Michael Somare	kina (3.00 = $1)	2,437	1,353
Samoa	184,000	Head of State Malietoa Tanumafili II; Prime Minister Sailele Malielegaoi Tuila'epa	tala (2.63 = $1)	14	113
Solomon Islands	517,000	Governor General Nathaniel Waena; Prime Minister Sir Allan Kemakeza	dollar (7.31 = $1)	74	67
Tonga	107,000	King Taufa'ahau Tupou IV; Prime Minister Lavaka ata Ulukalala	pa'anga (1.96 = $1)	27	86
Tuvalu	11,000	Governor General Filoimea Telito; Prime Minister Maatia Toafa	Australian dollar (1.29 = $1)	1	79
Vanuatu	218,000	President Kalkot Mataskelekele; Prime Minister Ham Lini	vatu (110.62 = $1)	27	138

*Exchange rates as of September 2005 or latest available data.   [†]Latest available data.

gans marched through the capital, Nuku'alofa, to the residence of King Taufa'ahau Toupou IV, the leader of the last monarchy in the Pacific Islands. The protesters demanded that the king dismiss his son, who was the prime minister, as well as all the Cabinet ministers. They also asked for the modernization of the Tongan constitution. The king's nephew, Prince Tu'ipelehake, supported the prodemocracy movement, which sought a fully elected parliament with no royal Cabinet appointments. The prodemocracy demands were largely ignored by the government.

Papua New Guinea. Joseph Kabui was inaugurated on June 15 as president of the first *autonomous* (self-ruled) government of Bougainville, a Papua New Guinea province. Part of the agreement establishing the autonomous government gave Bougainvilleans the right to vote on *secession* (separation) of Bougainville from the rest of Papua New Guinea. Rebels had fought for Bougainville independence since 1988. Francis Ona, the leader of the Bougainville Revolutionary Army, died in July 2005.

Vanuatu, a nation of about 218,000 people, marked 25 years of independence in 2005 from the *condominium* (joint control) government of France and the United Kingdom. The current prime minister, Ham Lini, is the younger brother of Walter Lini, who led the country to independence and became its first prime minister.

In June, the Australian development agency AusAID agreed to a five-year, $25-million (Australian dollars) grant to Vanuatu. The funds were to be used to improve agriculture, tourism, and services to rural communities.

Federated States of Micronesia. The ADB gave a negative economic report in 2005 to the Federated States of Micronesia, comparing the country's performance with that of other Pacific Island nations. ADB noted that the Federated States received $2.4 billion in aid from 1987 to 2003, but its GDP increased during the same period by less than 2 percent in all of the four states that make up the country. Nearly 28 percent of all households were below the poverty line in 2005.

Marshall Islands. In August, the U.S.S. *Boxer* visited Majuro, capital of the Marshall Islands. The crew engaged in a variety of community projects, including providing medical and dental services and renovating school buildings.

In September, the finance minister submitted to the Parliament a 2006 budget totaling more than $146 million, the largest in Marshall Islands history. The United States was expected to provide almost $100 million and Taiwan, $10 million of the total. Education accounted for the largest expenditure.

Palau. Koror, the Palau capital, hosted the South Pacific Mini-Games from July 24, 2005, to August 4, 2005. Eighteen nations participated.

■ Eugene Ogan

See also **Australia; New Zealand.**

Painting. See **Art.**

Pakistan. A massive earthquake struck northern Pakistan and India on Oct. 8, 2005, triggering what Prime Minister Shaukat Aziz called "a disaster of unprecedented proportions in Pakistan's history." Officials said the 7.6-magnitude quake killed more than 73,000 Pakistanis, injured 69,000 others, and left more than 3 million people homeless.

The earthquake was centered in the western Himalayas in the Jammu and Kashmir region, which is disputed by Pakistan and India. The quake destroyed whole towns and left many mountain roads impassible, isolating ravaged areas as winter began.

Relief efforts under the direction of Pakistan's army began slowly, and the rugged terrain limited the ability of relief workers to reach marooned villagers. The United Nations (UN) estimated that up to 1.5 million people were stranded without proper winter shelter, and food, medicine, and shelter were slow in being provided. Helicopters, which were the only way to reach many of the devastated areas, were sent by the United States armed forces and by other countries. It took relief teams months to reach some isolated villages.

Terrorism. Pakistan's president, Pervez Musharraf, claimed several times in 2005 that his government had destroyed the ability of the al-Qa`ida terrorist network to operate from Pakistan. After the terrorist attacks on the United States on Sept. 11, 2001, U.S. and allied forces believed they had driven al-Qa`ida and Taliban extremists into rugged areas along Pakistan's border with Afghanistan.

Musharraf continued in 2005 to take measures to crack down on Islamic militants. On July 29, he announced that all foreign students attending Islamic religious schools called madrasahs had to leave the country. The ban was enacted after allegations that suspects

Pakistani soldiers clear rubble from a collapsed building in Islamabad, the capital, after a 7.6-magnitude earthquake struck the region on October 8. More than 73,000 Pakistanis died in the quake, which was centered in Kashmir, a region claimed by both Pakistan and India.

involved in suicide bombings in London on July 7 had visited or studied at religious seminaries in Pakistan. Musharraf's statement was met with widespread skepticism in Pakistan as well as among Western nations that he could or would halt terrorists' use of Pakistan as a base.

In July, Pakistani authorities began a campaign to register the nation's 12,000 madrasahs in an effort to control them and the militant groups that operated many of the schools. Experts noted that textbooks remained in use that seemed to encourage martyrdom for the Islamic cause.

Violence continued in 2005 between Pakistan's Sunni Muslim majority and Shiah Muslim minority. On March 19, a Shiah shrine in the province of Balochistan was bombed, killing 43 people. Balochistan lies along Pakistan's border with Afghanistan and is known for harboring a strong Taliban presence. A bombing on May 27 at a shrine sacred to both Sunnis and Shiites in Islamabad, the capital, killed at least 20 people. On May 30, five people died in an attack on a Shiah mosque in the southern port of Karachi. The attack touched off riots that left at least six people dead.

Local government elections in August were marred by violence between rival political factions. At least 40 people were killed in the conflicts.

Candidates who were nominally independent, but were actually backed by a party allied to Musharraf, swept most seats. Candidates tied to religious groups, especially extremist ones, fared poorly. Many observers thought the elections had been rigged and that voting rules had been widely flouted. However, most political experts agreed that the election results indicated that Musharraf could win reelection in 2007. On May

17, 2005, a spokesperson for the president announced Musharraf's intention of running again, "because Pakistan needs his leadership."

According to Pakistan's constitution, however, the country's next president has to be a civilian elected by parliament. Opposition leaders suggested that Musharraf was subverting Pakistani law and consolidating his power base to eventually rule Pakistan as a dictator. They also asserted that Musharraf was not sharing power with parliament or his Cabinet. Observers regarded the Pakistan Peoples Party, headed by Benazir Bhutto, an exiled former prime minister, as the only viable political threat to Musharraf's position.

Economy. Prime Minister Shaukat Aziz announced on May 17, 2005, that Pakistan's economy was growing at the fastest rate in 20 years. Aziz attributed the 8.35-percent growth rate to policies set by Musharraf after he took power in a 1999 *coup* (overthrow).

On June 6, 2005, the government announced an almost 35-percent increase in spending on developing public infrastructure during fiscal year 2005, which began in July. The government also increased military spending by 16 percent in 2005.

■ Henry S. Bradsher

See also Asia; Disasters; India; Islam; Terrorism.

Palau. See Pacific Islands.

Paleontology. Dinosaur bones are relatively dense, compared with other kinds of fossilized bones, and they have been known to preserve excellent microscopic details. Still, scientists were surprised by a report in March 2005, by a team of paleontologists led by Mary Schweitzer of North Carolina State University at Raleigh, that described remains of soft tissues—and possibly even blood cells—inside the leg bone of a small *Tyrannosaurus rex.* The fossils of this *carnivorous* (meat-eating) dinosaur dated from the Late Cretaceous Period, approximately 70 million years ago, and were uncovered in Montana.

After dissolving the hard, mineralized material of the *T. rex* bone fragments, the paleontologists found remnants of soft tissues floating in the resulting solution. The tissues were slender, flexible tubes. Enlarged images of the tubes formed by scanning electron microscopy showed details that were almost identical to the blood vessels found in the bones of modern ostriches. The scientists discovered—to their great surprise—round, reddish-brown structures inside the tubes, which they identified as the possible remains of blood cells.

The scientists stated that the discovery and examination of other soft tissues like the ones found in this study might help paleontologists better understand how different species of dinosaurs were related to one another, as well as how dinosaurs are related to living animals. One possibility resulting from the study of these topics would be the discovery of intact *DNA* inside fossilized dinosaur bones. DNA, or deoxyribonucleic acid, is the molecule that makes up genetic material. The discovery of such ancient DNA would likely reveal important clues about the biology of prehistoric animals.

Schweitzer's team hoped additional research would also help them understand how the soft tissues were preserved over tens of millions of years. Normally, such tissues decay within a few months following the death of an animal. Perhaps these remnants survived, speculated the researchers, because they were deeply imbedded in unusually dense bone.

Plesiosaur bottom feeders. Scientists announced in October that two newly discovered specimens of *plesiosaurs,* extinct long-necked marine reptiles, contained clues about the last meals eaten by these animals. Paleontologists Colin McHenry, Alex Cook, and Steve Wroe, all of Queensland Museum in Australia, reported that the preserved fecal material, or *bromalites,* of these specimens contained abundant *gastroliths* (gizzard stones), which the plesiosaurs had to

have picked up some 180 miles (300 kilometers) away from their burial site.

According to the scientists, these gastroliths were gulped down from near-shore gravels and used to grind the food of the plesiosaurs—in the same digestion technique used by many modern birds. The gut contents of the plesiosaurs contained the remains of *crinoids* (sea lilies) and *gastropods* (snails), which lived on the Cretaceous sea bottom. This discovery showed that plesiosaurs could have used their long necks to grasp prey off the sea bottom.

Dinosaur embryos. A discovery reported in July provided insights into the early development of dinosaurs. A team of paleontologists led by Robert Reisz of the University of Toronto at Mississauga described a dinosaur nest with seven fossilized eggs from South Africa. The nest was dated to approximately 190 million years ago, during the Jurassic Period. Six of the eggs contained bones, which were the remains of the oldest dinosaur *embryos* (unborn organisms) ever recovered. The scientists identified the bones as belonging to the genus *Massospondylus,* a group of *herbivorous* (plant-eating) dinosaurs.

The embryos in the eggs were either toothless or had only weakly developed teeth, which demonstrated that they could not have nipped the tough vegetation that formed the diet of these dinosaurs. The discovery indicated that hatchling dinosaurs—at least in this species—required parental care.

Venomous mammals. Few living mammals have

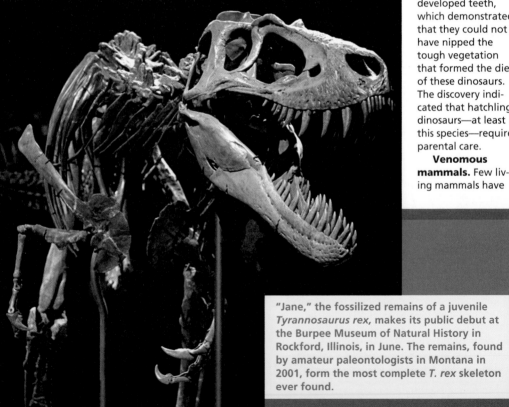

"Jane," the fossilized remains of a juvenile *Tyrannosaurus rex,* makes its public debut at the Burpee Museum of Natural History in Rockford, Illinois, in June. The remains, found by amateur paleontologists in Montana in 2001, form the most complete *T. rex* skeleton ever found.

venom (poison) to help them subdue prey or ward off predators. However, a discovery announced in June indicated that some prehistoric mammals might have used venom for these purposes.

Richard Fox and Craig Scott, paleontologists at the University of Alberta in Edmonton, Canada, described the *canine teeth* (fangs) of *Bisonalveus browni,* a small, mouse-sized mammal that lived 60 million years ago in Wyoming. They noted that each of these teeth bears a groove along one side that widens to form a circular area at the tooth's base. They surmised that this circular depression represents the site of a venom gland and that the venom ran along the groove to the sharp tip of the tooth—as is the case in rattlesnake teeth.

The Canadian scientists noted that the *B. browni* teeth resemble those of certain living shrews that are capable of injecting venom to immobilize insect prey. The researchers speculated that early mammals, which were perhaps not as quick and agile as modern mammals, might have greatly benefited from having the ability to inject venom into their prey. Conversely, the later evolution of more advanced mammals may have lessened the need for venom production among mammals.

■ Carlton E. Brett

Panama. President Martin Torrijos Espino's efforts to trim government spending and position Panama to invest in the modernization of the Panama Canal provoked protest in 2005. More than 80,000 workers walked off the job in early June when the Panamanian Congress approved an increase in payroll taxes and raised the retirement age as part of the president's budget-cutting program. The strike, which shut down public schools and many businesses, cost Panama $80 million in lost revenue, economists estimated.

In July, Torrijos—whose approval rating had plummeted to 23 percent—postponed the imposition of the cost-saving measures. The president also postponed a referendum, originally scheduled for November 2005, that would have put the issue of upgrading the aging 1914 Panama Canal to Panamanian voters.

United States President George W. Bush met with President Torrijos in Panama City in November 2005. Bush endorsed Torrijos's plans to widen the canal and pledged to seek U.S. Congressional approval of a stalled, bilateral free-trade pact between Panama and the United States.

■ Nathan A. Haverstock

See also **Latin America.**

Papua New Guinea. See Asia; Pacific Islands.

Paraguay. See Latin America.

in 2005 included those listed below, who were all from the United States unless otherwise indicated.

Abdullah, *ahb DUL lu* (1923?–   ), became the king and prime minister of Saudi Arabia on Aug. 1, 2005. He came to power after the death of his half brother King Fahd.

Abdullah was named heir to the throne by the Saudi royal family in 1982, when Fahd became king and prime minister. In the mid-1990's, Fahd suffered a stroke, and his health began to decline. As crown prince, Abdullah became increasingly responsible for governing the country. In 2000, he assumed the title of *regent* (one who governs in place of the king).

As regent, Abdullah supported moderate reforms within Saudi Arabia. He played a major role in the government's decision in 2005 to allow elections for half the seats on the country's municipal councils. Abdullah also played a leadership role in trying to find a peaceful settlement to the Israeli-Palestinian conflict. Political analysts expected Abdullah to maintain close relations with the United States.

Abdullah ibn Abd al-Aziz was born in Riyadh, the capital of Saudi Arabia. He is one of the many sons of Ibn Saud, who established the Kingdom of Saudi Arabia in 1932 and from whose descendants all Saudi monarchs have been chosen. Abdullah spent part of his youth living with Bedouin tribes in the Saudi deserts. In 1962, Abdullah was appointed commander of the National Guard, which handles internal security. He retains that post as king.

See also **Saudi Arabia.**

Ahmadinejad, Mahmoud, *ah MAH dih nee ZHAHD, mah MOO* (1956–   ), a hard-line Islamic conservative, took office as president of Iran on Aug. 3, 2005, after winning a landslide victory over a moderate opponent on June 24. A former mayor of Tehran, Iran's capital, Ahmadinejad benefited from the strong support of the Islamic clerics who control Iran's government. As a candidate, Ahmadinejad attacked government corruption, promised to improve life for Iran's lower classes, and stressed his simple lifestyle and commitment to traditional Islamic values. In October 2005, he caused an international furor with his comment that Israel must be "wiped off the map."

Ahmadinejad was born in Garmsar, near Tehran, the child of a blacksmith. He earned a doctoral degree in civil engineering from Iran University of Science and Technology in Tehran.

While at the university, Ahmadinejad helped organize a radical student organization, some of whose members seized the United States embassy in Tehran in 1979 and held a number of U.S. citizens there hostage until 1981. After Ahmadinejad's election, several former hostages identified him as one of their captors. He denied the charge, and in July 2005, U.S. officials reported finding no evidence for Ahmadinejad's involvement with the hostages.

In the 1980's, during Iran's war with Iraq, Ahmadinejad served in the Revolutionary Guards, a military force dedicated to preserving Iran's Islamic government. He has held a number of government posts, including governor of the northwestern province of Ardabil. In 2003, he was appointed mayor of Tehran by that city's governing council. As mayor, he reversed many changes that moderate mayors before him had put into effect. He resigned as mayor in 2005 to run for president.

See also **Iran**.

Alsop, Marin

(1956–), a critically acclaimed director, became the first woman named as music director of a major United States orchestra, the Baltimore Symphony Orchestra (BSO), in July 2005. She was to serve as music director designate for the BSO's 2006-2007 concert season and become music director for the 2007-2008 season. Although the classical music community applauded her appointment, most of the BSO's musicians publicly opposed her selection. They argued that the committee should have considered additional candidates. In September 2005, Alsop won a "genius award" from the John D. and Catherine T. MacArthur Foundation.

Alsop, the daughter of professional musicians, was born in New York City on Oct. 16, 1956. She decided to become a conductor at the age of 9, while watching the renowned U.S. conductor Leonard Bernstein lead one of his famous Young People's Concerts.

Alsop attended Yale University in New Haven, Connecticut, from 1973 to 1975. In 1978, she was awarded a master's degree in violin from New York City's Juilliard School, which denied her admission to its conducting program. Unable to find work as a classical conductor, Alsop in 1984 used her personal savings to establish the Concordia Chamber Orchestra, for which she served as artistic director. In 1988,

Alsop won the Leonard Bernstein Conducting Fellowship to the Tanglewood music festival in Massachusetts. Her work there attracted widespread notice, including that of Bernstein, who became her mentor.

Beginning in 1989, Alsop served as music director for a number of orchestras, including the Eugene (Oregon) Symphony Orchestra, the Colorado Symphony Orchestra in Denver, and the Long Island (New York) Philharmonic. In 2002, she was appointed principal conductor of the Bournemouth Symphony Orchestra in Poole in the United Kingdom, becoming the first woman to direct a major British orchestra. She also has appeared as a guest conductor with many other orchestras in the United States and Europe.

See also **Classical music**.

Marin Alsop

Benedict XVI

Benedict XVI (1927–), a German-born theologian known as an uncompromising defender of traditional Roman Catholic beliefs, was elected pope on April 19, 2005. Since 1981, the former Cardinal Joseph Ratzinger had served as the head of the Congregation for the Doctrine of the Faith, which works to promote and uphold accepted Catholic teachings.

Benedict XVI was born Joseph Alois Ratzinger on April 16, 1927, in Marktl am Inn in the German state of Bavaria. He began his religious life at age 12 at St. Michael's Seminary in Traunstein. During World War II (1939-1945), he was drafted into the German army, serving from 1943 until he deserted in the spring of 1945.

Ratzinger began preparing for the priesthood in 1945 and was ordained in 1951. He earned a doctoral degree in theology at the University of Munich in 1953. He then taught at a number of universities. As a young theologian, Ratzinger contributed to the work of Vatican Council II (1962-

1965), an *ecumenical* (general) council that produced the most far-reaching reforms within the church in 1,000 years.

In March 1977, Ratzinger became archbishop of Munich and Freising, and in June, Pope Paul VI appointed him a cardinal. In 1981, John Paul II appointed him prefect of the Congregation for the Doctrine of the Faith. Ratzinger was elected dean of the Sacred College of Cardinals, the body comprising all the cardinals, in 2002.

By choosing the name Benedict, the pope placed his pontificate under the inspiration of Saint Benedict of Nursia, the founder of the Benedictine order. The Benedictines played a major role in the religious and cultural revival of Europe after the Germanic invasions of the 400's.

Benedict has written numerous books on theology. They include *The Spirit of the Liturgy* (2000) and *Values in Times of Upheaval* (2005). He also wrote an autobiography, *Milestones: Memoirs 1927-1977* (1998).

See also **Roman Catholic Church.**

Bolton, John (1948–   ), a harsh critic of the United Nations (UN), became U.S. ambassador to that international group on Aug. 1, 2005. President George W. Bush named Bolton to the post during Congress's summer recess after Democrats in the Senate had twice blocked efforts to bring Bolton's nomination to a vote.

Democratic senators had argued that Bolton's highly critical attitude toward the UN would seriously interfere with his ability to work effectively with the world community. Bolton also came under attack for what opponents charged was an abrasive attitude toward subordinates who disagreed with him while he served as Bush's undersecretary for arms control and national security from 2001 to 2005. The recess appointment allowed Bolton, who was highly regarded by many conservatives, to remain as ambassador only until January 2007.

John Robert Bolton was born on Nov. 20, 1948, in Baltimore, Maryland. He earned a bachelor's degree in 1970 and a law degree in 1974, both from Yale University in New Haven, Connecticut. From 1974 to 1981, he worked for a private law firm in Washington, D.C. In 1981, he became general counsel for the U.S. Agency for International Development, returning to private practice in 1983.

In 1985, Bolton joined the U.S. Department of Justice as an assistant attorney general, leaving that office for private practice in 1993. From 1997 to 2001, he also held the post of senior vice president for the American Enterprise Institute, a conservative think tank in Washington, D.C.

See also **United Nations.**

Chertoff, Michael (1953–   ), a former prosecutor for the U.S. Department of Justice, was sworn in on Feb. 15, 2005, as the second secretary of the Department of Homeland Security (DHS). As an assistant attorney general in the Justice Department's criminal division, Chertoff helped draft antiterrorism policies for the administration of President George W. Bush. In September, Chertoff became the object of criticism when the response by the Federal Emergency Management Agency, which is part of the DHS, proved inadequate during the Hurricane Katrina disaster.

Chertoff was born on Nov. 28, 1953, in Elizabeth, New Jersey. He received a bachelor's degree in 1975 and a law degree in 1978, both from Harvard University in Cambridge, Massachusetts. From 1979 to 1980, he worked as a law clerk for Supreme Court Justice William J. Brennan and then entered private practice for three years. In 1983, he joined the Justice Department, rising from assistant U.S. attorney for southern New York in 1987 to U.S. attorney for New Jersey in 1994. From 1994 to 1996, he served as special counsel for a U.S. Senate committee investigating charges of financial misconduct by President Bill Clinton and his wife, Hillary Rodham Clinton. Chertoff then returned to private practice until 2003, when he was named to the U.S. Court of Appeals for the Third Circuit.

See also **Terrorism; United States, Government.**

Christo (1935–   ), a Bulgarian-born American environmental artist, and his French-American wife, **Jeanne-Claude** (1935–   ), celebrated the footpaths of New York City's Central Park in

Christo (right) and Jeanne-Claude

Patrick J. Fitzgerald

Fitzgerald, Patrick J.

(1960–   ), an aggressive prosecutor with a reputation for impartiality, won high praise in 2005 for his work directing an inquiry into the public disclosure of the identity of a Central Intelligence Agency (CIA) undercover operative in 2003. In October 2005, Fitzgerald announced the indictment of I. Lewis "Scooter" Libby, then chief aide to U.S. Vice President Dick Cheney, on charges relating to the investigation, which was ongoing at year's end. While serving as special counsel in the CIA probe, Fitzgerald retained his post as U.S. attorney for the Northern District of Illinois.

Fitzgerald was born on Dec. 22, 1960, in the Brooklyn section of New York City. He received a bachelor's degree in 1982 from Amherst College in Amherst and a law degree in 1985 from Harvard Law School in Cambridge, both in Massachusetts. After a three-year stint in private practice, he joined the U.S. Department of Justice as assistant U.S. attorney for the Southern District of New York. While in that position, he helped prosecute a number of high-profile cases, including the 1995 trial of Egyptian cleric Sheik Omar Abel Rahman and others convicted of conspiring to bomb United Nations headquarters in New York City. Fitzgerald was appointed U.S. attorney for Northern Illinois in 2001.

See also **Newspapers; People in the news** (I. Lewis "Scooter" Libby); **United States, Government of the.**

February 2005 with a vibrant art project titled *The Gates.* The two artists are known for creating temporary, large-scale, public installations involving natural landscapes and buildings. *The Gates* consisted of 7,500 steel-supported frames that stood 16 feet (5 meters) tall and were made of *saffron* (orange-yellow) vinyl. Hung with flowing saffron fabric panels, the gates wound along 23 miles (37 kilometers) of the park's curving pathways. The artists described the 16-day, $20-million installation as "a golden river appearing and disappearing through the bare branches of the trees."

Christo was born Christo Vladimirov Javacheff in Gabrovo, Bulgaria, on June 13, 1935, to a family of industrialists. From 1953 to 1956, he studied at the Fine Arts Academy in Sofia, Bulgaria. In 1957, he fled then-Communist Czechoslovakia for the West and studied briefly at the Vienna (Austria) Fine Arts Academy.

Jeanne-Claude was born Jeanne-Claude Denat de Guillebon, also on June 13, 1935, to a French military family in Casablanca, Morocco. She received a bachelor's degree in Latin and philosophy from the University of Tunis in Tunisia in 1952. Christo and Jeanne-Claude immigrated to the United States in 1964.

Christo and Jeanne-Claude began working together in 1961 on the installation *Stacked Oil Barrels, Dockside Packages at Cologne Harbor* in France. Their collaborations, chiefly done using fabric or plastic, include *Wrapped Museum of Contemporary Art, Chicago* (1969); *Running Fence, Sonoma and Marin Counties, California* (1976); *Surrounded Islands, Biscayne Bay, Greater Miami, Florida* (1983); *The Umbrellas, Japan-U.S.A.*; and *Wrapped Reichstag, Berlin* (1995).

See also **Architecture; New York City.**

Foxx, Jamie

(1967–   ), a highly successful stand-up comedian and television actor, won an Academy Award for best actor on Feb. 27, 2005, for his dynamic portrayal of music legend Ray Charles in *Ray* (2005). Foxx had also been nominated for best supporting actor for his performance as a mild-mannered cabdriver forced to drive a hit man from murder to murder in *Collateral* (2004).

Jamie Foxx, whose birth name was Eric Bishop, was born on Dec. 13, 1967, in Terrell, Texas. A piano student at an early age, Foxx won a music scholarship to U.S. International University in San Diego and studied classical piano at the Julliard School in New York City. While in San Diego, he began auditioning at comedy clubs using the name Jamie Foxx, purportedly because Jamie was perceived to be a woman's name, and women were more likely to be picked from lists of potential performers on open-mike nights.

From 1991 to 1994, he appeared on the television comedy show "In Living Color," where he won notice for his role as Ugly Wanda. From 1996 to 2001, he starred as a bellhop trying to find work as an actor in "The Jamie Foxx Show." He made his motion-picture debut in *The Truth About Cats and Dogs* (1996). His other film credits include *Any Given Sunday* (1999), *Ali* (2001), *Breakin' All the Rules* (2004), *Stealth* (2005), and *Jarhead* (2005).

See also **Motion pictures.**

Gonzales, Alberto R., *guhn ZAH lihz,*

(1955–), a long-time legal adviser to George W. Bush, was sworn in as U.S. attorney general on Feb. 3, 2005. He is the first Hispanic American to head the U.S. Department of Justice.

Gonzales served as President Bush's White House Counsel before being named attorney general. As White House counsel, he worked to expand Bush's power to conduct war. In the early 2000's, he helped draft legal policies extending presidential authority to restrict the legal rights of enemy combatants, including U.S. citizens, during the war on terrorism.

Alberto R. Gonzales was born on Aug. 4, 1955, in San Antonio, Texas, to Mexican immigrants. He served in the U.S. Air Force from 1973 to 1975 and studied at the Air Force Academy in Colorado Springs, Colorado, from 1975 to 1977. He earned a bachelor's degree from Rice University in Houston in 1979 and a law degree from Harvard University in Cambridge, Massachusetts, in 1982. Later that year, Gonzales joined a Houston law firm, where he specialized in corporate law.

In 1995, Bush, then governor of Texas, named Gonzales as his general counsel. Gonzales served in that position until 1997, when he became the Texas secretary of state. In 1999, Bush appointed Gonzales to the Texas Supreme Court. In 2001, after Bush was elected president of the United States, Gonzales left the court to become the president's chief counsel. He remained in that position until Bush named him to the Cabinet.

See also **Cabinet, U.S.**

Gutierrez, *goo TYEHR rehs,* Carlos M.

(1953–), a Cuban-born American business execu-

tive, was sworn in as U.S. secretary of commerce on Feb. 7, 2005. When nominated for the post, Gutierrez was chairman of the board and chief executive officer (CEO) of the Kellogg Company, where he had begun his business career in the mid-1970's selling cereal from a truck.

Gutierrez was born on Nov. 14, 1953, in Havana, Cuba. In 1960, his family fled Cuba for the United States after his father, a successful businessman, was briefly detained by the Communist government of Fidel Castro. Gutierrez became a U.S. citizen in 1966.

In the 1970's, the family moved to Mexico City, and in 1975, Gutierrez began working for Kellogg. By 1984, he had risen through company ranks to

Alberto Gonzales

become general manager of Kellogg's Mexican operations. In 1989, he was named CEO of Kellogg Canada. Beginning in 1990, he held various executive positions with Kellogg at the company's headquarters in Battle Creek, Michigan, becoming president and CEO in 1999. In 2000, he became chairman of the board. At Kellogg, Gutierrez significantly boosted sales, though he drew criticism for closing the company's flagship factory in Battle Creek.

See also **Cabinet, U.S.**

Jean, Michaëlle,

zhahn, mee shah EHL,
(1957–), a Haitian-born journalist, became governor general of Canada on Sept. 27, 2005. She was the first black person appointed to that post. She was also the first person from the province of Quebec to serve in that office since 1990. Some Canadians criticized Jean's appointment, raising concerns that she might be sympathetic to Quebecers seeking independence from Canada and questioning her dual French and Canadian citizenship. Jean subsequently renounced her French citizenship, which she had gained on marrying her French-born husband. In her first speech as governor general, Jean called for national unity.

Jean was born in Port-au-Prince, Haiti, in 1957. In 1968, her family fled the regime of dictator Francois Duvalier and settled in Quebec. In 1984, Jean received a bachelor's degree in literature and Italian and Hispanic languages from the University of Montreal in Quebec. She also studied at univer-

Michaëlle Jean

sities in Florence, Milan, and Perugia, Italy. She speaks fluent English, French, Haitian Creole, Italian, and Spanish.

From 1979 to 1987, Jean worked with Quebec shelters for women and children who were victims of domestic violence. In 1988, she joined the Canadian Broadcasting Corporation, hosting a number of English- and French-language news programs, including "The Passionate Eye" and "Grands Reportages." In 2004, she started her own interview program, "Michaëlle." Jean has received several awards for journalism, including the 1995 Amnesty International Journalism Award and the 2000 Galaxi Award for best information program host.

Jean has also worked on a number of documentary films with her husband, filmmaker Jean-Daniel Lafond. These include *Haiti dans tous nos reves* (*Haiti in All Our Dreams*, 1995) and *L'heure de Cuba* (*Last Call for Cuba*, 1999).

See also **Canada.**

Jeanne-Claude. See **Christo** (page 283).

Libby, I. Lewis "Scooter" (1950–), chief of staff to Vice President Dick Cheney, was charged on Oct. 28, 2005, with five felony counts of lying to federal agents and a federal grand jury investigating the 2003 public disclosure of the identity of a Central Intelligence Agency undercover agent. Libby resigned from his positions in the administration of President George W. Bush immediately after the indictment was announced. Libby had also served both as an assistant to the president and as Cheney's national security adviser. On Nov. 3, 2005, Libby pleaded not guilty to the charges.

Libby was born on Aug. 22, 1950, in New Haven, Connecticut. He received a bachelor's degree from Yale University, also in New Haven, in 1972 and a law degree from Columbia University in New York City in 1975. In 1981, Libby joined the U.S. State Department as a speechwriter. From 1982 to 1985, he served as the director of special projects in the department's Bureau of East Asian and Pacific Affairs. In 1990, he moved to the Department of Defense, first becoming the principal deputy undersecretary for strategy and resources and then, in 1992, the deputy undersecretary for policy. In 2001, after working at an international law firm, he joined Cheney's staff.

See also **People in the news** (Patrick Fitzgerald); **United States, Goverment of the.**

Merkel, Angela (1954–), a physicist raised in Communist East Germany, was sworn in as the first female chancellor of Germany on Nov. 22, 2005. She became the leader of a "grand coalition" government that was formed only after lengthy negotiations between Merkel's Christian Democrats and the opposition Social Democrats. Neither party won enough seats to form a majority government in parliamentary elections held in September.

The former Angela Kasner was born on July 17, 1954, in Hamburg. Her family soon moved to East Germany. At the University of Leipzig, she earned a bachelor's degree in physics in 1978 and completed a doctoral degree in physics in 1986. From 1978 to 1990, she worked as a researcher at the Central Institute of Chemical Physics of the Academy of Sciences in East Berlin.

Merkel became involved in politics in 1989, joining the democratic opposition to the Communist government of East Germany. In 1990, as the two Germanys moved toward reunification, she joined the center-right Christian Democratic Union (CDU). Later in 1996, she won election to the Bundestag, the lower house of parliament, in the first national elections held in a reunified Germany. In 1991, she became minister for women and youth, holding that position until becoming minister of the environment in 1994. In 1998, she was elected general secretary of the CDU, rising to leader of the party in 2000.

See also **Germany.**

Negroponte, John D. (1939–), a career foreign service officer, on April 21, 2005, was sworn in as the first U.S. director of national intelligence. In that position, he had responsibility for overseeing all 15 U.S. intelligence agencies and advising President George W. Bush on intelligence issues affecting national security. Congress established the intelligence director's position in 2004 on the recommendation of the independent commission that investigated the terrorist attacks in the United States on Sept. 11, 2001.

John Dimitri Negroponte was born on July 21, 1939, in London, the son of a Greek-American shipping magnate. In 1960, he received a bachelor's degree from Yale University in New Haven, Connecticut, and joined the U.S. Foreign Service. In 1968 and 1969, he served on the U.S. delegation to peace talks, held in Paris, aimed at ending the Vietnam War (1957-1975). From 1973 to 1977, he held diplomatic posts in Ecuador and Greece. In 1981, Negroponte was appointed U.S. ambassador to Honduras. He later served as ambassador to Mexico and the Philippines.

In 1997, Negroponte left the Foreign Service for a top post with the McGraw-Hill Companies, an international information services corporation. In 2001, he returned to government service as the U.S. ambassador to the United Nations. In 2004, he was appointed ambassador to Iraq.

See also **United States, Government of the.**

Patrick, Danica (1982–), finished fourth

in the 2005 Indianapolis 500, the highest placing by any woman in the history of the race. Patrick also became the first woman driver to lead the race, a position she held for 19 of the race's 200 laps. Patrick is one of only four women to have competed in the Indy 500.

Danica Patrick

Danica Patrick was born on March 25, 1982, in Beloit, Wisconsin, and raised in Roscoe, Illinois, the daughter of a mechanic. She became a kart-racing enthusiast at age 10 after a family outing at a kart track and soon began racing competitively. In 1994, she won the World Karting Association's Manufacturer's Cup title in the Yamaha Sportsman class and the first of three Grand National Championships.

In 1998, she began racing formula cars, making her European debut in the Formula Vauxhall Winter Series. In 2000, she finished second in the Formula Ford Festival at Brands Hatch, England, the best finish by an American in that race. In 2004, she achieved the fastest qualifying speed at a Toyota Atlantic Championship race in Portland, Oregon, becoming the first female driver to earn a pole position in that series.

See also **Automobile racing.**

Reid, Harry (1939–), a soft-spoken but

blunt Nevada politician, took office as Democratic minority leader in the U.S. Senate on Jan. 4, 2005. Reid was elected to the post unanimously in November 2004, after winning his third campaign for the Senate. A political moderate, Reid is known for his tenacity and formidable parliamentary skills.

Harry Mason Reid was born on Dec. 2, 1939, in the mining town of Searchlight, Nevada. He earned a bachelor's degree from Utah State University in Logan in 1961 and a law degree from George Washington University in Washington, D.C., in 1964.

From 1964 to 1966, Reid worked as city attorney for Henderson, Nevada. He served as a member of the Nevada State Assembly in 1969 and 1970 and as lieutenant governor of Nevada from 1970 to 1974, when he mounted his first, and unsuccessful, run for the U.S. Senate. From 1977 to 1981, Reid headed the Nevada Gaming Commission. He won a seat in the U.S. House of Representatives in 1982 and was reelected in 1984. In 1986, Reid made his second run for the Senate and won. He served as Senate Democratic *whip* (assistant leader) from 1999 to 2005.

See also **Congress of the United States; Democratic Party.**

Roberts, John G., Jr. (1955–), a

judge with a reputation for brilliance and an exacting approach to legal opinions, was sworn in as chief justice of the U.S. Supreme Court on Sept. 29, 2005. Roberts succeeded Chief Justice William Rehnquist, who died on September 3. In July, President George W. Bush nominated Roberts to fill the seat being vacated by retiring Associate Justice Sandra Day O'Connor. Following Rehnquist's death, President Bush nominated

Roberts for post of chief justice.

John Glover Roberts was born on Jan. 27, 1955, in Buffalo, New York, and grew up in Long Beach, Indiana. He earned a bachelor's degree in 1976 and a law degree in 1979, both from Harvard University in Cambridge, Massachusetts. He then worked as a law clerk for Rehnquist, then an associate Supreme Court justice.

From 1982 to 1986, Roberts served as a legal adviser to President Ronald Reagan. From 1989 to 1993, he worked as principal deputy solicitor general under President George H. W. Bush. From 1986 to 1989 and from 1993 to 2003, Roberts worked for a private law firm, quickly rising to partner. While working as deputy solicitor general and in private practice, Roberts argued 39 cases before the Supreme Court. In 2003, President George W. Bush named him a federal appeals court judge.

See also **Deaths; Supreme Court of the United States.**

John G. Roberts, Jr.

Rove, Karl (1950–   ), chief political adviser to President George W. Bush, became assistant to the president and deputy chief of staff for policy in February 2005. Rove had served as chief strategist for Bush's gubernatorial and presidential campaigns since 1993. In his new post, Rove gained responsibility for coordinating domestic policy, economic policy, national security, and homeland security. Many political experts regard Rove as the "architect" of George W. Bush's political career.

Karl Rove was born on Dec. 25, 1950, in Denver. In 1971, he left his studies at the University of Utah in Salt Lake City to become executive director of the College Republicans, the student branch of the Republican Party. He was elected national chairman of the organization in 1972. During the 1970's, Rove helped Republicans wrest political control of Texas from the Democrats. In 1980, Rove worked for George H. W. Bush's vice presidential campaign. From 1981 to 1999, Rove served as president of Karl Rove and Associates, a political consulting firm based in Austin. After wining the presidency in 2000, Bush named Rove senior White House adviser.

See also **Republican Party; United States, Government of the.**

Sheehan, Cindy (1957–   ), the mother of a U.S. Army soldier killed in Iraq, helped mobilize opposition in 2005 to the Iraq War, which began in 2003. Sheehan's 24-year-old son, Casey, died on April 4, 2004, in an ambush near Baghdad.

Sheehan, who lived in Vacaville, California,

made national headlines in August 2005, when she maintained a roadside vigil for 26 days outside President George W. Bush's ranch near Crawford, Texas. Sheehan asserted that she would remain near the ranch until the president personally explained his reasons for invading Iraq. Sheehan had met with Bush in June 2004, during one of his regular meetings with relatives of troops killed in the line of duty.

Sheehan, who in 2004 helped found the peace advocacy group Gold Star Families for Peace, attracted a number of supporters in 2005 to her campaign. However, she also drew sharp criticism from supporters of the war as well as from many families of military personnel serving in Iraq, including some members of her own family. Her opponents argued that her efforts were dishonoring U.S. forces.

In late August, Sheehan joined an antiwar bus tour that traveled to 25 states. In September, she spoke at an antiwar march on Washington, D.C., that drew an estimated 100,000 participants.

Spellings, Margaret (1957–), a longtime policy adviser to President George W. Bush, was sworn in as secretary of education on Jan. 20, 2005. As assistant to the president for domestic policy during this first term, Spellings was one of the principal authors of the No Child Left Behind Act of 2001, which significantly expanded the role of the federal government in public education in the United States.

Spellings was born on Nov. 30, 1957, in Ann Arbor, Michigan. At a young age, she moved with her family to Houston. She earned a bachelor's degree in political science from the University of Houston in 1979.

During the 1980's, Spellings worked as an aide in the Texas state legislature and as the associate executive director of the Texas Association of School Boards. In 1994, Bush asked her to work as the political director of his campaign for governor of Texas. After winning that office, Bush named her his chief education adviser. After Bush won the presidency in 2000, Spellings became the president's chief education adviser.

See also **Education.**

Stewart, Jon (1962–),

a comedian known for his sharp wit, collected two Emmy Awards on Sept. 18, 2005, for his satirical news program, "The Daily Show with Jon Stewart." The show won for outstanding variety, music, or comedy series and for outstanding writing for variety, music, or comedy program. Described by Stewart as a "fake news program," the show also has collected several prestigious journalism awards.

Stewart was born Jon Stewart Liebowitz in New York City on Nov. 28, 1962. His family soon moved to Lawrenceville, New Jersey. In 1984, he received a bachelor's degree from William and Mary College in Williamsburg, Virginia.

Stewart first appeared on television in 1989 in the comedy series "Short Attention Span Theater," moving up to host from 1990 to 1992. In 1993, he starred in the short-lived comedy series "The Jon Stewart Show." In 1999, Stewart took over as host of "The Daily Show." He has also appeared in a number of motion pictures, including *Mixed Nuts* (1994), his film debut, and *Death to Smoochy*

(2002). He is the coauthor of *The Daily Show with Jon Stewart Presents America (The Book): A Citizen's Guide to Democracy Inaction* (2004).

See also **Television.**

Yushchenko, Viktor Andriyovich

YOOSH chehn kaw, VEEK tawr ahn DREE yoh vihch (1954–), was inaugurated as president of Ukraine on Jan. 27, 2005, following a tumultuous campaign. Yushchenko's presidency, however, was seriously damaged in 2005 by political struggles with his prime minister and by charges of corruption against some of his closest advisers.

Yushchenko was born on Feb. 23, 1954, in Khoruzhivka, Ukraine, then a republic of the Soviet Union. He graduated from the Ternopil Academy of National Economy in 1975. He then began a career as a banker in the Ukrainian branch of the Soviet Union's State Bank.

In 1993, after Ukraine declared its independence from the Soviet Union, Yushchenko became the governor of the National Bank of Ukraine. He helped guide the country through a difficult transition from a government-controlled economy to a free-market economy.

In 1999, Yushchenko was appointed prime minister. In 2001, members of Ukraine's parliament opposed to Yushchenko's attempted economic reforms voted to remove him from office. He then became the leader of Our Ukraine, a reform coalition.

In 2004, while running for president, Yushchenko suffered an illness that left his face swollen and scarred. Medical tests later revealed that he had been poisoned with dioxin, a highly toxic, synthetically produced chemical.

In the election, held in October 2004, Yushchenko and his opponent, Prime Minister Viktor Yanukovych, each won about 40 percent of the vote. Ukraine's Central Election Commission declared Yanukovych the winner after a November runoff election. However, international observers reported widespread election fraud. Yushchenko's supporters filled the streets of Ukraine's largest cities to protest the results. In early December, Ukraine's Supreme Court *annulled* (canceled) the results of the runoff and ordered a second runoff. Yushchenko won that election with about 52 percent of the vote.

See also **Russia: A Special Report; Ukraine.**

■ Barbara A. Mayes

Jon Stewart

Peru experienced substantial economic growth during 2005, expanding its *gross domestic product* (GDP) by about 5 percent. (GDP is the value of all goods and services produced in a country in a given year.) Most of the gain in GDP, according to economists, was due to high world prices for Peru's copper, gold, silver, and zinc—mineral exports whose value in 2005 topped $16 billion, double the value of these exports in 2001.

In an interview in September 2005, President Alejandro Toledo, Peru's first chief executive of *indigenous* (native Indian) ancestry, expressed satisfaction over some of his administration's achievements. Nearing the end of a five-year presidential term begun in 2001, Toledo acknowledged, however, that his administration had made little headway in tackling widespread poverty in Peru. An estimated 54 percent of Peruvians lived on less than $2 a day in 2005, and 68 percent lived without electric power. Especially hard-pressed, analysts observed, were the people living under hazardous conditions in Peru's far-flung mining communities, which produced much of the country's wealth.

Scandals. Critics alleged that President Toledo was besieged by family members and associates seeking favors and jobs when he took office in 2001. In time, congressional probes resulted in formal charges against a brother of the president and ongoing investigations against other Toledo family members. In one of the most potentially damaging investigations, a congressional committee was looking into allegations that Toledo family members had forged voters' names on petitions to get Toledo's name on the ballot for the 2001 presidential election. The accumulation of scandals surrounding Toledo eroded his support, driving his approval rating below 10 percent by 2005.

Protests against mining companies operating in Peru led to at least 27 separate incidents across the country during 2005. One of the most violent episodes occurred in August at the Majaz mine in the Andes Mountains in the northern department of Piura. Protesters there alleged that the mine, owned by London-based Monterrico Metals, was polluting a major *aquifer* (underground river) that supplies water to surrounding communities. In two days of confrontations between the protesters and police, at least one protester was killed and scores of others were injured.

Antimining protesters received encouragement, analysts suggested, from an April court ruling in which Judge Rosario Alfaro ordered government agencies to develop a public health plan to alleviate environmental pollution caused by a United States-owned smelter. Smelting operations of the St. Louis, Missouri-based Doe Run Company, carried on at La Oroya, a town about 100 miles (160 kilometers) inland from Lima, the capital, allegedly were pouring tons of lead and other toxic metals into the air. In his ruling, the judge cited studies showing that 99.9 percent of children living in or near La Oroya tested positive in late 2004 for harmful levels of lead. Critics faulted the Toledo administration for granting Doe Run an exemption in 2004 that allowed the company to delay its compliance with Peruvian pollution standards for up to four years.

Presidential contenders. Peruvian disillusionment with President Toledo contributed to an early emergence of presidential contenders leading up to elections scheduled for April 2006. The front-runner in late 2005 was Lourdes Flores Nano, head of the hard-line conservative Popular Christian party. Two disgraced former presidents, each wanted for trial in Peru, were angling for presidential comebacks. Alan Garcia Perez (1985–1990) waged his campaign from the safety of exile in Colombia. Alberto Fujimori Kenya (1990–2000), who had been campaigning in exile from a Web site, was arrested in November 2005 in Santiago, Chile. The governments of Chile and Peru then entered into negotiations for the extradition of Fujimori to Peru to face various human rights charges.   ■ Nathan A. Haverstock

See also **Latin America.**

Petroleum and gas. See Energy Supply.

Philadelphia. Federal prosecutors in 2005 convicted 10 of 12 people charged with conspiracy, fraud, or extortion in a widespread probe of city government practices. Among them was former city treasurer Corey Kemp, who was sentenced on July 19 to 10 years in prison for welfare, bank, and tax frauds.

One of the two defendants not convicted, Ronald White, an attorney, died of complications related to cancer before his trial. The other, Denis Carlson, an investment banker, was acquitted of lying to Federal Bureau of Investigation (FBI) agents. White had worked for the city and was a fund-raiser for Mayor John F. Street. The FBI built much of its case from wiretapped conversations on White's phone. The mayor was not charged with any crime, and he claimed that he had done nothing wrong. However, the indictment alleged that he had instructed his staff to award business to White or firms that White backed if the firms appeared to be qualified.

Abuse by priests. A grand jury issued a 418-page report accusing past leaders of the Philadelphia Roman Catholic Archdiocese of covering up four decades or more of sexual abuse of minors by priests. The report noted that archdiocese officials had a pattern of moving priests suspected of abusing parishioners to other posts instead of punishing them.

More than 800,000 people gather near the Philadelphia Museum of Art for a Live 8 music concert on July 2, 2005. Promoters hoped that the concert, one of nine such musical events worldwide, would increase public awareness of the financial plights of developing countries, particularly the nations of sub-Saharan Africa.

"[I]n its callous, calculating manner, the archdiocese's handling of the abuse scandal was at least as immoral as the abuse itself," stated the grand jury report, issued September 21 and released by district attorney Lynne Abraham. It continued: "What we have found were not acts of God, but of men who acted in His name and defiled it." At least 63 priests abused hundreds of victims over the years, the report detailed.

The grand jury did not recommend criminal charges. The statute of limitations had run out, and the church hierarchy did not report abuses until it was too late for prosecutors to build cases. The report asked for legislative changes abolishing the statute of limitations for sexual abuse of children.

The jury began its examination in 2002, more than a year before Cardinal Justin Rigali became leader of the Philadelphia Archdiocese. Church officials countered, with a 70-page response, that the report was a "vile, mean-spirited diatribe." Rigali noted, however, that the archdiocese "acknowledges and completely repents mistakes made in the handling of some cases."

Live 8 concert. More than 800,000 people streamed into Center City, Philadelphia's downtown, on July 2, 2005, for the only concert in the United States in the worldwide Live 8 event. The popular-music concerts, in nine cities, called on the leaders of the world's richest countries to put an end to poverty and debt in developing countries.

The concert, on the grounds of the Philadelphia Museum of Art and extending down the Benjamin Franklin Parkway, began at noon with comments from rapper, television personality, and movie actor Will Smith, a Philadelphia native.

Transit strike. A weeklong transit strike shut down buses, subways, and trolleys and ended on November 7 when the union agreed to a contract.

Benjamin Franklin tercentenary. A special commission prepared throughout 2005 for the 300th birthday of Benjamin Franklin, the founding father whose name is synonymous with Philadelphia. Franklin was born on Jan. 17, 1706.

The commission organized an exhibit, *Benjamin Franklin: In Search of a Better World,* that opened on Dec. 15, 2005, at the National Constitution Center. It was scheduled to run through April 30, 2006. The organizers planned to move the exhibition to St. Louis, Missouri, then on to Denver, Colorado; Houston; Atlanta, Georgia; and Paris.

Two city leaders die. Robert Montgomery Scott, former president of the Philadelphia Museum of Art, died Oct. 12, 2005. Edmund Bacon, a city planner who modernized much of downtown Philadelphia, and the father of actor Kevin Bacon, died October 14.

■ Howard S. Shapiro

See also **City; Popular Music; Roman Catholic Church.**

Philippines. Opponents of Philippine President Gloria Macapagal-Arroyo tried unsuccessfully in 2005 to remove her from office through impeachment. Macapagal-Arroyo, who had moved up from the vice presidency in 2001, won a six-year term as president by more than 1 million votes in a 2004 election. However, political enemies accused her of rigging the vote to win the election.

In June 2005, Macapagal-Arroyo's opponents made public a recording of a telephone conversation that took place during the vote counting in 2004. On the recording, a woman talking with an election commissioner asks if her lead could fall below 1 million votes and expresses concern about poll results in the south. The commissioner replies, "We will do our best," without explanation. After weeks of public furor, Macapagal-Arroyo acknowledged in a television address on June 27 that she had phoned an election commissioner but said she was only trying to protect her votes, not influence the outcome. She denied any illegality and apologized for a "lapse in judgment" in having made the phone call.

Macapagal-Arroyo's opponents seized on the issue, as well as several other charges of corruption, to try to remove her from office. To vote-rigging and corruption accusations, they added

other charges, including *graft* (the awarding of contracts in which an officeholder has an interest).

Protests. Trying to imitate "people power" demonstrations that had driven Filipino presidents from office in 1986 and 2001, opponents of Macapagal-Arroyo organized protest rallies in 2005. None drew the hundreds of thousands of people who had mobbed Manila, the capital, on the earlier occasions, and Macapagal-Arroyo was able to muster supporters for her own large rallies. Bishops of the nation's dominant Roman Catholic Church, who had been influential in turning the public against former presidents, refused to side with Macapagal-Arroyo's opponents.

Ten officials quit after Macapagal-Arroyo asked her entire Cabinet to resign on July 7. They said they had planned to resign because she could no longer govern effectively while facing the accusations. Former President Corazon Aquino joined them in calling for the president to resign. Macapagal-Arroyo refused, saying she should be judged by the nation's Congress, where her supporters controlled both houses.

In late August, the justice committee of the lower house took up three impeachment charges. Committee members who supported the charges were in the minority, and they walked out on the proceedings. The remaining members rejected the charges in a nearly unanimous vote on August 31. After almost 24 hours of continuous debate, the lower house voted 158 to 51 on September 6 to uphold the committee's decision, ending the impeachment proceedings against Macapagal-Arroyo.

Changing government. On July 25, Macapagal-Arroyo, in her annual State of the Nation speech to Congress, called for the government to change to a parliamentary system. The new system would replace the president, who often had trouble getting laws through a divided and chaotic Congress, with a prime minister backed by the lower house's largest political grouping. A parliamentary system would allow for a change of national leaders without the turmoil that had accompanied the removal of presidents in 1986 and 2001.

Arguing that this would lead to more effective government, Macapagal-Arroyo said the two houses of Congress should turn themselves into a constituent assembly to amend the Philippine Constitution. If adopted, her plan would end her presidency short of its 2010 term. However, many Filipino politicians were skeptical. The upper house of Congress was considered likely to turn down the changes, which would limit its power. Some critics said any constituent assembly should be freshly elected rather than coming from Congress.

Terrorism continued to plague the Philippines in 2005. On February 14, bombs exploded in Manila and in two southern cities, killing 11 people and wounding some 130 others. Police blamed Abu Sayyaf, an Islamic fundamentalist group that authorities linked with the al-Qa`ida terrorist network. An Indonesian and two Filipinos were sentenced to death in October for their participation in the bombings.

A different form of terrorism stalked Filipino journalists who reported on corruption or angered local bosses. The New York City-based Committee to Protect Journalists announced on May 2, 2005, that the Philippines had become the world's "most murderous" country for journalists, with 66 individuals killed in the country since 1986.

Economy. The Philippine Supreme Court approved on Oct. 18, 2005, an increase from 10 to 12 percent in the value-added tax, a tax on goods as they pass through the production and sales cycles. Corporate taxes were also raised. These measures, which had been challenged by corporations, were expected to yield about $1.8 billion annually beginning in 2006. They were intended to help the government reduce a national debt of some $70 billion, half of it owed to foreigners, and to eliminate a budget deficit within five years.

■ Henry S. Bradsher

See also **Asia; Terrorism.**

Physics.

Physics. The United Nations declared 2005 the "International Year of Physics" to mark the 100th anniversary of Albert Einstein's *annus mirabilis* (miracle year). In 1905, the 26-year-old Einstein, while working as a patent examiner, wrote five papers that ushered in the modern age of physics and forever altered human understanding of the universe.

Scientists and physics students from around the world celebrated in 2005 with hundreds of ceremonies, conferences, museum displays, publications, and research projects, many of which were targeted at young people to promote interest in careers in physics.

Reconstructing the quake. The earthquake of Dec. 26, 2004, which caused the subsequent devastating tsunami, was the largest seismic event in 40 years, according to research released in May 2005. A group of 40 scientists from 30 institutions around the world published three comprehensive papers on the quake in the journal *Science*. The physicists used data from geological instruments around the globe to build computer models of the quake and reconstruct what happened.

The study confirmed that the earthquake occurred in a "subduction zone" where the floor of the Indian Ocean plunges under the geological plate that underlies Southeast Asia. According to the physicists' computer models, the ocean floor moved as much as 50 feet (15 meters) along a crack 960 miles (1,545 kilometers) long. The quake released as much energy as the combined force of all other earthquakes that have occurred since 1980. In fact, one of the earthquake's aftershocks, on March 28, 2005, was the second greatest earthquake in 40 years.

Light from tiny bubbles. Physicists have known since the 1930's that when very high frequency sound passes through liquids, tiny bubbles are formed and some of these bubbles emit light. Theorists had explained this effect by assuming that the sound waves cause rapid contraction of these bubbles, which heats the vapor inside them to very high temperatures.

In March 2005, researchers David Flannigan and Kenneth Suslick of the University of Illinois at Urbana-Champaign found that the temperature in these bubbles rises above 26,500 °F (14,700 °C), which confirmed the long-held theory. The temperature is several times as hot as the surface of the sun—hot enough to strip electrons from the atoms in the bubble and form a state of matter called plasma. The plasma emitted a spectrum of light that enabled the researchers to measure the temperature inside the bubbles.

Fusion in France. The last obstacle to an international effort to build a nuclear fusion reactor was removed in June 2005 when the partner nations agreed to build the reactor in Cadarache in southern France. The United States and several other nations had preferred a site in Japan. The project is known as ITER, a Latin word meaning "the way." Nearly all of the world's developed nations participated in the project.

Since the 1950's, physicists have sought to control the release of energy from the fusion of deuterium, an *isotope* (form) of hydrogen that is abundant and relatively cheap. However, to get the deuterium nuclei close enough to undergo fusion, a deuterium plasma must be raised to very high temperatures, comparable with those in the interior of the sun.

Physicists had found it difficult to confine a plasma at these temperatures, and until the ITER proposal, it had been impossible to hold a plasma long enough to generate as much energy as went into heating it. ITER is expected to produce 10 times as much energy as it uses to achieve fusion.

The project was expected to cost about $5 billion to build, with a completion date of 2016. It will consist of a giant, doughnut-shaped machine, called a tokamak, in which plasma is confined by a strong magnetic field. ITER will produce about 500 megawatts of power, as much as a large electric power plant. If ITER succeeds, fusion may produce a substantial portion of the world's power by the end of the 2000's. ■ Robert H. March

See also **Physics: A Special Report.**

Light quanta

Atoms

Relativity

$E=mc^2$

1905—
EINSTEIN'S
MIRACLE
YEAR

In 1905, Albert Einstein wrote four papers that ushered in the modern age of physics. One hundred years later, his theories continue to shape scientific thought and profoundly affect everyday life.

By Alfred J. Smuskiewicz

Scientists from around the world celebrated in 2005 the 100th anniversary of Albert Einstein's revolutionary breakthroughs in physics. In 1905, Einstein made a series of scientific discoveries that transformed human understanding of the universe and laid the foundation of modern physics. The reverberations of Einstein's so-called *annus mirabilis* (miracle year or year of marvels) continue to shake the world of science and technology.

In 1905, Albert Einstein was a 26-year-old clerk in the Swiss Federal Patent Office in Bern. The simple job left the German-born graduate student the time to work on a *dissertation* (formal paper needed to obtain a doctoral degree) in physics. He also pursued what he called "thought experiments," mental models of physics problems that he solved by intuition. From March to September, Einstein's thought experiments and mathematical equations led to four revolutionary papers that broke with classical physics and solved several of the most troubling scientific problems of his day.

The study of physics was in a state of disorder at the beginning of the 1900's. In the late 1800's, physicists discovered flaws in ideas that had been accepted as truth since the time of the English scientist Sir Isaac Newton (1642-1727). Since 1687, scientists had accepted from Newton's theories that observers moving at a constant *velocity* (speed in a particular direction) are governed by the same laws of physics as observers at rest. Many scientists also believed that all objects moved within a substance—ether—that filled all space.

The theory of electricity and magnetism developed by the Scottish scientist James Clerk Maxwell (1831-1879) suggested that visible light and other forms of electromagnetic waves travel through ether like ripples on a pond. According to Newton's theories, the speed of electromagnetic waves depends on how fast an observer is traveling compared with the ether. However, experiments conducted in the 1880's proved that electromagnetic waves travel at the same speed whether an observer is moving or at rest.

Another problem troubling physicists in the early 1900's involved the photoelectric effect, in which a beam of light shown on a metal plate causes the plate to release *electrons* (negatively charged particles) as an electric current. Physicists did not understand how light waves could explain the quantity and speed of electrons ejected from the plate.

Four revolutionary theories

Einstein addressed the photoelectric effect in March 1905 in the first of his four 1905 papers. He reasoned that the effect could happen only if light exists not just as waves of energy, but also as *quanta* (basic units of radiant energy). These quanta—known as photons—collide with electrons in the atoms that make up metal, knocking the electrons from the atoms. Einstein's model predicted the correct quantity and speed of the ejected electrons. Scientists have since proved that all forms of electromagnetic energy (such as light, radio transmissions, and X rays) exist as both waves and particles. Einstein won the 1921 Nobel Prize in physics for explaining the photoelectric effect.

In May 1905, Einstein explained another bewildering phenomenon, *Brownian motion.* Scientists previously had observed Brownian motion—jerky, irregular movement of microscopic particles suspended in liquids and gases—but did not understand it. Einstein showed that microscopic collisions of atoms within liquids and gases accounted for the jittery movement. Philosophers had theorized for thousands of years that atoms were tiny units that make up matter, but Einstein's analysis in combination with experiments conducted later by other scientists provided the first conclusive evidence that atoms do, in fact, exist.

Einstein is most famous for his theories of relativity. The first of these—the special theory of relativity—appeared in June 1905. In this paper, Einstein firmly rejected the idea of a mysterious, invisible ether spreading throughout space. He substituted the radical concept of spacetime, a four-dimensional combination of the three dimensions of space (length, width, and height) with the dimension of time. According to Einstein's theory, space and time are not separate entities. Instead, they are intertwined, forming a kind of fabric throughout the universe.

Measurements of space and time, according to Einstein's special theory of relativity, are not constant. They are relative—that is, they change—depending on an observer's position and velocity or frame of reference. The changing nature of space and time, however, would be apparent only to an observer moving near the speed of light, which is 186,282 miles (299,792 kilometers) per second.

A fundamental aspect of the special theory of relativity is the absoluteness of the speed of light. The speed is not affected by an observer's motion in any particular direction, as many scientists had assumed. In addition, Einstein established that nothing can move faster than the speed of light. It is the absolute cosmic speed limit.

Einstein imagined the relationship among different observers, space, and time with thought experiments. For example, imagine two spaceships moving relative to each other at a speed close to the speed of

The author:
Alfred J. Smuskiewicz is a free-lance writer specializing in science and medicine.

Light quanta

Einstein's first discovery changed human understanding of light.

The connection between electricity and light is something now taken for granted. A scanner at the supermarket (below) instantly registers the prices of grocery items by bouncing light off the bar code and turning it into an electrical signal. Solar panels (left) convert light from the sun into electric power. Inside these devices, light shines on metal surfaces, causing electrons to flow from the metal as an electric current. Einstein explained this phenomenon, known as the photoelectric effect, in his first paper of 1905.

Einstein proposed that light is made up of tiny particles of energy called *quanta*. When each light quantum—also known as a *photon*—strikes a metal atom, it causes the atom to eject some electrons. Einstein created the mathematical equations that relate the amount of incoming photons to the quantity of outgoing electrons. In the case of a bar code scanner, more photons reflect from the lighter areas of the bar code. As these patterns of photons hit the scanner, they produce a unique electrical signal for each item in the store.

light. Aboard each ship is a clock that is visible to passengers on both ships. According to the special theory of relativity, passengers on one ship would see the clock in the other ship running more slowly than their own clock—even though both are moving at the same rate when seen at rest. This phenomenon is known as time dilation. Passengers on each ship would also see the other ship becoming shorter than their own—though both ships are the same length when seen at rest. This effect is called length contraction.

In time dilation, an observer at rest sees time passing more slowly for a traveler as that traveler's speed approaches the speed of light. The "twin paradox" illustrates this idea. One brother stays on Earth for several decades, while his twin takes a trip in a spaceship, traveling close to light speed, for the same period. When the astronaut twin returns home, he finds his brother is an old man, but the astronaut is only a few months older than when he left on his trip.

In length contraction, an observer at rest sees a moving object shrink along its direction of motion as the object's speed approaches the speed of light. The "pole in the barn paradox" demonstrates this concept. A farmer takes a pole that is 20 feet (6 meters) long and throws it at near light speed into a barn that is 10 feet (3 meters) long. If the pole were at rest, it would not fit in the barn, but because the rapidly moving pole has a shorter length, the farmer finds that it does fit.

Einstein's final revolutionary paper appeared in September 1905. This paper, which followed from the principles of special relativity,

Atoms

Einstein's second breakthrough revealed the true nature of matter.

What is matter made of? For thousands of years, scientists and philosophers wondered whether matter was composed of basic building blocks or whether it could be broken into infinitely small pieces. In the early 1900's, scientists struggled to understand an effect called Brownian motion—the jittery movements of tiny particles suspended in gases and liquids. In May 1905, Einstein explained this motion in terms of collisions between the suspended particles and the atoms of the surrounding gases and liquids. With his second revolutionary paper, Einstein established that matter was indeed composed of atoms. In the 100 years since Einstein's discovery, scientists have developed the ability to manipulate matter at the atomic level or below—a field called nanotechnology. In one striking example, physicists at Cornell University in Ithaca, New York, used nanotechnology to create a guitar (left) only 0.4 thousandths of an inch (0.01 centimeter) long —the size of a single cell. This nanoguitar has six strings, each of which is only about 100 atoms thick.

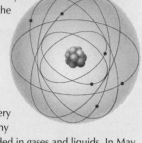

featured history's most famous mathematical equation, now written as $E=mc^2$. The equation is an expression of the idea that an object at rest has an energy E equal to the object's mass m times the speed of light c multiplied by itself. The equation is a mathematical way of saying that energy can change into mass, and mass can change into energy. Einstein described how the conversion of matter from one form to another can release energy. For example, when hydrogen is converted into helium within the sun, some mass is turned into the heat and light energy that makes life possible on Earth.

Physics' new foundation

The four major Einstein papers published in 1905 form the foundation of modern physics. However, the special theory of relativity raised a serious new problem with Newton's theories. Newton theorized that the force of gravity is somehow instantly transmitted between widely separated objects, such as Earth and the sun. However, if nothing can move faster than the speed of light, gravity could not work according to Newton's explanation.

In 1915, Einstein proposed a new explanation for gravity—the general theory of relativity—which agreed with his special theory of relativity. According to the general theory of relativity, gravity exists between objects as a distortion, or curve, in the fabric of space-time. The distortion is caused by massive objects, such as the sun, so that less massive objects, such as Earth, get trapped in a space-time curve around the more massive objects. According to the general theory of relativity, time moves more slowly closer to a massive object than it does farther away. Einstein's general theory of relativity combined space, time, and gravity, providing scientists with a full understanding of space-time.

Einstein's papers, and his later work on gravity, led to many new areas of scientific research. Einstein, however, disapproved of some of the paths this research took.

Quantum mechanics, the field of physics that describes the behavior of atoms and subatomic particles, grew directly out of Einstein's principle that light comes in distinct quanta. Investigators in quantum mechanics have discovered that the microscopic world works differently from the world commonly experienced by most human beings. Experiments have shown that physics cannot make definite predictions about the motion of subatomic particles. For example, physicists employ quantum mechanics to estimate the probability that an electron is in a specific place within an atom but cannot pinpoint that location with certainty. In quantum mechanics, all possibilities for the electron's position are valid.

Einstein, who believed in the power of science to make definite predictions and arrive at conclusive answers, held grave doubts about quantum mechanics. He did not believe that physicists could only calculate probabilities for the subatomic realm. Expressing his reservations about the hazy nature of quantum mechanics, he wrote, "I am at all events convinced that He [God] does not play dice." Einstein spent the last 25 years of his life trying unsuccessfully to develop a so-called unified field theory, partly to resolve what he saw as the flaws in quantum theory.

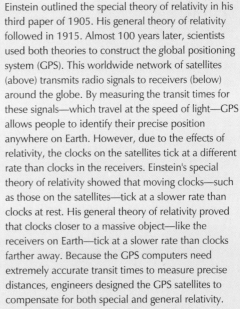

Relativity

Einstein's theories altered human perceptions of space and time.

Einstein outlined the special theory of relativity in his third paper of 1905. His general theory of relativity followed in 1915. Almost 100 years later, scientists used both theories to construct the global positioning system (GPS). This worldwide network of satellites (above) transmits radio signals to receivers (below) around the globe. By measuring the transit times for these signals—which travel at the speed of light—GPS allows people to identify their precise position anywhere on Earth. However, due to the effects of relativity, the clocks on the satellites tick at a different rate than clocks in the receivers. Einstein's special theory of relativity showed that moving clocks—such as those on the satellites—tick at a slower rate than clocks at rest. His general theory of relativity proved that clocks closer to a massive object—like the receivers on Earth—tick at a slower rate than clocks farther away. Because the GPS computers need extremely accurate transit times to measure precise distances, engineers designed the GPS satellites to compensate for both special and general relativity.

Einstein's unified field theory would have been a "theory of everything" that united all ideas about forces and matter into a single, comprehensive theory. Many physicists continue the quest for such a "theory of everything" by attempting to unify the principles of quantum mechanics, which describes the world of the very tiny, with those of Einstein's general theory of relativity, which describes the very large. In one version of such a unified theory, scientists propose that superstrings, tiny loops of energy, make up all particles of matter and explain all the forces in the universe. If superstring theory is correct, the universe would have at least 10 dimensions—6 more than the 4 familiar dimensions of space-time.

The puzzle of dark energy remains another area of research that is heavily based on Einstein's discoveries. Scientists use the term dark energy to describe a mysterious form of energy that causes galaxies to spread farther and farther apart at an accelerating rate. Since scientists discovered the accelerating expansion of the universe in the late 1990's, they have struggled to explain what kind of invisible force might be driving it. Many physicists point out that Einstein's general theory of relativity suggests that empty space might actually have some form of energy that could affect galaxies. Einstein called this unknown force the cosmological constant—though he later retracted the proposal.

Applying Einstein's theories

During the past 100 years, Einstein's ideas about atoms, mass, energy, time, space, light, and gravity made modern physics possible and led to numerous practical technological breakthroughs—both beneficial and harmful.

Scientists can harness nuclear energy, the energy released by changes in the *nuclei* (cores) of atoms, because Einstein discovered that mass and energy are interchangeable. In a nuclear reactor, the *fission* (splitting) of uranium nuclei releases energy that is converted largely into heat. Einstein's $E=mc^2$ equation also led to the development of nuclear weapons. In fact, Einstein wrote a letter to United States President Franklin D. Roosevelt in 1939, shortly before the outbreak of World War II (1939-1945), warning that German scientists might be developing an atomic bomb. The letter resulted in the Manhattan Project, a U.S. scientific undertaking that led to the production of the first atomic bomb in 1945. In the years before his death in 1955, Einstein urged nations to give up nuclear weapons and to establish controls on nuclear energy.

Einstein also contributed to technology based on a more benign form of energy—solar energy—by discovering that light occurs as particles called photons. Solar cells are based on the fact that photons from the sun force electrons to flow through layers of conductive material in the cells, producing an electric current.

Among the most widely appreciated technological outcomes of Einstein's explanation of the photoelectric effect are such consumer electronic devices as compact disc players, remote controls, and digital cameras. Einstein's explanation enabled engineers to combine electronic circuits with light, which is essential to the workings of these devices.

Einstein's ideas about the relativity of space and time also have practical

E=mc²

Einstein's fourth revolutionary paper unleashed the nuclear age.

Nuclear energy—from the peaceful power generation of a nuclear reactor (below) to the terrifying destruction of a nuclear bomb (above)—followed directly from Einstein's fourth paper of 1905. With the most famous equation in history, $E=mc^2$, Einstein showed that even a small amount of *mass* (quantity of matter) contains an enormous amount of energy. Scientists have put this equation into practice by converting part of the tiny *nuclei* (cores) of atoms into energy. All large commercial nuclear power plants, and some early nuclear weapons, produce energy by splitting the nuclei of uranium atoms. These devices fire a subatomic particle called a neutron at a uranium nucleus, breaking it into two fragments. The combined mass of the two pieces is less than the mass of the original nucleus. According to Einstein's equation, the missing mass is converted into energy—mostly an enormous amount of heat—and other particles. These particles cause more uranium atoms to split, which releases even more energy. The combined energy output can power entire cities—or destroy them.

applications. The global positioning system (GPS), a worldwide navigation system that uses radio signals broadcast by satellites, involves both the special and general theories of relativity. Because of the combination of effects predicted by these theories, scientists knew that clocks on the navigation satellites would tick faster than ground clocks. Before the satellites were launched, technicians slightly slowed the rate at which the clocks ticked—so that, when the clocks sped up in orbit, they ticked at the same rate as ground clocks.

By establishing the existence of atoms, Einstein contributed to the development of nanotechnology—the manipulation of individual atoms and molecules to create larger structures. Industry now uses nanotechnology to create strong but lightweight and long-lasting metal, plastic, and ceramic materials. Other nanotechnology-based products include some stain-resistant fabrics, advanced sunscreens, and tiny mechanical devices.

The United Nations celebrated Einstein's miracle year by declaring 2005 the "International Year of Physics." In January, scientists and physics students from around the world gathered at the United Nations Educational, Scientific and Cultural Organization (UNESCO) headquarters in Paris to celebrate Einstein's genius and legacy. At the "Physics for Tomorrow" conference, Nobel Prize winners joined with the next generation of scientists in discussing the challenges today's physicists, like Einstein before them, faced at the dawn of a new century.

Poetry. The appreciation of poetry as a spoken art was cultivated in schools across the United States in 2005. The National Endowment for the Arts (NEA) in Washington, D.C., in conjunction with the Poetry Foundation in Chicago, organized a national initiative called Poetry Out Loud. The NEA is an independent agency of the U.S. government that promotes and assists individuals and organizations in a wide range of artistic endeavors. The Poetry Foundation is a nonprofit organization that publishes *Poetry* magazine as well as promoting poetry through a variety of programs.

The program, which was launched in the spring of 2005 in both Washington, D.C., and Chicago before expanding to cities nationwide, is a poetry competition based on memorization and performance, similar to a poetry slam. However, in poetry slams participants often perform work that they have written, while in Poetry Out Loud students select poems by an established poet for their recitation. Each participating classroom sent one winning student to a schoolwide competition. The winner of each school competition will advance to state and then national finals, to be held in Washington, D.C., in May 2006, where a total of $50,000 will be awarded in scholarships and school stipends. Program organizers, who estimated that 250,000 students will participate in Poetry Out Loud in the 2005-2006 season, described the initiative as designed to help students "master public speaking skills, build self-confidence, and learn about their literary heritage."

Pulitzer Prize. In April 2005, the Pulitzer Prize for poetry went to U.S. Poet Laureate Ted Kooser for his collection *Delights & Shadows.* Kooser was born in Ames, Iowa, in 1939 and spent much of his life as an executive for an insurance company. His poetry, which often features images and situations of life centered in rural Nebraska, is often praised for its clarity. Kooser, who was named Poet Laureate in August 2004, was appointed in April 2005 to a second one-year term in the position.

The collected Wilbur. Among the poetry books selected by *The New York Times* as a notable book of the year in 2005 was *Collected Poems: 1943-2004* by former U.S. Poet Laureate Richard Wilbur. In addition to his acclaimed work as a poet, Wilbur, who won Pulitzer Prizes for his collections *Things of This World* (1956), and *New and Collected Poems* (1988), is also renowned for his translations of French authors. His translations of the French playwright Molière are considered by many to be among the finest translations of Molière in English.

Wilbur is a poet of great formal mastery, employing the age-old techniques of traditional verse, such as meter and rhyme, to powerful effect. Wilbur writes affectingly about love in such poems as "For C.," from his collection *Mayflies* (2000), and in one of his best-known poems "Love Calls Us to the Things of This World." The poem considers a scene in which laundry has been hung up to dry on a clothesline, and it concludes with the speaker imagining the clothes being taken down and the people who might wear them: "Bring them down from their ruddy gallows; / Let there be clean linen for the backs of thieves; / Let lovers go fresh and sweet to be undone / And the heaviest nuns walk in pure floating / Of dark habits, / keeping their difficult balance."

A miniaturist in verse. Kay Ryan's *The Niagara River* was another book of note in 2005. Ryan, whose poems are typically brief, with short intermittently rhymed lines, received the 2004 Ruth Lily Poetry Prize from Chicago's Poetry Foundation. Often in her work, apparently whimsical ruminations are darkened by a caustic wit that lends them weight, and her playful humor frequently masks a hidden melancholy. Despite the spare quality of her language, Ryan's poems address a wide range of concerns, including how difficult it can be to help others ("Atlas") or the way that many of our best intentions often go awry ("Home to Roost"). Ryan's poems are distinctive in their ability to provoke laughter and poignant emotion simultaneously. ■ David Yezzi

See also **Pulitzer Prizes.**

Poland. Polish voters endorsed a political shift to the right in parliamentary and presidential elections in 2005. In September, voters gave the right-of-center Law and Justice Party the largest number of seats in the Polish parliament, and in October they elected the party's candidate as president. Behind these political developments were twin brothers, Lech and Jaroslaw Kaczynski. Lech was elected Poland's president and Jaroslaw led the Law and Justice Party in 2005.

Parliamentary elections. The Law and Justice Party emerged from the September parliamentary elections with 27 percent of the popular vote and 155 seats out of 460 in the lower house of parliament. The closest competitor, the centrist Civic Platform Party, took 24 percent of the popular vote, winning 130 seats.

Presidential election. Lech Kaczynski, the mayor of Poland's capital, Warsaw, came from behind in polls to win the October 23 runoff presidential election against the Civic Platform candidate, Donald Tusk. Kaczynski campaigned on upholding traditional moral values and eliminating government corruption. In a report issued in October, Transparency International, a Berlin-based organization dedicated to combating governmental and institutional corruption, cited Poland as the most corrupt nation in the European Union (EU), which Poland joined in 2004.

During the presidential campaign, Kaczynski alleged that his opponent's grandfather had served in Nazi Germany's army during World War II (1939-1945). The claim was technically true, but Tusk's grandfather had only served briefly when drafted and later joined the Polish resistance movement. According to some pollsters, the revelation may have boosted Kaczynski to victory.

In parliament, Jaroslaw Kaczynski's Law and Justice legislative bloc turned to several small rightist parties to form a coalition after failing to reach an agreement with Civic Platform leaders. On Oct. 31, 2005, President Lech Kaczynski tapped legislator Kazimierz Marcinkiewicz to form a government. (Jaroslaw Kaczynski, who as Law and Justice leader would have been an obvious choice, declined to be a candidate to avoid any appearance of impropriety.) Marcinkiewicz's government won a vote of confidence in parliament in early November.

Foreign policy experts predicted that Poland's new leaders would seek closer ties with the United States. In late 2005, President Kaczynski hinted that Poland might extend its participation in the U.S.-led peacekeeping operations in Iraq beyond early 2006. The previous government had scheduled a February 2006 pullout of the 1,700 Polish troops serving in Iraq.   ■ Sharon L. Wolchik

See also **Europe; Iraq.**

Pollution. See Environmental Pollution.

Popular music. Illegal downloading, unauthorized CD burning, and other forms of music piracy accounted for a 6.5-percent decline in CD shipments in the first half of 2005, according to the Recording Industry Association of America (RIAA). The RIAA is a Washington, D.C.-based trade organization that represents the recording industry in the United States.

Legal digital sales of music, which rose by 154 percent in 2005, helped to offset the decline in CD shipments. In the first six months of 2005, Internet users downloaded nearly 149 million digital singles, compared with just under 59 million in the first half of 2004. During the same period, over 5 million full-length albums were downloaded from legal Internet music sites, compared with 1.5 million albums downloaded in the first six months of 2004.

Top sellers. Rapper 50 Cent's second album, *Massacre*, was released in March 2005—a week earlier than scheduled due to piracy concerns. The album sold more than 4.7 million copies to become the year's best-selling album, according to Nielsen SoundScan, a

GRAMMY AWARD WINNERS IN 2005

Record of the Year, "Here We Go Again," Ray Charles and Norah Jones

Album of the Year, *Genius Loves Company,* Ray Charles and Various Artists

Song of the Year, "Daughters," John Mayer

New Artist, Maroon5

Pop Vocal Performance, Female, "Sunrise," Norah Jones

Pop Vocal Performance, Male, "Daughters," John Mayer

Pop Performance by a Duo or Group with Vocal, "Heaven," Los Lonely Boys

Traditional Pop Vocal Album, *Stardust...The Great American Songbook Volume III,* Rod Stewart

Solo Rock Vocal Performance, "Code of Silence," Bruce Springsteen

Rock Performance by a Duo or Group with Vocal, "Vertigo," U2

Hard Rock Performance, "Slither," Velvet Revolver

Metal Performance, "Whiplash," Motörhead

Rock Song, "Vertigo," Bono, The Edge, and Larry Mullen

Rock Album, *American Idiot,* Green Day

Alternative Music Album, *A Ghost Is Born,* Wilco

Rhythm-and-Blues Vocal Performance, Female, "If I Ain't Got You," Alicia Keys

Rhythm-and-Blues Vocal Performance, Male, "Call My Name," Prince

Rhythm-and-Blues Performance by a Duo or Group with Vocal, "My Boo," Usher and Alicia Keys

Rhythm-and-Blues Song, "You Don't Know My Name," Alicia Keys, Harold Lilly, and Kanye West

Rhythm-and-Blues Album, *The Diary of Alicia Keys,* Alicia Keys

Contemporary Rhythm-and-Blues Album, *Confessions,* Usher

Rap Solo Performance, "99 Problems," Jay-Z

Rap Performance by a Duo or Group, "Let's Get It Started," The Black Eyed Peas

Rap Album, *The College Dropout,* Kanye West

Rap Song, "Jesus Walks," Miri Ben Ari, C. Smith, and Kanye West

Contemporary Jazz Album, *Unspeakable,* Bill Frisell

Jazz Vocal Album, *R.S.V.P. (Rare Songs, Very Personal),* Nancy Wilson

Jazz Instrumental, Solo, "Speak Like a Child," Herbie Hancock

Jazz Instrumental Album, Individual or Group, *Illuminations,* McCoy Tyner with Gary Bartz, Terence Blanchard, Christian McBride, and Lewis Nash

Large Jazz Ensemble Album, *Concert in the Garden,* Maria Schneider Orchestra

Country Album, *Van Lear Rose,* Loretta Lynn

Country Song, "Live Like You Were Dying," Tim Nichols and Craig Wiseman

Country Vocal Performance, Female, "Redneck Woman," Gretchen Wilson

Country Vocal Performance, Male, "Live Like You Were Dying," Tim McGraw

Country Performance by a Duo or Group with Vocal, "Top of the World," Dixie Chicks

Country Vocal Collaboration, "Portland Oregon," Loretta Lynn and Jack White

Country Instrumental Performance, "Earl's Breakdown," Nitty Gritty Dirt Band Featuring Earl Scruggs, Randy Scruggs, Vassar Clements, and Jerry Douglas

British vocalist Annie Lennox performs in July 2005 at the Live 8 concert in London, the main show of nine simultaneous concerts staged around the world to raise awareness of poverty in Africa.

White Plains, New York, company that tracks the sales of music and music video products throughout the United States and Canada. Rhythm and blues and pop singer Mariah Carey's *The Emancipation of Mimi*, released in April, was the second-most successful album of 2005. The album, hailed as Carey's true comeback album after her critically panned 2001 film, *Glitter*, produced her biggest mainstream Top 40 hit since 1997, "It's Like That." Another song from the album, the ballad "We Belong Together," also reached the top of the charts and was one of the most popular songs of the summer. The three remaining top five albums of 2005 were Green Day's Grammy-winning *American Idiot* and *Breakaway* by Kelly Clarkson, two 2004 releases, and *The Documentary* by The Game.

Landmark copyright case. The United States Supreme Court ruled unanimously in June 2005 that companies that produced file-sharing, or peer-to-peer, software could be held legally responsible when people use that software to illegally download music and movies. The court concluded that companies that actively encourage their users to engage in illegal downloading could be held liable for copyright infringement. Grokster Ltd. of Nevis, West Indies, and Stream-Cast Networks Inc. of Woodland Hills, California,

the distributor of the Morpheus file-sharing software, were the defendants in the case. Movie studios, record labels, music publishers, and songwriters brought the suit. The decision sent the cases against the two companies back to a lower court in Los Angeles.

Country music's resurgence in popularity continued in 2005. Albums by Big & Rich, Brooks & Dunn, Kenny Chesney, Montgomery Gentry, Toby Keith, Martina McBride, Jo Dee Messina, Brad Paisley, Rascal Flatts, LeAnn Rimes, George Strait, and Gretchen Wilson reached the top 10 on the *Billboard* magazine Top 200 chart. A new generation of country artists was credited with revitalizing the genre through a more traditional sound that was heard in such hit songs as Wilson's "When I Think About Cheatin'," Messina's "My Give a Damn's Busted," and Lee Ann Womack's "I May Hate Myself in the Morning."

Garth Brooks released a single, "Good Ride Cowboy," in October that broke the record for highest debut on the *Billboard* country chart. The old record had been set by Brooks himself in 1991. Brooks had retired from touring and had not had a new single on the radio since 2003.

Bruce Springsteen released *Devils & Dust*, his first album in three years, in April 2005. The album featured songs played with *acoustic* (non-electric) instruments and was recorded without his signature backup ensemble, the E Street Band. Critics praised the album's stark musical arrangements and dramatic storytelling. A 30th anniversary edition of Springsteen's classic 1975 album *Born to Run* was released in November 2005.

Comedy records. Two comedy albums debuted in the *Billboard* Top 10 in 2005, an unprecedented achievement. *Blue Collar TV* co-star Larry the Cable Guy's *The Right to Bare Arms*, released in March, set a record for first-week sales for a comedy album with 92,000 copies. *Retaliation*, by Dane Cook, a comedian popular with college students, debuted at No. 4 on the *Billboard* Top 200 chart in July, making it the highest charting debut for a comedy record since Steve Martin's *A Wild and Crazy Guy* in 1978.

Trapped in the Closet. R. Kelly's album, *TP.3 Reloaded*, released in July 2005, was Kelly's fifth No. 1 album. It featured his biggest hit in two years, "Trapped in the Closet," a five-"chapter" song about a man who is having an affair and becomes embroiled in a series of outrageous romantic revelations.

Live 8. Nine simultaneous concerts took place in July 2005, in advance of the Group of Eight (G8) summit in Scotland. (The G8 is an informal organization of eight industrialized nations that plays a major role in raising issues and setting priorities in the global community.) The concerts were designed to raise awareness of global poverty and to encourage the world's richest nations to cancel debts and increase aid to developing countries.

The concerts were held in Berlin; Johannesburg, South Africa; London; Moscow; Paris; Philadelphia; Rome; Tokyo; and near Toronto. Among the musical highlights was the reunion of the legendary rock band Pink Floyd. Other artists who appeared included Coldplay, Elton John, 50 Cent, Madonna, Paul McCartney, Will Smith, Joss Stone, U2, and Kanye West. The concert was organized by Bob Geldof, who in 1985 staged the all-star benefit concert Live Aid to raise money for African famine relief.

National Recording Registry. In April 2005, the Library of Congress designated 50 U.S. recordings "culturally, historically, or aesthetically important." Among the recordings were Thomas "Fats" Waller's *Ain't Misbehavin'* (1929), Glenn Miller and His Orchestra's *In the Mood* (1939), James Brown's *Live at the Apollo* (1955), John Coltrane's *Giant Steps* (1959), John Williams's *Star Wars* soundtrack (1977), and Nirvana's seminal grunge rock album *Nevermind* (1991).

Rare jazz recording. Tapes of a long-lost 1957 Carnegie Hall jazz concert featuring pianist Thelonious Monk and saxophonist John Coltrane were discovered in January 2005 by an audio preservationist at the Library of Congress. Monk and Coltrane played together for six months in 1957, and only a few recordings of their collaboration were known to exist. *Thelonious Monk Quartet with John Coltrane at Carnegie Hall* was released on CD in September 2005 to critical acclaim.

Rock legends who came to prominence in the 1960's completed new recordings in 2005. In September, the Rolling Stones released *A Bigger Bang*; Paul McCartney released his solo album *Chaos and Creation in the Backyard*; and Neil Young released *Prairie Wind*, an album in the spirit of his classic *Harvest* (1972). Stevie Wonder released *A Time to Love*, his first album in a decade, in October. Neil Diamond released *12 Songs*, his first recording in four years, in November.

Several Bob Dylan collections of early and previously unissued recordings were marketed to coincide with the September 2005 public television broadcast of the Martin Scorsese-directed biographical documentary *No Direction Home*.

The albums enjoyed more critical than commercial success, but the rock legends were among the year's most popular concert attractions.

Cream reunites. One of the most popular bands of the 1960's, Cream, performed together for the first time since their farewell concert in 1968. Guitarist Eric Clapton, bassist Jack Bruce, and drummer Ginger Baker performed a reunion concert in May 2005 at London's Royal Albert Hall. The group also performed at Madison Square Garden in New York City in October.

■ Donald Liebenson

See also **Internet; Philadelphia.**

Population.

Population. The total world population reached an estimated 6.5 billion in July 2005 and continued to grow at an annual rate of 1.2 percent, announced the United Nations (UN) Population Division in a report released in February. Division *demographers* (statisticians who study human populations) projected an addition of 2.6 billion people over the next 45 years, bringing the total world population to 9.1 billion by 2050. The UN estimate was based on a projection under which fertility rates would decline from 2.65 children per woman in 2005 to 2.05 children by 2050. If fertility rates remain at 2.65 children per woman, the world population is expected to reach 10.6 billion by 2050. However, if the rates decline to 1.55 children per woman, the total would be 7.7 billion people by midcentury.

The population in developed regions, which stood at a total of 1.2 billion people in 2005, was expected to change little in the coming decades, except in countries that accept a significant inflow of foreign migrants. The population in less developed regions was expected to rise steadily from 5.3 billion in 2005 to 7.8 billion by 2050.

On average, the world population grew by 76 million people annually from 2000 to 2005, with eight countries—Bangladesh, China, Congo (Kinshasa), Ethiopia, India, Nigeria, Pakistan, and the United States—accounting for half of the total.

Life expectancy. Health services and nutrition have improved in many countries over time, increasing the age to which people can expect to live. Global life expectancy at birth stood at 46 years from 1950 to 1955; rose to 65 years from 2000 to 2005; and was expected to continue rising, to 75 years, from 2045 to 2050.

An aging population. As people live longer, their number increases over time. The UN Population Division projected that the number of people age 60 years or over would triple by 2050, from 672 million to nearly 1.9 billion. The number of people 80 years old or over was expected to rise even more dramatically, from 86 million in 2005 to 394 million in 2050.

Decline in fertility rates. On Sept. 8, 2005, the UN Population Division published "Population Challenges and Development Goals." The document highlighted the fact that the continued decline in fertility rates, which began in the 1970's and 1980's, has had a beneficial effect on development. The number of dependent children in the population has fallen, while the number of people of working age has risen. As long as this trend continues—assuming that jobs remain available—developing countries can reap the benefits of increased production and lower costs that are associated with the decreasing proportion of dependent children. ■ J. Tuyet Nguyen

Portugal. Portugal's left-of-center Socialist Party returned to power in February 2005. The country's Socialist president, Jorge Sampaio, had called an election one year ahead of schedule, after the ruling center-right Social Democratic Party lost popular support.

The new prime minister, José Sócrates, planned to fight unemployment—which European Union economists forecast at 7.4 percent in 2005—with increased spending on education. Sócrates hoped to change Portugal's economy from one dominated by low-skill, low-pay sectors to one capable of competing with the modern, technology-based economies of Europe, such as Finland's.

Wildfires burned over 740,000 acres (300,000 hectares) of forest in 2005, claiming the lives of 11 firefighters and at least 12 civilians. Drought and a shortage of advanced firefighting aircraft contributed to the rapid spread of the fires.

The economy grew by only 0.4 percent in 2005. Soaring deficits forced the government to announce budget-tightening measures aimed at public sector employees in October, leading to strikes and demonstrations. ■ Jeffrey Kopstein

See also **Europe.**

President of the United States.
See **United States, President of the.**

Prince Edward Island. See Canadian provinces.

Prisons. The adult prison population in the United States continued to grow in 2004 but at a slower rate than in previous years, the Department of Justice (DOJ) reported on Oct. 23, 2005. The number of adult detainees held in federal and state prisons rose by 1.9 percent from Dec. 31, 2003, to Dec. 31, 2004. This percentage was slightly below the 2003 rate and well below the average annual increase of 3.2 percent since 1995. Nevertheless, the number of adults in U.S. prisons in 2004 reached a record 1,496,629. That figure represented 1 in every 109 men and 1 in every 1,563 women in the United States.

In 2004, federal prisons were operating at about 40 percent above capacity, and prisons in 24 states also were operating at or above capacity. Incarceration rates increased by at least 5 percent in 10 states, led by Minnesota (up by 11.4 percent). Eleven states reported lower prison populations, led by Alabama (down by 7.3 percent). About half of the men and one-third of the women in state prisons were serving time for a violent crime. About half of federal inmates were imprisoned because of a drug law violation.

Women, juveniles, and minorities. The number of female prisoners in federal and state prisons in 2004 rose by 4 percent—more than twice the rate for men—to 104,848, according to the DOJ. As of Dec. 31, 2004, women accounted for 7 percent of all prisoners, up from 6.1 percent in 1995. Juvenile corrections facilities held 102,338 children and teen-agers in 2002 (the latest year for which statistics were available), down from 110,284 in 2000. In 2004, about 41 percent of all inmates were black, down from 44 percent in 2003. Hispanics accounted for 19.2 percent of inmates, up slightly from 2003. About 34 percent of inmates were non-Hispanic white, down from 35 percent in 2003.

Probation and parole. In 2004, the number of adults on *probation* (a period of supervision in the community following a conviction) grew by 0.2 percent, the smallest annual increase since the DOJ began keeping such records in 1979. About one-fourth of all probationers had been convicted of a drug offense. The number of adults on *parole* (a period of conditional supervised release following a prison term) grew by 2.7 percent in 2004. About half of parolees were released because of mandatory sentencing statutes or good-behavior regulations.

Death row. The number of inmates awaiting execution in federal and state prisons in 2004 fell for the fourth consecutive year, to 3,315. However, the number of women on death row rose in 2004 to 52, 5 more than in 2003. All 59 inmates executed in 2004 were men. ■ Barbara A. Mayes

See also **Courts; Crime; State government.**

Prizes. See Nobel prizes; Pulitzer Prizes.

Billy Graham preaches moderation and tolerance of other faiths in June in New York City. The ailing evangelist referred to the occasion as his last "crusade."

Protestantism. The prominence of evangelical Christians in public life in recent years—from their involvement in controversies surrounding United States Supreme Court nominees in 2005 to the so-called "Christian vote" in the 2004 presidential election—disturbed many nonevangelical Christians. Various Roman Catholics, mainstream Protestants, and African American church members voiced resentment over the way the media appeared to lump all Christians into a single catchall designation that did not reflect the wide-ranging opinions of the majority. Evangelical Christians, in turn, often were offended by an apparent assumption that all fundamentalists, Billy Graham-style evangelicals, Pentecostals, Southern Baptists, and other members of conservative bodies think, act, and vote alike.

The Washington, D.C.-based National Association of Evangelicals claimed in 2005 that about 25 percent of the U.S. adult population was associated with evangelical churches. Larry Eskridge of the Institute for the Study of American Evangelicals at Wheaton College, in Wheaton, Illinois, suggested that as many as 33 percent of all U.S. adults were evangelicals. The figures are difficult to prove or refute. In the 2000 census, 76.7 percent of adults in the United States identified themselves as Christian—25.4 percent as Catholic and 45.1 percent as Protestant. About 35 percent of Protestants further identified themselves as belonging to mainstrean congregations.

Evangelicals varied greatly in their beliefs and causes in 2005. Rick Warren, the best-selling author of *The Purpose-Driven Life*, engaged in an aspect of evangelicalism that is often overlooked, humanitarianism. In March 2005, Warren traveled to Rwanda to promote antipoverty programs and help rebuild that war-torn, largely Catholic nation. Warren also joined well-known evangelicals Tony Campolo, Ron Sider, and Jim Wallis in support of progressive social programs. World-famous evangelist Billy Graham expressed moderation and friendliness to other faiths in his last "crusade," which took place in New York City in June.

The *megachurch,* a huge congregation that incorporates entertainment and the personal needs of members, has become a phenomenon of the modern evangelical movement. In 2005, more than 1,200 U.S. congregations had weekly attendance of more than 2,000 people, according to the Hartford Institute for Religion Research in Connecticut. In July, the largest congregation in the United States, the Lakewood Church of Houston, led by Pastor Joel Osteen, moved into a former sports arena with a seating capacity of 16,000.

A more militant face of evangelicalism remained visible in 2005 as well. In August, televangelist Pat Robertson called for the assassination of Venezuelan President Hugo Chávez, a statement that was condemned by most of his fellow believers. In 2005, evangelical groups continued to aggressively oppose stem cell research and gay marriage while promoting "faith-based" businesses and displays of the Ten Commandments.

Homosexuality. Mainstream denominations remained torn in 2005 by internal disagreement over ordination policies and the blessing by clerics of gay unions. The Episcopal Church (U.S.A.) continued this debate, despite having ordained an openly gay bishop in 2003. In January 2005, church bishops apologized for the "pain, hurt and damage caused ... by certain actions of our church" in an effort to remain in the Anglican community. In August, the Evangelical Lutheran Church in America upheld policies against ordaining gay clergy and voted against blessing gay unions. The highest court of the United Methodist Church defrocked an openly lesbian minister in November and reinstated another minister who had been suspended for refusing to allow a gay man to join a congregation.

Israel controversy. Two Protestant groups disputed matters related to Israel in 2005. The Presbyterian Church (U.S.A.) debated "initiat[ing] a process of phased, selective divestment in multinational corporations operating in Israel." The World Council of Churches encouraged its 347 member churches to adopt a similar policy. These actions evoked criticism from more militant evangelicals, who regarded the prosperity of Israel as a necessary factor to the return of Jesus Christ.

■ Martin E. Marty

Psychology. See Mental Health.

Public health officials and government leaders worldwide stepped up efforts in 2005 to prepare for a global influenza *pandemic* (simultaneous epidemics). In particular, officials worried that the highly *pathogenic* (disease-causing) H5N1 strain of avian influenza (bird flu) could *mutate* (change genetically), leading to rapid person-to-person transmission. Such a virus, to which people have no immunity, could claim millions of lives. In November, United States President George W. Bush unveiled an influenza preparedness plan that focused on funding vaccine research and stockpiling flu vaccine and antiviral drugs.

In 2005, Cambodia and Indonesia joined China, Thailand, and Vietnam in reporting laboratory-confirmed human cases of H5N1 infection. From mid-December 2004 through early December 2005, the five countries reported 91 cases and 37 deaths, compared with 44 cases and 32 deaths in Thailand and Vietnam only from late 2003 through mid-2004. In 1997, 18 cases of bird flu and 6 deaths in Hong Kong became the first known instances of human infections with the H5N1 virus. Health officials believed that most victims developed bird flu after direct contact with infected birds, though in a few cases, human-to-human transmission seemed possible.

New Orleans hospital closed. In September 2005, Louisiana officials announced that Hurricane Katrina had left Charity Hospital, the main source of free medical care in New Orleans, permanently uninhabitable. In 2001 (the latest year for which data were available), the hospital provided 90 percent of all uncompensated inpatient care and 95 percent of all uncompensated outpatient care in New Orleans, according to the Louisiana State University Health Sciences Center. Hospital staff were treating patients at other sites.

Polio. An international campaign to immunize an estimated 100 million children in west and central Africa in 2004 and 2005 apparently halted a polio epidemic that had been sweeping through the region since mid-2003. In 2005, Afghanistan, India, Niger, Nigeria, and Pakistan continued to report new cases of polio. Ethiopia, Yemen, and nine other countries that had been free of polio reported new cases in 2005. The United States reported five polio cases in Minnesota.

Indonesia in 2005 mounted a major polio eradication campaign in response to the largest recorded polio epidemic in that country's history. As of November 1, the World Health Organization had confirmed 295 polio cases in Indonesia caused by a strain of the virus traceable to Nigeria. Since 2003, 18 polio-free countries had become re-infected with this strain. For 12 months in 2003 and 2004, an Islamic-dominated state in Nigeria had halted polio immunizations there, amid charges that the vaccine was dangerous.

Immunizations essential. Numerous studies have found no link between autism and vaccines against measles and other so-called childhood diseases, top officials from three major U.S. public health agencies asserted at a press conference in July 2005. Autism is a serious medical disorder characterized by a limited ability to communicate and interact with other people. Some researchers, parents, and public officials have linked an apparent, unexplained increase in autism rates since the late 1990's to a mercury-based preservative commonly used in vaccines until 2001.

Chemical survey. A dramatic drop in Americans' overall exposure to secondhand smoke was reported in July 2005 by researchers at the Centers for Disease Control and Prevention (CDC) in Atlanta, Georgia. CDC researchers said that blood levels of cotinine, a chemical produced by the body from environmental tobacco smoke, had plunged by about 70 percent in children and nonsmoking adolescents and adults since the early 1990's. Cotinine levels in African Americans were twice as high as those in non-Hispanic whites or Mexican Americans. CDC researchers also credited the elimination of lead from nearly all U.S. engine fuels with reducing the percentage of U.S. children with elevated lead levels from 4.4 to 1.6.

■ Barbara A. Mayes

See also **Agriculture; Asia; Indonesia; Medicine.**

Puerto Rico. Anibal Acevedo Vila of the Popular Democratic Party was sworn in for a four-year term as governor on Jan. 2, 2005, following the closest election in the Commonwealth of Puerto Rico's history. Although Acevedo pledged to conduct "a shared government," his political opponents from the New Progressive Party, bitter over their loss in a gubernatorial contest that was decided by the courts, proved unwilling to cooperate. They used their majorities in both houses of Puerto Rico's legislature to promote their own pro-statehood agenda and thwart Acevedo's legislative program.

On March 31, the legislature passed a bill that would have scheduled a referendum for July 2005 to petition the U.S. Congress for the right to hold a future binding referendum on Puerto Rico's status. Options to be put before the voters included U.S. statehood, existing commonwealth status with expanded autonomy, or outright independence. Governor Acevedo, who in his 2004 election campaign endorsed a plan to reform the existing commonwealth arrangement, vetoed the bill.

In retaliation, opposition legislators rejected Acevedo's proposals to trim government spending to reduce a projected $1.3-billion deficit for fiscal year 2005 (July 1–June 30, 2006). A key part of that plan was a reduction of the workweek for nonessential public employees to four days. In July 2005, the legislature instead passed a budget with a $1-billion deficit, which Acevedo vetoed, calling it "a great lie." The result was a political impasse, and the government continued to operate on the basis of the 2004 budget.

Threat to rain forest. In early 2005, Ariel Lugo, director of the International Institute of Tropical Forestry in San Juan, the capital, issued a report warning of the threat posed by urbanization to El Yunque, a 29,000-acre (11,745-hectare) rain forest in northeastern Puerto Rico. The report revealed that local municipal authorities for years had granted numerous variances to environmental rules. The result, according to Lugo, was a 2,100-percent increase in urbanization on a greenbelt around the forest that was theoretically protected by existing regulations.

Puerto Rican separatist killed. Filiberto Ojeda Ríos, a leader of the island's independence movement, was shot and killed by Federal Bureau of Investigation agents during a raid on his hideout in southwestern Puerto Rico on Sept. 23, 2005. A fugitive from justice, Ojeda jumped bail in 1990 while awaiting trial for his participation in a 1983 armed robbery in West Hartford, Connecticut. News of Ojeda's killing triggered demonstrations by 500 of his followers in San Juan on the night of his death. ■ Nathan A. Haverstock

See also **Latin America.**

Pulitzer Prizes in journalism, letters, drama, and music were announced on April 4, 2005, by Columbia University in New York City on the recommendation of the Pulitzer Prize Board.

Journalism. The prize for breaking news went to the staff of *The Star-Ledger* of Newark, New Jersey, for coverage of the resignation of New Jersey's governor following an adulterous, homosexual affair. *The Los Angeles Times* won the public service prize for exposing racial injustice and medical incompetence at a major public hospital in Los Angeles. Kim Murphy of the *Times* and Dele Olojede of *Newsday* on Long Island, New York, shared the prize for international reporting. Murphy wrote on Russia's struggles with terrorism and other internal problems. Olojede examined Rwanda 10 years after the mass slaughter of Tutsi.

Nigel Jacquiss of *Willamette Week* in Portland, Oregon, won the investigative reporting award for exposing the sexual abuse of a teen-age girl by a former governor. The national reporting prize went to Walt Bogdanich of *The New York Times* for articles about corporate denials of responsibility for fatal accidents at railway crossings. Tom Philp of *The Sacramento* (California) *Bee* won the editorial writing prize for advocating the reclamation of a flooded California valley.

Amy Dockser Marcus of *The Wall Street Journal* won the beat reporting prize for articles on cancer survivors. The *Journal's* Joe Morgenstern received the criticism prize for his film reviews. The *Chicago Tribune's* Julia Keller won the feature writing prize for her harrowing account of a deadly tornado in Illinois. A series on stem cell research won Gareth Cook of the *Boston Globe* the prize for explanatory journalism. The prize for commentary went to Connie Schultz of *The Plain Dealer* in Cleveland, Ohio, for columns on underprivileged people. Nick Anderson of *The Courier-Journal* in Louisville, Kentucky, won for editorial cartooning. Deanne Fitzmaurice of the *San Francisco Chronicle* was recognized for her feature photography. The award for breaking news photography went to the staff of the Associated Press for its coverage of combat in Iraqi cities.

Letters, drama, and music. Marilynne Robinson won the fiction prize for her novel *Gilead*. David Hackett Fischer won the history award for *Washington's Crossing*. The biography prize went to Mark Stevens and Annalyn Swan for *De Kooning: An American Master*. Ted Kooser won the poetry prize for *Delights & Shadows*. The general nonfiction prize went to Steve Coll for *Ghost Wars: The Secret History of the CIA, Afghanistan, and Bin Laden*. John Patrick Shanley won the drama prize for *Doubt, a Parable*. Composer Steven Stucky won the music prize for "Second Concerto for Orchestra." ■ Barbara A. Mayes

Quebec. See Canadian provinces.

Radio. The explosive growth of satellite radio and alternative sources for listening to music as well as new audience-measurement technology converged in 2005 to raise new questions about the United States radio industry's future as a leading entertainment and advertising medium.

Satellite radio. In 2005, XM Satellite Radio of Washington, D.C., and smaller rival Sirius Satellite Radio of New York City attracted 6.8 million paid subscribers just four years after its launch. Satellite radio delivers radio programming via satellite in much the same way as subscription satellite television services. XM reported in September that it had 5 million subscribers and had more than doubled its subscription base in a year. Sirius also reported rapid growth, with a customer base of 1.8 million people paying $12.95 a month for 120 channels.

A report issued by Kagan Research of Monterey, California, in 2005 projected that satellite radio would have 46.8 million subscribers and annual revenues of $7.6 billion by 2014. By comparison, the New York City-based Radio Advertising Bureau, which chronicles U.S. advertising spending, said the commercial radio industry had revenues of slightly more than $20 billion in 2004, the most recent year for which comprehensive figures were available.

New media. A report in 2005 from Paragon Media Strategies, a Denver-based research firm, that examined the impact of satellite radio also explored how other "new media" sources might affect radio listenership. Paragon studied the use of Apple's iPod and similar digital music players, Internet radio listenership, and *podcasting* (a method of publishing audiofiles to the Internet and allowing users to subscribe to a digital file feed) in the survey of 400 teen-agers and adults. Ninety-seven percent listened to traditional radio, 52 percent listened to radio on the Internet, and 20 percent both owned and used a digital music player. Only 1 percent of respondents said they had downloaded programming from the Internet, or "podcasted," according to Paragon.

Personal People Meter. The U.S. radio industry found itself mired in a debate about new technology to measure listenership, the Personal People Meter, which was introduced in 2004 by New York City-based Arbitron, Inc., the primary source of radio ratings data throughout the country. Traditionally, radio ratings reflected data from "diaries" in which Arbitron asked volunteers to record what stations they tuned in during different times of the day. Researchers often doubted the accuracy of the information from those diaries because few people were willing to make precise entries throughout the day. The Personal People Meter, an electronic device about the size of a cell phone, was designed to be carried in a pants pocket or a purse where it could pick up encoded signals from radio stations, recording precise data about what station or stations an Arbitron volunteer heard. A study in 2005 by the Radio Advertising Bureau and Arbitron said advertisers would increase spending by as much as $414 million a year if the technology was adopted.

Jack. While 10,972 (4,759 AM; 6,213 FM) commercial stations across the country struggled with questions about a decline in the number of listeners, a new format on 21 stations—commonly referred to as "Jack"—attracted both listeners and media attention in 2005. In what seemed to be a rejection of the conventional wisdom in the industry—that each station must have a tightly structured format (country music, "oldies," or news/talk, for example)—"Jack" offered huge playlists of music that seemed to be randomly selected. One radio station executive likened it to selecting shuffle play on an iPod, creating a stream of music that seemed to have no cohesive theme. The format was completely automated and usually eliminated disc jockeys, news, weather, traffic reports, and at least part of the hourly commercial load.   ■ Gregory Paeth

See also **Computer; Newspaper; State government; Telecommunications; Television.**

Republican Party.

Republican candidates fared poorly in off-year elections on Nov. 8, 2005, specifically gubernatorial elections in New Jersey and Virginia. In California, four ballot initiatives promoted by Republican Governor Arnold Schwarzenegger were soundly defeated.

Corzine victorious. In New Jersey, United States Senator Jon Stevens Corzine, a Democrat, defeated Republican businessman Douglas Forrester in the governor's race. Corzine replaced acting Governor Richard J. Codey, who assumed the office when James E. McGreevey resigned in 2004 after admitting that he had had an extramarital homosexual affair. The race between Forrester and Corzine in 2005 grew highly negative, with accusations of marital philandering. On substantive issues, both candidates called for a reduction in the state's property taxes and pledged to restore honor to state government, which some claimed was rife with corruption and *patronage* (the power to give jobs or favors). Political experts noted that the negativity of the campaign appeared to turn off many voters.

Virginia governor's race. Democratic Lieutenant Governor Timothy M. Kaine defeated former state Attorney General Jerry W. Kilgore, a Republican, in the race for Virginia governor. As the race began, Kilgore led in voter polls. However, Kaine's campaign steadily picked up momentum. Experts suggested that the momentum was fed by voter resentment over U.S. President George W. Bush's handling of the Iraq War and the economy. In an attempt to give the campaign a boost, Bush campaigned for Kilgore the day before the election. Kilgore aides later claimed that Bush energized state Republicans and boosted Kilgore's support. However, Democrats asserted that the Bush visit spurred state Democrats and independents to turn out in force on election day.

California ballot initiatives voted down. Voters in California sent an unmistakable message to Governor Schwarzenegger by rejecting ballot initiatives to overhaul and reform state government. Voters overwhelmingly turned down Schwarzenegger's proposals to slow the growth of state spending; to reform the way state legislative and congressional districts were drawn, removing them from the range of the state legislature; to require teachers to work longer before achieving tenure; and to limit political spending by public employee unions.

Washington state election challenge. In 2005, Republicans tried to overturn the 2004 gubernatorial election of Democrat Christine Gregoire. On June 6, 2005, state Judge John Bridges rejected Republican claims that Gregoire's election win over Republican Dino Rossi had been clouded by fraud. Rossi had been the apparent winner by 261 votes in the November 2004 election. However, a subsequent machine recount reduced his lead to 42 votes. Democrats successfully petitioned for a hand recount in December. On December 23, a recount put Gregoire ahead by 130 votes. On December 30, Republican Secretary of State Sam Reed certified Gregoire as the winner.

DeLay indicted. A Texas grand jury charged House Majority Leader Tom DeLay (R., Texas) on September 28 with criminal conspiracy for allegedly funneling corporate contributions into state election campaigns in 2002. On October 3, a grand jury indicted DeLay on multiple charges for money laundering. (A judge dismissed the conspiracy charge on December 6.) Texas law prohibits the use of corporate funds in state elections. The 2002 elections, which gave the Republican Party a majority in the Texas House of Representatives for the first time in more than 100 years, allowed the Republicans to redraw congressional districts. Consequently, Texas voters elected five additional Republicans to the U.S. House of Representatives in 2004. Under indictment, DeLay stepped aside as majority leader. (House rules bar lawmakers under criminal indictment from holding leadership posts.) Republicans elected House Whip Roy Blunt of Missouri to temporarily serve as majority leader.

The indictments, brought by Travis County, Texas, District Attorney Ronnie Earle, alleged that a Texas-based political action committee that DeLay helped create had transferred $190,000 in corporate funds to the Republican National Committee (RNC) in Washington, D.C. The RNC on Oct. 4, 2002, allegedly then donated $190,000 to seven Republican candidates for seats in the Texas House of Representatives. If found guilty, DeLay faced up to two years in jail and a possible fine of $100,000.

Texas state Judge Bob Perkins was originally to preside over the case. DeLay demanded a different judge, however, claiming that Perkins, a Democrat, was partisan. Perkins was removed from the case on November 1 and replaced by Senior Judge Pat Priest. However, Priest was also a Democrat.

Fund-raising. From January through September, the RNC raised $81.5 million, with $34 million in the bank, according to the Federal Election Commission, an independent regulatory agency of the U.S. government based in Washington, D.C. The Democratic National Committee raised $42 million during the same period, with $6.8 million in the bank.

■ Geoffrey A. Campbell

See also **Cabinet, U.S.; Congress of the United States; Democratic Party; Elections; State government; United States, Government of the; United States, President of the.**

Roman Catholic Church. Pope John
Paul II, one of the longest-reigning pontiffs in history, died on April 2, 2005. When he was elected, the Polish-born Karol Józef Wojtyla became the first non-Italian pope in 456 years. During his reign, John Paul traveled more miles than all previous popes added together. After his death, mourners stood in line for hours to pay their respects as he lay in state in St. Peter's Basilica.

A new pope. A conclave of 115 cardinals, which opened on April 18, 2005, in Rome, took only one day and four ballots to choose German Cardinal Joseph Ratzinger as the 265th pope. Cardinal Ratzinger took the name Benedict XVI.

Ratzinger had gained worldwide acclaim during the previous papacy as the head of the powerful Congregation for the Doctrine of the Faith. As chief doctrinal officer, Ratzinger disciplined scores of theologians and thinkers, silencing some and declaring others unfit to teach in Catholic universities. His election was seen by many as a continuation of the papacy of John Paul II. Benedict is seen as a pope who was expected to be less flashy in his public appearances, less of a traveler, and more attentive to the nuts and bolts of governance.

World Youth Day. Benedict XVI's debut on the international stage took place in Cologne, Germany, in mid-August for World Youth Day. Although created by John Paul II, the event

Pope Benedict XVI, the newly elected head of the Roman Catholic Church, greets throngs of well-wishers from a balcony of St. Peter's Basilica in the Vatican on April 19, 2005. Benedict XVI was the first German to be elected pope in more than 500 years.

allowed the new pope to display his more understated style and to show that he would pull no punches in his message to youth. He advanced the theme of "dictatorship of relativism," which had become a hallmark of his election week in April. "There can be no false compromise," he warned, "no watering down of the Gospel."

During his visit to Cologne, Benedict also reached out to Jews and Muslims. He was seen as reaffirming John Paul's bold interfaith initiatives while noting that genuine differences over matters of faith and truth cannot be overlooked.

Gay men in seminaries. Among the issues left over from the John Paul II papacy was a document regarding the admission of homosexuals to seminaries. The document, released in November, states that the church "cannot admit to the seminary . . . those who practice homosexuality, present deeply rooted homosexual tendencies, or support so-called gay culture." Nevertheless, the final decision on admitting a specific candidate is left to the discretion of local bishops, seminary rectors, and superiors of religious orders.

Meeting with dissident. Benedict XVI surprised many conservatives and liberals in the church when he met on September 24 with the liberal Swiss theologian Father Hans Küng, an outspoken critic of the Vatican and of Ratzinger as head of the Congregation of the Doctrine of the Faith. The two, however, were old friends and former colleagues. Küng and Benedict both described the four-hour meeting as cordial.

Clergy sex abuse. In the United States, the effects of the clergy sex abuse scandal continued to disrupt church life. By June, church expenditures to pay victims suing for damages had topped $1 billion, according to reports by the Associated Press. Some dioceses were forced to sell off assets to pay for damages. In Boston, several schools and churches were closed. At least three dioceses—Tucson, Arizona; Portland, Oregon; and Spokane, Washington—declared bankruptcy. Court proceedings were underway to determine whether parish assets and those of other properties tied to the church could be used to settle diocesan debts.

A grand jury investigation into the Archdiocese of Philadelphia reported on September 21 that two former archbishops had orchestrated a cover-up spanning 40 years that shielded from prosecution at least 63 priests who had sexually abused hundreds of children. No criminal charges were brought because of a statute of limitations.

On October 12, the Archdiocese of Los Angeles released a report that outlined accusations against 126 priests dating back nearly 50 years and involving more than 500 alleged victims. The settlement negotiations that prompted the release of the document continued. ■ Thomas W. Roberts

See also **Deaths: A Special Report; People in the news** (Benedict XVI); **Philadelphia.**

Romania. The right-of-center coalition government of Prime Minister Calin Tariceanu, formed in late December 2004, survived a no-confidence vote in June 2005. Tariceanu had been chosen by President Traian Basescu to form a government even though his Justice and Truth Alliance Party had trailed the Socialist Party in November 2004 parliamentary elections. Upon taking office, Tariceanu promised to work for reforms urged by the European Union (EU), which Romania was scheduled to join in 2007. On April 25, 2005, Romanian leaders signed the EU accession treaty, the final step in the long process of applying for EU membership. The EU retained the right to delay membership for one year if the Romanian government lagged on reforms.

Heavy rains and flooding afflicted much of Romania in the spring and again in July. Floods inundated 20,000 residences and 247,000 acres (100,000 hectares) of farmland and damaged or destroyed 400 bridges throughout the country.

In October, economists predicted that growth in Romania's *gross domestic product* (GDP), the value of all goods and services produced in a country in one year, would meet the government's stated target of 5.5 percent. In 2004, GDP had grown by 8.4 percent.   ■ Sharon L. Wolchik

See also **Disasters; Europe.**

Rowing. See **Sports.**

Russia. President Vladimir Putin's government expanded its influence over Russian political and economic institutions in 2005. In foreign policy, the Russian government faced serious challenges by neighboring post-Soviet countries. Chechen separatists also continued to concern the Putin government, as violence sparked by the conflict spread throughout the northern Caucasus region.

Economy. Russia's economic growth slowed slightly in 2005, to 5.5 percent from nearly 7 percent in 2004, according to the International Monetary Fund, a United Nations affiliate that assists nations experiencing financial difficulties. High international prices for oil and gas contributed significantly to this steady growth. Russia was the world's leading natural gas exporter and second-largest oil exporter in 2005. As of November 1, Russia held more than $150 billion in foreign currency reserves and its stabilization fund (which collects the government's windfall energy profits) had reached some $38 billion. The stabilization fund held less than $4 billion when it was created in January 2004. Russia used this unexpected revenue to pay down its foreign debt ahead of schedule. Russia's foreign debt declined from 90 percent of *gross domestic product* (GDP) in 1998 to only 18 percent as of November 2005. (GDP is a measure of the value of all goods and services produced in a country in a given year.)

Russian President Vladimir Putin (left) and United States President George W. Bush take a ride in Putin's 1956 Volga before a state dinner on May 8. The GAZ M21 Volga, the most luxurious car that a Soviet citizen was permitted to own, was developed in the early 1950's to showcase the vitality of the Soviet Union's post-World War II economy.

Despite these positive developments, the Russian government faced difficulties in implementing its economic policies in 2005. The most significant setback occurred in January, as thousands of demonstrators across Russia protested changes to Soviet-era social benefits programs for retirees, veterans, the disabled, and other select groups. The new system introduced on January 1 replaced in-kind benefits such as free public transportation, prescription medicine, and telephone access, with fixed cash payments. Demonstrators argued that inflation would eat away the cash payments' value over time and that the payments were already too low to cover essential services. The size and scope of the demonstrations dwarfed similar protests that occurred when the State Duma (parliament) first passed the law in August 2004. Demonstrations opposing the measure took place in all but a handful of Russia's 89 administrative units. Initial delays in disbursing the cash payments intensified the social unrest.

In response, many regional leaders began restoring in-kind benefits on their own. After a week of protests, Putin on January 17 criticized his government for its botched implementation of the reforms. The federal government subsequently restored some in-kind benefits and raised pensions, tapping oil revenues to do so. The massive protests shook the government deeply and made it reluctant to introduce additional spending cuts and fiscal reforms in 2005.

State-business relations. The Russian government increased its influence over the largest Russian companies in 2005, primarily at the expense of the private businessmen known as Russia's "oligarchs." The government both removed Yukos, once Russia's largest oil company, from the hands of founder and CEO Mikhail Khodorkovsky and strengthened the economic position of the state gas monopoly Gazprom.

On Dec. 19, 2004, the Russian government auctioned off Yuganskneftegaz, the main production subsidiary of Yukos, to cover Yukos's tax liabilities. The buyer was an unknown company, Baikal Finance Group. On December 22, state-owned oil company Rosneft announced the purchase of Baikal Finance Group, bringing Yuganskneftegaz under state control. Khodorkovsky's lawyers immediately protested the auction. Debt and legal concerns forced the cancellation of Rosneft's planned merger with Gazprom on May 17, 2005.

On May 31, a Moscow court sentenced Khodorkovsky and codefendant Platon Lebedev to nine years' imprisonment for embezzlement and tax evasion. The verdict followed the March 30 sentencing of former Yukos head security officer Alexei Pichugin to 20 years in prison for murder

A woman holding a portrait of fallen Yukos oil magnate Mikhail Khodorkovsky and a man dressed as the Grim Reaper with the face of Vladimir Putin hold a mock funeral for justice on June 5 in St. Petersburg. Khodorkovsky was sentenced to nine years in jail for embezzlement and tax evasion.

and attempted murder. Russian authorities had arrested all three men in 2003. It took the court 12 days to read the entire verdict, which ran over 1,000 pages. On Sept. 7, 2005, Khodorkovsky announced plans to run for a seat in the State Duma during a December 4 by-election in Moscow but election laws prevented him from doing so after an appellate court upheld his conviction on September 22. The appellate court reduced Khodorkovsky and Lebedev's sentences to eight years each. Both Khodorkovsky and Lebedev were sent to labor camps in Siberia in October. Despite widespread international condemnation over Khodorkovsky's trial and sentencing, foreign investors retained interest in Russia during 2005. Government tax revenues from domestic businesses also increased significantly after the Yukos affair.

Gazprom once again played a leading role in the Russian government's energy policies. In June, the government increased its shareholding in Gazprom to just over 50 percent. Dmitri Medvedev, chairman of Gazprom's board of directors and Putin's chief of staff, stated that this would allow Gazprom to "block decisions that put the economic interests of the country at risk." Gazprom further expanded its influence in June when its subsidiary Gazprom-Media purchased a controlling stake in the leading Russian newspaper *Izvestiya* from oligarch Vladimir Potanin's Interros group. Finally, on September 28, Gazprom agreed to purchase 72 percent of the powerful Sibneft oil company from oligarch Roman Abramovich's Millhouse Capital for some $13 billion. The acquisition nearly quadrupled Gazprom's annual oil extraction capabilities.

Mikhail Fradkov named a relative unknown, Igor Fedorov, as acting head of the Chamber on October 29. When complete, the Public Chamber will have 126 members representing both governmental and nongovernmental organizations. Leading Russian human rights groups refused to participate in the new institution, arguing that it would serve only as a mouthpiece for the Putin government.

Russian political debate in 2005 increasingly revolved around the March 2008 presidential elections. Putin repeatedly denied that he would seek to amend the Russian Constitution in order to run for a third term. The Constitution now permits presidents to serve only two terms. World chess champion Garry Kasparov announced on March 10, 2005, that he would retire from professional chess to lead an anti-Putin political movement called the United Civic Front. On September 14, former Prime Minister Mikhail Kasyanov announced his intention to run for the presidency in 2008 as a regime opponent.

Perpetually feuding liberal parties Yabloko and the Union of Right Forces presented on Nov. 1, 2005, a joint party list for the December 4 Moscow City Duma elections. Analysts saw this move as a first step toward the parties' likely and unprecedented cooperation in the upcoming State Duma and presidential elections.

Politics. The Putin government introduced important changes to Russia's electoral laws and political institutions in 2005. Liberal opponents accused Putin of undemocratically strengthening his hold over the political system and announced new initiatives challenging the regime.

Putin signed a law on May 19 overhauling the electoral rules for the 450-member State Duma. As of the December 2007 elections, the Duma will be chosen entirely by proportional representation. Parties must pass a 7-percent threshold to gain seats in the Duma, and electoral blocs will be banned. Under the current rules, voters elect half of the Duma members through single-member districts and half through proportional representation, with a 5-percent threshold. Analysts expected the new legislation to benefit United Russia, the government-supported party that dominated the Duma in 2005. Opinion polls indicated that only United Russia and the Communist Party could definitively clear the higher threshold.

On April 4, 2005, Putin signed a law creating the Public Chamber. The new institution will make recommendations on public policy to the government. The government first raised the idea of forming a Public Chamber after a deadly hostage crisis in the southern town of Beslan in September 2004 led to widespread denunciations of government policies and responsiveness. The Public Chamber held its first meeting on Oct. 1, 2005. Prime Minister

Chechnya. The persistent separatist conflict in Chechnya raged on and spilled over into the surrounding northern Caucasus in 2005. Chechen resistance leader and former president Aslan Maskhadov declared a unilateral cease-fire in early February, and later in the month he called for talks to resolve the conflict. However, pro-Russian forces killed Maskhadov in Chechnya on March 8. The new Chechen resistance leader, Abdul-Khalim Sadulayev, declared his intention to fight Russian influence throughout the northern Caucasus. Repeated terrorist attacks claimed lives across the region throughout 2005. The deadliest took place in October in Nalchik, the capital of the Kabardino-Balkaria Republic. Numerous armed fighters of the Caucasus Front (an umbrella resistance organization associated with Sadulayev and Chechen terrorist Shamil Basaev) attacked government facilities in Nalchik on October 13, leading to bloody clashes with government forces.

Despite the persistent violence, the Russian government held parliamentary elections in Chechnya on November 27. The pro-Russian United Russia party won 61.5 percent of the vote, which Putin claimed would help restore order to the region. International observers dismissed the results as being flawed.   ■ Juliet Johnson

See also **Europe; Russia: A Special Report.**

Rwanda. See Africa.

President Vladimir Putin
refocuses foreign relations
in an attempt to restore
Russia's waning influence.

RUSSIA
in the Post-Soviet World

By Juliet Johnson

Three former republics of the Soviet Union underwent major power shifts from 2003 to 2005 and established new governments in open defiance of the government of Russia. In 2003, widespread protests in Georgia forced President Eduard Shevardnadze to resign. In late 2004, a disputed election in Ukraine led reform candidate Viktor Yushchenko to defeat the Russia-backed candidate, Viktor Yanukovych, in a highly contested runoff election. Antigovernment protests in Kyrgyzstan in March 2005 forced President Askar Akayev to flee his country for his own safety.

These three changes of governments, known collectively as the "colored revolutions," were essentially peaceful and resulted in the displacement of pro-Russian leaders. All three involved Western influence, particularly the influence of nongovernmental organizations (NGO's), which supported parallel vote-counts, monitored the elections, and funded opposition to the incumbent regimes. All three proved to be major reversals for the president of Russia, Vladimir Putin.

Putin found himself on the defensive in the aftermath of these changes, and he reacted angrily to what he considered Western interference in local affairs. The dispute over the fraud-ridden presidential election in Ukraine triggered an angry torrent of old-fashioned Cold War-style rhetoric. Bristling at perceived Western interference in his own "backyard," Putin denounced the administration of United States President George W. Bush as dictatorial in its international relations. Putin accused the West of acting like a "kind but strict uncle" that dared to lecture Russia, and he openly ridiculed President Bush's plans for national elections in Iraq in early 2005. The Bush administration responded in kind. United States Secretary of State Condoleezza Rice, speaking to reporters on her way to Moscow for an official visit in April, chastised Putin's government for policies that she characterized as "setbacks" and expressed her concern that Russia was "reverting back to Soviet times."

Russian President Vladimir Putin (opposite page, center) entertains leaders of the former Soviet republics during a Commonwealth of Independent States meeting in Moscow in 2004.

The near abroad

Russian officials refer to that "backyard"—that is, the former republics of the Soviet Union in Europe and Central Asia—as the "near abroad." They consider the near abroad within Russia's sphere of influence, an area where Russia continues to wield considerable power. Russia controls the region's major transportation routes; is the key trading partner for most post-Soviet nations; supplies energy to these countries; and has the region's largest military force. In addition, an estimated 25 million ethnic Russians live in the former Soviet republics. According to international affairs experts, President Putin fully expects the West to recognize and respect Russia's extensive interests in these countries. However, recent events, including the colored revolutions, have challenged Russia's predominant influence in the region and have strained relations with the United States and Europe.

Georgia's Rose Revolution. Widespread fraud tainted Georgia's parliamentary elections in November 2003 and triggered large-scale, but peaceful, protests in the capital, Tbilisi. The student group *Kmara* (Enough Is Enough) mobilized the protests. (Kmara was modeled on the student organization that ousted Serb leader Slobodan Milosevic in the wake of similarly tainted elections in Serbia in 2000.) Mikhail Saakashvili, a U.S.-educated lawyer, quickly formed an opposition coalition in Georgia in 2003 to demand the resignation of President Eduard Shevardnadze. Shevardnadze accepted the inevitable and stepped down on November 23. His resignation cleared the way for new elections, and Saakashvili swept to victory in the presidential election in January 2004. In parliamentary elections in March, Saakashvili's

The author:
Juliet Johnson is an associate professor of political science, specializing in Russia and the former Soviet republics, at McGill University in Montreal, Canada.

National Movement-Democratic Front captured a large majority of seats. The elections completed the Rose Revolution, named after the roses that protesters in Tbilisi had carried as a symbol of nonviolence. The Bush administration hailed Saakashvili's victory as a step forward for democracy.

Putin took a far dimmer view of the political transition in Georgia and blamed the West for sparking it. In particular, the Putin administration blamed the Open Society Institute (OSI) for funding Kmara. (Founded by U.S. philanthropist George Soros, the OSI is a New York City-based foundation that promotes democratic governance, human rights, and economic reform.) Putin's suspicions about Georgia's political transition and its leaders were not unfounded. Upon taking power, Saakashvili immediately sought to lessen Russian military and economic influence in Georgia. In particular, Saakashvili pressured Russia to dismantle its military bases in the Georgian cities of Batumi and Akhalkalaki. Eventually, Putin agreed to these demands and promised to shut down both bases by the end of 2008.

Saakashvili also quickly adopted a pro-Western foreign policy. His aim was to acquire Western support to topple Russian-backed separatist governments in three *autonomous* (self-governing) regions of Georgia— South Ossetia, Abkhazia, and Adzharia.

Tensions between Georgians and the ethnic groups, including many Russians, in these three regions began in the 1990's. The people of South Ossetia, an area in north-central Georgia, declared themselves independent in 1990. Fighting broke out between the Ossetians and Georgians after the government in Tbilisi ruled the declaration invalid. Both sides agreed to a cease-fire in 1992 without actually settling the status of South Ossetian independence.

Fighting broke out between Georgians and Abkhazians in 1992 after Abkhazia, a region in the northwest, declared that its laws took precedence over those of Georgia. Abkhazian forces drove the Georgians out by late 1993, but again the status of independence was never settled.

President Mikhail Saakashvili carries the symbol of Georgia's Rose Revolution as he is welcomed in triumph in Batumi, capital of Adzharia, in May 2004. His arrival in the city ended a struggle with Adzharian leader Aslan Abashidze, who was backed by Russia, for control of the region, which historically has been part of Georgia.

Adzharia, in the southwest, enjoyed nearly complete independence since the breakup of the Soviet Union in 1991. Saakashvili's predecessor, Shevardnadze, burned by the military conflicts in Abkhazia and South Ossetia, refrained from interfering in the internal affairs of Adzharia as long as it maintained nominal loyalty to his government in Tbilisi. Saakashvili moved on Adzharia after its leader, Aslan Abashidze, sent out troops to prevent Saakashvili from campaigning in Batumi, the Adzharian capital, in the run-up to the March 2004 parliamentary elections. Following massive anti-Abashidze protests in Batumi and under pressure from Saakashvili, Abashidze fled to Moscow on May 6, ceding control over Adzharia to Saakashvili's government in Tbilisi.

Flush with this victory, Saakashvili stepped up pressure on South Ossetia and Abkhazia to recognize his government's authority. The regions' leaders proved more intractable and turned firmly toward Russia in their efforts to maintain their autonomy. The Putin government responded to Saakashvili's policies by maintaining preferential visa standards for the breakaway regions and extending offers of Russian citizenship to most of the residents.

Ukraine's Orange Revolution. The so-called Orange Revolution that toppled a pro-Russian regime in Ukraine in late 2004 proved an even greater blow to Russian interests and expectations. When no presidential candidate polled more than 50 percent of the vote in the October election, a runoff became inevitable between the two candidates with the highest results—Prime Minister Viktor Yanukovych and opposition leader and former Prime Minister Viktor Yushchenko. The Russian government actively supported Yanukovych in the belief that he would maintain existing close political and economic ties with Russia and protect the interests of Russian-speaking Ukrainians. The governments of the United States and Western Europe preferred the challenger, Yushchenko, and many Ukrainian NGO's, such as the Western-financed student group *Pora* (It's Time), worked on behalf of the opposition.

Although the Ukrainian Central Electoral Commission declared Yanukovych the victor in the November runoff, the official result became a joke in the face of reports of massive fraud. Ukrainian NGO's as well as a number of international organizations, including the Parliament of the European Union (EU) and the North Atlantic Treaty Organization (NATO), condemned the balloting. A voter turnout rate of 97 percent in the pro-Yanukovych region of Donetsk represented the clearest example of fraud but was far from the only one. Pora and other groups supporting Yushchenko responded with peaceful protests in Kiev, the capital. The number of protesters eventually climbed into the hundreds of thousands as an enormous tent city bedecked in orange (the color of Yushchenko's campaign) spread over Kiev's Independence Square.

Yanukovych and outgoing President Leonid Kuchma, under intense domestic and international pressure, entered into European-mediated negotiations with Yushchenko and discussed holding a new election. Putin, who had congratulated Yanukovych on his victory, ridiculed the idea of yet another runoff. The Ukrainian parliament then passed a nonbinding resolution declaring the election results invalid. On December 3, the Ukrainian Supreme Court overturned the results of the

Viktor Yushchenko takes the oath of office as president of Ukraine in Kiev, the capital, in January 2005. He assumed office after multiple rounds of voting, massive public demonstrations, and an attempt on his life that left Yushchenko disfigured. His triumph humiliated Putin, who had openly backed the loser, Viktor Yanukovych.

November race and ordered a rerun of the second round. On December 26, Yushchenko defeated Yanukovych with more than 52 percent of the vote in balloting watched intently by international monitors.

Putin reacted strongly to Yanukovych's loss, again blaming Western interference for the outcome. (Pora did receive funding from the Open Society Institute and from Freedom House, a Washington, D.C.-based nonpartisan organization that works to advance political and economic freedom.) According to experts, Putin viewed the Orange Revolution as a Western attempt to undermine Russia's legitimate interests and draw Ukraine away from the Russian sphere of influence.

Yushchenko, in his first speech upon taking the presidential oath, declared "Our place is in the European Union," confirming Putin's worst fears. The new Ukrainian leadership also expressed interest in joining NATO and enhancing economic ties with the EU. However, Yushchenko did recognize Ukraine's long-standing economic and security ties with Russia and confirmed that Ukraine would not challenge an agreement that allowed Russia to station its Black Sea Fleet along Ukraine's Crimean peninsula. (After the collapse of the Soviet Union, Ukraine and Russia divided the naval fleet in the Crimea and signed an agreement allowing Russia to keep a base there until 2017.) Despite these assurances, Putin's government felt humiliated over the Orange Revolution, and Russian-Ukrainian relations cooled considerably. Putin showed his continuing displeasure in September 2005 when his government endorsed a plan to build a gas pipeline to Germany under the Baltic Sea, bypassing an existing pipeline across Ukraine and Poland.

Kyrgyzstan's Tulip Revolution. Disputed parliamentary elections in Kyrgyzstan in February and March 2005 led to countrywide demonstrations and the eventual resignation of President Askar Akayev. The spontaneous demonstrations began the southern Kyrgyz cities of Osh and Jalal-Abad. Protesters in Osh quickly occupied regional administration buildings, a police station, and an airport. In the capital, Bishkek, demonstrators marched in silk scarves holding pink and yellow tulips. (The silk symbolized Bishkek's heritage as a city on the ancient Silk Road, and pink and yellow became the colors of the revolution.) After police in Bishkek broke up a rally and detained journalists, students, and NGO leaders, the protests grew more widespread and violent. When demonstrators occupied government offices, President Akayev fled first to Kazakhstan and then to Moscow.

Confusion ensued as the newly elected parliament and the previous parliament both asserted legitimacy. After negotiations, the newly elected parliament assumed power and named Kurmanbek Bakiev, a popular leader from southern Kyrgyzstan, acting president and prime minister. President Akayev agreed to resign and signed the official papers at the Kyrgyz embassy in Moscow on April 3. In July, Bakiev was elected president in a landslide. He selected Felix Kulov, a popular politician who had been jailed under Akayev, to serve as prime minister.

Bakiev, unlike his counterparts in Georgia and Ukraine, quickly expressed his intention of maintaining close ties with Russia. He reassured the Russian government that he supported maintaining a Russian military base at Kant. In October, Bakiev also agreed to allow a U.S. military base to remain in Kyrgyzstan. After the terrorist attacks on the United States on Sept. 11, 2001, the Kyrgyz government, with Russian acquiescence, gave the United States permission to open an air base at Bishkek's Manas International Airport. The Russian government followed suit in 2003 and stationed Russian forces at Kant, only 20 miles (30 kilometers) from Manas. International affairs experts speculated that while Russia wanted to combat Islamic militants in the area, it also wanted to prevent the United States from establishing a lone military presence in Kyrgyzstan.

The Tulip Revolution represented a more complex political transition than the revolutions in Georgia and Ukraine. No united opposition

A U.S. Air Force crew member walks the wing of an American KC 135 tanker plane at the Manas International Airport in Bishkek, capital of Kyrgyzstan, in 2005. After the Tulip Revolution in March, the new Kyrgyz government remained allied with Russia but agreed in October to allow the United States to continue to operate the strategically important air base in Bishkek.

existed to spark and harness the demonstrators, sporadic violence erupted throughout the country, and opposition leaders were no more pro-Western than Akayev. The opposition forces in Kyrgyzstan had received relatively little Western encouragement and support. Nevertheless, the earlier events in Georgia and Ukraine led the increasingly concerned Russian government to interpret Kyrgyz events in a similarly pro-Western, anti-Russian light. Many Russians decried Western interference in Kyrgyz politics, and the Russian government became preoccupied with preventing similar revolutions in other former Soviet republics.

Other regional challenges

The colored revolutions put President Putin's government on the defensive throughout the former Soviet Union. The leaders of the Baltic countries, Estonia, Latvia, and Lithuania, which had been annexed by the Soviet Union prior to World War II (1939-1945), reinforced their rejection of Russia and its influence by joining the EU in May 2004. Russian concerns with Islamist movements and political unrest in authoritarian former republics in Central Asia were sharpened in May 2005 when Uzbekistan violently put down public protests in the city of Andijon. Lingering conflicts in Abkhazia and South Ossetia—as well as between Armenia and Azerbaijan—troubled Putin's government as well. However, Western condemnation of Russia's relationship with Belarus, its controversial military presence in Moldova, and the ongoing conflict in Chechnya proved particularly challenging for the Putin government.

Belarus. Russia has a closer political, economic, and military relationship with Belarus than with any other near abroad country. Leaders of the two governments regularly have discussed forming a federation. Russia is Belarus's main trading partner, while the much smaller Belarus is Russia's second-largest trading partner. More importantly, Belarus is a key western transit route for Russian oil and gas shipments. Despite its proximity to the West, the government of Belarus has expressed no interest in joining the EU or NATO. In 2001, Belarus and Russia adopted a joint military doctrine and have held regular joint military exercises. Such close cooperation led successive Russian governments to support the authoritarian Belarusian leader Aleksandr Lukashenko.

Lukashenko, nevertheless, proved to be an increasing headache for the Putin government. Lukashenko's ever-growing authoritarianism attracted both negative Western attention and emboldened the Belarusian opposition. No opposition candidates actually won in the October 2004

A police-helmeted protester brandishes a police truncheon in triumph outside a government building in Bishkek, Kyrgyzstan's capital, during the "Tulip Revolution" in March 2005. When protesters occupied government headquarters on March 24, President Askar Akayev fled to Moscow and the protection of his ally, Putin.

Belarusian parliamentary elections, and voters simultaneously approved a constitutional amendment that allowed Lukashenko to run again in 2006. Western observers were not, however, fooled by the results, which were soundly condemned as having been rigged. The U.S. Congress responded by passing the Belarus Democracy Act, which called for the promotion of democracy in Belarus through aid to political parties, NGO's, and the independent media. The legislation also blocked U.S. agencies from giving financial aid to Belarus.

Although weak, the Belarusian opposition declared its intent to challenge Lukashenko in the 2006 presidential elections and cited Ukraine's revolution as an inspiration and model. While Lukashenko's downfall seemed unlikely, Putin, according to international affairs experts, feared that a repeat of the events in Ukraine could bring down Russia's closet ally and turn yet another near abroad country toward the West.

Moldova. Russia also faced reverses in Moldova in 2005. The Moldovan Communist Party, which was once firmly pro-Russian, successfully campaigned on an anti-Russian platform before parliamentary elections in March. The party's leader, Vladimir Voronin, objected to Russia's continuing military presence in Moldova's separatist Trans-Dniester region. Voronin and other party members viewed Russian military forces, which have been in Trans-Dniester since the Soviet collapse, as a partisan force supporting the Trans-Dniestrian government. Voronin earned the Russian government's particular enmity by actively courting Georgian President Saakashvili and Ukrainian President Yushchenko during the election campaign. Although suspicious Western governments kept Voronin at arm's length and criticized his party's behavior during the campaign, Russia clearly felt that it had lost another ally in the region. The Putin government responded by declaring that it would not withdraw troops from Trans-Dniester until leaders from Moldova and Trans-Dniester reached a definitive settlement.

An elderly man cleans mortar from old bricks for reuse in Groznyy, the Chechen capital, in 2004. More than 10 years of conflict between Chechnya and the government of Russia left Groznyy in ruins. Attempts by Western governments to intervene in the conflict strained relations with Russia.

Chechnya. The 11-year conflict in Chechnya, a breakaway region of Russia, not only continued in 2004 and 2005 but spread further outside Chechen borders. In September 2004, Russia suffered its worst terrorist attack to date when Chechen separatists took an entire school hostage in the North Ossetian town of Beslan. The result—the deaths of more than 300 people, including many children—shocked the world. Putin's government was harshly criticized for its handling of the crisis and came under increased pressure to bring the Chechen conflict to an end.

In March 2005, pro-Russian forces in Chechnya killed separatist leader Aslan Maskhadov. Russian officials hailed Maskhadov's removal as a step forward in their battle against the separatists, but his death actually deepened the conflict. It left the insurgency in the hands of leaders with little interest in a negotiated settlement. Maskhadov's handpicked successor, Abdul-Khalim Sadulayev, declared in May his intention to extend the conflict throughout the northern Caucasus. Maskhadov's death also raised the profile of Shamil Basaev, the Chechen responsible for the Beslan and other terrorist attacks. In July, Russian Defense Minister Sergei Ivanov responded by announcing Russia's intention of opening military facilities in Dagestan and Karachayevo-Cherkessia, in the northern Caucasus. International affairs experts noted in 2005 that Putin remained extremely sensitive to Western criticism of Russian policies in Chechnya and that he continued to frame the conflict as part of the broader international struggle against Islamist terrorism. The U.S. television network ABC particularly incensed Putin's government in July when it aired an interview with Shamil Basaev on the "Nightline" news program. Russian officials compared the airing of the Basaev interview with granting air time to al-Qa`ida terrorist leader Osama bin Laden.

Russia and the West

Foreign relations between Russia and the United States and Russia and the EU have grown tenser since Vladimir Putin became president in 2000. Western leaders criticized Russia for rolling back democratic practices, particularly Putin's attempts to strengthen his own position by weakening the authority of regional officials. He also drew criticism for seizing assets from the country's largest oil company, Yukos, and arresting its major stockholder, Mikhail Khodorkovsky, on charges of fraud and tax evasion. Putin, in turn, resented Western interference in the near abroad and the continuing criticism of the Chechen conflict.

Russia and the West, particularly the United States, did find common ground in the fight against terrorism. Under Putin, Russia also solidified its membership in the elite Group of Eight (G8), an international economic and political organization that also includes Canada, France, Germany, Italy, Japan, the United Kingdom, and the United States. Russia assumed the rotating G8 presidency in January 2006.

The United States. Initial good relations between President Bush and President Putin began to sour after the Bush administration voiced concern over the growing authoritarianism of Putin's government. In turn, Putin condemned the U.S. role in promoting regime change within the former Soviet Union. His government had already grown suspicious of U.S. motives in promoting NGO's when it banned American Peace

Corps volunteers from Russia in December 2002 on the grounds that they were spying. Russian leaders believed that financial assistance from Western—and in particular U.S.—NGO's sparked the colored revolutions. While Putin's government could do little to prevent such activity outside Russia's borders, it put domestic NGO's under increased scrutiny, which complicated their relationships with Western donors. At the same time, the Russian government declared its intention to counter the efforts of non-Russian NGO's by promoting and funding pro-Russia societal groups.

Putin also surprised the Bush administration by refusing to support U.S. intervention in Iraq in March 2003 and by agreeing in February 2005 to supply Iran with fuel for a nuclear reactor. The Russian and U.S. governments also were often at odds over energy matters. The Bush administration strongly supported constructing the Baku-Tbilisi-Ceyhan pipeline, which will pump Caspian oil west through Azerbaijan, Georgia, and Turkey. The line bypasses Russia completely.

The European Union. Russia and Europe, interdependent on economic and security matters, have maintained a better relationship during Putin's presidency than Russia and the United States. After the breakup of the Soviet Union, Europe became Russia's main energy market and accounted for over half of its foreign trade. In May 2004, Russia and the EU concluded an agreement that promised EU support for Russia's bid to join the World Trade Organization if Russia agreed to ratify the Kyoto Protocol. (The Kyoto Protocol is a global agreement to set limits on the emission of carbon dioxide and other greenhouse gases. Russia ratified the protocol in November 2004, fulfilling the last requirement for it to take effect.)

Russian-EU relations were not completely harmonious. Putin rejected European calls for joint peacekeeping efforts in Moldova. It refused to allow the Organization for Security and Co-operation in Europe (OSCE) to mediate an end to the conflict in Chechnya. (The OSCE is a 55-nation regional security organization.) And the Russian government only grudgingly accepted the fact that former Soviet republics had been granted membership in the EU and NATO.

A new multilateral course

Russia under Putin has pursued two interrelated foreign policy goals—to establish a secure political and economic sphere of influence in the near abroad; and again to be recognized as a great power. The Putin government has experienced setbacks in both ambitions. International affairs experts note, however, that these setbacks have only reinforced Putin's belief in the importance of his aims. To that end, his government has adopted a new *multilateral* (involving three or more countries) approach to foreign relations.

The Russian government responded to setbacks in the near abroad nations by attempting to forge new links with these countries. The Commonwealth of Independent States (CIS), an organization to coordinate economic and security policies among Russia and the former republics, was no longer a useful administrative body by the time Putin became president in 2000. Different national interests and widespread concern over Russian domination had led to the CIS losing importance since its formation in 1991. In its place, Russia increasingly turned to narrower agreements.

In April 2003, Russia formed the Collective Security Treaty Organization (CSTO) with Armenia, Belarus, Kazakhstan, Kyrgyzstan, and Tajikistan specifically to combat terrorism. The Russian air base at Kant in Kyrgyzstan represented one of the fruits of this agreement. CSTO participants also planned another Russian base for Tajikistan. Russia also became more active on the economic front, pressing for the consolidation of a "common economic space" among Belarus, Kazakhstan, Russia, and Ukraine.

President Vladimir Putin meets with U.S. Secretary of State Condoleezza Rice in Moscow in April 2005. Before the meeting, Secretary Rice publicly chastised Putin for authoritarian policies that she characterized as "reverting back to Soviet times." Putin had refused to back the United States in the war in Iraq in 2003 and repeatedly accused Western leaders, including U.S. President George W. Bush, of interfering in Russia's sphere of influence.

As relations with the Western powers cooled, Russia reached out to China, particularly through the Shanghai Cooperation Organization (SCO). China, Kazakhstan, Kyrgyzstan, Russia, Tajikistan, and Uzbekistan forged the SCO in June 2001 to maintain regional peace, security, and stability and strengthen economic and cultural relations. In August 2005, Russia and China conducted their first joint military exercises. The Chinese military represents one of the most important markets for Russian arms, making Russia's interest in the relationship both strategic and commercial. Putin appreciated an international partner that did not criticize his increasingly authoritarian domestic politics. China also expressed little interest in challenging Russia's influence in the near abroad. In response, Putin assured Chinese officials in 2005 that a key multibillion-dollar Siberian oil pipeline would go to China first and only later serve Japan. International affairs experts noted that Putin viewed energy resources as a significant asset in strengthening Russia's international influence, and he expected Russian oil and gas companies to use their resources to enhance Russian power.

The experts also noted that Putin needed more than a multilateral approach to foreign relations to succeed internationally. They pointed out that if Russia is to restore its sphere of influence and position as a great power, the Russian government must resolve conflicts on post-Soviet territory, particularly in breakaway Chechnya; it must combat political and economic instability and repression in neighboring countries, such as Belarus and Uzbekistan; and it must compete economically with China, the European Union, and the United States for influence and markets. All three are daunting challenges, particularly for a man who has pledged to be one of the few leaders in Russian history to voluntarily give up power when his term of office ends in 2008.

Safety. In 2005, mold posed a threat to people in Louisiana and Mississippi working to restore or demolish residences and businesses that had suffered severe flood damage because of Hurricane Katrina. Mold spores, which thrive in moist areas, may cause nasal or respiratory problems in people with asthma, allergies, or other breathing problems or in those with weakened immune systems. In New Orleans, tens of thousands of structures became waterlogged after flood waters breached the city's levees in early September. A number of government agencies, including the Centers for Disease Control and Prevention (CDC) in Atlanta, Georgia, and the Louisiana Department of Health and Hospitals in Baton Rouge, offered guidelines for safely removing mold from residences and other structures. CDC officials also urged health experts in the Gulf Coast area to monitor incidences of nasal and respiratory problems.

Safer highways. The number of Americans dying in highway accidents has fallen to its lowest level since the government began keeping records in 1966, the National Highway Traffic Safety Administration (NHTSA) reported in August 2005. NHTSA officials said that in 2004, 42,636 people were killed in traffic accidents, a 16-percent decline over the 1966 fatality rate.

NHTSA officials attributed the drop, in part, to increased use of safety belts. A record 82 percent of Americans regularly used seat belts in 2005, a 34-percent increase over the number in 1997, the United States Department of Transportation reported in September. By 2005, 22 states and the District of Columbia had adopted primary safety belt laws, which allow law enforcement officers to issue a safety-belt citation after observing an unbelted driver or passenger. Some states allow officers to cite an unbelted motorist only after stopping a driver for another violation.

Blood alcohol standard. The United States in 2005 gained a nationwide standard for the minimum blood alcohol content (BAC) for a person to be charged for driving while intoxicated. The BAC is the percentage of alcohol in a person's bloodstream. On August 1, Minnesota became the last state to adopt a BAC of 0.08 percent.

Fire deaths. The number of fires and the number of people killed by fire in the United States dropped slightly in 2004, the U.S. Fire Administration (USFA) reported in September 2005. The USFA said that 3,900 people died in 2004, compared with 3,925 people in 2003. The total number of fires also dropped, from 1.58 million in 2003 to 1.55 million in 2004. Residential fires accounted for 26.5 percent of all fires. In two-thirds of U.S. residential fires, smoke alarms were missing or not working, the USFA reported. ■ Barbara A. Mayes

See also **Disaster Special Report; Public health.**

Saudi Arabia. In April 2005, Saudi Crown Prince Abdullah ibn Abd al-Aziz Al Saud and United States President George W. Bush issued a joint statement on U.S.-Saudi relations that included U.S. support for Saudi Arabia's accession to the World Trade Organization (WTO). The WTO oversees global trade agreements and arbitrates disputes among member nations.

By September, U.S. and Saudi officials had concluded a bilateral market-access agreement leading the way to Saudi Arabia's full membership in the WTO. The conditions of membership required Saudi Arabia to enact revisions in many of its trade policies, including the lowering of its tariff and nontariff trade barriers.

Oil exports and revenues. Saudi Arabia supplied the United States with 1.5 million barrels per day of crude oil, or 15 percent of U.S. imports, during the period from January to May 2005. The U.S. Department of Energy estimated that, due to rising oil prices, Saudi net oil export revenues for 2005 would increase to $150 billion.

Despite a larger than expected revenue surplus, Saudi Arabia continued to face a number of serious economic and social challenges in 2005. These challenges included an estimated $175 billion in public debt and an unemployment rate of approximately 13 percent for Saudi nationals.

Terrorism and security. The Saudi government reported in 2005 that it had, during 2004, added $2.5 billion to the $5.5 billion it had spent on national security in 2003. The rise in expenditures was prompted by an increased terrorist threat to the kingdom's many oil pipelines, oilfields, and ports.

Terrorist attacks in Saudi Arabia decreased from 2004 to 2005. However, the U.S. embassy in Riyadh, the capital, and U.S. consulates in Jidda and Dhahran closed for two days in August because of credible reports of terrorist threats against Westerners.

Municipal elections. In 2005, for the first time in its history, Saudi Arabia held municipal elections. These elections, in which women were not allowed to participate, took place in three phases: in February in the Riyadh region; in March in the south and east; and in April in the north and west.

Death of King Fahd. On August 1, King Fahd ibn Abd al-Aziz Al Saud died at the age of 84. The king had been incapacitated by a stroke since 1995. Crown Prince Abdullah, who had been the de facto ruler for the past decade, was named by the Al Saud family to succeed the late king.

■ Mary-Jane Deeb

See also **Deaths; Energy; Middle East; People in the news** (Abdullah); **Terrorism.**

School. See **Education.**

Senegal. See **Africa.**

The shrouded body of Saudi King Fahd ibn Abd al-Aziz Al Saud is carried by his sons through Riyadh, the capital of Saudi Arabia, on Aug. 2, 2005. The king, who had died the previous day at age 84, was replaced on the throne by his halfbrother, Crown Prince Abdullah.

Serbia and Montenegro. The union of Serbia and Montenegro, the remnant of the former Yugoslavia, endured in 2005, but its future survival appeared uncertain in the face of a strong independence movement in Montenegro. Within Serbia, the dominant partner in the union, political developments reflected an ongoing struggle that pitted pro-Western leaders willing to cooperate with international institutions, such as the European Union (EU) and the North Atlantic Treaty Organization (NATO), against nationalists who continued to resist any compromises. Late in 2005, the United Nations (UN) launched formal talks on the future status of Kosovo, technically a Serbian province but since 1999 administered by UN officials.

Political life in Serbia continued to be dominated by disagreements over cooperation with the International Tribunal for War Crimes in The Hague, Netherlands. The Tribunal, as well as the EU and NATO, demanded that Serbian officials turn over alleged war criminals from the wars surrounding Yugoslavia's breakup in the 1990's. International officials were particularly concerned with Bosnian Serb leader Radovan Karadzic and Serbian General Ratco Mladic, who allegedly participated in a 1995 massacre of Muslims in Srebrenica, Bosnia. Tribunal and UN officials alleged that Karadzic and Mladic were in hiding under protection of Serbian nationalists.

In June 2005, Serbian Prime Minister Vojislav Kostunica and Pero Bukejlovic, prime minister of the Republika Srpska, the Serbian enclave within Bosnia, issued a statement condemning the Srebrenica massacre. Despite this gesture, neither political entity delivered any high-ranking indictee to the War Crimes Tribunal in 2005.

EU talks. Despite dissatisfaction over Serbia's record on arresting war criminals, EU ministers in early October scheduled talks with leaders of Serbia and Montenegro on a stabilization and association agreement, the first step in applying for EU membership. At the opening of the talks on October 10, EU officials emphasized that progress on the application would depend on cooperation with the War Crimes Tribunal.

Union status. Javier Solana, foreign policy chief of the EU, in April persuaded leaders of Serbia and Montenegro to extend legislative terms in the union's joint parliament. The decision ended a constitutional crisis caused by Montenegro's refusal to hold parliamentary elections before holding a referendum on independence. The leaders also agreed not to dissolve the union before 2006, when Montenegro was expected to hold a referendum on independence. Montenegro is the junior partner in the union, with only one-fifteenth the population of Serbia.

Kosovo. Multiparty talks sponsored by the UN on the status of Kosovo began in Pristina, Kosovo, in November. Kosovo's population is mainly Albanian Muslim, with a small Serb minority. NATO forces ended a conflict between Serbian forces and Kosovar Albanian guerrillas in 1999 and installed a UN-led administration.

Officials of Serbia entered the talks determined to reject independence, while Kosovar Albanian representatives insisted on an independent Kosovo. Another difficult issue involved the status of 100,000 ethnic Serbs who had fled Kosovo during the conflict. Martti Ahtisaari, the UN-appointed mediator of the talks, was granted wide powers to enforce rules requiring the parties to reach agreement before disbanding.

Economy. Two international financial organizations—the London-based European Bank for Reconstruction and Development and the World Bank, a Washington, D.C.-based UN affiliate—reported in 2005 that Serbia and Montenegro was the top reformer among European transition countries. However, high inflation and unemployment continued to pose economic challenges. According to economists, Serbia's economy grew at a rate of 4.8 percent in 2005.   ■ Sharon L. Wolchik

See also **Europe**.

Seychelles. See **Africa**.

Sierra Leone. During 2005, Western diplomats repeatedly expressed dissatisfaction over President Ahmad Tejan Kabbah's failure to tackle rampant corruption in Sierra Leone. Kabbah had overseen Sierra Leone's transition to peace following the end of its civil war (1992-2002) and had won reelection in 2002. The civil war, which pitted the Revolutionary United Front (RUF) against Kabbah's internationally recognized government, had led to the deaths of at least 100,000 Sierra Leonans.

Kabbah's critics in 2005 did not accuse him of personal corruption, but they faulted him for failing to take action against dishonest officials in his administration and in his ruling Sierra Leone People's Party. Analysts familiar with local conditions noted that government corruption was leading to widespread cynicism among Sierra Leone's population, especially when pay for teachers or supplies and medicines for hospitals disappeared, which happened routinely.

International affairs experts noted the chilling effect that Sierra Leone's corruption was apparently having on international donors. Sierra Leone, which is ranked by the United Nations (UN) as the least developed country in the world, relied on Western donors for about two-thirds of its national budget in 2005, with the greatest share contributed by the United Kingdom. When the G8 leaders—a group of eight countries with advanced industrialized economies—considered a program of debt cancellation for 18 poor nations in February, Sierra Leone did not make the list.

The UN peacekeeping mission in Sierra Leone, called UNAMSIL, remained in the country until December 2005, when the 2,000 remaining UN troops were withdrawn. At the height of peacekeeping operations in the early 2000's, UNAMSIL had numbered 17,500 troops.

Following the UN withdrawal, a British-trained army and police force remained to provide security. The United Kingdom had maintained a military presence in Sierra Leone since President Kabbah requested help in 2000 to shore up a UN force under attack by RUF forces.

UN investigator convicted. A court in Freetown, the capital, convicted Australian Peter Halloran on Feb. 21, 2005, of sexually molesting an underage female servant and sentenced him to 18 months in jail. Halloran was working for the UN as chief investigator for the UN Special Court for Sierra Leone (SCSL). The SCSL, presided over by Sierra Leonan and UN-appointed judges, was created to investigate and try individuals who allegedly committed war crimes and human rights offenses during Sierra Leone's civil war.   ■ Simon Baynham

See also **Africa**.

Singapore. Sellapan Rama Nathan was declared president of Singapore for a second six-year term on Aug. 17, 2005, after officials disqualified all three challengers. Nathan, 81 years old, first won the office in 1999 under similar circumstances. In both elections, he was backed by the People's Action Party (PAP), which has tightly controlled the government since the small island nation became independent in 1965.

In 2005, Singapore continued to moderately loosen government control over public conduct. The government had in the past refused to permit gambling casinos. On April 18, Prime Minister Lee Hsien Loong announced plans to build two casinos in an effort to increase tourism and create jobs. Singapore's share of Asian tourism had declined, and officials turned to casino gambling as a way of luring more people. The plan met with opposition from religious leaders.

The island's prosperity, based on shipping and reinforced by manufacturing, was threatened by the move of production lines to China, where wages were much lower in 2005. Lee, who also served as finance minister, announced on August 8 that he expected the next five years to be better economically than the last five.

■ Henry S. Bradsher

See also **Asia**.

Skating. See Hockey; Ice skating; Sports.

Skiing. Bode Miller of the United States had a historic season in 2005, becoming the first American skier in 22 years to win the Alpine World Cup overall title. The women's title chase was decided by the smallest margin since 1992, with Anja Paerson of Sweden defeating Janica Kostlic of Croatia by only three points to take the crown on March 13 in Lenzerheide, Switzerland.

Miller set a blistering pace, winning six of the first 10 races in the 2005 season. He clinched the title on March 12, 2005, in Lenzerheide with a second-place finish in the final slalom event. Miller finished with 1,648 points, followed by Austria's Benjamin Raich, who collected 1,454 points. Miller's overall title was the first for a skier from the United States since Phil Mahre and Tamara McKinney won in 1983.

Miller also took the super-giant slalom (super-G) title, becoming the first American to win that event since it was introduced in 1986. Raich captured both the giant slalom and slalom titles, and Austria's Michael Walchhofer won the downhill title.

In the women's competition, Tanja Poutiainen of Finland took both the slalom and giant slalom titles, while Austria's Michaela Dorfmeister won the super-G. Austria's Renate Goetschl won the downhill title for the fourth time in her career.

World Alpine Championships. Miller and Raich ruled the men's field at the World Alpine Championships, which were held in Bormio, Italy, in early February. The two men captured four of the five events. In the women's competition, Kostelic and Paerson completely dominated, taking all five events.

Raich won the combined and slalom, took silver in the giant slalom, and claimed bronze in the super-G. Miller won the super-G and downhill but crashed in the other three events. Miller and American Dahron Rahlves made history in the downhill by becoming the first skiers from the United States to take gold and silver in the same world championship event.

Kostelic took gold in the combined, slalom, and downhill, while Paerson won the super-G and giant slalom.

Cross-country. On March 19, 2005, Axel Teichmann became the second German in two years to win the overall title when he finished seventh in Falun, Sweden. Marit Bjoergen of Norway won the women's overall title.

Nordic combined. Finland's Hannu Manninen defended his World Cup combined title in 2005. Norway won the Nordic combined team title at the World Championships in Oberstdorf, Germany.

Ski jumping. Finland's Janne Ahonen won the overall World Cup ski jumping title for the second straight year by finishing fourth in Lillehammer, Norway, in March. ■ Michael Kates

Bode Miller of the United States competes during the super-G final in an Alpine World Cup event in Lenzerheide, Switzerland, in March 2005. Miller later became the first American since 1983 to win the World Cup overall title.

Slovakia.

Slovakia. The right-of-center coalition government of Prime Minister Mikulas Dzurinda pressed for completion of reforms in Slovakia's pension and health care systems in 2005. However, widespread dissatisfaction with market-oriented reforms enacted by the Dzurinda government since coming to power in 2002, and increasing activity on the part of opposition politicians, stymied parts of the government's agenda.

Opposition leaders, including Robert Fico of *Smer* (New Direction), argued that the government's reforms benefited mainly Slovakia's wealthiest citizens. In June 2005, Fico introduced a no-confidence motion in parliament, but the Dzurinda government mustered enough votes to defeat it. In September, opposition and independent members of parliament boycotted sessions, denying the government a quorum and halting parliamentary business for one week. In December elections, opposition parties won most of Slovakia's regional governorships.

During 2005, the Slovakian parliament made minor amendments to six laws passed in 2004 that had fundamentally reformed Slovakia's health care system. In October 2005, the legislators approved a law that liberalized regulation of Slovakia's spa industry, based in several warm-spring "spa towns." Legislators debated, but did not pass, a bill that would have reduced the number of regional public health offices from 36 to 8. Parliament also made minor changes in 2005 to sweeping pension reforms passed in 2004.

Pollsters reported in November 2005 that Prime Minister Dzurinda's Slovak Democratic and Christian Union would poll 6.5 percent of votes if elections were to be held. In the same poll, Dzurinda's four-party coalition would muster less than 30 percent of votes. Analysts predicted that Dzurinda's government would survive until June 2006 general elections but observed that it lacked political capital to enact further reforms.

Slovakia's economy in 2005 continued to outpace economies of most other nations in the European Union (EU). The government in November announced a third-quarter annual growth rate of 6.2 percent, exceeding the projections of most economists. Unemployment remained high, however, hovering above 16 percent.

Foreign policy. In May, Slovakia joined four other member nations of the EU—Germany, Latvia, Lithuania, and Poland—in forming a rapid reaction force. The development was part of an EU strategy to maintain up to 13 such units, each numbering 1,500 troops, that could be deployed quickly to support peacekeeping activities in international trouble spots. ■ Sharon L. Wolchik

See also **Europe**.

Slovenia. See Europe.

Soccer. The United States men's soccer team made significant strides in 2005, qualifying for the 2006 World Cup finals and claiming eighth place in the Fédération Internationale de Football Association (FIFA) rankings. Mexico won its first world title at any level with its victory in the 2005 Under-17 World Championship. Also in 2005, soccer fans mourned the death of George Best, one of soccer's all-time great players.

International soccer. Most international soccer fans in 2005 focused their attentions on the zonal competitions for the 2006 World Cup, to be held in Germany. The U.S. team qualified for the World Cup finals on Sept. 3, 2005, by defeating Mexico 2-0 in Columbus, Ohio. Among the top teams to qualify were Argentina and Brazil from the South American zone and England, France, Italy, and the Netherlands from the European zone. As the host country, Germany qualified automatically. The 32 finalists are scheduled to meet from June 9 through July 9, 2006. On Dec. 9, 2005, at the draw for the 2006 World Cup in Leipzig, Germany, the United States just missed being seeded and drew tough opponents including the Czech Republic and Italy.

Brazil defeated Argentina 4-1 on June 29, 2005, to take the FIFA Confederations Cup. The competition, held in Germany from June 15 to June 29, included teams from all the world soccer zones. The participants were Argentina, Australia, Brazil, Germany, Greece, Japan, Mexico, and Tunisia. Germany finished at the top of Group A, edging Argentina on goal difference on June 21. Mexico topped Group B, with Brazil three points behind in second place.

However, Brazil made the final by defeating Germany 3-2, and Argentina advanced after taking a 6-5 decision on penalties over Mexico after the two teams were tied at 0-0 in regulation. Germany won the match for third place, defeating Mexico 4-3 at Leipzig on June 29. Brazil forward Adriano scored five goals in the tournament, earning the Golden Shoe award for being the top scorer. Adriano also won the Golden Ball, awarded to the best player of the tournament.

As of December 2005, Brazil (840 points) topped the men's FIFA World Rankings. The Czech Republic (796 points) and the Netherlands (791 points) stood second and third, respectively. The United States (767) placed eighth, up three places from 2004.

Argentina won the FIFA World Youth Championship, which took place in the Netherlands from June 10 to July 2, 2005. Argentina defeated Nigeria 2-1 in the final, held July 2 in Utrecht, Netherlands, behind the playmaking skills of Lionel Messi, who scored twice. Messi scored six goals in the tournament and was awarded both the Golden Shoe and Golden Ball awards.

Argentina emerged as the winner despite losing to the United States in the first round. Of the three sides from the Confederation of North, Central American, and Caribbean Association Football (CONCACAF), only the U.S. team reached the knockout stages, where it lost to Italy 3-1. Brazil took third place.

At the FIFA Under-17 World Championship held in Peru from September 16 to Oct. 2, 2005, Mexico defeated Brazil 3-0 in the final to take its first ever FIFA world championship. Mexico's star striker Carlos Vela scored six goals in the tournament and claimed the Golden Shoe award. Brazil's forward Anderson won the Golden Ball. The Netherlands defeated Turkey 2-1 in the match for third place.

International club competitions. Costa Rica club Deportivo Saprissa defeated Pumas UNAM (Mexico) 3-2, on aggregate, in the final of the 2005 CONCACAF Champions Cup in May. Deportivo won the first leg 2-0 in Costa Rica on May 4 and lost the second leg 2-1 in Mexico on May 11.

In the European Champions League, Liverpool (England) defeated AC Milan (Italy) in the final on May 25 in Istanbul. Milan led 3-0 at halftime, but Liverpool made a sensational recovery in the second half to tie the score 3-3 and went on to win the game 3-2 on penalties.

Deportivo and Liverpool met in the final of the 2005 FIFA World Club Championship in December. Liverpool defeated São Paulo 1-0 on a goal by Mineiro.

In the Copa Libertadores, two teams from Brazil—São Paulo and Atletico Paranaense—met in the two-legged final. It was the first time in the 46-year history of the competition that two teams from the same country reached the final. The first leg, which ended in a 1-1 tie, was played in Porto Alegre, Brazil. São Paulo overpowered Atletico Paranaense in the second leg, which was held on July 14 in São Paulo, Brazil. São Paulo won the contest 4-0 to take the trophy 5-1 on aggregate scoring.

Major League Soccer (MLS). The Los Angeles Galaxy took their second MLS title in four years on Nov. 13, 2005, defeating the New England Revolution 1-0 in extra time in the final at Pizza Hut Park in Frisco, Texas. The Galaxy's last title came in 2002, also against the New England Revolution. That game was also decided 1-0 in extra time. In the 2005 final, the Galaxy's Guillermo "Pando" Ramirez scored the winning goal off of a corner kick by teammate Landon Donovan in the 107th minute.

The MLS expanded to 12 teams in 2005 with the addition of Real Salt Lake (Utah) and Chivas U.S.A. (Los Angeles). As a result of the expansion, eight teams made the play-offs. In the opening round of the Eastern Conference playoffs, the top-seeded New England Revolution lost the first game 1-0 to the fourth-seeded MetroStars (New Jersey), and then fell behind 1-0 in the return leg. However, the Revolution fought back with three goals in the last 22 minutes to clinch a 3-2 victory that took them into the final. The Chicago Fire cruised to a 4-0 aggregate win over D.C. United in their semifinal, but the Revolution defeated the Fire 1-0 in the Eastern Conference championship game.

In the Western Conference semifinals, the Los Angeles Galaxy defeated the fourth-seeded San Jose Earthquakes 4-2 on aggregate. The Colorado Rapids got past FC Dallas 5-4 on penalty kicks. However, the Rapids lost to the Galaxy 2-0 in the Western Conference final.

Women's soccer. The United States women's team maintained its winning form in 2005. The U.S. team got off to a terrific start, sweeping the Algarve Cup in Portugal in March. The team held opponents scoreless in eight consecutive games. In the European Women's Championship held June 19 in Blackburn, England, Germany defeated Norway 3-1.

In the FIFA women's world rankings as of December 21, Germany was on top with 2,234 points; the U.S. team was second with 2,184 points; and Norway was third with 2,100 points.

Laws. The International Football Association Board (IFAB) in February 2005 made some minor changes to soccer's laws. The body decided to experiment with a new technology that would determine for certain whether or not a ball has crossed the goal-line. The system uses a prototype ball with an embedded electronic chip. The system was used at the FIFA Under-17 World Championship, but authorities in late 2005 decided the technology was not yet ready.

In an effort to make play safer, the IFAB made it mandatory for officials to dismiss players who make dangerous tackles from the front or side instead of just from behind. The new laws went into effect on July 1.

Ronaldinho, a star player with Brazil and FC Barcelona, took his second consecutive FIFA men's World Player of the Year in December. Birgit Prinz of Germany took the women's award for the third year in a row.

Best dies. George Best, an Irish soccer star whom many considered one of the best players of all time, died Nov. 25, 2005, at the age of 59. Best, a goal-scoring winger, played for England's Manchester United in 1968 when the team became the first English club to win the European Cup. Best was renowned for his amazing ability to make deceptive moves with his body while dribbling the ball. ■ Norman Barrett

See also **Deaths.**

BENEFIT OF DOUBT

How secure are American entitlements?

By Emily Friedman and
Scott Thomas

United States President George W. Bush, in his 2005 State of the Union address, vowed to reform Social Security, which he characterized as "headed for bankruptcy." He proposed the creation of personal investment accounts as part of the "guiding ideal of liberty for all." In April, he traveled to a federal building in Parkersburg, West Virginia, peered into the bottom drawer of a filing cabinet containing U.S. Treasury bonds held by the Social Security trust funds, and said, "Imagine—the retirement security for future generations is sitting in a filing cabinet." He later declared, "There is no [social security] 'trust fund,' just IOU's. . . .It's time to strengthen and modernize Social Security for future generations with growing assets that you can control."

In March, Alan Greenspan, chairman of the Federal Reserve System (the Fed), the nation's central bank, warned the House of Representatives Budget Committee that the costs connected to the aging of the "baby boom" generation—specifically the costs of Social Security and Medicare—would likely drive up budget deficits, possibly to "unsustainable levels." (The baby boom generation was born from 1946 to 1964.)

In October 2005, U.S. Department of Health and Human Services (HHS) officials announced that Florida had been granted permission to radically alter its Medicaid program. Under the new plan, the state would cap the amount spent on each beneficiary and launch a pilot program that would shift most enrollees into private managed care health insurance plans. (Managed care refers to an insurer that limits costs by controlling the type of care provided to patients.) Health care experts characterized the pilot program as the initial step in transferring complete authority over the state's Medicaid system to a private corporation.

Political leaders who opposed President Bush's proposal to reform Social Security and the other entitlement programs responded with skepticism to the president's and Fed chairman's claims. (Entitlements are programs in which the law requires payment of benefits to any person who meets the eligibility standards.) They claimed that Bush was exaggerating the severity of the problem to either undermine or privatize the country's main entitlements programs—Social Security, a pension program for people age 65 and older; Medicare, a health care system for people 65 and older; and Medicaid, a health care system for low-income residents. What is the truth about federal entitlements? Are these programs teetering toward extinction?

SOCIAL SECURITY

Social Security provides retired workers and some other workers and their families with a stable monthly income. Social Security payments help to replace income lost as a result of retirement, unemployment, disability, or the death of a spouse or parent. More than 45 million U.S. workers, primarily elderly people, receive monthly benefits. The system provides about two-thirds of all beneficiaries with the majority of their income and is the sole source of income for about one-fifth of beneficiaries. The system also covers unemployment insurance and workers' compensation.

Social Security came into existence in the United States as part of the New Deal, President Franklin Roosevelt's legislative program to counteract the Great Depression, the worldwide economic downturn in the 1930's. Congress passed the Social Security Act and President Roosevelt signed it into law in 1935. The Federal Insurance Contribution Act (FICA) taxes that fund Social Security were first levied in 1937. Originally, the system provided benefits only to retired workers in commerce and industry. In 1939, Congress amended the act to benefit wives and dependent children of deceased workers. In 1950, the system was expanded to cover many farm and domestic workers, nonprofessional self-employed workers, and many state and municipal employees. Coverage became nearly universal in 1956, when lawyers and other professionals came under the system.

President Franklin D. Roosevelt, surrounded by Cabinet members and congressional leaders, signs legislation creating Social Security at a ceremony at the White House in 1935. Social Security, which has been widened in scope numerous times, is one of the most popular U.S. government programs in history.

The Social Security trust funds

The part of Social Security that covers old-age, survivors, and disability benefits is financed by the FICA payroll tax. Each worker's annual income, up to a certain fixed amount, is subject to the tax. Employers deduct the FICA tax from workers' pay each pay period, add an equal contribution, and send the amount periodically to the U.S. Department of the Treasury. Self-employed individuals also pay the FICA tax. The Treasury Department distributes most of the money to the Old-Age and Survivors Insurance Trust Fund and the Disability Insurance Trust Fund, which pay the appropriate benefits.

The Social Security trust funds consist of more than $1.7 trillion worth of special-issue Treasury bonds; that is, a certificate issued by the government promising to pay back money it has borrowed. The $1.7 trillion is the result of a FICA tax surplus; that is, more money came in than was needed to pay benefits. At the recommendation of Alan Greenspan and congressional leaders, more taxes were collected than needed to build up reserves against the eventual retirement of the baby boom generation. By law, this surplus was invested in Treasury bonds. The Treasury Department used the money from the sale of the bonds to finance the everyday operation of the federal government. As a result, the trust funds own part of the national debt—in fact, nearly 25 percent.

According to economists, the special-issue bonds held by the Social Security trust funds are as secure as any other U.S. government bond. Governments, of course, have defaulted on debt. Bonds issued by the Confederate States of America famously became worthless even before the South lost the Civil War (1861-1865). How likely is it that the U.S. government would default on its promises to creditors? Not likely if measured by the value of U.S. bonds on financial markets. Treasury bonds are

The authors:
Emily Friedman is a health policy and ethics analyst.
Scott Thomas is the managing editor of *The World Book Year Book*.

considered essentially risk free on markets around the world. No Treasury bond in modern times has been *discounted* (devalued) for fear that the debt would go unpaid. Economists note that if the U.S. government were to default on any portion of its debt—including the bonds held by Social Security trust funds—the effect on world markets would be staggering and likely to trigger a worldwide economic crisis. The government, therefore, has little choice but to honor the bonds in the trust funds.

Social Security demographics

The U.S. labor force was greatly enlarged from the mid-1960's through the mid-1980's by the entry of the baby boom generation. Also, low birth rates in the 1920's and 1930's resulted in a relatively small population of retirees in the 1980's and 1990's. As a result, the labor force that finances Social Security was about three times as large as the population of beneficiaries in 2005. It is expected to remain so until about 2010. According to a 2005 report issued by the trustees that oversee Social Security, the trust funds are expected to grow until about 2025. However, soon after 2025, the large number of baby boom retirees will begin to draw down the funds. The Social Security Administration estimates that costs will exceed income in approximately 2027. If nothing is done to correct the imbalance, these funds may be depleted in 2041, according to some government estimates. (The Congressional Budget Office calculates that the trust funds will not run dry until 2052.) In 2005, each Social Security beneficiary was supported by three workers paying FICA taxes. Only two workers will be supporting each beneficiary in 2041, according to Social Security Administration estimates. Will this push the system into bankruptcy as President Bush has predicted?

The Social Security Administration projects that program costs will exceed income from FICA taxes in approximately 2027. If nothing is done to correct the imbalance, the trust funds will be emptied sometime between 2041 and 2052.

Reforming the system

President Bush's proposed solution to Social Security's financial problems involved the creation of personal investment retirement accounts. As outlined in his plan, approximately one-third of participating individuals' FICA tax money would be diverted into private stock market accounts. He proposed that the money be invested in relatively low-risk *mutual fund* accounts. (A

Social Security current and projected financial status

Income
Costs

Dollars (in billions)

Year

Source: Social Security Administration statistics compiled in 2005.

mutual fund is an investment company that pools funds from many investors and uses the money to buy stocks and other securities.)

While President Bush did not provide details on what impact the diversion of FICA taxes would have, politicians who opposed the plan happily volunteered that private accounts would radically change Social Security. Under the current system, the younger generation pays the cost of supporting the older generation. The private account system would allow the younger generation to hold onto at least part of its FICA deductions, depriving the older generation of that support. Some economists predicted that shifting this cash away would result in one of two outcomes—the government would be forced to borrow $2 trillion in the next 10 years to plug the gap; or the government would be forced to substantially cut benefits.

Members of Congress who opposed the plan suggested various alternatives—increasing tax rates; changing the ways benefits are calculated; enlarging the system's base by expanding the categories of workers who participate; reducing benefits for higher-income workers; raising the percentage of benefits that are subject to income taxes; even allowing the Social Security Administration to invest funds in stocks and other investments.

The solutions most often proposed involved raising the ceiling on the payroll taxes above the current limit and raising the retirement age. Under rules in effect in 2005, people do not pay FICA tax on annual incomes above $90,000. While the average U.S. worker pays FICA taxes on his or her entire income, the chief operating officer of a corporation who makes several million dollars a year pays FICA taxes only on a small percentage of that income. With a record 2.5 million U.S. citizens holding assets in excess of $1 million in 2005, lifting the current cap obviously would raise substantial revenue. Political experts noted, however, that President Bush, who consistently opposed tax hikes, would likely veto any increase in the FICA cap. The age at which U.S. workers qualify for Social Security benefits already has been lifted once. In 2003, the retirement age of 65 began to increase gradually. It will rise by two months per year to age 66 by 2009 and remain fixed through 2020, then increase gradually to age 67 by 2027.

Social Security is often referred to as the "third rail" of U.S. politics. The phrase alludes to the highly charged third rail that powers an electric train. One touches a third rail at great peril. The vast majority of the American public met President Bush's private accounts proposal with skepticism.

In 2005, the Social Security trust funds contained $1.7 trillion in U.S. Treasury bonds. The funds are expected to grow until about 2025, when large numbers of the baby boom generation will be collecting benefits. In 2005, each beneficiary was supported by three workers. Only two workers will support each beneficiary by 2040.

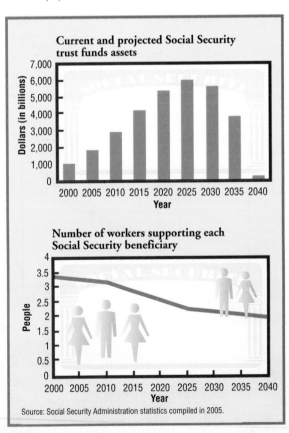

Current and projected Social Security trust funds assets

Dollars (in billions) — Year: 2000, 2005, 2010, 2015, 2020, 2025, 2030, 2035, 2040

Number of workers supporting each Social Security beneficiary

People — Year: 2000, 2005, 2010, 2015, 2020, 2025, 2030, 2035, 2040

Source: Social Security Administration statistics compiled in 2005.

Social Security has worked without major problems since the 1930's. Nearly everyone has a parent, grandparent, or some relative who receives benefits from the system; and nearly everyone over a certain age has paid into the system for years and fully expects to, in turn,

become a beneficiary. By the end of 2005, political experts had declared the president's proposal essentially dead. Members of Congress who faced reelection in 2006 had little appetite for reconfiguring one of the most popular government programs in U.S. history. The problem, of course, is that the financial crisis posed by the aging and retirement of the baby boom generation will not disappear simply because politicians lack the will to fix it. A time bomb has been set, and it is ticking away toward 2017, when benefits will exceed income, and the 2040's, when the trust funds will likely become insolvent.

President Lyndon B. Johnson signs Public Law 89-97, creating Medicare and Medicaid on July 30, 1965. The ceremony took place at the Truman Presidential Library in Independence, Missouri, with former President Harry S. Truman and Bess Truman (seated and standing, far right) in attendance. Truman, who proposed universal health care in 1948, was issued the first Medicare card.

MEDICARE

On July 30, 1965, President Lyndon B. Johnson signed a bill that became Public Law 89-97, establishing the two most important public health insurance programs in U.S. history. The successful passage by Congress of the bill was the culmination of decades of work on the part of many people. The idea of public payment for the health care expenses of some or all U.S. citizens goes back at least as far as President Theodore Roosevelt. His unsuccessful 1912 campaign for president on the Progressive ticket included a proposal for "health insurance legislation" to cover the medical costs for working class people. In 1934, President Franklin Roosevelt considered including health care coverage in his Social Security proposal, but strong opposition, especially from the American Medical Association (AMA), led him to give up the idea. (The AMA is a Chicago-based professional society of physicians.) Roosevelt revived the concept in 1944 and planned to send a message to Congress urging passage of a bill for universal coverage, but he died before it was completed.

After Franklin Roosevelt's death, President Harry S. Truman announced in his 1948 State of the Union address, "This great nation cannot afford to allow its citizens to suffer needlessly from the lack of proper medical care." He urged Congress to enact "a national health program." Congress did not respond. In 1960, Congress did pass the Kerr-Mills Act, which provided grants to states to help pay for the health care costs of citizens over 65 with low incomes.

Although few states took full advantage of the Kerr-Mills funding, public interest in the program convinced some members of Congress that a means of paying for health care costs of the elderly was needed. Advocates for the poor and some members of Congress believed that low-income citizens needed such assistance as well. Others advocated universal, government-paid coverage, which was not politically feasible. The still-powerful AMA opposed any health program for the elderly, let alone a universal one. In addition, private health insurance for employed people had become common during and after World War II (1939-1945), making the need for a universal program appear less acute.

Wilbur Mills (D., Arkansas), the then-powerful chairman of the House of Representatives Ways and Means Committee and co-author of the Kerr-Mills Act, worked with President John F. Kennedy in the early 1960's to pass a bill providing coverage to seniors and some low-income people. After Kennedy's assassination in 1963, Mills and President Lyndon Johnson continued the effort. The mood of the country after President Kennedy's death and Johnson's keen understanding of Congress, gained during his years as majority leader of the Senate, suddenly made passage of health care legislation possible. Congress passed the bill despite continued opposition from the AMA, and Johnson signed it at the Harry S. Truman Presidential Library in Independence, Missouri, with former President Truman and his wife Bess Truman in attendance. The Trumans received the first two Medicare enrollment cards.

How Medicare works

Medicare, a health insurance program that covers nearly all legal U.S. residents age 65 and older, went into effect in 1966 as a two-part program. Part A covers most hospital costs for beneficiaries. Part B is an optional program that pays for physician care and some other services. Nearly all beneficiaries choose to join it. Part B is funded by premiums paid by beneficiaries and by large annual contributions from the federal government. The program is managed by the Centers for Medicare and Medicaid Services, a part of the HHS.

In 1972, Congress expanded Medicare to include people with disabilities under 65 who receive federal income assistance and persons who have serious kidney disease. In 1988, Congress broadened the program further by adding coverage for prescription drugs used outside hospitals and limiting what beneficiaries had to pay for some services. In 1989, Congress repealed this coverage in response to political opposition.

Congress passed legislation in 1997 that allowed beneficiaries to completely opt out of Medicare in favor of a private health insurance plan with premiums paid for by Medicare. This benefit is known as Part C. The new law stipulated that for a beneficiary to qualify for Part C he or she must join a managed care plan. In 2005, 12 percent of beneficiaries belonged to Part C.

Congress expanded Medicare again in 2003 with coverage for prescription drugs used outside hospitals. Known as Part D, this benefit, which went into effect in

Medicare, a federally funded health insurance program, covers nearly all citizens age 65 and older.

January 2006, specifies private insurance coverage for prescription drugs; that is, participants must join a drug plan operated by a private insurance company. Part D is not free. In addition to the premiums beneficiaries pay for the drug benefit, they must pay a $250 deductible; 25 percent of prescription costs between $250 and $2,250; and 100 percent of costs between $2,250 and $5,100. Medicare picks up 95 percent of costs exceeding $5,100. Under the new program, low-income beneficiaries receive help covering the cost of the deductible. Part D is an optional program.

Despite the expansions, Medicare does not cover all health costs. Benefits for nursing home and other long-term care for people with chronic illness are limited. Medicare does not pay for dental care. (For much of its history, it did not pay for preventive care, such as physical examinations, or for certain diagnostic tests.) In 2002, AARP estimated that Medicare paid only 45 percent of beneficiaries' total medical costs. (AARP, originally the American Association of Retired Persons, is a private, nonprofit membership organization, based in Florida, that addresses the needs of older people in the United States.) As a result, 71 percent of beneficiaries have additional health insurance to cover gaps in the program. Some of the supplementary insurance plans are private; others are public through the Medicaid program.

Medicare funding problems

Medicare is funded by a combination of payroll taxes; interest on surplus funds; beneficiary premiums; and federal general revenue funds. Historically, these revenue sources were sufficient to keep the program solvent, though beneficiary premiums were increased several times since 1966.

Two major forces threaten Medicare. Americans live longer than they once

The trustees of the Medicare program predicted in their 2005 annual report that costs would exceed revenue beginning in 2012. The trust fund will likely run out of money by 2019, unless new sources of revenue are found. Medicare costs keep rising in relation to the gross domestic product because of ever increasing health care costs.

Current and projected Medicare financial status

Current and projected Medicare trust fund assets

Medicare costs as a percentage of GDP*

*GDP (gross domestic product): total value of all goods and services produced in a country in a given year.

Source: Medicare Boards of Trustees statistics compiled in 2005.

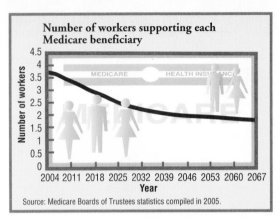

Number of workers supporting each Medicare beneficiary

Source: Medicare Boards of Trustees statistics compiled in 2005.

In 2005, every Medicare beneficiary was supported by the payroll taxes of nearly four U.S. workers. Each beneficiary will be supported by only two workers by 2067, according to Medicare Boards of Trustees estimates.

The care of 46 percent of all elderly residents of U.S. nursing homes was paid by Medicaid in 2003. Medicare benefits for nursing home and other long-term care for people with chronic illnesses are limited.

did, and health care costs rise faster than the rate of inflation. In 1965, the life expectancy for the average U.S. citizen was 70.2 years. In 2005, life expectancy was 77.6 years, and the country had more than twice as many citizens over age 65 as it had in 1966. The problem will become acute as the 76 million members of the baby boom generation begin to become eligible for the program in 2011. Medicare trustees predicted in their 2005 annual report that costs will exceed revenue in 2012 and the Medicaid trust fund will run out of money by 2019. Health care experts noted that the Part D prescription benefit will likely accelerate the problem. According to government estimates, Part D will add $724 billion to Medicare expenses between 2006 and 2015.

Short-term fixes

The future of Medicare is the subject of intense public debate. Supporters of the traditional program insist that cost containment measures, greater efficiencies, and increased contributions from the federal general revenue funds can largely solve the problem. Supporters of private-sector approaches to health care for the aged suggest that more Medicare beneficiaries should opt out of the traditional program for Part C, private coverage. According to the private-sector advocates, who include President Bush, the private health plans would result in greater efficiency and savings than the public program if more beneficiaries were to enroll in the private plans. However, many health care experts question this argument because private health plans spend considerably more to administer their Medicare programs than does the federal government.

Some politicians and heath care experts have suggested that Medicare beneficiaries with higher incomes should pay more. (They will pay higher Part B premiums than lower-income beneficiaries pay beginning in 2007.) Political leaders also have proposed that Medicare should only be available to low-income Americans and that all other seniors should purchase private coverage on their own. Other analysts have suggested that benefits will have to be trimmed to save the program. Senator Edward Kennedy (D., Massachusetts) has argued the opposite. He has proposed that Medicare should be expanded to cover all Americans, regardless of their age.

An important consideration in this debate for politicians is Medicare's public appeal. Medicare is among the most popular of government programs. It largely benefits senior citizens, a higher percentage of whom vote than do members of other age groups. Whatever solution is found for Medicare's long-term challenges will have to be acceptable to the 42 million people it covers today and the 78 million people it will cover by 2030.

MEDICAID

Medicaid is a federal program that works in cooperation with state governments to partly finance medical assistance to needy people. Medicaid was the "other" part of Public Law 89-97. During the campaign for passage of the bill, public attention was focused largely on Medicare. Medicaid was almost an afterthought. Ironically, that afterthought became the nation's largest public health insurance program. Medicaid pays for some or most of the health care expenses of more than 52 million people. While a federal program, Medicaid nevertheless is administered by the states. The decentralization was the result of a political reality. Because Medicare was to be federally controlled, state governors wanted a program that was under their power. However useful the decentralization may have been politically in 1965, it has produced many complications.

By the early 1980's, each state, as well as the District of Columbia and territories, had set up its own Medicaid system, resulting in 53 different programs. The Medicaid law also allowed the federal government to grant waivers to change how programs are organized, what services are covered, and who is eligible. By 2005, 19 states had expanded eligibility through such waivers. State control over Medicaid came at a cost. State governments became partially responsible for the funding. The federal government contributes between 40 and 60 percent of Medicaid costs, depending on the wealth of the state. Poorer states receive a greater percentage than richer states.

People with chronic illnesses who need nursing home care—which includes the elderly and disabled—are responsible for the largest growth of Medicaid spending. The provision in the original Medicaid bill authorizing coverage of *indigent* (needy) nursing home patients was considered a minor benefit in 1965, when life expectancy was shorter.

Medicaid has long faced another challenge: it costs much more than expected. At the time of its passage, little information was available on how many low-income people might need coverage. One 1965 estimate provided to Congress projected that 3 million people would be eligible. The program's complexity continues to make precise numbers about enrollment difficult to determine. In 1990, the estimated figure was 24.1 million; in 2003, it was 52.4 million; and in 2004, it was 57.3 million. Total Medicaid spending in 2003 was estimated to be $266 billion.

Medicaid was originally designed to cover people who received "welfare" payments from the federal government or the state, a system that went back to the Great Depression. Welfare recipients were mostly low-income mothers and children. Medicaid also was required to cover Medicare payments for low-income beneficiaries and the costs of long-term care for sick older people. The original

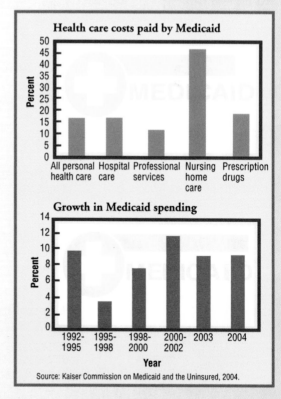

Source: Kaiser Commission on Medicaid and the Uninsured, 2004.

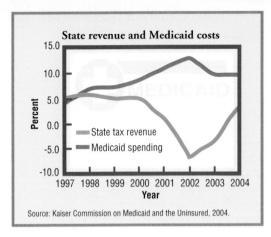

State revenue and Medicaid costs

Percent

— State tax revenue
— Medicaid spending

Year: 1997 1998 1999 2000 2001 2002 2003 2004

Source: Kaiser Commission on Medicaid and the Uninsured, 2004.

State revenues (above), hurt by a downturn in the economy that began in 2000, declined while Medicaid costs escalated due to sharply higher medical costs. Officials reined in costs by cutting benefits and people from rolls. The disabled and elderly (below), who account for 25 percent of enrollees, receive nearly 70 percent of all benefits.

legislation also allowed the states to cover other groups, but using only state money. In 1996, Congress dissolved the tie between welfare payments and Medicaid. A person or family could be eligible for one but not the other, depending on state regulations.

Over time, legislation was passed making other groups eligible for benefits—more low-income women and children; some people with disabilities, including those who need community-based services but for whom long-term, institutional care is unnecessary; and low-income people up to age 21. In 1997, Congress established the State Children's Health Insurance Program (SCHIP) and provided some federal funds for its implementation. SCHIP allowed states to provide Medicaid coverage for children whose families made too much money to qualify for Medicaid but who could not afford private insurance. Some states enrolled these children in Medicaid. Others established separate programs. Congress also allowed states to enroll beneficiaries in private insurance plans called health maintenance organizations with premiums paid by Medicaid. At least 60 percent of all Medicaid beneficiaries belonged to such plans in 2005, though the states by and large maintain oversight and control over benefits and services.

Medicaid and nursing home care

People with chronic illnesses who need nursing home care are responsible for the highest growth in Medicaid spending. The provision in the original law authorizing states to cover the care of *indigent* (needy) nursing home patients was considered a minor benefit. No one in 1965 expected that many people would need this protection. The great irony of Medicaid is that while the largest percentage of the beneficiaries in 2005 were low-income families, the largest percentage of spending was on long-term care for the disabled and elderly. According to the Kaiser Commission on Medicaid and the Uninsured, 60 percent of all residents of nursing homes received some Medicaid benefits in 2003. Typically, even middle-class people in long-term care end up on Medicaid because nursing home costs exhaust their life savings and can force the sale of their residences. (Annual nursing home care averaged $60,000 in the United States in 2005.)

Controlling Medicaid costs

As the number of people eligible for Medicaid grew, the program became ever more expensive for the states. Economic swings deepened the problem. In bad financial times, tax revenues shrank while the number of

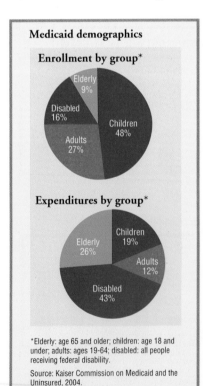

Medicaid demographics

Enrollment by group*

Elderly 9%
Disabled 16%
Adults 27%
Children 48%

Expenditures by group*

Children 19%
Elderly 26%
Adults 12%
Disabled 43%

*Elderly: age 65 and older; children: age 18 and under; adults: ages 19-64; disabled: all people receiving federal disability.

Source: Kaiser Commission on Medicaid and the Uninsured, 2004.

recipients grew as people lost jobs and employer-provided health insurance. The problem became acute in the early 2000's, when growth in Medicaid enrollment, rapidly rising health care costs, and a financial recession in the U.S. economy threatened to sink state economies. Although the crisis began to ease in 2004 and 2005, many state governments continued to reduce Medicaid rolls. Tennessee, which at one point had a higher percentage of its population on Medicaid than any other state, dropped nearly 200,000 people from its program in mid-2005. Less drastic but still major reductions were made to rolls in Mississippi, Missouri, Oregon, and other states. The government of South Carolina followed the lead of Florida in 2005 in asking the Bush administration for a waiver to transfer complete authority over the state's Medicaid program to private insurers.

Congress also cut Medicaid funding in 2005. Both houses passed a budget resolution mandating $10 billion in cuts in federal spending on Medicaid over the next five years. Michael Leavitt, secretary of HHS, which administers Medicaid, appointed a commission to determine how these cuts would be made. House and Senate Democrats, some Republican senators, and members of the National Governors Association refused to participate in the commission because they were not accorded voting rights. The commission's two most significant proposed changes involved cutting reimbursements for Medicaid prescription drug benefits and allowing states to increase and enforce the co-payments that higher income beneficiaries pay.

Health care experts predicted in 2005 that Medicaid funding almost certainly would be reduced both on state and federal levels but warned that the role of Medicaid in U.S. health care could not be overstated. In 2003, Medicaid paid for 17 percent of all personal health care in the nation; 17 percent of all hospital care; 12 percent of health care professional services; 19 percent of all prescription drug costs; and 46 percent of all nursing home costs. Medicaid had been a laboratory for state experimentation in a wide variety of areas—finding alternatives to nursing home care; the coordination of care for children; and the creation of public-private partnerships in providing insurance to vulnerable people.

In 2005, Medicaid covered more people than any other single insurance plan, public or private. Many of these people were poor, sick or both. Political decisions made about this program, as well as the other entitlements, have major implications for the health and welfare of the nation; for how many people in the United States end up completely uninsured; for how states are able to shape public health insurance; and for how much creativity there will be in the U.S. health care system.

Mississippians gather inside the State Capitol in Jackson in June 2004 to protest plans to cut 65,000 people from the state's Medicaid rolls. In 2005, a number of states drastically lowered Medicaid funding, and the U.S. Congress cut federal funds for the program by $10 billion over five years.

South Africa. President Thabo Mbeki on June 14, 2005, dismissed Jacob Zuma, widely regarded as his heir-apparent, from the post of deputy president. (In South Africa, the deputy president is a member of the Cabinet, appointed by the president.) Zuma was deeply implicated in a corruption scandal involving his financial advisor and business partner, Schabir Shaik, who on June 8 had been sentenced to a 15-year jail sentence for attempted bribery. Shaik was found guilty of soliciting bribes from a French company to pay Zuma to help win a large defense contract in 1999. Hilary Squires, the judge presiding in the Shaik trial, said that he found "convincing and overwhelming evidence of a corrupt relationship" between Shaik and Deputy President Zuma. On June 20, 2005, prosecutors brought corruption charges against Zuma himself. In November, the executive council of the African National Congress (ANC), the ruling party of Mbeki and Zuma, issued a statement that Zuma was under investigation separately on an allegation of rape.

Mbeki's dismissal of Zuma provoked a succession crisis for the ANC. Constitutional provisions prohibit Mbeki, whose presidential term ends in 2009, from running again for president, and most ANC leaders had regarded Zuma as the president's likely successor. On June 22, 2005, President Mbeki promoted Minister of Energy Affairs Phumzile Mlambo-Ngcuka as deputy president, opening the way for the 49-year-old ethnic Zulu to become a leading presidential contender and possibly the nation's first woman president. Political analysts noted, however, that Zuma, one of the ANC's most popular Zulu politicians, could still be a candidate for president in 2009.

Travelgate. The dismissal of Zuma was accompanied in 2005 by revelations of another scandal, dubbed "Travelgate" by local media and described as the biggest corruption scandal in South Africa's *postapartheid* history (the period since apartheid, the system of strictly enforced racial segregation, which was ended in 1994). Prosecutors announced on Jan. 21, 2005, that 40 members of parliament (MPs), mostly from the ANC—which in 2005 held 279 seats in the 400-member National Assembly—would be charged with fraud. They stood accused of illegally misusing official travel expenses totalling approximately $3 million. Prosecutors obtained the first convictions in the case on March 18, when a Johannesburg court found five ANC MPs guilty of fraud. Other convictions followed.

Riots. Police armed with rubber bullets, stun grenades, and tear gas confronted rioters in black townships of Cape Town and other South African communities in June 2005 in scenes reminiscent of 1980's antiapartheid riots. Analysts said that the violence, unlike that of the 1980's, was directed at the predominantly black leadership of the ruling ANC, the result of frustration over unrelieved poverty and high rates of unemployment (over 40 percent in 2005). At the same time, South Africans living in substandard conditions waited on a construction backlog of at least 260,000 new houses.

The NNP disbands. The political party that introduced apartheid and enforced racial segregation in South Africa for nearly half a century disbanded and apologized for its racist policies on April 10, 2005. The New National Party (NNP) renamed from the old National Party (NP) in 1997, voted itself out of existence after several electoral defeats. In the 2004 general elections, it took only 1.65 percent of the national vote. Officials with the main opposition Democratic Alliance (DA) said their party would attempt to pick up NNP's support base.

Gun laws tightened. New firearms legislation went into force in January 2005, requiring all legally held guns in South Africa to be relicensed over a five-year period. Critics of the new law claimed that it was an attempt to disarm law-abiding citizens while doing nothing to stop criminals from using guns in violent crimes. However, police officials alleged that many licensed owners did not know how to use or secure their weapons and that many legally obtained firearms were falling into criminal hands. In 2005, at least 2.5 million registered owners possessed 4.5 million legal guns in South Africa, with up to 4 million illegal guns also in circulation. In 2005, South Africa had one of the world's highest murder rates, at 43 murders per 100,000 population. Criminology experts estimated that nearly half of the approximately 20,000 murders reported annually were gun-related.

Capital name change. One of South Africa's most famous place names was cast into history on May 26, when a national commission on geographical names decided that the capital, Pretoria, would henceforth be known as Tshwane. The new name honors an African chief who once ruled the surrounding area. Pretoria was founded in 1855 by white Afrikaners and named for Andries Pretorius, an Afrikaner military leader who successfully fought off Zulu warriors and British troops. Afrikaners are South African citizens of Dutch descent.

New chief justice. On June 1, 2005, Pius Langa, a former shirt factory worker and later a lawyer defending victims of apartheid, became South Africa's first black chief justice following his appointment in April by President Mbeki. Langa had been deputy chief justice since November 2001. ■ Simon Baynham

See also **Africa**.

South America. See **Latin America**.

Space exploration. The United States National Aeronautics and Space Administration (NASA) resumed human spaceflight in 2005 for the first time since the loss of the space shuttle Columbia in 2003. However, continuing safety concerns with the shuttle fleet and damage to critical ground facilities in the path of Hurricane Katrina in August 2005 raised questions about when—and how many more times—the aging space planes would fly.

In 2005, NASA announced plans for sending astronauts to the moon and Mars; NASA's Mars Exploration Rovers kept on roving long beyond their estimated lifetimes; China sent two astronauts into space; and one European spacecraft landed on Saturn's moon Titan, while another began searching beneath the surface of Mars for underground lakes of life-supporting water.

Return to flight. The space shuttle Discovery lifted off from Kennedy Space Center, Florida, on July 26, 2005, after a series of delays prompted by heightened safety concerns in the wake of the Columbia disaster. The July launch appeared perfect. However, images captured by a camera aboard the shuttle's external fuel tank revealed a piece of insulating foam peeling off the tank. Cameras had been installed to monitor the condition of the tank after it was determined that foam falling from the tank during Columbia's last mission had fatally damaged the orbiter.

The piece lost during Discovery's launch did not appear to strike the shuttle's delicate thermal protection system. Inspection with cameras aboard the International Space Station (ISS) showed only minor debris damage to the orbiter. Nevertheless, the incident revealed that NASA engineers had failed to correct the problem that destroyed Columbia. A second shuttle flight planned for fall 2005 was postponed until the foam problem could be resolved. Future shuttle flights were further delayed after August 29, when Hurricane Katrina slammed into New Orleans, where the shuttle's tanks are built. Although damage to the assembly facility was minor, the storm scattered the facility's employees.

International Space Station. Fortunately for the U.S.-Russian crews who live on the ISS, Discovery left enough food, water, clothing, fuel, and equipment to keep the orbiting laboratory functioning well into 2006. In addition, Discovery crew members Stephen K. Robinson of NASA and Soichi Noguchi of the Japanese Aerospace Exploration Agency replaced a malfunctioning altitude control gyroscope on the ISS. The repair eliminated the need for the station to use precious fuel for its thrusters to keep the station's solar arrays pointed at the sun. Nevertheless, without a set schedule of shuttle flights, smaller Russian Soyuz crew capsules and Progress cargo vehicles were the only supply link to the ISS, limiting its operations and halting station assembly altogether.

On Oct. 3, 2005, a Soyuz spacecraft brought a new crew to the space station—Expedition 12, consisting of astronaut William McArthur and cosmonaut Valery Tokarev. They were accompanied by the third tourist to fly in space, U.S. millionaire scientist Gregory Olsen. Olsen reportedly paid the Russian Space Agency $20 million for a seat on the Soyuz and the opportunity to conduct science experiments aboard the ISS for a week. Olsen returned to Earth on October 10 with Expedition 11 cosmonaut Sergei Krikalev and astronaut John Phillips. Krikalev and Phillips had been on the ISS since April, having replaced the Expedition 10 crew, astronaut Leroy Chiao and cosmonaut Salizhan Sharipov. Krikalev set a new career record for total days spent working in space—803.

Exploration vision. On September 19, NASA announced plans for the future of the U.S. space program, involving a push to the moon with new technology that may help human beings reach Mars. The shuttle was to be retired in 2010, after completing as much of the remaining space station assembly as possible. Meanwhile, NASA engineers were to start developing two new rockets based on existing shuttle technology. One was to carry astronauts to space. The other, larger rocket was to carry the equipment and supplies needed to get the astronauts to the surfaces of the moon and Mars and sustain them while they explore. NASA set 2012 as the date to begin flying a six-seat Crew Exploration Vehicle (CEV) similar to the Apollo capsule, the first generation of lunar spaceships. At first, the CEV is to fly to the space station, where crews will continue developing techniques for successfully living and working in space. By 2018, the CEV is to fly four astronauts to the moon for the first time since 1972.

Robotic explorers. Although human activity in space was limited in 2005, robotic explorers entered a kind of golden age. One of the year's most spectacular achievements took place in January, when a small European probe named for Dutch astronomer Christiaan Huygens (1625-1695) parachuted through the orange clouds of Titan, Saturn's largest moon. The Huygens probe had ridden piggyback to Titan on NASA's Cassini spacecraft. Huygens sent back the first pictures ever taken of Titan's surface. Clearly visible was a coastline with rivers running into what may be a supercold hydrocarbon sea, its semisolid surface dotted with ice pebbles. Huygens continued to return data and close-up images for some 70 minutes after it unexpectedly survived the impact of landing.

At Mars, the European Space Agency's Mars Express orbiter sent back spectacular three-dimensional images of the surface below. In July, controllers unfurled a set of boom antennas on Mars

Discovery—the first shuttle to return to space since the loss of the Columbia in 2003—lifts off from the Kennedy Space Center at Cape Canaveral, Florida, on July 26, 2005 (right) for a flight to the International Space Station. During the mission, astronaut Steve Robinson (below) rode the station's robotic arm to an area below the shuttle. There, he removed thermal protection tile gap fillers that mission control experts feared might cause higher-than-normal temperatures during the shuttle's return to Earth.

The United States resumed human space flight in 2005 and, with the European Space Agency, sent probes to explore comets and other planets.

On July 4, 2005, NASA's Deep Impact spacecraft reached Tempel 1—81 million miles (130 million kilometers) from Earth—and photographed the comet's topography (below, left). Moments later, the spacecraft released an impact probe that was designed to collide with the comet (below, right). By analyzing the crater that formed, scientists hoped to learn more about comets, which contain debris dating from the time that the solar system formed.

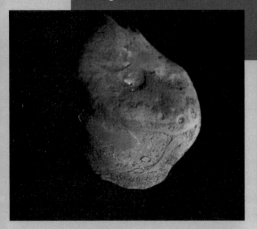

Saturn looms in the background as its small icy satellite, Dione, hovers above one of the planet's rings in an image captured by the Cassini spacecraft in October 2005. Cassini, a mission developed jointly by the National Aeronautics and Space Administration, the European Space Agency, and the Italian Space Agency, was launched in 1997 and reached Saturn in 2004.

Boulders lie strewn about the surface of Titan, Saturn's largest moon, in one of the first images ever taken by a spacecraft that has landed on another planet's satellite. The spacecraft, Huygens, was carried to Titan by Cassini and parachuted to the planet's surface in January 2005.

Express that allowed them to use radar to search for underground water that could support life.

On the surface of Mars, the two U.S. Mars Exploration Rovers—Spirit and Opportunity—continued to work long after their planned 90-day service life passed. Spirit traveled some 3 miles (5 kilometers) from its landing site in the giant Gusev Crater, climbing to the top of a low ridge named the Columbia Hills in honor of the lost space shuttle. On the other side of the planet, Opportunity escaped from sandy terrain that ensnared it for five weeks. The rover continued traveling toward craters similar to the one called Endurance, which it explored soon after its January 2004 landing.

On Aug. 12, 2005, an Atlas V rocket launched NASA's Mars Reconnaissance Orbiter (MRO)—equipped with a powerful camera—on a 15-month journey to Mars. After it settles into orbit, the MRO will take the highest resolution images of the surface of Mars ever collected from orbit.

China in space. On October 12, a Long March rocket carried two Chinese astronauts, Fei Junlong and Nie Haisheng, into space. The flight, aboard the Shenzhou VI spacecraft, marked the country's second human space flight. Yang Liwei was the first Chinese astronaut to fly in space when he orbited Earth for 21½ hours in 2003.

■ Frank Morring, Jr.

See also **Astronomy.**

Spain. The minority government led by Prime Minister José Luiz Rodríguez Zapatero's Socialist Party faced a challenge in 2005 by a call for greater autonomy by Catalonia, a region in northeast Spain. In September, Catalonia's parliament passed a constitutional statute that would give the region the right to raise taxes, form an independent legal system, and refer to itself as a "nation."

The proposal, which required the approval of the national government in Madrid, caused a conflict for Zapatero. The main opposition, the conservative People's Party, maintained that any granting of increased autonomy to Catalonia could lead to new demands for autonomy from Spain's other regions—especially the terrorism-plagued Basque region. However, the Socialists needed the support of Catalonia's left-wing politicians—who overwhelmingly supported greater autonomy—to maintain their parliamentary majority. Although political observers suggested the Catalonian law was likely to be struck down in its present form in the national parliament, they indicated that there may be room for compromise in matters of taxation and self-administration. A decision was expected in 2006.

Basque terrorist talks. In May 2005, Zapatero announced that he would seek to negotiate an end to terrorism in the Basque country with representatives of various Basque political organi-

Spanish soldiers bear the caskets of 17 fallen comrades toward a waiting plane at Herat Air Base in Afghanistan for the journey home to Spain. The men were killed on August 16 when their NATO helicopter collided in midair with another helicopter during training exercises south of the city of Herat.

zations. The Basque terrorist group ETA, whose initials stand for Basque Homeland and Freedom in the Basque language, has been fighting for an independent Basque homeland in northern Spain and southwestern France since the late 1960's. The violence has claimed more than 800 lives. Spain's supreme court suspended Batasuna, the ETA's political wing, in 2002.

On May 17, 2005, the Spanish parliament approved Zapatero's plan to engage in talks with ETA if the group would renounce violence. Nevertheless, the plan was highly controversial. The People's Party accused Zapatero of "betraying the dead" and "surrendering parliament." In June, an estimated 850,000 people demonstrated in Madrid to protest the decision. Throughout 2005, ETA continued low-level violence. In December, the group released a statement in an internal newsletter that the governments of Spain and France must make the first moves by stopping all armed forces action in the Basque region.

Economy. According to European Union (EU) economists, Spain's economy grew by 3.4 percent in 2005, well above the 1.5 percent average for the 25 EU nations. Unemployment remained high at 9.2 percent but represented an improvement over 2004, when it stood at 11.0 percent. ■ Jeffrey Kopstein

See also **Europe**.

Sports.
On July 24, 2005, Lance Armstrong of the United States accomplished something no other cyclist had ever done, winning the Tour de France for the seventh straight time. Armstrong, who announced before the race that he intended to retire when the race was over, capped a season of several outstanding performances in 2005.

Eldrick "Tiger" Woods reclaimed his title as the No. 1 golfer in the world with 2005 proving to be one of his best seasons. Woods won two major titles, the Masters and the British Open, and finished in the top four of the remaining two majors. He took second at the U.S. Open and fourth at the PGA Championship. With his victories, Woods moved to third all-time with 10 major titles, trailing Jack Nicklaus (18) and Walter Hagen (11). Ironically, while Woods appeared to have made a successful comeback after three tough seasons, he saw his record streak of *making the cut* (qualifying for the final two rounds) in 142 consecutive tournaments end in May at the Byron Nelson Classic.

In women's golf in 2005, Annika Sorenstam became the first woman since Pat Bradley in 1986 to capture the year's first two major championships. She also broke a Ladies Professional Golf Association (LPGA) record by winning five consecutive tournaments.

In tennis in 2005, Roger Federer of Switzerland became the first man since Don Budge in 1937-1938 to win both Wimbledon and the U.S. Open in consecutive years. The Williams sisters—Venus and Serena—returned to top form, with Serena taking the Australian Open and Venus winning Wimbledon.

In professional team sports, the San Antonio Spurs captured their third title in seven years in the National Basketball Association (NBA); the New England Patriots won their second consecutive Super Bowl in the National Football League (NFL); and the Chicago White Sox overcame 88 years of disappointment to win Major League Baseball's World Series.

The National Hockey League (NHL) in 2005 became the first North American professional sports league to cancel an entire season because of a labor dispute. As a result, the NHL did not award a Stanley Cup for the first time since the 1918-1919 season when an influenza epidemic forced the league to cancel its finals. NHL team owners and players reached a new labor agreement in July 2005, and the 2005-2006 season began as scheduled.

Tour de France. On July 5, 2005, Lance Armstrong took the lead in the fourth stage of the Tour de France when his Discovery Channel team set a record with an average speed of 35.54 miles (57.20 kilometers) per hour, easily topping the previous best of 34.06 miles (54.81 kilometers) per hour. During that team time trial stage, then-leader David Zabriskie of the United States was involved in a crash and suffered multiple cuts and a torn uniform but was not seriously injured.

Once in the lead, Armstrong and his team never faltered during the 21-stage, 2,232.7-mile (3,593-kilometer) race through France and part of Germany, finishing ahead of Italy's Ivan Basso by 4 minutes, 40 seconds, on July 24 in Paris. The margin of victory was Armstrong's second smallest of his seven wins. During the final stage, three of Armstrong's teammates slipped and crashed on the French capital's rain-slick streets, but Armstrong avoided the crash and breezed to the finish. Organizers made a rare decision to stop the clock with seven laps to go because of the slippery conditions. The only stage Armstrong won was the second to last stage, a 34.5-mile (55.5-kilometer) time trial.

In August, a French sports newspaper claimed it had found evidence that urine samples from Armstrong's first Tour victory in 1999 had tested positive for erythropoietin (EPO), an illegal performance-enhancing hormone. Armstrong vigorously denied the allegations. There was no way to verify the newspaper's claims. Armstrong said the allegations might motivate him to cancel his retirement, but in September he confirmed that he would remain in retirement.

The year of the woman. Race car driver Danica Patrick, a 23-year-old rookie on the Indy Racing League (IRL) circuit, made history when she nearly won the Indianapolis 500 in May 2005. First, Patrick qualified for the fourth position, the best ever starting position earned by a woman. During the race, Patrick became the first woman to take the lead in the Indy 500. She nearly won, but settled for fourth place, the best finish ever by a woman. Also during 2005, Patrick won the *pole position* (starting position earned by the driver with the fastest qualifying times) three times.

Michelle Wie, a 15-year-old golfer from the United States, made waves with her quest not only to play against men but to try to qualify for the Masters. The Masters is one of the most prestigious events in golf and is held annually at Augusta National, a private course in Augusta, Georgia, on which women are not allowed to play. In July, Wie, an amateur, failed in her attempt to gain an automatic berth, which is granted to the winner of the men's U.S. Amateur Public Links, when she lost in the quarterfinals. Wie had previously played in several men's tournaments but failed to make the cut in any of them.

NCAA mascots. In August, the National Collegiate Athletic Association (NCAA) issued a decree effective Feb. 1, 2006, banning the use of Native American mascots and imagery by sports teams during post-season tournaments. NCAA officials said the ban was an attempt to rid American collegiate sports of symbols and nicknames deemed "hostile or abusive." Schools not conforming with the policy would be barred from hosting post-season tournaments.

BALCO scandal. In July 2005, all four defendants involved in a steroid scandal that rocked the sports world and involved several high-profile professional athletes pleaded guilty. The defendants included Victor Conte, founder of the Bay Area Laboratory Co-Operative (BALCO); James Valente, vice president of BALCO; Greg Anderson, personal trainer to baseball star Barry Bonds; and track coach Remi Korchemny.

In October, Conte was sentenced to four months in prison and four months of house arrest. Anderson was sentenced to three months in prison and three months of home confinement. Valente was sentenced to probation. In November, Korchemny was sentenced to probation. The guilty pleas allowed high-profile athletes from major sports, as well as some Olympic athletes, to avoid being called to testify.

Members of the United States Congress held hearings periodically during the spring and summer of 2005 on steroid use and testing in U.S. professional sports leagues, particularly in professionial baseball. Angered by the lack of uniformity of testing and the lack of severe punishments for violators, lawmakers threatened to impose Olympic-style testing and sanctions on all professional leagues in the United States. Among other things, these sanctions were to include mandatory two-year suspensions for the first positive steroid test.

Awards. Gymnast Paul Hamm received the 75th annual James E. Sullivan Award in April 2005. The award is presented by the Amateur Athletic Union to the best U.S. amateur athlete for performances in the previous year. Hamm was honored for his gold-medal performance in the all-around men's competition at the 2004 Summer Olympic Games. Hamm is only the second gymnast, after Kurt Thomas in 1979, to win the award.

Equestrian. 2005 World Cup Final individual show jumping champion: Meredith Michaels Beerbaum, Germany; dressage champion: Anky van Grunsven, the Netherlands.

Gymnastics. Men's all-around champion: Hiroyuki Tomita, Japan. Women's all-around champion: Chellsie Memmel, United States.

Luge. Germany dominated the World Championships held in Park City, Utah, in February, winning six of the nine individual medals and the team title. Armin Zoeggeler of Italy won the men's singles event, Sylke Otto of Germany won the women's singles title, and Germans Andre Florschutz and Torsten Wustlich won the men's doubles event.

Marathon. On April 18, Catherine Ndereba of Kenya became the first woman to win the Boston Marathon four times, finishing in 2 hours, 25 minutes, and 13 seconds. Ndereba also won in 2000, 2001, and 2004. In 2005, Hailu Negussie became the first Ethiopian man to win the Boston Marathon since 1989, finishing in 2 hours, 11 minutes, and 45 seconds.

Rodeo. Ryan Jarret of Summerville, Georgia, won the All-Around World Champion Cowboy title at the 2005 Wrangler National Finals Rodeo, held from December 2 to December 11 in Las Vegas, Nevada.

Rowing. The German club Dortmund Rowing Center won the marquee Grand Challenge Cup on July 3 at the Henley Royal Regatta in Henley-on-the-Thames, England, beating a British team from Oxford University by two-thirds of a length. A team from Cambridge University in Cambridge, England, captured the Ladies' Challenge Plate, beating England's Leander Club by nearly two boat lengths.

Sled-dog racing. On March 26, 2005, Robert Sorlie of Norway won his second Iditarod Trail Sled Dog Race, finishing the 1,100-mile (1,770-kilometer) trip across Alaska from Anchorage to Nome in 9 days, 18 hours, 39 minutes, and 31

Lance Armstrong of the United States, accompanied by his children, waves his final farewell to fans in Paris after winning the Tour de France on July 24. Armstrong, who announced his retirement in April, is the only man in history to win the grueling race seven consecutive times.

seconds. The victory was Sorlie's second Iditarod win in three years.

Soap Box Derby. Stephanie Inglezakis, 16, of Stow, Ohio, won the Masters Division of the 68th All-American Soap Box Derby held in Akron, Ohio, on July 30. Inglezakis is the 22nd female winner.

Speed skating. Shani Davis became only the fourth American to win the men's overall title at the World All-Around Speedskating Championships on Feb. 6, 2005, in Moscow. Davis also broke world records in the 1,500-meter race and for overall points with 149,359. Germany's Anni Friesinger swept all four of her races to capture a third world overall title. Friesinger won the 500-meter, 1,500-meter, 3,000-meter, and 5,000-meter events.

Triathlon. Australians took the men's and women's world championships on September 11 in Gamagori, Japan. Peter Robertson captured his third men's title with a time of 1 hour, 49 minutes, and 32 seconds. Emma Snowsill won her second title with a time of 1 hour, 58 minutes, and 3 seconds.

Other champions:

Archery. World Outdoor Championships: men's compound, Morgan Lundin, Sweden; women's compound, Sofya Goncharova, Russia;

men's recurve, Jae Hun Chung, South Korea; women's recurve, Sung Jin Lee, South Korea; men's team compound, United States; women's team compound, France; men's team recurve, South Korea; women's team recurve, South Korea.

Badminton. Men's singles: Taufik Hidayat, Indonesia; men's doubles: Tony Gunawan and Howard Bach, United States; women's singles: Xie Xingfang, China; mixed-doubles: Nova Widianto and Lilyana Natsir, Indonesia.

Biathlon. Ole Einar Bjoerndalen of Norway won four gold medals to lead the way at the world championships held in March in Hochfilzen, Austria. Germany's Uschi Disl won two golds to lead the women competitors.

Bobsledding. World championships: men's two-man, pilot Pierre Lueders, Canada; men's four-man, pilot Andre Lange, Germany; women's two-person, pilot Sandra Kiriasis, Germany.

Curling. Men's world champion: Canada; women's world champion: Sweden.

Fencing. Team world champion: France.

Field hockey. Champions Trophy men's gold medal: Australia; women's gold medal: the Netherlands.

Handball, team. Men's world champion: Spain; women's champion: Russia.

Lacrosse. Men's National Collegiate Athletic

Association champion: Johns Hopkins University; women's champion: Northwestern University.

Modern pentathlon. World championships: men's individual, Qian Zhenhua, China; men's team, Russia; women's individual, Claudia Corsini, Italy; women's team, Russia.

Motorcyle racing. FIM Grand Prix MotoGP champion: Valentino Rossi, Italy.

Skeleton. World championships: men, Jeff Pain, Canada; women, Maya Pedersen, Switzerland.

Snowboarding. World championships: men's parallel slalom and giant parallel slalom, Jasey Jay Anderson, Canada; men's halfpipe, Antti Autti, Finland; men's cross, Seth Wescott, United States; women's parallel slalom, Daniela Meuli, Switzerland; women's giant parallel slalom, Manuela Riegler, Austria; women's halfpipe, Doriane Vidal, France; women's cross, Lindsey Jacobellis, United States.

Water polo. World champions: men, Serbia; women, Hungary.

Weightlifting. Women's 165-pound (75-kilogram) gold: Miran Jang, South Korea. Men's 231-pound (105-kilogram) champion: Dmitry Klokov, Russia. ■ Michael Kates

See also **Automobile racing; Baseball; Golf; Hockey; Ice skating; Skiing; Swimming; Tennis.**

Sri Lanka.
Mahinda Rajapakse, a 60-year-old leftist lawyer who had served as prime minister since April 2004, became president of Sri Lanka on Nov. 19, 2005. Rajapakse took office two days after narrowly winning election over Ranil Wickremesinghe of the conservative United National Party (UNP). Rajapakse was supported by his Sri Lanka Freedom Party (SLFP), the Marxist Janatha Vimukthi Peramuna (JVP), and a party of Buddhist monks.

Rajapakse had forged an electoral alliance with the JVP and the monks by promising to renegotiate a cease-fire agreement made in 2002 with the Liberation Tigers of Tamil Eelam (LTTE) and to rescind an aid-sharing deal with them. The LTTE had been fighting a guerrilla war since 1983 to win independence for Sri Lanka's minority of Hindu Tamils. The JVP and the monks opposed any concessions to the LTTE, voicing strong nationalism on behalf of the island nation's majority Buddhist Sinhalese population.

As prime minister in 2002, Wickremesinghe had helped negotiate the cease-fire and a plan for regional *autonomy* (local government) for Tamils. He continued to back a compromise in the civil war that had taken more than 64,000 lives. Rather than help him win the presidential election, however, the hard-line LTTE pressured Tamils not to vote.

The LTTE leader, Velupillai Prabhakaran,

threatened on Nov. 28, 2005, to renew "our struggle for national liberation to establish self-government" in Tamil-inhabited areas unless Rajapakse made satisfactory new political proposals.

Tsunami. Rajapakse's predecessor as president, Chandrika Kumaratunga of the SLFP, disagreed with Rajapakse in 2005 on how to distribute aid to those affected by a tsunami that struck the country on Dec. 26, 2004. Kumaratunga's government had agreed to allow the LTTE to distribute some of the $3 billion received by Sri Lanka as aid for recovery.

The tsunami killed more than 31,000 people on the island, displaced 1 million others, and devastated houses, farms, fishing fleets, and road and rail systems on the east and south coasts. However, the nation's economic growth, which was slowing down before the tsunami, showed new vigor in 2005.

Kumaratunga's decision to let the LTTE help distribute aid angered the JVP, which quit Prime Minister Rajapakse's coalition government, leaving it without a majority in parliament. However, with a presidential election in the offing, the opposition UNP did not try to vote the government out of office, which would have mandated parliamentary elections. ■ Henry S. Bradsher

See also **Asia.**

State government.
Hurricane Katrina, which hit the Gulf Coast on Aug. 29, 2005, killing more than 1,200 people, flooding New Orleans, and forcing mass evacuations, overshadowed other state developments as the nation rallied to extend aid to Alabama, Florida, Louisiana, and Mississippi. At year's end, officials for states affected by Katrina were still determining the full cost of the disaster, awaiting more federal assistance, and mapping out their future.

Disaster costs. In 2005, federal law required states to pay a portion of Federal Emergency Management Agency (FEMA) assistance, which meant Mississippi owed up to $172 million and Louisiana as much as $3.7 billion. FEMA is a United States government agency that helps communities prepare for and recover from natural and human-made disasters.

Following Katrina, Louisiana and Texas sustained major damage from Hurricane Rita, which made landfall along the Gulf Coast on September 24. Faced with a $1-billion shortfall as a result of Katrina and Rita, the Louisiana legislature met in a special session in November. The legislature approved a plan to cut more than $600 million in spending, mostly in health care services and education. The state also planned to tap its "rainy day" fund and some surplus funds to make up the budget shortfall. The legislature approved a state takeover of any New Orleans school that

SELECTED STATISTICS ON STATE GOVERNMENTS

State	Resident population*	Governor†	Legislature† House (D)	(R)	Senate (D)	(R)	State tax revenue‡	Tax revenue per capita‡	Public school expenditure per pupil§
Alabama	4,530,182	Bob Riley (R)	63	42	25	10	$ 7,018,000,000	$1,550	$ 6,990
Alaska	655,435	Frank Murkowski (R)	14	26	8	12	1,288,000,000	1,970	10,040
Arizona	5,743,834	Janet Napolitano (D)	21	39	12	18	9,606,000,000	1,670	5,470
Arkansas	2,752,629	Mike Huckabee (R)	72	28	27	8	5,581,000,000	2,030	6,200
California	35,893,799	Arnold Schwarzenegger (R)	48	32	25	15	85,721,000,000	2,390	7,820
Colorado	4,601,403	Bill F. Owens (R)	35	30	18	17	7,051,000,000	1,530	8,100
Connecticut	3,503,604	M. Jodi Rell (R)	99	52	24	12	10,291,000,000	2,940	11,900
Delaware	830,364	Ruth Ann Minner (D)	#15	25	13	8	2,375,000,000	2,860	10,330
Florida	17,397,161	Jeb Bush (R)	36	84	14	26	30,768,000,000	1,770	7,040
Georgia	8,829,383	Sonny Perdue (R)	#80	99	22	34	14,571,000,000	1,650	8,500
Hawaii	1,262,840	Linda Lingle (R)	41	10	20	5	3,849,000,000	3,050	9,050
Idaho	1,393,262	Dirk Kempthorne (R)	13	57	7	28	2,648,000,000	1,900	6,740
Illinois	12,713,634	Rod Blagojevich (D)	65	53	#32	26	25,491,000,000	2,000	10,440
Indiana	6,237,569	Mitch Daniels (R)	48	52	17	33	11,957,000,000	1,920	8,730
Iowa	2,954,451	Tom Vilsack (D)	49	51	25	25	5,133,000,000	1,740	7,480
Kansas	2,735,502	Kathleen Sebelius (D)	42	83	10	30	5,284,000,000	1,930	7,560
Kentucky	4,145,922	Ernie Fletcher (R)	57	43	**15	23	8,463,000,000	2,040	7,720
Louisiana	4,515,770	Kathleen Blanco (D)	#67	37	24	15	8,026,000,000	1,780	7,550
Maine	1,317,253	John Baldacci (D)	††76	73	19	16	2,897,000,000	2,200	10,740
Maryland	5,558,058	Robert Erlich (R)	98	43	33	14	12,315,000,000	2,220	9,760
Massachusetts	6,416,505	Mitt Romney (R)	#139	20	34	6	16,699,000,000	2,600	11,320
Michigan	10,112,620	Jennifer Granholm (D)	52	58	16	22	24,061,000,000	2,380	8,910
Minnesota	5,100,958	Tim Pawlenty (R)	66	68	#35	31	14,735,000,000	2,890	9,240
Mississippi	2,902,966	Haley Barbour (R)	75	47	28	24	5,125,000,000	1,770	6,450
Missouri	5,754,618	Matt Blunt (R)	66	97	11	23	9,120,000,000	1,580	7,450
Montana	926,865	Brian Schweitzer (D)	50	50	27	23	1,626,000,000	1,750	8,030
Nebraska	1,747,214	Dave Heineman (R)	unicameral (49 nonpartisan)				3,640,000,000	2,080	7,620
Nevada	2,334,771	Kenny Guinn (R)	26	16	9	12	4,739,000,000	2,030	7,100
New Hampshire	1,299,500	John Lynch (D)	147	253	8	16	2,005,000,000	1,540	9,570
New Jersey	8,698,879	Jon Corzine (D)	48	32	22	18	20,981,000,000	2,410	11,500
New Mexico	1,903,289	Bill Richardson (D)	42	28	23	19	4,002,000,000	2,100	7,230
New York	19,227,088	George E. Pataki (R)	104	46	27	35	45,834,000,000	2,380	12,880
North Carolina	8,541,221	Mike Easley (D)	63	57	29	21	16,576,000,000	1,940	6,960
North Dakota	634,366	John Hoeven (R)	27	67	15	32	1,229,000,000	1,940	7,030
Ohio	11,459,011	Robert Taft (R)	38	61	11	22	22,476,000,000	1,960	9,570
Oklahoma	3,523,553	Brad Henry (D)	44	57	26	22	6,427,000,000	1,820	6,270
Oregon	3,594,586	Ted Kulongoski (D)	27	33	18	12	6,103,000,000	1,700	7,910
Pennsylvania	12,406,292	Ed Rendell (D)	93	110	20	30	25,347,000,000	2,040	9,640
Rhode Island	1,080,632	Don Carcieri (R)	59	16	33	5	2,409,000,000	2,230	10,640
South Carolina	4,198,068	Mark Sanford (R)	50	74	19	27	6,804,000,000	1,620	8,160
South Dakota	770,883	Mike Rounds (R)	19	51	10	25	1,063,000,000	1,380	7,640
Tennessee	5,900,962	Phil Bredesen (D)	53	46	16	17	9,536,000,000	1,620	6,730
Texas	22,490,022	Rick Perry (R)	63	87	12	19	30,752,000,000	1,370	7,140
Utah	2,389,039	Jon Huntsman, Jr. (R)	19	56	8	21	4,189,000,000	1,750	5,250
Vermont	621,394	James Douglas (R)	‡‡83	60	21	9	1,767,000,000	2,840	11,640
Virginia	7,459,827	Tim Kaine (D)	§§39	58	16	24	14,233,000,000	1,910	8,850
Washington	6,203,788	Christine Gregoire (D)	55	43	26	23	13,895,000,000	2,240	8,450
West Virginia	1,815,354	Joe Manchin III (D)	68	32	21	13	3,749,000,000	2,070	9,450
Wisconsin	5,509,026	Jim Doyle (D)	39	60	14	19	12,531,000,000	2,270	9,880
Wyoming	506,529	Dave Freudenthal (D)	14	46	7	23	1,505,000,000	2,970	10,200

*July 1, 2004, estimates. Source: U.S. Census Bureau.
†As of November 2005. Source: National Governors' Association; National Conference of State Legislatures; state government officials.
‡2004 figures. Source: U.S. Census Bureau.
§2004-2005 estimates for elementary and secondary students in fall enrollment. Source: National Education Association.

#One independent.
**One undecided, one independent.
††One Green Party, one independent.
‡‡Six Progressive Party, one independent.
§§Three independents.

failed to meet academic standards, a temporary suspension of the 4-percent sales tax for individuals, and a temporary suspension of state residential building codes. Before the session, Governor Kathleen Blanco, a Democrat, appointed the Louisiana Recovery Authority to oversee the recovery.

The disaster had a profound effect on the economy of the region. In September, Louisiana's unemployment rate climbed to 11.5 percent, the highest level for any state in 25 years. The hurricane destroyed Mississippi's 13 Gulf Coast floating hotel-casinos, which employed some 14,000 people and paid millions of dollars in taxes. In an October session, the Mississippi legislature voted to allow the casinos to be rebuilt on land.

Elections. Democrats won the only two governors' races in 2005. On November 8, Virginia's Democratic lieutenant governor, Timothy M. Kaine, defeated Republican Jerry W. Kilgore to succeed Democrat Mark R. Warner as governor. In New Jersey, U.S. Senator Jon Stevens Corzine beat Republican businessman Douglas Forrester in the governor's race.

Nationwide, voters on November 8 passed just 2 of 18 citizen-initiated ballot measures. In Washington state, citizens voted "yes" to require governmental audits and to ban smoking in public places. Voters also agreed to a 9.5-cent per gallon hike in the gasoline tax, approved by the Washington legislature in April. California voters rejected four initiatives championed by Republican Governor Arnold Schwarzenegger.

Voters in Maine, New York, and Ohio approved bond issues on November 8 to fund economic development or transportation; New Jersey voters endorsed the election of the state's first lieutenant governor in 2009; and Maine voters retained a state law banning discrimination against gays in housing, job, and school matters.

Constitutional bans on gay marriage were passed in Kansas in April 2005 and in Texas in November. Colorado voters in November lifted state spending limits temporarily, forfeiting $3.7 billion in tax refunds.

Revenue. State revenues generally rebounded in 2005, exceeding predictions in 42 states, according to a survey released in 2005 by the National Governors Association and National Association of State Budget Officers, both based in Washington, D.C. According to the survey, Arizona, Arkansas, Montana, and Virginia had large surpluses.

On April 27, the U.S. Census Bureau reported that tax collections by state governments rose to $593 billion in fiscal 2004 (April 2004-March 2005), an 8.1-percent, or $44-billion, rise over 2003. According to the bureau, all 50 states brought in more tax revenues in 2004 than in 2003, with general sales taxes rising 7.5 percent

to $198 billion and state income taxes increasing 8.5 percent to $197 billion.

States passed various pieces of legislation in 2005 designed to increase revenue. North Carolina legalized a state lottery and hiked the cigarette tax by 30 cents a pack. Kentucky increased cigarette taxes from 3 cents to 30 cents a pack. A new Ohio law mandated the taxing of corporate sales rather than profits. Washington also raised taxes on cigarettes, large estates, and liquor. The government of Illinois announced in 2005 that funding for state pension systems would be cut by $2.3 billion in 2005 and 2006. Alaska shifted to a 401(k)-style pension plan for state employees in 2005, replacing a defined benefit plan based on years of service. In August, the Texas Parks and Wildlife Department announced that it would close nine state parks to save money.

Georgia and Hawaii bucked the trend. With the price of gasoline at a record high in September 2005, Georgia Governor Sonny Perdue temporarily suspended the state's taxes on gasoline. Hawaii capped the wholesale price of gasoline.

Medicaid. States continued in 2005 to attempt to control the cost of funding Medicaid, the state-federal health care program that served some 53 million disabled, low-income, and elderly Americans in 2005. Medicaid funding accounted for some 22 percent of state budgets in 2005. Most states attempted to curb costs by limiting provider payments, controlling prescription drug costs, and promoting managed care. Tennessee and Missouri reduced the number of people eligible for Medicaid in 2005. Tennessee dropped nearly 200,000 people from TennCare, the state's health insurance program for the poor and uninsured. Missouri eliminated 22,020 low-income parents from Medicaid. Florida Governor Jeb Bush launched a test program in 2005 to eventually move most of the state's 2.2 million Medicaid recipients onto privately operated managed-care health plans funded with a combination of state and federal money. Michigan reduced Medicaid copayments in 2005 if recipients practiced measurable healthy behavior, such as exercising.

Three states increased health insurance coverage for residents in 2005. Maine established a program to help small businesses buy health insurance for employees. Massachusetts was trying to extend insurance coverage to all uninsured residents, estimated at 500,000, and Illinois established a single managed-care plan for all uninsured children in the state.

Criminal law. The Missouri legislature passed a bill in 2005 that requires released child-sex offenders to wear global positioning system devices so authorities could track their whereabouts. Three other states—Florida, Ohio, and Oklahoma—passed similar laws in 2005 restricting the movement of convicted sex offenders.

The governors of Arizona and New Mexico issued emergency declarations that freed up state funds to tackle problems caused by illegal immigration, such as crime and drug trafficking. The Arizona legislature also authorized the arrest of people caught smuggling illegal immigrants across the border and the seizure of vehicles driven by illegal immigrants. The state also banned local government job services for illegal immigrants.

Ethics. Charges of political wrongdoing surfaced in several states in 2005. Kentucky Governor Ernie Fletcher, a Republican, in August issued blanket pardons to members of his administration under grand jury investigation. In September, he was forced to dismiss nine employees who had violated state law governing the hiring of state employees. In Ohio, Governor Bob Taft, a Republican, pleaded no contest to violating state ethics laws for accepting expensive gifts and various kinds of entertainment. Taft is the great-grandson of President William Howard Taft and the grandson and son of U.S. senators. ■ Elaine Stuart McDonald

See also **Democratic Party; Disasters; Elections; Republican Party; Social Security: A Special Report; Supreme Court of the United States.**

Stocks and bonds.

Stocks and bonds. The United States stock market climbed in late 2005 to a higher peak than it had achieved in a similar year-end rally in 2004. The economy grew more than 4 percent in the third quarter of 2005, overcoming the devastation caused by Gulf Coast hurricanes and resultant high energy prices.

During the first nine months of 2005, higher energy costs—crude oil prices jumped 40 percent from January to September—jeopardized corporate profits and consumer optimism. However, as 2005 drew to a close, warmer-than-usual temperatures led to reduced oil prices and a boost in consumer confidence.

The Standard & Poor's (S&P) 500 Index, a benchmark of 500 large-company U.S. stocks, was up about 4 percent for the year through November. The Dow Jones Industrial Average, an index of 30 major companies, had gained about 1 percent. The S&P 600 Index of small-company stocks was up nearly 7 percent.

Bonds erode. Thirteen rounds of increases in short-term interest rates by the Federal Reserve System, the central bank of the United States, finally began to affect long-term interest rates, including mortgage rates. The more than fourfold increase in short-term rates, which took them from 1 percent in June 2004 to 4.25 percent in December 2005, was designed to preempt price inflation, which nonetheless crept higher in 2005.

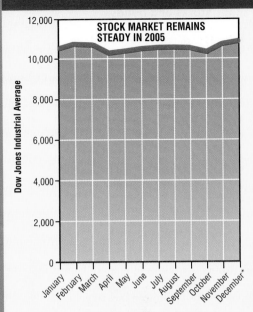

Closing month averages for 2005
* December figure is as of the 16th.

The Dow Jones Industrial Average fluctuated little throughout 2005. After a slight dip in autumn following the Gulf Coast hurricanes, the market rebounded with a year-end rally.

The yield on 10-year U.S. Treasury notes, which represents a benchmark interest rate for many home mortgages, climbed to nearly 4.5 percent by late November from slightly more than 4.2 percent at the beginning of the year. The rate hike, which reduces the value of existing bond securities, seemed like a small increase, but it was enough to heighten fears of a "bubble" in the housing market.

Winners and losers. Shares of homebuilders, one of the hottest sectors of the stock market in the first half of 2005, retreated in the second half of the year. Nonetheless, two of the biggest homebuilders, KB Home, based in Los Angeles, and Pulte Homes Inc. of Bloomfield, Michigan, were up more than 25 percent for the year.

Energy prices skyrocketed in late 2005 after Gulf Coast hurricanes damaged U.S. oil refineries, resulting in limited U.S. gasoline supplies. Shares of Valero Energy Corp., a San Antonio, Texas-based petroleum refining and marketing company, climbed 120 percent between January and November, making it one of the biggest gainers in the S&P 500 Index. Sunoco Inc., headquartered in Philadelphia, and Houston-based National Oilwell Varco Inc. and Marathon Oil Corp., were also among the best performers in the index.

Industrial companies, which consume energy,

suffered in turn. Stock of Ford Motor Co. of Dearborn, Michigan, was down 41 percent through November. General Motors Corp. of Detroit, Michigan, was one of the worst performers in the Dow Industrials, down 37 percent. Delphi Corp. of Troy, Michigan, the largest U.S. auto parts supplier, raised Wall Street's concerns about the auto industry when it filed for bankruptcy in October.

Technology stocks, favored by many active investors, produced mixed results in 2005. Apple Computer Inc. of Cupertino, California, maker of the popular iPod line of digital media players, jumped more than 90 percent, a strong performance in the S&P 500 Index. Computer equipment manufacturer Hewlett-Packard Co., based in Palo Alto, California, rebounded from a poor showing in 2004 to become a top performer among the Dow Industrials in 2005, up 45 percent.

However, International Business Machines Corp., headquartered in Armonk, New York, lost ground, down 16 percent. Gateway Inc., an Irvine, California-based computer merchant, fell 49 percent. Intel Corp. of Santa Clara, California, the leading maker of semiconductors and a bellwether for the technology industry, rallied strongly in the first half of 2005 but began to lose ground in July. Shares recovered to a 19 percent gain for the year, as of late November.

Technology stock enthusiasts will remember 2005 for one company—Google Inc., a provider of search services for Internet users. The Mountain View, California-based company first issued public shares using a controversial on-line auction, in August 2004, at $85 a share. Against widespread predictions of trouble, the price began to climb—and multiplied—to $428 by late 2005.

International markets. Despite greater risk and comparatively less-transparent market forces, many investors sought higher gains in so-called emerging markets. As was the case in 2004, investors found the best opportunities in Central and South America. The Mexican Bolsa Index of major companies was up 28 percent in 2005 in U.S. dollar terms; the leading Brazilian stock market index, the Bovespa Index, rose 42 percent in 2005. Top mutual fund performers between late 2004 and late 2005 included several Latin American funds with returns of more than 60 percent.

However, returns in other countries were hurt by the stronger dollar and a cooling of economic growth. Stocks traded on China's Shanghai Stock Exchange were down 11 percent through November. Stocks in Europe were up only modestly in dollar terms, hurt by political troubles and weakened currencies. ■ Bill Barnhart

See also **Disasters: A Special Report; Economics, U.S.; Economics, World; Energy supply; International trade; Transportation.**

Sudan. The Sudanese government and the Sudan People's Liberation Movement (SPLM) signed a "comprehensive peace agreement" on Jan. 9, 2005. John Garang de Mabior, chairman of the SPLM, a southern rebel group that had waged war against the government for 21 years, said that the agreement included a "one-country-two-systems model" for Sudan. The agreement granted the southern part of the country political *autonomy* (limited self-governance), as well as a share of Sudan's oil industry income.

The agreement was scheduled to be renegotiated in 2011, at which time the southern Sudanese would decide if they wanted to remain part of Sudan or secede and form an independent state. The agreement also emphasized good governance and the democratic representation of all Sudanese.

Darfur and the United Nations. A series of United Nations (UN) Security Council resolutions regarding Darfur, a western region where conflict between government forces and two rebel groups began in 2003, were issued in March 2005. Resolution 1590 established a UN Mission in Sudan (UNMIS) for a six-month period to foster peace in Darfur in coordination with the mission of the African Union, an association of African nations.

Resolution 1591 called upon the Sudanese government to end offensive military flights over Darfur and criticized the government for violating cease-fire agreements and committing human rights abuses. Resolution 1593 referred the Darfur situation to the prosecutor of the International Criminal Court (ICC), a permanent court in The Hague, Netherlands.

In September, Security Council Resolution 1627 extended the mandate of UNMIS until March 2006. The resolution also called upon the African Union's mission to continue to foster peace and stability in Darfur. However, following a spike in violence and kidnappings in October 2005, the UN ordered all of its "nonessential" staff out of Darfur.

Prosecutor's findings. The ICC prosecutor, Luis Moreno Ocampo, began his investigation in June 2005. He determined that there were numerous cases of human rights abuses that were admissible in the ICC. The prosecutor collected more than 3,000 documents from a variety of sources that demonstrated that grave crimes had been committed in Darfur, including the killing of thousands of civilians, the displacement of 1.9 million people, and the destruction and looting of many houses and villages.

Vice president's death. Sudanese Vice President John Garang died on July 30 when the Ugandan military helicopter in which he was flying crashed in the hills south of New Site,

Sudanese President Umar Hasan Ahmad al-Bashir (right) congratulates John Garang, leader of the Sudan People's Liberation Movement, on becoming first vice president on July 8 in Khartoum. The appointment was part of a peace agreement with the rebel group, ending a 21-year civil war. Garang's death in a helicopter crash on July 30 sparked riots among his followers who refused to believe that the crash was an accident.

Uganda. The vice president had been shuttling back and forth between Sudan and Uganda for meetings with Ugandan President Yoweri Musevini.

The confirmation of Garang's death two days later led to riots when angry southerners in Khartoum, Sudan's capital, accused the Sudanese government of assassinating Garang. The demonstrators burned cars, threw stones, and attacked Sudanese Arabs, killing more than 40 people and injuring 300 others.

World leaders urged the Sudanese factions to continue pursuing the peace process to diffuse the violence. General Salva Kiir, the new leader of the SPLM, also called for calm and vowed to pursue the peace agreement.

Rebellion in eastern Sudan. A rebellion led by the armed wings of the Beja Congress, Rashaida Free Lions, and Justice and Equality Movement threatened to undermine the African Union's peace initiatives in Sudan. In this eastern front, rebels engaged government soldiers in combat in June near the town of Tokar, south of Port Sudan on the Red Sea. The conflict, combined with seasonal floods, had the potential of displacing as many as 200,000 people in eastern Sudan, according to UN sources.

■ Mary-Jane Deeb

See also **Middle East; United Nations.**

Supreme Court of the United States.

In 2005, the Supreme Court of the United States handed down opinions in 80 cases involving a wide range of issues, including church-state relations, the death penalty, the Internet, and property rights and eminent domain. The retirement of one justice and the death of another in 2005 changed the makeup of the Supreme Court for the first time in 11 years. President George W. Bush's subsequent Supreme Court nominations prompted widespread speculation that a long-established balance between conservatives and liberals would be tipped to the right.

Changes on the Court. Justice Sandra Day O'Connor, the first woman to serve on the Supreme Court, announced on July 1 that she would retire. O'Connor's retirement, after serving 24 years, was the first change in the court's makeup since 1994. Judicial experts had long argued that O'Connor was the most influential of the nine justices. Often described as a "swing vote," O'Connor voted with liberals on such issues as abortion, voting rights, church-state separation, and sex discrimination; she joined the conservative justices in confirming the rights of the states, supporting limits on affirmative action, and ending the vote count in the 2000 presidential election.

President Bush, on July 19, 2005, nominated John G. Roberts, Jr., a federal appeals judge, to

1986. As chief justice, he had led the court in a conservative direction.

On Sept. 5, 2005, Bush renominated Roberts as chief justice. His confirmation hearings began on September 12, and the Senate Judiciary Committee quickly voted 13 to 5 to recommend that the Senate confirm his nomination. Roberts won confirmation as chief justice on September 29 by a Senate vote of 78 to 22.

President Bush nominated his own White House counsel, Harriet Miers, to replace O'Connor as associate justice on October 3. Her nomination was widely criticized, not by liberal Democrats, but by conservative Republicans, who accused the president of *cronyism* (appointing close friends to government positions). Conservative columnists pointed out that Miers had never served as a judge and was inexperienced in the field of constitutional law. The president suggested that conservatives should accept his judgment regarding her qualifications, while Vice President Dick Cheney assured radio audiences that Miers was a devout fundamentalist Christian. After three weeks of national debate, Harriet Miers withdrew her nomination in what political experts described as a major embarrassment for the president.

On October 31, President Bush nominated Samuel Alito, who had served as a federal appeals judge for 15 years, for the position vacated by O'Connor. The nomination of a known conservative with a broad background in constitutional law pleased conservatives without sparking an angry reaction from liberals. The chairman of the Senate Judicial Committee, Arlen Specter (R., Pennsylvania), scheduled Alito's confirmation hearing for January 2006.

Property rights versus eminent domain. On June 23, 2005, the Supreme Court, in a 5-to-4 decision, ruled that governments can, under certain circumstances, employ the constitutional power of *eminent domain* to seize private property to turn over to private developers. (Eminent domain is the power of a government to take

replace O'Connor as an associate justice. Roberts had served as a law clerk for Chief Justice William H. Rehnquist when Rehnquist was an associate justice. Roberts also worked in the U.S. Department of Justice during President Ronald W. Reagan's administration and later was appointed principal deputy to the solicitor general of the United States. As a government and private lawyer, Roberts argued 39 cases before the Supreme Court.

Chief Justice Rehnquist died on September 3, before the Senate Judiciary Committee began confirmation hearings on Roberts's nomination. Rehnquist had been an associate justice on the Supreme Court since 1972 and chief justice since

private property for public use after paying the owner a fair market price.) The court decided against a group of homeowners who had resisted plans by city officials in New London, Connecticut, to clear working-class housing for commercial development. Justice John Paul Stevens wrote in the majority opinion that government can use eminent domain to acquire private property for private development if that development serves a public good. In the dissent, Justice O'Connor charged that, "the fallout from this decision will not be random. The beneficiaries are likely to be those citizens with disproportionate influence and power in the political process."

Religious displays. In two separate 5-to-4 rulings on June 27, the court ruled that some displays of the Ten Commandments on public property are constitutional while others are not. Five justices ruled that a granite monument bearing the Ten Commandments on the grounds of the Texas State Capitol was just 1 of 17 monuments and 21 historical markers on display and, therefore, was not a government endorsement of religion. In a separate case, five justices decided that framed copies of the Ten Commandments displayed on interior walls of two Kentucky courthouses did promote religion and, therefore, did violate the concept of separation of church and state established in the First Amendment to the Constitution.

Gender discrimination. A March 29 ruling held that coaches who face retaliation when they complain about gender discrimination against their teams could sue their employers over the mistreatment. The decision expanded the scope of Title IX of the Education Amendments of 1972. Title IX barred sex discrimination in educational programs receiving federal funds, including high schools and colleges. However, it usually had been enforced through lawsuits by players or coaches who claimed they were victims of discrimination. By a 5-to-4 vote, the court ruled that a coach in Birmingham, Alabama, could sue after he was reassigned when he complained that his high school girls' basketball team was unfairly treated compared with the boys' team.

Controlled substances. The Supreme Court, in a 6-to-3 decision, determined on June 6 that federal authorities may prosecute sick people who use prescribed marijuana for pain management. Writing for the majority, Justice Stevens emphasized that the decision was not a judgment on the potential medical benefits of marijuana but a clarification of the hierarchy of federal and state laws. The court ruled that the federal drug-banning law overruled laws in 10 states that allow the use of marijuana for medical purposes. Stevens noted that the use of marijuana for medical purposes can only be legalized

if the U.S. Congress rescinded the appropriate provisions of the Controlled Substances Act, which was part of the Comprehensive Drug Abuse Prevention and Control Act of 1970.

Capital punishment. On March 1, 2005, the court abolished the death penalty for criminals who committed a murder before the age of 18. In a 5-to-4 decision, the court declared that capital punishment for juvenile killers was unconstitutional on the grounds of being "cruel and unusual" punishment. Writing for the majority, Justice Anthony Kennedy noted, "Our society views juveniles … as categorically less culpable than the average criminal."

Sentencing. The court, in a 5-to-4 decision, ruled on January 12 that federal judges no longer needed to abide by sentencing guidelines. The decision applied to an 18-year-old federal sentencing guideline system that was designed to bring conformity to federal court sentences for similar crimes. The sentencing guidelines could stand, the court ruled, as long as they were "advisory," not mandatory. Writing for the majority, Justice Stephen Breyer noted that juries, not judges, should consider the various factors that can add years to a defendant's prison sentence.   ■ Geoffrey A. Campbell

See also **Courts; Deaths; People in the News** (John G. Roberts); **United States, President of the.**

Sweden. A final report by the Swedish Disaster Commission on Dec. 2, 2005, harshly criticized Prime Minister Goran Persson's Social Democratic Party (SAP) government for its response to the Dec. 26, 2004, tsunami in Southeast Asia. More than 500 Swedes died in the disaster and thousands of others were stranded in Thailand. Opposition groups called for Persson to dismiss ministers for not sending help quickly enough. Persson, who has served as prime minister for 10 years, accepted responsibility for the mistakes made but refused to fire any ministers. Persson's SAP has ruled Sweden for all but 9 years of the past 73.

Sweden continued to enjoy economic growth and a generous welfare system in 2005. However, the SAP endured several scandals involving housing benefits for party members and the manipulation of membership lists for youth organizations to receive higher subsidies. None of the scandals affected the government's popularity until the December report.

Sweden's economy grew by 2.5 percent in 2005, but unemployment remained a significant problem. European Union economists estimated unemployment at 6.8 percent. However, most observers maintained that the number was actually higher because of make-work schemes and early retirement.   ■ Jeffrey Kopstein

See also **Europe.**

Swimming. Michael Phelps of the United States and Grant Hackett of Australia shared the spotlight at the 2005 World Championships in Montreal, Canada, in July. Phelps won five gold medals and one silver, and Hackett took five medals—three gold—and set a new world record. The U.S. women's team captured 32 medals—15 of them gold—the most since 1982.

World Championships. Phelps, who won a record-tying eight medals, including six gold, at the 2004 Summer Olympic Games in Athens, dropped two events at the 2005 World Championships to work on events in which he had less experience. Although he failed to qualify in those two events, he won gold medals in the 200-meter freestyle, 200-meter individual medley, 800-meter freestyle relay, the 400-meter freestyle relay, and the 400-meter medley relay. He took silver in the 100-meter butterfly.

Hackett won a record fourth straight 1,500-meter freestyle title on the final day of competition. He also won the 400-meter and 800-meter freestyles, breaking the world record in the 800 with a swim of 7 minutes, 38.65 seconds. Hackett won silver in the 200-meter freestyle and bronze in the 800-meter freestyle relay.

Jessica Hardy of the United States swam the 100-meter breaststroke semifinal in 1:06.20, breaking the world record set in 2003 by Leisel Jones of Australia by 0.17 second. However, Hardy settled for silver in the final, with Jones taking the gold. Jones swept the 100- and 200-meter breaststroke events, setting a new world record in the 200 with a time of 2:21.72.

Several other swimmers set world records at the World Championships, including South Africa's Roland Schoeman in the 50-meter butterfly final (22.96); American Aaron Peirsol in the 200-meter backstroke final (1:54.66); Poland's Otylia Jedrzejczak in the 200-meter butterfly final (2:05.61); and Australia's Jade Edmistone in the 50-meter breaststroke final (30.45).

Other world records. Janine Pietsch of Germany set a world record in the 50-meter backstroke on May 25, 2005, in Berlin, with a time of 28.19 seconds. She broke the 28.25 mark set by fellow German Sandra Voelker in 2000.

Peirsol broke his own 100-meter backstroke record on April 2, 2005, in Indianapolis, with a time of 53.17 seconds.

Short-course records. On February 11 in East Meadow, New York, Ryk Neethling of South Africa smashed a world record he had set only a month earlier in the 100-meter individual medley, swimming the race in 51.52 seconds. His time was nearly a half-second faster than the time he posted in Moscow in January.

On March 13 in Stockholm, Anna-Karin Kammerling of Sweden trimmed 0.03 second off her own world-record time in the 50-meter butterfly with a time of 25.33. ■ Michael Kates

Grant Hackett of Australia competes at the World Championships, held July 16-31 in Montreal, Canada. Hackett won five medals during the competition, including three gold, and set a world record in the 800-meter free-style with a time of 7 minutes, 38.65 seconds.

Switzerland. On June 5, 2005, Swiss voters approved a referendum on joining the Schengen treaty, which allows for passport-free travel within most countries of the European Union (EU). The voters also approved an EU agreement for handling asylum seekers. A further referendum in September paved the way for citizens from the EU's 10 newest member nations to work in Switzerland. Such support of EU policies surprised many observers because, in 2001, voters had rejected a proposal on Switzerland's joining the EU.

Economists with the Organization for Economic Cooperation and Development (OECD), an association of 30 nations headquartered in Paris, forecast that the Swiss economy would grow by 1.2 percent in 2005. The country's unemployment rate was estimated to stand at 4.1 percent, well below the 8.7 percent average of the 25 EU nations.

Swiss engineers in April completed blasting a new tunnel under the Alps. The Lötschberg tunnel begins just east of Adelboden and ends east of Leuk. When completed in 2007, the tunnel will allow rail traffic to travel from Germany to Italy, transporting goods much more easily and safely than the current practice of hauling goods over roads through treacherous mountain passes.

■ Jeffrey Kopstein

See also **Europe.**

Syria. On Nov. 1, 2005, the government of Syria granted permission to members of a United Nations (UN) inquiry team to question relatives of Syria's president, Bashar al-Assad, in connection with the assassination of former Prime Minister Rafik Hariri of Lebanon. Hariri, an opponent of Syrian domination of Lebanon, had been murdered in Beirut, Lebanon's capital, on February 14 in a car bombing. On October 20, an interim UN report implicated two of President Assad's relatives, who were also government officials, in the assassination. Syrian cooperation with the UN investigation came after the UN Security Council voted unanimously on October 31 to impose sanctions if Syrian officials continued to mislead the investigators.

Hariri's murder galvanized Lebanese opposition to Syria's control of Lebanon. At a March rally of 1.5 million people in Beirut, protesters called for the complete withdrawal of Syrian troops from Lebanon. Syria also came under intense international criticism for its occupation of Lebanon. The pressure led to the withdrawal of Syrian troops in April.

Iraq war. The government of the United States condemned Syria in 2005 for supporting insurgents in Iraq, who launched hundreds of attacks against Iraqi civilians and coalition forces during the year. Syria was accused of harboring Iraqis who were members of the Baath Party, the party once led by deposed Iraqi dictator Saddam Hussein, as well as the ruling party in Syria. Many experts in terrorism believed that these Baathists helped finance and support the Iraqi insurgents.

United States officials claimed that Syria allowed *Jihadists* (Islamic "holy warriors") from Arab countries to enter Iraq and be trained for suicide bombings and other terrorist operations. Iraq's defense minister, Saud al-Dulaimi, claimed in September, "We know the terrorists have no other gateway into Iraq but Syria."

Calls for reform. In June 2005, more than 200 Syrian intellectuals, human rights activists, and opposition leaders sent a signed open letter to the congress of the Syrian Baath Party calling for major reforms in Syria's political institutions. The congress, however, recommended only modest reforms, such as laws to authorize new political parties and publications.

The Syrian government subsequently ordered the closure of the Atassi Forum, which was Syria's only open political forum. In September, the European Parliament, the main advisory body to the European Union, passed a resolution demanding the immediate release from prison of two opposition members of the Syrian parliament.

■ Marius Deeb

See also **Iraq; Lebanon; Middle East.**

Taiwan took steps in 2005 to make the government more democratic. Voting in parliamentary elections was changed, and new requirements were instituted for approving constitutional amendments by a majority of all eligible voters. The 300-member National Assembly, a separate body from parliament, adopted the changes on June 7. It also abolished itself, leaving future constitutional changes to popular referendums.

One change, scheduled to take effect in 2007, reduced parliament's size from 225 seats to 113. Another change reduced each constituency to one directly elected member of parliament and one chosen proportionally by political party affiliation. Some constituencies had had as many as 10 lawmakers.

Both the Democratic Progressive Party (DPP) of Taiwanese President Chen Shui-bian and the main opposition party, the Kuomintang (KMT), favored limited constituencies. The requirement of popular voting on future constitutional amendments angered China, which claimed sovereignty over Taiwan. Chinese officials feared the setting of a precedent with referendums.

The National Assembly was chosen in a May 14, 2005, election in which only 23.4 percent of voters bothered to cast ballots. The DPP, which had failed to win control of parliament in elections on Dec. 11, 2004, won 42.5 percent of the

2005 assembly vote, compared with only 38.9 percent for the KMT.

The KMT had ruled Taiwan from 1949, when KMT leaders fled China after losing the civil war, until its candidate, Lien Chan, lost the presidential election to Chen Shui-bian in 2000. Lien stepped down as KMT leader in 2005, leading to the KMT's holding the party's first leadership election in its 110-year history. In the July contest, Ma Ying-jeou, the popular 55-year-old mayor of Taipei, Taiwan's capital, defeated parliamentary speaker Wang Jin-pyng. International affairs experts considered Ma a strong presidential candidate for 2008. In municipal elections held on Dec. 3, 2005, the KMT and its allies won control of 17 of Taiwan's 23 local governments. Some experts suggested that the outcome was a vote of no confidence in Chen's government.

Contacts with China varied in 2005, as Taiwan continued to worry about the Communist nation's growing military strength and threatening attitude. Lien Chan met with Chinese President Hu Jintao in April, and James Soong of the opposition People First Party visited China in May. Both leaders emphasized the need for close ties with China.

■ Henry S. Bradsher

See also **Asia; China.**

Tajikistan. See Asia.

Tanzania. See Africa.

Taxation. The United States Congress sought in 2005 to use the federal tax code to alleviate some of the financial burden imposed on citizens by natural disasters. The Congress also attempted through changes in tax law to encourage charitable giving to natural-disaster survivors.

Hurricane Katrina. Congress and President George W. Bush approved legislation in September amending federal tax law to allow individuals and families to withdraw tax-free up to $100,000 from retirement accounts, such as 401K's, if they had sustained losses in such federally declared natural disasters as the Gulf Coast after being hit by Hurricane Katrina on August 29. The legislation also temporarily removed limitations on the tax deductions individuals and corporations could take for cash contributions to charitable organizations made between August 28 and December 31. In addition, the legislation allowed a personal tax exemption for individuals who provided free housing to people displaced by Hurricane Katrina.

Tsunami donations. On January 7, President Bush signed into law a measure allowing individuals to deduct from their taxes in 2004 charitable cash contributions they made in January 2005 for the relief of victims in areas devastated by the Dec. 26, 2004, tsunami.

Disaster funds. Lawmakers approved legislation in April 2005 allowing victims of natural dis-

asters to receive certain federal monetary assistance tax-free. The measure amended the Internal Revenue Code to exclude federal funds for disaster victims from gross income. The law also provided for favorable tax treatment to people who sold or transferred their property to the government as part of disaster mitigation efforts.

Proposed tax rates. A *bipartisan* (both parties) panel submitted to the Bush administration on November 1 a report recommending a simplification of the U.S. tax code. Suggestions included reducing the number of tax brackets from six to four and setting the top rate at 33 percent, down from 35 percent; repealing the alternative minimum tax, which was designed to force people who use loopholes and tax shelters to pay at least minimum taxes, but actually increased taxes for moderate-income families; cutting by nearly 50 percent the top rate on *capital gains* (profit from the sale of securities or real estate); removing all tax on stock dividends; reducing mortgage-interest deductions for the highest-income taxpayers; converting the mortgage-interest deduction to a 15 percent credit for all homeowners; and ending the federal deduction on state and local tax payments. ■ Geoffrey Campbell

See also **Congress of the United States; Disasters: A Special Report; Economics, U.S.; United States, Government of the.**

Telecommunications. A momentous shift occurred in the telecommunications industry in 2005. According to a July report issued by the United States Federal Communications Commission (FCC), the number of cell phones in use in the United States grew to 181 million, surpassing the 178 million wired phones in use. (The FCC is an independent government agency that regulates communication by radio, television, wire, satellite, and cable.) The wireless triumph underscored the forces remaking the traditional phone industry.

Internet telephony, also known as Voice over Internet Protocol (VoIP), also continued to gain ground in the market. In September, San Jose-based eBay Corporation acquired Skype Technologies S.A., a Luxembourg-based company that gives away software enabling people to make free calls using the Internet. The online auction company planned to integrate the Skype service into its auctions for calls between buyers and sellers.

So long distance. Declining long-distance revenues led to a historic merger in January, when San Antonio-based SBC Communications Inc. bought New York City-based AT&T Corp. The purchase of AT&T, an American icon once known as "Ma Bell," by a carrier that was once a small part of the Bell empire triggered further consolidation.

In March, MCI Inc., an Ashburn, Virginia-based long-distance company, agreed to be purchased

The Motorola ROKR E1 phone, released in September 2005, was the first mobile phone to enable users to download and play music files from Apple's iTunes online music store. The phone holds up to 100 songs and features a color screen that can display CD cover art as a song is playing.

companies, which had been required to share DSL lines with competitors.

Other disputes remained unresolved in 2005. SBC and Verizon, which planned to offer video services on their networks in 2006, argued that they should not need to acquire cable TV franchise approval in each municipality where they offer service, as had been required for cable operators. The law could slow by years their plans to offer consumers more choices, they claimed. The carriers sought a change in federal law that would waive municipal approval requirements and pursued statewide franchising in Texas and other states.

911. In May 2005, the FCC ruled that VoIP service providers by November must enable customers who dial 911 to reach a public safety operator. Cable TV operators who use VoIP to offer voice service had little problem with the order because their service uses phones in a fixed location. However, Internet phone service offered by others, such as Vonage Holdings Corp. of Edison, New Jersey, posed a more difficult problem because of mobility. A Vonage customer can use the service with a phone and portable computer any place a broadband connection is available.   ■ Jon Van

See also **Computer; Electronics; Internet.**

by Verizon Communications Inc., a New York City-based carrier. Verizon's move provoked Denver-based Qwest Communications International Inc., which had also been interested in MCI, to stage a bidding war that ultimately failed, though it did drive up the amount Verizon paid for MCI. SBC and Verizon bought the one-time powerhouse long-distance carriers to acquire their optical fiber networks and lucrative corporate customers, not their consumer long-distance business.

Wireless. The wireless carriers continued to innovate in 2005. Verizon Wireless unveiled new technology that enabled cell phones to receive data at speeds comparable with those available to digital subscriber line (DSL) customers with landline connections. The higher speeds were intended to make cell phones more useful to business people and to support new consumer applications, such as handheld video.

Cell phone makers sought to market phones to ever younger customers. In July, the Walt Disney Co., the entertainment conglomerate based in Burbank, California, announced plans for phone packages designed specifically for families that will provide service using the Sprint wireless network.

FCC rulings. Regulators eliminated rules in 2005 that telecom companies claimed hampered their ability to compete with cable operators in providing a full suite of voice, data, and video services. In June, the U.S. Supreme Court upheld FCC rulings that freed cable TV operators from opening their systems to competitors. In August, the FCC extended the same freedom to telephone

Television. Perceived government inaction in the wake of Hurricane Katrina, which hit the Gulf Coast of the United States on Aug. 29, 2005, emboldened television news journalists to more directly question authorities and inject personal feelings into their broadcasts. The breakout hit of the summer television season was a celebrity ballroom dancing competition, while another series, cancelled two years earlier, returned to prime time. By mid-2005, three major news anchors were no longer on the air.

News anchors made headlines in 2005. By the middle of the year, three anchors, who had been major forces in television news for decades, had left their posts. NBC anchor Tom Brokaw retired at the end of 2004; Dan Rather signed off as anchor of the "CBS Evening News" in March 2005; and ABC anchor Peter Jennings went off the air in April and died of lung cancer on August 7.

Rather stepped down exactly 24 years to the day that he replaced legendary news broadcaster Walter Cronkite. Rather was embroiled in a controversial 2004 broadcast in which documents used in a story about President George W. Bush's service in the Texas Air National Guard during the Vietnam War (1957-1975) could not be authenticated. Rather signed off his final newscast with the word: "Courage." CBS News Chief Washington Correspondent Bob

Johnny Carson
"...a very heartfelt goodnight."

Television talk show host Johnny Carson, hailed as "the king of late night," died on Jan. 23, 2005, at age 79. An icon of popular culture, Carson hosted "The Tonight Show" from 1962 to 1992. He was best known for his nightly monologues and for launching the careers of a generation of stand-up comedians.

John William Carson was born on Oct. 23, 1925, in Corning, Iowa. He first entertained audiences at the age of 14 performing a magic act as "The Great Carsoni." After high school, Carson served in the United States Navy during World War II (1939-1945) as an ensign aboard the U.S.S. *Pennsylvania*. Following the war, he attended the University of Nebraska in Lincoln and worked part-time as an announcer at a local radio station before graduating in 1949. Two years later, he moved to Los Angeles, where he became a staff announcer at KNXT-TV. Carson, an avid fan of comedian Jack Benny, created a Sunday afternoon comedy show, "Carson's Cellar," that attracted the attention of Benny as well as Red Skelton and Groucho Marx, all of whom appeared on the show. Skelton, who had his own national television show, hired Carson as a writer. In 1954, Carson stepped in as host after Skelton injured himself. In 1955, he was offered his own show, "The Johnny Carson Show," which was not successful. Carson moved to New York City, and in 1957, he was hired as the host of the game show, "Do You Trust Your Wife?" (later called "Who Do You Trust?"). The announcer, Ed McMahon, became Carson's sidekick for three decades on "The Tonight Show." McMahon's signature "Tonight Show" intro, "Here's Johnny," became a catch phrase for a generation of Americans. Selected to replace Jack Paar as host of NBC's "Tonight Show," Carson's first broadcast was on Oct. 1, 1962.

Unlike the volatile and controversial Paar, Carson returned "The Tonight Show" to the kind of comedy entertainment show it had been under the original host, Steve Allen. Carson created and portrayed a gallery of memorable comedy characters, including soothsayer Carnac the Magnificent, feisty Aunt Blabby, and sleazy TV huckster Art Fern.

Carson's nightly monologue, which he always concluded with a free and easy pantomimed golf swing, satirized events and notable figures of the day and was considered a social and political barometer for the nation. One critic called it "America's bedtime story." Perhaps Carson's greatest legacy was as a promoter of upcoming stand-up comedians. Drew Carey, Jay Leno, David Letterman, and Jerry Seinfeld were among those who got their first breaks on "The Tonight Show" stage.

Carson was renowned for his wit and his ability to adlib. When asked how he became a star, he famously replied, "I started in a gaseous state and then I cooled."

Schieffer replaced Rather, who rejoined "60 Minutes" as a correspondent.

Television news reporters covering Hurricane Katrina and its destructive aftermath began to question authorities more directly and show their emotions in the wake of the storm's destruction of New Orleans. During one interview, CNN's Anderson Cooper criticized Senator Mary L. Landrieu (D., La.) on air. When she offered congratulatory praise for her colleagues, Cooper interrupted, "I've been seeing dead bodies in the streets here in Mississippi. And to listen to politicians thanking each other and complimenting each other ... there are a lot of people here who are very upset ... Do you get the anger that is out here?" The 24-hour news network considered Cooper a ratings draw and promoted him in November to fill the prime time slot formerly occupied by more traditional journalist Aaron Brown. Brown resigned from the network following CNN's decision.

Greta Van Susteren, the host of the Fox Channel nightly news program, "On the Record w/Greta Van Susteren," earned her best-ever ratings with her reports on Natalee Holloway, a teen-ager who disappeared in Aruba in May 2005. Van Susteren devoted show after show to the case. Journalists on other networks, including Nancy Grace on CNN, also dedicated entire shows to Holloway's disappearance. Critics raised questions about the disproportionate

Carson's timing and delivery were seemingly effortless. He could be at his funniest salvaging a gag that bombed by making a joke at his own expense. As a host, Carson's unflappable style and self-effacing Midwestern sensibilities made him a dependable, reassuring presence for viewers. He was as adept at interviewing ordinary people as he was politicians and Hollywood notables.

Carson became one of television's most powerful figures. During his tenure, "The Tonight Show" generated an estimated 20 percent of NBC's profits, which made him a formidable figure with the network. Through the decades, he successfully fended off many competitors, including Joey Bishop, Dick Cavett, Joan Rivers, Alan Thicke, and Arsenio Hall. Carson earned seven Emmy Awards and a George Foster Peabody Award. In 1972, he orchestrated the show's move from New York City to Burbank, California. Carson also earned plaudits for his role as emcee of the Academy Awards, which he hosted five times between 1979 and 1984. He was inducted into the Television Hall of Fame in 1987.

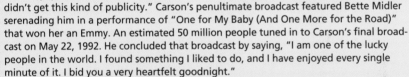

Carson announced his retirement in 1992. The countdown to his final broadcast became a national event, leading him to quip, "the Soviet Union's end didn't get this kind of publicity." Carson's penultimate broadcast featured Bette Midler serenading him in a performance of "One for My Baby (And One More for the Road)" that won her an Emmy. An estimated 50 million people tuned in to Carson's final broadcast on May 22, 1992. He concluded that broadcast by saying, "I am one of the lucky people in the world. I found something I liked to do, and I have enjoyed every single minute of it. I bid you a very heartfelt goodnight."

Carson made few television appearances after he retired. He provided his own voice for a 1993 episode of the animated series "The Simpsons" and made several cameos on the "Late Show with David Letterman." Shortly before his death, it was revealed that Carson occasionally contributed jokes to Letterman's monologues. "I left at the right time," he told an interviewer in 2002. "You've got to know when to get ... off the stage, and the timing was right for me. The reason I really don't go back or do interviews is because I just let the work speak for itself." ■ Donald Liebenson

news coverage of the disappearances of young, attractive white females, compared with the media attention paid to missing young African American or Hispanic women. In August, sports and talk show host Bob Costas protested the coverage by refusing to appear as a substitute host for Larry King on CNN if the Holloway case was the topic.

Ted Koppel anchored his last broadcast of ABC's news program "Nightline" on Nov. 22, 2005. Koppel was the original host of "Nightline," which began in 1980 as a series of late-night news specials during the Iran hostage crisis. He was replaced by ABC News White House correspondent Terry Moran, "Primetime Live" correspondent

Cynthia McFadden, and "20/20" correspondent Martin Bashir.

Spring shows. "Grey's Anatomy" was a breakout hit for ABC. The medical drama about first-year hospital interns and their supervisors debuted in March 2005 in the time slot that had been occupied by the Emmy Award-winning legal series, "Boston Legal." "Grey's Anatomy" was so popular that ABC pulled "Boston Legal" from its schedule until the fall.

"Family Guy," Seth MacFarlane's controversial animated series about a dysfunctional Rhode Island family, returned to network television with new episodes in May 2005. Fox had cancelled the series in 2002 but made the decision to resurrect

Television newscasters Peter Jennings (left) and Dan Rather (right) gather at the Museum of Television and Radio in New York City in February 2005 to honor fellow newscaster Tom Brokaw (center), who retired as anchorman of NBC's "Nightly News" on Dec. 1, 2004. Rather retired later in 2005, and Jennings died in August.

it after reruns of the series's first three seasons on Cartoon Network's Adult Swim programming block developed a cult following. Solid sales of the show's first season on DVD further demonstrated its popularity.

Series finales. Three notable television series ended in 2005. The CBS series "Everybody Loves Raymond," starring Ray Romano, finished its ninth and final season as the top-rated comedy on television. In the final episode, broadcast in May, Ray had a fleeting near-death experience that united the normally combative Barone family.

The UPN series "Star Trek: Enterprise" went off the air in May after four seasons, marking the first time in nearly two decades that there was not a "Star Trek" series in active production.

HBO's "Six Feet Under," about a family of undertakers, ended in August after five seasons. The show, which was credited with bringing the reality of death to television audiences, ended with one character having a vision of how all of the show's characters would die.

Dave Chappelle, the star of Comedy Central's highest-rated series, "Chappelle's Show," mysteriously halted production of the third season of the sketch series in April 2005. Chappelle disappeared from public view and later surfaced in South Africa. In an interview with *Time* magazine in May, Chappelle cited stress as a reason for the abrupt end of the show. In December, Comedy

TOP-RATED U.S. TELEVISION SERIES

The following were among the most-watched television series for the 2004-2005 regular season, which ran from Sept. 20, 2004, to May 25, 2005.

1. "CSI" (CBS)
2. "American Idol" (Tuesday) (FOX)
3. "American Idol" (Wednesday) (FOX)
4. "Desperate Housewives" (ABC)
5. "CSI: Miami" (CBS)
6. "Without a Trace" (CBS)
7. "Survivor: Palau" (CBS)
8. "Survivor: Vanuatu" (CBS)
9. "Grey's Anatomy" (ABC)
10. "Everybody Loves Raymond" (CBS)
11. "NFL Monday Night Football" (ABC)
12. "Two and a Half Men" (CBS)
13. "Apprentice 2" (NBC)
14. "E.R." (NBC)
15. (tie) "Lost" (ABC)
    "Cold Case" (CBS)
17. "60 Minutes" (CBS)
18. "Law and Order: SVU" (NBC)
19. (tie) "Apprentice 3" (NBC)
    "Medium" (NBC)

EMMY AWARD WINNERS IN 2005

COMEDY

Best Series: "Everybody Loves Raymond"

Lead Actress: Felicity Huffman, "Desperate Housewives"

Lead Actor: Tony Shalhoub, "Monk"

Supporting Actress: Doris Roberts, "Everybody Loves Raymond"

Supporting Actor: Brad Garrett, "Everybody Loves Raymond"

DRAMA

Best Series: "Lost"

Lead Actress: Patricia Arquette, "Medium"

Lead Actor: James Spader, "Boston Legal"

Supporting Actress: Blythe Danner, "Huff"

Supporting Actor: William Shatner, "Boston Legal"

OTHER AWARDS

Miniseries: "The Lost Prince"

Reality/Competition Series: "The Amazing Race"

Variety, Music, or Comedy Series: "The Daily Show with Jon Stewart"

Made for Television Movie: "Warm Springs"

Lead Actress in a Miniseries or Movie: S. Epatha Merkerson, "Lackawanna Blues"

Lead Actor in a Miniseries or Movie: Geoffrey Rush, "The Life and Death of Peter Sellers"

Supporting Actress in a Miniseries or Movie: Jane Alexander, "Warm Springs"

Supporting Actor in a Miniseries or Movie: Paul Newman, "Empire Falls"

Central executives announced that they were in the process of constructing episodes out of the material Chappelle had filmed and planned to air them in 2006.

Summer hits. "Dancing with the Stars," a competition series that paired celebrities with professional dancers, was a surprise hit during summer 2005. More than 22 million viewers watched the July finale, when "General Hospital" star Kelly Monaco and her partner, Alec Mazo, scored an upset victory over popular "Seinfeld" co-star John O'Hurley and Charlotte Jorgensen. Many viewers complained that O'Hurley should have been declared the winner and raised questions about the judging. A dance-off rematch, which O'Hurley won, was broadcast in September. The scripted series "The Closer" was a critical and ratings success for basic cable network TNT. Kyra Sedgwick starred as a woman who specializes in getting confessions from crime suspects. "Over There," the first television series set during the Iraqi conflict, also performed well in the ratings for the FX network.

Fall season. "Everybody Hates Chris," a series on the UPN network, became one of the most critically acclaimed shows of the 2005-2006 season. Comedian Chris Rock narrated the sitcom, which is based on his childhood in 1980's Brooklyn. NBC, which had dropped to fourth place in the ratings, enjoyed success with the quirky series "My Name Is Earl," starring Jason Lee as a petty crook who wins the lottery and decides to make amends to all the people he had previously hurt.

ABC's "Commander in Chief," starring Geena Davis as the first female president of the United States, was the only new program to premiere in the Top 10. "Prison Break," a dramatic series about a man who hatches an elaborate plan to break his framed brother out of prison, was a hit for the Fox network.

"The Late Show with David Letterman" received its highest ratings in more than 11 years on Dec. 1, 2005, after TV talk show host Oprah Winfrey appeared on the show for the first time in more than 16 years. Through the years, Letterman had made many jokes about a perceived feud with Winfrey, who claimed she felt she had been made sport of in previous appearances. Her return coincided with the opening night of the Broadway musical *The Color Purple,* which Winfrey had backed.

■ Donald Liebenson

See also **People in the news** (Jon Stewart).

Tennis. Roger Federer of Switzerland in 2005 became only the second man to win both the United States Open and Wimbledon in consecutive years. Don Budge accomplished the same feat in 1937 and 1938. The Williams sisters of the United States—Venus and Serena—reasserted themselves as dominant forces on the women's tour in 2005, grabbing two of the four Grand Slam tournament titles and seizing the spotlight from the young Russian stars who had captured three of the major titles in 2004.

Australian Open. Serena Williams defeated Lindsay Davenport of the United States to win her second Australian Open title on Jan. 29, 2005. The Australian Open was Williams's first Grand Slam title since taking Wimbledon in 2003 and her seventh title overall. Williams dropped the first set to Davenport and fought through a rib injury to win 2-6, 6-3, 6-0. Williams, who said she hurt herself lunging for a ball in the first set, won the last nine games of the match.

In the men's bracket, Marat Safin of Russia boomed 18 aces and rallied after losing the first set to defeat Australian Lleyton Hewitt 1-6, 6-3, 6-4, 6-4 on Jan. 30, 2005. The victory marked Safin's second Grand Slam title. Zimbabwe's Wayne Black and Kevin Ullyett won the men's doubles title; Australian Alicia Molik and Russian Svetlana Kuznetsova won the women's doubles;

Roger Federer of Switzerland returns Andre Agassi's serve during the men's title match at the U.S. Open in New York City on Sept. 11, 2005. Federer eventually overpowered Agassi, who at 35 years of age was the oldest finalist in more than 30 years.

and the Australian pair of Scott Draper and Samantha Stosur won the mixed doubles.

French Open. On June 4, Justine Henin-Hardenne of Belgium throttled Mary Pierce of France 6-1, 6-1 in the tournament's most one-sided women's final since 1988. It was Henin-Hardenne's second French Open crown and her first win since a knee injury and a blood virus forced her out of competition for seven months.

Spain's Rafael Nadal became the first man to win the French Open on his first attempt since Mats Wilander did so in 1982. At the age of 19, Nadal also was the youngest champion since Michael Chang won in 1989. Nadar topped unseeded Mariano Puerta of Argentina 6-7, 6-3, 6-1, 7-5. However, in December, tennis officials banned Puerta for eight years for testing positive for stimulants. It was his second offense.

Spain's Virginia Ruano Pascual and Argentina's Paola Suarez won the women's doubles title; Sweden's Jonas Bjorkman and Max Mirnyi of Belarus won the men's doubles; and Slovakia's Daniela Hantuchova and France's Fabrice Santoro won the mixed doubles.

Wimbledon. Venus Williams captured her third Wimbledon title in six years on July 2, 2005. Williams defeated Davenport 4-6, 7-6, 7-4, 9-7. Seeded 14th, Williams not only became the lowest-seeded woman to win a Wimbledon title, she became the first woman since 1935 to win a final match despite facing a match point. The 2-hour, 45-minute match was the longest in Wimbledon history for a wom-en's championship.

On July 3, 2005, Federer easily dismissed Andy Roddick of the United States in straight sets, 6-2, 7-6, 6-4 in a very quick match that lasted only 1 hour, 41 minutes. It was Federer's third consecutive Wimbledon title. One of the biggest surprises of the tournament came in the men's doubles. Australian Stephen Huss and South African Wesley Moodie, playing in just their second tournament together, became the first qualifiers ever to capture a Wimbledon title. The pair stunned Bob and Mike Bryan of the United States 7-6, 6-3, 6-7, 6-3. Zimbabwe's Cara Black and South Africa's Liezel Huber won the women's doubles title, while Mary Pierce of France and India's Mahesh Bhupathi won the mixed doubles title.

U.S. Open. The top-seeded Federer toppled American Andre Agassi, the seventh seed, 6-3, 2-6, 7-6, 6-1, on September 11. Belgium's Kim Clijsters won her first Grand Slam title with a 6-3, 6-1 straight set victory over Pierce on September 10. The Bryan twins captured the men's doubles title; American Lisa Raymond and Australian Samantha Stosur won women's doubles; and Hantuchova and Bhupati won the mixed doubles crown.

■ Michael Kates

Terrorism increased at an alarming rate around the globe in 2005. More than 3,000 documented incidents produced at least 5,000 fatalities. While terrorism affected virtually every region of the world, the Middle East remained the world's center of terrorism, with attacks averaging more than six a day in 2005.

Middle East. Israel, the West Bank, and Gaza were second only to Iraq in the number of terrorist acts carried out in 2005, with 53 people killed and 179 others injured. While Hamas was the most active of Palestinian militant groups, Islamic Jihad attacks were the most consistently fatal. In one of the deadliest attacks of 2005, a suicide truck bombing at the main crossing between Israel and Gaza killed 9 people and wounded 15 others on January 13. Authorities attributed the attack to the al-Fatah Martyrs' Brigade. A suicide bombing carried out by Islamic Jihad in the Israeli port of Hadera on October 26 killed 5 Israelis and wounded some 21 others. Israel responded with raids that killed one Islamic Jihad leader.

On February 14, former Lebanese Premier Rafik Hariri was assassinated in a massive bombing in Damascus that killed at least 20 other people. A United Nations investigation implicated Syrian officials, triggering international pressure on Syria to cooperate in tracking down the killers.

Bombings in the Egyptian resort of Sharm al-Sheikh on July 23, the height of the tourist season, killed 64 people and injured more than 200 others. A group linked to the al-Qa'ida terrorist network claimed responsibility.

Three nearly simultaneous suicide bombings in United States-owned hotels in Amman, Jordan, on November 9 killed at least 56 people and injured nearly 100 others. The most lethal of the attacks was carried out in a ballroom during a wedding reception attended primarily by Jordanians. The al-Qa'ida in Iraq terrorist group, led by the Jordanian-born militant Abu Musab al-Zarqawi, claimed responsibility for the attacks.

Africa. Members of the Lord's Resistance Army (LRA) ambushed a bus on July 10 in Uganda, killing at least 14 passengers before setting the bus on fire. In October, the Interna-

The wreckage of a double-decker bus litters a London street after a suicide terrorist bombing on July 7, 2005. The attack was one of four almost simultaneous explosions that killed 52 people and wounded some 700 others on London's public transportation system.

tional Criminal Court in The Hague, Netherlands, issued arrest warrants for crimes against humanity for senior LRA leaders, who for years waged regular, deadly attacks on private citizens in Uganda.

An unsuccessful attempt on the life of Prime Minister Ali Ghedi Mohamed of Somalia in a stadium in Mogadishu, the capital, on May 3 nevertheless killed 15 people and wounded 38 others.

Asia. A series of devastating bomb attacks in India's capital, New Delhi, on October 29 killed at least 58 people and maimed more than 200 others. Security experts attributed the attacks, which took place in crowded markets a day before major Hindu and Muslim holidays, to Lashkar-e-Taiba, a Pakistani group opposed to peace between India and Pakistan. On June 13, a car bomb exploded outside a high school in Pulwama, Pakistan, killing 16 people and injuring 100 others. The attack, allegedly intended for a police force camp next to the school, was attributed to Muslim forces fighting against Indian control of several Kashmiri states.

In Afghanistan on June 1, a suicide bombing of a Kandahar mosque during the funeral of an anti-Taliban cleric left 21 Afghans dead and 52 others injured.

On May 28, 22 people were killed and some 50 others wounded in two explosions in a busy market in Tentena on the Indonesian island of Sulawesi. The second blast was timed to take place as people gathered to assist victims of the first.

The nearly simultaneous detonation on October 1 of three bombs on the Indonesian resort island of Bali killed 23 people and injured more than 100 others. The attacks were allegedly connected to the al-Qa`ida-linked Jemaah Islamiyah.

In the Philippines, an unknown group blew up the General Santos City public market on January 12, killing 17 people.

Europe. Four suicide bombers attacked London's public transportation system on July 7, killing 52 people and leaving 700 injured. The Secret Organization of al-Qa`ida in Europe claimed responsibility for the city's most violent single day since World War II (1939-1945).

Russia. Unidentified terrorist groups targeted utilities and transportation systems in Russia with multiple attacks in 2005. On October 13, guerillas associated with Chechen leader Shamil Basaev attacked Nalchik in southern Russia, killing at least 130 people, including 94 militants.   ■ Richard E. Rubenstein

See also **Middle East; Syria; United Kingdom.**

Thailand. Prime Minister Thaksin Shinawatra of Thailand led his Thai Rak Thai political party to a landslide victory in parliamentary elections on Feb. 6, 2005. The party won 376 out of 500 seats in the dominant lower house of parliament.

Political observers attributed the victory to Thaksin's carrying out 2001 election promises of providing cheap health care, forgiving farmers' debts, and improving the country's economy. Thaksin also benefited from the dominance of private and state-controlled media. His popularity also was aided by public approval of his response to the tsunami that struck the country on Dec. 26, 2004.

Violence continued in 2005 to plague three southern, Muslim-majority provinces of predominantly Buddhist Thailand. Political observers blamed the trouble, which resulted in the deaths of some 1,000 people since January 2004, on militant separatists, government neglect, and reactions to police and army abuses.

Thaksin promised in March 2005 to set up a peace panel to address grievances in the area. However, after a major rebel attack on July 14, he signed an emergency decree giving authorities new powers to combat the trouble. The political opposition in parliament countered that the powers violated constitutional human rights guarantees and would only fuel the violence.   ■ Henry S. Bradsher

See also **Asia; Biology.**

Theater audiences in 2005 mourned the passing of two of America's finest contemporary dramatists—Arthur Miller, author of *Death of a Salesman,* and August Wilson, whose best-known work, *Fences,* like *Salesman,* portrays an American family and the often difficult relationships between fathers and sons. The mournful note sounded for these two writers gave way late in the year to widespread acclaim for the United Kingdom's renowned dramatic master, the 75-year-old playwright, poet, and *polemicist* (writer of controversies) Harold Pinter. In October, the Swedish Academy in Stockholm awarded Pinter the Nobel Prize in literature, which carried a purse of $1.3 million (723,000 British pounds) and was widely considered to be the highest honor bestowed on a living writer.

Pinter and the "Pinteresque." As a measure of Pinter's profound impact on the theater, the *Oxford English Dictionary* in 2005 added the word *Pinteresque.* The word connoted, as Robert McCrumb had written in *The Observer* newspaper, "an intoxicating cocktail of menace, erotic fantasy, obsessive jealousy, family hatred, and mental disequilibrium." Spare, often fragmentary speech, as well as the frequent use of non sequiturs and pregnant pauses, marked Pinter's distinctive style, which by the mid-1960's

Arthur Miller
Attention Must Be Paid

Arthur Miller was a giant of the American stage. Despite the uneven reception of a number of his later efforts, Miller's most acclaimed work, *Death of a Salesman,* continues to hold a place among the landmark plays of the 20th century. His wrenching portrayal of the plight of Willy Loman, a traveling salesman ruinously down on his luck, was written with astonishing speed over six weeks and received rave reviews and a slew of awards, including the 1949 Pulitzer Prize for drama. Miller's play gives eloquent voice to the elusiveness of the American dream. Loman's wife, admonishing the couple's two adult sons for belittling their father, concludes that "attention must be paid." It would be cruel to ignore his suffering. Loman's struggle recalls the despair that, years earlier, engulfed America during the Depression, a period through which Miller himself lived and which he viewed as the most defining moment in American history, rivaled only by the Civil War.

Miller, who died on Feb. 10, 2005, at his residence in Roxbury, Connecticut, at the age of 89, achieved a reputation as an American master, alongside playwrights like Eugene O'Neill and Tennessee Williams. Born in New York City in 1915, Miller began writing plays at the University of Michigan in Ann Arbor, where he won several awards for his early work. In 1944, his first Broadway production, *The Man Who Had All the Luck,* fared poorly, closing after only a few performances. His first success on Broadway came in 1947, with *All My Sons,* which endures as one of his most celebrated works. The play examines a family's concealment of shoddy business practices that led to the deaths of innocent soldiers during wartime.

When *Death of a Salesman* opened on Broadway in 1949, with Lee J. Cobb as Willy Loman, critics proclaimed it a contemporary masterpiece. Another of Miller's most frequently revived plays, *The Crucible,* was not as well-received when it premiered in 1953. The play constitutes Miller's response to the Communist witch hunts of the 1950's led by Wisconsin Senator Joseph R. McCarthy. Miller was called in front of the House Un-American Activities Committee and refused to reveal the names of associates who may have been Communists. He was cited with contempt of Congress, though the citation was later revoked.

Another autobiographical aspect of *The Crucible* is John Proctor's confession to his wife of an extramarital affair, which mirrored the real-life affair that Miller was having at the time with actress Marilyn Monroe, whom he married in 1956. Miller wrote the screenplay to the film *The Misfits* (1961) for Monroe, but the marriage did not last. Two of Miller's later plays recall his troubled relationship with Monroe—*After the Fall* (1964), which depicts a character named Maggie, whose drug addiction and blond coiffure recall Monroe; and Miller's last play, *Finishing the Picture* (2004), which recounts the making of *The Misfits*.

Numerous noteworthy plays followed *Death of a Salesman*, including *A View from the Bridge* (1955), about the tragic fate of two immigrant brothers in New York City; and *The Price* (1968), which incorporates material suggestive of Miller's Jewish heritage and describes the separate fortunes of two brothers, one a successful doctor, the other a cop who sacrificed a more illustrious career to look after his ailing father. Although Miller never again achieved the success of *Death of a Salesman*, his tale of the unsung everyman solidified his place in American drama. ■ David Yezzi

August Wilson
King of the Hill

Widely considered the foremost African American playwright, August Wilson was one of America's finest playwrights, period. While no one of his plays achieved the heights of acclaim enjoyed by Arthur Miller's *Death of a Salesman* or Eugene O'Neill's *Long Day's Journey into Night*, Wilson's 10-play cycle of the African American experience displays a consistency of excellence unique in American theater. Arguably the finest poetic voice since Tennessee Williams, Wilson found in the colloquial speech of his inner-city characters a soaring and resonant music all his own.

Wilson died of cancer on Oct. 2, 2005, in his adopted city of Seattle, Washington. He was 60 years old. The recipient of two Pulitzer Prizes and a Tony Award, Wilson began writing *Jitney* (1982), the first play in his epic cycle, in 1979, and completed the cycle shortly before his death, with *Radio Golf*. All of Wilson's plays, except for *Ma Rainey's Black Bottom* (1984) about a Chicago blues singer, are set in the Hill District of Wilson's native Pittsburgh, and all of them, save *Jitney* and *Radio Golf*, appeared on Broadway during a time when other dramatists fared better in off-Broadway houses.

Wilson left school at age 15, relying on his own reading for his education in the arts. He frequently spoke of the "four B's" that influenced him as a writer: the blues, the Argentine writer and poet Jorge Luis Borges, the politically outspoken American playwright and poet Amiri Baraka, and the American artist Romare Bearden. Wilson enjoyed a longtime collaboration with the director Lloyd Richards, who for many years ran the Yale Repertory Theater, where many of Wilson's plays were produced prior to their appearance on Broadway. Wilson's plays were not huge commercial successes, yet they remained a benchmark of literary drama in an increasingly difficult commercial climate.

Fences (1985), the popular favorite among Wilson's plays, won the Pulitzer Prize for drama in 1987 and featured James Earl Jones as Troy Maxson, a former baseball player who works as a garbage man. Troy's brutality toward his wife and son contribute to the complexity of Wilson's portrait of an African American patriarch in the 1950's. Other notable characters from Wilson's plays include Bynum, a "conjure man" in *Joe Turner's Come and Gone* (1986), who consoles lost souls and awaits supernatural portents, and Aunt Esther from *Gem of the Ocean* (2003), a wise spiritual guide nearly 300 years old. Wilson's characters eloquently denounce racial oppression in the United States, yet their passionate speeches are more poetic arias than hectoring rants. The other plays in Wilson's cycle include *The Piano Lesson* (1987), *Two Trains Running* (1990), *Seven Guitars* (1995), and *King Hedley II* (2000). Since the 1980's, numerous prominent actors have appeared, and occasionally made their reputations, in Wilson's plays, including Angela Basset, Charles S. Dutton, Laurence Fishburne, Delroy Lindo, Phylicia Rashad, and Leslie Uggams.

In the weeks before Wilson's death, it was announced that the Virginia Theatre on Broadway in New York City would be renamed in Wilson's honor. Two weeks after his death, the theater was renamed. Wilson's daughter Sakina Ansari conveyed the playwright's thoughts upon hearing that a theater was to be renamed in his honor, saying that the dedication was the capstone "to the measure and meaning of my life."

■ David Yezzi

established him as a bold and unique new voice. Even Pinter's earliest plays, including most notably *The Birthday Party* (1957), *The Caretaker* (1959), and *The Homecoming* (1964), exemplified Pinter's particular brand of menace.

Many theatergoers considered the plays of Pinter's middle period—such as *Betrayal* (1978), which relates the story of an adulterous relationship in reverse chronological order, and *No Man's Land* (1975), the hilarious and decidedly creepy encounter between a successful writer and a failed poet—to represent Pinter's strongest work. In recent years, Pinter's plays have become more political in nature, a change that certain critics felt represented a diminution of Pinter's artistic powers compared with his earlier plays.

Despite Pinter's recent battle with cancer of the esophagus, his artistic output continues without interruption. In October 2005, the British Broadcasting Corporation (BBC) featured a radio drama based on Pinter's later plays, including *Mountain Language* (1988) and *Ashes to Ashes* (1996). Pinter had collaborated with composer James Clarke to create the radio drama. Pinter's recent work regularly depicts scenes of interrogation and implied torture, and Pinter, an imposing figure with a resonant voice, often performs in and directs his own plays. In addition to acting on stage, Pinter has worked as a character actor in supporting film roles, such as Sir Thomas Betram in the 1999 film adaptation of Jane Austen's *Mansfield Park*.

Beyond his work as a writer, Pinter receives a great deal of attention as a public figure. An outspoken opponent of the war in Iraq, he remained a stern critic of the governments of both United States President George W. Bush and United Kingdom Prime Minister Tony Blair in 2005. In his December speech at the Nobel award ceremony, Pinter accused the United States of using "a vast tapestry of lies" to justify the war in Iraq. Earlier in 2005, before he won the Nobel Prize, Pinter announced that he would no longer write plays, choosing instead to work in such other forms as poetry and political polemic. However, his nearly 30 plays, written over 5 decades, extended the tradition of innovative playwriting advanced by fellow Nobel laureate Samuel Beckett and will constitute his enduring legacy as a writer.

Kevin Spacey at the Old Vic. In Kevin Spacey's second season as artistic director of the Old Vic theater in London, the two-time Oscar-winning actor, best known for his roles in such Hollywood films as *American*

Beauty and *The Usual Suspects,* received mixed reviews for his leadership of the historic venue. While the announcement of Spacey's appointment generated a great deal of media attention in 2004, the response to his first season—featuring productions of Maria Goos's *Cloaca* directed by Spacey and a new version of the pantomime *Aladdin,* starring the acclaimed actor Sir Ian McKellen as Widow Twankey—was decidedly tepid. Also on offer at the Old

TONY AWARD WINNERS IN 2005

Best Play, *Doubt*

Best Musical, *Monty Python's Spamalot*

Best Play Revival, *Glengarry Glen Ross*

Best Musical Revival, *La Cage aux Folles*

Best Special Theatrical Event, *Billy Crystal 700 Sundays*

Leading Actor in a Play, Bill Irwin, *Who's Afraid of Virginia Woolf?*

Leading Actress in a Play, Cherry Jones, *Doubt*

Leading Actor in a Musical, Norbert Leo Butz, *Dirty Rotten Scoundrels*

Leading Actress in a Musical, Victoria Clark, *The Light in the Piazza*

Featured Actor in a Play, Liev Schreiber, *Glengarry Glen Ross*

Featured Actress in a Play, Adriane Lenox, *Doubt*

Featured Actor in a Musical, Dan Fogler, *The 25th Annual Putnam County Spelling Bee*

Featured Actress in a Musical, Sara Ramirez, *Monty Python's Spamalot*

Direction of a Play, Doug Hughes, *Doubt*

Direction of a Musical, Mike Nichols, *Monty Python's Spamalot*

Book of a Musical, Rachel Sheinkin, *The 25th Annual Putnam County Spelling Bee*

Original Musical Score, Adam Guettel, *The Light in the Piazza*

Orchestrations, Ted Sperling, Adam Guettel, and Bruce Coughlin, *The Light in the Piazza*

Scenic Design of a Play, Scott Pask, *The Pillowman*

Scenic Design of a Musical, Michael Yeargan, *The Light in the Piazza*

Costume Design of a Play, Jess Goldstein, *The Rivals*

Costume Design of a Musical, Catherine Zuber, *The Light in the Piazza*

Lighting Design of a Play, Brian MacDevitt, *The Pillowman*

Lighting Design of a Musical, Christopher Akerlind, *The Light in the Piazza*

Choreography, Jerry Mitchell, *La Cage aux Folles*

Regional Theater, Theatre de la Jeune Lune, Minneapolis

Lifetime Achievement, Edward Albee, producer, writer, and director

Vic in 2005 were the British premiere of Dennis McIntyre's *National Anthems* followed by a revival of *The Philadelphia Story,* both starring Spacey. Susannah Clap derided this lineup in *The Observer* as "First, a dull Dutch play, then a second-rate American one. [Then] a revival of a creaky vehicle," characterizing the entire season as "undistinguished."

Such lackluster critical response was accompanied by mediocre sales for *Cloaca,* which played to half-full houses, though *Aladdin* fared better, opening to a healthy advance sale of 1.2 million pounds (about $2.1 million). Spacey received further criticism from audiences for leaving the cast of *The Philadelphia Story* early in the play's run for a film role. By the end of 2005, however, Spacey's critical fortunes rebounded, with regard to both his acting and his leadership of the Old Vic. Spacey's modern-dress interpretation of the title role in Shakespeare's *Richard II,* directed by Trevor Nunn, received glowing notices. Theater critics considered the production and Spacey's portrayal in particular as a return to form for the Old Vic, where great productions of Shakespeare have long been a mainstay.

Doubt wins Pulitzer. Perhaps the greatest critical success on Broadway in 2005 was John Patrick Shanley's drama *Doubt,* directed by Doug Hughes. The play featured the acclaimed actress Cherry Jones as a nun who accuses a priest, played by Brian F. O'Byrne, of sexual misconduct in 1964. The play received the 2005 Pulitzer Prize for drama, making Shanley one of only a few writers to win both a Pulitzer and an Academy Award, which Shanley received in 1988 for his screenplay of *Moonstruck.* Also the recipient of the 2005 Tony Award for best play, *Doubt* was among several of Shanley's works produced in New York City during the 2004-2005 season. Also produced were *Sailor's Song* at the LAByrinth Theater and *Danny and the Deep Blue Sea* at Second Stage Theatre.

The success of *Doubt,* which moved to the Walter Kerr Theatre from an earlier run at the Manhattan Theatre Club, defied the typical difficulties of producing nonmusical plays on Broadway. The average cost of mounting a new Broadway play was $2 million in 2005, according to Jesse McKinley in *The New York Times.* With such steep overhead, it was not surprising that a nonmusical play had not turned a significant profit in recent years. In light of these harsh economic realities, *Doubt*'s staying power boded well for the presence of serious literary drama on Broadway.

■ David Yezzi

See also **Nobel prizes.**

Toronto in 2005 benefited financially from tax revenues provided to the city from federal and provincial sources. The emergence of details of city officials' past scandals and a series of shootings cast a less positive light on the city.

Finances. Mayor David Miller surprised subway riders on September 7, when he boarded a train carrying a giant novelty check for $24.5 million under his arm. (All amounts are in Canadian dollars.) The check symbolized a historic change in the financing of Canadian cities. The federal government once had balked at giving cities a fixed share of tax revenues, but in 2005 undertook to provide cities with a 1.5-cent-per-liter share from the federal gas tax, to rise to 5 cents a liter by 2009.

Miller's subway ride sent a message that the city's overburdened transit system was at last getting outside help. The hard-pressed Toronto Transit Commission had been forced to increase fares in February 2005 from $2.25 to $2.50.

The check was part of the national campaign for additional urban support, called "The New Deal for Cities," which began with Toronto's political and business leaders in 2002. After years of crippling budget deficits and with Canadian cities expanding rapidly, the campaign's officials hoped in 2005 that the monetary support would make the cities more competitive internationally.

MFP scandal. Early in September, Madame Justice Denise Bellamy delivered her report on the MFP scandal. Bellamy had been engaged by the Toronto City Council to investigate how the city's contracts with outside consultants and its obligations to MFP Financial Services Ltd., a computer leasing company, based in nearby Mississauga, Ontario, had ballooned from around $40 million to more than $80 million. For three years, Bellamy studied 124,000 pages of documents and held public hearings, with 156 witnesses.

Bellamy's investigation revealed that parts of Toronto's administration had been chaotic in the years following amalgamation, when the Ontario provincial legislature voted to merge the six municipalities that made up the metropolitan federation of Toronto into a single city in 1997. Bellamy's 2005 report showed that many government employees in the newly combined city had been confused about their responsibilities and that controls over spending had been lax. Bellamy also revealed that lobbyists had lavished treats on politicians and civil servants and then tried to cover their tracks.

Shootings. Toronto, which long prided itself on being one of the safest cities in North America, suffered a rash of violent incidents involving guns over the summer and fall of 2005. In November, Amon Beckles, an 18-year-old, was shot and killed on the steps of a Toronto church. He was attending the funeral of a friend who had been murdered a few days earlier.

Beckles's death was Toronto's 48th gun homicide in 2005. Some of the killings appeared to grow out of a gang war among drug dealers. However, on October 24, a gunfight took place in front of a busy midtown subway station and a stray bullet narrowly missed the driver of a van. Gun incidents in the city's nightclub and entertainment district and on the edge of the stylish Cabbagetown neighborhood followed. A shoot-out on Yonge Street on December 26 killed a teen-age girl—the 52nd firearm-related death in Toronto in 2005—and left six other people injured. The spread of gunfire brought demands for tougher penalties for crimes involving fire-arms and demands from Prime Minister Paul Martin that the United States do more to curb the entry of illegal guns into Canada.

The film industry. In October, the Toronto Film Studios announced that it would build a massive $275-million "film village" on city-owned land near the waterfront by 2007. The studios hired British architect Will Alsop to design the new complex. The film studio announcement came a month after the Toronto International Film Festival celebrated its 30th year by showing 335 films in 10 days. ■ David Lewis Stein

See also **Canada; Canadian provinces; City.**

Toys and games. Consumers in the United States were treated to an early Christmas in 2005, with retailers beginning their holiday sales and promotions sooner than in previous years. Traditionally, many U.S. consumers begin shopping on the first day after Thanksgiving, commonly known as "Black Friday" among retail-ers, as it helps to put store sales "in the black," a favorable position in accounting terminology. Fearing that holiday shoppers, worried by the high prices of gasoline and home heating oil, would make fewer shopping trips, many stores began discounting prices on toys and other traditional holiday gifts as early as the day after Halloween.

A holiday campaign beginning on November 1 was the earliest start in the history of Wal-Mart Stores of Bentonville, Arkansas, the largest retailer of toys. For Wal-Mart and other retailers, holiday spending accounts for 25 to 40 percent of their annual sales, and they sought to reach the earliest holiday shoppers with low prices.

New game system. Video game players lined up early outside retail stores across the United States on November 22 to purchase the newly re-leased Xbox 360 game system by Microsoft Corp. of Redmond, Washington. In addition to improved high-definition graphics, the Xbox 360 allowed players to listen to music, view photos, watch DVD's, and play electronic puzzle and card games.

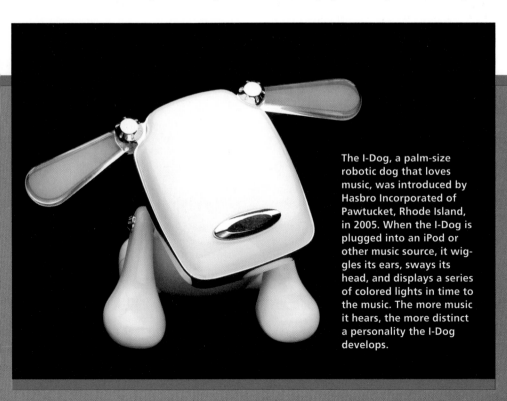

The I-Dog, a palm-size robotic dog that loves music, was introduced by Hasbro Incorporated of Pawtucket, Rhode Island, in 2005. When the I-Dog is plugged into an iPod or other music source, it wig-gles its ears, sways its head, and displays a series of colored lights in time to the music. The more music it hears, the more distinct a personality the I-Dog develops.

The I generation. With more and more children joining the Internet generation, toy manufacturers responded by incorporating features that appeal to children's tastes in electronics, music, entertainment, and fashion. Pixel Chix are virtual friends that live inside a 3-D handheld game designed in the shape of a house. Made by Mattel Incorporated of El Segundo, California, the animated Pixel Chix can engage a child in play with games on five different levels or with requests for help in choosing activities, outfits to wear, or things to eat. If a child ignores her Pixel Chix pal, the pal will tap her foot, clear her throat, and eventually fade from the screen.

Also introduced in 2005, I-Dog from Hasbro Incorporated of Pawtucket, Rhode Island, is a palm-sized robotic dog that loves to listen to music. Plugged into an iPod or other music source via a headphone jack, I-Dog's ears wiggle, its head sways, and its puppy face lights up in time to the music, changing its "personality" with the length of play time and the type of music played.

Nine inches (23 centimeters) tall, the three-legged iZ is the ultimate fusion of music and toy with a personality all its own. Made by Zizzle LLC of Bannockburn, Illinois, iZ plugs into a music source. Twisting iZ's ears creates new combinations of rhythm and lead tracks. Pressing its belly changes the music's beat.

Do you Sudoku? Not since the Rubik's Cube craze of the 1970's has a puzzle so captured the imagination of enthusiasts worldwide as Sudoku did in 2005. A number logic puzzle that originated in the United States as Number Place in 1979, Sudoku first became popular in the mid-1980's in Japan. (*Sudoku* means "number" and "unique" in Japanese.) The puzzle consists of a grid of 81 squares, or nine 3-by-3 boxes. Each puzzle comes with some numbers in place. A player solves the puzzle by filling the grid with numbers so that every row, column, and box contains the digits 1 through 9 without repeating a number. The puzzle appeared in newspapers in the United Kingdom in 2004, then spread to the United States in 2005. In addition to appearing in daily newspapers worldwide, Sudoku puzzles became available on the Internet, as applications for mobile phones, in several best-selling books, and on a handheld electronic version featuring 100,000 different puzzles made by Techno Source USA of New York City.

Monster mashed. In 2005, Hasbro announced that Mr. Potato Head had joined the dark side, introducing the best-selling spud of more than 50 years as Darth Tater just in time for the release of the latest Star Wars film, *Revenge of the Sith*. Plastic potato body and parts, including helmet, cape, face plate, and lightsaber, allow children to dress up their favorite tuber as the Star Wars villain.

■ Diane P. Cardinale

Track and field. Asafa Powell of Jamaica became the fastest man on Earth on June 14, 2005, when he broke the men's 100-meter world record, becoming only the fourth non-American to hold the 100-meter record since 1912.

Powell ran a time of 9.77 seconds at the Tsiklitiria Super Grand Prix in Athens, one hundredth of a second better than American Tim Montgomery's record of 9.78 set in 2002. In 2004, Montgomery's name surfaced during an investigation of an illegal steroid ring. As a result, in December 2005 Montgomery's former record time was wiped out by the Court of Arbitration for Sport.

World championships. The United States captured 14 gold medals at the 2005 world championships, a nine-day event held in August in Helsinki, Finland. The team finished with 25 medals, one shy of the record it set in Tokyo in 1991. The Russian team finished with 20 medals, 7 of them gold.

Despite the success of the U.S. runners, many observers were disappointed in the relay teams, two of which failed to qualify for the finals despite being favorites. American men made history in the 200-meter event, making the United States the first country to sweep the top four places in an event. The feat was later duplicated by the Ethiopian women in the 5,000-meter race.

Justin Gatlin of the United States became only the second sprinter to sweep the 100-meter and 200-meter races at a world championship. Maurice Greene of the United States accomplished the same feat in 1999. Gatlin won the 200-meter race in 20.04 seconds, 0.16 second ahead of Wallace Spearmon of the United States. Gatlin had won the 100-meter in 9.88 seconds, 0.17 second faster than Jamaica's Michael Frater, the largest margin of victory in the event since the world championships began in 1983.

However, Gatlin's goal of three gold medals ended when the team dropped the baton in the 4x100-meter relay. The U.S. women's 4x400-meter relay team was disqualified when Suziann Reid failed to stay in her lane.

Ethiopian women, led by 20-year-old Tirunesh Dibaba, swept the medals in the 10,000-meter run on the championship's opening day. Later, they took the top four places in the 5,000-meter event. Dibaba pulled away in the final 300 meters of the 5,000 to win in 14:38.59, becoming the first woman to take both events.

Bryan Clay of the United States captured the decathlon with 8,732 points, 211 more than Olympic gold medalist and world record holder Roman Sebrle of the Czech Republic. Clay had won the silver medal at the 2004 Summer Olympic Games.

Three athletes—all women—broke world records during the world championships. Osleidys

United States sprinters (from left to right) Justin Gatlin, Tyson Gay, John Capel, and Wallace Spearmon sweep the top four places in the 200-meter race at the world championships in Helsinki, Finland, on Aug. 11, 2005. The team was the first in history to take the top four places in a single event.

WORLD TRACK AND FIELD RECORDS ESTABLISHED IN 2005

Event	Holder	Country	Where set	Date	Record
MEN INDOOR					
400 meters	Kerron Clement	U.S.A.	Fayetteville, Arkansas	March 12	44.57
WOMEN INDOOR					
Pole vault	Yelena Isinbayeva	Russia	Madrid	March 6	4.90 m
5,000 meters	Tirunesh Dibaba	Ethiopia	Roxbury, Mass.	January 29	14:32.93
4x200-meter relay	Russia	Russia	Glasgow, Scotland	January 29	1:32.41
MEN OUTDOOR					
100 meters	Asafa Powell	Jamaica	Athens	June 14	9.77
10,000 meters	Kenenisa Bekele	Ethiopia	Brussels	August 26	*26:17.53
Half marathon	Samuel Wanjiru	Kenya	Rotterdam, Neth.	September 11	*59.16
30-kilometer race	Takayuki Matsumiya	Japan	Kumamoto, Japan	February 27	1:28:00
WOMEN OUTDOOR					
25-kilometer race	Deena Kastor	U.S.A.	Chicago, Illinois	October 9	*1:21:57
30-kilometer race	Deena Kastor	U.S.A.	Chicago, Illinois	October 9	*1:38:29
Pole vault	Yelena Isinbayeva	Russia	Helsinki	August 12	5.01m
Decathlon	Austra Skujyte	Lithuania	Columbia, Missouri	April 15	8,358 points
Hammer throw	Tatyana Lysenko	Russia	Moscow	July 15	*77.06 m
Javelin throw	Osleidys Menendez	Cuba	Helsinki	August 14	71.70 m
20-kilometer walk	Olimpiada Ivanova	Russia	Helsinki	August 7	1:25:41

m = meters
* = not yet ratified.   Source: International Association of Athletics Federation (IAAF).

Menendez of Cuba shattered her own javelin mark with a throw of 235 feet, 3 inches (71.7 meters), breaking her 2001 record by 7 inches (17.8 centimeters). Russian pole vaulter Yelena Isinbayeva made a vault of 16 feet, 5.25 inches (5.01 meters), breaking her own mark set in July 2005.

Olimpiada Ivanova of Russia shaved 41 seconds off of the 20-kilometer (12.4-mile) walk mark set in 2001 and equaled in 2003 with a time of 1 hour, 25 minutes, and 41 seconds.

Hitting the jackpot. Triple-jumper Tatyana Lebedeva of Russia won the triple jump in the final event of the $1 million Golden League in Berlin on Sept. 4, 2005. By completing her sweep in that event, Lebedeva captured the $1 million jackpot, which goes to athletes who sweep their events at all six Golden League meets.

Other world records. Kenenisa Bekele of Ethiopia set a world record in the 10,000 meters at the Memorial Van Damme in Brussels on August 26. He finished in 26 minutes, 17.53 seconds, breaking his previous record of 26 minutes, 20.31 seconds set in June 2004. Tatyana Lysenko of Russia set a women's record in the hammer throw with a toss of 252 feet, 10 inches (77.06 meters) on July 15, 2005, in Moscow.

■ Michael Kates

Transit. See Transportation.

Transportation. United States President George W. Bush signed into law legislation on Aug. 10, 2005, that reauthorized the funding of highways and public transportation for the period 2004 to 2009. Officially known as the 2005 Safe, Accountable, Flexible, and Efficient Transportation Equity Act, or SAFETEA-LU, it replaced the 1998 Transportation Equity Act for the 21st Century (TEA-21), which had expired in 2003. In the intervening years, federal funding continued through 12 temporary extensions while the administration and the U.S. Congress debated the size of the funding package.

Ultimately, a compromise was reached that authorized $286.4 billion over the six-year period. The majority of the funds were transferred to individual states to support construction and maintenance of highways and public transit facilities. The act drew extensive criticism, particularly after cost estimates to rebuild New Orleans in the aftermath of Hurricane Katrina became known in September 2005. Critics pointed out that SAFETEA-LU contained funding for more than 6,000 specific projects—representing almost 9 percent of the total budget—that were inserted at the request of individual legislators. Some of these projects were considered "pork barrel" schemes that would raise support for the legislator from his or her constituents yet did little to improve transportation.

Terrorism. On July 7, 2005, bombs exploded on three subway trains and a double-decker bus in London, killing 52 people as well as the 4 bombers. The attack marked the first time that suicide bombers had struck in Western Europe. An investigation revealed that the bombers, who held radical Islamic beliefs, were citizens of the United Kingdom, born of immigrant families. A group calling itself the Secret Organization of Al-Qa`ida in Europe claimed responsibility for the attacks.

On July 21, a similar plot was foiled when the bombs failed to explode. Police subsequently apprehended the four bombers and began to investigate whether they were linked to the July 7 attackers. Parts of the London subway system were closed for one month because of the devastation. The fear of further attacks resulted in the deployment of extra police to guard the transit system.

In the United States, the attacks prompted the Department of Homeland Security to temporarily raise its color-coded terror threat level for public transit from yellow, or "elevated," to orange, or "high." In New York City, police officers began random bag searches of subway riders. Several months later, New York City officials reported that they had received the most specific threat to date of a planned attack on the city's subway system. Police officers on October 7 conducted random searches of bags and baby strollers, the means by which an explosive was to have been planted.

Amtrak in April withdrew from service all 20 of its high-speed Acela trains in the Northeast Corridor, its main East Coast route between Boston, New York, and Washington, D.C. (Amtrak is the semipublic corporation that provides intercity passenger rail transportation in the United States.) The agency had discovered cracks in the trains' brakes. Acela trains, which can operate at speeds up to 150 miles (241 kilometers) per hour, have experienced problems since their introduction in the United States in 2000. Some engineers believe the problems stem from modifications made to the trains to meet U.S. safety standards. Amtrak substituted aging conventional trains until replacement brakes could be manufactured. Acela trains resumed normal service in September 2005.

Members of Congress resisted a budget proposal by President Bush to eliminate operating subsidies to Amtrak for the fiscal year starting October 1. Had the subsidy been removed, Amtrak would have been forced to shut down many long-distance routes and look to individual states for support for other services. Nevertheless, on September 27, Amtrak announced nationwide increases in ticket prices, to offset rising fuel costs. In addition, on October 12, Amtrak's board of directors reported that they had authorized joint federal-state management of the Northeast Corridor, the most heavily traveled portion of the system.

On November 9, the board dismissed Amtrak President David L. Gunn because of his opposition to the Bush administration's proposal to break up the passenger rail service.

Trucking. The U.S. trucking industry began to feel the impact of rising fuel costs even before hurricanes Katrina and Rita damaged oil shipping and refining facilities along the Gulf Coast. In 2002, the U.S. Environmental Protection Agency had passed regulations that required the addition of extra parts to diesel engines to control emissions. The parts increased the weight of the engines, decreasing fuel efficiency.

Throughout 2005, the industry also faced a global shortage of refining capacity and strong global demand for diesel fuel. By October 10, the price of diesel fuel had hit an all-time high in the United States of more than $3.00 per gallon. Prices were expected to rise even higher in 2006, when strict new federal regulations on the sulfur content of motor fuel were to go into effect. Industry analysts predicted that the higher costs would eventually be passed on to consumers of the various goods that trucking companies haul.   ■ Ian Savage

See also **Disasters: A Special Report; Terrorism; United Kingdom.**

Trinidad and Tobago. See Latin America.

Tunisia. See Middle East.

Turkey. Negotiations concerning the accession of Turkey to the European Union (EU) began in Luxembourg in October 2005, when the 25 EU foreign ministers met with Turkish Foreign Minister and Deputy Prime Minister Abdullah Gul. The negotiations were expected to last as long as 10 years.

United States breaks deadlock. The U.S. government played a major role in 2005 in breaking a deadlock that had threatened Turkey's accession talks with the EU. Austrian officials had insisted that Turkey be offered a "privileged partnership" with the EU rather than full membership—an offer that Turkish officials rejected. United States Secretary of State Condoleezza Rice persuaded Austrian leaders to drop their objections to membership talks for Turkey.

Cyprus dispute. In July, Turkish officials signed a document that extended a Turkey-EU customs accord to the 10 new EU member nations, including Cyprus. Turkey has never recognized Cyprus as a single nation under the control of the Greek Cypriot government. A provision attached to the document declared, "Turkey will continue to regard the Greek Cypriot authorities as exercising authority, control, and jurisdiction only in the territory south of the buffer zone [in Cyprus] ... and as not representing the Turkish Cypriot people ... "

The Turkish declaration upset Greek Cypriots, who had hoped that the document would constitute Turkey's recognition of the Republic of Cyprus as a nation and full EU member. Despite this concern, the EU's European Commission ruled that Turkey's recognition of Cyprus was not a prerequisite to Turkey's accession negotiations.

European reaction. According to international affairs analysts, a key factor in voters' rejections of the EU constitution in France and the Netherlands in May and June, respectively, was their opposition to Turkey's entry into the EU. Eurobarometer polls in 2005 showed that some 51 percent of Europeans opposed Turkish membership in the EU, while only 35 percent were in favor of Turkey's accession.

The case of Orhan Pamuk. On December 19, Turkish writer Orhan Pamuk was charged by a Turkish court with "denigrating the Turkish national identity." Pamuk had told a Swiss interviewer that Turkey was responsible for Armenian *genocide* (the systematic extermination of a cultural or racial group) that took place in 1915, in the waning days of the Ottoman Empire. EU officials strongly criticized the Turkish government for Pamuk's arrest   ■ Mary-Jane Deeb

See also **Europe; France; Netherlands.**

Turkmenistan. See Asia.

Tuvalu. See Pacific Islands.

Uganda. Hopes for peace in northern Uganda were dashed in 2005 as a promised truce between government troops and rebel guerrillas of the Lord's Resistance Army (LRA) failed to materialize. On January 2, Ugandan President Yoweri Museveni announced that the Ugandan Army would resume all-out war against the rebels only two days after peace talks between the government and the LRA, led by Joseph Kony, collapsed.

The LRA is a cult that advocates "Christian rule" but in practice has carried out a campaign of terror against civilians in a 19-year rebellion. In 2005, human rights groups estimated that the insurgency had resulted in the deaths of thousands of people and the abduction of some 20,000 children to serve as slaves and fighters for the LRA. About 1.5 million people also have been displaced in the region since 1986. During 2005, a series of short-lived cease-fires were brokered by peace negotiators, but none held, and the LRA intensified its campaign of terror among northern Uganda's Acholi ethnic population. Reports of such atrocities as mutilation and amputation continued to surface in 2005.

Referendum. In a nationwide referendum on July 28, 2005, Ugandans voted overwhelmingly to end a ban on independent political parties that had been in effect since President Museveni's National Resistance Movement (NRM) seized power in 1986. According to results released by Uganda's electoral commission, 92 percent of voters cast "yes" ballots in favor of reestablishing multiparty politics in preparation for general elections, scheduled for March 2006. The electoral commission reported that 47 percent of eligible voters had turned out for the referendum.

President Museveni had previously submitted the issue of multiparty politics to the voters in a June 2000 referendum. His admonition that political pluralism would unleash ethnic divisiveness and violence secured a "no" vote.

Opposition politicians dismissed the 2005 referendum as a charade and urged their supporters to boycott the poll. They claimed that Museveni's turnabout on the issue of political pluralism was a ploy to appease Western donors. The opposition also alleged that Museveni manipulated parliamentary leaders in 2005 to pass a law abolishing presidential term limits, which enabled him to run for reelection in 2006. Political analysts predicted a heated election campaign in 2006, to be fought along multiparty lines for the first time since elections in 1980.

Death. Milton Obote died on Oct. 10, 2005, in Johannesburg, South Africa. He had led the political movement that resulted in Uganda's independence from the United Kingdom in 1962.

■ Simon Baynham

See also **Africa.**

Viktor Yushchenko gives his inaugural address at the parliament building in Kiev, Ukraine's capital, on January 23. Yushchenko became president after a series of contested elections and popular protests that became known as the Orange Revolution.

Ukraine began 2005 with a new president after 2004's Orange Revolution swept presidential challenger Viktor Yushchenko to power over Prime Minister Viktor Yanukovich. Yushchenko declared his intention to move toward membership in the European Union (EU), the North Atlantic Treaty Organization (NATO), and the World Trade Organization (WTO); to crack down on corruption; and to preserve Ukrainian national unity. However, the government soon encountered roadblocks in carrying out Yushchenko's reform program.

The first public signs of tension appeared in May 2005, as Yushchenko criticized his popular prime minister Yuliya Tymoshenko for her decision in April to place price caps on oil. Yushchenko reversed this policy after Russian oil companies responded by reducing their exports to Ukraine, causing fuel shortages. Yushchenko and Tymoshenko's conflicting economic philosophies led to continued disagreements in the following months. On September 8, Yushchenko dismissed Tymoshenko and her Cabinet after she had clashed with several of her Cabinet members. He then named economist Yuri Yekhanurov acting prime minister. Parliament confirmed Yekhanurov on September 22.

■ Juliet Johnson

See also **Europe; People in the news** (Viktor Yushchenko); **Russia: A Special Report.**

Unemployment. See Economics; Labor.

United Arab Emirates. See Middle East.

UNITED KINGDOM

In 2005, Prime Minister Tony Blair's Labour Party government won an unprecedented third term in office; the United Kingdom (U.K.) succeeded in its bid to host the 2012 Olympic Games; London was attacked by British suicide bombers; and the heir to the British throne, Prince Charles, married for the second time.

Terrorism. After the terrorist attacks on New York City and Washington, D.C., on Sept. 11, 2001, Blair's Labour government (first elected in 1997) supported United States President George W. Bush's "war on terror." The U.K. provided troops for both the war in Afghanistan and the war in Iraq. Nevertheless, British public opinion remained divided about the wars, and many British people were concerned that the country might itself become a target for terrorist activity launched by Islamic fundamentalist groups.

In December 2004, the Law Lords (the final court of appeal in the U.K.) had ruled that the detention of suspects without trial was illegal. (Nine foreign suspects had been detained in the U.K. following the U.S. terrorist attacks.) In March 2005, Parliament passed Home Secretary Charles Clarke's Prevention of Terrorism bill, which stated that British and foreign suspects would be subject to "control orders," including house arrest, the withdrawal of a passport, and electronic monitoring. Civil rights campaigners and some members of Parliament (MP's) denounced what they considered to be an infringement of civil liberties. As part of a compromise, the bill was to remain in force for only a year, after which it would be subject to review.

Iraq. Blair's government came under increasing pressure in 2005 to release the advice that its attorney general, Lord Goldsmith, had provided about the legality of the war in Iraq prior to the invasion in 2003. (A one-page summary of the advice had been made public in 2003.) The government eventually agreed to publish the full document in April 2005.

Lord Goldsmith advised that the invasion could be justified under an existing United Nations (UN) resolution. However, he qualified his opinion by saying that it would be safer to obtain a second UN resolution supporting the war. (The attempt to do so, which Blair supported, failed.) Blair insisted that the report demonstrated that his government's action had been legal under international law. Nevertheless, critics charged that the report should have been made available earlier and that Goldsmith's support for the war was more qualified than the public had been led to believe.

Economy. In the March 2005 budget, Chancellor of the Exchequer Gordon Brown maintained that he remained committed to increasing public spending. He also announced that the national minimum wage (which the Labour government had introduced) would increase from £4.85 to

The heir to the British throne, Prince Charles, and his wife, the former Camilla Parker-Bowles, leave St. George's Chapel in Windsor following a service of Prayer and Dedication blessing their marriage on April 9. Parker-Bowles took the title Duchess of Cornwall upon her marriage to Charles, the Prince of Wales.

£5.05 ($8.69) per hour in October.

During the summer, financial analysts criticized a move by Brown to manipulate his self-imposed "golden rule," which states that expenditures should be balanced by revenue over the course of an economic cycle. Brown changed the date at which the current economic cycle began from 1999 to 1997, which allowed the public finances to remain in balance. In his November 2005 prebudget report, Brown accepted that economic growth in the U.K. in 2005 would be only 1.75 percent, down from the 3 to 3.5 percent he had predicted earlier in the year and the weakest economic performance in a decade.

Collapse of Rover. The government was embarrassed in April when the U.K.'s only British-owned car manufacturing company, MG Rover, collapsed. About 5,000 jobs at the company's plant in Birmingham were lost following the failure of a partnership bid by a Chinese company, Shanghai Automotive Industrial Corporation. MG Rover's assets were subsequently purchased by another Chinese automaker, Nanjing Automobile Corp.

Election campaign. The prime minister announced in April that the general election would be held on May 5. (Under British law, the governing party sets the date of the election, which must take place within five years of the last election, subject to the government commanding a majority in Parliament). Labour was widely expected to win the election, despite the fact that many of its followers had opposed the prime minister's decision to support the United States in the Iraq War and to commit troops to the effort.

The Conservatives (the largest opposition party) were led by Michael Howard, whose strategy included promises to improve public services as well as the controversial issue of restricting immigrants

and asylum seekers. Critics charged Howard with both racism and hypocrisy, as he was the son of Jewish immigrants.

The Liberal Democrats, the main center party led by Charles Kennedy, campaigned on a pledge to increase income tax rates for high earners. The party emphasized that it was the only main party to oppose the Iraq War (though the party supported British troops once fighting began).

Election. In the May 5 general election, Blair was returned to power but with a dramatic reduction in Labour's majority (from 166 seats over the other parties' combined totals in the 2001 election to 65 seats in 2005). Of the 646 seats in parliament, Labour won 354; the Conservatives took 196; and the Liberal Democrats, 62. (The remaining seats went to smaller parties.) The turnout rose slightly, to 61.5 percent of the electorate from 59.4 percent in 2001.

Although Blair achieved a working majority and a third consecutive term in power for Labour (the first time the party had ever managed to capture three subsequent terms), many Labour voters had clearly opted to support other parties, particularly the Liberal Democrats. Labour's share of the popular vote (35.2 percent) was the lowest for a winning party in modern times.

The election also delivered mixed news to the Conservatives. Although they gained 33 seats, their share of the vote rose by only 0.6 percent, suggesting they had yet to make the necessary advances for a return to power.

In local elections also held on May 5, the Conservatives did better than in the general election, gaining 152 additional seats and 7 new councils. The Liberal Democrats gained 40 new seats and 3 more councils. However, Labour won three of the four mayoral elections. The party was embarrassed in April when six of its councilors in Birmingham lost their seats after a court found them guilty of falsifying mailed-in votes during the 2004 local elections.

Conservatives. Michael Howard's announcement on the day after the election that he would resign as leader of the Conservatives triggered a leadership election. In the opening rounds of the contest, former Conservative Chancellor of the Exchequer Kenneth Clarke and *shadow* Foreign Secretary Liam Fox were eliminated. (A shadow

Londoners celebrate in Trafalgar Square on September 13 the victory of England's cricket team over Australia in the Ashes tournament. The English-Australian classic, which began in 1882, was dubbed "the Ashes" by a London newspaper that proclaimed the death of British cricket in the face of Australian victory—"The body will be cremated, and the ashes taken to Australia."

secretary is a member of the opposition whose duty is to criticize the government in power and prepare to form a new government.) The choice was between the shadow home secretary, David Davis, and the new shadow education secretary, David Cameron. On December 6, Cameron was elected as leader of the party.

Cabinet reshuffle. Blair announced several changes to his Cabinet the day after the election. David Blunkett returned as work and pensions secretary. The former home secretary had been forced to leave the government in December 2004, after newspaper revelations that he had fast-tracked a visa for his former mistress's nanny. Blunkett was forced to resign again in November 2005 after failing to properly register his business dealings during his time away from the Cabinet. Blunkett was replaced by John Hutton.

Blair launched a new legislative program on May 17 when the queen opened the new session of Parliament. The program included controversial measures such as the introduction of national identity cards and a law outlawing the incitement of religious hatred. Plans to hold a referendum on the new European Constitution were postponed after the French and Dutch rejected the document in referenda in May and June.

Olympic bid. In July, the International Olympic Committee announced that London had won its bid to host the 2012 Olympic Games. The plan promised to help regenerate much of the city's East End. Celebrations were cut short, however, by the London bombings, which took place the day after the Olympic committee announced its decision.

London bombings. On the morning of July 7, 2005, three bombs exploded on the London Underground public transportation system and a fourth, on a London bus. Fifty-two civilians, as well as the 4 bombers, were killed, and 700 people were injured. The police determined that the explosions had been detonated by British suicide bombers and launched a major investigation into possible accomplices. Within days, the bombers were identified from closed-circuit television footage as Muslims who had been born in the U.K. Muslim leaders in Britain condemned the bombings and promised to assist with the suppression of extremist groups, including foreign-born clerics who were thought to be inciting violence in the U.K.

On July 21, further bombings were attempted on the London Underground, but the bombs, which had been left on trains, failed to explode. The following day, a Brazilian man, Jean Charles de Menezes, was shot dead on a train in Stockwell, South London. The police had been trailing Menezes because they had information that suggested he might be a suicide bomber. Within 24 hours, it became clear that Menezes was innocent and merely lived in the same block of flats as one of the suspects who had been under surveillance. The Metropolitan Police Commissioner, Sir Ian Blair, apologized but insisted that the police must be ready to shoot suspected suicide bombers. (British police are usually unarmed.) Four Muslims were apprehended and charged in connection with the July 21 attempted bombings, and a fifth suspect was captured in Rome.

Blair's government promised new measures to combat terrorism in 2005. However, it had difficulty gaining parliamentary support in November for a measure that would allow the police to detain suspected terrorists for 90 days without being charged while they were under investigation. Labour rebels, together with the opposition parties, argued that the legislation was a threat to civil liberties. Blair's government suffered its first major defeat in Parliament when the bill was voted down, 322 to 291. Forty-nine Labour MP's voted against the government and supported an alternative measure calling for a maximum of 28 days' detention without charge.

Faced with a serious blow to his authority, Blair responded, "Sometimes it is better to do the right thing and lose, than to win doing the wrong thing." Opponents and journalists argued that the vote suggested that Blair would not remain in power for long and that future rebellions by Labour's own MP's would make it difficult for the government (with its smaller majority) to get its legislative program passed by Parliament.

Railways. A manslaughter trial of the owners of Balfour Beatty, a company responsible for railway track maintenance, ended in a verdict of "not guilty" in July. Charges had been brought against the owners following the Hatfield rail crash of 2000, in which 4 people died and 102 others were injured during a derailment caused by a cracked rail. The owners were subsequently fined in October 2005 for "sustained industrial negligence."

The owners of the engineering firm Jarvis were found not guilty of manslaughter in October. Charges had been brought against Jarvis following the 2002 Potters Bar crash, in which 7 people died and 76 others were injured in a derailment caused by loose bolts.

Deaths. Two former prime ministers died in 2005. Edward Heath, a Conservative, who died at age 89, had governed Britain from 1970 to 1974. James Callaghan (Labour), who died at age 92, had run the country from 1976 to 1979.

Two leading Labour politicians died in 2005. Robin Cook, the former Labour foreign secretary and leader of the House of Commons, who had resigned from the Cabinet because of his opposition to the Iraq War, died at age 59 in August. Marjorie (Mo) Mowlam died at age 55 in August. Mowlam had been Blair's first secretary of state for Northern Ireland and had helped achieve the Good

Friday agreement of 1998 that produced a cease-fire in the province.

Royal wedding. In February 2005, the heir to the British throne, Prince Charles, announced that he would marry his long-term partner, Camilla Parker-Bowles. The couple chose a civil rather than a religious ceremony, as Parker-Bowles was divorced. Princess Diana, Charles's former wife who was killed in an automobile accident in 1997, had blamed Charles's relationship with Parker-Bowles for the break-up of her own marriage to Charles.

The wedding took place on April 9, 2005, one day later than originally planned so that the prince could attend the funeral of Pope John Paul II in Rome. The wedding was held in Windsor Guildhall, with Prince Charles's son William and Camilla's son, Tom, acting as witnesses. Charles's mother, Queen Elizabeth II, did not attend the wedding. However, she was present at a subsequent service in Windsor Castle at which the Archbishop of Canterbury blessed the marriage.

Charles's new wife took the title of Duchess of Cornwall. Should Charles ascend to the throne, she is to be known as "Princess Consort," rather than "Queen." In November, Charles and Camilla traveled to the United States on their first tour as a couple. ■ Rohan McWilliam

See also **Europe; Iraq; Northern Ireland.**

United Kingdom, Prime Minister of.

Tony Blair in May 2005 became the first Labour Party leader to win a third successive term in office. On February 4, Blair had set a record as the longest-serving Labour prime minister in British history. In 2004, he had announced that he intended to serve a full term if reelected but would retire before a fourth election.

Critics considered the loss of nearly two-thirds of Labour's majority in the 2005 election as a rebuff for Blair, even though the party had won. Many Labour supporters objected to Blair's support of the United States in the Iraq War and voted for other parties. Following the July 7 terrorist bombings in London, critics also claimed that Blair's support for the Iraq War had made the United Kingdom a target for terrorists. Blair, however, insisted that he would continue to introduce reforms in public services—particularly health and education, which he considered his legacy—and to protect national security.

Blair's standing was damaged in November when one of his leading allies, Work and Pensions Secretary David Blunkett, was forced to resign from the government for a second time. Shortly afterwards, his government suffered its first defeat in Parliament (over a counter-terrorism bill) since it was elected in 1997. ■ Rohan McWilliam

See also **United Kingdom.**

Queen Elizabeth II congratulates Prime Minister Tony Blair at Buckingham Palace on May 6, the day after Blair's Labour Party won an unprecedented third term in office.

United Nations. The United Nations (UN) General Assembly opened a three-day summit on Sept. 14, 2005, to mark the 60th anniversary of the world organization, which was founded on Oct. 24, 1945. The meeting was attended by some 150 presidents and prime ministers in the largest gathering of government leaders in history.

The summit concluded with the adoption of a World Summit outcome document, the aim of which was to reform the aging organization and speed up implementation of a 2000 program known as the Millennium Development Goals. The goals include reducing world poverty by half, halting the spread of HIV/AIDS, and universalizing primary education by 2015. In opening the summit, UN Secretary-General Kofi Annan said the document would achieve "vital breakthroughs" in areas such as the global fight against terrorism and protecting populations against genocide, war crimes, ethnic cleansing, and crimes against humanity. Reform-minded governments and non-governmental organizations expressed frustration that the outcome document had largely failed in providing impetus in bringing education to all young people, decisively fighting poverty, and ending nuclear proliferation.

The outcome document included approval for the establishment of a new Human Rights Council and a Peacebuilding Commission to help countries emerging from conflict. Reform was left to the General Assembly session presided over by President Jan Eliasson, a Swedish diplomat. Tensions erupted over details of reform, with a majority of delegates refusing to relinquish to the secretary-general the power to decide on UN programs.

Oil-for-food scandal. The Independent Inquiry Committee, established to investigate charges that UN officials were guilty of corruption and accepting bribes in the oil-for-food program, issued its final report on Oct. 27, 2005. The committee was headed by former U.S. Federal Reserve Chairman Paul Volcker. The oil-for-food program had been established in 1996 to allow the Iraqi government to sell oil and use the proceeds to purchase humanitarian goods for Iraqis affected by UN sanctions. The UN had imposed sanctions on Iraq in 1990, after then-president Saddam Hussein invaded Kuwait.

According to the report, $64 billion of oil was sold through the program from 1997 to 2003, and $34.5 billion of humanitarian goods were purchased. Hussein's regime received $229 million for "oil surcharges," and 148 companies involved in the transactions were paid $1.5 billion in kickbacks.

In addition, Annan was alleged to have used his position to influence the selection in 1998 of a Swiss-based company—at which his son, Kojo, was employed—to provide inspection services to the program. On March 29, 2005, the committee cleared Annan of any wrongdoing. Nevertheless, the investigators criticized Annan for failing to adequately scrutinize his son's possible conflict of interest in the matter. Annan denied having had knowledge of the awarding of contracts to companies doing business with the program.

On August 8, a former director of the program, Benon Sevan of Cyprus, was accused of "illicit activities" in collusion with a Middle East-based petroleum company. Sevan allegedly sold for profit Iraqi oil that was intended for the humanitarian program. Sevan served as director of the $64-billion program from 1996 to 2003.

UN Security Council. Several proposals to overhaul the UN in 2005 included expanding the Security Council to make it more representative. In May, Brazil, Germany, India, and Japan signed a draft resolution demanding that six new permanent members be added to the council—the four countries themselves and two additional African countries. The African Union, comprising 53 members, also called for two permanent seats in the council. The United States opposed changing the composition of the council, preferring that the UN first carry out reforms of its management and secretariat. Because of the lack of consensus, proposals to enlarge the council remained stalled.

On October 10, the UN General Assembly elected five new members for the Security Council—Congo (Brazzaville), Ghana, Peru, Qatar, and Slovakia. Those nations were to begin a two-year term in January 2006, joining the council's permanent members—China, France, Russia, the United Kingdom, and the United States; and five nonpermanent members elected in 2004—Argentina, Denmark, Greece, Japan, and Tanzania.

Africa. On March 31, 2005, the UN Security Council adopted a resolution demanding that the International Criminal Court at The Hague prosecute those responsible for the killing of civilians in Sudan's Darfur region. The decision was based on findings by an international commission of inquiry that concluded that the killing amounted to crimes against humanity and war crimes but not genocide. The UN estimated that more than 180,000 people were killed and about 2 million displaced from 2003 to 2005 by fighting between Arab militias and two African rebel groups.

Nuclear nonproliferation. On October 7, the Norwegian parliament awarded the Nobel Peace Prize to the International Atomic Energy Agency and its director, Mohamed ElBaradei. The UN nuclear watchdog agency, based in Vienna, Austria, strives to ensure that nuclear science is used for peaceful purposes to serve humanity.

■ J. Tuyet Nguyen

See also **Nobel prizes; Sudan.**

United States, Government of the.

The United States continued to wage war in Iraq through 2005. The U.S.-led coalition, joined by newly trained Iraqi forces, engaged in guerrilla action against loyalists of former Iraqi President Saddam Hussein's Baath Party and Islamic militants who had infiltrated into Iraq largely through Syria. At the end of 2005, some 2,150 U.S. soldiers had died in Iraq since the war began in 2003.

Intelligence assessment. President George W. Bush on Feb. 17, 2005, named U.S. Ambassador to Iraq John Negroponte director of national intelligence. His mission was to oversee the 15 intelligence operations conducted by the U.S. government, including the Federal Bureau of Investigation and the Central Intelligence Agency (CIA). The U.S. Congress created the position in 2004 in legislation based upon recommendations in *The 9/11 Commission Report* issued by the National Commission on Terrorist Attacks upon the United States.

The Commission on Terrorist Attacks issued its final report on Dec. 5, 2005, on the federal government's progress in making the nation secure from terrorist attacks. Chairman Thomas Kean, a former Republican governor of New Jersey, and Vice Chairman Lee Hamilton, a former Democratic congressman from Indiana, gave the government "more F's than A's" on achieving the recommendations issued in 2004. Both men expressed concerns that the United States remained at risk for terrorist attacks because the government had yet to enact most of the commission's recommendations —including reallocating security funds for cities most at risk, that is, cities like New York and Washington, D.C., that have symbolic landmarks; allowing police and fire departments to communicate across radio spectrums; and screening cargo loads on passenger planes. The commission did give the Bush administration an "A–" for curbing terrorist financing.

Intelligence failings. On March 31, 2005, the Commission on the Intelligence Capabilities of the United States Regarding Weapons of Mass Destruction reported to President Bush that U.S. spy agencies had been "dead wrong" in their assessments of Iraqi weapons of mass destruction. The commission was established to examine how and why various agencies failed to uncover errors in intelligence reports used by the Bush administration to justify the Iraq War. The authors of the report found that the nation's spy apparatus was deeply flawed and urged a complete overhaul. The commission recommended that Director Negroponte be given greater control over all intelligence operations.

Homeland security. Richard L. Skinner, inspector general of the Department of Homeland Security, issued a report on April 19 that was highly critical of the Transportation Security Administration (TSA), the agency responsible for

Demonstrators march outside the White House in July, demanding that President George W. Bush end a cover-up of who in his administration exposed Valerie Plame as a Central Intelligence Agency operative. In October, vice presidential advisor I. Lewis Libby, Jr., not presidential advisor Karl Rove, was indicted for allegedly obstructing justice and perjuring himself before a grand jury in the "Plamegate" investigation.

protecting the nation's transportation systems. According to the report, TSA officials had spent hundreds of thousands of dollars on unnecessary art, decorations, and kitchens at a TSA "security center" in Herndon, Virginia, an office used by 79 full-time employees.

In October, federal auditors and procurement specialists disclosed that a corporation with a contract to improve the security of the U.S. transportation system appeared to be overbilling the TSA by millions of dollars. Auditors alleged that the project was costing double the anticipated amount per month and was far from complete.

Hurricane fallout. Michael D. Brown, head of the Federal Emergency Management Agency (FEMA), resigned on September 12 amid mounting criticism of FEMA's response to Hurricane Katrina, which devastated the Gulf Coast on August 29. FEMA, a Department of Homeland Security agency, helps communities prepare for and recover from natural and human-made disasters. Department Secretary Michael Chertoff had removed Brown from oversight of relief efforts on September 9 and replaced him with U.S. Coast Guard Vice Admiral Thad W. Allen. Brown's resignation coincided with news reports that he had inflated his resume, had little experience in disaster relief, and

had organized horse shows before being appointed to FEMA. The federal response to the Katrina disaster led to widespread media speculation about Homeland Security's effectiveness in the face of future terrorist attacks.

Skyscraper safety. The National Institute of Standards and Technology (NIST) issued a report on June 23 recommending the adoption of new rules in the planning, construction, and operation of skyscrapers. The NIST is a nonregulatory federal agency that promotes innovation and industrial competitiveness by advancing measurement science, standards, and technology. The suggestion for new rules grew out of a federal study of the collapse of the World Trade Center towers in New York City on Sept. 11, 2001. The authors of the report suggested better evacuation strategies in the nation's tallest buildings, stronger elevators and stairways, and improved methods of testing a building's fireproofing.

Separation of powers upheld. The Court of Appeals for the District of Columbia Circuit ruled on May 10, 2005, that Vice President Dick Cheney did not have to testify about the formulation of Bush administration energy policies. The ruling held that the administration was under no obligation to divulge the names of people who had

FEDERAL SPENDING   United States budget for fiscal 2005*

Billions of dollars

National defense	493.9
International affairs	34.4
General science, space, technology	24.5
Energy	0.6
Natural resources and environment	26.2
Agriculture	28.4
Commerce and housing credit	7.4
Transportation	68.1
Community and regional development	25.1
Education, training, employment, and social services	97.9
Health	250.4
Social security	523.3
Medicare	298.6
Income security	347.6
Veterans' benefits and services	70.2
Administration of justice	39.7
General government	17.7
Interest	184.1
Undistributed offsetting receipts	−65.2
Total budget outlays	**2,472.9**

*Oct. 1, 2004, to Sept. 30, 2005.
Source: U.S. Department of the Treasury.

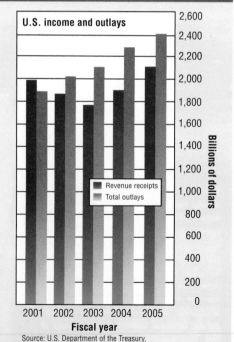

U.S. income and outlays

Revenue receipts
Total outlays

Billions of dollars

Fiscal year
2001 2002 2003 2004 2005

Source: U.S. Department of the Treasury.

SELECTED AGENCIES AND BUREAUS OF THE U.S. GOVERNMENT*

Executive Office of the President
President, George W. Bush
  Vice President, Richard B. Cheney
  White House Chief of Staff, Andrew H. Card, Jr.
  Presidential Press Secretary, Scott McClellan
  Assistant to the President for Domestic Policy,
    Claude A. Allen
  Assistant to the President for National Security Affairs,
    Stephen J. Hadley
  Director, Office of Science and Technology Policy,
    John H. Marburger III
  Council of Economic Advisers—Vacant†
  Office of Management and Budget—
    Josh B. Bolten, Director
  Office of National Drug Control Policy—
    John P. Walters, Director
  U.S. Trade Representative, Robert J. Portman

Department of Agriculture
Secretary of Agriculture, Michael O. Johanns

Department of Commerce
Secretary of Commerce, Carlos M. Gutierrez
  Bureau of Economic Analysis—J. Steven Landefeld, Director
  Bureau of the Census—Charles Louis Kincannon, Director

Department of Defense
Secretary of Defense, Donald H. Rumsfeld
  Secretary of the Air Force, Michael W. Wynne
  Secretary of the Army, Francis J. Harvey
  Secretary of the Navy, Gordon R. England
  Joint Chiefs of Staff—
    General Richard B. Myers, Chairman
    General Teed Michael Moseley, Chief of Staff, Air Force
    General Peter J. Schoomaker, Chief of Staff, Army
    Admiral Michael G. Mullen, Chief of Naval Operations
    General Michael W. Hagee, Commandant, Marine Corps

Department of Education
Secretary of Education, Margaret Spellings

Department of Energy
Secretary of Energy, Samuel Wright Bodman

Department of Health and Human Services
Secretary of Health and Human Services,
  Michael O. Leavitt
  Office of Public Health and Science—Cristina Beato,
    Acting Assistant Secretary
  Centers for Disease Control and Prevention—
    Julie Louise Gerberding, Director
  Food and Drug Administration—Lester M. Crawford,
    Commissioner
  National Institutes of Health—Elias A. Zerhouni, Director
  Surgeon General of the United States, Richard H. Carmona

Department of Homeland Security
Secretary of Homeland Security, Michael Chertoff
  Bureau of Citizenship and Immigration Services—
    Alfonso Aguilar, Acting Director
  U.S. Coast Guard—Admiral Thomas H. Collins, Commandant
  U.S. Secret Service—W. Ralph Basham, Director
  Federal Emergency Management Agency—R. David Paulison,
    Acting Director

Department of Housing and Urban Development
Secretary of Housing and Urban Development,
  Alphonso R. Jackson

Department of the Interior
Secretary of the Interior, Gale A. Norton

Department of Justice
Attorney General, Alberto R. Gonzales
  Federal Bureau of Prisons—Harley G. Lappin, Director
  Drug Enforcement Administration—
    Karen P. Tandy, Administrator
  Federal Bureau of Investigation—
    Robert S. Mueller III, Director
  Acting Solicitor General, Paul D. Clement

Department of Labor
Secretary of Labor, Elaine L. Chao

Department of State
Secretary of State, Condoleezza Rice
  U.S. Ambassador to the United Nations, John R. Bolton

Department of Transportation
Secretary of Transportation, Norman Y. Mineta
  Federal Aviation Administration—
    Marion C. Blakey, Administrator

Department of the Treasury
Secretary of the Treasury, John W. Snow
  Internal Revenue Service—Mark W. Everson, Commissioner
  Treasurer of the United States, Anna Escobedo Cabral
  Office of Thrift Supervision—John M. Reich, Director

Department of Veterans Affairs
Secretary of Veterans Affairs, R. James Nicholson

Supreme Court of the United States
Chief Justice of the United States, John G. Roberts, Jr.
  Associate Justices—
    John Paul Stevens   David H. Souter
    Sandra Day O'Connor‡   Clarence Thomas
    Antonin Scalia   Ruth Bader Ginsburg
    Anthony M. Kennedy   Stephen G. Breyer

Congressional officials
President of the Senate pro tempore, Ted Stevens
Senate Majority Leader, William H. Frist
Senate Minority Leader, Harry Reid
Speaker of the House, J. Dennis Hastert
Acting House Majority Leader, Roy Blunt
House Minority Leader, Nancy Pelosi
Congressional Budget Office—Douglas Holtz-Eakin, Director
Government Accountability Office—David M. Walker, Comptroller
  General of the United States
Library of Congress—James H. Billington, Librarian of Congress

Independent agencies
Central Intelligence Agency—Porter J. Goss, Director
Commission on Civil Rights—Gerald A. Reynolds, Chairperson
Commission of Fine Arts—Earl A. Powell III, Chairperson
Consumer Product Safety Commission—
  Harold D. Stratton, Jr., Chairperson
Corporation for National and Community Service—
  Stephen Goldsmith, Chairman
Environmental Protection Agency—Stephen L. Johnson, Administrator
Equal Employment Opportunity Commission—
  Cari M. Dominguez, Chair
Federal Communications Commission—Kevin J. Martin, Chairman
Federal Deposit Insurance Corporation—
  Donald E. Powell, Chairman
Federal Election Commission—Scott E. Thomas, Chairman
Federal Reserve System Board of Governors—
  Alan Greenspan, Chairman‡
Federal Trade Commission—Deborah Platt Majoras, Chairman
General Services Administration—Stephen A. Perry, Administrator
National Aeronautics and Space Administration—Michael D. Griffin,
  Administrator
National Endowment for the Arts—Michael Dana Gioia, Chairman
National Endowment for the Humanities—Bruce Cole, Chairman
National Labor Relations Board—Robert J. Battista, Chairman
National Railroad Passenger Corporation (Amtrak)—
  David Hughes, Acting President and CEO
National Science Foundation—Arden L. Bement, Jr., Director
National Transportation Safety Board—
  Mark V. Rosenker, Acting Chairman
Nuclear Regulatory Commission—Nils J. Diaz, Chairman
Peace Corps—Gaddi H. Vasquez, Director
Securities and Exchange Commission—
  Christopher Cox, Chairman
Selective Service System—William A. Chatfield, Director
Small Business Administration—Hector V. Barreto, Jr., Administrator
Smithsonian Institution—Lawrence M. Small, Secretary
Social Security Administration—Jo Anne Barnhart, Commissioner
U.S. Postal Service—John E. Potter, Postmaster General

*As of Dec. 31, 2005.   †Vacant seat to be filled in 2006.
‡Retirement planned for 2006.

been consulted during the formulation of the energy policy in 2001. The Sierra Club, a San Francisco-based environmental group, and Judicial Watch, a Washington, D.C.-based public interest law firm, filed the lawsuit in an attempt to force the vice president to reveal how the energy policy had been crafted and who had participated. The two groups claimed that under the Federal Advisory Committee Act the public was entitled to know the extent to which oil and gas and public utilities executives had helped craft the policy. In an 8-0 decision, the appeals court held that no disclosure was necessary.

Corporation for Public Broadcasting. The inspector general of the Corporation for Public Broadcasting (CPB) reported on Nov. 15, 2005, that the former CPB chairman, Kenneth Y. Tomlinson, had broken federal law and violated the CPB rules and code of ethics in his efforts to promote a conservative agenda. CPB, a private, nonprofit organization that promotes public television and radio in the United States, is charged by law to insulate programming from politics. After an internal investigation, CPB Inspector General Kenneth A. Konz concluded that Tomlinson had exceeded his authority in his determination to address what Tomlinson viewed as a liberal bias in public broadcasting. Konz documented numerous occasions in which Tomlinson circumvented CPB contracting procedures, including hiring consultants to monitor the political leanings of guests on "Now with Bill Moyers" and attempting to raise funds for a public television program featuring conservative editorial writers from *The Wall Street Journal*. Tomlinson resigned as chairman on November 3.

No Child Left Behind. The Government Accountability Office (GAO), an independent agency in the legislative branch of the U.S. government, ruled on September 30 that the U.S. Department of Education had violated federal law when it paid commentator and columnist Armstrong Williams $240,000 to offer favorable publicity to the No Child Left Behind program initiated in 2001. The law establishing No Child Left Behind requires states to identify poorly performing public schools and allow children in those schools to transfer to better-performing public schools in the same districts. An internal Education Department inquiry into the contract with Williams found on April 15, 2005, that the arrangement was ill-advised and a waste of money but did not violate federal law. However, GAO officials determined that the contract violated a federal law that bars the government from secretly spreading propaganda.

Plamegate. The Bush administration found itself embroiled in controversy in 2005 over the leak of the name of an undercover CIA operative. Special prosecutor Peter Fitzgerald, on October 28,

indicted Vice President Dick Cheney's chief of staff, I. Lewis "Scooter" Libby, Jr., on charges that Libby had obstructed justice, made false statements, and committed perjury while testifying before a federal grand jury. Libby resigned after being indicted. The charges revolved around whether Libby in 2003 purposely revealed to journalists the fact that Valerie Plame worked secretly at the CIA. A federal law prohibits exposing the identity of a covert agent.

Plame's position at the CIA was revealed in July 2003 in a syndicated column by Robert D. Novak, who claimed to have gotten the information from "senior administration officials." Political experts suggested that she had been exposed to discredit or punish her husband, Joseph C. Wilson IV, a diplomat. Novak's column appeared days after Wilson had written an opinion piece in *The New York Times* accusing the administration of twisting intelligence to justify going to war in Iraq. Wilson criticized President Bush for claiming in his 2003 State of the Union address that deposed Iraqi President Saddam Hussein had obtained uranium in Niger for atomic weapons. Sent to Niger by the CIA in 2002, Wilson had disproved that claim before the president made his speech. The president's justification for going to war was based on assertions that Hussein had weapons of mass destruction and was developing nuclear weapons.

A number of journalists were ordered to testify about their knowledge of Plame. On July 6, 2005, a federal judge had a *New York Times* reporter, Judith Miller, jailed after she refused to reveal who had told her of Plame's CIA connection. After spending several weeks in jail, Miller did testify that I. Lewis Libby had been her source. A second journalist, *Time* magazine reporter Matthew Cooper, avoided jail time by cooperating with Fitzgerald. Bob Woodward, a prominent journalist with *The Washington Post*, testified in November that a member of the Bush administration, though not Libby, had revealed Plame's identity to him before Novak had published the story.

Prosecutor Peter Fitzgerald's investigations continued through the end of 2005. He refused to confirm or deny whether more indictments would be handed down.

Federal Reserve chairman. On October 24, President Bush named Ben Bernanke to succeeded Alan Greenspan as chairman of the Federal Reserve System (the Fed), the nation's central bank. Bernanke served on the Fed's board of governors for nearly three years before being named chairman of the president's Council of Economic Advisers. ■ Geoffrey A. Campbell

See also **Armed forces; Congress of the United States; Newspaper; People in the news** (Michael Chertoff; Peter Fitzgerald; I. Lewis Libby, Jr.); **State government; United States, President of the.**

United States, President of the.

On Jan. 20, 2005, George W. Bush took the oath of office to begin his second term as president. In his inaugural address, the president proclaimed the United States to be a worldwide liberator committed to aiding oppressed nations.

After winning reelection in November 2004, the president stated that he had earned "political capital" in the campaign and intended to "spend it" rebuilding Iraq, waging the war on terror, and reforming Social Security and the U.S. tax code.

Social Security. On Feb. 2, 2005, the president, in his State of the Union address, proposed creating personal Social Security accounts that would be invested in stock market mutual funds. In March, he launched a "60 stops in 60 days" campaign to sell his plan to the public. The plan, however, met with little public enthusiasm, and political experts had declared it "dead" by mid-summer.

Bolton nomination. On August 1, President Bush, using his power to make appointments while Congress was in recess, appointed John Bolton ambassador to the United Nations (UN). The nomination had been held up in the Senate because Democrats objected to the fact that Bolton often had expressed contempt for the UN.

Political troubles. In early September, the president returned to Washington, D.C., after a Texas vacation, to find a political storm brewing over the government's response to victims of Hurricane Katrina, which had devastated the Gulf Coast and New Orleans on August 29. According to political experts, the failure of the Federal Emergency Management Agency to respond in a timely fashion proved politically disastrous for the president.

The troubles continued. During the week of October 24, the number of soldiers killed in the Iraq War climbed to more than 2,000; Harriet Miers, Bush's nominee to replace Justice Sandra Day O'Connor on the U.S. Supreme Court, was forced to withdraw in the face of mounting criticism that she lacked the necessary experience; and a federal grand jury indicted Vice President Dick Cheney's chief of staff, I. Lewis Libby, Jr., on charges that he had obstructed justice and committed perjury during an investigation of who in the Bush administration had revealed the identity of a Central Intelligence Agency operative. By mid-November, President Bush's public approval rating had fallen to the lowest level of his presidency, with 60 percent of people polled disapproving of his performance in office.

■ Geoffrey A. Campbell

See also **Congress of the United States; Disasters: A Special Report; Republican Party; Social Security: A Special Report; Supreme Court; Taxation; United States, Government of the.**

George W. Bush is sworn in for a second time as the 43rd president of the United States on January 20. In his 21-minute address, the president proclaimed the United States to be a worldwide liberator— "The survival of liberty in our land increasingly depends on the success of liberty in other lands."

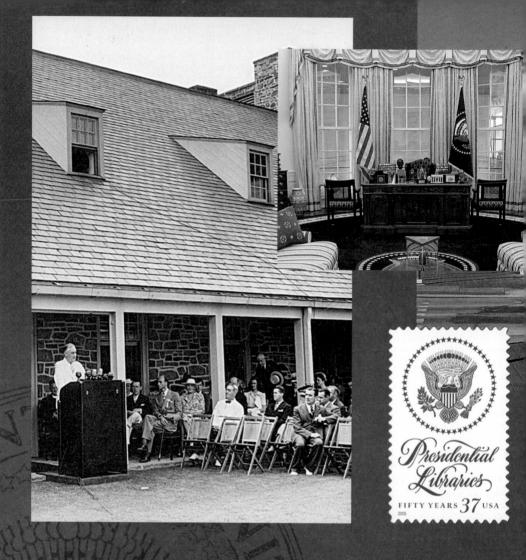

PRESERVING LEGACIES

By Michael J. Devine

THE DIRECTOR OF THE
HARRY S. TRUMAN
PRESIDENTIAL LIBRARY
OFFERS AN INSIDER'S
VIEW OF A RAREFIED
WORLD.

Franklin D. Roosevelt (opposite page, far left) speaks at the dedication of his presidential library at Hyde Park, New York, in 1941. A replica of the Oval Office (opposite page, center) as the room looked during Bill Clinton's administration (1993-2001) is a permanent exhibit at the William J. Clinton Presidential Library and Museum in Little Rock, Arkansas. A 2005 U.S. postage stamp (opposite page, bottom) commemorates the 50th anniversary of the Presidential Libraries Act of 1955.

The Abraham Lincoln Presidential Library and Museum (top left) opened in Springfield, Illinois, in 2005. A 1966 photograph of Lyndon B. Johnson (top right) catches the 36th president in a contemplative mood. Former President Ronald W. Reagan (above, second from left) poses with President George H. W. Bush and former Presidents Jimmy Carter, Gerald R. Ford, and Richard M. Nixon at the dedication of the Ronald Reagan Presidential Library and Museum in Simi Valley, California, on Nov. 4, 1991.

Presidential libraries are not really libraries in the traditional sense; rather they are archives, repositories, and museums. They hold the official documents of a president and presidential administration, the president's personal papers, and materials including gifts from foreign governments and from the people of the United States pertaining to the president's life and era. The libraries also house photos, film, audiotapes, and in the newer libraries, extensive electronic records. All presidential libraries offer visitors exhibits and displays about presidents and their legacies. Presidential historian Michael Beschloss observed that "walking into one of the [presidential] libraries is almost like walking into a president's autobiography." Indeed, the location of the library, its architectural style, and its exhibits and programs all reflect the individual president's character and qualities.

The mission of presidential libraries is to preserve all the historical materials of the presidents they represent and to make these materials available to the public for both research and enjoyment. While scholars use the collections of presidential libraries for research, the general public visits the museum exhibits and participates in a wide range of public and educational programming. Behind impressive entranceways and exhibition galleries, professional archivists and curators arrange and describe extensive and complex collections of historical materials. Experts review *classified* (secret) presidential papers to determine if they can be declassified without disclosing government secrets or compromising national security. Scholars study the presidents' papers and artifacts for endeavors that range from doctoral dissertations to books and documentary films. Younger scholars use the collections for classroom assignments and innovative school projects. However, the vast majority of visitors to the presidential libraries are school groups and tourists who view the museum exhibits or attend a public event, such as a lecture or policy forum. Furthermore, the amazing expansion of the Internet has made presidential libraries and their extraordinary collections available to millions of people throughout the world. All presidential libraries offer information on Web sites about their holdings, exhibits, and programs.

Preserving the record

How presidential libraries came into being is a complex story that begins with George Washington. When the nation's first president left office in 1797, he packed all his official papers, which were considered his personal property, into two trunks, placed them on the back of a stagecoach, and took them to his Virginia estate, Mount Vernon. Washington planned to build a modest library at Mount Vernon to house his small archive and use it as a place to write and meet with important guests. However, he died before carrying out his plan.

Subsequent presidents during the 1800's and early 1900's made various plans, or no plans at all, for the proper care and disposition of official papers. The papers of John Adams and his son, John Quincy Adams, for example, found a superb home in the Massachusetts Historical Society in Boston. The children of President Rutherford B. Hayes donated their father's residence, Spiegel Grove, to the state of Ohio. In return, the state in 1916 built an attractive library on the grounds at

The author:
Michael J. Devine is director of the Harry S. Truman Presidential Library in Independence, Missouri.

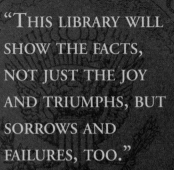

"THIS LIBRARY WILL SHOW THE FACTS, NOT JUST THE JOY AND TRIUMPHS, BUT SORROWS AND FAILURES, TOO."

LYNDON B. JOHNSON, AT THE DEDICATION OF HIS LIBRARY, MAY 22, 1971

Visitors to the Lyndon Baines Johnson Library and Museum in Austin, Texas (above), examine portraits of former first ladies, a permanent exhibit at the largest of the presidential libraries. The libraries typically showcase both permanent and temporary exhibits and provide scholars with access to historic documents.

President Franklin D. Roosevelt's study (above) at the Roosevelt Library contains a portrait of his mother, Sara Delano Roosevelt, and one of his custom-made wheelchairs. Roosevelt used the room as a part-time office and broadcast a "fireside chat" radio address from there during World War II (1939-1945). The grave of President Richard M. Nixon (right) is at the Richard Nixon Library & Birthplace in Yorba Linda, California. The library is on a parcel of land once owned by the president's father and includes the house in which Nixon was born (background) in 1913.

Spiegel Grove to house and display materials documenting Hayes's Civil War record and his services as a member of Congress, governor of Ohio, and president of the United States. The Library of Congress eventually purchased the papers of George Washington, Thomas Jefferson, Andrew Jackson, and other presidents of the 1800's from their relatives or heirs. However, the papers of several presidents—notably John Tyler, Zachary Taylor, and Franklin Pierce—were lost or destroyed.

Robert Todd Lincoln, son of Abraham Lincoln, withheld many of his father's papers from the public for decades after his father's death in 1865. Robert Lincoln wanted to preserve his family's privacy and was concerned about the sensitive and emotional state of his grieving mother. He allowed only a few people—Judge David Davis and Lincoln's White House secretaries, John G. Nicolay and John Hay—to examine and use the papers. Sadly, Robert Lincoln's excessive secretiveness only caused speculations that the Lincoln family had something to hide, which they did not. By the time Robert Lincoln finally turned over most of his father's presidential papers to the Library of Congress in 1919 (with the condition that they not be opened until 21 years after his death), many of the former president's private and nonpresidential papers had been

Former President Harry S. Truman (left) greets fellow Missourian Thomas Hart Benton at the unveiling of *Independence and the Opening of the West*, at the Truman Library in 1961. The mural, in the library's entrance hall, interprets the early history of Truman's hometown, Independence, Missouri.

scattered across the country. They are housed to this day in such diverse institutions as Brown University in Providence, Rhode Island; the Huntington Library in San Marino, California; the Chicago Historical Society; the Abraham Lincoln Presidential Library and Museum in Springfield, Illinois; and the National Archives and Records Administration (NARA), a federal government agency in College Park, Maryland.

In 1903, the Library of Congress established a presidential papers collection and began trying to persuade recent presidents and their families to donate their presidential papers to the government. Some presidents or their families agreed—most notably, Theodore Roosevelt, William H. Taft, and Edith Bolling Wilson, the widow of Woodrow Wilson—but others were not so cooperative. After President Warren G. Harding died in office in 1923, his widow, Florence Kling Harding, spent several weeks in the White House burning as many of her late husband's papers as she could find. Perhaps Mrs. Harding was worried that the papers might contain information that would link her husband, his friends, and maybe even herself to the scandals that eventually blighted her husband's legacy. Unfortunately, until the 1930's, more than 150 years after the founding of the republic, the critical and sensitive issue of the preservation of the records of U.S. presidents was still left largely to chance.

FDR sets a precedent

The haphazard preservation of presidential records finally ended in 1939, when President Franklin D. Roosevelt (FDR) set an example that has been followed, with some modifications, ever since. Roosevelt and his family decided to donate a parcel of land on their property at Hyde Park, New York, along with Roosevelt's presidential papers to the National Archives (now NARA), which would administer his presidential library. The building was constructed with privately donated money. Roosevelt was still president when the library was dedicated on June 30, 1941, and he frequently used his office at the library during the remaining four years of his life. However, since he died in office, he never had the opportunity to retire to his library to write his memoirs as he had intended.

In 1953, President Harry S. Truman expressed his intention to donate the records of his administration to the National Archives and establish a presidential library on the model of the Roosevelt Library. The Harry S. Truman Presidential Library was built in Truman's hometown, Independence, Missouri.

On Aug. 12, 1955, President Dwight D. Eisenhower signed the Presidential Libraries Act into law. The legislation allowed the government to accept future presidential libraries. Over the next 25 years, the papers of Herbert Hoover, Eisenhower, John F. Kennedy, Lyndon B. Johnson, Gerald R. Ford, and Jimmy Carter were donated to federally managed presidential libraries built with private and state and local government funds.

The Nixon tapes

In 1974, Richard M. Nixon, following his resignation from the presidency, agreed to donate his presidential materials to the federal government. However, he demanded that his office tape recordings, the recordings that had become notorious in the Watergate scandal of 1973-1974, as well as certain papers, be destroyed. Their destruction was unacceptable to NARA as well as to the U.S. Department of Justice, still investigating Nixon administration activities. The U.S. Congress responded with the Presidential Records and Materials Preservation Act (1974), which President Ford signed into law. The legislation established the government's complete control over Nixon's presidential papers and required that they remain deposited in the Washington, D.C., area, so they could be readily available for investigations

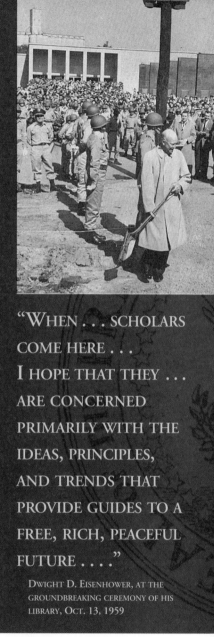

"WHEN . . . SCHOLARS COME HERE . . . I HOPE THAT THEY . . . ARE CONCERNED PRIMARILY WITH THE IDEAS, PRINCIPLES, AND TRENDS THAT PROVIDE GUIDES TO A FREE, RICH, PEACEFUL FUTURE . . . ."

DWIGHT D. EISENHOWER, AT THE GROUNDBREAKING CEREMONY OF HIS LIBRARY, OCT. 13, 1959

Artist Veryl Goodnight's bronze statue *The Day the Wall Came Down*, at the George H. W. Bush Presidential Library and Museum at College Station, Texas, commemorates the fall of the Berlin Wall in 1989, which took place during Bush's presidency. The five horses, leaping over actual rubble from the wall, symbolize freedom.

An actor interacts with a hologram image of Abraham Lincoln (below, left) in an interactive exhibit at the Abraham Lincoln Presidential Library and Museum in Springfield, Illinois. A series of such exhibits offer visitors an interpretation of Lincoln's life and presidency during the U.S. Civil War (1861-1865).

Caroline Kennedy Schlossberg, daughter of President John F. Kennedy, shows a group of school-children visiting the Kennedy Library in Boston a collection of dolls given to her during her father's presidency. Gifts from heads of state to presidents and their family members typically are turned over to presidential libraries for public display.

A replica of the Oval Office as the room looked during Gerald R. Ford's presidency is displayed at the Ford Library in Grand Rapids, Michigan. Period re-creations of the office are featured at a number of presidential libraries, including the Truman, Carter, Reagan, and Clinton facilities.

"THE OVAL OFFICE IS MORE THAN A SYMBOL. IT'S A TRUE SEAT OF POWER IN THE EXECUTIVE BRANCH OF OUR GOVERNMENT."

GERALD R. FORD

and legal proceedings. The Nixon situation ultimately led to the passage in 1978 of the Presidential Records Act, which made most presidential materials, referred to as "presidential records," government property. The legislation ended the private property tradition that had been in effect since George Washington's time.

The evolving nature of presidential libraries

The funding, nature, and operation of presidential libraries has evolved greatly since 1939 and will continue to do so. As the nation and its government have grown over the past 60 years, so too have presidential administrations and presidential libraries. The Truman Library was built in 1957 at a cost of $1.7 million. By comparison, the William J. Clinton Presidential Library and Museum in Little Rock, Arkansas, which opened in 2004, cost more than $165 million. While the Truman Library contains about 15 million pages of records and documents, the Clinton Library holds about 100 million pages. In addition, the Clinton Library maintains nearly 20 million pages of electronic records, along with huge collections of audiovisual materials that were unimaginable in Truman's era. The cost of operating presidential libraries also has jumped dramatically and now covers expenses associated with high-tech exhibits and an abundance of education and outreach activities. The library staffs now include marketing and membership departments. Newer libraries offer upscale dining facilities, elaborate gift shops, and other visitor amenities. None of this was envisioned when the first presidential libraries were established in the 1940's and 1950's. As a result, both the older and newer libraries in the NARA system have become increasingly dependent on their private foundations to secure funding from individuals, corporations, and *philanthropic* (charitable) organizations for improved facilities, new exhibits, educational programs, Web sites, and even basic program and operating costs. Private funding and income from admissions, gift shops, and facility

Bill Clinton hosts President George W. Bush and three former presidents and their families at the dedication of the William J. Clinton Presidential Library and Museum in Little Rock, Arkansas, in November 2004—(from left to right) Rosalyn Carter, Jimmy Carter, Barbara Bush, George H. W. Bush, Laura Bush, George W. Bush, Chelsea Clinton, Hillary Clinton, and Bill Clinton.

"THIS IS MOSTLY THE STORY OF WHAT WE, THE PEOPLE, CAN DO WHEN WE WORK TOGETHER."

BILL CLINTON, AT THE DEDICATION OF HIS LIBRARY, NOV. 19, 2004

rental provide 30 percent or more of the annual operating costs of presidential libraries.

The expansion of the federal system of presidential libraries has sometimes generated criticism from legislators, scholars, and the public. More than a few legislators and government watchdog groups claim that managing a network of archival institutions scattered throughout the nation is too costly. These critics maintain that a single centralized location for the papers of all the nation's presidents would be more efficient. Some historians charge that the library exhibits tend to overstate the achievements of the president whose legacy they interpret. They argue that presidential libraries contribute to the notion of supreme presidential power, which scholars call the "imperial presidency"—or at least present the office of the presidency as greater than the other coequal branches of the federal government, the legislature and judiciary. The influence of the libraries' private foundations in setting priorities for individual libraries also has been questioned by some critics who have noted that the former presidents, their families, friends, and prominent benefactors seem to influence the direction of presidential libraries and the types of displays they offer to the public.

Former President Ronald W. Reagan presents Mikhail Gorbachev, former leader of the Soviet Union, with the Reagan Freedom Medal at the Reagan Library in Simi Valley, California, in May 1992. Former presidents often use their libraries when hosting current and former heads of state and other dignitaries.

Despite such criticism, the current practice of establishing presidential libraries is likely to remain in place. In recent years, delegates from China, the Czech Republic, Germany, South Korea, Taiwan, and other nations have toured presidential libraries and conferred with NARA officials about the possibility of establishing in their own countries institutions much like the U.S. presidential library system.

Behind the scene politics

In serving researchers and in providing public and academic programs, presidential libraries strive to maintain an objective, *nonpartisan* (in support of no political party), and professional approach. Objectivity is not easy, however. Presidential libraries, by their very nature, deal with the lives and careers of people immersed in partisan political activity. The benefactors who contribute the funding to build the libraries and provide operational revenue tend to be people who favored the policies of the president whose library they support. Of course, the family, friends, and benefactors of each former president want their president's library to present the legacy in a favorable light. In particular, when the former president or influential family members are still alive, the library exhibits and programs at times border on *hagiography* (a biography that idolizes its subject). Many years must go by before a presidential library can assess its president through its exhibits and public programs with objectivity.

Humidity- and temperature-controlled archives at the Jimmy Carter Library and Museum (top) in Atlanta, Georgia, preserve Carter's presidential papers, which are accessible to historians and other scholars by appointment. The archives at the John F. Kennedy Library and Museum in Boston include artwork and furniture once owned by President Kennedy and his family.

Moreover, the accurate presentation of the lives and deeds of most recent presidents is further complicated by a lack of documentary information. Important documents usually remain restricted for decades. The records of a president's family and close associates may not be placed in the library collections or opened to public scrutiny for many years. For example, more than 1,300 letters that Harry S. Truman wrote prior to and during his presidency were not placed in the Truman Library until 30 years after he left the White House. Highly personal and revealing, the letters were stashed in the attic of Truman's Independence, Missouri, house and apparently forgotten. Archivists of the Truman Library were shocked to discover this treasure trove after the death in 1982 of Bess Truman, Harry Truman's widow.

The Presidential Records Act of 1978 *mandates* (specifies) that papers of recent presidents be opened fairly quickly after a president leaves office. In reality, though, scholars find it difficult to gain prompt access to immense collections of presidential materials, filled with national security information and sensitive personal and political information. In addition, President George W. Bush issued an executive order in 2002 that allows a serving president, a former president, or that former president's spouse, children, or heirs to withhold from public access those documents for which "executive privilege" is claimed. (President Bush's order has been challenged in the federal courts.)

Additional libraries

Not all presidential libraries are a part of the NARA system. The Hayes Presidential Center, Inc., a nonprofit group, operates the Rutherford B. Hayes Presidential Center, which was, in some ways, the prototype for all presidential libraries. In 2005, the Illinois Historic Preservation Agency opened a new facility to house the collections of the Illinois State Historical Library, which included, among its extensive holdings, a fine collection of Lincoln memorabilia. The result is a spectacular new installation, the Abraham Lincoln Presidential Library and Museum in Springfield, Illinois. The Lincoln Library was funded by state, federal, and private sources. Recently, the Stark County Historical Society in Canton, Ohio, which holds among its collections significant William McKinley papers, renamed one of its facilities the Wm. McKinley Presidential Library & Museum. The Woodrow Wilson Birthplace in Staunton, Virginia, following construction of a new building, has renamed itself a presidential library.

The dedication of the Clinton Library in November 2004 added an 11th library to the NARA system. In addition, Congress has authorized NARA to acquire and manage the privately operated Nixon Library and to relocate Nixon's presidential materials to Yorba Linda, California. President George W. Bush will decide in 2006 where in Texas to locate his presidential library.

At the present rate of growth, 25 to 30 presidential libraries could exist in the NARA system by the 2050's. These libraries will give even more insight into the complexities of the nation's leaders and will help to teach visitors the remarkable history of the United States. The size and technical developments of these future presidential libraries cannot even be imagined.

PRESIDENTIAL LIBRARIES MANAGED BY THE NATIONAL ARCHIVES AND RECORDS ADMINISTRATION (NARA)

George Bush Presidential Library and Museum
1000 George Bush Drive W
College Station, Texas 77845

Jimmy Carter Library and Museum
441 Freedom Parkway
Atlanta, Georgia 30307

William J. Clinton Presidential Library and Museum
1200 President Clinton Avenue
Little Rock, Arkansas 72201

Eisenhower Presidential Library and Museum
200 SE Fourth Street
Abilene, Kansas 67410

Gerald R. Ford Presidential Library and Museum
Library: 1000 Beal Avenue
               Ann Arbor, Michigan 48109

Museum: 303 Pearl Street NW
                Grand Rapids, Michigan 49504

Herbert Hoover Presidential Library and Museum
210 Parkside Drive
P.O. Box 488
West Branch, Iowa 52358

Lyndon Baines Johnson Library and Museum
2313 Red River Street
Austin, Texas 78705

John F. Kennedy Library and Museum
Columbia Point
Boston, Massachusetts 02125

Richard Nixon Library & Birthplace
(scheduled to be transferred to NARA control in 2006)
18001 Yorba Linda Boulevard
Yorba Linda, California 92886

Ronald Reagan Presidential Library and Museum
40 Presidential Drive
Simi Valley, California 93065

Franklin D. Roosevelt Presidential Library and Museum
4079 Albany Post Road
Hyde Park, New York 12538-1999

Harry S. Truman Presidential Library
500 W. U.S. Highway 24
Independence, Missouri 64050

PRESIDENTIAL LIBRARIES (NOT MANAGED BY NARA)

Rutherford B. Hayes Presidential Center
Spiegel Grove
Fremont, Ohio 43420

Abraham Lincoln Presidential Library and Museum
212 N. Sixth Street
Springfield, Illinois 62701

Wm. McKinley Presidential Library & Museum
800 McKinley Drive NW.
Canton, Ohio 44708

Woodrow Wilson Presidential Library
18-24 N. Coalter Street (P.O. Box 24)
Staunton, Virginia 24402

Uzbekistan. Massive protests in the eastern city of Andijon in May 2005 challenged Uzbek president Islam Karimov's 14-year rule. The events began on May 10, when several thousand demonstrators gathered to protest the trial of 23 local businessmen who were alleged to be Muslim extremists. On the night of May 12, several dozen armed men stormed the local prison, freeing several hundred prisoners. Gunmen attacked an army barracks and a police station, taking police and government officials hostage. In response, government forces on May 13 opened fire on the growing crowd of protesters in the city center. While government sources claimed 187 deaths resulted, human rights groups estimated a death toll of 1,000. Hundreds more fled across the nearby border into Kyrgyzstan. The government immediately ordered foreign journalists to leave the city and blocked Uzbeks from access to many foreign television news channels and Internet sites. The Uzbek government subsequently cracked down on dissent within Uzbekistan.

On September 20, the government put 15 men on trial for organizing protests in Andijon. Prosecutors alleged that the men belonged to outlawed militias. All 15 entered guilty pleas. On November 14, the court found the 15 men guilty and gave them prison sentences of between 14 and 20 years.

Foreign relations. The events in Andijon had significant foreign policy consequences for Uzbekistan. Although the Uzbek government accused Islamic extremists of provoking the violence, Western journalists and international organizations condemned the Karimov regime for using excessive force against unarmed demonstrators. The United States and several international organizations called for an independent investigation into the violence. On July 29, the Uzbek government demanded that U.S. troops leave the Karshi-Khanabad air base by the end of the year. The air base had served as a hub for U.S.-led missions into neighboring Afghanistan since late 2001. The final U.S. troops left on Nov. 21, 2005.

On October 3, European Union foreign ministers agreed to ban arms sales to Uzbekistan and bar many Uzbek government officials from traveling to Europe. Although Karimov had previously maintained friendly diplomatic relationships with both Russia and the Western powers, the aftermath of the Andijon protests turned Karimov's attention toward Russia. He signed a military and strategic alliance with Russia on November 14 that committed Russia to protect Karimov's regime from domestic or foreign threats. International affairs experts suggested that Karimov and Russian President Vladimir Putin feared the influence of foreign religious and political organizations. ■ Juliet Johnson

See also **Asia; Russia: A Special Report.**

Vanuatu. See Pacific Islands.

Venezuela. With petroleum prices at record highs in 2005, President Hugo Chavez Frias was able to earmark $6 billion in oil revenues—triple the amount in 2004—to fund domestic welfare, invest in health and literacy, and subsidize prices of basic foods for the nation's poor. His policies of using oil revenues to promote social change boosted Chavez's approval rating among Venezuelans to 70 percent or higher during the year.

The Chavez administration also used windfall oil revenues to court good relations with neighbors. Through a new initiative dubbed PetroCaribe, Venezuela began supplying poor Caribbean nations with deeply discounted oil in 2005. Cash-poor small nations in the region were able to repay some of the cost with their surplus bananas, rice, and sugar, which Venezuela needed to feed its people, and to finance the balance on advantageous terms. Venezuela's treasury purchased bonds from neighbors, including Argentina and Ecuador, to offset declining investments from the United States.

Foreign oil companies. To support his ambitious social agenda, President Chavez tightened government control of foreign companies, which extracted and marketed 42 percent of the country's oil. He hiked the taxes on their profits and demanded that they enter into joint-venture agreements to make Petroleos de Venezuela, the state-owned oil company, the majority partner in their operations.

Threat to press freedom. Venezuela's government changed the nation's criminal code in March 2005 to include crimes described by legal experts as "poorly defined offenses," such as demeaning the "honor" of public officials. Reporters Without Borders, a Paris-based journalist advocacy group, characterized the revisions as "a big step backwards" for freedom of the press.

Venezuela-U.S. relations. In April, Venezuela terminated a 35-year-old military cooperation agreement with the United States and ordered four U.S. military advisers out of the country, alleging that they were agitating for rebellion. In July, President Chavez claimed that the United States had plans to invade Venezuela.

Relations between Chavez and the administration of U.S. President George W. Bush took a bizarre turn in August when U.S. religious broadcaster Pat Robertson, a vocal supporter of President Bush, suggested that U.S. agents assassinate Chavez to stop Venezuela from becoming a "launching pad for Communist infiltration and Muslim extremism." Although a U.S. Department of State official called Robertson's comments "inappropriate," the incident fueled speculation about secret U.S. plans to remove Chavez from office. ■ Nathan A. Haverstock

See also **Latin America.**

Vermont. See State government.

Vice President of the United States. See United States, Government of the.

Vietnam. The death toll from avian flu rose above 40 in Vietnam in 2005, making it the country hardest hit by the virus. Officials said the 42nd Vietnamese victim of the bird flu had been hospitalized after his family bought a prepared chicken from a market. He died on October 29.

In 2005, Vietnam's government expanded a program to vaccinate fowl. The program involved vaccinating some 60 million birds on small farms before winter, when the virus seems to spread most dangerously. However, health officials worried that wild birds might continue to harbor the virus and spread it back into flocks of chickens, ducks, and other domestic fowl.

In January, government officials announced a plan to create 1.6 million jobs in 2005 in an attempt to lower the unemployment rate to below 5.4 per-cent in urban areas and lower the country's poverty rate to 7 percent. Officials declared in March that every family had an obligation to observe a limit of two children. The announcement signaled the government's growing concern that the existing two-child policy was increasingly being ignored and larger families would make it harder to achieve economic progress. Officials worried that the population would exceed a targeted 88 million in 2010.

■ Henry S. Bradsher

See also **Asia; Public health.**

Vital statistics. See **Census; Population.**

Fireworks over Ho Chi Minh City (formerly Saigon) on April 29 mark the 30th anniversary of the end of the Vietnam War (1957-1975), which resulted in the unification of the country under a Communist government.

Baseball fans at Robert F. Kennedy Memorial Stadium cheer the unveiling of an enormous American flag at the Washington Nationals' first home opener on April 14. The game against the Arizona Diamondbacks, which the Nationals won, was the first Major League Baseball game played in the nation's capital since 1971.

Washington, D.C. Major League Baseball returned to the nation's capital for the first time since 1971 when on April 14, 2005, the Washington Nationals, in their first home game, beat the Arizona Diamondbacks 5 to 3. The Nationals, which had been the Montreal Expos before moving to Washington, D.C., finished the 2005 season with a perfectly split record of 81 wins and 81 losses.

City officials tried for years to bring a team back to Washington, where professional baseball was last played by the Senators in 1971. Even after Major League Baseball awarded the city a team in 2004, Mayor Anthony A. Williams said the deal was "close to dying" because initial cost estimates to build a new stadium ballooned. Washington's District of Columbia council and baseball officials salvaged the deal by agreeing to a privately financed new stadium. Until a new stadium is built, the Nationals were scheduled to play at Robert F. Kennedy Memorial Stadium, which was refurbished to conform to Major League Baseball standards.

The new stadium was planned for a location south of Capitol Hill, near the Anacostia River, and budgeted to cost $535 million. A groundbreaking date was not announced in 2005, but other development in the neighborhood began, including two 14-story towers to be used as a hotel and residences. The $110-million project is on the site of an old warehouse and abandoned row houses. The United States Department of Transportation began building new offices near the stadium site, and a developer announced plans for a complex of offices, shops, restaurants, residences, and a park.

Taxicabs with meters. First-time visitors to Washington were often surprised to find taxicabs unequipped with mileage meters that figure the cost of a ride, as in other major cities. Instead, a zone system set cab fares for different areas of the city.

In October 2005, the D.C. Taxicab Commission launched an eight-month experiment by installing meters in a small number of cabs. The zone system has been in place since the U.S. Congress banned meters in 1933. A switch to meters would make short rides in the city less expensive than they are under the current system. The shortest zoned ride in the city's downtown cost $7 in 2005, about $2 more than a metered ride under the commission's experimental taxicab fares.

Martin Luther King, Jr., memorial. The foundation overseeing the development of a new national memorial in Washington, D.C., to civil rights leader Martin Luther King, Jr., had raised about $40 million by the end of 2005 and was seeking $60 million more for the project. Congress authorized the memorial in 1996, and the federal government approved the location, a 4-acre (1.6-hectare) plot between the Lincoln and Jefferson memorials. The groundbreaking was scheduled for late 2006 with construction to be completed in 2008.

Walter Reed Center to close. An independent commission reviewing U.S. Department of Defense plans for various military installations recommended in 2005 closing Walter Reed Army Medical Center. The medical center has been a Washington, D.C., institution where ordinary soldiers as well as generals and U.S. presidents had received medical treatment for nearly a century. The hospital complex is located on 113 acres (45 hectares) in Northwest Washington, a neighborhood of very expensive real estate. Officials suggested that the land be developed to add to the

end of January, Boston had received 43.3 inches (110 centimeters), the city's snowiest month since record keeping began in 1892.

Damp weather persisted in the Southwest into March 2005. In California, heavy rains in late February caused more than 200 mudslides near Los Angeles and led to at least nine deaths. More than 37 inches (94 centimeters) of rain fell on Los Angeles during the water year that began in July 2004, the second-highest total since record keeping began in 1877. Arizona, Nevada, and New Mexico in 2005 each had the wettest winters on record. The rains alleviated a drought that had plagued the Southwest for a number of years. In contrast, winter in the Northwest was dry, with 72 percent of the region experiencing drought.

A late winter storm crossed the Northeast on March 7 and 8, 2005, depositing more than 2 feet (0.6 meters) of snow in northern Maine. The storm also gave New York City a seasonal total of 40 inches (102 centimeters), the first time on record that the city received at least 40 inches (102 centimeters) of snowfall in three consecutive winters.

Spring floods and snows. A potent storm carried heavy rain and snowfall to the Northeast on April 2 and 3. Two to six inches (5 to 15 centimeters) of rain fell on ground already saturated from previous rains and recent snow melt, leading to severe flooding in parts of New York, New Jersey, and Pennsylvania. At least 12,000 residents had to be evacuated from along the Delaware River, with 3,200 residences damaged in New Jersey alone. Crests on parts of the Delaware River were the second highest on record.

The same storm blanketed parts of northwestern Pennsylvania and upstate New York under more than 2 feet (0.6 meters) of snow, bringing down power lines and closing Interstate 90. The 6.6 inches (16.8 centimeters) that fell in Cleveland, Ohio, on April 24 brought the city's seasonal total to over 105 inches (267 centimeters), the highest on record.

Several deluges occurred on the eastern Gulf Coast in spring. Pensacola, Florida, received 25.15 inches (63.88 centimeters) of rain from March 31 to April 12. With a total of 24.46 inches (62.1 centimeters) for the month of April, the city set a record for its wettest month.

After a very dry winter, the Northwest experienced its second-wettest spring on record. By May, the area under moderate to severe drought had shrunk to 41 percent, compared with 63 percent at the end of winter.

Frequent episodes of chill in May affected a wide area of the country from the Plains to the Northeast. More than a dozen records were set for lowest May temperature, including 13 °F (-11 °C) on May 2 at Aberdeen, South Dakota, and 27 °F (-3 °C) on May 3 in Fort Wayne, Indiana. In the

city's tax base. Critics pointed out that moving the medical facilities out of Washington and into suburban Maryland, as Defense Department officials proposed, would cost the city as many as 5,000 federal jobs. The Defense Department planned to close the historic hospital—as well as other military bases—by 2011.

■ Howard S. Shapiro

See also **Baseball; Zoos.**

Water. See **Environmental pollution.**

Weather. The 2005 hurricane season in the Atlantic produced more storms than had occurred in any other year since record keeping began in 1851. Twenty-seven named storms formed—including a record 14 hurricanes—and one storm, Katrina, produced one of the greatest natural disasters in the history of the United States.

Wet winter. The year began with wet weather in the Southwest States as a series of moist weather systems swept inland from the Pacific. Between Dec. 26, 2004, and Jan. 10, 2005, Los Angeles recorded 16.97 inches (43.1 centimeters) of rain, the city's wettest 15-day period on record. In the Northeast, more than 2 feet (0.6 meters) of snow blanketed parts of the area on January 22 and 23. Boston's Logan Airport closed as 23 inches (58.4 centimeters) of snow fell on the city. By the

FOCUS ON ■ WEATHER

Weather in 2005 was
characterized by a
record-breaking
number of storms
and by both extreme
drought and rainfall.

A cornfield near Centerville, Illinois,
withers from a summer drought
that in July 2005 extended from
east Texas to the Great Lakes. The
drought destroyed corn, soybeans,
and rice crops and stressed city
trees and shrubbery.

Hurricane Wilma, the most powerful storm ever recorded in the Atlantic Ocean, with winds of 175 miles (282 kilometers) per hour, batters Mexico's Yucatan Peninsula on October 21. Wilma caused the deaths of a dozen people in Mexico and Cuba before it weakened and made landfall on the south-west coast of Florida near Naples. An additional 30 people were killed in Florida as the storm crossed the state. Wilma was one of 27 named storms that formed in the Atlantic during the 2005 hurricane season, breaking the previous record of 21 storms set in 1933.

Floodwaters unleashed by heavy rains destroy a section of Route 10 in Gilsum, New Hampshire, on October 9. By the end of the month, weeks of torrential rain had inundated many parts of the Northeast with more than 12 inches (30 centimeters) of water, causing the deaths of 12 people and forcing the evacuation of thousands of residents.

People flee as a wildfire approaches the village of Lapa do Lobo, about 186 miles (300 kilometers) north of Lisbon, Portugal, on October 2. By the end of October, wildfires in central and northern Portugal had destroyed an estimated 740,000 acres (300,000 hectares) of forest and agricultural land—the second worst fire season on record—and caused the deaths of 18 people.

Northeast, the month was the 10th coldest on record since 1895.

In contrast, late May 2005 brought record heat to the West. More than 400 daily record highs were set or tied from May 20 to 25. Temperatures in El Paso, Texas, twice reached 105 °F (41 °C), the highest May temperature on record, and in Las Vegas, Nevada, topped 100 °F (38 °C) on nine straight days from May 20 to 28, breaking the previous May record of seven straight days.

Tornadoes. For the first time since record keeping began in 1950, no tornado-related deaths occurred during the height of the season (from April to June) despite more than 500 twisters. However, five separate tornado outbreaks led to 27 deaths in November 2005, including 23 deaths near Evansville, Indiana, on the 12th.

The summer of 2005 will be remembered in the United States for extreme heat. In the West, both Las Vegas and Denver tied their all-time maximum daily temperatures. Las Vegas reached 117 °F (47 °C) on July 19; Denver recorded 105 °F (41 °C) on July 20. In the East, New Jersey had its warmest summer since record keeping began in 1895. Averaged across the nation, the summer of 2005 was the 10th warmest on record.

The Atlantic hurricane season of 2005 was unprecedented in how early it began, the high intensity of the storms in the Gulf of Mexico, and the damage that they caused in the United States. The first named tropical storm, Arlene, formed in the western Caribbean on June 9. Arlene crossed western Cuba before making landfall near Pensacola on June 11 with winds of 60 miles (97 kilometers) per hour.

The season's first hurricane, Dennis, formed in the eastern Caribbean on July 6. The storm swept ashore near Cienfuegos, Cuba, as the strongest Atlantic hurricane recorded so early in the year, a Category 4. (A Category 4 hurricane, according to the Saffir-Simpson hurricane classification system, generates winds of 131 to 155 miles [210 to 249 kilometers] per hour.) Dennis had weakened to a Category 3 storm, with winds of 111 to 130 miles (179 to 209 kilometers) per hour when it made landfall near Pensacola on July 10. Nevertheless, Dennis caused less damage than Category 3 Hurricane Ivan, which struck the same area in 2004.

As Dennis dissipated, Tropical Storm Emily formed in the eastern Atlantic in the second week of July. Emily became a Category 4 hurricane as it moved through the Caribbean, striking Jamaica. The storm made a second landfall in Mexico about 75 miles (121 kilometers) south of Brownsville, Texas, as a Category 3 hurricane on July 20. By the end of July, seven Atlantic storms had been named, a record for so early in the season.

Katrina, a storm destined to become one of the most destructive acts of nature on record in the United States, made landfall in Florida near North Miami Beach on August 25 as a Category 1 hurricane, with winds of 74 to 95 miles (119 to 153 kilometers) per hour. The storm moved southwest across Florida, where it was blamed for 11 deaths.

Over the eastern Gulf, Katrina intensified into the fourth strongest hurricane since record keeping began in 1851. The eye of the hurricane slammed into the southeastern Louisiana coast on Aug. 29, 2005, with winds of 127 miles (204 kilometers) per hour. The storm center passed just east of New Orleans before moving into Mississippi. The *storm surge* (a sudden rise of ocean water that accompanies a hurricane at landfall) reached 20 to 30 feet (6 to 9 meters) along parts of the Mississippi coast, destroying all structures close to the beachfront.

In New Orleans, the combination of heavy rain and roiling waters in Lake Ponchartrain caused the levee system to fail at several points. Water inundated about 80 percent of the city, and thousands of stranded people had to be rescued by boat and helicopter in the days following the storm. Hurricane Katrina caused at least 1,200 deaths in Mississippi and Louisiana, as well as economic losses estimated at $100 billion to $200 billion.

Hurricane Rita, which formed in the eastern Atlantic, intensified as it swept by the Florida Keys on September 20 and 21. In the central Gulf of Mexico, the storm grew to be the third strongest hurricane on record. Rita made landfall near the Texas-Louisiana border on September 24 as a Category 3 storm, with peak winds of 120 miles (193 kilometers) per hour. The storm surge flooded much of the southwestern Louisiana coast.

In October, Hurricane Wilma became the most powerful storm ever recorded in the Atlantic, with winds of 175 miles (282 kilometers) per hour. At least 12 people were killed in Mexico and Cuba before Wilma weakened and struck the southwest coast of Florida near Naples as a Category 3 storm on October 24. The hurricane crossed Florida, causing more than 30 deaths and extensive damage.

In all, 27 named storms formed in the Atlantic in 2005, breaking the previous record of 21 storms set in 1933. After the U.S. National Hurricane Center exhausted its list of 21 names, meteorologists began using letters of the Greek alphabet—from Alpha to Zeta—to name the storms.

Autumn floods. A series of storms that began on Oct. 7, 2005, brought record rain to the Northeast. Flooding led to the deaths of 12 people, while thousands of others were evacuated. New York City had its wettest October, with 16.78 inches (42.6 centimeters) of rain. In Providence, Rhode Island, October was the wettest of any month, with 15.38 inches (39.06 centimeters) of rain.

■ Fred Gadomski and Todd Miner
See also **Disasters: A Special Report.**

Weightlifting. See Sports.

Welfare. United States Department of Health and Human Services (HHS) Secretary Mike Leavitt announced on Feb. 9, 2005, that 1.96 million families received Temporary Assistance for Needy Families (TANF) benefits from June 2003 to June 2004, a 3-percent decrease from the previous year. (TANF is a program that provides cash assistance and helps with child-care services for low-income workers and the unemployed.) During the same period, 4.72 million individuals received TANF benefits, a 4.4-percent decrease.

TANF funding expired in 2002. The program subsequently remained in operation through a series of temporary extensions.

Energy aid. Leavitt disclosed on Jan. 31, 2005, that the government would provide an extra $100 million in emergency aid to state, territorial, and tribal governments under the Low Income Home Energy Assistance Program. The program annually helps some 4.5 million low-income families heat and cool their residences.

Marriage programs. A review of marriage and relationship programs conducted by the HHS Administration for Children and Families (ACF), released February 10, revealed that the programs do help couples improve communication and sustain healthy relationships. ACF is a federal program that promotes social and economic success for families. In 1996, researchers for Congress found that stable marriages help families become and remain economically self-sufficient. President George W. Bush's budget request for 2006 included $100 million in matching funds to states and tribes to develop healthy marriage programs.

On June 13, 2005, HHS released a report analyzing healthy marriage demonstration projects and grant activities. The goal of the initiative was to help couples have broader access to voluntary marriage education services.

Child abuse and neglect. The ACF reported on April 1 that an estimated 906,000 children across the United States had been abused or neglected in 2003. According to statistics culled by the National Child Abuse and Neglect Data System, 12.4 out of every 1,000 children in the country were victims of abuse or neglect, compared with 12.3 out of 1,000 children in 2002.

Head Start. Initial findings of a study released June 9, 2005, on the Head Start program found that more than 900,000 children enrolled in the program from 2002 to 2003 showed some improvements in such areas as prereading, prewriting, vocabulary, and health but still lagged behind children who came from economically advantaged families. Head Start is a federal program that provides educational, social, and health services to young children from the nation's lowest-income families. ■ Geoffrey A. Campbell

See also **Social Security: A Special Report.**

West Indies. At a July 2005 summit in St. Lucia, leaders of the Caribbean Community (CARICOM) member nations reconfirmed their support for the creation of a single-market economy within the association of 15 small Caribbean countries. They set Jan. 1, 2006, as the target date by which trade tariffs were to be harmonized and borders opened to free migration of skilled workers—in effect, implementing the regional free market. The only CARICOM nation that did not sign the accord was the Bahamas, whose leaders, analysts suggested, feared being deluged by immigrants from poorer neighbors.

PetroCaribe. In a September 2005 summit at Montego Bay, Jamaica, leaders of nine Caribbean nations, all hard-hit by mounting costs of fuel imports, signed an energy initiative offered by Venezuelan President Hugo Chavez Frias. Under the plan, called PetroCaribe, Venezuela would supply 13 Caribbean nations (including four earlier signatories) with 190,000 barrels of oil per day on highly favorable terms.

Because Venezuela imports more than 80 percent of its food, Chavez encouraged nations producing agricultural surpluses to pay for a portion of their fuel imports with commodities such as bananas, rice, and sugar. Under the terms of PetroCaribe, participating nations could finance 40 percent of the cost of Venezuelan oil imports over 25 years at an annual interest rate of 1 percent. Venezuela also pledged $50 million a year to establish a new social development fund to finance social programs in the Caribbean region.

Only two CARICOM nations declined Venezuela's PetroCaribe offer. Trinidad and Tobago, an oil producer, met its own energy needs in 2005 and supplied oil to neighbors, including Barbados. The prime minister of that small island country, Owen Arthur, said that Barbados was already receiving adequate supplies of energy. His political opponents, however, charged that he had buckled under to pressure from the United States not to participate in an initiative sponsored by Chavez, with whom the administration of President George W. Bush was at odds.

Dominican Republic prison riot. In early March 2005, rival gangs rioted and torched the prison where they were incarcerated in Higuey, a town in the eastern Dominican Republic. Originally built to house 80 inmates, the facility held 426 men when fighting broke out among prisoners armed with guns, knives, and machetes. Dominican authorities reported that 136 prisoners died in the riot. ■ Nathan A. Haverstock

See also **Latin America; Venezuela.**

Yemen. See Middle East.

Yukon Territory. See Canadian territories.

Zambia. See Africa.

Zimbabwe. President Robert Mugabe celebrated 25 years of independence on April 18, 2005, by telling Western officials to stay out of Zimbabwe's internal affairs and leave Africa to Africans. Mugabe's statement followed the sixth electoral victory of his ruling Zimbabwe African National Union-Patriotic Front (ZANU-PF) since Mugabe led the country to independence in 1980. Soon after the 2005 victory celebration, Mugabe's government launched a so-called "cleanup" of urban neighborhoods that left hundreds of thousands of people homeless.

Elections. Mugabe's ZANU-PF won a landslide victory in parliamentary elections on March 31. ZANU-PF took 78 of the National Assembly's elective seats, while the opposition Movement for Democratic Change (MDC), headed by Morgan Tsvangirai, won 41 seats. A constitutional provision that allows the president to appoint 30 additional members enabled ZANU-PF to rack up a two-thirds majority in the 150-member parliament. Analysts predicted that Mugabe would use the lopsided majority to amend the constitution to allow him to run for president again upon expiration of his term in 2008.

International reaction. South Africa and some other African nations accepted Zimbabwe's 2005 elections as valid. Critics noted, however, that the Mugabe regime had barred international election monitors. An independent election-monitoring organization within Zimbabwe, the Zimbabwe Support Network, alleged widespread electoral fraud by ZANU-PF. Officials of the United States, the United Kingdom, and the European Union (EU) called on the Mugabe government to answer charges of election fraud.

Sanctions extended. On Feb. 21, 2005, the EU renewed for one year so-called "smart sanctions" targeted against Mugabe and 94 of his inner circle of close aides. The measures were first introduced in 2002 when Mugabe expelled the head of the EU election observer team prior to the March 2002 presidential elections.

"Cleanup" campaign. In May 2005, the Mugabe regime launched "Operation Clean out the Filth," in which government troops demolished urban neighborhoods after driving the residents onto the streets. Spokespersons for the government claimed that the campaign was

A boy sifts through the rubble of buildings demolished by Zimbabwean government troops in a township near Harare, the capital, in June. The government's campaign to demolish the urban housing of the poor, which officials said was needed to clean up squalor and fight crime, left 700,000 Zimbabweans homeless in 2005.

directed against crime and a burgeoning black market economy. Government opponents, however, claimed it was directed against city and township precincts that backed the MDC in the March elections and compared the policy with Pol Pot's forced depopulation of Phnom Penh and other Cambodian cities during that Khmer Rouge leader's 1970's reign of terror in Cambodia. People dislocated by Mugabe's campaign were given little or no assistance and were forced to retreat to the countryside to seek shelter and forage for food.

On July 22, 2005, the United Nations (UN) issued a report condemning the Mugabe government's "indiscriminate and unjustified" forced relocation of some 700,000 Zimbabweans. In a separate statement, UN Secretary-General Kofi Annan said that the leaders responsible for the policy would be held "fully accountable for their actions."

Economic turmoil. Analysts said that the forced relocation policy had harmed Zimbabwe's already ramshackle economy. By the end of 2005, the country was experiencing a 400-percent inflation rate and severe shortages of food, fuel, and other commodities. Unemployment hovered above 70 percent. As the country experienced a fifth year of poor harvests, international relief organizations estimated that 4 million Zimbabweans would need food aid during 2005.

Zimbabwe's economy had begun a long-term decline in 2000 when the Mugabe government, opting for a land reform policy of confiscation rather than planned buyouts, started seizing white-owned commercial farms and awarding them to ZANU-PF political associates. The result of this policy, which hurt more than helped most black farm workers, was the collapse of the country's agricultural sector.   ■ Simon Baynham

See also **Africa.**

Zoology. See Biology.

Zoos. Employees of zoos and aquariums along the Gulf Coast scrambled to save animals from Hurricane Katrina in August 2005. The Audubon Aquarium of the Americas in New Orleans, Louisiana, lost almost 10,000 fish and other aquatic animals when Hurricane Katrina disabled its life support system after the staff was evacuated. After the storm, other zoos took in the Audubon Aquarium's handful of survivors, including sea otters and penguins. New Orleans's Audubon Zoo, located on higher ground than the aquarium, was severely battered, but its staff remained and only three animals—two otters and a raccoon—died. The zoo had reinforced housing and an emergency food supply. Employees of the Marine Life Oceanarium in Gulfport, Mississippi, recaptured, with the help of scientists from the National Marine Fisheries Service, eight Oceanarium dolphins that Hurricane Katrina had washed into the Gulf of Mexico.

Lincoln Park Zoo. In July, the American Zoo and Aquarium Association (AZA)—a nonprofit organization that accredits all zoos in the United States and is based in Silver Spring, Maryland—released a report, recommending changes for the treatment of animals at the Lincoln Park Zoo in Chicago. Employees of the zoo asked for the report after 12 animals, including 2 of the zoo's 3 African elephants, had died since the previous October. AZA reported no gross negligence, but the deaths sparked debate on the purpose of zoos.

Jaws revisited. Employees of the Monterey Bay Aquarium in California released a great white shark back into the Pacific Ocean in March 2005, after the shark killed two other sharks in the exhibit. The great white, a 6-foot (1.8-meter) long female, had been captured by a fisherman in August 2004 and held by the aquarium for 198 days. The previous record of holding a great white in captivity was 16 days.

Marine exhibits. On Nov. 23, 2005, an aquarium billed as the world's largest opened in Atlanta, Georgia. The Georgia Aquarium housed more than 100,000 animals, including two whale sharks, the largest species of fish. The animals inhabited tanks totaling 8 million gallons (30 million liters) of water.

The Great Barrier Reef exhibit at the Fort Worth (Texas) Zoo also opened in May. Located in the zoo's Australian Outback section, the exhibit contained 86 species of Australian sea life, ranging from sharks to corals.

Into the forest. The San Diego and St. Louis (Missouri) zoos unveiled major exhibits with tropical forests in 2005. In June, San Diego opened Monkey Trails and Forest Tales. Covering 3 acres (1.2 hectares), the exhibit was the largest and

A baby hippopotamus snuggles up to a giant tortoise at the Haller Wild-life Park outside Mombassa, Kenya, in February 2005. Orphaned by the Dec. 26, 2004, tsunami, Owen, the hippo, adopted the century-old male tortoise as a mother substitute upon being placed in the park.

most elaborate in the zoo's history. Visitors trekked through multilevel habitats similar to forests in Africa and Asia with monkeys, a rare pygmy hippopotamus, Visayan warty pigs, and clouded leopards.

The Donn & Marilyn Lipton Fragile Forest opened in May at the St. Louis Zoo. Covering 35,000 square feet (3,250 square meters), the exhibit featured landscaped environments for orangutans and chimpanzees, including a habitat cut by streams, with huge deadfall trees and forest vegetation. Visitors could focus on a single ape with a binocular-like scope that identified the particular animal.

The Tennessee Aquarium's Ocean Journey exhibit, which opened in Chattanooga in April, also featured a tropical forest, one of three sections that stressed the connection between water and land environments. Ocean Journey showcased a replica of a famed reef system in the Gulf of Mexico. Holding 618,000 gallons (2.3 million liters) of sea water, it offered a living coral ecosystem, with sharks, sea turtles, sting rays, and schooling fish. The tropical rain forest section, 30 feet (9.1 meters) high, highlighted hundreds of butterflies flying freely among tall tropical plants and exotic flowers.

Endangered wolves. The Wolf Woods exhibit, which opened at the Cincinnati (Ohio) Zoo in May 2005, featured a pair of Mexican gray wolves, the most endangered subspecies of gray wolf in North America. Four male and four female Mexican wolves were born in May at Stone Zoo, in Stoneham, Massachusetts, part of the Boston-based Zoo New England.

In April, five red wolves were born at the North Carolina Zoo in Asheboro and three others were born at the Roger Williams Park Zoo in Providence, Rhode Island. The U.S. Fish and Wildlife Service captured the few red wolves still in the wild in 1980. Captive breeding allowed the red wolves to be reintroduced on a North Carolina refuge, where about 100 survived in 2005.

Panda production. Giant pandas at the National Zoo in Washington, D.C., and the San Diego Zoo produced cubs in 2005. The Washington cub arrived in July and the San Diego youngster, in August. Later in August, a panda born at the San Diego Zoo gave birth to twin cubs at a panda research center in China.

Small zoos, big births. Not all significant births of animals in danger of becoming extinct took place at major zoos. In March, three Amur tiger cubs, a male and two females, were born at the Potter Park Zoo in Lansing, Michigan. The Beardsley Zoo in Bridgeport, Connecticut, welcomed cubs of the same species in April.

■ Edward R. Ricciuti

See also **Disasters: A Special Report.**

Index

How to use the index

This index covers the contents of the 2004, 2005, and 2006 editions.

McCarthy, Cormac, **06:** 235
McCartney, Robert, 06: 274
MediaNews Group Inc., 06: 272
Medicaid, 06: 335, 343-345, 356
Medicare, 06: 339-342
Medicine, 06: *251-252,* **05:** *270,* **04:** *276;* blood clots, **06:** 103; geology, **06:** 193; Nobel Prize, **06:** 68, 273; Reed Center closing, **06:** 408-409. See also **Genetic engineering; Health care issues; Mental health; Public health**
Megachurches, 06: 307
Mehlis, Detlev, 06: 233
Mekong River, 06: 81
Memoirs of a Geisha (film), **06:** 259
Memorial to the Murdered Jews of Europe, 06: 50, 194 (il.)
Mercosur, 06: 231
Meri, 06: 47
Merkel, Angela, 06: 193, 195, *286*
Mesa Gisbert, Carlos, 06: 84, 229
Mesic, Stipe, 06: 134
Messi, Lionel, 06: 332
Messick, Dale, 06: 143
Methamphetamines, 06: 166
Metropolitan Museum of Art, 06: 54, 55
Metropolitan Opera (New York City), **06:** 111
Mexico, 06: *253,* **05:** *271-272,* **04:** *277-278;* immigration, **06:** 204; table, **06:** 230
MFP Financial Services Ltd., 06: 376
MG Rover (company), **06:** 384
Mice, 06: 82
Michael L. Printz Award, 06: 247
Michigan, 06: 356; table, **06:** 355
Michigan Opera Theatre, 06: 111
Micronesia, Federated States of, 06: 277-278; table, **06:** 277
Microsoft Corp., 06: 114, 377-378
Middle East, 06: *254-256,* **05:** *273-276,* **04:** *278-281;* Latin American summit, **06:** 228
Miller, Frank, 06: 239, 242
Miller, Judith, 06: 271, 392
Miller, Laura, 06: 135
Miller, Reggie, 06: 78
Million Dollar Baby (film), **06:** 260-261 (il.)
Mills, Sir John, 06: 143, 144 (il.)
Mining, 06: 101, 290; disasters, **06:** 156
Minneapolis (Minnesota), **06:** 50
Minnesota, table, **06:** 355
Mississippi, 06: 161 (il.), 354, 356; table, **06:** 355
Missouri, 06: 356; table, **06:** 355
Mladic, Ratco, 06: 329
Montana, 06: 356; table, **06:** 355
Montana, Allison "Tootie," 06: 143
Montenegro. See Serbia and Montenegro
Monterey Bay Aquarium, 06: 415

Each index entry gives the edition year and the page number or page numbers—for example, **McCartney, Robert.** This means that information on this person may be found on the page indicated in the 2006 edition.

When there are many references to a topic, they are grouped alphabetically by clue words under the main topic. For example, the clue words under **Medicine** group the references to that topic under several subtopics.

A page number in italic type means that there is an article on this topic on the page or pages indicated. For example, there is an Update article on **Mexico** on page 253 of the 2006 edition. The page numbers in roman type indicate additional references to this topic in other articles in the volumes covered.

The indications (il.) or (ils.) mean that the reference on this page is to an illustration or illustrations only, as in *Million Dollar Baby* in the 2006 edition.

The "see" and "see also" cross-references refer the reader to other entries in the index. For example, information on Montenegro will be found under the **Serbia and Montenegro** heading.

A

Abashidze, Aslan, 06: 320
Abbas, Mahmoud, 06: 216, 228, 254, 05: *324*
ABC (network), 06: 365, 367
Abdullah (king of Saudi Arabia), 06: *281,* 328
Abdullah II (king of Jordan), 06: 221
Abdullah Azzam Brigades, 06: 174, 254
Abe, Shinzo, 06: 220
Abitibi Consolidated, Inc., 06: 99
Abkhazia, 06: 193, 319-320
Abortion, 06: 123, 150, 167, 175, 214
Abraham Lincoln Presidential Library and Museum, 06: 395 (il.), 400-401 (il.), 405
Abramoff, Jack, 06: 117
Abu Ghraib Prison, 06: 52, 201
Academy Awards, 06: 258, 284, 367
Aceh (Indonesia), 06: 56, 63, 207-208
Acela trains, 06: 380
Acevedo Vila, Anibal, 06: 309
Acholi, 06: 381
ACT (test), 06: 172
Adamo, Mark, 06: 111
Adams, Don, 06: 138
Adams, John (composer), 06: 111
Adams, John (president), 06: 396
Adams, John Quincy, 06: 396
Adams, Mason, 06: 138
Adelphia Communications Corp., 06: 125
Adolescents, 06: 166
Advani, Lal Krishna, 06: 206
Adzharia, 06: 319-320
Afghanistan, 06: *37,* 05: *37,* 04: *37;* disasters, 06: 155-157; military operations, 06: 52, 62; table, 06: 58. See also Terrorism
AFL-CIO, 06: 227
Afleet Alex (horse), 06: 199-200
Africa, 06: *38-43,* 05: *38-43,* 04: *38-43*
African Americans: biographies, 06: 202, 250, 374; employment, 06: 225; health, 06: 44, 167; prisons, 06: 306
African National Congress, 06: 346
African Union, 06: 38, 42
Aging, 06: 306
Agriculture, 06: *43-44,* 05: *43-44,* 04: *43-44;* farm subsidies, 06: 209. See also Food
Agriculture, U.S. Department of, 06: 43, 44, 89, 186
Ahern, Bertie, 06: 214
Ahmadinejad, Mahmoud, 06: 210-211, 256, *281-282*
Ahmed, Abdullah Yusuf, 06: 43
Ahtisaari, Martti, 06: 330
AIDS, 06: 39, *44-45,* 388, 05: *45,* 04: *44-45*
Air Force, U.S. See Armed forces
Air Line Pilots Association, 06: 225
Airbus Industrie, 06: 71
Airlines. See Aviation
Airports, 06: 105, 135, 322. See also Aviation
Akayev, Askar, 06: 224, 316, 321-323
Akmatbayev, Ryspek, 06: 225
Akmatbaev, Tynychbek, 06: 225
Alabama, 06: 354; table, 06: 355
Aladdin (play), 06: 375-376
Alaska, 06: 116, 356; table, 06: 355
Albania, 06: *45,* 249, 05: *45,* 04: *45;* table, 06: *182*
Albert, Eddie, 06: 138
Alberta, 06: 97-98
Alcohol, 06: 166, 328
Alderson, Samuel W., 06: 138
Aleman Lacayo, Arnoldo, 06: 272
Alexander, Shana, 06: 138
Algeria, 06: *45,* 05: *45-46,* 04: *45;* table, 06: 40
Al-Ghad Party, 06: 173
Aliens. See Immigration

Alimony, 06: 102
Alito, Samuel, 06: 360
Aliyev, Ilham, 06: 72
All My Sons (play), 06: 373
Allawi, Ayad, 06: 211, 05: *324-325*
Allen, Patrick, 06: 85
Alliance for the Future of Austria, 06: 67
Alliance of Motion Picture and Television Producers, 06: 226
Al-Qa`ida. See Qa`ida, Al-
Al-Sistani, Grand Ayatollah Ali, 06: 215, 05: *325*
Alsop, Marin, 06: 111, *282*
Alvarez Solon, Vivian, 06: 63
Amazon Basin, 06: 87, 121-122
America West Airlines, 06: 71
American Academy of Pediatrics, 06: 252
American Ballet Theater, 06: 136
American Federation of Television and Radio Artists, 06: 226
American Indian Probate Reform Act (2004), 06: 207
American Institute of Architects, 06: 50
American League. See Baseball
American Library Association, 06: 233
American Medical Association, 06: 339-340
American Splendor (film and novel), 06: 239, 244 (il.)
American Tragedy, An (Picker), 06: 111
Americans with Disabilities Act (1990), 06: 155
America's Cup, 06: 83
Amman (Jordan), 06: 33 (il.)
Amnesty International, 06: 201
Amtrak, 06: 380-381
Anderson, Alfred, 06: 138
Anderson, Greg, 06: 352
Anderson, Jack, 06: 138
Andorra, table, 06: 182
Angelopoulos-Daskalaki, Gianna, 05: *325*
Angina pectoris, 06: 103
Angola, 06: 39, 42; table, 06: 40
Animals. See Biology; Ocean; Paleontology; Zoos
Annan, Kofi, 06: 42, 115, 388
Annan, Kojo, 06: 388
Annus mirabilis, of Einstein, 06: 293, 295-301
Antarctica, 06: 196, 276
Anthropology, 06: *45-46,* 05: *46-47,* 04: *46-47*
Anti-Semitism, 06: 150
Antigua and Barbuda, table, 06: 230
Antioxidants, 06: 187
Antispyware programs, 06: 131
Antivirus programs, 06: 131
Apartheid, 06: 346
Apes, 06: 82, 121
Apple Computer, Inc., 06: 113-114, 175, 209
Aquino, Corazon, 06: 292
Arabs. See Islam; Middle East
Arafat, Yasir, 06: 176, 05: *274*
Archaeology, 06: *47-48,* 05: *47-49,* 04: *47-49*
Archery, 06: 353
Archibald Prize, 06: 68
Architecture, 06: *48-50,* 05: *49-50,* 04: *49-53.* See also Building and construction
Arctic ice, 06: 196
Arctic National Wildlife Refuge, 06: 101
Argentina, 06: *50-51,* 228, 231, 05: *50-51,* 04: *53;* soccer, 06: 332, 333; table, 06: 230
Arizona, 06: 204, 356, 357; table, 06: 355
Arizona Cardinals, 06: 88
Arkansas, 06: 356; table, 06: 355
Armed forces, 06: *51-53,* 201, 288, 05: *51-54,* 04: *54-56;* Korea, South,

06: 223-224; mental health, 06: 252-253. See also Defense, U.S. Department of; Iraq War; and specific countries
Armenia, 04: *56;* table, 06: 58
Armstrong, Lance, 06: 351, 353 (il.)
Army Corps of Engineers, U.S., 06: 164
Art, 06: *53-55,* 283-284, 05: *54-55,* 04: *56-58*
Art Institute of Chicago, 06: 54-55
Arthur Ravenel, Jr., Bridge, 06: 87
Ashcroft, John, 06: 233
Ashes tournament, 06: 124, 385 (il.)
Ashton, Frederick, 06: 136
Asia, 06: *56-59,* 05: *56-60,* 04: *58-63*
Asian Americans, 06: 225
Asian Art Museum (San Francisco), 06: 55
Asian Development Bank, 06: 276, 278
Aso, Taro, 06: 220
Assad, Bashir al-, 06: 363
Associated Press, 06: 187
Association of Flight Attendants, 06: 225
Association of Southeast Asian Nations, 06: 262
Astronomy, 06: *60-61,* 05: *59-62,* 04: *62-75.* See also Space exploration
Athens (Greece). See Olympic Games
Atkins Nutritionals Inc., 06: 186
Atkinson, Ted, 06: 138
Atlanta Symphony Orchestra, 06: 111
Atlantic Ocean, 06: 195
Atomic bomb. See Nuclear weapons
Atomic Energy Agency, 06: 273
Atoms, 06: 298
AT&T Corp., 06: 364
Audubon Aquarium of the Americas, 06: 415
Audubon Zoo, 06: 415
Aumann, Robert J., 06: 273
Australia, 06: *62-66,* 124, 05: *62-67,* 04: *76-80*
Australia, Prime Minister of, 06: *66,* 05: *67,* 04: *81.* See also Howard, John
Australian Open, 06: 369-370
Australian rules football, 06: *67,* 05: *67,* 04: *81*
Austria, 06: 47, *67,* 181, 05: *68,* 04: *81;* table, 06: 182
Autism, 06: 308
Automobile, 06: *68-70,* 05: *69-71,* 04: *82-85;* Canada, 06: 100; economics, 06: 170; Houston traffic program, 06: 201; hybrid, 06: 68 (il.), 177; labor issues, 06: 227; safety, 06: 328; United Kingdom, 06: 384
Automobile racing, 06: *70,* 287, 352, 05: *71,* 04: *85-86*
Avian influenza, 06: 44, 308, 407
Aviation, 06: *71-72,* 05: *72-73,* 04: *87;* crashes, 06: 155-156; Fossett, Steve, 06: 269-270; hurricane impact, 06: 169; labor issues, 06: 225-226. See also September 11 terrorist attacks
Aviator, The (film), 06: 259, 261 (il.)
Awami League, 06: 72
Axum obelisk, 06: 266-267
Azerbaijan, 06: *72,* 05: *73,* 04: *88;* table, 06: 58
Aziz, Shaukat, 06: 278, 279

B

Ba Jin, 06: 138
Baath Party, 06: 211, 363
Baby boom generation, 06: 335, 342
Bach, Johann Sebastian, 06: 111
Bachelet, Michelle, 06: 105
Bacon, Edmund, 06: 292

Bacteria, 06: 273
Badawi, Abdullah bin Ahmad, 06: 251
Badminton, 06: 353
BAE Systems, 06: 71
Baghdad (Iraq), 06: 21 (il.), 211
Bahamas, 06: 413; table, 06: 230
Bahcall, John N., 06: 138
Bahrain, table, 06: 256
Baker, Tom, 06: 86
Bakhit, Marouf al-, 06: 221
Bakiev, Kurmanbek, 06: 225, 322
Balanchine, George, 06: 136
Baldry, "Long" John, 06: 138
Balfour Beatty (company), 06: 386
Bali, 06: 62, 63, 372
Balkenende, Jan Peter, 06: 263
Ballet. See Dance
Baltic states, 05: 74
Baltimore Symphony Orchestra,
 06: 111
Bancroft, Anne, 06: 138
Banda Aceh (Indonesia), 06: 207 (il.)
Bangladesh, 06: 72, 124, 05: 74, 04: 88;
 shipwrecks, 06: 156; table, 06: 58
Bank, 06: 73-74, 05: 73-74, 04: 88-89;
 identity theft, 06: 128-131
Bank of America Corp., 06: 74
Bank of Italy, 06: 219
Bankruptcies, 06: 71, 73, 169, 170,
 225-226
Banny, Charles Konan, 06: 42
Banville, John, 06: 235
Barbados, table, 06: 230
Barker, Ronnie, 06: 138
Bartholomew, Patriarch, 06: 168
Basaev, Shamil, 06: 325
Baseball, 06: 74-77, 276, 05: 76-79,
 04: 89-92
Basescu, Traian, 06: 313
Bashir, Umar Hasan Ahmad al-,
 06: 359 (il.)
Basketball, 06: 77-80, 227, 05: 79-82,
 04: 92-95
Basques, 06: 350-351
Batman, 06: 241 (il.), 242
Batukaev, Aziz, 06: 225
Bauman, Joe, 06: 77
Bay Area Laboratory Co-Operative,
 06: 352
Baylor University, 06: 80
Beckham, David, 04: 306-307
Beckles, Amon, 06: 376-377
Beethoven, Ludwig van, 06: 111
Beirut (Lebanon), 06: 232 (il.)
Bel Geddes, Barbara, 06: 138
Belarus, 06: 80, 323-324, 05: 82,
 04: 96; table, 06: 182
Belgium, 06: 80, 05: 83, 04: 96; table,
 06: 182
Belize, table, 06: 230
Bellamy, Denise, 06: 376
Bellow, Saul, 06: 138, 234, 236-237
Benedict XVI, 06: 221 (il.), 222, 282-283,
 311-312
Benenson, Peter, 06: 138
Benin, table, 06: 40
Benjamin, Joel, 06: 104
Benson, Renaldo "Obie," 06: 138
Benzene, 06: 179
Berenger, Paul, 06: 251
Berenstain, Stan, 06: 138
Berger Perdomo, Oscar, 06: 198
Berisha, Sali, 06: 45
Berlusconi, Silvio, 06: 218
Bernanke, Ben S., 06: 73, 170, 392
Beslan (Russia), 06: 325
Best, George, 06: 138, 333
Bethe, Hans Albrecht, 06: 138
Bextra (drug), 06: 167
Bharatiya Janata Party, 06: 206
Bhutan, 06: 58-59; table, 06: 58
Bhutto, Benazir, 06: 279
Biathlon, 06: 353

Bicycle racing. See Cycling
BiDil (drug), 06: 167
Bin Husin, Azahari, 06: 62, 208
Biobased Products Preferred
 Procurement Program, 06: 44
Biology, 06: 81-82, 05: 83-87, 04: 96-98
Bird flu. See Avian influenza
Bird in Space (Brancusi), 06: 54
Birri, Nabih, 06: 232
Birth control. See Contraception
Bishkek (Kyrgyzstan), 06: 224, 321-323
Bisonalveus browni (animal), 06: 281
Black, Conrad, 06: 272
Blackfeet Indians, 06: 206
Blair, Tony, 06: 180, 383-387, 387,
 05: 397, 04: 396
Blanchett, Cate, 06: 68, 261 (il.)
Blanco, Kathleen, 06: 164
Bloch Bauer, Ferdinand, 06: 53
Blogging, 06: 210
Blood alcohol content, 06: 328
Blood clots, 06: 103
Bloomberg, Michael, R., 06: 264
Blum, Geoff, 06: 74 (il.)
Blunkett, David, 06: 386, 387
Boating, 06: 83, 05: 87, 04: 98-99
Bobsledding, 06: 353
Bochner, Lloyd, 06: 138
Bodman, Samuel W., 06: 89
Boeing Co., 06: 71, 227
Boger, David, 06: 68
Bolaños Geyer, Enrique, 06: 231, 272
Bolivia, 06: 84, 228, 229, 231, 05: 87;
 table, 06: 230
Bolkiah, Haji Hassanal, 06: 58
Bolshoi Ballet, 06: 137
Bolton, John, 06: 283, 393
Bond, James, 06: 259
Bond, Ruth Clement, 06: 138
Bond, Tommy, 06: 138
Bonds. See Stocks and bonds
Bonds, Barry, 06: 352, 05: 325-326
Bonobos, 06: 121
Books. See Literature; Literature for
 children; Poetry
Booth, Wayne, 06: 139
Bosnia-Herzegovina, 06: 84-85, 05: 88,
 04: 100; table, 06: 182
Boston Symphony Orchestra, 06: 111
Botswana, 06: 39; table, 06: 40
Bougainville, 06: 277
Bouteflika, Abdelaziz, 06: 45
Bovine spongiform encephalopathy.
 See Mad cow disease
Bowl Championship Series, 06: 187
Bowling, 06: 85-86, 05: 88, 04: 100
Boxer, U.S.S. (ship), 06: 278
Boxing, 06: 86, 05: 88-89, 04: 101
Bozize, François, 06: 38
Brain lateralization, 06: 82
Branch, Deion, 06: 188
Brancusi, Constantin, 06: 54
Brando, Marlon, 05: 283
Brazil, 06: 87, 228, 229, 231, 05: 89-90,
 04: 101-102; soccer, 06: 332, 333;
 table, 06: 230
Breakfast on Pluto (film), 06: 262
Breast cancer, 06: 252
Bremer, L. Paul, III, 04: 307
Breton, Thierry, 06: 192
Bridges, 06: 87, 116
Brin, Sergey, 04: 307
British Broadcasting Corp., 06: 375
British Columbia, 06: 98
Broadband connections, 06: 209
Brody, Adrien, 04: 307-308
Brokaw, Tom, 06: 365, 368 (il.)
Brokeback Mountain (film), 06: 258
Broken Flowers (film), 06: 259
Brooks, Garth, 06: 304
Brothers Grimm, The (film), 06: 258
Brown, Clarence "Gatemouth," 06: 139
Brown, Gordon, 06: 383-384

Brown, Michael D., 06: 160-164, 390
Brown, Oscar, Jr., 06: 139
Brownian motion, 06: 296
Brunei, 06: 58; table, 06: 58
Bryan, William Jennings, 06: 267-268
BTK killer, 06: 125
Bubbles, 06: 293
Buckovski, Vlado, 06: 249
Building and construction, 06: 87-89,
 05: 90-92, 04: 102-103; costs,
 06: 357. See also Architecture
Bukejlovic, Pero, 06: 85, 329
Bulgaria, 06: 47, 89, 05: 92, 04: 104;
 table, 06: 182
Burials, 06: 47
Burkina Faso, table, 06: 40
Burma. See Myanmar
Burns, William J., 06: 234
Burundi, 06: 38; table, 06: 40
Bush, Barbara, 06: 402 (il.)
Bush, George Herbert Walker, 06: 395
 (il.), 402 (il.); library, 06: 400 (il.)
Bush, George Walker, 06: 185 (il.), 313
 (il.), 393, 402 (il.), 05: 403, 04: 409;
 appointments and nominations, 06:
 73, 89, 170, 199, 286-288, 359-360;
 Brussels visit, 06: 181; National
 Guard service, 06: 210, 365
 policies and issues: agriculture, 06: 43,
 44; armed forces, 06: 51, 53; avian
 flu, 06: 308; Bolivia, 06: 84; Canada,
 06: 96; disaster responses, 06: 115,
 116, 164, 168, 364; education, 06:
 172; environment, 06: 101, 122, 178;
 faith-based initiatives, 06: 221; immigration, 06: 204, 253; intelligence, 06:
 389; Korea, North, 06: 223; labor, 06:
 227; Latin America, 06: 209, 231;
 Libya, 06: 234; Macedonia, 06: 249;
 Panama, 06: 281; Russia, 06: 316,
 325-326; Saudi Arabia, 06: 328; Social Security, 06: 335-345; transportation, 06: 380; Venezuela, 06: 406
Bush, Laura, 06: 402 (il.)
Bush, Reggie, 06: 187, 189 (il.)
Business identity theft, 06: 130
Byrd, Robert C., 06: 117 (il.)
Byrd amendment, 06: 183-184

C

Cabinet, U.S., 06: 89, 05: 92, 04: 104
Cable television, 06: 365
Cabrera Infante, Guillermo, 06: 139
Calatrava, Santiago, 06: 50
Caldecott Medal, 06: 247
California, 06: 102, 178; ballot initiatives,
 06: 154, 174-175, 311, 356; table,
 06: 355
Calipari, Nicola, 06: 218
Callaghan, James, 06: 139, 386
Cambodia, 06: 89, 05: 92, 04: 104;
 table, 06: 58
Cameroon, table, 06: 40
Canada, 06: 90-96, 285-286, 05: 93-98,
 04: 105-111; football, 06: 189
Canada, Prime Minister of, 06: 97, 05:
 99, 04: 111. See also Martin, Paul
Canada Winter Games, 06: 101
Canadian Mounted Police, 06: 97-98
Canadian provinces, 06: 97-100,
 05: 99-102, 04: 112-115
Canadian territories, 06: 101, 05: 103,
 04: 115-116
Canadian War Museum, 06: 49 (il.)
Canal, 06: 87
Cancer, 06: 68, 167, 251-252
Cape Verde, table, 06: 40
Capel, John, 06: 379 (il.)
Capital punishment, 06: 306, 361
Capote (film), 06: 259
Cappuccilli, Piero, 06: 139
CardSystems Inc., 06: 113
Carey, Mariah, 06: 304

Caribbean Community, 06: 413
Carlson, Denis, 06: 290
Cars. See **Automobile**
Carson, Johnny, 06: 139, *366-367*
Carter, Elliot, 06: 111
Carter, Jimmy, 06: 395 (il.); library, **06:** 402 (il.)
Carter, Rosalyn, 06: 402 (il.)
Casa delle Liberta, 06: 218
Casey, George W., Jr., 06: 51
Casinos, 06: 257
Cassel, Marcus, 06: 189 (il.)
Cassini (spacecraft), **06:** 60, 347, 349 (il.)
Castro, Fidel, 06: 134
Catalonia, 06: 350
Caterpillars, 06: 82
Catfish, 06: 81
Cathedral, 06: 88
Caucasus, 06: 315, 325
CBS (network), **06:** 210, 365, 366, 368
Cedar Revolution, 06: 232, 233, 254
Celebrex (drug), **06:** 167
Cellular telephones, 06: 72, 175, 364-365
Census, 06: *102,* 05: *104,* 04: *116.* See also **Population**
Census Bureau, U.S., 06: 102
Centers for Disease Control and Prevention, U.S., 06: 44, 252, 308, 328
Centers for Medicare and Medicaid Services, 06: 340
Central African Republic, 06: 38; table, **06:** 40
Central America. See **Latin America**
Central American-Dominican Republic Free Trade Agreement (2005), **06:** 44, 209, 227, 231
Central Intelligence Agency, 06: 271, 284, 286, 389, 392
Central Park (New York City), **06:** 283-284
Cervical cancer, 06: 68
Chad, table, **06:** 40
Chair Car (Hopper), **06:** 54
Chappelle, Dave, 06: 368-369
Charity Hospital (New Orleans), **06:** 198, 308
Charles, Dame Eugenia, 06: 139
Charles, Prince, 06: 383 (il.), 387
Charles, Ray, 05: *338*
Charleston (South Carolina), **06:** 87
Chauvin, Yves, 06: 274
Chavez Frias, Hugo, 06: 51, 228, 406, 413
Chechnya, 06: 315, 325
Chemistry, 06: *102-103,* 05: *104-105,* 04: *117;* Nobel Prize, **06:** 273-274
Chemotherapy, 06: 251-252
Chen Shui-bian, 06: 106, 363, 364
Chen Gonzales, Hilda, 06: 50
Cheney, Dick, 06: 51, 271, 284, 286, 390-392
Chertoff, Michael, 06: 89, 108, *283,* 390
Chess, 06: *103-104,* 05: *105-106,* 04: *118*
Chibitty, Charles, 06: 139
Chicago (Illinois), **06:** *104-105,* 415, 05: *106-108,* 04: *118-119*
Chicago Skyway, 06: 105
Chicago Symphony Orchestra, 06: 111
Chicago White Sox, 06: 74-76, 105
Chiche Gonzales, Hilda, 06: 50
Chicken Soup for the Soul (magazine), **06:** 251
Child support, 06: 102
Children, 06: 186-187, 305, 413; Africa, **06:** 38; lead poisoning, **06:** 193. See also **Adolescents; Education; Literature for children; Toys and games**
Childs, David, 06: 48
Chile, 06: *105,* 05: *109,* 04: *119;* table, **06:** 230
Chimpanzees, 06: 47, 81, 121

China, 06: 56, *105-107,* 05: *109-111,* 04: *120-122;* AIDS, **06:** 45; disasters, **06:** 107, 156-157, 179; economy and trade, **06:** 170, 171, 208; expressway, **06:** 88-89; space exploration, **06:** 350; table, **06:** 58
relations with: Europe, **06:** 181; Japan, **06:** 220; Russia, **06:** 327. See also **Taiwan**
China National Offshore Oil Corp., 06: 171
Chinese Communist Party, 06: 105
Chirac, Jacques, 06: 181, 191-192
Chisholm, Shirley, 06: 139
Chissano, Joaquim, 06: 39
Chocolate, 06: 187
ChoicePoint, Inc., 06: 113
Cholmondeley, Thomas, 06: 223
Chongzun Expressway, 06: 88-89
Chrétien, Jean, 06: 90-91, 97, 04: *111*
Christian Democratic Union, 06: 193, 195, 286
Christianity, 06: 218, 221-222. See also **Eastern Orthodox Churches; Protestantism; Roman Catholic Church**
Christie's, 06: 54
Christo, 06: 50, 265 (il.), *283-284*
CIA. See **Central Intelligence Agency**
Ciampo, Carlo Azeglio, 06: 218
Cincinnati (Ohio), **06:** 174
Cité Soleil (Haiti), **06:** 198
Citigroup (company), **06:** 73
City, 06: *108-110,* 05: *111-114,* 04: *122-125*
Civil rights, 06: 202, 04: *125-126.* See also **Human rights**
Civil unions. See **Same-sex marriage**
Clark, Helen, 06: 266
Clark, Wesley, 04: *308*
Clarke, Kenneth, 06: 385
Class action lawsuits, 06: 116
Classical music, 06: *111-112,* 282, 05: *114-116,* 04: *126-128;* Pulitzer Prizes, **06:** 309
Clemens, Roger, 06: 74
Clements, Vassar, 06: 139
Climate change. See **Global warming**
Clinton, Bill, 06: 218; library, **06:** 385 (il.), 402, 405
Clinton, Hillary, 06: 402 (il.)
Cloaca (Goos), **06:** 375-376
Cloning, 06: 81
Close, Chuck, 06: 54
Clothing, 06: 208. See also **Fashion**
CNN (network), **06:** 366
Coast Guard, U.S., 06: 163 (il.)
Coatzacoalos River, 06: 178 (il.)
Cobell, Elouise, 06: 206, 05: *326*
Cocaine, 06: 84
Cochran, Johnnie, 06: 139
Cocoons, 06: 82
Coetzee, J. M., 06: 234
Coll, Steve, 06: 235
Collective Security Treaty Organization, 06: 327
College Board, 06: 172
Colleges. See **Basketball; Education; Football**
Collins, Max Allan, 06: 239, 243-244
Colombia, 06: *113,* 228, 05: *116,* 04: *128-129;* shipwreck, **06:** 156; table, **06:** 230
Colorado, 06: 175, 356; table, **06:** 355
Coltrane, John, 06: 305
Columbia (space shuttle), **06:** 347
Comedy, 06: 305
Comet. See **Tempel 1**
Comic books, 06: 238-245
Comix, 06: 240
"Commander in Chief" (TV program), **06:** 369

Commerce, U.S. Department of, 06: 89, 169, 170, 285
Commercial identity theft, 06: 130
Commission on Terrorist Attacks, 06: 389
Commonwealth Heads of Government Meeting, 06: 66
Commonwealth of Independent States, 06: 326-327
Communication Workers of America, 06: 226
Communism, 06: 149
Commwarrior (computer virus), **06:** 175
Comoros, table, **06:** 40
Compact discs, 06: 303
Companhia Vale do Rio Doce (company), **06:** 87
Computer, 06: *113-114,* 05: *117-123,* 04: *129-130.* See also **Electronics; Internet**
Conference of Mayors, U.S., 06: 108
Congo (Brazzaville), table, **06:** 40
Congo (Kinshasa), **06:** *114-115,* 121, 05: *124,* 04: *130;* table, **06:** 40
Congress of the United States, 06: *115-120,* 05: *124-129,* 04: *130-137*
issues: Amtrak, **06:** 380; armed forces, **06:** 51-52; labor, **06:** 227; Medicare/Medicaid, **06:** 198, 338-345; Puerto Rico, **06:** 309; steroid abuse, **06:** 352. See also **Democratic Party** (U.S.); **Elections; Republican Party**
Congress Party (India), **06:** 206
Connecticut, table, **06:** 355
Conroy, Frank, 06: 139
Conservation, 06: 101, *121-122,* 05: *129-130,* 04: *138-139*
Conservative Party: Canada, **06:** 91, 92; United Kingdom, **06:** 384-386
Constantine the Great, 06: 48 (il.)
Constitution: European Union, **06:** 180, 191-192, 263; Iraq, **06:** 180, 211-213; Kenya, **06:** 223; Nigeria, **06:** 272-273
Consumer Price Index, 06: 169
Conte, Victor, 06: 352
Continued Dumping and Subsidy Offset Act (2000), **06:** 183-184
Contraception, 06: 167
Contract with God, A (Eisner), **06:** 240
Cook, Dane, 06: 305
Cook, Robin, 06: 139, 386
Cooke, Alistair, 05: *345*
Cooper, Anderson, 06: 366
Copyright, 06: 116, 304
Corby, Schapelle, 06: 62-63
Corn, 06: 43
Corporation for Public Broadcasting, 06: 392
Corzine, Jon Stevens, 06: 154, 174, 310
Costa Rica, 06: 231; table, **06:** 230
Costas, Bob, 06: 367
Costello, Peter, 06: 64, 66
Côte d'Ivoire, 06: 42; table, **06:** 40
Cotton, 06: 43, 44
Council on American-Islamic Relations, 06: 215
Country music, 06: 304
Courts, 06: *123,* 05: *131,* 04: *139-140;* separation of powers, **06:** 390-392. See also **Supreme Court of the United States**
Coutts, Russell, 06: 83
Covic, Dragan, 06: 85
Craig, Daniel, 06: 259
Crawford, Lester, 06: 199
Cream (band), **06:** 305
Creationism, 06: 173
Crede, Joe, 06: 74 (il.)

Credit cards, 06: 73, 128-131
Credit reports, 06: 131
Creeley, Robert, 06: 139
Crew Exploration Vehicle, 06: 347
Crick, Francis, 05: 84-85
Cricket, 06: *124*, 385 (il.), 05: *132-133*, *04: 140-141*
Crime, 06: *125-133*, 05: *133-134*, 04: *141-142*; El Salvador, 06: 176; Toronto, 06: 376-377. See also Courts; Identity theft; Police; Prisons; Terrorism; and specific country and city articles
Criminal identity theft, 06: 128-129
Crist, Ray, 06: 139
Croatia, 06: *134*, 181, 05: *134-135*, 04: *142-143;* table, 06: 182
Crows, 06: 275
Crumb, Robert, 06: 244
Crystallography, 06: 102
Cuba, 06: *134*, 228, 231, 05: *135*, 04: *143;* table, 06: 230
Cummings, Constance, 06: 139
Cunningham, Randy "Duke," 06: 117
Curling, 06: 353
Customs and Border Protection, U.S., 06: 204
Cutler, Lloyd N., 06: 139
Cycling, 06: 351, 353 (il.)
Cyclones, 06: 196
Cyprus, 06: 381; table, 06: 256
Czech Republic, 06: *135*, 199, 05: *135-137*, *04: 143-144;* table, 06: 182

D

DaimlerChrysler, 06: 69-70
Daley, Richard M., 06: 104-105
Dallas (Texas), 06: *135-136*, 05: *137*, *04: 144-145*
Dallas Center for the Performing Arts Foundation, 06: 135-136
Dallas/Fort Worth International Airport, 06: 135
Dance, 06: *136-137*, 05: *138-139*, *04: 145-147*
Dancer, Stanley, 06: 139
"Dancing with the Stars" (TV program), 06: 369
Danielpour, Richard, 06: 111
Dantzig, George Bernard, 06: 139
Darfur, 06: 254-255, 358, 388
Dark energy, 06: 300
Dark Knight series (Miller), 06: 241 (il.), 242
Darrow, Clarence, 06: 267-268
Davenport, Guy, 06: 139
Davis, Hope, 06: 244 (il.)
Davis, Ossie, 06: 139
Day, Pat, 06: 200
Dean, Howard, III, 06: 154, 04: *308-309*
Death of a Salesman (Miller), 06: 372, 373
Death penalty. See Capital punishment
Deaths, 06: *138-153*, 05: *140-148*, *04: 147-159*
Deaths and Entrances (Graham), 06: 136
Dee, Sandra, 06: 139-140
Deep Impact (spacecraft), 06: 60-61, 349 (il.)
Deep Throat, 06: 272
Defense, U.S. Department of, 06: 52, 106, 176, 408-409
Defense Advanced Research Projects Agency, U.S., 06: 176
Defense Base Closure and Realignment Commission, 06: 52
Delaware, table, 06: 355
DeLay, Tom, 06: 117, 311
Delights & Shadows (Kooser), 06: 302
Delli Colli, Tonino, 06: 140
Delorean, John, 06: 140
Deloria, Vine, Jr., 06: 140
De los Angeles, Victoria, 06: 140

Delphi Corp., 06: 69, 170
Delta Air Lines Inc., 06: 71, 72, 169
Del Tredici, David, 06: 111
Demetrios, 06: 168
Democratic National Committee, 06: 154
Democratic Party: Albania, 06: 45; Japan, 06: 220
Democratic Party (U.S.), 06: *154*, 287, 05: *149-150*, 04: *160;* judicial nominees, 06: 123. See also Elections
Democratic Progressive Party, 06: 106, 363-364
Denker, Arnold, 06: 140
Denmark, 06: 101, *155*, 05: *150-151*, 04: *161;* table, 06: 182
Dennis, Clarence, 06: 140
Denver (Ohio), 06: 175
Denver, Bob, 06: 140
Denver, University of, 06: 199
Depression (illness), 06: 253
Detroit (Michigan), 06: 174
Detroit Spurs, 06: 77-78
Deuterium, 06: 293
Devils & Dust (recording), 06: 304
de Young Museum, 06: 49 (il.), 50
Diamond, David, 06: 140
Diamonds, 06: 101
Diana, Princess, 06: 387
DiCaprio, Leonardo, 06: 261 (il.)
Didion, Joan, 06: 237
Dietary Guidelines for Americans, 06: 186
Diets, 06: 186, 252
Digital cameras, 06: 175-176
Dinosaurs, 06: 279-281
Dione (satellite), 06: 349 (il.)
Dirceu de Oliveira e Silva, Jose, 06: 87
"Dirty war," in Argentina, 06: 51
Disability, 06: *155*, 198, 345, 05: *151*, *04: 161*
Disasters, 06: *155-165*, 05: *152-155*, *04: 162-164;* city planning, 06: 108; congressional action, 06: 115-116; Houston explosion, 06: 201; tax assistance, 06: 364. See also Aviation; Earthquakes; Fires; Hurricanes; Railroads; Shipwrecks; Tsunami; Weather
Discovery (space shuttle), 06: 347, 348 (il.)
Disease. See Health care issues; Medicine; Mental health; Public health
District of Columbia. See Washington, D.C.
Djibouti, table, 06: 40
DNA, 06: 102
Doctor Atomic (Adams and Sellers), 06: 111
Dogs, 06: 81, 99-100
Doha round, 06: 209
Doll, Sir Richard, 06: 140
Dolphins (mammals), 06: 82, 275
Dominica, table, 06: 230
Dominican Republic, 06: 231, 413; fire, 06: 156; table, 06: 230
Don Quixote (Balanchine), 06: 136
Donald, Rod, 06: 266
Doohan, James, 06: 140
Dos Santos, Lucia de Jesus, 06: 140
Doubt (Shanley), 06: 376
Dover (Pennsylvania), 06: 173
Dow Jones Industrial Average, 06: 357
Drama. See Theater
Dresden (Germany), 06: 88
Drought, 06: 64, 410 (il.)
Drucker, Peter, 06: 140
Drug abuse, 06: 166, 05: *155-156*, *04: 164-165;* sports, 06: 76, 351, 352. See also Marijuana
Drug trafficking: Afghanistan, 06: 37;

AIDS, 06: 44-45; Australia, 06: 62-63; Bolivia, 06: 84; Canada, 06: 97-98; Colombia, 06: 113
Drugs, 06: *167*, 05: *156-157*, 04: *165-166;* Canada, 06: 99; depression, 06: 253; Medicare program, 06: 198, 340-341
Drunken driving, 06: 328
Duhalde, Eduardo, 06: 50
Duisenberg, Willem, 06: 140
Duma, 06: 315
Dumpster diving (crime), 06: 130
Duncan, Tim, 06: 77-78
Dunne, Peter, 06: 266
Durand, Asher B., 06: 53-54
Durkan, Mark, 06: 274
Dwarfism, Island, 06: 45-46
Dworkin, Andrea, 06: 140
Dylan, Bob, 06: 305
Dzurunda, Mikulas, 06: 332

E

E-mail, 06: 128
E=mc^2, 06: 298
Eagle Nebula, 06: 61 (il.)
Earthquakes, 06: 192-193; Asia, 06: 30 (il.), 56, 156, 192, 205, 278, 293. See also Tsunami
East Timor, 06: 58; table, 06: 58
Easter Rising (1916), 06: 214
Eastern Orthodox Churches, 06: 152, 168, 05: *157-158*, 04: *166*
Eastwood, Clint, 06: 260 (il.)
eBay Corp., 06: 364
Ebbers, Bernard, 06: 125
Eberhart, Richard, 06: 140
Ebola, 06: 121
Ebony (magazine), 06: 250
Economics, United States, 06: *168-170*, 05: *158-160*, 04: *166-168;* census data, 06: 102
Economics, World, 06: *170-171*, 05: *158-160*, 04: *166-168;* Nobel Prize, 06: 273. See also Bank; Labor and employment; Manufacturing; Unemployment and specific country articles
Ecuador, 06: *171*, 228, 229, 05: *160*, 04: *168;* table, 06: 230
Education, 06: *172-173*, 05: *160-173*, 04: *168-181;* Canada, 06: 98, 101; China, 06: 106; disabilities, 06: 155; Head Start, 06: 413; poetry, 06: 302
Education, U.S. Department of, 06: 89, 172, 288-289
Education Amendments (1972), 06: 361
Edwards, John, 05: *326-327*
Edwards, Ralph, 06: 140
Egypt, 06: 38, *173-174*, 254, 05: *174-175*, 04: *182;* table, 06: 256. See also Terrorism
Egypt, Ancient, 06: 47, 173 (il.)
Einstein, Albert, 06: 293, *294-301*
Eisenhower, Dwight D., 06: 399
Eisenman, Peter, 06: 50, 88, 194
Eisner, Will, 06: 140, 240
ElBaradei, Mohamed, 06: 273, 388
Elections, 06: *174-175*, 05: *174-178*, *04: 182-183;* state, 06: 154, 174, 310-311, 356; voter turnout, 06: 102. See also Democratic Party (U.S.); Republican Party; United States, President of the; and specific country, province, and city articles
Électricité de France (company), 06: 51
Electricity, 06: 297
Electromagnetic waves, 06: 295-296
Electronics, 06: 175-176, 05: *179*, 04: *183-184*. See also Computer; Telecommunications
Electrons, 06: 296
Eliasson, Jan, 06: 388

Elizabeth II, **06:** *96, 97,* 266, 387
Ellis, Bret Easton, **06:** 235
El Salvador, **06:** *176,* 231, **05:** *179,*
   04: *184;* table, **06:** 230
Emancipation of Mimi, The (recording),
   06: 304
Embryos, Dinosaur, **06:** 280
Eminent domain, **06:** 108-110, 360-361
Emirates Palace, **06:** 88 (il.)
Emmy Awards, **06:** 369
Empey, Sir Reg, **06:** 274
Employment. See Labor and
   employment
Energy, U.S. Department of, **06:** 89
Energy supply, **06:** 116, *176-177,* 413,
   05: *180-181,* **04:** *184-185;* prices,
   06: 357-358. See also Natural gas;
   Petroleum
Engineering. See Building and
   construction
England. See United Kingdom
England, Lynndie R., **06:** 52, 201
Enkhbayar, Nambaryn, **06:** 57
Enron Corp., **06:** 74
Environmental pollution, **06:** *178-179,*
   05: *181-182,* **04:** *185-186;* Canada,
   06: 91, 93; court ruling, **06:** 123;
   Malaysia, **06:** 251; Peru, **06:** 290
Environmental Protection Agency,
   06: 123
Equatorial Guinea, table, **06:** 40
Equestrian events, **06:** 352
Eritrea, **06:** 42; table, **06:** 40
Estonia, table, **06:** 182
ETA (group), **06:** 351
Ether theory, **06:** 295
Ethiopia, **06:** 42, 157, 266-267; table,
   06: 40
EU. See European Union
Europe, **06:** *180-184,* **05:** *183-187,*
   04: *187-191;* economy, **06:** 170-171;
   floods, **06:** 157
Europe Central (Vollmann), **06:** 236-237
European Aeronautic Defense and
   Space Company, **06:** 71
European Central Bank, **06:** 171
European Commission.
   See European Union
European Space Agency,
   06: 60, 347-350
European Union, **06:** 71-72, 180-184, 209
   members: Austria, **06:** 67; Czech Republic, **06:** 135; France, **06:** 191, 192; Germany, **06:** 195; Greece, **06:** 197; Hungary, **06:** 203; Ireland, **06:** 214; Italy,
   06: 218; Netherlands, **06:** 263; Poland,
   06: 302; Portugal, **06:** 306; Slovakia,
   06: 332; Spain, **06:** 351; Sweden, **06:**
   361; Switzerland, **06:** 363
   relations with: Albania, **06:** 45; Bosnia-
   Herzegovina, **06:** 84; Bulgaria, **06:**
   89; Croatia, **06:** 134; Indonesia, **06:**
   207; Libya, **06:** 234; Macedonia, **06:**
   249; Myanmar, **06:** 262; Romania,
   06: 313; Russia, **06:** 326; Serbia and
   Montenegro, **06:** 329; Syria, **06:** 363;
   Turkey, **06:** 381; Uzbekistan, **06:** 406;
   Zimbabwe, **06:** 414-415
Euthanasia, **06:** 150
Evangelical Christians, **06:** 307-308
"Everybody Hates Chris" (TV program),
   06: 369
"Everybody Loves Raymond" (TV pro-
   gram), **06:** 368
Everything, Theory of, **06:** 300
Evolution, **06:** 172-173
Eyadema, Gnassingbe, **06:** 42, 140

F

Fahd (king of Saudi Arabia), **06:** 140,
   328-329
"Family Guy" (TV program), **06:** 367-368
Family Stone, The (film), **06:** 258-259

Farm and farming. See Agriculture
Farrell, Suzanne, **06:** 136
Fashion, **06:** *184-185,* **05:** *187-188,*
   04: *191-193*
Fatah, **06:** 371
Fazio, Antonio, **06:** 219
FBI. See Federal Bureau of Investigation
FCC. See Federal Communications
   Commission
Federal Aviation Administration, **06:** 72
Federal Bureau of Investigation, **06:** 125,
   135, 174, 389
Federal Communications Commission,
   06: 72, 364, 365
Federal Emergency Management
   Agency, **06:** 29 (il.), 108, 160-164,
   168, 354, 390, 393
Federal Insurance Contribution Act
   (1937), **06:** 336
Federal Reserve System, **06:** 73,
   169-170, 357, 392
Federal Trade Commission, **06:** 127,
   132, 133
Federation Internationale de Football
   Association, **06:** 332, 333, **05:** 359
Federer, Roger, **06:** 351, 369-370
Fedorov, Igor, **06:** 315
Fei Junlong, **06:** 350
Felt, W. Mark, **06:** 272
FEMA. See Federal Emergency
   Management Agency
Fences (Wilson), **06:** 372, 374
Fencing, **06:** 353
Fernandez de Kirchner, Cristina, **06:** 50
Ferrer, Fernando, **06:** 264
Fertility rates, **06:** 306
Fianna Fail, **06:** 214
FICA taxes, **06:** 336-338
Fico, Robert, **06:** 332
Fiedler, John, **06:** 140
Field hockey, **06:** 353
50 Cent, **06:** 303-304
Fiji, table, **06:** 277
Filibuster, **06:** 123
Films. See Motion pictures
Financial identity theft, **06:** 128
Finland, **06:** *185,* **05:** *189,* **04:** *193;* table,
   06: 182
Firearms. See Gun laws
Fires, **06:** 156, 306, 328, 411
First Nations, **06:** 99-101
Fischer, Bobby, **06:** 103-104
Fish, **06:** 81
Fishing industry, **06:** 99, 179
Fission, Nuclear, **06:** 300
Fitzgerald, Geraldine, **06:** 140
Fitzgerald, Patrick J., **06:** 104-105, *284*
Fitzgerald, Peter, **06:** 392
Flemings, **06:** 80
Fletcher, Arthur, **06:** 140
Fletcher, Ernie, **06:** 357
Flip-flops, **06:** 185 (il.)
Floods, **06:** 156-157; Guatemala, **06:** 198;
   India, **06:** 205 (il.), 206; Romania, **06:**
   313; U.S., **06:** 26 (il.), 158-165, 409-
   412. See also Hurricanes; Tsunami
Floren, Myron, **06:** 140
Flores (island), **06:** 45
Florida, **06:** 102, 199, 354, 356-357; table,
   06: 355
Flu. See Influenza
Fokine, Michel, **06:** 136
Fontana, Carlo, **06:** 111
Food, **06:** *186-187,* **05:** *189-190,* **04:** *193-*
   194; Africa, **06:** 39, 42; Korea, North,
   06: 223; labor issues, **06:** 226. See
   also Agriculture
Food and Drug Administration, **06:** 167,
   199
Food Guide Pyramid, **06:** 186
Football, **06:** 88, *187-191,* **05:** *190-194,*
   04: *194-197.* See also Australian
   rules football; Soccer

Foote, Shelby, **06:** 140-141
Ford, Bill, **06:** 69
Ford, Gerald R., **06:** 395 (il.), 401 (il.)
Ford Made in America (Tower),
   06: 112
Ford Motor Co., **06:** 69, 170, 227
Fordham Spire, **06:** 104 (il.)
Foreshore and Seabed Act (2004),
   06: 266
Forests, **06:** 121-122, 415-416. See
   also Rain forests
Forman, James, **06:** 141
Forrester, Douglas, **06:** 154, 174, 310
Fort Worth Zoo, **06:** 415
Fossett, Steve, **06:** 269-270
Fossils, **06:** 45-47, 279-280
Fowles, John, **06:** 141
Fox, Liam, **06:** 385
Fox Quesada, Vicente, **06:** 253
Foxx, Jamie, **06:** 260 (il.), *284-285*
Fradkov, Mikhail, **06:** 315
France, **06:** 180-182, *191-192,* **05:** *194-*
   195, **04:** *198-199;* table, **06:** 182
Franklin, Benjamin, **06:** 292
Franklin, Gretchen, **06:** 141
Franklin D. Roosevelt Presidential
   Library and Museum, **06:** 394 (il.),
   397 (il.), 399
Frattini, Franco, **06:** 234
Freas, F. K., **06:** 141
Free Aceh Movement, **06:** 207
Free Trade Agreement of the
   Americas, **06:** 209, 231
Freedom Tower, **06:** 48
French Open, **06:** 360
French Quarter (New Orleans), **06:** 164
Frist, Bill, **04:** *309*
Fruits Basket (novel series), **06:** 245 (il.)
Fry, Christopher, **06:** 141
Fujimori Kenya, Alberto, **06:** 290
Fungus, **06:** 44
Fur, **06:** 184

G

Gabon, table, **06:** 40
Gambia, table, **06:** 40
Game theory, **06:** 273
Games. See Toys and games
Gandhi, Sonia, **05:** *327*
Ganji, Akbar, **06:** 211
Gannett Company, Inc., **06:** 272
Garang de Mabior, John,
   06: 254, 358-359
García Márquez, Gabriel, **06:** 234
García Pérez, Alan, **06:** 290
Gardasil (drug), **06:** 68
Garden District (New Orleans),
   06: 164
Gardening, **05:** *196,* **04:** *199-200*
Gas, Natural. See Natural gas
Gas del Sur (program), **06:** 228
Gasoline. See Petroleum
Gates, The (art), **06:** 50, 265 (il.),
   283-284
Gatlin, Justin, **06:** 378
Gay, Tyson, **06:** 379 (il.)
Gay marriage. See Same-sex marriage
Gaza Strip, **06:** 216-217, 254, 371
Gazprom (company), **06:** 314
Gbagbo, Laurent, **06:** 42
General Motors Corp., **06:** 69, 170, 227
General theory of relativity,
   06: 298-299
Genetic engineering, **06:** 81, 103
Genetically modified crops, **06:** 43-44
Genome, **06:** 82
Geology, **06:** *192-193,* **05:** *196-197,*
   04: *200-201*
George H. W. Bush Presidential
   Library and Museum, **06:** 400 (il.)
Georgia (country), **06:** *192-193,* 318-
   320, **05:** *197-198,* **04:** *202;* table,
   06: 58

Georgia (state), **06:** 356; table, **06:** 355
Georgia Aquarium, **06:** 415
Gerald R. Ford Presidential Library and Museum, **06:** 401 (il.)
Germany, **06:** 180-182, *193-195*, 286, **05:** *198-199*, **04:** *202-203;* cathedral, **06:** 88; soccer, **06:** 332; table, **06:** 182
Get a Life (Gordimer), **06:** 234
Getty Museum, J. Paul, **06:** 248
Gezeichneten, Die (Schreker), **06:** 112 (il.)
Ghana, **06:** 38; table, **06:** 40
Ghost Wars (Coll), **06:** 235
Giacomo (horse), **06:** 200
Giamatti, Paul, **06:** 244 (il.)
Gilead (Robinson), **06:** 235
Githongo, John, **06:** 222
Giulini, Carlo Maria, **06:** 141
Glaciers, **06:** 179
Glass, Bob, **06:** 86
Glauber, Roy J., **06:** 274
Global Positioning System, **06:** 274, 299, 301
Global warming, **06:** 64, 178, 179, *195-196*, 276
Gnassingbe, Faure, **06:** 42
Goldsmith, Lord, **06:** 383
Golf, **06:** *196-197*, 257, 351, 352, **05:** *200-201*, **04:** *203-204*
Gomery, John, **06:** 90-91
Gonzales, Alberto, **06:** 89, 123, *285*
Good Friday Agreement (1998), **06:** 274
Good Night, and Good Luck (film), **06:** 259
Goodale, Ralph, **06:** 90-91, 96
Google Inc., **06:** 114, 233, 358
Gorbachev, Mikhail, **06:** 149, 151 (il.), 403 (il.)
Gordimer, Nadine, **06:** 234
Gordon, Bruce, **06:** 201
Gorillas, **06:** 82, 121
Gorshin, Frank, **06:** 141
Gotham Glory (Del Tredici), **06:** 111
Government Accountability Office, **06:** 392
GPS. See Global Positioning System
Graham, Billy, **06:** 307
Grammy Awards, **06:** 112, 303
Grand Turk (ship), **06:** 267 (il.)
Graner, Charles A., Jr., **06:** 201
Grant, Joe, **06:** 141
Graphic novels, **06:** *238-245*, 259
Gravity, **06:** 298
Gray, L. Patrick, III, **06:** 141
Great apes, **06:** 121
Great Britain. See United Kingdom
Greece, **06:** *197*, **05:** *201*, **04:** *205;* air crash, **06:** 155; Eastern Orthodox Church, **06:** 168; table, **06:** 182
Greenhouse gases, **06:** 178, 196, 276
Greenspan, Alan, **06:** 73, 170, 335
Gregoire, Christine, **06:** 154, 311
Grenada, table, **06:** 230
"Grey's Anatomy" (TV program), **06:** 367
Griffin, Jimmy, **06:** 141
Grizzly Man (film), **06:** 259
Grodnikov, Vasily, **06:** 80
Grokster, Ltd., **06:** 209-210
Gross, Stanislav, **06:** 135
Gross domestic product, **06:** 168-170
Ground Zero (New York), **04:** *50-52*
Group of Eight, **06:** 38, 171, 178, 305, 325, 330
Groznyy (Chechnya), **06:** 324 (il.)
Grubbs, Robert H., **06:** 273-274
Gruner+Jahr (company), **06:** 251
Grunwald, Henry A., **06:** 141
Guantanamo Bay (Cuba), **06:** 37, 201
Guatemala, **06:** 48, *198*, 231, **05:** *201*, **04:** *205;* table, **06:** 230
Guebuza, Armando, **06:** 39
Guerrero, Lalo, **06:** 141
Guggenheim Bilbao Museum, **06:** 55 (il.)
Guinea, table, **06:** 40

Guinea-Bissau, table, **06:** 40
Gul, Abdullah, **06:** 45, 381
Gulf Intracostal Waterway, **06:** 159, 162 (il.)
Gun laws, **06:** 116, 346
Gutierrez, Carlos M., **06:** 89, *285*
Gutierrez, Lucio Edwin, **06:** 171, 229
Guyana, table, **06:** 230
Gyanendra Bir Bikram Shah Dev, **06:** 262
Gymnastics, **06:** 352

H

Haas, Karl, **06:** 141
Habib, Mamdou, **06:** 62
Hackers, **06:** 127
Hackett, Grant, **06:** 362
Hackworth, David, **06:** 141
Hagedorn, Horace, **06:** 141
Hagen, Kevin, **06:** 141
Hain, Peter, **06:** 274
Haiti, **06:** *198*, **05:** *202-211*, **04:** *205;* table, **06:** 230
Hajed, Sheikh Hasina, **06:** 72
Hall, John L., **06:** 274
Hallaren, Mary A., **06:** 141
Halloran, Peter, **06:** 330
Halonen, Tarja, **06:** 185
Hamas, **06:** 371
Hamm, Paul, **06:** 352, **05:** *327*
Hans Island, **06:** 101
Hänsch, Theodor W., **06:** 274
Harding, Warren G., **06:** 398-399
Hardy, Jessica, **06:** 362
Hariri, Rafik, **06:** 141, 232-233, 254, 363, 371
Harman, Sabrina, **06:** 201
Harper, Stephen, **06:** 92
Harry Potter and the Half-Blood Prince (Rowling), **06:** 246
Hate crimes, **06:** 125
Haute couture. See Fashion
Haver, June, **06:** 141
Hawaii, **06:** 102, 356; table, **06:** 355
Hayes, Rutherford B., **06:** 396, 398, 404
Head Start program, **06:** 413
Health and Human Services, U.S. Department of, **06:** 186, 199, 252, 335, 340, 345, 413
Health care issues, **06:** *198-199*, **05:** *212*, **04:** *206;* Canada, **06:** 92; China, **06:** 106-107; congressional action, **06:** 116; dietary guidelines, **06:** 186. See also Drugs; Medicaid; Medicare; Medicine; Mental health; Public health
Health-South Corp., **06:** 125
Heart failure, **06:** 167
Heath, Sir Edward, **06:** 141, 386
Heath, Percy, **06:** 141
Hefley, Joel, **06:** 116-117
Heinäluoma, Eero, **06:** 185
Heisman Trophy, **06:** 187
Helicobacter pylori, **06:** 273
Helms, Chet, **06:** 141
Henderson, Skitch, **06:** 142
Henin-Hardenne, Justine, **06:** 370
Henkes, Kevin, **06:** 247
Hepburn, Katharine, **04:** *286-289*
Herceptin (drug), **06:** 167
Herman, George, **06:** 142
Heroin, **06:** 44-45
Hezbollah, **06:** 232, 254
Hicks, David, **06:** 62
Hieroglyphs, **06:** 48
Highways, **06:** 88-89, 116, 328
Hildegarde, **06:** 142
Hilleman, Maurice, **06:** 142
Himalayan Mountains, **06:** 278
Hinduism, **06:** 205
Hippopotamus, **06:** 416 (il.)
Hirohito, **06:** 220
Hirschfeld, Al, **04:** *382-383*

Hispanic Americans, **06:** 102, 225, 248, 285, 306
History of Violence, A (film), **06:** 239, 259
Hmong, **06:** 59
Ho Chi Minh City (Vietnam), **06:** 407 (il.)
Hockey, **06:** *199*, 226-227, 351, **05:** *212-214*, **04:** *206-208*
Hokusai Manga, **06:** 243
Holliger International Inc., **06:** 272
Holloway, Natalee, **06:** 366-367
Holmes, Ray, **06:** 142
Holocaust, **06:** 50, 194 (il.), 222, 256
Homeland Security, U.S. Department of, **06:** 72, 89, 108, 283, 389-390
Homelessness, **06:** 136
Homicide, **06:** 125
Hominids. See Anthropology
Homo florensiensis, **06:** 45-46
Homo sapiens, **06:** 46-47
Homosexuality, **06:** 92, 201-203, 308, 312. See also Same-sex marriage
Honda Motor Co., **06:** 68 (il.), 70
Honduras, **06:** 231; table, **06:** 230
Hong Kong (China), **06:** 107
Hood, Jay W., **06:** 201
Hope, Bob, **04:** *156-159*
Hopper, Edward, **06:** 54
Horn, Shirley, **06:** 142
Horse racing, **06:** *199-200*, **05:** *214-215*, **04:** *208-209*
Hospitals. See Medicine; Public health
Hotel Association of Washington, D.C., **06:** 226
House of Representatives, U.S. See Congress of the United States
Housing, **06:** 169-170, 248
Houston (Texas), **06:** *200-201*, **05:** *214-215*, **04:** *209-210*
Houston Astros, **06:** 74-76, 200-201
Houston Grand Opera, **06:** 111
Howard, John, **06:** 62-64, *66*, **05:** *67*, **04:** *81*
Howard, Michael, **06:** 384-386
Hu Jintao, **06:** 106, 107, 364, **04:** *309*
Human rights, **06:** 201-203, **05:** *216-217*, **04:** *210-211;* Africa, **06:** 38, 39; Argentina, **06:** 51; China, **06:** 106; Iran, **06:** 211; John Paul II's views, **06:** 152; Turkey, **06:** 381. See also Civil rights
Human Rights Council, **06:** 388
Hun Sen, **06:** 89
Hungary, **06:** 180, 203, **05:** *217*, **04:** *211-212;* table, **06:** 182
Hunter, Bob, **06:** 142
Hunter, Evan, **06:** 142
Hurricane Katrina, **06:** 26 (il.), 157, *158-165*, 179, 409, 412; government actions, **06:** 52, 115-116, 364; television coverage, **06:** 365-366
impact on: city planning, **06:** 108; Dallas, **06:** 136; economy, **06:** 168-169; energy supply, **06:** 176, 209; federal government, **06:** 390, 393; Houston, **06:** 200; libraries, **06:** 233; mental health, **06:** 252; newspapers, **06:** 272; safety, **06:** 328; state government, **06:** 354-356; transportation, **06:** 380; zoo, **06:** 415
Hurricane Rita, **06:** 108, 164, 179, 412
impact on: climate, **06:** 179; economy, **06:** 169; energy supply, **06:** 176, 209, 381; Houston, **06:** 200; state government, **06:** 354
Hurricanes, **06:** 179, 195, 198, 409-412; Dennis, **06:** 134, 198, 412; Emily, **06:** 412; Wilma, **06:** 169, 411, 412. See also Hurricane Katrina; Hurricane Rita
Hussey, Ruth, **06:** 142
Hutu, **06:** 38

Huygens (spacecraft), 06: 60, 347, 349 (il.)
Hybrid cars, 06: 68 (ils.), 177
Hyundai Motor Co., 06: 70

I

I-Dog (toy), 06: 377-378
Iakovos, Geron, 06: 142
Ice, in polar regions, 06: 179, 196, 276
Ice skating, 06: 203, 05: 217-218, 04: 212-213
Iceland, table, 06: 182
Idaho, table, 06: 355
Identity cloning, 06: 129
Identity theft, 06: 113, 126-133
Illinois, 06: 356; table, 06: 355
Immigration, 06: 204, 05: 218-219, 04: 213; to Australia, 06: 63; to Austria, 06: 67; to Canada, 06: 99; to Denmark, 06: 155; to Libya, 06: 234; to Netherlands, 06: 263-264; to U.S., 06: 204, 253, 357
Immunizations, 06: 308
Implants, Surgical, 06: 103
India, 06: 124, 204-206, 05: 219-221, 04: 214-215; disasters, 06: 30 (il.), 56, 155-157; poaching, 06: 121; table, 06: 58; terrorism, 06: 371
Indian, American, 06: 99-101, 206-207, 05: 221-223, 04: 215-216
Indian Ocean, 06: 56. See also Tsunami
Indian Probate Reform Act (2004), 06: 207
Indiana, table, 06: 355
Indianapolis 500, 06: 70, 287
Indonesia, 06: 56-57, 207-208, 215 (il.), 05: 224-225, 04: 217; Australia relations, 06: 62-63, 66; disasters, 06: 156; excavations, 06: 45; libraries, 06: 233; public health, 06: 308; table, 06: 58; terrorism, 06: 208, 372
Influenza, 06: 308. See also Avian influenza
Insulza, José Miguel, 06: 231
Intelligent design, 06: 172-173
Inter-American Development Bank, 06: 113
Interest rates, 06: 73, 169-171, 357
Interior, U.S. Department of the, 06: 206
International Association of Machinists and Aerospace Workers, 06: 225-227
International Atomic Energy Agency, 06: 210, 251
International Congress on Islamic Feminism, 06: 214
International Cricket Council, 06: 124
International Criminal Court, 06: 181, 231, 255, 358, 371, 388
International Energy Agency, 06: 176-177
International Football Association, 06: 333
International Monetary Fund, 06: 51, 134, 170, 209, 313
International Olympic Committee, 06: 276
International Space Station, 06: 347
International trade, 06: 208-209, 05: 225-226, 04: 217-218
International Tribunal for War Crimes, 06: 329
Internet, 06: 209-210, 364, 05: 226-227, 04: 219-220; aircraft, 06: 72; Canadian drugs, 06: 99; Census Bureau site, 06: 102; search engines, 05: 118-123; security, 06: 127, 130-132
Internet & American Life Project, 06: 209
Iowa, table, 06: 355
iPod, 06: 114 (ils.), 175, 209, 310, 378
Iran, 06: 210-211, 256, 281-282, 05: 227,

04: 220; disasters, 06: 156; European Union relations, 06: 182; table, 06: 256
Iraq, 06: 13 (il.), 21 (il.), 211-213, 255-256, 05: 228-241; armed forces, 06: 51; European Union relations, 06: 181-182; oil-for-food program, 06: 388; stampede, 06: 157; table, 06: 256. See also Terrorism
Iraq War (2003-), 06: 51, 212, 213, 255-256, 05: 228-241, 04: 221-240; human rights, 06: 201; intelligence failings, 06: 389; mental health of troops, 06: 252-253; newspaper controversies, 06: 271
role or position of: armed forces, 06: 53; Australia, 06: 62; Canada, 06: 96; Italy, 06: 218; Pinter, Harold, 06: 375; Poland, 06: 303; Sheehan, Cindy, 06: 288; Syria, 06: 363; United Kingdom, 06: 383, 387
Ireland, 06: 214, 05: 242, 04: 241; table, 06: 182
Irish Republican Army, 06: 274
Ishiguro, Hiroshi, 06: 271 (il.)
Ishiguro, Kazuo, 06: 235
Islam, 06: 152, 214-215, 05: 242-243, 04: 242; Australia, 06: 62; Bangladesh, 06: 72; Egypt, 06: 173-174; Europe, 06: 181; France, 06: 191; India, 06: 205; Italy, 06: 218; Netherlands, 06: 263-264; Roman Catholic Church relations, 06: 312; United Kingdom, 06: 386
Islamic Jihad, 06: 371
Islamic Society of North America, 06: 214
Israel, 06: 216-218, 222, 254, 308, 05: 243-244, 04: 243-244; El Salvador relations, 06: 176; Iran relations, 06: 211, 256; table, 06: 256; terrorism, 06: 371. See also Judaism
Italy, 06: 218-219, 05: 245, 04: 244-245; table, 06: 182
Ivory Coast. See Côte d'Ivoire

J

J. P. Morgan Chase (bank), 06: 73-74
Jack (radio format), 06: 310
Jackson, Michael, 06: 125
Jafari, Ibrahim Aleshaiker al-, 06: 213, 255
Jamaat-ul-Mujahideen, 06: 72
Jamaica, table, 06: 230
James E. Sullivan Award, 06: 352
Jammu and Kashmir, 06: 56, 204-205, 278
Jane (fossil), 06: 280 (il.)
Janeway, Elizabeth, 06: 142
Japan, 06: 56, 219-220, 05: 246-247, 04: 246-247; agriculture, 06: 44; economy, 06: 171; table, 06: 58; train wreck, 06: 157
Japanese Aerospace Exploration Agency, 06: 347
Japanese encephalitis, 06: 157
Jarhead (film), 06: 259
Jazz, 06: 270-271, 305
Jean, Michaëlle, 06: 93-96, 285-286
Jeanne-Claude, 06: 50, 265 (il.), 283-284
Jemaah Islamiyah, 06: 372
Jennings, Peter, 06: 142, 365, 368 (il.)
Jerusalem, 06: 168
Jews. See Judaism
Jimmy Carter Library and Museum, 06: 404 (il.)
Jimmy Corrigan, The Smartest Kid on Earth (Ware), 06: 242 (il.), 243
Johanns, Mike, 06: 43, 89
John (Close), 06: 54
John F. Kennedy Library and Museum, 06: 401 (il.), 404 (il.)

John Paul II, 06: 18 (il.), 142, 148-153, 311
Johnson, John H., 06: 250
Johnson, Leavander, 06: 86
Johnson, Liz, 06: 85-86
Johnson, Lyndon B., 06: 339, 395 (il.), 397 (il.)
Johnson, Philip, 06: 50, 142
Johnson Publishing Co., 06: 250
Johnson-Sirleaf, Ellen, 06: 42
Jones, Norah, 04: 309
Jordan, 06: 33 (il.), 221, 05: 248, 04: 247; table, 06: 256
Joyon, Francis, 06: 83
Judaism, 06: 152, 221-222, 05: 248-249, 04: 248; memorial, 06: 50, 194 (il.); Roman Catholic Church relations, 06: 312
Jugnauth, Pravind, 06: 251
Justice, U.S. Department of, 06: 89, 123, 233, 285, 306
Justice and Peace Law (Colombia), 06: 113
Juveniles, in prison, 06: 306

K

Kabbah, Ahmad Tejan, 06: 330
Kabila, Joseph, 06: 114-115
Kabui, Joseph, 06: 277
Kaczynski, Jaroslaw, 06: 302-303
Kaczynski, Lech, 06: 302-303
Kadare, Ismail, 06: 236
Kadima (party), 06: 217-218, 254
Kain, Karen, 06: 137
Kaine, Timothy M., 06: 154, 174, 310-311
Kampuchea. See Cambodia
Kansas, 06: 173, 175, 356; table, 06: 355
Karadzic, Radovan, 06: 329
Karamanlis, Costas, 06: 197
Karimov, Islam, 06: 406
Karpinski, Janis, 06: 52, 201
Karume, Amani, 06: 42-43
Karzai, Hamid, 06: 37
Kashmir. See Jammu and Kashmir
Kasparov, Garry, 06: 103, 315
Katrina, Hurricane. See Hurricane Katrina
Kazakhstan, 06: 222, 05: 249, 04: 248; table, 06: 58
Keeling, Charles D., 06: 142
Kefaya Movement, 06: 173
Kelly, R., 06: 305
Kemp, Corey, 06: 290
Kempner, Nan, 06: 142
Kennan, George F., 06: 143
Kennedy, Charles, 06: 384
Kennedy, Edward, 06: 342
Kennedy, John F., 06: 401 (il.), 404 (il.)
Kennedy, Rosemary, 06: 143
Kennedy Center (New York City), 06: 137
Kennedy Space Center, 06: 347
Kentucky, 06: 356, 357; table, 06: 355
Kenya, 06: 38, 43, 222-223, 05: 250, 04: 249; table, 06: 40
Kerr-Mills Act (1960), 06: 339-340
Kerry, John Forbes, 05: 328
Khachiyan, Leonid, 06: 143
Khmer Rouge, 06: 89
Khodorkovsky, Mikhail, 06: 314, 325
Kibaki, Mwai, 06: 222, 223
Kidman, Nicole, 04: 310
Kilby, Jack, 06: 143
Kilgore, Jerry W., 06: 154, 174, 310-311
Killen, Edgar Ray, 06: 203
Kilpatrick, Kwame, 06: 174
Kim Jong-il, 06: 223
Kindred Spirits (Durand), 06: 53-54
King, Martin Luther, Jr., 06: 408
King Kong (film), 06: 258
Kirchner, Nestor, 04: 50-51, 310

Kiribati, table, 06: 277
Kirov Ballet, 06: 136
Klaus, Vaclav, 06: 135
Klimt, Gustav, 06: 53
Klitschko, Vitali, 06: 86
Knight Ridder Inc., 06: 272
Koizumi, Junichiro, 06: 171, 219-220
Kony, Joseph, 06: 381
Kooser, Ted, 06: 302
Koppel, Ted, 06: 367
Koran. See Qur'an
Korchemny, Remi, 06: 352
Korea, North, 06: 223, 223, 05: 250,
　04: 250; table, 06: 58
Korea, South, 06: 223, 223-224, 229-
　231, 05: 251, 04: 251; table, 06: 58
Kosovo, 06: 329, 330
Kostelic, Janica, 06: 331
Kostov, Hari, 06: 249
Kostunica, Vojislav, 06: 134, 329
Kozlowski, Dennis, 06: 125
Kroger Co., 06: 226
Ku Klux Klan, 06: 203
Kuchma, Leonid, 06: 320
Kulov, Felix, 06: 225, 322
Kumaratunga, Chandrika, 06: 354
Küng, Hans, 06: 312
Kuomintang, 06: 363-364
Kurds, 06: 211, 255
Kuwait, table, 06: 256
Kwan, Michelle, 06: 203
Kyoto Protocol, 06: 64, 91, 93, 178, 326
Kyrgyzstan, 06: 224-225, 321-323,
　04: 251; table, 06: 58

L

Labor and employment, 06: 225-227,
　05: 252-254, 04: 251-253; airlines,
　06: 71; Australia, 06: 64; automo-
　biles, 06: 69; New York City, 06: 34
　(il.); Philadelphia, 06: 292; Social Se-
　curity, 06: 337
Labor Party (Israel), 06: 217
Labor Statistics, U.S. Bureau of,
　06: 225
Labour Party: New Zealand, 06: 266;
　United Kingdom, 06: 383-385, 387
La Corona site, 06: 48
Lacrosse, 06: 353-354
Ladies Professional Golf Association,
　06: 196, 197
Lagerfeld, Karl, 06: 184
Lagos, Ricardo, 06: 105
Lake Pontchartrain, 06: 159
Lamberth, Royce, 06: 206
Lambiel, Stephanie, 06: 203
Landrieu, Mary L., 06: 366
Langa, Pius, 06: 346
Lange, David, 06: 266
Langford, Francis, 06: 143
Lantos, Tom, 06: 234
Laos, 06: 59; table, 06: 58
Larry the Cable Guy, 06: 305
La Scala, 06: 111
Lashkar-e-Taiba, 06: 371
LaSorda, Tom, 06: 70
Latham, Mark, 06: 64
Latheef, Jennifer, 06: 58
Latin America, 06: 228-231, 05: 254-
　258, 04: 254-258; economy and
　trade, 06: 171, 209; floods, 06: 157;
　stocks, 06: 358
Latvia, table, 06: 182
Layton, Jack, 06: 91-92
Lead poisoning, 06: 193
Leavitt, Michael O., 06: 89, 199, 413
Lebanon, 06: 22 (il.), 232-233, 254,
　05: 258-259, 04: 258; table, 06: 256
Lebedev, Platon, 06: 314
Lebedeva, Tatyana, 06: 380
LeDoux, Chris, 06: 143

Lee, Eugene, 06: 143
Lehman, Ernest, 06: 143
Lennon, John, 06: 270
Lennox, Annie, 06: 304 (il.)
Leslie, Michelle, 06: 63
Lesotho, table, 06: 40
Lester, William, 06: 143
Letterman, David, 06: 367, 369
Libby, I. Lewis "Scooter," 06: 271, 284,
　286, 392, 393
Liberal Democratic Party: Japan,
　06: 171, 219-220; United Kingdom,
　06: 384-385
Liberal National Party, 06: 64
Liberal Party: Canada, 06: 90-92, 97, 98;
　Denmark, 06: 155
Liberation theologians, 06: 149
Liberation Tigers of Tamil Eelam,
　06: 354
Liberia, 06: 42; table, 06: 41
Libeskind, Daniel, 04: 50-52
Library, 06: 233, 05: 259, 04: 258-260;
　presidential, 06: 394-405
Library of Congress, 06: 305
Libya, 06: 38, 234, 05: 260, 04: 260;
　table, 06: 41
Liechtenstein, table, 06: 182
Lien Chan, 06: 106, 364
Life expectancy, 06: 306
Light, 06: 61, 293, 296-297
Light therapy, 06: 253
Likud Party, 06: 217
Lincoln, Abraham, 06: 398; library and
　museum, 06: 395 (il.), 400-401 (il.),
　405
Lincoln Park Zoo (Chicago), 06: 415
Lini, Ham, 06: 277
Lini, Walter, 06: 277
Lipponen, Paavo, 06: 185
Liquefied natural gas, 06: 177
Literature, 06: 234-245, 373, 05: 261-
　263, 04: 261-269; Nobel Prizes, 06:
　273; Pulitzer Prizes, 06: 309. See also
　Poetry; Theater
Literature for children, 06: 246-247, 05:
　264-265, 04: 270-271
Lithuania, table, 06: 183
Live 8 (concert), 06: 291-292, 305
Locke, Vince, 06: 239
Locusts, 06: 42, 255 (il.)
London (England), 06: 276, 375-376; ter-
　rorist attack, 06: 25 (il.), 62, 215, 371
　(il.), 372, 380, 386
Long Beach (Mississippi), 06: 161 (il.)
Loong, Lee Hsien, 06: 330
Lopez, Al, 06: 77
Lopez Obrador, Andres Manuel, 06: 253
Lord's Resistance Army (Uganda), 06:
　371, 381
Los Angeles (California), 06: 14-15 (il.),
　248-249, 05: 266, 04: 272-273
Louisiana, 06: 168-169, 354-356; table,
　06: 355. See also New Orleans
Love Field (airport), 06: 135
Loyalist Party, 06: 274
Lubetzky, Seymour, 04: 259
Luge, 06: 352
Lukashenko, Aleksandr,
　06: 80, 323-324
Lula da Silva, Luiz Inacio,
　06: 87, 228, 231
Lunar Park (Ellis), 06: 235
Lung cancer, 06: 251-252
Luxembourg, 06: 381; table, 06: 183
Lyndon Baines Johnson Library and
　Museum, 06: 397 (il.)
Lysistrata (Adamo), 06: 111

M

Ma Ying-jeou, 06: 364
Maasai, 06: 222, 223
Maathai, Wangari, 05: 329

Mac Mini (computer), 06: 113-114
MacAdam, Kevin, 06: 100
Macapagal-Arroyo, Gloria, 06: 292
MacArthur, Ellen, 06: 83
MacArthur Fellowship, 06: 111
MacDonald, Rodney, 06: 99
Macedonia, 06: 249, 05: 266-267,
　04: 273; table, 06: 183
Machimura, Nobutaka, 06: 220
MacLane, Saunders, 06: 143
Mad cow disease, 06: 44, 96
Madagascar, 06: 39; table, 06: 41
Magazine, 06: 249-251, 05: 267-268,
　04: 273-274
Maine, 06: 175, 356; table, 06: 355
Major League Baseball. See Baseball
Major League Soccer. See Soccer
Malacca, Strait of, 06: 56-57
Malawi, 06: 39; table, 06: 41
Malaysia, 06: 56-57, 251, 05: 268, 04:
　274; table, 06: 59
Maldives, 06: 57-58; table, 06: 59
Mali, table, 06: 41
Mallory, Mark, 06: 174
Malone, Karl, 06: 78
Malta, table, 06: 183
Mammals, 06: 281
Man Booker Prize, 06: 234-236
Manas International Airport, 06: 322
Manga, 06: 243-244
Manitoba, 06: 99
Manufacturing, 06: 170, 05: 268-269,
　04: 274-275
Maoists, 06: 262
Maori Party, 06: 266
Maps, 06: 233, 270 (il.)
Mara Salvatrucha (gang), 06: 176
Marathon, 06: 352
Marburg virus, 06: 42
March of the Penguins (film), 06: 258
Margaret Garner (Danielpour), 06: 111
Marijuana, 06: 97-98, 175, 361
Marine Corps, U.S. See Armed forces
Marinin, Maxim, 06: 203
Marriage, 06: 413. See also Same-sex
　marriage
Mars, 06: 347-350
Mars Express (spacecraft), 06: 347-350
Marshall, Barry J., 06: 68, 273
Marshall Islands, 06: 278; table, 06: 277
Martha Graham Company, 06: 136
Martin, Barney, 06: 143
Martin, Jimmy, 06: 143
Martin, Paul, 06: 90-92, 97, 05: 328-329
Maryland, table, 06: 355
Maskhadov, Aslan, 06: 315, 325
Massachusetts, 06: 356; table, 06: 355
Massacre (recording), 06: 303-304
Massospondylus, 06: 280
Mastercard International, 06: 113
Masters of African-American
　Choreography (dance), 06: 137
Masters Tournament, 06: 196-197, 352
Match Point (film), 06: 258
Matisse, Henri, 06: 55
Matter, 06: 298
Mauritania, 06: 42, 255 (il.); table, 06: 41
Mauritius, 06: 38, 251, 05: 269-270, 04:
　275-276; table, 06: 41
Maus (Spiegelman), 06: 240
Maxwell, James Clerk, 06: 295
Mayans, 06: 47-48
Mayne, Thom, 06: 50
Mayo, Virginia, 06: 143
Mazzanti, Vince, Jr., 06: 86
Mbeki, Thabo, 06: 38, 42, 346
MBNA Corp., 06: 74
McAleese, Mary, 06: 214
McArthur, William, 06: 347
McCain, John, 06: 206
McCarthy, Cormac, 06: 235
McCarthy, Eugene, 06: 143
McCartney, Robert, 06: 274

McCartney, Stella, 06: 184
McCormick, Pat, 06: 143
McCrumb, Robert, 06: 372
McDonald, Robert, 06: 270
McEwan, Ian, 06: 235
McGahan, Andrew, 06: 68
McGuinty, Dalton, 06: 93
McGwire, Mark, 06: 76
MCI Inc., 06: 364-365
McKibbon, Al, 06: 143
McMahon, Ed, 06: 366
Me and You and Everyone We Know (film), 06: 259
MediaNews Group Inc., 06: 272
Medicaid, 06: 198, 335, 343-345, 356
Medicare, 06: 198, 339-342
Medicine, 06: *251-252,* 05: *270,* 04: *276;* blood clots, 06: 103; geology, 06: 193; Nobel Prize, 06: 68, 273; Ontario, 06: 100; Reed Center closing, 06: 408-409. See also Genetic engineering; Health care issues; Mental health; Public health
Megachurches, 06: 307
Mehlis, Detlev, 06: 233
Mekong River, 06: 81
Memoirs of a Geisha (film), 06: 259
Memorial to the Murdered Jews of Europe, 06: 50, 194 (il.)
Memories of My Melancholy Whores (García Márquez), 06: 234
Menezes, Jean Charles de, 06: 386
Mental health, 06: 125, *252-253,* 05: *271,* 04: *277*
Merchant, Ismail, 06: 143
Mercosur, 06: 231
Meri, 06: 47
Merkel, Angela, 06: 193, 195, *286*
Mesa Gisbert, Carlos, 06: 84, 229
Mesic, Stipe, 06: 134
Messi, Lionel, 06: 332
Messick, Dale, 06: 143
Methamphetamines, 06: 166
Metropolitan Museum of Art, 06: 54, 55
Metropolitan Opera (New York City), 06: 111
Mexico, 06: *253,* 05: *271-272,* 04: *277-278;* table, 06: 230; U.S. immigration, 06: 204, 253
MFP Financial Services Ltd., 06: 376
MG Rover (company), 06: 384
Mice, 06: 82
Michael L. Printz Award, 06: 247
Michigan, 06: 356; table, 06: 355
Michigan Opera Theatre, 06: 111
Mickelson, Phil, 06: 196-197
Micronesia, Federated States of, 06: 277-278; table, 06: 277
Microsoft Corp., 06: 114, 377-378
Middle East, 06: *254-256,* 05: *273-276,* 04: *278-281;* Latin American summit, 06: 228
Miers, Harriet, 06: 360, 393
Mikan, George, 06: 78, 143
Mikerevic, Dragan, 06: 85
Mi'kmaq Indians, 06: 99
Miles Franklin Literary Award, 06: 68
Millennium Development Goals, 06: 388
Millennium Ecosystem Assessment, 06: 178-179
Millennium Park (Chicago), 06: 105
Miller, Arthur, 06: 143, 372, *373-374*
Miller, Bode, 06: 331
Miller, David, 06: 376
Miller, Frank, 06: 239, 242
Miller, Judith, 06: 271, 392
Miller, Laura, 06: 135
Miller, Reggie, 06: 78
Million Dollar Baby (film), 06: 260-261 (il.)
Mills, Sir John, 06: 144
Milov, Vadim, 06: 104
Mining, 06: 101, 290; disasters, 06: 156

Minneapolis (Minnesota), 06: 50
Minnesota, table, 06: 355
Mississippi, 06: 161 (il.), 354, 356; table, 06: 355
Missouri, 06: 198, 356; table, 06: 355
Mr. and Mrs. Smith (film), 06: 258
Mr. Potato Head, 06: 378
Mladic, Ratco, 06: 329
Mlambo-Ngcuka, Phumzile, 06: 346
Modern pentathlon, 06: 354
Mogadishu (Somalia), 06: 43
Mohamed VI (king of Morocco), 06: 45
Mohamed, Ali Ghedi, 06: 371
Mohammed, Sheik, 06: 200
Mold, 06: 328
Moldova, 06: *257,* 324, 05: *277;* table, 06: 183
Monaco, table, 06: 183
Mongolia, 06: 57; table, 06: 59
Monk, Thelonious, 06: 305
Montana, 06: 356; table, 06: 355
Montana, Allison "Tootie," 06: 144
Montenegro.
See Serbia and Montenegro
Monterey Bay Aquarium, 06: 415
Montgomery, Tim, 06: 378
Montreal (Quebec), 06: *257,* 05: *277,* 04: *281-282*
Moog, Robert, 06: 144
Moon, 06: 347
Moon, Myung, 06: 229-231
Moore, Constance, 06: 144
Moore, Michael, 05: *329*
Morales, Evo, 06: 84, 229
Morgenthau, Robert M., 06: 264
Morita, Pat, 06: 144
Morning-after pill, 06: 167
Morocco, 06: 45; table, 06: 41
Morpheus (software), 06: 304
Morris, Howie, 06: 144
Morrison, Philip, 06: 144
Mortgage loans, 06: 169-170
Morton, Arnold, 06: 105
Moss, Kate, 06: 184
Motion pictures, 06: *258-262,* 284-285, 05: *278-283,* 04: *282-289;* graphic novels, 06: 239; labor issues, 06: 226; Toronto, 06: 377
Motley, Constance Baker, 06: 144
Motorcycle racing, 06: 354
Motorola ROKR E1 telephone, 06: 365 (il.)
Mount Rushmore National Memorial, 06: 269
Moussaoui, Zacarias, 06: 123
MovieFlix.com, 06: 209-210
Mowlam, Marjorie "Mo," 06: 144, 386
Moynihan, Daniel Patrick, 04: *136-137*
Mozambique, 06: 39-42; table, 06: 41
Mubarak, Hosni, 06: 173-174, 254
Mudslides, 06: 409
Muftis, 06: 214
Mugabe, Robert, 06: 38-39, 414-415
Multinational Forces (Iraq), 06: 180
Mumbai (India), 06: 205 (il.)
Mummies, 06: 47
Munich (film), 06: 259
Murder, 06: 125
Murphy, Paul, 06: 274
Museums, 06: 49 (il.), 50, 05: *284-295.* See also Art
Museveni, Yoweri, 06: 381
Musharraf, Pervez, 06: 204-205, 278-279
Music. See Classical music; Popular music
Muslim Brotherhood, 06: 174
Muslim-Croat Federation, 06: 84
Muslims. See Islam; Shiah Muslims; Sunni Muslims
Muti, Riccardo, 06: 111
Mutual funds, 06: 337-338
MX missiles, 06: 53

"My Name is Earl" (TV program), 06: 369
Myanmar, 06: *262,* 05: *296,* 04: *290;* table, 06: 59
MyPyramid, 06: 186

N
Nadal, Rafael, 06: 370
Namibia, table, 06: 41
Nanotechnology, 06: 298, 301
Nanotubes, 06: 103
Narayanan, Kocheril Raman, 06: 144
Narodnaya Volya (newspaper), 06: 80
NASA. See National Aeronautics and Space Administration
NASCAR, 06: 70
Nathan, Sellapan Rama, 06: 330
National Action Plan on Safety and Security in America's Cities, 06: 108
National Aeronautics and Space Administration, 06: 60, 61, 195, 276, 347-350
National Archives and Records Administration, 06: 398, 399, 402-405
National Association for the Advancement of Colored People, 06: 201, 202
National Basketball Association. See Basketball
National Book Awards, 06: 236-237
National Collegiate Athletic Association, 06: 77, 80, 352
National Council on Disability, 06: 155
National Endowment for the Arts, 06: 302
National Football League. See Football
National Gallery of Art, 06: 55
National Guard, U.S., 06: 53, 163 (il.), 164, 210, 365
National Highway Traffic Safety Administration, 06: 328
National Hockey League, 06: 199, 226-227
National Institute of Mental Health, 06: 167
National League. See Baseball
National League of Cities, 06: 108
National Party (New Zealand), 06: 266
National People's Congress (China), 06: 106
National Recording Registry, 06: 305
National Resistance Movement, 06: 381-382
Nationalist Party (Taiwan), 06: 106
Nation's Report Card, 06: 172
Native Americans.
See Indian, American
NATO. See North Atlantic Treaty Organization
Natural gas, 06: 176-177, 228
Nauru, table, 06: 277
Navy, U.S. See Armed forces
Nazarbayev, Nursultan, 06: 222
NBC (TV network), 06: 367
Nebraska, table, 06: 355
Neethling, Ryk, 06: 362
Negro Digest (magazine), 06: 250
Negroponte, John D., 06: *286-287,* 389
Nelson, Gaylord, 06: 144
Nepal, 06: 157, *262,* 05: *296;* table, 06: 59
Netherlands, 06: *263-264,* 05: *297,* 04: *290;* table, 06: 183
Nevada, table, 06: 355
Never Let Me Go (Ishiguro), 06: 235
New Brunswick, 06: 99
New Democratic Party (Canada), 06: 91-92, 98
New England Patriots, 06: 187-188
New Hampshire, table, 06: 355
New Jersey, 06: 154, 174, 310, 356; table, 06: 355

New London (Connecticut), 06: 108-110
New Mexico, 06: 102, 357; table, 06: 355
New National Party, 06: 346
New Orleans (Louisiana), 06: 26 (il.), *158-165;* architecture, 06: 48; congressional aid, 06: 115-116; economy, 06: 168-169; health issues, 06: 198, 308, 328; Houston, refugees to, 06: 200; state funds, 06: 354-356; transportation, 06: 380; zoo, 06: 415. See also Hurricane Katrina
New Orleans Convention Center, 06: 160
New Orleans Times-Picayune, 06: 272
New Partnership for Africa's Development, 06: 38
New York (state), 06: 156, 356; table, 06: 355
New York City, 06: *264-265,* 05: *298-299,* 04: *291-292;* architecture, 06: 48-50, 283-284; dance, 06: 136, 137; strike, 06: 34 (il.); terror threat, 06: 380
New York Times, The, 06: 272, 392
New Zealand, 06: 124, *266,* 05: *299,* 04: *292;* table, 06: 277
Newbery Medal, 06: 247
Newfoundland and Labrador, 06: 93, 99
News bytes, 06: *266-271,* 05: *299-302,* 04: *293-296*
Newspaper, 06: *271,* 05: *303,* 04: *296;* Pulitzer Prizes, 06: 309
Newsweek (magazine), 06: 249
Newton, Sir Isaac, 06: 295, 298
Niagara River, The (Ryan), 06: 302
Nicaragua, 06: 231, *272,* 05: *303,* 04: *297;* table, 06: 230
Nichols, Jack, 06: 144
Nicholson, R. James, 06: 89
Nicklaus, Jack, 06: 196
Nie Haisheng, 06: 350
Niger, 06: 39 (il.), 42; table, 06: 41
Nigeria, 06: 38, *272-273,* 05: *303-304,* 04: *297;* disasters, 06: 156; table, 06: 41
"Nightline" (TV program), 06: 367
Niinistö, Sauli, 06: 185
9/11 Commission Report, 06: 389
911 (emergency number), 06: 365
Nissan Motor Co., 06: 70
Nixon, Richard M., 06: 395 (il.), 397 (il.), 399-402
Nkurunziza, Pierre, 06: 38
No Child Left Behind Act (2001), 06: 172, 288-289, 392
No Country for Old Men (McCarthy), 06: 235
Nobel Prizes, 06: 68, 234, *273-274,* 372, 05: *305,* 04: *297-298*
Nonsmall cell lung cancer, 06: 251-252
Nonsteroidal anti-inflammatory drugs, 06: 167
Norodom Sihamoni, 05: *329*
North, Sheree, 06: 144
North American Aerospace Command, 06: 96
North Atlantic Treaty Organization, 06: 37, 96, 181, 249, 329, 330
North Carolina, 06: 356; table, 06: 355
North Carolina, University of, 06: 77, 80
North Dakota, 06: 99; table, 06: 355
North Korea. See Korea, North
Northern Ireland, 06: *274,* 05: *306,* 04: *298-299*
Northwest Airlines Corp., 06: 71, 169, 225-226
Northwest Territories, 06: 101
Norton, Gale, 06: 206
Norway, 06: *275,* 05: *306-307,* 04: *300;* table, 06: 183
Notre Dame, University of, 06: 187
Nour, Ayman, 06: 254
Nova Scotia, 06: 93, 99
Novak, Robert D., 06: 271, 392
Nowak-Jezioranski, Jan, 06: 144

Nuclear energy, 06: 210-211, 293, 300-301
Nuclear weapons, 06: 53, 300-301, 388; Iran, 06: 182, 210-211; North Korea, 06: 223
Nuclei, 06: 300
Nucleotides, 06: 82
Nuevo Laredo (Mexico), 06: 253
Nunavut, 06: 101
Nursing homes, 06: 344
Nye, Louis, 06: 144

O

Obama, Barack, 05: *330*
Obasanjo, Olusegun, 06: 38, 42, 272-273
Obesity, 06: 186-187, 252
Obituaries. See Deaths
Obote, Milton, 06: 381
O'Brien, George H., Jr., 06: 144
Observatories, Space, 04: *64-75*
Ocampo, Luis Moreno, 06: 358
Occidental Petroleum Corp., 06: 234
Ocean, 06: 179, *275-276,* 05: *307,* 04: *300-301.* See also Geology
O'Connor, Sandra Day, 06: 359
O'Hare International Airport, 06: 105
Ohio, 06: 356-357; table, 06: 355
Ohrid agreement (2001), 06: 249
Oil. See Petroleum
Ojeda Rios, Filiberto, 06: 309
Oklahoma, 06: 175, 357; table, 06: 355
Old Vic (theater), 06: 375-376
Olsen, Gregory, 06: 347
Olsen, John, 06: 68
Olympic Games, 06: *276,* 05: *308-319,* 04: *301;* British Columbia, 06: 98; London, 06: 386; Montreal, 06: 257; New York City, 06: 265
Oman, table, 06: 256
Omega Financial (company), 06: 130
On Beauty (Smith), 06: 235
On Human Dignity (John Paul II), 06: 152
On Human Life (John Paul II), 06: 152
Ontario, 06: 93, 99-100, 215
Open Society Institute, 06: 319
Opium, 06: 37
Opportunity (spacecraft), 06: 350
Orange Order, 06: 274
Orange Revolution, 06: 80, 320-321, 382
Orangutans, 06: 121
Orbach, Jerry, 05: *145*
Oregon, table, 06: 355
Organisation for Security and Co-Operation in Europe, 06: 224
Organization for Economic Co-operation and Development, 06: 227
Organization of American States, 06: 198, 231, 272
Organization of the Petroleum Exporting Countries, 06: 177
Orthodox Churches. See Eastern Orthodox Churches
"Oscars." See Academy Awards
Ossetia, South. See South Ossetia
Ottawa, 06: 98
Owen, Mickey, 06: 144

P

Paar, Jack, 06: 366, 05: *382*
Pacific Islands, 06: *276-278,* 05: *320-321,* 04: *302-303*
Padilla, Jose, 06: 123
Paerson, Anja, 06: 331
Page, Larry, 04: *307*
Paisley, Ian, 06: 274
Pakistan, 06: 124, 204-205, *278-279,* 05: *322,* 04: *303-304;* disasters, 06: 56, 155-157; table, 06: 59; terrorism, 06: 371

Pakistan Peoples Party, 06: 279
Palacio, Alfredo, 06: 171, 229, 231
Palau, 06: 278; table, 06: 277
Paleontology, 06: *279-281,* 05: *322-324,* 04: *304-305*
Palestinians, 06: 168, 176, 216-218, 254, 371
Palmeiro, Rafael, 06: 76
Palmer, Mick, 06: 63
Pamuk, Orhan, 06: 381
Pan American Games, 04: *306*
Panama, 06: *281,* 05: *324,* 04: *306;* table, 06: 230
Panama Canal, 06: 281
Pandas, 06: 416
Papua New Guinea, 06: 277; table, 06: 277
Paraguay, 06: 229-231; table, 06: 230
Parker-Bowles, Camilla, 06: 383 (il.), 387
Parks, Rosa, 06: 144, *202*
Parks, Suzan-Lori, 04: *310-311*
Parole, 06: 306
Paroubek, Jiri, 06: 135
Paterno, Joe, 06: 187
Patient Safety and Quality Improvement Act (2005), 06: 116
Patrick, Danica, 06: 70, *287,* 352
Patten, Edward, 06: 144
Paul Revere's Ride (Del Tredici), 06: 111
Peabody Essex Museum (Salem), 06: 55
Peace Prize, Nobel, 06: 273
Peck, M. Scott, 06: 144
Peer-to-peer networks, 06: 209-210
Pekar, Harvey, 06: 239, 244
Penguins, 06: 276
Penn, Sean, 05: *330*
Pennsylvania, table, 06: 355
Pennsylvania State University, 06: 187
Pensions, 06: 135
People in the news, 06: *281-289,* 05: *324-332,* 04: *306-314.* See also Deaths; News bytes
People's Party (Austria), 06: 67
Pepi II, 06: 47
Perdue, Frank, 06: 144
Peres, Shimon, 06: 217-218, 254
Peretz, Amir, 06: 217, 254
Perphenazine (drug), 06: 167
Perry, Elwood L. "Buck," 06: 144
Persepolis (Satrapi), 06: 241
Personal People Meter, 06: 310
Persson, Goran, 06: 361
Peru, 06: 228, 231, *290,* 05: *332-333,* 04: *314-315;* air crash, 06: 155; table, 06: 230
Peters, Winston, 06: 266
PetroCaribe (program), 06: 228, 413
Petroleum: aviation, 06: 71; Azerbaijan, 06: 72; Canada, 06: 101; Cuba, 06: 134; Ecuador, 06: 171; Houston, 06: 201; Iraq oil-for-food program, 06: 388; Latin America, 06: 228; Libya, 06: 234; market, 06: 169-171, 176-177, 208-209, 356, 357, 381; Nigeria, 06: 273; Norway, 06: 275; oil spill, 06: 178 (il.); Saudi Arabia, 06: 328; Ukraine, 06: 382; Venezuela, 06: 406; West Indies, 06: 413. See also Natural gas
Petrosur (program), 06: 228
Pettigrew, Pierre, 06: 96
Phelps, Michael, 06: 362, 05: *330-331*
Philadelphia (Pennsylvania), 06: *290-292,* 05: *333,* 04: *315*
Philadelphia Eagles, 06: 187-188
Philippines, 06: *292-293,* 05: *334-335,* 04: *316;* table, 06: 59
Phillips, John, 06: 347
Phishing (computing), 06: 128, 130
Photoelectric effect, 06: 296, 297, 300
Photons, 06: 297
Physics, 06: *293-301,* 05: *335-336,* 04: *317;* Nobel Prize, 06: 274
Piano, Renzo, 06: 55

Picker, Tobias, 06: 111
Pietsch, Janine, 06: 362
Pinochet Ugarte, Augusto, 06: 105
Pinter, Harold, 06: 273, 372-375
Piracy: electronic, 06: 209-210, 303, 304; ship, 06: 43, 56-57
Pit bulls, 06: 99-100
Pixel Chix (toy), 06: 378
Plame, Valerie, 06: 271, 392
Planets, 06: 60-61
Plasma (physics), 06: 293
Plesiosaurs, 06: 280
Pluto, 06: 60
Poaching, 06: 121
Podcasts, 06: 209, 310
Poetry, 06: *302,* 05: *336,* 04: *317-318*
Poetry Out Loud (program), 06: 302
Poland, 06: *302-303,* 05: *337,* 04: *318;* table, 06: 183
Polgar, Susan, 06: 104
Police, 06: 84, 249
Polio, 06: 208, 308
Pollution. See **Environmental pollution**
Popcorn, 06: 102-103
Pope. See **Benedict XVI; John Paul II**
Popular music, 06: *303-305,* 05: *337-340,* 04: *318-322*
Population, 06: *305-306,* 05: *340,* 04: *322;* cities, 06: 109-110. See also **Census**
Portillo Cabrera, Alfonso, 06: 198, 231
Portugal, 06: *306,* 05: *341,* 04: *322-323;* table, 06: 183
Post-traumatic stress disorder, 06: 252
Poultry, 06: 44
Powell, Asafa, 06: 378
Prehistoric people. See **Anthropology; Archaeology**
Presbyterian Church, 06: 308
President, U.S. See **United States, President of the**
Presidential libraries, 06: *394-405*
Presidential Libraries Act, 06: 399
Presidential Records and Materials Preservation Act, 06: 399
Presidents Cup, 06: 257
Pretorius (South Africa), 06: 346
Price, Rod, 06: 144
Prices. See **Economics, United States; Economics, World**
Prince Edward Island, 06: 100
Prisons, 06: *306,* 05: *341,* 04: *323;* Dominican Republic, 06: 413. See also **Abu Ghraib Prison**
Pritzker Prize, 06: 50
Prius (car), 06: 68 (il.)
Probation, 06: 306
Prodi, Romano, 06: 218
Professional Golfers' Association, 06: 196-197
Prostate surgery, 06: 252
Protection of Lawful Commerce Act (2005), 06: 116
Protestantism, 06: 274, *307-308,* 05: *342,* 04: *323-324*
Proxmire, William, 06: 144-145
Pryor, Richard, 06: 145
Pseudoephedrine, 06: 166 (il.)
Public Chamber (Russia), 06: 315
Public health, 06: *308,* 05: *342-343,* 04: *325;* Medicare/Medicaid, 06: 339-345; Montreal, 06: 257. See also **AIDS; Food; Health care issues; Medicine**
Public transportation. See **Transportation**
Puerto Rico, 06: *309,* 05: *343,* 04: *325-326;* table, 06: 230
Pulitzer Prizes, 06: 112, 235, 302, *309,* 05: *344,* 04: *326*
Purpose-Driven Life, The (Warren), 06: 307

Pushkin Museum of Fine Arts, 06: 53
Putin, Vladimir, 06: 313-327
Pyinmana (Myanmar), 06: 262

Q

Qadhafi, Muammar Muhammad al-, 06: 38
Qa`ida, Al-, 06: 37, 62, 123, 254, 278-279, 371-372; in Europe, 06: 215, 380
Qatar, 06: 214, 217; table, 06: 256
Quanta, 06: 296-297
Quantum mechanics, 06: 299-300
Quebec, 06: 96, 100, 285-286
Qur'an, 06: 37, 201, 214
Qwest Communications, 06: 226

R

Rabin, Yitzhak, 06: 218
Radcliffe, Ted, 06: 145
Rader, Dennis, 06: 125
Radio, 06: 209, *310,* 05: *344-346,* 04: *326-327*
Raffarin, Jean-Pierre, 06: 192
Rafsanjani, Ali Akbar Hashemi, 06: 210
Raich, Benjamin, 06: 331
Railroads, 06: 380-381, 386; disasters, 06: 157. See also **London**
Rain forests, 06: 87, 121-122, 309
Rainier III, 06: 145
Rainsy, Sam, 06: 89
Raitt, John, 06: 145
Rajapakse, Mahinda, 06: 354
Ramgoolam, Navin, 06: 251
Ramgoolam, Seewoosagur, 06: 251
Rape, 06: 125
Rasmussen, Anders Fogh, 06: 155
Rather, Dan, 06: 210, 365-366, 368 (il.)
Ratzinger, Joseph. See **Benedict XVI**
Rau, Cornelia, 06: 63
Ravenscroft, Thurl, 06: 145
Ray (film), 06: 260 (il.), 284
Rayner, Richard Piers, 06: 244
Reagan, Ronald W., 06: 395 (il.), 403 (il.), 05: *404-409*
Recording Industry Association of America, 06: 303
Rehn, Olli, 06: 134
Rehnquist, William H., 06: 145, 360
Reid, Harry, 06: *287*
Relativity, 06: 296-300
Religious displays, 06: 361
Rembrandt, 06: 53
Republican Party, 06: *310-311,* 05: *346-347,* 04: *327-328.* See also **Elections**
Republika Srpksa, 06: 84
Rhode Island, table, 06: 355
Rice, 06: 43
Rice, Condoleezza, 06: 89, 213, 216-217, 316, 327 (il.)
Rice, Jerry, 06: 188
Richard II (Shakespeare), 06: 376
Richard Nixon Library & Birthplace, 06: 397 (il.)
Ricoeur, Paul, 06: 145
Rigali, Justin, 06: 291
Rigas, John J., 06: 125
Right to die, 06: 17 (il.), 198-199
Riou, Vincent, 06: 83
Rita, Hurricane. See **Hurricane Rita**
Road to Perdition, The (Collins), 06: 239, 243-244
Robbery, 06: 125
Robert F. Kennedy Memorial Stadium, 06: 408
Roberts, John G., Jr., 06: *287-288,* 359-360
Robertson, Pat, 06: 307, 406
Robinson, Marilynne, 06: 235
Robinson, Steve, 06: 348 (il.)
Robinson, V. Gene, 04: *311*
Robots, 06: 176, 271 (il.), 347-350
Rock, Chris, 06: 369

Rock music, 06: 305. See also **Popular music**
Rock School (film), 06: 262
Rodeo, 06: 352
Rodino, Peter W., 06: 145
Rodríguez Veltzé, Eduardo, 06: 229
Roehrig, Kelli, 06: 79 (il.)
Rogers, Fred, 04: *375*
Roh Moo-hyun, 06: 223-224, 04: *311*
Rojas, Victor Alfonso, 06: 204
Roman Catholic Church, 06: 274, 290, *311-312,* 05: *347-348,* 04: *328-329.* See also **Benedict XVI; John Paul II**
Romania, 06: *313,* 05: *349,* 04: *329;* Eastern Orthodox Church, 06: 168; table, 06: 183
Rome (Italy), 06: 219 (il.)
Rome, Ancient, 06: 48 (il.)
Roosevelt, Franklin D., 06: 300, 336, 394 (il.), 399
Rose, Jeremy, 06: 200
Rose Revolution, 06: 193, 318-320
Rosoff, Meg, 06: 247
Rossi, Dino, 06: 154, 311
Rossi, Jim, 06: 145
Rossner, Judith, 06: 145
Rotblat, Joseph, 06: 145
Rothschild, Dame Miriam, 06: 145
Rove, Karl, 06: *288,* 389 (il.)
Rowand, Aaron, 06: 74 (il.)
Rowing, 06: 352
Royal Dutch/Shell Group, 06: 234
Rudolph, Eric, 06: 123
Rumsfeld, Donald, 06: 249
Rush, Geoffrey, 06: 68
Rushdie, Salman, 06: 234-236
Russell, Nipsey, 06: 145
Russia, 06: *313-327,* 05: *349-351,* 04: *330-345;* China relations, 06: 106; table, 06: 59; terrorism, 06: 325, 372; Uzbekistan relations, 06: 406
Russian Space Agency, 06: 347
Rwanda, 06: 38; table, 06: 41
Ryan, Kay, 06: 302

S

Saakashvili, Mikhail, 06: 193, 318-320
Sabin, Roger, 06: 245
Sabine Lake, 06: 165 (il.)
Saca, Elias Antonio (Tony), 06: 176
Sacramento Monarchs, 06: 80
Sadr, Moqtada al-, 06: 215
Sadulayev, Abdul-Khalim, 06: 315, 324
Safe, Accountable, Flexible, and Efficient Transportation Equity Act (2005), 06: 380
Safe Clear (program), 06: 201
Safety, 06: *328,* 05: *342-343,* 04: *325.* See also **Identity theft; Public health**
Safin, Martin, 06: 369
Saikley, Charlie, 06: 145
St. Paul's Cathedral (London), 06: 54 (il.)
St. Peter's Square, 06: 153 (il.)
St. Petersburg (Russia), 04: *332-345*
St. Kitts and Nevis, table, 06: 230
St. Lucia, table, 06: 230
St. Vincent and the Grenadines, table, 06: 230
Salvation Army, 06: 270
Same-sex marriage, 06: 90 (il.), 92, 175, 201-203
Samoa, table, 06: 277
Sampaio, Jorge, 06: 306
Sample, Johnny, 06: 145
Samuel, Audwin M., 06: 108
San Antonio Spurs, 06: 77-78
San Francisco (California), 06: 49 (il.), 50
San Francisco Ballet, 06: 137
San Francisco Opera, 06: 111
San Marino, table, 06: 183

Sanader, Ivo, 06: 134
Sanchez, Martin, 06: 86
Sanchez de Lozada, Gonzalo, 06: 84, 231
Sanderson, Mike, 06: 83
São Tomé and Príncipe, table, 06: 41
Sariska National Park (India), 06: 121
Sarkozy, Nicolas, 06: 191
Saskatchewan, 06: 100
SAT (test), 06: 172
Satellite radio, 06: 310
Satellites, Artificial, 06: 276, 299
Satrapi, Marjane, 06: 241-242
Saturday (McEwan), 06: 235
Saturn, 06: 347, 349 (il.)
Saudi Arabia, 06: 281, *328*, 05: *352*, 04: *346;* table, 06: 256
Saunders, Dame Cicely, 06: 145
SBC Communications Inc., 06: 364
Scanlon, Michael, 06: 117
Schell, Maria, 06: 145
Schelling, Thomas C., 06: 273
Schengen treaty, 06: 363
Schenkel, Chris, 06: 145
Schiavo, Michael, 06: 198-199
Schiavo, Terri, 06: 145, 198-199
Schilling, Kurt, 06: 76 (il.)
Schistosomiasis, 06: 107
Schizophrenia, 06: 167
Schlossberg, Caroline Kennedy, 06: 401 (il.)
Schmeling, Max, 06: 146
Schreker, Franz, 06: 112 (il.)
Schrock, Richard R., 06: 273-274
Schröder, Gerhard, 06: 181, 193, 195
Schumacher, Michael, 06: 70
Schwarzenegger, Arnold, 06: 154, 175, 178, 311, 356
Scopes, John, 06: 267-268
Scopes trial, 06: 267-268
Scott, Robert Montgomery, 06: 292
Screen Actors Guild, 06: 226
Scrushy, Richard, 06: 125
Sea, The (Banville), 06: 235
Sea-viewing Wide Field-of-view Sensor, 06: 276
Seabourn Spirit (ship), 06: 43
Search engines, 05: *118-123*
Seasonal affective disorder, 06: 253
Security. See Safety; Terrorism
Security Council. See United Nations
Segregation, 06: 202
Sellars, Peter, 06: 111
Senate, U.S. See Congress of the United States
Senegal, table, 06: 41
Sentencing guidelines, 06: 361
September 11 terrorist attacks, 06: 123, 225, 390; memorials, 04: *50-52*
Serbia and Montenegro, 06: 134, *329-330*, 05: *352-353*, 04: *347-348;* table, 06: 183
Sergeyev, Konstantin, 06: 136
Serra, Richard, 06: 55 (il.)
Settle, Mary Lee, 06: 146
Sevan, Benon, 06: 388
Sex discrimination, 06: 361
Sexual abuse, 06: 290, 312, 330, 356
Seychelles, table, 06: 41
Shaik, Schabir, 06: 346
Shalimar the Clown (Rushdie), 06: 234-236
Shalom, Silvan, 06: 217
Shanghai (China), 06: 58 (il.), 106-107 (il.)
Shanghai Cooperation Organization, 06: 327
Shanley, Patrick, 06: 376
Shari`ah, 06: 215
Sharon, Ariel, 06: 216-218, 254
Sheard, Michael, 06: 146
Sheehan, Cindy, 06: *288*
Sher Bahadur Deuba, 06: 262
Shevardnadze, Eduard, 06: 316, 318

Shiah Muslims, 06: 211, 213, 215, 255, 279
Shibicky, Alex, 06: 146
Shipping industry, 06: 249
Ships, 06: 56-57, 155, 270
Shipwrecks, 06: 156
Short, Bobby, 06: 146
Shoulder surfing, 06: 130
Sierra Leone, 06: *330*, 05: *353*, 04: *348;* table, 06: 41
Simon, Claude, 06: 146
Simon, Danny, 06: 146
Simon, Simone, 06: 146
Sin, Cardinal Jaime, 06: 146
Sin City (film), 06: 239, 259
Singapore, 06: 56-57, *330*, 05: *353*, 04: *348;* table, 06: 59
Singh, Manmohan, 06: 121, 204-205, 05: *331*
Siniora, Fouad, 06: 232, 254
Siniscalco, Domenico, 06: 218
Sinn Fein, 06: 274
Sirius Satellite Radio, 06: 310
Sistani, Ali. See al-Sistani, Grand Aya-tollah Ali
"Six Feet Under" (TV program), 06: 368
Skeleton (sport), 06: 354
Skiing, 06: *331*, 05: *354*, 04: *349*
Skimming (crime), 06: 130
Skinner, Richard L., 06: 389
Skype Technologies S.A., 06: 364
Skyscrapers, 06: 390
Slavkov, Ivan, 06: 276
Sled-dog racing, 06: 352
Sleeping Beauty (Sergeyev), 06: 136
Slovakia, 06: *332*, 05: *355*, 04: *350;* table, 06: 183
Slovenia, table, 06: 183
Slow Man (Coetzee), 06: 234
Slutskaya, Irina, 06: 203
Smiley, E. Forbes, III, 06: 233
Smiley, Richard, 06: 146
Smith, Jimmy, 06: 146
Smith, Zadie, 06: 235
Smoking, 06: 100, 123, 166, 308
Snapple Beverage Corp., 06: 266
Snow, 06: 409
Snow, John W., 04: *311-312*
Snowboarding, 06: 354
Soap Box Derby, 06: 352-353
Soccer, 06: 332-333, 05: *356-357*, 04: *350-351*
Social Democratic Party: Austria, 06: 67; Germany, 06: 193, 195; Sweden, 06: 361
Social Security, 06: *334-345*, 393, 05: *358*, 04: *352;* identity theft, 06: 128-131
Social Security Act (1935), 06: 336
Social Security Administration, 06: 337
Socialist Party: Bulgaria, 06: 89; Portu-gal, 06: 306
Sócrates, José, 06: 306
Softball, 06: 276
Solar energy, 06: 300
Solomon Islands, table, 06: 277
Solyom, Laszlo, 06: 203
Somalia, 06: 43; table, 06: 41
Songhua River, 06: 179
Sorenstam, Annika, 06: 196, 197, 351, 04: *312*
Sosa, Sammy, 06: 76
Sotheby's, 06: 54
South Africa, 06: 38, 42, 124, *346*, 05: *358-359*, 04: *352-353;* table, 06: 41
South America. See Latin America
South Carolina, table, 06: 355
South Dakota, table, 06: 355
South Korea. See Korea, South
South Ossetia, 06: 193, 319-320
South Pacific Mini-Games, 06: 278
Southern California, University of, 06: 187

Soybeans, 06: 43, 44
Soyuz (spacecraft), 06: 347
Space exploration, 06: *347-350*, 05: *359-362*, 04: *353-357*. See also Astronomy
Space-time, 06: 296-297
Spacey, Kevin, 06: 375-376
Spain, 06: *350-351*, 05: *363*, 04: *357;* table, 06: 183
Spartacus (Grigorovich), 06: 116
Spearmon, Wallace, 06: 379 (il.)
Special theory of relativity, 06: 296-298
Speed of light, 06: 296-297
Speed skating, 06: 353
Spellings, Margaret, 06: 89, 172, *288-289*
Spencer, John, 06: 146
Spiegelman, Art, 06: 240, 245
Spirit (spacecraft), 06: 350
Spitzer, Eliot, 04: *312-313*
Spitzer Space Telescope, 06: 61
Sponges, 06: 275
Sports, 06: *351-354*, 05: *364-367*, 04: *358-361*. See also Olympic Games and specific sports
Springsteen, Bruce, 06: 304
Squid, Giant, 06: 275 (il.)
Srebrenica Massacre, 06: 85 (il.)
Sri Lanka, 06: 124, *354*, 05: *367*, 04: *361;* table, 06: 59
Standard & Poor's 500 index, 06: 357
Stanishev, Sergei, 06: 89
"Star Trek: Enterprise" (TV program), 06: 368
Star Wars: Episode III-Revenge of the Sith (film), 06: 258
Starr, Ringo, 06: 270
State, U.S. Department of, 06: 89
State Children's Health Insurance Program, 06: 344
State government, 06: *354-357*, 05: *367-370*, 04: *361-364;* Medicaid, 06: 344-345. See also Elections
Stavenhagen, Rudolfo, 06: 266
Steroids, 06: 76, 352
Stewart, Jon, 06: *289*
Stewart, Tony, 06: 70
Stockdale, James B., 06: 146
Stocks and bonds, 06: 337-338, *357-358*, 05: *370-371*, 04: *365-366*
Stoltenberg, Jens, 06: 275
Storm surges, 06: 412
Storms, 06: 156-157, 409-412. See also Hurricanes; Tornadoes; Tsunami
Stram, Hank, 06: 146
Strawberry Field (school), 06: 270
Street, John F., 06: 290
Strikes. See Labor and employment
Stronach, Belinda, 06: 92
Stucky, Steven, 06: 112
Succeeding Against the Odds (John-son), 06: 250
Successor, The (Kadare), 06: 236
Sudan, 06: 254-255, *358-359*, 388, 05: *372*, 04: *366;* table, 06: 41
Sudoku (puzzle), 06: 378
Suez SA (company), 06: 51
Sugar, 06: 134
Suicide bombings. See Terrorism
Sumatra, 06: 56, 63, 156, 192
Sun Microsystems, Inc., 06: 114
Sunni Muslims, 06: 211, 213, 215, 279
Super Bowl, 06: 187-188
Superdome, 06: 158-160
Supreme Court of the United States, 06: 123, *359-361*, 05: *373-374*, 04: *366-368;* Roberts nomination, 06: 287-288
issues: cable TV, 06: 365; copyrights and piracy, 06: 210, 304; disability law, 06: 155; eminent domain, 06: 108-110; right to die, 06: 199

Suriname, table, 06: 230
Suzuki, Ichiro, 06: 77
Swank, Hilary, 06: 260-261 (il.)
Swartz, Mark, 06: 125
Swaziland, 06: 39; table, 06: 41
Sweden, 06: *361,* 05: *374,* 04: *368-369;* table, 06: 183
Swift Satellite, 06: 61
Swimming, 06: 257, *362,* 05: *375,* 04: *370*
Switzerland, 06: *363,* 05: *376,* 04: *371;* table, 06: 183
Sydney Swans, 06: 67
Sylphides, Les (Fokine), 06: 136
Sylvia (Ashton), 06: 136
Syria, 06: 254, *363,* 05: *376,* 04: *371;* Lebanon occupation, 06: 232-233, 254; table, 06: 256
Syriana (film), 06: 259

T

Taft, Bob, 06: 357
Taiwan, 06: 106, *363-364,* 05: *377,* 04: *372;* table, 06: 59
Tajikistan, table, 06: 59
Talabani, Jalal, 06: 228
Taliban, 06: 37, 52, 278
Tamils, 06: 354
Tange, Kenzo, 06: 146
Tantaquidgeon, Gladys, 06: 146
Tanzania, 06: 42-43, 80; table, 06: 41
Tanzi, Calisto, 06: 219
Tariceanu, Calin, 06: 313
Tariffs. See **Taxation**
Taxation, 06: *364,* 05: *378,* 04: *372;* Germany, 06: 195; Medicare/Medicaid, 06: 341-345; Philippines, 06: 293; Social Security, 06: 335-345; state government, 06: 356
Taxicabs, 06: 408
Taya, Ould, 06: 42
Team handball, 06: 353
Teamsters Union, 06: 227
Tectonic plates, 06: 192
Teen-agers. See **Adolescents**
Telecommunications, 06: *364-365,* 05: *378-379,* 04: *373-374;* Australia, 06: 64; labor issues, 06: 226. See also **Computer; Internet**
Telephones, 06: 72, 175, 364-365
Telescopes, Space, 04: *64-75*
Telesur (network), 06: 228
Television, 06: 289, *365-369,* 05: *379-382,* 04: *374-377;* Internet, 06: 209; labor issues, 06: 226; Latin America, 06: 228-229; public, 06: 392; telecom companies, 06: 365
Telstra (company), 06: 64
Tempel 1 (comet), 06: 60-61, 349 (il.)
Temporary Assistance for Needy Families, 06: 115-116, 187
Ten Commandments, 06: 361
Tennessee, 06: 198, 356; table, 06: 355
Tennis, 06: 351, *369-370,* 05: *383,* 04: *378-379*
Termonti, Giulio, 06: 218
Terrorism, 06: *371-372,* 05: *383-384,* 04: *379;* Afghanistan, 06: 37, 371-372; Australia, 06: 62; aviation, 06: 72; Bangladesh, 06: 72; Egypt, 06: 174, 254, 371; India, 06: 206; Indonesia, 06: 208, 372; Iraq, 06: 213, 215, 371; Italy, 06: 218; Jordan, 06: 221, 254; Myanmar, 06: 262; Nigeria, 06: 273; Pakistan, 06: 278-279, 371; Philippines, 06: 293; Russia, 06: 325, 372; Saudi Arabia, 06: 328; Spain, 06: 350-351; Syria, 06: 363; Uganda, 06: 381; United Kingdom, 06: 25 (il.), 62, 215, 371 (il.), 372, 380, 383, 386; United Nations resolution, 06: 388; U.S., danger to, 06:

204, 264, 380, 389; U.S. court rulings, 06: 123. See also **September 11 terrorist attacks**
Texas, 06: 102, 156, 175, 354, 356; table, 06: 355
Texas, University of, 06: 77, 187
Texas City (Texas), 06: 201
Textiles, 06: 208
Thai Rak Thai (party), 06: 372
Thailand, 06: 56-57, *372,* 05: *384,* 04: *380;* art, 06: 55; table, 06: 59
Thaksin Shinawatra, 06: 372
Theater, 06: *372-376,* 05: *384-386,* 04: *380-383*
Theophilos III, 06: 168
Theron, Charlize, 05: *331*
Thompson, Hunter S., 06: 146
Thorpe, Ian, 05: *331*
Three Illusions for Orchestra (Carter), 06: 111
Tigers, 06: 121, 416
Time, 06: 296
Time (magazine), 06: 249
Titan (moon), 06: 60, 347, 349 (il.)
Tobacco. See **Smoking**
Togo, 06: 42; table, 06: 41
Tokarev, Valery, 06: 347
Toledo, Alejandro, 06: 231, 290
Tolkien, J. R. R., 04: *265-269*
Tomlinson, Kenneth Y., 06: 392
Tomlinson, LaDainian, 06: 188
Tonga, 06: 276-277; table, 06: 277
"Tonight Show, The," 06: 366-367
Tony Awards, 06: 375
Tools, 06: 82, 275
Topalov, Veselin, 06: 103
Tornadoes, 06: 412
Toronto (Ontario), 06: *376-377,* 05: *387,* 04: *384-385*
Torrijos Espino, Martin, 06: 281
Tortoise, 06: 416 (il.)
Toti, Andrew, 06: 146
Totmianina, Tatiana, 06: 203
Touch the Sound (film), 06: 259
Toulouse-Lautrec, Henri de, 06: 55
Toupou, Taufa'ahau, IV, 06: 277
Tour de France, 06: 351, 353 (il.)
Tower, Joan, 06: 112
Toyota Motor Co., 06: 68 (il.), 70
Toys and games, 06: *377-378,* 05: *387-388,* 04: *385-386*
TP.3 Reloaded (recording), 06: 305
Track and field, 06: *378-380,* 05: *389-390,* 04: *386-388*
Trade. See **Economics, United States; Economics, World; International trade**
Trafalgar, Battle of, 06: 266
Trains. See **Railroads**
Trans-Dniester, 06: 257
Transitional National Assembly (Iraq), 06: 211, 213, 255
Transportation, 06: *380-381,* 05: *390-391,* 04: *388-389;* disabled, 06: 155; New York City, 06: 34 (il.), 264, 265; Toronto, 06: 376. See also **Automobile; Aviation; Highways; Railroads**
Transportation Security Administration, 06: 72, 389-390
Trastuzumab (drug), 06: 167
Travelgate scandal, 06: 346
Treasury, U.S. Department of the, 06: 336-337
Tremblay, Gérald, 06: 257
Triathlon, 06: 353
Trilafon (drug), 06: 167
Trimble, David, 06: 214, 274
Trinidad and Tobago, table, 06: 230
Tripoli (Lebanon), 06: 22 (il.)
Trophy art, 06: 53
Troxell, Terry, 06: 83
Trucking industry, 06: 381

Trucks, Light. See **Automobile**
Truman, Harry S., 06: 339-340, 403-404
Tsang, Donald, 06: 107
Tshwane (South Africa), 06: 346
Tsunami, 06: 56-58; earthquake studies, 06: 192, 293; Swedish aid, 06: 361; U.S. aid, 06: 116, 364
impact on: Australia, 06: 62, 63; immigration, 06: 204; Indonesia, 06: 208; Sri Lanka, 06: 354
Tuberculosis, 06: 107
Tueni, Jubran, 06: 233
Tulip Revolution, 06: 224, 321-323
Tung Chee-hwa, 06: 107
Tunisia, table, 06: 41
Turkey, 06: *381,* 05: *391,* 04: *390;* European Union relations, 06: 180-181; Greece relations, 06: 197; table, 06: 183
Turkmenistan, table, 06: 59
Tutankhamun, 06: 173 (il.)
Tutsi, 06: 38
Tuvalu, table, 06: 277
TV. See **Television**
TV Brazil, 06: 229
TV Guide (magazine), 06: 249-250
Twenty20 (game), 06: 124
Tyco International Ltd., 06: 125
Tymoshenko, Yuliya, 06: 382
Tyrannosaurus rex, 06: 279-280
Tyson, Mike, 06: 86

U

UB313 (planet), 06: 60
Uganda, 06: 358-359, 371, *381-382,* 05: *391,* 04: *391;* table, 06: 41
Ukraine, 06: 80, 289, 320-321, *382,* 05: *392,* 04: *391;* table, 06: 183
Ulcers, 06: 273
Ulster Unionist Party, 06: 274
UN. See **United Nations**
Unemployment, 06: 84, 184, 191, 227; U.S., 06: 169, 170, 356
UNESCO, 06: 301
UNICEF, 06: 38
Unification Church, 06: 229-231
Unified field theory, 06: 299-300
Union of Right Forces, 06: 315
UNITE HERE, 06: 226, 227
United Airlines, 06: 72, 225
United Arab Emirates, 06: 88 (il.); table, 06: 256
United Automobile Workers, 06: 69, 227
United Food and Commercial Workers International Union, 06: 226, 227
United Iraqi Alliance, 06: 211, 213
United Kingdom, 06: 180-182, *383-387,* 05: *393-397,* 04: *392-396;* cricket, 06: 124; Sierra Leone mission, 06: 330; table, 06: 183. See also **London; Northern Ireland; Terrorism**
United Kingdom, Prime Minister of, 06: *387,* 05: *397,* 04: *396.* See also **Blair, Tony**
United Nations, 06: *388,* 05: *397-398,* 04: *396-397;* Bolton appointment, 06: 283; Millennium Ecosystem Assessment, 06: 178-179; population studies, 06: 305; World Food Program, 06: 39, 42, 223
actions in: Afghanistan, 06: 37; Cambodia, 06: 89; China, 06: 106; Congo (Kinshasa), 06: 114-115; Haiti, 06: 198; Iran, 06: 210-211; Iraq, 06: 213; Lebanon, 06: 232-233, 254; New Zealand, 06: 266; Pakistan, 06: 278; Serbia and Montenegro, 06: 329, 330; Sierra

Leone, **06:** 330; Sudan, **06:** 254-255, 358; Syria, **06:** 363; tsunami region, **06:** 56; Zimbabwe, **06:** 415. See also International Monetary Fund; UNICEF; World Trade Organization
United Self-Defense Forces of Colombia, **06:** 113
United States: moments in time, **04:** *402-407;* western frontier life, **04:** *472-480.* See also specific topics
United States, Government of the, **06:** 389-392, **05:** *398-402,* **04:** *398-401 relations with:* Afghanistan, **06:** 37; Bolivia, **06:** 84; Canada, **06:** 96; China, **06:** 106, 208; Colombia, **06:** 113; European Union, **06:** 181-183; India, **06:** 205-206; Italy, **06:** 218; Korea, North, **06:** 223; Korea, South, **06:** 223; Latin America, **06:** 231; Libya, **06:** 234; Myanmar, **06:** 262; Nicaragua, **06:** 272; Russia, **06:** 325-326; Saudi Arabia, **06:** 328; Syria, **06:** 363; Turkey, **06:** 381; Uzbekistan, **06:** 406; Venezuela, **06:** 406. See also Armed forces; City; Congress of the United States; Courts; Elections; Iraq War; Supreme Court of the United States
United States, President of the, **06:** 393-405, **05:** *403-409,* **04:** *409;* libraries, **06:** 394-405. See also Bush, George Walker
Universities. See Basketball; Education; Football
University Hospital (New Orleans), **06:** 198
University of... See under keyword, as in Texas, University of
Uri (party), **06:** 222
Uribe Velez, Alvaro, **06:** 113
Uruguay, **06:** 228, 231; table, **06:** 230
U.S. News & World Report (magazine), **06:** 249
U.S. Open, **06:** 360
US Airways Group, **06:** 71, 169, 225
USA Patriot Act (2001), **06:** 233
Utah, table, **06:** 355
Uzbekistan, **06:** *406,* **05:** *410,* **04:** *409;* table, **06:** 59

V
V-22 Osprey (aircraft), **06:** 52
Vajpayee, Atal Bihari, **06:** 204-205
Valente, James, **06:** 352
Vall, Ely Ould Mohamed, **06:** 42
Vandross, Luther, **06:** 147
Van Gogh, Theo, **06:** 263
Vanhanen, Matti, **06:** 185
Van Susteren, Greta, **06:** 366
Vanuatu, **06:** 277; table, **06:** 277
Vasher, Nathan, **06:** 188
Vatican Council, Second, **06:** 148-153
Vázquez, Tabaré, **06:** 231
Velocity, **06:** 295
Vendee Globe (race), **06:** 83
Venezuela, **06:** 51, 228, 231, *406,* **05:** *410,* **04:** *409;* air crash, **06:** 155; Cuba relations, **06:** 134; table, **06:** 230
Venom, **06:** 281
Verhofstadt, Guy, **06:** 80
Verizon Communications Inc., **06:** 365
Verizon North Inc., **06:** 226
Vermont, table, **06:** 355
Vernon, John, **06:** 147
Veterans Affairs, U.S. Department of, **06:** 89
Video cameras, **06:** 175-176
Vietnam, **06:** *407,* **05:** *410,* **04:** *409;* table, **06:** 59

Vikings, **06:** 270
Villaraigosa, Antonio, **06:** 248
Villepin, Dominique de, **06:** 191-192
Vioxx (drug), **06:** 167, 199
Virginia, **06:** 154, 174, 310-311, 356; table, **06:** 355
Viruses, Computer, **06:** 175
Voice over Internet Protocol, **06:** 364, 365
Volcker, Paul, **06:** 388
Volkswagen Beetle, **06:** 68 (il.)
Vollmann, William T., **06:** 236-237
Von Eschenbach, Andrew, **06:** 199
Voris, Roy "Butch," **06:** 147
Voronin, Vladimir, **06:** 257, 324

W
Wadud, Amina, **06:** 214
Wages. See Census; Labor and employment
Wagner, John, **06:** 239
Wagoner, Rick, **06:** 69
Wal-Mart, **06:** 377
Walk the Line (film), **06:** 259
Walker Art Center, **06:** 50, 54
Walloons, **06:** 80
Walsh, Kay, **06:** 147
Walter Reed Center, **06:** 408-409
Walters, Barbara, **05:** *331-332*
Wangchuck, Jigme Khesar Namgyel, **06:** 59
Wangchuck, Jigme Singye, **06:** 58-89
War of the Worlds (film), **06:** 258
Ware, Chris, **06:** 242 (il.), 243
Warner, John, **06:** 117 (il.)
Warren, J. Robin, **06:** 68, 273
Warren, Rick, **06:** 307
Warrick, Ruth, **06:** 147
Washington (state), **06:** 154, 311, 356; table, **06:** 355
Washington, D.C., **06:** *408-409,* **05:** *411-412,* **04:** 410-411
Washington, George, **06:** 396
Washington Nationals, **06:** 408
Washington Post, The, **06:** 271-272
Water polo, **06:** 354
Waterfalls, **06:** 268-269
Watergate, **06:** 399
Weapons of mass destruction, **06:** 234, 389
Weather, **06:** *409-412,* **05:** *412-414,* **04:** *411-414.* See also Disasters; Floods; Global warming; Hurricanes; Storms; Tsunami
Web logs, **06:** 210
Weber, Dick, **06:** 147
Weightlifting, **06:** 354
Weir, Johnny, **06:** 203
Weir, Mike, **06:** 257
Weizman, Ezer, **06:** 147
Welfare, **06:** 343-345, *413,* **05:** *414-415,* **04:** *414*
Wen Jiabao, **06:** 106-107
West Bank, **06:** 216, 371
West Coast Eagles, **06:** 67
West Indies, **06:** 124, *413,* **05:** *415,* **04:** *415*
West Virginia, table, **06:** 355
Westmoreland, William C., **06:** 147
Wheat, **06:** 43
Wheldon, Dan, **06:** 70
Whiskeytown National Recreation Area, **06:** 268-269
White, Bill, **06:** 201
White, Ronald, **06:** 290
White Settlement (Texas), **06:** 175
Wie, Michelle, **06:** 352
Wiesenthal, Simon, **06:** 147
Wilbur, Richard, **06:** 302
William J. Clinton Presidential Library and Museum, **06:** 395 (il.), 402
Williams, Anthony A., **06:** 408

Williams, Dudley, **06:** 137
Williams, Marvin, **06:** 78 (il.)
Williams, Serena, **06:** 369-370, **04:** *313*
Williams, Venus, **06:** 369-370
Wilson, August, **06:** 147, 372, *374*
Wilson, Earl, **06:** 147
Wilson, Joseph C., IV, **06:** 271, 392
Wimbledon, **06:** 360
Winchell, Paul, **06:** 147
Wind, Herbert Warren, **06:** 147
Winfrey, Oprah, **06:** 369
Wireless communication, **06:** 72, 364-365
Wisconsin, **06:** 175, 355; table, **06:** 355
Wise, Robert, **06:** 147
Wojtyla, Karol Józef. See John Paul II
Wolesi Jirga, **06:** 37
Wolfowitz, Paul, **04:** *313*
Wolves, **06:** 416
Women: employment, **06:** 225; prisons, **06:** 306; rights, **06:** 214, 224, 361. See also Abortion; specific sports
Woode, Jimmy, **06:** 147
Woodpeckers, Ivory-billed, **06:** 122
Woods, Eldrick "Tiger," **06:** 196, 351
Woods, Rose Mary, **06:** 147
Woodward, Bob, **06:** 271-272
Woolley, Catherine, **06:** 147
World Council of Churches, **06:** 308
World Cup (soccer), **06:** 332
World Series, **06:** 74-75, 105, 200
World Trade Center, **06:** 48-50, 390, **04:** *50-52*
World Trade Organization, **06:** 44, 71-72, 183-184, 209, 328
World War II, **06:** 53, 150-151. See also Holocaust
World Wide Web. See Internet
World Youth Day, **06:** 311-312
WorldCom Inc., **06:** 73-74, 125
Wright, Robert, **06:** 147
Wright, Teresa, **06:** 147
Wright Amendment (1975), **06:** 135
Wriston, Walter, **06:** 147
WWF, **06:** 121-122
Wyoming, table, **06:** 355

X
Xbox game system, **06:** 377-378
XM Satellite Radio, **06:** 310

Y
Yabloko party, **06:** 315
Yanukovych, Viktor, **06:** 316, 320-321
Yao Ming, **04:** *313-314*
Year of Magical Thinking, The (Didion), **06:** 237
Yemen, table, **06:** 256
Young, Sophia, **06:** 79 (il.)
Yuan, **06:** 171, 208
Yukon, **06:** 101
Yukos (company), **06:** 314, 325
Yushchenko, Viktor Andriyovich, **06:** *289,* 316, 320-321, 382

Z
Zambia, table, **06:** 41
Zanzibar, **06:** 42-43
Zapatero, José Luiz Rodríguez, **06:** 350, **05:** *332*
Zarqawi, Abu Musab al-, **06:** 33 (il.), 215, 221, 254, 371
Zhao Ziyang, **06:** 107, 147
Zhou Yongkang, **06:** 105
Zhvania, Zurab, **06:** 193
Zia, Khaleda, **06:** 72
Zimbabwe, **06:** 38-39, 124, 171, *414-415,* **05:** *415-416,* **04:** *415;* table, **06:** 41
Zoellick, Robert, **06:** 272
Zoos, **06:** 415-416, **05:** *416,* **04:** *416*
Zuma, Jacob, **06:** 346

Acknowledgments

The publishers acknowledge the following sources for illustrations. Credits read from top to bottom, left to right, on their respective pages. An asterisk (*) denotes illustrations and photographs created exclusively for this edition. All maps, charts, and diagrams were prepared by the staff unless otherwise noted.

8 © Ali Jasim, Reuters
9 © Michael Ainsworth, *Dallas Morning News*/Corbis
10 NASA/JPL
13 © Faleh Kheiber, Reuters
14 © David McNew, Getty Images
17 © Chris Greenberg, ZUMA Press
18 © Reuters
21 © Akram Saleh, Reuters
22-25 AP/Wide World
26 © Chris Graythen, Getty Images
29 AP/Wide World
30 © Amit Bhargava, Corbis
33 AP/Wide World
34 © Mario Tama, Getty Images
39 © AFP/Getty Images
46 © Peter Brown
48 © AFP/Getty Images
49 © Mark Darley, Corporation of the Fine Arts Museums; Harry Foster, CMC
54 © Jonas Borg, UPPA/ZUMA Press
55 © AFP/Getty Images
57 © Alessandro Digaetano, Polaris Images
60-61 NASA
63 © Bill Hearne, Newspix
67 © Robert Jaeger, Reuters
68 © Tim Boyle, Getty Images; Honda; Volkswagen; Toyota
71 AP/Wide World
74 © Tim Boyle, Getty Images
76 © Win McNamee, Getty Images
78 © Ryan McKee, Getty Images
79 © Andy Lyons, Getty Images
81 AP/Wide World
83 © Peter Macdiarmid, Getty Images
85 AP/Wide World
88 © Otto Pohl
90 © Jim Young, Reuters
97 © Simon Hayter, Getty Images
98 AP/Wide World
104 © Fordham Company/Getty Images
107 © AFP/Getty Images
112 Bernd Uhlig, Salzburg Festival
114 Apple Computer, Inc.
117 © Chip Somodevilla, Getty Images
122 AP/Wide World
126 Art Explosion
130 © Igors Irbe, SuperStock
137 Damir Yusupov, Bolshoi Ballet
138 © Embassy/Kobal Collection
139 © Universal/Kobal Collection; AP/Wide World
140 © Hulton Archive/Getty Images; © CBS/Getty Images
141 © Warner Bros./Kobal Collection; AP/Wide World
142 AP/Wide World; © Time Life Pictures/Getty Images; AP/Wide World
143 © The Sporting News/ZUMA Press
144 Kobal Collection; © KPA/ZUMA Press
145 AP/Wide World; © Jason Reed, Reuters; AP/Wide World
146 © Getty Images
147 AP/Wide World; © Reuters
148 © AFP/Getty Images
150 © ITF/ZUMA Press
151 © AFP/Getty Images; © Luciano Mellace, Reuters
152 © AFP/Getty Images
153 AP/Wide World
158 NOAA; © Thomas Haley, Sipa Press
159 © Mark Wilson, Getty Images;

© Michael Ainsworth, *Dallas Morning News*/Corbis
160 AP/Wide World
161 © Smiley N. Pool, *Dallas Morning News*/Corbis
162 AP/Wide World
163 © Thomas Haley, Sipa Press; AP/Wide World
164 © Shawn Thew, Sipa Press; © Erich Schlegel, *Dallas Morning News*/Corbis
165 © Reuters/Corbis; © David L. Ryan, Reuters
166 AP/Wide World
173 © Kenneth Garrett, National Geographic Image Collection
177 © AFP/Getty Images
178 AP/Wide World
180 © AFP/Getty Images
185 AP/Wide World
186 U.S. Department of Agriculture
188 © Ben Chen, ZUMA press
191 © Eric Travers, Sipa Press
194-197 AP/Wide World
202 © Joe Raedle, Getty Images; © Corbis/Bettmann
205-207 AP/Wide World
210 © Reuters
212 © Ali Jasim, Reuters; AP/Wide World
213 AP/Wide World
215 © AFP/Getty Images
216 © Eddie Gerald, ZUMA Press
217 © Ricki Rosen, Corbis
219 AP/Wide World
221 © AFP/Getty Images
224 © Vasily Shaposhnikov, ZUMA Press
226 © Cory Ryan, Getty Images
229 AP/Wide World
232 © AFP/Getty Images
237 © Jeff Lowenthal, Lebrecht
238-239 © PhotoDisc
240 AP/Wide World
241 © PhotoDisc
242-243 From JIMMY CORRIGAN by Chris Ware, copyright © 2000, 2003 by Chris Ware. Used by permission of Pantheon Books, a division of Random House, Inc.
244 Kobal Collection
247 AP/Wide World
248 © J. Emilio Flores
250 © Corbis/Bettmann
255 © AFP/Getty Images
260-261 ZUMA Press
263 © Ronald Fleurbaaij, Reuters
264 © Matthew Peyton, Getty Images
267 © Peter Macdiarmid, Getty Images
268 Watson Davis, Smithsonian Institution; AP/Wide World
269 AP/Wide World
270 © Peter Macdiarmid, Getty Images
271-275 AP/Wide World
278 © Faisal Mahmood, Reuters
280 AP/Wide World
282 © Bournemouth Symphony Orchestra/Getty Images
283 © Stephen Chernin, Getty Images
284-285 AP/Wide World
286 © Chris Wattie, Reuters
287 © AFP/Getty Images
288 © Kevin Lamarque, Reuters
289 © Scott Gries, Getty Images
291 AP/Wide World

294 © The Hebrew University of Jerusalem; AP/Wide World
297 © John Mead, Photo Researchers; © Chuck O'Rear, Corbis
298 D. Carr and H. Craighead, Cornell University
299 AP/Wide World; © Corbis
301 © Corbis/Bettmann; © David Burnett, Photo Researchers
304 © AFP/Getty Images
307 © Keith Bedford, Reuters
312 © Arturo Mari, Getty Images
313-315 © AFP/Getty Images
317-319 AP/Wide World
321 © Gleb Garanich, Reuters
322-323 AP/Wide World
324 © Adlan Khasanov, Reuters
327 © AFP/Getty Images
329 AP/Wide World
331 © AFP/Getty Images
334 AP/Wide World; © MPI/Getty Images
336-337 AP/Wide World
339 Lyndon B. Johnson Presidential Library
340 © Brand X Pictures/Alamy Images
341-342 © PhotoDisc/Getty Images
345 AP/Wide World
348 AP/Wide World; NASA
349 NASA/JPL
350 AP/Wide World
353 © Bernard Papon, Reuters
359-362 AP/Wide World
365 Motorola, Inc.
367 © NBC/ZUMA Press
368 © ZUMA Press/Corbis
370-374 AP/Wide World
377 Hasbro, Inc.
379 AP/Wide World
382 © Vasily Fedosenko, Reuters
383 AP/Wide World
385 © Tom Shaw, Getty Images
387 © ROTA/Getty Images
389 AP/Wide World
393 © Win McNamee, Getty Images
394 Franklin D. Roosevelt Presidential Library and Museum; William J. Clinton Presidential Library and Museum
395 Abraham Lincoln Presidential Library and Museum; © David Hume Kennerly, Getty Images; Yoichi R. Okamoto, Lyndon B. Johnson Presidential Library
397 Franklin D. Roosevelt Presidential Library and Museum; Lyndon B. Johnson Presidential Library;
© David McNew, Getty Images
398-399 © Time Life Pictures/Getty Images
400 George Bush Presidential Library; Abraham Lincoln Presidential Library and Museum
401 © Brian Snyder, Reuters; Gerald R. Ford Library and Museum
402 © AFP/Getty Images
403 Ronald Reagan Presidential Library and Museum
404 Jimmy Carter Presidential Library and Museum; © Time Life Pictures/Getty Images
407 © Desmond Boylan, Reuters
408 © Jonathan Ernst, Reuters
410 NOAA; AP/Wide World
411 AP/Wide World; © AFP/Getty Images
414 AP/Wide World
416 © AFP/Getty Images